Vodou Songs in Haitian Creole and English

VODOU SONGS

in Haitian Creole and English

Chante Vodou
an kreyòl ayisyen ak angle

BENJAMIN HEBBLETHWAITE

With the editorial assistance of

Joanne Bartley, Chris Ballengee,
Vanessa Brissault, Erica Felker-Kantor, Andrew Tarter,
Quinn Hansen, and Kat Warwick

TEMPLE UNIVERSITY PRESS
Philadelphia

TEMPLE UNIVERSITY PRESS
Philadelphia, Pennsylvania 19122
www.temple.edu/tempress

Published 2012

Harold Courlander songs: Courtesy of the Emma Courlander Trust.

Songs from the Werner A. Jaegerhuber collection "Complaintes haïtiennes": Courtesy of Anna Maria Etienne (Jaegerhuber).

Laura Boulton recording of a Vodou ceremony in 1947: ATL 13270, side A, pp. 1–5; ATL 13271, side A, pp. 10–15; ATL 13271, side B, pp. 15–21; ATL 13272, side A, pp. 21–26. Courtesy of Aaron Fox and Ana Ochoa, Department of Music, Columbia University.

Oungan Max Gesner Beauvoir songs: Courtesy of Oungan Max Gesner Beauvoir.

Mythologie Vodou songs: From Milo Marcelin, *Mythologie Vodou (Rite Arada),* vols. 1–2 (Pétionville: Éditions Canapé Vert, 1950).

Le sacrifice du tambour songs: From Jacques Roumain, *Le sacrifice du tambour-Assôtô(r)* (Port-au-Prince: Imprimerie de l'État, 1943; repr., Port-au-Prince: Éditions Presses Nationales d'Haïti, 2007).

Formation ethnique songs: From Jean Price-Mars, *Formation ethnique, folk-lore et culture du peuple haïtien,* 2d ed. (Port-au-Prince: Imprimerie N.A. Théodore, 1956).

Library of Congress Cataloging-in-Publication Data

Hebblethwaite, Benjamin.
Vodou songs in Haitian Creole and English / Benjamin Hebblethwaite ; with the editorial assistance of Joanne Bartley . . . [et al.].
p. cm.
Includes bibliographical references and index.
ISBN 978-1-4399-0601-9 (cloth : alk. paper)
ISBN 978-1-4399-0602-6 (pbk. : alk. paper)
ISBN 978-1-4399-0603-3 (e-book)
1. Vodou music—History and criticism. 2. Vodou music—Texts. I. Bartley, Joanne. II. Title.

ML3197.H43 2011
782.3'9675—dc22 2011015298

∞ The paper used in this publication meets the requirements of the American National Standard for Information Sciences—Permanence of Paper for Printed Library Materials, ANSI Z39.48-1992

Printed in the United States of America

121916P

This book is dedicated to my first Haitian friend, J.L.

On cold days in West Lafayette, Indiana,
you blessed me with your knowledge of Vodou
and you shared your beautiful Haitian Creole language with me.

I miss you.

CONTENTS

——*

ACKNOWLEDGMENTS

——*

THE HARD WORK, patience, and generosity of many friends and colleagues made the compilation and publication of this book possible. I had the privilege of working with outstanding Creolist students at the University of Florida, and I thank them for their unshakable support and friendship. Their contributions had a profound impact on this project and enriched my life.

I began the work with Joanne Bartley, who was enrolled as an undergraduate student in Haitian Creole courses at the University of Florida. She worked on transcription, orthographical modernization, translation, and editorial tasks for Chapters 4 and 5 and for Appendix A: Dictionary of Vodou Terms. Chris Ballengee, a University of Florida doctoral candidate in ethnomusicology, typed J.L.'s songs and texts for Chapter 6, and together we translated them. Erica Felker-Kantor, a graduate student in Latin American studies at the University of Florida and a Haitian Creole Foreign Language and Area Studies (FLAS) scholar, helped translate Courlander's songs for Chapter 8. The University of Florida graduate students and Haitian Creole FLAS scholars Andrew Tarter (in anthropology) and Quinn Hansen (in linguistics) extracted headwords and definitions for Appendix A from Bryant Freeman and Jowel Laguerre, *Haitian-English Dictionary* (Lawrence, Kan.: Institute of Haitian Studies, 2004). The University of Florida's Enhancing the Humanities Scholarship generously funded the work of these two students, for which we extend our sincere thanks. Kat Warwick, an undergraduate student in engineering and a Haitian Creolist at the University of Florida, created entries on the Catholic saints for Appendix A. Vanessa Brissault, an undergraduate linguistics major at the University of Florida, typed the first draft of Appendix B: Outline of Haitian Creole Grammar.

I thank Oungan Max Gesner Beauvoir for granting permission to use a selection of songs from *Le grand recueil sacré ou répertoire des chansons du vodou haïtien* (Port-au-Prince: Edisyon Près Nasyonal d Ayiti, 2008) and for his kind words of encouragement. I am grateful to Anna Maria Etienne (Jaegerhuber) for granting me permission to use Werner A. Jaegerhuber's texts in Chapter 3 and to Michael Largey at Michigan State University for putting me in touch with her. I thank Aaron Fox and Ana Ochoa at Columbia University for granting me permission to include the Laura Boulton material in Chapter 5. I thank my friend J.L. for sharing with me the songs in Chapter 6. I am indebted to Oungan Nelson Marcenat, who patiently participated in interviews and checked facts during our conversations in 2008 and 2009. His contribution was invaluable to our presentation of Vodou, and his warmth and wisdom greatly enlivened my research. I thank Mike Courlander and the Emma Courlander Trust for granting me permission to use songs from Harold Courlander's unpublished 1939–1940 manuscript (from the University of Michigan Special Collections Library) in Chapter 8. I am also grateful to Marilyn Graf at the Indiana University Archives of Traditional Music and Kate Hutchens at the University of Michigan Special Collections Library, who went to great lengths to help me secure manuscripts and permissions. I thank Richard Phillips and Paul Losch at the University of Florida's Latin American Collection for constantly helping me obtain essential materials. I extend my gratitude to Laurie Taylor at the Digital Library Center and Sophia Krzys Acord at the Center for Humanities and the Public Sphere at the University of Florida for their support of our work. I am grateful to Gerald Murray for sharing many insights into Vodou with me.

I am indebted to Hannah Covert, Carmen Diana-Deere, Philip Williams, and Richmond Brown at the Center for Latin American Studies at the University of Florida, who supported the creation of the "Introduction to Haitian Vodou" class and this book project. I acknowledge the generous award of $3,500 from the Center for Latin American Studies toward the completion of this book. Michou Phenelus and Rachael Bruce, students in my classes, made various corrections to the manuscript. I thank Mary Watt (chair of the Department of Languages, Literatures, and Cultures) and my colleagues and friends at the University of Florida for their encouragement. I thank Samantha Nader and the University of Florida's Club Creole for kindly inviting me to speak about this book.

Jacques Pierre at Duke University has patiently answered my questions about Vodou for several years—*yon kokennchenn mèsi, frè m!* Albert Valdman at the Indiana University Creole Institute mentored me for years and helped cultivate in me the skills needed to bring this project to fruition—*mèsi bòs Albè!* Deborah Jenson and Laurent Dubois at Duke University enthusiastically received the manuscript and graciously invited me to present the work-in-progress at Duke in November 2009. The Haitian Studies Association asked me to present the book project at its annual conference in November 2009 and

November 2010, after which the participants shared constructive feedback. I thank Liesl Picard at Florida International University for asking me to present the book project at a lecture for the Haitian Summer Institute in July 2010. I am grateful to Michel DeGraff at the Massachusetts Institute of Technology, who has encouraged and inspired me. I thank Armin Schwegler at the University of California, Irvine, for his valuable suggestions and corrections on numerous Kikongo etymologies in Appendix A. I thank Oungan Michelet Tibosse Alisma of the temple Société Linto Roi in Miami for warmly inviting me to Vodou ceremonies and for sharing many insights. I am profoundly grateful to Jérôme Soimaud—photographer of Vodou and consummate artist—for his many clarifications, corrections, and for this book's brilliant cover art, which he drew and designed. I thank Jerry and Yvrose Gilles, whose published work and correspondence helped me dramatically improve the book—*chapo ba, djakout nou chaje kou Legba!*

I am deeply grateful to Micah Kleit, Joan Vidal, Lynne Frost, Susan Deeks, Amanda Steele, Gary Kramer, and the staff at Temple University Press for their sharp eyes, professionalism, enthusiasm, and friendliness.

I thank my wife, Changhee; my daughters, Chloe and Ellie; and my friends, who shared their love with me and made many sacrifices so that I could work serenely. I thank my brothers, Antony and Paul, who encouraged me throughout this project. I thank Bondye (Mawou-Lisa), who made Vodou: *Nanpwen anyen la pase Bondye o!* (Oh there is nothing here but God!).

Any inaccuracies that remain are my own.

Ayibobo!—Bilolo!

CHAPTER 1

The World of Vodou Songs

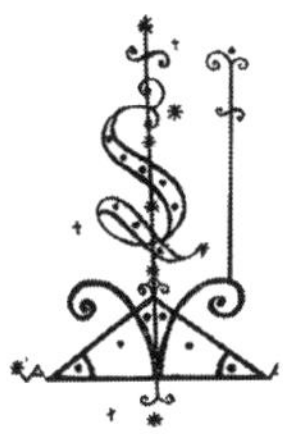

The Roots of Vodou

Vodou is the hereditary spiritual tradition of African descendants in Haiti (Jil and Jil 2009). Throughout the ages, Vodou has been transmitted by the elders to the children:

Depi m piti, m ap chante pou lwa yo.
Se pa ti nèg ki te montre m chante o.
Adje, kite m montre chante Bondje!
Depi nan vant manman m,
gwo lwa m yo reklame mwen. Bilolo![1]

Since I was small, I have been singing for the lwa.[2]
Oh it wasn't a little guy who showed me how to sing.
Oh heavens, let me teach God's songs!
Ever since my mother's womb,
my great lwa have claimed me. Bilolo!

Vodou, or serving the *lwa* (spiritual beings and forces), is a religion, philosophy, culture and way of life that comes mainly from two major regions in Africa: Dahomey (Benin, Nigeria) and the Kongo. Dahomey was a large African kingdom and empire that spanned three centuries until the French invasion and colonization in 1892.[3] It included parts of the countries currently known as Ghana, Togo, Nigeria, and Benin, the seat of its power. Fon, Yorùbá, and Ewe were the three important Dahomian ethnolinguistic groups in the early colonial period of Saint-Domingue (c. 1680–1750; see Bellegarde-Smith 2006). The second major influence came from the Kongo, which supplied the majority of slaves in the late colonial period (c. 1750–1791). On the eve of the Haitian Revolution in 1791, the Kongo population equaled the Dahomian population (Jil and Jil 2009: 199). Among the hundreds of African ethnolinguistic groups transported on French slave vessels to Saint-Domingue were the Adja, Akan, Ayizo, Bambara, Edo, Fulah, Hwla, Igbo, Igala, Mayi, Mede, Moudong, Nago,

Ouatchi, Petwo, Rada, Savalou, Seneka, Wangòl, and Yagba communities (see Blier 1995: 83; Jil and Jil 2009; Rigaud 1953: 26; Yai 2008: 234). Vodou songs are important historical records in their preservation of these and many other African ethnic, cultural, and geographical terms. In Africa today, descendants maintain traditions related to Haitian Vodou and provide a rich source for comparing traditions (see Brand 2000a: 15; Monsia 2003; Rouget 1991, 2001: v).

The first wave of slaves shipped to Haiti came from the kingdom of Dahomey and its peripheries (Jahn 1961: 29–30).[4] Slavery became a national industry in Dahomey, in Saint-Domingue, and, financially and managerially, in France (Métraux 1958: 20). The torture of slavery and the spiritual resources needed to survive and overcome it remain a permanent meditation in Vodou songs:

Si pa te gen Lwa,[5] nou tout nou ta neye!	If there weren't Lwa, as for us, we'd all drown!
Si pa te gen Lwa, nou tout nou ta peri o, nan peyi letranje.	If there weren't Lwa, as for us, oh we'd all perish in foreign countries.
Nou soti nan Ginen,	We come from Ginen,
men nan men, pye nan pye!	hand bound to hand, foot bound to foot!
Nou prale yon kote, lè n rive, n a va posede!	We'll go to a place, when we arrive, we'll own it!
Anba kal negriye, nou prale yon kote,	In the hold of the slave ship, we're going somewhere,
tou benyen, tou poudre ak Gwo Lwa a,	all bathed and powdered with the Great Lwa,
n ape navige!	we're sailing!
(Beauvoir 2008b: 335)	

Although African influences are fundamental and tangible in Vodou, they are creolized or blended into a coherent Haitian Creole religious and cultural system (Michel 2006: 30). Comparatively, Vodou shares traits with Korean shamanism and with the old religions of Greece and Rome (Castor 1998: 28; Métraux 1958: 23).[6] Those religious systems involve piety and sacrifices to deities and ancestors, patterns familiar to Vodouists. Today the Atlantic perimeter is home to diverse groups that inherited, maintain, or adopted African religions and philosophies (Murrell 2010: 1). Vodou songs are a testament to the tenacity and genius of the ancestors who taught and practiced these ancient traditions in the dreadful conditions of Saint-Domingue.

Orientation, Motivation, Methods, and Structure of the Book

Vodou songs constitute the living memory of a Vodou community. They belong not to a fixed tradition but to one that is constantly evolving. Changes, clarifications, additions, and subtractions shape the corpora of Vodou songs through time. Songs are created, retained, transformed, and forgotten. Revelation cannot be frozen in a book, because it "is a continual process" in Vodou (see Laguerre

1980: 22). Each community has its own tradition of songs that members acquire; the songs form a profound religious and cultural heritage that traverses the ages and refreshes the present. Vodou songs accompany organized ritual, dance, drumming, and interactions between people and the lwa who ride the *chwal* (horses or vessels of the lwa; Laguerre 1980: 22). Scholars provide some insight into the meaning of Vodou songs and their words; at the same time, they have various interpretations because they speak to people in different ways.

The primary goal of this volume is to introduce readers of English and Haitian Creole to the language, mythology, philosophy, origins, and culture of Vodou through source songs. The provision of all texts bilingually in Haitian Creole and English gives readers a tool to study the Haitian Creole source language in addition to the English target language. Remarkably, the most important materials about Vodou, the sacred songs of the religion, largely have been unavailable in English. The publication of Vodou songs in Haitian Creole and English is crucial for understanding the Vodouist's perspective. We are motivated by the notion that people who are studied should be able to express themselves, since they are their own experts (Brown 1991: 14). There are several excellent English-language scholarly accounts of aspects of Vodou religion and culture, whereas few publications have focused on editing Vodou songs and contextualizing them lexicographically.[7] Alfred Métraux (1958: 16) pointed this out when he said Vodou was still awaiting a good folklorist who would take the trouble to fix the rich oral traditions of the religion. Harold Courlander (1939–1940), Jacques Roumain (1943), Milo Marcelin (1950a, 1950b), Milo Rigaud (1953), Michel Laguerre (1980), Max Beauvoir (2008a, 2008b), and Dyeri Jil and Ivwoz Jil (2009), among others, are very much the "Homeric folklorists" for whom Métraux called. Several of these important collections are out of print or include no English, however. This volume includes a diverse range of sources to stitch together a representative collection of Vodou sacred literature. The bilingual heart of this book aims to be a gate between Haitian Creole and English-speaking communities and a foundation for the growth of more scholarly and exegetical work on Vodou songs.

As a Haitian Creolist and a student of religion, my point of view is that the sacred songs of Haitian Vodou are exceptional religious, linguistic, historical, and cultural treasures that deserve preservation, translation, and interpretation. Source texts are the starting points for the study of religion and culture. One cannot understand Judaism or Islam if the Hebrew Scriptures or the Qur'an are left unexamined. Similarly, one cannot grasp Rastafari if one does not study reggae music lyrics. Over millennia, Vodou religion has maintained itself via *oral* traditions. Since the 1940s, however, significant efforts have been dedicated to collecting Haitian Creole materials, but few of those pioneering works have been made available in English translation.[8] Many other important

Vodou source texts remained in manuscript form in personal collections or in sound recordings in library collections. This book makes available a diverse range of hard-to-find or unpublished sources to provide a springboard for advancing research on Vodou.

The songs collected here belong to profound traditions. They include invocations, acclamations, poetry, prayers, *langaj* (West African language fragments), formulas, terms, and proverbs; as a whole, they provide a panoramic view of Vodou religion and Haitian history. Scholars working on sacred texts employ various exegetical methods to elucidate their meanings. This book employs explanations and interpretations that focus on the origins, history, culture, audience, genre, and linguistic dimensions of the sources. Exegesis is the practice, procedure, and method employed to understand a text (Porter and Clarke 2002: 6). Exegesis aims to "read out," as opposed to "read into," a text's meaning (Porter and Clarke 2002: 5). Exegetes are concerned with discovering the meaning that authors intend for their audience and are concerned not with "truth" but, rather, with scientific fact (Kümmel 1972: 111; Porter and Clarke 2002: 7). Exegesis is interpretation and understanding that come from the "subjective context" of a text (Cohen 2001: 239). This means that exegesis compares a text with its *own* cultural traditions and those that are relevant to it.[9] In that way, Haitian Vodou is best compared with African Vodou and the religious traditions of the African diaspora.

Our work is inspired by works in linguistic, ethnographic, anthropological, and mythological research, which present the source language and the target language in a side-by-side format to give readers the opportunity to study and compare both languages. Wilhelm Bleek and Lucy Lloyd's (1911) collection of Khoisan folklore from South Africa, Elsie Clews Parsons's (1933, 1936) volumes on Antillean Creole folklore, Robert Hall's (1953) collection of Haitian Creole-English bilingual texts, Nsuka Zi Kabwiku's (1986) materials on the Kongo, John Mason's (1992) collection of Cuban Yorùbá-English Santería songs, and Akínyẹmí Akíntúndé's (2004) work on Yorùbá royal poetry are just a few examples of what this book aspires to.

Chapter 2 offers historical songs from Serge Fuertès's *Wòl Vodou nan Bwa Kayiman* (1992) and Max Beauvoir's *Le grand recueil sacré ou répertoire des chansons du vodou haïtien* (2008). In Chapter 3, the songs found in Jacques Roumain's *Le sacrifice du tambour-Assôtô(r)* (1943) and two small collections (Jaegerhuber 1950; Price-Mars 1956) appear updated in the official spelling. In Chapter 4, the songs that were originally collected by Marcelin (1950a, 1950b) appear updated in the official spelling. Chapter 5 includes the previously unpublished transcriptions of a Vodou ceremony recorded by Laura Boulton in 1947.[10] Chapter 6 comes from the handwritten, unpublished manuscript of J.L., a Haitian immigrant who had only recently arrived in the United States when

I met him in 1996–1997. Assorted songs I collected in 1999, 2000, 2008, and 2009 on trips to Belle-Rivière, Haiti, are given in Chapter 7. Chapter 8 presents fifty songs that Courlander recorded and transcribed during his fieldwork in Haiti in 1939–1940. Appendix A provides a detailed inventory and analysis of Vodou terminology. Appendix B provides an outline of Haitian Creole grammar through illustrative sentences drawn from Vodou songs and texts.

Textualization and Vodou's View of Revelation

There are many questions about how the *textualization* of orally transmitted songs fits into larger interpretations of Vodou, which include the analysis of possession performances, ritual, drumming, dance, aesthetics, objects, architecture, and much else. One of the objectives of this chapter is to suggest ways in which readers can approach these songs, which are already once and often twice removed from their ritual context as written documents and, for many readers, as translations. Issues of context and interpretation are raised by the settling of these songs into written form. This chapter and Appendix A: Dictionary of Vodou Terms strive to provide explanations that help situate the texts in their original world.

There are important differences in the sacred literature of Vodou compared with other religions. While other religions are heavily organized around a *written* text, Vodou, until recently, has centered on songs that are sung and memorized and not written down. A complex process of translation exists between cultures in all ethnographic writing (Price 2002: 21). Books can freeze songs and traditions that otherwise exist in a flowing oral current that sustains communal worship. In the process of writing down Vodou texts, the religion enters a stage of codification, and books like this one run the risk of appearing to assemble a Vodou canon.

Vodou songs are revealed or inspired in the moment by the lwa themselves.[11] They belong to "sacred oral tradition" that is not *closed* but *open*. The tradition of Vodou cannot be boxed into a canon, because the lwa are living and forever revealing themselves to their followers. Revelation occurs at an individual, familial, or community level and is not universal or uniform. A Vodou community in northern Haiti may have significant differences in the relationships, songs, and traditions of a given lwa—in addition to a layer of commonalities—when compared with a community in southern Haiti. Vodou is not a centralized religion but one with local expressions.

This collection is not a Vodou bible. While religions such as Islam and Judaism are organized around sacred written texts, Vodou is organized around oral traditions. Vodou is lived and practiced through music, dance, song, visual symbolism, ritual, liturgy, and possession. This is an early collection of the fragments of Vodou religion because so little is known about the collective repertoire of Vodou songs. In an age in which Vodou risks becoming a dwindling minority religion, a work such as this helps preserve ancient historical traditions and enrich the study and practice of Vodou (Murrell 2010: 91). The sections that follow examine Vodou through the lens of song. While this chapter cannot provide an exhaustive study of the types and content of Vodou songs, it does try to explore some of their most salient meanings and functions to open the way to further research.

Vodou in Haiti

In the next paragraphs, my goal is to introduce basic notions about Vodou as they are reflected in songs.[12] Vodou religion reinforces group solidarity, provides physicians for the sick, and offers regular worship and recreation in the community (Laguerre 1980: 26). In Haitian Creole, the term *Vodou* broadly refers to the religion and its culture. In the Fon language of Benin, *vodun* refers to a "divinity of the Fon pantheon" and is equivalent to the word *lwa* in Haitian Creole (Höftmann 2003: 376).[13] As J.L.'s song 22 shows, most Haitians simply refer to this religion of young and old as *sèvi lwa* (serving the lwa):

Jan w wè m piti an, m sèvi gwo lwa.	You may see me as puny, but I serve great lwa.
Nan demanbre m lakou lakay	In my family's Vodou ceremony in the home yard
granmoun: granmoun, timoun, timoun.	of the elders: elders, children, children.

The two basic types of Vodou are public and domestic. Public Vodou involves an *ounfò* (temple) where ceremonies are held by an *oungan* (priest), *bòkò* (priest of divination), or *manbo* (priestess). If a priest or priestess is responsible for a fully functional temple, he or she will collaborate with ritual personnel, musicians, initiates, choir leaders, singers, patrons, and a loyal uninitiated following. Other Vodou priests focus on healing and do not have temple facilities but maintain a sacred space with an altar.

Domestic Vodou, which involves ceremonies that take place on ancestral family land, is considered the most important locus for the transmission of Vodou tradition (Laguerre 1980: 36). Domestic services take place on the *lakou* (agricultural compound) of the extended family (Fleurant 2006a: 60). In that context, traditions and songs are preserved through knowledgeable family members. J.L.'s song 14 points out how the *lakou* is the heart of Vodou transmission:

Se vre lakou a ban m rele lwa yo.	It's true the yard gave me the invocation of the lwa.
Lè m rele lwa yo, lwa yo tande mwen.	When I call the lwa, the lwa hear me.

Domestic rituals are carried out either by an oungan/bòkò or manbo in the family or one invited and remunerated for officiating. There are both household ceremonies and extended-family ceremonies (Laguerre 1980: 25). Only a small number of the servants of the lwa are actually members of a particular temple. Instead of being initiated, most Vodouists maintain family-based traditions on designated days annually or periodically (Murray 1984: 194). The song below shows how the hereditary dimension of Vodou traditions can emerge after the death of a family member:

Kòmanse m pral kòmanse. Depi manman m mouri, m pral kòmanse vre! Kòmanse m pral kòmanse, sèvis la kòmanse bèl o. (Beauvoir 2008b: 220)	I am certainly going to begin. Since my mother died, I'm truly going to begin! I am certainly going to begin oh the service has begun beautifully.

J.L.'s song 144 suggests the protective power of hereditary lwa:

Mwen gen yon bagay nan tèt mwen, se lè m angaje. Y a wè sa ki nan tèt mwen. M pral wè sa ki nan tèt mwen. Men lè m angaje, lwa manman m yo dechennen.	I have something in my head, it's when I'm in trouble. They will see what's in my head. I'm going to see what's in my head. But when I'm in trouble, my mother's lwa are unchained.

Vodou religion is rooted in the Haitian family, community, culture, history, and identity. The religion is part of everyday life through song, vocabulary, mythology, theology, philosophy, ritual, proverbs, stories, mentality, symbolism, and attire.[14] The Haitian Creole language and Haitian thinking are permeated with Vodou concepts, terminology, and wisdom.

Syncretism and Stratification in Vodou and Catholicism in Haiti

Haiti's religious culture is often described as syncretistic and stratified because many people practice both Vodou and Catholicism but assign them different roles. J.L.'s song 86, like many Vodou songs, shows this dual alliance and an underlying quest for unity:

Twa Patè, o twa Ave Mariya, nou kwè nan Dye a ki ban nou lavi a, men gen Ginen. Nan Ginen, o genyen lwa, genyen lwa o, nan Ginen lafanmi o, an nou met tèt ansanm pou n ka sove peyi a.	Three Paters, oh three Hail Marys, we believe in the God who gave us life, but there is Ginen. In Ginen, oh there are lwa, oh there are lwa, Oh the family is in Ginen, let's put our heads together so we can save the country.

There are some who stay planted exclusively in one faith tradition. These individuals are mostly Catholics, but there are also Vodou purists. As a result of colonial legacies, the Catholic Church has been linked to prestige, wealth, the government, and the urban elite, while Vodou has been linked to rural communities, family, and the working classes. At the same time, individuals from diverse social classes converge in Catholicism and Vodou. Many view the two religions as inseparable. J.L.'s song 14 begins by thanking his parish priest for assistance but goes on to assert the importance of the lwa:

Pè Larak, m ap di w mèsi,	Father Larak, I'm thanking you,
se pa lajan w ban mwen.	it's not about the money you gave me.
M vin di w mèsi.	I came to thank you.
Se vre lakou a ban m rele lwa yo.	It's true the yard gave me the calling of the lwa.
Lè m rele lwa yo, lwa yo tande mwen.	When I call the lwa, the lwa hear me.
Lè m pal a lwa yo,	When I speak to the lwa,
yo regle zafè mwen.	they take care of my problems.

In Saint-Domingue, enslaved Vodou practitioners living in the crucible of the Catholic and capitalist French colonial society were compelled through violence to camouflage Vodou, but in the process they achieved the survival of the religion, the subversion of Catholicism, and, ultimately, the demise of French rule (Beauvoir-Dominique 1995: 156). While forced to convert, Africans in the colony already had a deep tradition of *assembling* religion from diverse traditions. Anthropological fieldwork in a Haitian village shows how this culture continues. Some 85 percent ($N = 421$) of Gerald Murray's participants identified themselves as Catholic (Murray 1984: 193). Of this group, fewer than 30 percent identified themselves as *Katolik fran* (pure Catholics), while the remaining 70 percent stated that their families serve the lwa.

Until very recently, the Catholic Church's entanglements with the Haitian state limited the freedom and status of Vodou, and it resulted in the domination of Haitians by Christian rites and symbols (Murray 1984: 222). It is for this reason that, rather than simple syncretism, Catholicism and Vodou are highly stratified, and each religion is domain-specific (Murray 1984: 223). While they borrow elements from each other, at their cores they are not syncretistic. Haitian servants of the lwa may have a relationship with Catholicism in public and with Vodou at home; however, each faith tradition has its specific domain, relevance, and unique interpretation of the divine. Vodou and Catholicism have different leadership, sacred spaces, traditions, rituals, theologies, philosophies, gender and sexual philosophies, worldviews, and historical, geographical, and ethnic origins, among other divergences.[15]

Basic Ethical and Philosophical Principles in Vodou

Vodou religion, unlike Christianity, Islam, or Judaism, is not a prescriptive religion with laws and commandments. Vodou presents the ethical life through "trends" and "thematic modalities" in narrative oral myths, in songs, and in the possession performances of the lwa. Basic goals in Vodou include maintaining harmony and promoting love, justice, goodness, patience, forgiveness, cooperation, respect for the elders, and the instruction of positive values in children (Michel 2006: 28). Vodou priests and priestesses should *not* harm others, because that will alienate them from God:

Yo peye m lajan pou m fè mal,	They pay me money to do evil,
M pa vle!	I don't want to!
Si m fè mal, Bondje va vire do ban mwen.	If I do evil, God is going to turn against me.
(Beauvoir 2008b: 436)	

Vodou is concerned with reducing suffering while strengthening survival instincts. J.L.'s song 52 shows sympathy for the poor and expresses an understanding of what poverty drives people to do:

M te panse m te pòv, m te pòv o,	I thought I was poor, oh I was poor,
lè m gade, mwen wè gen pi mal;	when I looked, I saw there were worse off;
m pran kouraj o.	oh I mustered my courage.
Pandan m t ap kabicha,	While I was napping,
sa k te pi mal la vòlè kwi a.	the one worse off stole my calabash bowl.
Gad se nan kwi a	Look, it's in the calabash bowl
li fè tout afè li nan lavi sa.	that he takes care of all his business in this life.
Pa janm di ou pi mal,	Never say you're the worst off,
genyen pi mal.	there are those who are even worse off.

Vodou ethics are contextual because special instructions vary according to the nature of the advising lwa and the receiving horse (Brown 2006: 10). J.L.'s song 104 expresses a personal crisis in which his poverty and drinking are related to his refusal to properly serve Ogou, lwa of war, defense, energy, force, iron, metallurgy, and the like:

Si ou wè m malere, pa kritike mwen.	If you see that I'm poor, don't criticize me.
Si ou wè m bwè kleren, pa fawouche mwen.	If you see that I'm drinking rum, don't harass me.
Se yon lwa Ogou	It's an Ogou lwa
k ap fè m pase mizè sa.	who is making me endure this misery.
Li vle m sèvi l, men m poko vle sèvi l.	He wants me to serve him, but I don't want to yet.

Vodou songs capture Haiti's socioeconomic situation and address the moral way to live in the context of hardship:

Gran nèg ap travay pou yo rich o.	Oh the powerful work to be rich.
Malere ap travay pou santiman . . .	The poor work for the sake of feelings . . .
Malere, m dakò m se malere.	Poor, I agree I'm poor.
M pito mande charite pase m vòlè.	I'd rather beg than steal.
(Beauvoir 2008b: 203)	

The wisdom of prudence is a basic Vodouist outlook (Beauvoir 2008a). The Vodouist conforms to the will of the ancestors and the living family in the observation of customs. The next song suggests the dedication that Vodouists must show to hereditary lwa:

Lwa sa a se Lwa m,	These Lwa are my Lwa,
M pa gen anyen pou m ba yo!	I don't have anything to give them!
Lwa sa a se Lwa papa m,	These Lwa are my father's Lwa,
M pral mande pou m ba yo!	I'm going to beg in order to give to them!
Lwa sa a se Lwa manman m,	These Lwa are my mother's Lwa
M pral mande pou m ba yo!	I'm going to beg in order to give to them!
(Beauvoir 2008b: 257)	

Vodou is non-apostolic because it does not seek converts. Vodouists manifest their faith through the "emotional participation" in the sacred, which they accomplish by serving as the vessels of the lwa. The rites of religion are carried out through ceremonies, rituals, music, song, dance, dreams, possession, and a daily comportment that is religious. The emphasis on respect for others keeps Vodouists from engaging in "inquisitions," pogroms, and acts of *dechoukaj* (uprooting) under the "false and cruel pretext that he or she received from God the mission of converting all nations" (Beauvoir 2008b: 70). For a Vodouist, killing people in the name of God reduces the Supreme Being to the status of a vulgar, non-universal idol. Haitians believe that a high price is exacted from those who gain something through illegitimate means, and this keeps the use of negative sorcery under control (Brown 2006: 22). Vodou justice is expressed in the practices of altruism, interdependence with nature, generosity, hospitality, and labor exchange such as the *konbit* (collective reciprocal farming). The *way* to live is a central concern of Vodou ethics, philosophy, and spirituality.

Bondye (God) and the Lwa

This section looks at key theological concepts in Vodou and their expression in songs. Bondye (God), the lwa, the Marasa (Divine Twins), and the ancestors are worshiped in Vodou (Beauvoir 2008a: 69–73). Bondye is the creator and Supreme Being of the universe. Ubiquitous in Haiti, the word *Bondye* commonly occurs in fixed expressions such as "*si Bondye vle* (Lord willing)."[16] Vodouists believe that nothing exceeds the power of Bondye. The will of Bondye surpasses that of the lwa, the Marasa, and the ancestors (Beauvoir 2008b: 51; Murray 1984: 205). The lwa are living spiritual intermediaries between humans and God. The next song suggests that Bondye is distant with respect to human problems, and it accuses humans of only selfishly calling on Bondye when in need:

Lò nou nan mizè o, n ape rele Bondje!	When we're suffering, we're calling upon God!
Bondje nan somèy,	God is sleeping,
Ganga, Bondje pa tande . . .	Ganga, God doesn't hear . . .
. . . Lò nou nan byen,	. . . When you're doing well,
nou pa sonje genyen Bondje!	you don't remember that God exists!
Lò nou nan mizè, Ganga Kalounga,	When you are suffering, Ganga Kalounga,
n ape rele Bondje!	you're calling upon God!
(Beauvoir 2008b: 254)	

J.L.'s song 83 asserts Bondye's precedence, elevates Mary and the lwa, and criticizes humans:

Mari ou sen, ou se manman Bondye;	Mary, you are holy, you are God's mother;
nou se pechè, o lapriyè pou nou.	we are sinners, oh pray for us.
Avan n ap sèvi lwa yo, n rele Bondye avan.	Before we are serving the lwa, we first call upon God.
Mari ou sen, ou se manman Bondye.	Mary, you are holy, you are God's mother.
Nou se pechè, o lapriyè pou nou.	We are sinners, oh pray for us.

Marcelin's song 5 for Ayizan, lwa of Vodou temples, markets, public places, doors, gates, roads, shows that Bondye gives the lwa to Vodou followers:

Se Bondye ki ban mwen lwa a kenbe	It is God who gave me the lwa to hold on to.
Sa m a di lwa a, sa m a di o!	What shall I tell the lwa, oh what shall I say!

Many Vodou songs make no explicit reference to Bondye's superiority, but they uniformly list the Supreme Being first. The next song reflects the traditional order: Bondye, the Pwen (protective lwa), and the Marasa.

M sèvi Bondje, m sèvi Pwen an,	I serve God, I serve the Pwen,
Tchakou, tchakou, gwo Lwa yo avè mwen.	Tchakou, tchakou, the great Lwa are with me.
M sèvi Bondje,	I serve God,
m sèvi Twa plat Marasa.	I serve the Three plates of the Marasa.
Tchakou, tchakou,	Tchakou, tchakou,
nèg pa Bondje nan peyi a.	men are not Gods in this country.
(Beauvoir 2008b: 279)	

There is no doubt that the French etyma *bon* (good) and *Dieu* (God) fused together to form the Haitian Creole word for God, *Bondye/Bondje.*[17] However, there is substantial evidence from Benin and Nigeria that the notion of the Supreme Being was and remains a fundamental part of African Vodou and Orisha culture. In Yorùbáland, Olódùmarè is the Supreme Being who undergirds the world and the *orisha* (lwa; Mason 1992: 5). In Benin, Vodouists recognize Máwú, the female upper God who created all things with her masculine counterpart, Lisa. Together they form a pair of gendered and reproductive Supreme Gods (Brand 2000b: 67; Breure 2006: 282).[18]

The Lwa

Vodouists in West Africa and in Haiti serve various immaterial beings, powers, forces, and spirits (the *vodun* in Benin or the lwa, *pwen,* or *gad* in Haiti) that emanate from human ancestors and natural forces and appear before the family and community through possession (Rouget 2001: v). God created the lwa and nature; the lwa can *influence* God and nature. The lwa express themselves in the bodies and minds of human beings through possession,[19] healing, insights, secrets, the procurement of wealth, interpretations, wisdom and punishment, and the like (see Murray 1984: 209). In addition to possession, revelations may occur through channeling, dreams, oracles, signs, animals, plants, stones, water, trees, mirrors, and other forms. The lwa reflect the complex dimensions of the people who serve them:

> Each spirit [and each family of spirits], Petwo as well as Rada, has both constructive and destructive dimensions, and these change as the character of a lwa is applied to a particular life situation through the medium of possession performance. The lwa thus do not so much set examples for the living as they hold up mirrors that clarify certain aspects of the lives of those who serve them. (Brown 2006: 19)

Initiated Vodouists identify a *pe* or *badji* (altar) and ounfò where they worship and contact various lwa who form a pantheon. Marcelin's song 6 for Legba, the lwa who rules entries, crossroads, and paths, shows the centrality of the ounfò as a meeting place for the appearance of the lwa:

Papa Legba nan ounfò mwen!	Papa Legba is in my temple!
Atibon Lebga nan ounfò mwen!	Atibon Legba is in my temple!
Alegba Papa nan ounfò mwen!	Alegba Papa is in my temple!
Ou menm ki pote drapo nan Ginen!	It's you who bears the flag in Ginen!
Ou menm ki pote chapo nan Ginen!	It's you who wears the hat in Ginen!
Se ou menm k a pare solèy pou lwa yo.	It's you who will block the sun for the lwa.

Initiates have domestic practices such as the upkeep of an *ogatwa* (home altar), prayers, singing, rituals, and, occasionally, *kandjanhoun* or *demanbre* (ancestral celebrations). As in West Africa, many Vodouists also worship in front of "found altars," especially those that are majestic natural sites such as rocky cliffs, deep springs, rivers, and towering trees (Thompson 1993: 147). Other locations where Vodou rituals unfold include crossroads, cemeteries, riverbanks, springs, caves, at the seaside, and on the sea.

There are a great many lwa in Haitian Vodou. Oungan Max Beauvoir (2008a) recognizes 401 lwa, while Oungan Nelson Marcenat indicates that he has "251 lwa in his camp." In Ouidah, Benin, Christian Merlo (1940) gathered the names of 3,381 distinct *vodun* (lwa) in a town with a population of 9,381 people (cited in Blier 1995: 66). In Haiti, one could also record the names of hundreds of lwa. The common numerical formulas 100 + 1 = 101, 250 + 1 = 251, and 400 + 1 = 401, which are found in Haiti and West Africa, represent the expandability and rejuvenation of the Vodou pantheon. Numerical differences such as the 101, 251, or 401 lwa are a reflection of the fact that Vodou has a *heterogeneous,* not a *homogeneous,* orientation. Leadership and traditions in Vodou are local. Each Vodou priest or priestess, Vodou community, and Vodouist family and servant of the lwa has her or his own grouping of lwa based on the choices of the lwa, on personal influences, and on experiences. The knowledge of the lwa *evolves* over a lifetime as the lwa appear through the possessions of friends and family and through dreams. The repertoire of lwa cannot be fixed, because the individual, local, and national pantheons organically add or subtract lwa over the course of time.

Lwa rest in three domains: the sky, the earth, and under the water (Jil and Jil 2009). The next song illustrates these three realms and refers to Savalou, a town in Dahomey and modern Benin:

Vodou tè a, ey Savalou e!	Spirits of the earth, hey Savalou, yeah!
Vodou dlo a, ey Savalou e!	Spirits of the water, hey Savalou, yeah!
Vodou lè a, ey Savalou e!	Spirits of the air, hey Savalou, yeah!
(Beauvoir 2008b: 372)	

Trees are fundamental symbols in Vodou because they span the sky, earth, and water. Lwa inhabit trees (lwa Loko); take refuge in fresh water such as ponds, lakes, rivers or springs (e.g., lwa Djobolo Bosou and Simbi); make their home in the salty sea (e.g., lwa Agwe and Èzili); surge from the ground (lwa Azaka); and swirl around the heavens, trees, and waters (lwa Danbala Wèdo and Ayida Wèdo). Marcelin's song 38 shows Danbala's link to fresh water:

Ala lwa mache nan dlo,	Look how the lwa walks on water,
se Danbala o!	oh it's Danbala!
Ala lwa mache nan dlo,	Look how the lwa walks on water,
se Danbala o!	oh it's Danbala!
Papa Danbala se tèt dlo!	Papa Danbala is the water's spring!
Papa Danbala se tèt dlo! Abobo!	Papa Danbala is the water's spring! Abobo!

Similarly, Marcelin's song 78 refers to Agwe's home in the sea and alludes to the lwa's role as a naval warrior:

Agwe rete sou lanmè, li tire o!	Agwe stays at sea, oh he fires!
Li tire o, Agwe Tawoyo!	Oh he fires, Agwe Tawoyo!
Agwe rete sou lanmè,	Agwe stays at sea,
li tire o, li tire o, Agwe Tawoyo!	oh he fires, oh he fires, Agwe Tawoyo!

Every place on earth is inhabited by lwa, and they move at the speed of light.[20] The home base of the lwa and ancestors is Ginen (Africa). The lwa are symbolically linked to storms, rain, lightning, and thunder. Marcelin's song 193 captures the lwa Agawou's association with stormy weather:

Agawou se pa moun isit!	Agawou is not from here!
Agawou gwonde, gwonde,	Agawou rumbles, rumbles,
li gwonde loray!	he rumbles the thunder!
Agawou vante, vante,	Agawou blows, blows,
li vante van!	he blows the wind!
Agawou sòti lan Ginen,	Agawou comes from Ginen,
li vante, li gwonde!	he blows, he thunders!

Other lwa, such as the Gede family and its father and head, Bawon Samdi, are dead and dwell in cemeteries. Still others are sealed in clay jars in Vodou temples and at home shrines. J.L.'s song 137 shows the lwa Bawon Samdi's symbolization of death and the cemetery:

Bawon Samdi mèt simityè.	Bawon Samdi is the master of the cemetery.
Èske gen moun sou latè k pa ka mouri?	Is there anyone in the world who can't die?
Moun yo mache pale yo di yo se towo.	The people go around saying they are bulls.
Nan sèkèy la, Bawon, n a wè longè yo.	In the coffin, Bawon, we'll see how big they are.

Lwa can inhabit animals, such as snakes, birds, cows, and goats, or insects. They may dwell in stones, mountains, waterfalls, caves, or any impressive natural site. Upon being summoned, the lwa rise through the earth or descend from the sky—their *axis*, attractor, and symbolic tree is the *potomitan* (center post) in Vodou temples—and they possess the servants of the lwa who they have *reklame* (claimed) as their own (see Desmangles 2006: 46). J.L.'s song 159 shows how Vodouists may be claimed by the lwa from a tender age, and devotion to them sometimes results in persecution by intolerant sectors of society:

Depi m piti, gwo lwa yo reklame mwen	Since I was a child, great lwa have claimed me
pou m fè sèvis Ginen an.	in order that I hold Ginen services.
M pa konn pouki, mesye,	I don't know why, sir,
nèg yo vle manje mwen.	the guys want to destroy me.

The lwa possess animals prior to sacrifice; animals in that state are calm as the Vodouists brush, stroke, and oil them in preparation for their sacred death.[21] If animals consume the food offerings laid out for them, they acknowledge their readiness to be sacrificed (Hurbon 1993: 90). This tradition continues in Haiti and West Africa.[22]

One reason there are thousands of lwa in Haitian Vodou is that the religion has undergone a metamorphosis involving the "familialization" of the lwa (Murray 1984: 198). Familialization refers to the process by which the uniform Dan (Danbala) or Gou (Ogou) of Benin, *vodun* who are worshiped similarly by different kin groups, have been "fragmented" in Haiti so that a sibling group inherits separate "Danbala" or "Ogou" lwa from different sides of the family. This fragmentation has produced a system in which Haitian Vodouists serve an array of lwa, whereas initiates in Benin serve one, and only one, *vodun*.

The Danbala of family Y is not entirely the same as the Danbala of family Z, because through possession events family members turn into familial Danbalas and Ogous (Murray 1984: 198). Many participants in Murray's study had separate Danbala lwa on their father's and mother's sides of the family. In the village he worked in, each kin group maintained its own, separate contingent of locally served lwa. In this way, the Bosou lwa or the Danbala lwa share features throughout the community but also have family-specific traditions (Murray 1984: 199). The lwa Danbala in family X will have a different history of possession events from those in family Y. The accumulation of these different possession events gives rise to different traditions and lore about the respective lwa. Further evidence for this fragmentation is reflected in the plethora of names for any given lwa, such as the thirty-five distinct names for Ogou in Appendix A: Dictionary of Vodou Terms.

Marcenat sheds light on a formal approach. For him, each lwa belongs to a familial group of *seven*, and they form a *twoupo* (flock):

> Tout lwa yo se sèt yo ye. Legba, se sèt Legba k genyen yo. Tout, yo mache pa sèt. Ogou, sèt, Èzili, sèt, Legba, sèt, Danbala, sèt, Bawon, sèt, Azaka Mede, sèt, eh? Kouzen Zaka Mede, sèt, tout se sèt nèt.
>
> All lwa are seven. Legba, there are seven Legba who exist. All of them, they walk in sevens. Ogou, seven, Èzili, seven, Legba, seven, Danbala, seven, Bawon, seven, Azaka, seven, get it? Kouzen Zaka Mede, seven, each and every one is seven.

He illustrates this with the seven Ogou:

> Gen Ogoun Kafou wi, gen Ogou Badagi, gen Ogou Feray, gen Ogou Chango, gen Ogoun Balize, gen Ogou Fè, gen Sen Jak Majè ki fè sèt Ogou.
>
> There is indeed Ogoun Kafou, there is Ogou Badagi, there is Ogou Feray, there is Ogou Chango, there is Ogoun Balize, there is Ogou Fè, and there is Sen Jak Majè which makes seven Ogou.

When I asked Marcenat what place the Catholic Saint Sen Jak Majè (Saint James the Greater) had in the groupings, he stated that he was the *chèf bann nan* (chief of the group). The grouping of related lwa into a familial flock explains why the different members of, say, the Ogou flock can manifest many different attributes, for in every family there are different and complex personalities, outcomes, and tendencies.[23]

Marcelin's song 11 for Legba shows that Marcenat's division of lwa into flocks of seven draws from a broad tradition:

Vanyan Legba, sèt Legba Katawoulo yo. Vanyan Legba, Alegba-se, se nou de, ago, yè!	Courageous Legba, the seven Legba of the Katawoulo. Courageous Legba, Alegba's divine power, it is the two of us, ago, yeah!

In a related tradition, when Mawou-Lisa (the male and female Supreme Beings) created the earth, the couple first created *seven* lwa, the first being Danbala and the seventh being Legba. Each lwa was given the mastery of a domain and instructed to help humans (e.g., Ogou, iron; Legba, dance, music, and communication; and Ozanyen and Gran Bwa, healing; see Jil and Jil 2009: 60, 64).

Apologetics, which are the defense of ideas, are part of all religions. In the next song, sinners are admonished for their refutation of the lwa:

Nèg yo di pa gen Lwa, e,	The men say there are no Lwa, oh my,
pechè yo di pa gen lwa vre!	the sinners say there really are no Lwa!
Vivan yo di nanpwen Lwa!	The living say there are absolutely no Lwa!
Pechè yo di pa gen Lwa nan peyi sa a,	The sinners say there are no Lwa in this country,
e m konnen genyen Lwa nan demanbre!	and I know there are Lwa in the family rituals!

(Beauvoir 2008b: 330)

Composure and calm are expected of Vodouists. Emotion is reserved for war and possession (Blier 1995: 81). In possession, the servant of the lwa is the *chwal* who is ridden by the lwa. A lwa *monte* (mounts or rides) its *chwal.* The lwa *danse nan tèt* (dance in the heads) of Vodouists; they *pran* (take) them and *sele* (saddle) them, among other conceptualizations. The "exorbitant gaze" or "eyes-wide-open stare" is the primary sign of the "inner pressure" of the lwa (Thompson 1993: 150). When a lwa possesses a Vodouist, this individual's *ti bonnanj* (good little angel), which is a person's individual consciousness and personality, leaves the body, making way for possession by one or more lwa.[24] Mastering possession involves learning how to let go of and retrieve the ti bonnanj. The lwa and the ti bonnanj of inexperienced horses sometimes struggle, and the priest or priestess often use the *ason* (sacred rattle) to send away a lwa who can harm the human vessel (Brown 2006: 11).

The lwa is recognized or announces herself or himself to the community through the horse. The horse manifests the identity and traits of the possessing lwa. During the possession event, other Vodouists observe, protect, interact with, and sing to the lwa. Participants recognize the lwa, not the person who is possessed. The horse is viewed as inhabited by a divine being. The horse may soothsay, engage in oracular discourse, hiss as Danbala, stutter violently as Èzili Dantò, or nasalize speech as Gede (Beauvoir 2006; Brown 2006). Possession can occur in temples, in nature, or in the family setting, especially at appropriate times, such as the family *demanbre* or *kandjanhoun,* which are occasional but important Vodou celebrations. Possession in public Vodou tends to have a "performative" dimension, whereas in domestic Vodou it involves advice from the ancestors (Jil and Jil 2009: 321; Saint-Lot 2003). The characterizations "theater of possession" and "possession performance" describe how the possessed fill roles that are specific to the lwa (Consentino 1995: 40–41).

An *inappropriate* possession is typically related to conditions that are emotional, stressful, or abusive (see Beauvoir 2006; Célestin-Mégie 2003). For example, becoming possessed at school or in church can be a signal that the possessed individual is undergoing abuse. The lwa typically will appear not superfluously but, rather, when there is ritual, music, offerings, and symbolism that encourage their appearance. Marcenat maintains strict order at his annual celebrations; vicious or self-destructive lwa and drunken celebrants are expelled. To symbolize his authority over the lwa, he cracks a whip during the ceremony.

Vodouists serve the lwa to gain protection, fortune, social status, and wisdom. Serving them allows people to experience the depths of music, mythology, and trance. Marcelin's song 4 for Èzili is a cry to the lwa for help:

M angaje o! Èzili voye rele lwa yo, pou m wè si m a sove!	Oh I am in trouble! Èzili send for the lwa, so that I may be saved!

Individuals, families and communities evolve naturally with their own pantheons of lwa. Specific lwa are called on for shielding, intervention, advice, and possession performance depending on the situation, the sponsor, and the needs at hand (Marcelin 1950b: 125).

The servants of the lwa may identify with *nanchon* (nations), which are groupings of lwa that reflect the traditional ethnic origins of the Haitian people.[25] Beauvoir's Vodou liturgical text *Lapriyè Ginen* (The Ginen Prayer), which is oral tradition that he reconstructed through his consultations with several oungan, provides a list of *nanchon*: Rada, Ginen, Seneka, Ibo, Danwonmen, Mahi, Nago, Kaplaw-Kanga, Banda, Anmin, Kongo Fran, Kongo Savann, Kita, Mondong-Mousayi, Mandeng, Wangòl, Bizango, Zandò, Pemba, Boumba Mazwa and Petwo (Beauvoir 2008a: 109–110). Traditionally, each *nanchon* has its own pantheon, hierarchy, and traditions for serving the lwa. Oungan Alisma's temple in Miami, Société Roi Linto, has several *nanchon*-based ceremonies around the New Year: December 31 for the Petwo *nanchon,* January 1 for Rada, January 2 for Nago, and January 3 for Kongo.

The *rit* (rite) refers to the ways in which the lwa are served. Although I have just given the names of the twenty-one *nanchon* above, in contemporary Vodou there are two major divisions: the Rada rite, which includes the "cooler" lwa of Dahomey, and the Kongo-Petwo rite, which includes the "hotter" lwa from the Kongo, Angola, and Haiti (Fleurant 2007). Both rites are commonly observed—beginning with Rada and closing with Kongo-Petwo—in the course of single ceremonies. Different songs, drum rhythms, instrumentation, rituals, dances, attire, colors, *vèvè* (a mystical diagram traced with some kind of powder that represents a lwa or the lwa), and evocations are encountered in the different rites. At the same time, lwa in the same flock are served in *both* rites (e.g., Atibon Legba in the Rada rite and Legba Kalfou in the Kongo-Petwo rites). Again, this reflects the fact that "Legba" is a flock of lwa whose members have different personalities, tendencies, and affiliations. This could come about because lwa/*vodun* such as Legba, Danbala, and Ogou, among others, were worshiped in numerous ethnolinguistic communities in West Africa. The preexisting diversity of West African Vodou—and later, Central African Vodou—converged in Haiti and produced a *systematic blending* of traditions and communities where commonalities fused with local particularities.

Vodou Priests, Priestesses, and Specialists

The Vodou priesthood is composed of oungan or bòkò, if male, or manbo, if female. Many think that female priests and *ounsi kanzo* (initiates) are more numerous than the male cohort (Castor 1998: 37). The manbo and oungan are intermediaries between the community and the lwa. Some Vodouists align themselves with an oungan or manbo, while others maintain only domestic traditions. Initiates refer to their respective priest or priestess as *papa* (father) or *manman* (mother), and they, in turn, refer to their members as *pitit kay* (children of the house; Brown 2006: 7). Those who have received the care of the Vodou priest or priestess are *pitit fèy* (children of the leaves), a reference to herbal medicine (Métraux 1958: 62). Gender, sexual orientation, and race are generally of less importance than the oungan or manbo's cultural sphere, healing and psychotherapeutic services, wisdom, and mystical powers. Experience, philosophy, medical and psychological services (e.g., midwifery, bone setting, herbalism, remedies, intervention in mental illness or emotional crisis), community service, attention to the poor, and the ability to establish harmony and restore balance are all factors in the career and reputation of a Vodou oungan, bòkò, or manbo. The next song shows that sickness is a basic problem that people seek to cure with the help of a Vodou priest, here referred to as *gangan*, and the healing lwa Simbi:

Fèy yo, sove lavi mwen	Oh leaves, save my life
nan mizè mwen ye o.	from the misery I'm in.
Pitit mwen malad, mwen kouri kay gangan,	My child is ill, I run to the house of the gangan,
Simbi o.	oh Simbi.
Pitit mwen malad, mwen kouri kay gangan.	My child is ill, I run to the house of the gangan.
Si ou bon gangan, sove lavi mwen	If you're a good gangan, oh save my life
nan mizè mwen ye o.	from the misery I'm in.

Temple Vodou is generally a lowland and urban phenomenon in Haiti, whereas the highlands and mountains tend to be the terrain of healer oungan or manbo (see Smucker 1984). In his rural Haitian setting, Oungan Nelson Marcenat brings culture, well-being, and stability to his community. In accordance with his hereditary traditions, he does not demand large sums of money for his services. Generally, most rural oungan or manbo have no active congregation or *ounsi kanzo.* Marcenat is respected among local families and was introduced to me through several trusted friends. Marcenat, who focuses on treating illness and delivering babies, has no temple facility but works from his family's homestead, which includes three wattle-and-daub thatched dwellings, one of which serves as a Vodou room with a *pewon* (altar). In contrast, Oungan Alisma, in his urban Miami setting, has dozens of well-disciplined initiates and an ounfò for ceremonies and consultations.

The *ounsi kanzo* initiation is also a prerequisite for the initiation into the priesthood, except in the case of hereditary oungan and manbo. The next song evokes the continuity of tradition through initiation and touches on the competitive energy that can exist between the oungan and the *ounsi kanzo* initiates, some of whom aspire to be oungan or manbo themselves:

Se hounsi ki fè houngan, vèvè dlo.	It's hounsi who become houngan, water vèvè.
Houngan tonbe, hounsi leve, vèvè dlo.	The houngan falls, the hounsi rises, water vèvè.
Konbyen hounsi ki fè houngan, vèvè dlo?	How many hounsi become houngan, water vèvè?
Depi nan Ginen hounsi trayi houngan, vèvè dlo.	Since Ginen hounsi have betrayed houngan, water vèvè.

Oungan or manbo have encyclopedic knowledge of the lwa, their oral and song traditions, appropriate liturgies, rituals, symbols, and vèvè diagrams for ceremonies, and they have experience with and authority over possession. They are priests, healers, advisers, soothsayers, mediators, psychotherapists, horses of the lwa, organizers, and community references (see Métraux 1958: 54–55; Rouget 1991). As this song shows, Vodou leaders are highly esteemed by members of a temple:

Nou ranmèsi Papa Sobo, n ap ranmèsi yo,	We thank Papa Sobo, we thank them,
Vodou, nou ranmèsi nou la!	Vodou, we thank you right here!
M ranmèsi nou.	I thank you.
Houngan mwen la e, m a ranmèsi yo!	Hey my Houngan, I'll thank them!
M ranmèsi Manbo kay la, m ranmèsi yo!	I thank the Manbo of the house, I thank them!
(Beauvoir 2008b: 334)	

In rural Haiti, serving the lwa is more closely associated with family than an external center (Murray 1984: 203). Only an estimated 5 percent of all Vodouists are formally initiated as *pitit kay* or members of a temple community (Murray 1984: 203). Vodouist families periodically organize ceremonies on private land. Small Vodou huts demarcated with the Haitian flag are set up apart from other structures on ancestral land. Families organize *demanbre*

Vodou ceremonies and celebrations with rituals and possession, animal sacrifice, singing, drumming and feasting with ritual food, barbecue, soft drinks, and alcohol.

The flying of flags from the center of a private dwelling indicates the location of a Vodou priest or priestess in Haiti. The same practice continues today in Benin, West Africa.[26] Marcenat, for his part, considers the display of flags to be indiscreet and flashy. Instead, a *pens,* which is an iron rod that represents the lwa Ogou Fè, is planted in the ground of his courtyard and serves as the only visible Vodou symbol.

Oungan and manbo are generally of two basic types, the oungan/manbo ason and the oungan/manbo Ginen. A third type of Vodou specialist addressed later is the bòkò. The oungan/manbo ason have made all the required preparations, paid a significant fee, and undergone extensive training and initiation rituals that are required under the tutelage of an established oungan or manbo (Métraux 1958: 63; Murray 1984: 195). The oungan/manbo ason receive the *ason* (sacred rattle) on completion of this ritual. The *ason* is the priesthood's primary symbol of leadership, a rhythm instrument, and the tool used to call and send away the lwa. The next song shows how the *ason* represents the power and reputation of an oungan or manbo:

Ason an k nan men manbo a,	The ason that's in the manbo's hand,
yo di li gate.	they say it's spoiled.
Gade, l pa sa gate,	Look, it can't be spoiled,
m sèvi twò gwo Lwa.	I serve Lwa who are too great.
Medizan yo, malpalan yo,	Back-biters, slanderers,
yo met tèt ansanm.	they put their heads together.
(Beauvoir 2008b: 115)	

The second type of Vodou authority is the *oungan/manbo Ginen* (Ginen priest/priestess), who receives training and knowledge intuitively from a Vodou priest or priestess within the family and thus is not formally but experientially initiated.

Oungan/manbo ason typically have their own temple for rituals, feasts, and dances dedicated to the lwa and for consultations with fee-paying patients or clients (Murray 1984: 195). These temples range from a shack to an upscale structure. Oungan/manbo Ginen, by contrast, often have no indoor facilities for gatherings but are well respected by the community for their knowledge and healing services.

Oungan and manbo are involved in a folk healing system that combines medicinal and therapeutic treatments with mysticism and ritual. Vodouists seek to appease or gain the support of the lwa through ceremonies, rituals, offerings, animal sacrifice, songs, and prayers, among other methods (Murray

1984: 195). Country dwellers will often consult with more than one oungan or manbo to get a second opinion on an illness or problem (Murray 1984: 195, 203). Vodou priests have no qualms about directing their patients to Western medicine, but the sick often lack the means to pay for it. In addition to healing, priests and priestesses provide instruction to candidate initiates; give herbal baths, massage therapy, prayers, personalized rituals, card reading, channeling, counseling and advice, oracles, spells, charms, blessings, magic, baptism, burial, and weddings; lead pilgrimages; and may officiate at important annual ceremonies for specific households, to name just a few activities (see Franswa 2009: 6). They may be paid to employ *maji blan* (white magic) to effect some change or improvement for a paying client. Some oungan disassociate themselves from the selling of lwa, which they deem risky, and the use of *maji nwa* (black magic), which they claim the bòkò employs to no good end.[27]

The bòkò are said to work with both hands, which means they serve fiery and benevolent lwa and offer services dedicated to both. A Vodou bòkò I met in Leyogann in 2009 stated that his domains of magic and mysticism were *ni cho, ni frèt* (both hot [dynamic, quick, and dangerous] and cold [benevolent, slow, and safe]). The young bòkò in Leyogann had inherited a considerable temple facility and congregation from his recently deceased father. There are also Vodou priests who are oungan-bòkò because they have inherited both traditions. Bòkò, like oungan and manbo, often receive training, designation, and realization within the family. Bòkò are different from oungan and manbo because they buy and sell lwa; they work for money and personal advantages; they engage in divination as opposed to the oungan's interpretation; they serve benevolent and dangerous lwa; and they allow the expression of self-interest, vengeance, and ambition (Hurbon 1987: 161). On a personal level as someone who knows bòkò, oungan, and manbo, it is not obvious to me whether these generalizations in the literature are entirely accurate; a quantitative study is needed. Underlying their differences, oungan, manbo, and bòkò try to heal illness, to give advice and direction about everyday life, and have knowledge about the supernatural.[28] Oungan, manbo, and bòkò reflect different traditions in the Vodou system. In Benin, the *bokónõ* is an initiated individual who interprets the "Vodun Fa," a kind of mystical fortune-telling of Yorùbá origin that uses palm nuts. The *bokónõ* predicts the future for his clients (Brand 2000b: 23). In Benin, the Fa-reading *bokónõ* are distinct in name and function from the *vodunnò* (priest of Vodou divinities; see Höftmann 2003: 376). Thus, the division of labor in Vodou is parallel in Haiti and Benin, and this suggests the robust survival of African cultural heritage.

Several types of rituals are presided over by oungan and manbo.[29] In *healing rituals*, the oungan or manbo have direct contact with the sick patient they try to cure. In *propitiatory rituals*, songs, prayers, food, and drink are offered to the lwa to gain their favor or stop their attacks. In *preventative rituals,* songs, prayers, food, and drink are offered to avoid angering the lwa and to prevent illness and misfortune. In *community rituals,* songs, prayers, liturgy, and dances are organized to pay homage to and celebrate the lwa. These calendar-based ceremonies are given to specific lwa on a designated day (e.g., Èzili Dantò on July 16, Agawou on September 24, and Legba on December 11). In *initiatory rituals,* ceremonies are held to honor the entrance or completion of initiation. Finally, in *domestic rituals,* perhaps the most important of all rituals, food and drink are offered to family lwa and the departed family ancestors.

Vodou Sacred Spaces, Objects, and Signs

The ounfò is the sacred space of the lwa and a place for ritual, worship, and celebration, which take the form of prayer, liturgy, percussion, song, dance, and possessions.[30] Marcelin's song 6 rejoices over the appearance of Atibon Legba:

Atibon Lebga nan ounfò mwen!	Atibon Legba is in my temple!
Alegba Papa nan ounfò mwen!	Alegba Papa is in my temple!

The oungan or manbo, as noted, also use the ounfò for consultation and treatment, and he or she typically lives there with family. The *peristil* of the ounfò, which ranges from a modest place covered with thatch, corrugated metal, or tent canvas to an upscale home, is where ceremonies and rituals take place safe from the elements (Métraux 1972: 77–81).

The *potomitan* stands in the middle of the temple on a concrete base or is sometimes planted directly into the dirt. It serves as the sacred entryway for the lwa and the center around which ritual and dancing orbit. In Marcelin's song 3, the *potomitan* is linked to Atibon Legba, who is sometimes known as Legba Potomitan (Legba of the Center Post) because of his role in opening the way to the lwa:

Alegba, mache, non!	Alegba, get walking already!
N ape pote Atibon Legba,	We're carrying Atibon Legba,
n ape pote potomitan!	we're carrying the center post!
Alegba, mache non!	Alegba, get walking already!
Kote n bouke, se la n a poze	When we're tired, we'll set down
poto ki nan do n.	the post that is on our backs.

The walls of the Vodou ounfò are often painted with portraits of the lwa, the saints, vèvè, or representations of historical events such as the Bwa Kayiman Vodou ceremony of 1791, which helped set the war of independence into motion. Danbala Wèdo and Ayida Wèdo, the wedded serpent lwa, are often painted as if wrapped around the *potomitan*. The oungan and manbo trace vèvè diagrams that represent the lwa who are honored for the ceremony on the ground around the *potomitan*. Roumain's song 21 evokes the idea that the vèvè should be touched by the hands or the feet in dance as part of the encounter with the lwa:

O kreyòl yo di kon sa	Oh the creoles say that
yo va manyen vèvè Loko.	they're going to touch Loko's vèvè.
Se kreyòl jodi	It's the creoles today
ki montre Ginen chanson kreyòl.	who show the Ginen creole songs.
Mwen kriye: abobo!	I cry out: abobo!

Accompanied by rhythm and song, Vodouists dance around the *potomitan* while the lwa "mount" and "ride" the "horses" who serve them. In temple Vodou, horses are usually mounted at very specific points in ritual, typically late in the night. Usually, the officiating priest or priestess is ridden by the lwa being honored. Sometimes initiates may be mounted under the supervision of the priest or priestess. However, many emerging possessions among inexperienced initiates are blocked by the oungan or manbo by means of a vigorously shaken *ason*. Emerging possessions are welcome because they suggest the presence of the lwa; however, they are not allowed to overwhelm ritual order and the possession of the oungan or manbo. Spirited dancing is highly prized, as this song shows:

Nègès Katye Moren,	Women of Katye Moren,
Nègès ki gen talan pou yo danse Vodou!	Women who have a talent for Vodou dancing!
(Beauvoir 2008b: 330)	

In a separate room, the ounfò contains a sanctuary called the *sobagi/bagi/badji* where a stonework or concrete *pe* or *pewon* is located. J.L.'s song 29 addresses the protection provided by the *sobagi* and its lwa:

Byen viv o, mal viv o, m ta pito mande	Oh good living, oh dreadful living, I would rather ask
charite devan sobagi lwa m nan.	for charity before the sanctuary of my lwa.
Moun yo di lwa pa ban m lajan,	People say the lwa doesn't give me money,
men l proteje lan mwen.	but she protects me within.
Li sove lavi m e l sove lavi zanfan yo	She saves my life and she saves the lives of children
lè nèg yo vle manje mwen.	when the men want to destroy me.

The *sobagi* serves as a kind of "vestry" where those possessed go to obtain objects that represent the lwa who has possessed them (e.g., Zaka's *makout* bag, straw hat, and pipe; Legba's crutch; Bawon's tophat and sunglasses; Métraux

1972: 80). Typically, a *sobagi* is dedicated to a patron lwa; however, representations of other lwa also share the space. Other items such as Vodou flags are also kept in the *sobagi.* An additional space is the *djèvo* room, which on top of providing storage serves as a space for those undergoing the *kanzo* initiations or for ill patients in treatment.

Altars are elevated structures where religious rites and sacrifices are made. While some altars express "dense opulence," others at first glance appear spare and dusty but remain infused with symbolism (Brown 1991: 41). At the base of his three-tiered altar, Marcenat keeps the skull of a *Ginen* (Vodouist ancestor). On the altar itself he keeps his *ason,* human bones, knotted ropes, chromolithograph images, *pyè tonnè* (mystical stones that are often ax heads or arrowheads), bottles with remedies, images, *plat Marasa* (three linked plates with small jars), and the Bible. In the same hut, he also raises roosters for cockfighting.

Additional items commonly found on altars include Haitian flags, beaded Vodou flags that represent specific lwa, *govi* (clay jars that contain lwa and ancestors), bottles of rum, candles, a water basin, a sword, a saber or machete, statues, dolls, stones, oil, crosses, flags, iron work, perfume, powder, fabric, playing cards, photographs symbolic of the lwa, and food and drink offerings (Marcelin 1950a, 1950b). The song below addresses the use of flags in Vodou ritual and indicates that the master of ceremonies has the role of displaying them:

Houngan m ape dòmi e,
se veye l ape veye!
Laplas, kondui m ale.
Kondui m ale, Lapas, o Sayil o!
An arivan m, Laplas,
deplwaye drapo!
(Beauvoir 2008b: 207)

Hey my houngan is sleeping,
he's actually watching out!
Master of ceremonies, take me along.
Take me along, master of ceremonies, oh Sayil oh!
Upon arriving, master of ceremonies,
unfurl the flags!

At the Société Roi Linto temple in Miami, both Haitian and U.S. flags are displayed in ceremonies. Flags represent Vodou's military history, sociopolitical ambitions, and the nations in which Vodouists find themselves.

Human skulls and bones are readily available for sale to oungan and manbo at urban cemeteries in Haiti, where many families can afford to bury their deceased only temporarily. In rural Haiti, the dead are buried close by the living on family compounds. At first, cadavers are placed in chambers above ground, but once the bodies have completely decomposed, the skeletons are broken and thrown below the tomb into a communal pit. Thus, the bones of the ancestors can be taken for display from the communal pit. Marcenat notes that scrapings from the skull at the base of his altar are included in some remedies. The imagery and discourse of death remind the living of the ancestors (Jil and Jil 2009). The following song captures the mature view of death found in Vodou thought:[31]

Gwo manman Yanman e,	Hey big mother Yanman,
o m a rele manman Yanman o!	oh I'll call for mother Yanman oh!
Manman Yanman e,	Hey mother Yanman,
o m a rele manman Yanman e!	oh hey I'll call mother Yanman!
Ou te mèt bèl kou w bèl,	As beautiful as you may be,
fò w pase nan sèkèy!	you must pass through the coffin!
(Beauvoir 2008b: 207)	

Marcenat's yard is a dense mixture of medicinal and edible plants and trees that he uses to sustain his family, to produce remedies, and to feed his livestock. He is able to identify most of the plants and trees in the yard and describe their medicinal properties. He also engages in sharecropping to earn additional income and is an active collaborator in *konbit.*[32] Most rural oungan are farmers, and they raise animals for Vodou sacrifices and feasts, for the marketplace, to make leather goods, or for eggs or cockfighting (Métraux 1958).

Around many ounfò are placed other sacred objects such as the *pens* (iron rod) for Ogou, a small concrete basin for Danbala, a black cross for Bawon, or a symbolic tomb for the Gede (Métraux 1972: 81). In addition to these symbols and objects, the ounfò is surrounded by *pye repozwa* (resting trees for the lwa) and poultry, fowl, goats, pigs, cows, and other animals destined for sacrifice or sale (Métraux 1972: 81).

New Vodouists are instructed to acquire an ogatwa, which consists of a wooden altar box or niche containing items symbolic of the lwa served. Vodou initiates pray at their ogatwa and keep offerings within it to serve the lwa properly and ensure their protection, benefits, and appearance.[33] Vodouists also meet outside the temple. J.L.'s song 16 mentions his pilgrimage to the spectacular waterfall of Saut d'Eau and his petitions to the Our Lady of Mount Carmel (i.e., the Virgin Mary, who doubles as Èzili Dantò). They are both celebrated every July 16–17 at Saut d'Eau's Catholic Church and at the nearby waterfall, as well as at temples throughout Haiti and its diaspora on that date.

Vyèj mirak Sodo,	Virgin miracle of Saut d'Eau,
m vin lapriyè w.	I have come to pray to you.
Mwen vin mande w pou bay	I come to ask you to give
moun sa yo travay.	these people work.
Men nuit kou jou, mesye,	But night and day, my goodness,
y ape pale mal.	they are speaking badly.
Mwen santi m about o!	Oh I'm at the end of my rope!

The song reveals the importance of pilgrimages to sacred places in nature and expresses the hope placed in the Virgin and the beleaguered condition of its author.

Hierarchy and Roles in Vodou

Authority, social prominence, and experience are important in Vodou culture. Vodou is an initiatory religion that encourages people to pursue special instructions, training, and acculturation. Each successive rank in Vodou is attained through gradual assimilation, initiation, and recognition by the priest or priestess and the initiated community (Métraux 1972: 194). Initiation requires a lot of time on the part of priests and priestesses and therefore it is expensive. Individuals with high ranks and special roles have a long-standing relationship with the temple (Métraux 1958: 60). The candidates of Vodou initiation, the *ounsi bosal* (uninitiated Vodouists), undertake seven pilgrimages, participate in public and private rituals, purchase in advance all accessories and undergo a seven-day period of isolation during which they receive only small amounts of ritual food and drink and face a culminating symbolic ordeal such as contact with flame or hot cornmeal in the *ounsi kanzo* initiation.[34] These are not painful ordeals but ones that symbolize spiritual rebirth and empowerment. The education of the *ounsi* involves the learning of a repertoire of Vodou songs, the tradition and interpretation of the lwa, liturgy and ritual, among other objectives (Laguerre 1980: 34). Roumain's song 24 makes reference to the *hounsi kanzo* (initiated Vodouists) and the *ounsi bosal* (uninitiated Vodouists):

Houngan m ape travay, o.	Oh my houngan is working.
Loko ape dòmi, ape dòmi,	Loko is sleeping, is sleeping,
Djahountò, l ape dòmi.	Djahountò, he's sleeping.
Leve, leve, leve, hounsi kanzo.	Get up, get up, get up, hounsi kanzo.
Hounsi bosal, bay lè pou hounsi.	Hounsi bosal, leave the hounsi alone.
Kanzo pase.	The kanzo ceremony is over.
Leve, leve, leve, o Gwimakou,	Get up, get up, get up, oh Gwimakou,
houngan m ape travay.	my houngan is working.

Gilbert Rouget (2001: 33–46) photographically documents the seven-day *hunsi* isolation rituals in Dahomey (Benin) in the 1950s and 1960s, showing the continuity in Benin and Haiti. For the *ounsi kanzo* initiation, the culmination of preparations is the seven-day period of isolation (see Métraux 1972: 199). The period of time required for isolation has remained the same in Benin and Haiti over several centuries. The seclusion requires reflection and fasting and it is intended to be purifying, strengthening, mystical, and celebratory. While it is an isolation ritual, it is often undertaken in the company of other *ounsi* candidates. The objectives of the ascetic experience are to make the initiate a pure receptacle for the lwa, increase knowledge and discipline, heighten spirituality, and improve the health and good fortune of initiates. The initiation is one of the most important events for the Vodouist (Métraux 1972: 192; Rouget 1991: 112–131). Marcenat reports that his *ounsi* must spend seven days in isolation with no food or drink, but he adds that the *ounsi*'s lwa will provide some sustenance.[35]

The highest initiation in Vodou, the *asogwe* or *prizdèzye*, leads to the rank of oungan or manbo. In the case of Marcenat, it requires several pilgrimages to sacred Vodou-Catholic sites, twenty-one days of isolation, and months and sometimes years of training, depending on the individual. As the following song shows, an oungan must be serious and prepared for difficulties:

Zafè Houngan pa gen jwèt o!	Oh the Houngan's work is not a joke!
Lò yon nèg ap fè Houngan reziye w o.	When a guy becomes a Houngan, oh resign yourself.
Metye Houngan pa gen jwèt o!	Oh the career of the Houngan is not a joke!
Si w ranse, w ap mouri mal o.	If you're playing, oh you're going to die badly.
(Beauvoir 2008b: 214)	

In a context of limited resources and no central hierarchy, Vodou priests or priestesses may have to compete with each other. The next song addresses these problems and returns to the source:

Poukisa Houngan rayi Houngan?	Why do oungan hate oungan?
Poukisa Manbo rayi Manbo?	Why do manbo hate manbo?
Se pa lajan metye a gen ladan l,	It isn't money that the vocation has,
Se mistè ki fè mwen sèvi Lwa yo!	It is mystery which makes me serve the lwa!
(Beauvoir 2008b: 362)	

In his forty-three-year vocation as priest, Marcenat has trained eleven other oungan. The training and initiation of new oungan, manbo, and *ounsi* is part of the oungan's or manbo's livelihood, reputation, and influence. In some cases, a child is cultivated for the priesthood by family members who are priests or priestesses; in other cases, a person discovers her or his calling through personal mystical experiences. In the case of Marcenat, as an *oungan Ginen* he "intuitively" entered the priesthood through his mother, grandparents, and life experience; he was not formally initiated. It is possible for a prepubescent child to attain the priesthood and to employ the *ason*. Individuals who did not inherit the priesthood and its techniques directly through family members must be trained extensively by an oungan or manbo.

Other roles important in temple Vodou include the *oungenikon*, the leader of singing at a Vodou service. The oungenikon has the important role of learning, remembering, and transmitting a temple's repertoire of songs (Laguerre 1980: 34). In a ceremony, the oungenikon sings the first lines, and the *ounsi* initiates join their voices in unison (Métraux 1972: 186–192). Other roles include the *oungenikon katye mèt,* who is responsible for offerings and ritual accessories; the *laplas* (master of ceremonies), who is responsible for proper order and carries a saber, sword, or machete; the *pòt drapo* (flag bearers); the *tanbourinè/ountò* (drummers); and the *ogantye* (cowbell player; see Fleurant 2007: 79). The next song greets the drummers of the *hountò* (large drum) and *hountògi* (midsize drum):

Hountògi yo,	Hountògi drummers,
m ap di n bonswa, ayibobo!	I'm saying good evening to you, ayibobo!
M ape mande Hountò yo,	I'm asking the Hountò drummers,
kòman nou ye?	how are you?
(Beauvoir 2008b: 209)	

The *ounsi* initiates are responsible for assisting the Vodou priest or priestess in the preparations required for a Vodou ceremony. They are the lead singers and dancers at ceremonies: they stand around the *potomitan,* dress in clothes of the same color (white for Rada and colors for Kongo-Petwo), and ensure the right ambiance and energy. The next song's lyrics reflect several of the positions found in Vodou temples:

Manbo a kanpe, li vanyan,	The manbo stands, she is brave,
Hounsi mwen yo kanpe, yo vanyan,	my Hounsi initiates stand, they are brave,
Houndjènikon mwen leve,	my Houndjènikon choir leader rises,
Pòt drap yo leve, leve non.	the flag bearers rise, rise up now.
(Beauvoir 2008b: 209)	

Animal Sacrifice and Offerings to the Lwa

Vodouists serve the lwa by providing offerings in the form of sacrificed animals, food, drinks, perfume, money, and devotion, among other signs.[36] Animal sacrifice is the most important offering because it involves flowing blood and serves as a dramatic demonstration of the interrelationship of life and death. Marcelin's song 163 reveals the importance of flowing animal blood and shows the link between the possessed and the animal in its description of Ogou Feray killing a rooster:

Wòy, wòy!	Oh my, oh my!
Ogou Chango, nèg Feray o!	Ogou Chango, oh man of Feray!
San vèse, Feray, san vèse!	Blood is shed, Feray, blood is shed!
Ogou Feray touye,	Ogou Feray killed,
koklo Feray okon o.	oh Feray's rooster is dead.
N ape ba ou donon,	We will give you food,
Feray o!	oh Feray!
Sanyan, sanyan, sanyan!	Bleeding, bleeding, bleeding!
Gad jan n touye koklo la!	Look how he killed the rooster!
Sanyan, sanyan, sanyan!	Bleeding, bleeding, bleeding!

Lwa require a specific animal for sacrifice. Healthy cows, goats, chickens, guinea fowl, doves, among other animals, are offered to the lwa and are cooked and consumed by the servants of the lwa. The fur or plumage of the animal must correspond with the color tradition of the lwa to which they are offered (see Marcelin 1950a, 1950b; Métraux 1958). Animal blood and flesh are offered to feed, please, and placate the lwa. Flowing blood, the life force of all living animals, symbolizes the power, fragility, and essence of life. Sacrificial animal blood is collected in a *kwi* (calabash bowl), and the priest or priestess traces it to the lips or foreheads of Vodouists (Beauvoir 2008a, 2008b; Breure 2006; Métraux 1958: 156; Rouget 2001).[37] Animal blood is also mixed with other ingredients and cooked for consumption. *Migan,* for example, includes sacrificial blood that is cooked with tubers and other vegetables and is offered to children at Vodou ceremonies. This song for the lwa Ogou Fè describes children drinking *migan* and links the ritual food to consolation:

Frè Tijan, sonje bwè migan,	Brother Tijan, remember to drink migan,
o konsole!	oh be consoled!
Konsole o, timoun yo pral bwè migan an,	Oh be consoled, the children will drink the migan,
Fè, Ogou Fè, Ogou Fè, Ogou Fere.	Fè, Ogou Fè, Ogou Fè, Ogou Fere.
Bwè migan, bwè migan, o konsole!	Drink migan, drink migan, oh be consoled!
(Beauvoir 2008b: 185)	

Raw blood is consumed by those *chwal* possessed by the class of blood-drinking lwa such as Ogou Feray; it is a sign of the lwa's power. According to Marcenat, *dyab* (malicious lwa) also have a predilection for raw animal blood.[38] Historians report that the blood of a sacrificial pig was sipped during the revolutionary Bwa Kayiman ceremony in northern Haiti as part of an oath to fight French slavery and colonialism or to perish in the attempt (Fuertès 1992: 23).[39] Pigs are sacrificed in the Petwo rite but not in the Rada rite, which suggests that the Bwa Kayiman ceremony was a Petwo ceremony (Métraux 1958:

150). The aggressive warrior qualities of the Petwo lwa made them important in the war of independence.

Once an animal is sacrificed, a small portion is buried or scattered outside for the lwa, and the rest is cooked. Roumain's song 8 captures the digging of a "feeding hole" for the lwa Olicha Ogoun Chango:

Twou a, twou a,	The hole, the hole,
Olicha, n ap ofri w.	Olicha, we're offering to you.
N ape fouye twou Olicha.	We're digging a hole for Olicha.
Pou nou fouye twou Olicha	We must dig a hole for Olicha
pou nou ba li manje.	so that we can give him food.
N ape fouye twou Ogoun	We are digging the hole of Ogoun
pou nou ba li manje.	so that we can give him food.
N ape fouye twou Chango.	We are digging the hole of Chango.
Twou a, o twou a,	The hole, oh the hole,
twou Olicha.	the hole of Olicha.
Abobo!	Abobo!

A share of the cooked meat is for the lwa who is being honored in the ceremony. That lwa possesses one or more Vodouists and eats first, then distributes the food among those present. The lwa honored will bless the food and feed it to other practitioners. The lion's share of a sacrificed animal is for the community. Animal sacrifice and related songs and rituals render a feast sacred and align the community with the lwa who protect them and the animals that nourish them. Animal sacrifice is the heart of Vodou ritual and feasting.

Vodou Musicians and Instruments and Their Reflection in Songs

To gain insight into the songs, it is important to grasp some basic aspects of Vodou music. Traditional Vodou music is fundamentally vocal and percussive, but other instruments may be used. In *rasin* (roots or Vodou pop) music, traditional and electric instruments are used.[40] There one finds guitars, violins, banjos, accordions, synthesizers, and drum kits, in addition to traditional drums. In traditional Vodou music, the song *calls* the lwa whose presence is desired and explains what is expected of the lwa. The playing of rhythm instruments serves the function of *insisting on* the appearance of the lwa because it encourages dance, trance, and triggers possession (Comhaire-Sylvain 1951: 65). In describing the instruments, I start with the *ason* because it intertwines fundamental musical and symbolic properties in Vodou religion.

The *ason* is a small calabash gourd covered with a latticework of multicolored porcelain beads that are strung together with snake vertebrae. It is a rhythm instrument but also the means by which oungan and manbo call forth or placate the lwa, who are both encouraged and frightened by it because it can summon them or send them away (Brown 2006: 12). The *ason* is also used to bless Vodouists and ceremonies. When two or more oungan or manbo greet formally in a ceremony, the *ason* are employed in elaborate "mirroring" rituals.[41] The *hunsògo* or *asògò* used in the Vodou of Benin is likewise covered with snake vertebrae (Brand 2000b: 18; Rouget 2001: 18). The snake vertebrae represent Danbala Wèdo, the serpent lwa. The *ason* is also said to be the *lang Danbala* (tongue of Danbala). When the *ason* is shaken, it produces a sound that counterbalances the cadence of the *ogan* (iron cowbell). The *ason* is thus not only a musical instrument but also a sacred and ritual object. Oungan, manbo, bòkò, oungenikon, and laplas are the only members of the Vodou community who have the authority to use the *ason*. The *ason* can be used to trace kabalistic patterns in the air or shaken to communicate with the lwa or the oungenikon (Comhaire-Sylvain 1951: 65). Marcelin's song 158 describes how the *ason* that belongs to the healing lwa Osanj is borrowed by the oungan or manbo who serves him to *heal* a patient. Thus, the oungan or manbo's ason, the lwa, and herbal medicine are intimately involved in healing:

Osanj o! lese koule Mèt Osanj.	Oh Osanj! Let it be Master Osanj.
O lese koule!	Oh let it be!
Yo pran ason Osanj sèvi gerizon.	They take Osanj's rattle in order to heal.
O lese koule!	Oh let it be!
Yo pran badji Osanj sèvi gerizon.	They take Osanj's altar to use for healing.
O lese koule Mèt Osanj!	Oh let it be Master Osanj!
Osanj o! Lese koule, Mèt Osanj!	Oh Osange! Let it be, Master Osanj!

J.L.'s song 82 shows the ritual power of the *ason* to call forth the lwa and it reflects hereditary Vodou:

Lafanmi o,	Oh my kith and kin,
an n rasanble nan demanbre a,	let's assemble for the family's Vodou ceremony,
n pral fè seremoni an.	we're going to do the service.
Limen balenn nan—o an n rele lwa yo.	Light the candle—oh let's call the lwa.
Sonnen ason an—rele Papa Legba.	Shake the rattle—call Papa Legba.
Nan kafou a, o nou angaje.	At the crossroad, oh we're in trouble.
Papa Legba—louvri baryè pou lwa yo.	Papa Legba—open the gate for the lwa.

In addition to the *ason,* Vodou priests use the *klochèt* (bell) and the *siflèt* (whistle) to communicate with the lwa, the musicians, and the singers (Comhaire-Sylvain 1951: 66).

Vodou songs are accompanied by drumming, dancing, and possessions. J.L.'s song 97 celebrates the influence of drumming on dance and worship and describes the lighting of a candle at the base of the drum as a sign of respect:

Rasin sa se nan san nou l ye;	This root is right in our blood;
depi tanbou frape, tout moun leve danse.	as soon as drums beat, everyone gets up to dance.
Men rasin sa, m pral limen	Here are these roots, oh I'm going to light
yon balenn nan pye w o.	a candle at your feet.

Rada and Kongo-Petwo ceremonies are associated with overlapping and distinct rhythmic traditions that display significant complexity. Rada rhythms include *yanvalou, twarigòl, mayi,* and *zepòl,* while Kongo-Petwo rhythms include *kita sèch, kita mouye, boumba,* and *kongo sosyete* (Fleurant 2007). The Kongo-Petwo rhythms and corresponding dances are fast and aggressive. Similarly, the Kongo-Petwo lwa are more excitable than the Rada lwa and will go to greater lengths on behalf of their followers. Often special rhythms are linked to lwa, such as the triple beat of the Marasa Dosou Dosa, which mirrors the siblings who are the Marasa (Divine Twins) and the Dosou (male infant) or Dosa (female infant) born subsequently. Some rhythms, like the ubiquitous *yanvalou,* accompany an assortment of lwa. Vodou drumming is a "vibration" that helps call forth the lwa and "speaks the language of the lwa" (Fleurant 2007: 82–83). Marcelin's song 63 shows the role of drums in calling the lwa—in this case, Nouvèl:

Nouvèl o! Nouvèl o!	Oh Nouvèl! Oh Nouvèl!
Tanbou Vodou m rele Nouvèl o!	Oh my Vodou drums call Nouvèl!

The tightly organized, syncopated, and multilayered percussion in Vodou helps to induce trance and possession. At the same time, possession also occurs in the absence of music.[42]

Drums in the Rada rite include the big *oun,* the medium *ountò,* and the small *ountòki.* The *oun* is more commonly called the *manman tanbou* (mother drum) in Haitian Creole. The *manman* is played with one bare hand and a stick in the other hand, and it punctuates dance movements with its deep resonation. The *ountò,* also called the *segon* (second), and the *ountògi,* also called the *boula,* are both played with two sticks—one straight, and one curved—and produce a continuous and regular rhythmic pattern (Fleurant 2006b: 52,

2007: 79). *Ountò* refers to the drum, the drummer, and the lwa of drums, and all three are praised:

Rele Hountò nou, Ladogwesan,	Call our drummer, followers of the Heritage,
Hountò mwen solid o!	oh my drummer is strong!
M di Hountò Ogou Badagri,	I say Drummer of Ogou Badagri,
Hountò a ye,	let the Drummer be,
rele Hountò a, Ladogwesan.	call the Drummer, followers of the Heritage.
(Beauvoir 2008b: 211)	

The tall *asòtò* drum still exists in a few ounfò in Haiti.[43] Some of the songs from Roumain (1943) in this volume describe the rituals and liturgy associated with the *asòtò* drum and lwa. Roumain's song 1 addresses the Vodou priest's baptism of the *asòtò* drum, the primacy of God, and the origin of the drum and its lwa in Ginen. The inclusion of the Catholic Trinitarian formula in French in line 5 adds power to the *asòtò*:

Asòtò, Micho.	Asòtò, Micho.
N ape rele Jan.	We are calling Jean.
Jan Asòtò, n ape rele	Jean Asòtò, we are calling
pou nou batize tanbou Asòtò.	for you to baptize the Asòtò drum.
Dye le Pè, Dye le Fis, Dye le Sent Espri.	God the Father, God the Son, God the Holy Spirit.
Apre Bondye, m ap batize.	After God, I'm baptizing.
Ou sòti nan Ginen,	You come from Ginen,
ou vini wè kreyòl la yo.	you come to see the Creoles.
Nou kontan wè Asòtò Micho.	We are happy to see Asòtò Micho.
M ap batize Asòtò.	I'm baptizing Asòtò.

Drums, *ogan* (cowbells), and *ason* have many "mystical secrets within them" and form a "theological addition" because they help Vodouists relate with the lwa. The deep tones of the *manman tanbou* drum help dissolve the resistance between the Vodouist and the lwa, while the *kase* (rhythmic break) opens the way for the appearance of the lwa (Fleurant 2007: 80). The lwa love drumming; hence, a priest or priestess may trace a vèvè in the drums' honor and sprinkle them with sacrificial blood. The *ounsi* bow and kiss the earth in front of them (Métraux 1958: 163; Rouget 2001).

The drums are made from hollowed-out tree trunks. In Rada rites, they are covered with *po bèf* (cowskin), and in Kongo-Petwo rites, they are covered with *po kabrit* (goatskin). The securing of the skins with stakes is a Rada tradition, while the use of tension cords is a Kongo-Petwo tradition (Fleurant 2007: 80). Hard woods are used for Rada drums, while soft ones are used for Kongo-Petwo. The Rada and Kongo rites use three drums, and the Petwo rite uses two, referred to as the *ti baka* (little goblin) and the *gwo baka* (big goblin; Métraux 1958: 162). Bigger ceremonies have several drums. Vodou music, drumming, and rhythm are critical for the practice of the religion and the maintenance of balance with the lwa and nature (Courlander 1939; Dauphin 1986; Fleurant 1996, 2007; Wilcken 1992). For example, Marcelin's song 111 shows how drumming and the practice of Vodou can be linked to rainfall:[44]

Mwen se nèg Nago.	I am a Nago[45] man.
Tout tan tanbou Nago pa bat	As long as the Nago drum isn't beaten
lapli p ap tonbe!	the rain will not fall!
Mwen se nèg Nago!	I am a Nago man!

The *ogan* is used to keep the tempo by the *ogantye* (player of the cowbell; Fleurant 2007: 79). The *ogan* has a long mouth and a short mouth, which are struck with wooden sticks. In the past, there were blacksmiths who produced the traditional iron cowbells used in Vodou instrumentation. The different-size mouths produce different sounds and are struck alternately to create rhythmic variation. The original *ogan* has become less common, and in its place any two pieces of iron or even a glass bottle and a wooden drumstick can be used (Fleurant 2006b, 2007). Boulton's song 1 shows the importance of an ensemble of percussionists for the invocation of the lwa—in this case, Ayida Wèdo and her husband, Danbala Wèdo:

Wèdo, rele Wèdo ey.	Wèdo, hey, call Wèdo.
Wèdo gade Wèdo ey.	Wèdo, hey look at Wèdo.
N a prale wè yo.	We are going to see them.
Si n a dakò, Wèdo wè mwen.	If we shall be agreed, Wèdo sees me.
Laplas,	Master of ceremonies,
rele ogantye.	call the cowbell player.
Segondye rele boulaye.	The segondye drummer calls the boula drummer.
Boulaye,	Boula drummer,
pale ak manman tanbou a pou mwen.	talk with the mother drum for me.

Musicians provide the foundation for Vodou ritual and worship, and many songs show the recognition and respect they receive.

The Origin of Vodou Songs

The song texts of African religions in the Americas, such as those in Haiti, Cuba, Trinidad, and Brazil, have been published and analyzed only in recent times (Beauvoir 2008a, 2008b; Jil and Jil 2009; Marcelin 1950a, 1950b; Mason 1992; Roumain 1943; Verger 1999). In the English language, aside from

Laguerre (1980), few researchers have systematically gathered, translated, and interpreted a corpus of Vodou songs. In some New World traditions where songs are preserved in Yorùbá, Fon, Ewe, Kikongo, Kimbundu, or a mixture of languages, translation and interpretation require extensive multilingual and cultural specialization. In the case of Haiti, most songs are in Haitian Creole; however, significant West African language fragments and phrases are also used.[46] The frequent occurrence of *langaj* in Vodou songs shows that many were transmitted during the French colonial period (c. 1660–1803) when African languages were widely spoken. Much more work on numerous African languages is needed to better understand *langaj* in Haitian Vodou songs.

Songs are taught to people by the lwa and by other people.[47] They are revealed by the lwa so that their servants can best please them. The singing of songs invites the appearance of the lwa. Some songs are the creations of Vodouists who are inspired by aspects of the lwa. Others are revealed by the lwa through possession, trance, or dream. These revelations are discussed in homes and temples, and other practitioners are then taught the song. Sometimes a lwa will possess a horse and teach the congregation a new song about herself or himself. The songs can be sung to induce possession, to attain a spiritual state of mind, or for recreation and relaxation.

As Haitians move to the towns and cities, new songs emerge in those destinations as individuals integrate into new communities. By sharing songs and traditions, new members of the community create a niche for the lwa and traditions of their ancestors. The visits of friends and family to temples and domestic *demanbre* celebrations in various regions of Haiti also help diffuse songs.

The Content and Characteristics of Vodou Songs

Vodou songs have meanings that reflect material, philosophical, and mythological dimensions of the religion. Their content expresses Vodou theology, culture, and social structure (Carvalho 2008: 416). Sacred songs capture the poetic and musicological imagination of people; they reflect the spirit of their creators and deserve preservation and study (Carvalho 2008: 426). Vodou songs, like those of other African religions in the Americas, have a compressed structure and a coded message (Carvalho 2008: 426; Mason 1992; Verger 1999). They tell compact and cryptic stories and parables about the lwa and their servants. They have elliptical qualities that increase when the author or circumstances of the song are unknown (Laguerre 1980: 32). Their literary features may include rhyme, allusion, simile, alliteration, double entendre, allegory, onomatopoeia, reiteration, exclamation, invocation, prayer, chant, and dialogue. They include proverbs, parables, sayings, fixed expressions, spells, historical memories, esoteric knowledge, charms, West African language phrases, magical formulas, greeting formulas, leave-taking messages, blessings, curses, signs, oracles, praise, warnings, admonitions, comparisons, cosmologies, and relationships. Metaphor, epithet (e.g., calling the lwa Bawon Samdi *mèt simityè* [master of the cemetery]), enigmatic discourse, and defensive or confrontational rhetoric can be found in songs. The songs express emotions that pertain to the traditions of the lwa they address: love, fear, awe, violence, energy, jubilation, admiration, and respect (Laguerre 1980: 32). The lyrics express the view that all in Vodou is generated by and dependent on God (Mason 1992: 4, 182). Hierophanies or breakthroughs of the sacred, lyricism, moral guidance, paradoxes, rapturous emotion, and trance-inducing repetition mark the songs (Carvalho 2008: 426).

Vodou songs provide unique insight into the mythology of the lwa (Laguerre 1980: 29–30). The songs describe their personalities, their names, and what they appreciate and abhor, and they explain what the lwa's functions are (e.g., healing the sick, waging war, protection at sea, preparation for and acceptance of death, the creation of life, obtaining of prosperity, preservation of nature, fruitful farming, success in love). The songs can point out the color associated with the lwa (e.g., red and blue for Ogou and Èzili Dantò, black and purple for Gede, white for Danbala and Ayida). The next song for the serpent lwa Danbala reveals his enjoyment of sweet syrup:

Danbala, men lwa koulèv la ye,	Danbala, here is the snake lwa yeah,
Danbala, men lwa koulèv la, ba li siwo!	Danbala, here is the snake lwa, give him syrup!

Songs describe the families, friends, lovers, and relationships of the lwa. The lwa are referred to using kinship terms such as Papa Legba (Father Legba), Manman Brijit (Mother Brijit), Grann Èzili (Granny Èzili), and Kouzen Zaka (Cousin Zaka). The songs often maintain the ethnic and geographic origin of the lwa (e.g., Danwomen, Ibo, Kongo, Mede, Nago), and they convey their nature and characteristics. Vodou songs also speak about people and their needs and aspirations. They shed light on the congregation's experiences and history. Songs also refer to plants, trees, animals, and weather and draw from Haiti's agrarian and working-class cultures. Vodou songs simultaneously reflect the diversity and unity of the religion.

The Functions of Vodou Songs

The functions of Vodou songs are diverse (Laguerre 1980: 30–31). The songs educate people about the lwa and the nature of the religion. They have a liturgical function in the way they signal which phase a ceremony is traversing. The number and order of lwa and their respective songs are known prior to ceremonies: twenty-one, twenty-nine, or some other number of lwa may be evoked in cycles of three songs. Rhythm and songs create an atmosphere conducive to worship and the appearance of the lwa. Vodou songs are an expression of jubilation, and singing in chorus cements community unity. The singing of songs eliminates stress and purifies the mind. Vodou ceremonies, songs, and drumming occur in a relaxed and free ambiance that may include playing children, the drinking of alcohol, smoking, chatting, laughing, eating, and joyous and enthusiastic interactions. Haitian culture often weds formality to informality, and the Vodou setting exemplifies this with the precision and seriousness of ritual around the *potomitan* (center post [priests and priestesses, choir leader, singers, musicians]) and a rapturous audience around the periphery.

The Classification of Vodou Songs

Vodou songs can be classified into various types, genres, and themes. One way to look at them is to determine the role they play in ceremonies (Carvalho 2008: 431; Comhaire-Sylvain 1951: 61–87). Songs of *preparation* are sung to assure the lwa that their servants are dedicated or to prepare for distinct phases of ritual. Songs of *invocation* (i.e., *rele lwa* [calling the lwa] are sung to obtain the protection of specific lwa and to invite them to appear. Songs of *response* and *prayer* are sung once the lwa have possessed one or more Vodouists. Songs of response and prayer can be further classified into songs of demand, offering, thanksgiving, praise, criticism of the lwa, magic, and litany, which involves invocations and responses (Laguerre 1980: 33). Songs of *leave-taking* or *farewell* are sung when a lwa has overstayed her or his welcome or if it is feared that the temporarily departed soul of the possessed Vodouist, the ti bonnanj, has gone astray. In addition to these classifications, *booms* are cyclical songs reserved for special ceremonies that are held only once every seven years (Laguerre 1980: 33). Another way to classify Vodou songs is by their focus on the families of lwa and human-lwa interactions, which include songs of preparation and leave-taking (Laguerre 1980; Wilcken 1992: 94).

In the Rada rite, the songs of preparation are accompanied by rhythms such as *rada* or *yanvalou,* and dance steps involve bent knees and movements of the shoulders. The *rada* or *yanvalou* are calm and purifying dances that lead to the appearance of the lwa in a horse. In the next preparation song, Atibon Legba is asked to open the gate for the lwa:

Atibon Legba, louvri bayè pou mwen. Ago e!
Papa Legba, louvri bayè pou mwen.
Louvri bayè pou m kapab rantre.
Lò m a tounen, m a salouye lwa yo. Abobo.
(Comhaire-Sylvain 1951: 66)

Atibon Legba, open the gate for me. Ago hey!
Papa Legba, open the gate for me.
Open the gate so that I can come in.
When I return, I will greet the lwa. Abobo!

Songs of invocation are sung accompanied by a wide range of rhythms, which are selected according to the lwa called on or the type of ceremony under way. Rhythm types include *vodoun dawome, rada, nago, ibo, mayi, petwo kouran, kita chèch, moudong, yanvalou,* and *kongo fran* (Wilcken 1992). All present may dance, except to rhythms dedicated to Danbala, which are for only the oungan or manbo (Comhaire-Sylvain 1951: 66). Generally, the dancing is collective and not in pairs. The text below illustrates a song of invocation sung for Agwe, lwa of the sea:

Mèt Agwe, kote ou ye?	Master Agwe, where are you?
Ou pa wè mwen nan resif?	Don't you see that I am having difficulty?
Agwe Woyo, kote ou ye?	Agwe Woyo, where are you?
Ou pa wè mwen sou lanmè?	Don't you see that I am at sea?
Zaviwon yo nan men mwen.	The paddles are in my hands.
M pa sa tounen dèyè,	I cannot turn back,
m deja douvan,	I'm already out to sea,
m pa sa tounen dèyè.	I cannot turn back.
(Comhaire-Sylvain 1951: 67)	

In songs of response, the lwa expresses herself or himself through the voice of the person who is being ridden while the audience repeats the lwa's lines. The next song is part of a dialogue in which the audience is informed that a lwa different from the one expected is riding the horse:

Ogoun pa la, se mwen ki la.	Ogoun isn't here, it's me who is here.
Ogoun pa la. Chen an mòde mwen.	Ogoun isn't here. The dog bit me.
Ogoun pa la, se mwen Sobo.	Ogoun isn't here, it's me Sobo.
Ki fè chen an mòde w?	Who made the dog bite you?
Se mwen Sobo.	It's me Sobo.
(Comhaire-Sylvain 1951: 67)	

In the song of response below, Ogoun protests being forgotten by the audience:

Depi tan m la,	I have been here a long time,
depi tan m la, Ogoun Badagri,	I have been here a long time, Ogou Badagri,
mwen di nou lage mwen.	I say you forgot me.
Depi tan m la,	Since the time I have been here,
se kòd ki mare kòd.	it is rope that ties rope.
Depi tan m la,	I have been here for ages,
yo pa konnen mwen se Ogoun,	they don't know I'm Ogoun,
depi tan m la.	I have been here for ages.
(Comhaire-Sylvain 1951: 67–68)	

Many songs of response are accompanied by symbolic dances that are unique to specific lwa. For example, when Agwe, the lwa of the sea, possesses a follower, the horse can sing a response while performing a *dans Agwe* (Agwe dance), which involves arm movements that evoke the movement of waves or, for the lwa Danbala, a *yanvalou,* which involves a serpentine flow in the spine and neck (Comhaire-Sylvain 1951: 68).

Prayers sing praise to or beseech the lwa who has appeared. Prayers may complain of tragic events or misfortunes and they can beg the lwa for help. The next song is a prayer asking Bawon Samdi, lwa of the cemetery, for his support in farming:

Bawon Samdi, ride mwen.	Bawon Samdi, help me.
Lè m ap plante, ride mwen, Bawon Samdi.	When I'm planting, help me, Bawon Samdi.
Ride mwen lò m ap plante.	Help me when I'm planting.
Jou grenn nan leve,	The day the seed rises,
Bawon Samdi, ride mwen.	Bawon Samdi, help me.
Lò m ap plante, ride mwen,	When I'm planting, help me,
genyen mwen pou wou. Abobo.	my gain is for you. Abobo.
(Comhaire-Sylvain 1951: 68)	

Marcelin's song 129 illustrates the leave-taking or farewell song in its request for the departure of Ogou Badagri:

Tanpèt mare, lanmè move!	The storm is raging, the sea is troubled!
Ogou Badagri o se nèg politik!	Oh Ogou Badagri is a politician!
Glise koule, glise ale, fè wout ou!	Slip away, slip away, be on your way!
Ogou Badagri se nèg politik o!	Oh Ogou Badagri is a politician!

Likewise, the next song appears to request the departure of Gede Mazaka. Note that the mischievous Gede lwa have a reputation for coming late to a ceremony and overstaying their welcome:

Gede Mazaka, n ap kite won an ba yo!	Gede Mazaka, you're leaving the round for them!
Mazaka, ala yon Lwa ki rèd se Mazaka.	Mazaka, what a tough Lwa is Mazka.
(Beauvoir 2008b: 190)	

Songs reflect many domains within Vodou culture. They are dedicated to the lwa and the people in the Vodou community. They memorialize historical figures, ancestors, the living, and ritual objects such as the *ason,* machetes, candles, water, perfume, flags, drums, flour, and vèvè tracings. They address community matters or connect to historical events. Marcelin's song 23, for example, identifies the Emperor Dessalines, Haiti's first leader, and the lwa Loko and Agasou with the Vodou ounfò:

O Loko-De.
Lanperè Desalin o!
O kle ounfò a nan men nou.
Kle ounfò a nan men Agasou-miwa.
Kle ounfò a nan men nou.

Oh Loko-De.
Oh Emperor Dessalines!
Oh the temple's keys are in your hands.
The temple's keys are in the hands of Agasou-mirror.
The temple's keys are in your hands.

The next song, also for Dessalines, captures his quest to establish Haiti as a refuge for the black race and links him with the lwa Jan Pyè Ibo.[48]

Jan Pyè Ibo, Lanperè Desalin o!
Peyi sa pa pou blan,
peyi sa a se pou nèg li ye, tande.
(Beauvoir 2008b: 168)

Jan Pyè Ibo, oh Emperor Dessalines!
This country is not for whites,
this country is for blacks, you hear.

The inventories and diffusion of Vodou songs geographically have scarcely been studied (see Beauvoir 2008b; Marcelin 1950a, 1950b; Métraux 1958). Many Vodou songs enjoy wide diffusion across Haiti, which suggests that they belong to an old repertoire; others are known only locally. A significant local event may cause individuals or communities to create new songs with references to shared experience. The next song, from Beauvoir's temple, illustrates the expression of warning through music. It may refer to the appearance of a powerful lwa or an individual who is present at the *demanbre*:

Lakou a gen danje, adje!
Lakou sa a, gen danje nan demanbre.
E lakou sa a gen danje o,
lakou Bovwa a gen danje o!
(Beauvoir 2008b: 235)

The yard is dangerous, oh no!
This yard, there is danger in the ceremony.
Hey this yard is oh so dangerous,
oh Beauvoir's yard is dangerous!

A fair number of the songs in this volume are *chante pwen* (songs of reproach or satire) that express messages of correction, advice, self-defense, and criticism. Like other songs in J.L.'s collection, song 19 expresses frustration with a group of critical and unsavory individuals:

Gran Bwa e, men moun;
yo rayi mwen o, sa m fè yo?
M pa manje nan men yo;
m pa bwè dlo lakay yo.
Amwa, m Gran Bwa,
m deja Gran Bwa nan kò m.
Mwen konnen yo; m ap fout viv avè yo.

Hey Gran Bwa, here are the people,
oh they abhor me, what did I do to them?
I don't eat among them;
I don't drink water at their home.
As for me, I'm Gran Bwa,
I am already Gran Bwa in my body.
I know them; I'm fucking living with them.

The next *chante pwen* criticizes two-faced practitioners who disparage Vodou and yet turn to it in hard times:

Kou yo malad o,	Oh as soon as they're sick,
yo kouri kay Nago sa a!	they run to that Nago house!
Kou w wè gerizon yo, Nago se demon e.	When you see their recovery, hey Nago is a demon.
Nago se demon, Achade, Nago se demon e.	Nago is a demon, Achade, hey Nago is a demon.
Nago se satan, Achade, Nago se demon e.	Nago is satan, Achade, hey Nago is a demon.
Kou yo malad y al kay Achade,	When they're sick they go to Achade's house,
yo kouri kay Achade.	they run to Achade's house.
Kou w wè gerizon yo, li se demon e.	When you see they have healed, hey, he is a demon.
(Beauvoir 2008b: 227)	

The next *chante pwen* reflects the struggle of *houngan* healers in a world where hospitals and Western medical science constantly grow in prestige and legitimacy:

Makaya o, se pa vre,	Oh Makaya, it isn't true,
Makaya o, se pa vre!	Oh Makaya, it isn't true!
Timoun mouri nan lopital,	Children die in the hospital,
se pa janm lapenn.	it's never a pain.
Depi l mouri nan men Houngan,	If she dies in the hands of the Houngan,
se peche vre!	it's a real sin!
(Beauvoir 2008b: 285)	

The song reveals the risks and disappointments faced by traditional healers who attempt to treat the sick in a world where Western medicine is idealized. Of course, no Vodou priest or priestess opposes Western medicine, but access to it is limited, and people thus must seek out traditional healers (Jil and Jil 2009: 298–299).

The Interpretation and Transmission of Vodou Songs

The point of view in many Vodou songs is subtle. Vodou songs express "cryptic tricksterism," which involves the expression of multiple meanings, points of view, and interpretations (Brown 1987: 74). The lyrics may be the words of the congregation or they may be the words of the lwa, and the point of view can switch within a single song. In the song below, the lwa asserts that maturity and respect are required for his appearance:

Onè, onè o lamezon, anye!	Honor, oh honor to the house, oh yeah!
Si se granmoun ki la, m a rantre!	If adults are here, I'll come in!
Si se timoun ki la a, m a vire do m, m ale!	If children are here, I'll turn my back and go!
(Beauvoir 2008b: 345)	

The shortness and repetition of Vodou songs help reinforce central notions, promote memorization, and, through their circularity, trigger possession.[49] The Vodou song is typically built out of one or two verses with a brief chorus, if there is any chorus at all. Many lines are repeated, and variant words or lines are incrementally added. The compactness of Vodou songs mirrors Vodou's typology and the oral culture from which it arises (Beauvoir 2008b). Others suggest that the economy and concision of Vodou songs gives the priest or priestess the flexibility to use them according to the phase of ritual being traversed in a ceremony (Wilcken 1992: 98).

Vodou songs are the method adapted to Haitian culture for the expression of Vodou's "articulated thought" (Beauvoir 2008b: 14). Vodou songs express in a "simple and coherent manner conceptions that are cosmological, theological, and anthropological" (Beauvoir 2008b: 13). Vodou songs are the embodiment of Haiti's sacred literature; gasping them requires experience, reflection, and regular study.[50] Becoming initiated and practicing Vodou is the original and ancient way to enter and interpret the religion. Scholars should also employ exegetical methods and cross-religious and cultural comparison to analyze Vodou songs. Some songs are obscure or symbolic on a local level; time, perseverance, and patience are therefore needed to appreciate their meanings.

The two main spheres of transmission are the public temple and the private household. In temple-based Vodou, it is the role of the oungenikon and the priest or priestess to remember and disseminate songs. It is common that oungenikon and *ounsi* initiates in the choir receive songs from the lwa or create them and then introduce them at ceremonies (Métraux 1972: 187). Thereafter, the new songs may diffuse into other temples through visits and migration. Some songs originate as *chante pwen,* which are improvised by a participant at a ceremony (Métraux 1972: 188; Richman 2007, 2008). If the song is exceptional, the *ounsi* choir will pick up the melody and memorize the words. In future appearances of the lwa, the *ounsi* will sing the new song to whom they are dedicated.

Recruitment of other singers into the choir—and initiates into the temple—guarantees the continuity of tradition.[51] Vodou singers need to practice, memorize, and create material. Participation through singing is an important part of Vodou, and over time the members of a congregation will acquire the majority of important songs. Many children who participate in ceremonies also learn songs intuitively through experience rather than explicitly through initiation or study. When an oungenikon dies, a knowledgeable successor replaces her or him.

In domestic Vodou, the role of singing and remembering is maintained by one or more members of the family. J.L.'s collection in this volume contains many songs that originated in his household or are his personal creations. The songs indicate that he received this tradition from his mother and other members of his household. Those with knowledge work with inheritors who in turn preserve tradition and transmit it through their eventual family line. Individuals within the extended family of the *lakou* share a common repertoire in addition to individual repertoires gathered through experiences outside the *lakou.* The content and nature of the repertoires depend on the relationships the ancestors and the inheritors of the *lakou* have with the lwa. Song traditions are influenced by the integration of new family members through marriage, for example.

Naturally, some songs disappear or change over time.[52] The death of a temple member will sometimes result in the loss of songs as the protector lwa of the deceased will not necessarily be retained by the community. However, in November, when the ancestral dead are remembered in Haiti, many songs that have fallen into disuse once again surface in honor of the dead. Alterations may occur in songs because participants cannot hear the lyrics over the thunder of drumming. Furthermore, words or lines may be forgotten, and new words may be added to fill the gap or to embellish or clarify a text. Over the generations, songs may become incomprehensible and thus undergo alterations to increase relevance. New members may bring better-preserved versions of related songs into a community. No control is exerted over alterations, and participants are able to make them according to their knowledge, experience, and needs. The repertoire of songs in Vodou is organic in that it lives, reproduces, grows, ages, decays, dies, and is reborn through endless creative cycles. The repertoire of songs evolves as individuals reanalyze existing material, create new content, experience new revelations from the lwa, migrate to new communities, or pass away.

Songs are the cornerstone of worship and the foundation of memory in Vodou. Until the twentieth century, their transmission was mostly oral. Courlander (1939–1940), Roumain (1943), Jaegerhuber (1950), Marcelin (1950a, 1950b), Rigaud (1953), Price-Mars (1956), Laguerre (1980), Beauvoir (2008a, 2008b), Jil and Jil (2009), and this volume, among others, transmit songs through writing. In the course of textualization, Vodou is emerging as another "religion of the book"—or, more accurately, a religion of *books,* since the revelation of the lwa is living and cannot be reduced or closed into a *single* holy book. The great beauty of books is their ability to show people who did not inherit the tradition the towering contributions of the "African wing of the great family of humanity" (Jil and Jil 2009: 371).

Conclusion

My goal in this chapter has been to investigate basic aspects of the Vodou religion and culture to prepare readers for the songs and the details in Appendix A: Dictionary of Vodou Terms. I acknowledge the limits of my knowledge and experience, and I admit that I have only scratched the surface of this Caribbean and African religion. Readers in search of more depth will find it in the songs of this volume, in the appendixes, in the references and, most important, in the fellowship of Vodou oungan, bòkò, manbo, and initiates.

Authors who write about Vodou in English generally have pursued a research and publishing paradigm that emphasizes representing, analyzing, and commenting on the religion. There has been little investment in the systematic collection of *source texts* in Vodou's actual language, Haitian Creole, and their translation into English. Vodou lexicography has also been restricted to short glossaries. This book brings the latest linguistic methodologies to the writing down of Vodou sacred literature. Linguistic approaches include our sketch of Haitian Creole grammar, the orthographical modernization of all texts in the standard spelling of Haitian Creole, their translation, and the lexicographical and etymological research in the Dictionary of Vodou Terms.

Commentaries on Buddhism, Christianity, Islam, and Judaism, among other religions, are difficult to imagine without the in-depth consideration of sacred texts. Besides Courlander (1939–1940, 1960), Laguerre (1980) or Gilles and Gilles (2009), few scholars have attempted to collect or analyze a full corpus of original oral or written Vodou texts in a systematic way. This lacuna stands out even more when one considers the sheer volume of published Vodou documents that exists in Haitian Creole. This project represents fifteen years of collecting songs. The recording, transcription, and translation of Vodou materials will provide the public with a fresh understanding of the religion because the perspective of the practitioner is prioritized. Several thousand Vodou songs still need orthographical modernization (Courlander 1939–1940; Rigaud 1953; Laguerre 1980) or translation into English (Beauvoir 2008a, 2008b). The rich and living oral corpora of Haitian Vodou remain largely uncollected and unexamined. This book begins to fill the gap by preserving and disseminating several hundred original Haitian Creole texts, by providing English translations, and by including scholarly support chapters. Our objective is for this work to provide a multifaceted source and reference to readers from a wide array of research disciplines and backgrounds.

This volume provides the means to expand and improve research on Vodou and Haitian Creole. Our fusion of the Vodouist perspective and the scholarly perspective marries the illustration and defense of Vodou and Haitian Creole to its interpretation and analysis. This project is the latest of several books we have published that provide Haitian Creole alongside English and French. The Haitian community and students of Haiti benefit greatly from the availability of bilingual or trilingual books that use a side-by-side format as they provide the means for the accelerated study of the respective languages and cultures (see Hebblethwaite and Pierre 2001, 2005, 2010). We hope that the songs, texts, and scholarship published here will serve as an entryway to the deep contemplation and examination of the ancient and modern Vodou religion and the beautiful Haitian Creole language that soars with it.

CHAPTER 2

Historical Songs

THIS CHAPTER begins with two versions of the famous *Lapriyè Boukmann* (Boukmann's Prayer), which the Vodou priest Boukmann Dutty is said to have uttered on the eve of the Bwa Kayiman ceremony on August 14, 1791. Whether the text is faithful to Boukmann's actual words or has been expanded by oral tradition or a single author, *Lapriyè Boukmann* stands out as an extraordinary document. The theological orientation closely reflects Vodou thought. There is one true Bondje (God), who is good, the Bondje of Vodou. Like the lwa, Bondje is closely associated with nature. There is also a Bondje blan (white God), who is cruel and criminal. The crimes of the white God's followers require vengeance. The practice and images of the white God should be cast away. The religious, political, and military positions of the text likely reflect Haitian Vodouist thinking of the revolutionary period.

Lapriyè Boukmann clearly shows the slaves' frustration with life in the colony. The white God is identified as *the* major obstacle to *libète* (freedom). The fact that the text considers the religion of Europeans to be the enemy of African slaves suggests that a Vodou priest was the source of the document. The deep antagonisms reflected in it seem inevitable, considering the historical situation. Boukmann's racial and religious polarization was essentially part of his military strategy. Today, most modern Haitians do not view Catholicism and Vodou as strictly racial, even if some racial associations remain.

Chan lagè (War Song) is undated but is probably from the Haitian revolutionary period. The war is described in the future, which suggests that the song was sung to encourage valiant fighting. Today in Vodou, the term *nanchon* refers to a Vodou rite or tradition associated with a specific place in West

Africa—that is, *nanchon Rada* (Dahomian traditions), *nanchon Nago* (Yorùbá traditions), or *nanchon Kongo* (Kongo traditions). In this song, however, the *nanchon* are amalgamated as "war nations."

The final song, *Batay la angaje* (The Battle Continues), is a modern text. I include it in this chapter because it provides an overview of some of the main historical challenges that Vodou has faced since Haiti won its independence from France.

Chante istorik

Lapriyè Boukmann

Bondje ki fè solèy
ki klere nou anwo,
ki souleve lanmè,
ki fè gwonde loray.
Bondje la, zòt tande, kache nan yon nyay,
e la a, li gade nou,
li wè tou sa blan an fè.
Bondje blan an mande krim
e pa nou vle byenfè.
Men Dje pa nou an ki si bon
òdonnen nou vanjans.
Li va kondui bra nou,
Li va ban n asistans.
Jete pòtre Dje blan an
ki swaf dlo nan je nou.
Koute lalibète
ki pale nan kè nou tout.
(Beauvoir 2008a: 44)

Historical Songs

Boukmann's Prayer

God who created the sun
that shines on us from above,
who raises the sea,
who makes thunder rumble.
God is there, you hear, hidden in a cloud,
and there, he looks at us,
he sees all that the whites do.
The white God asks for crimes
and ours wants good deeds.
But our God who is so good
commands us to seek vengeance.
He will lead our arms,
He will give us assistance.
Throw away the image of the white God
who is thirsty for our tears.
Listen to the freedom
that speaks in all of our hearts.

Lapriyè Boukmann

Bondye ki fè solèy
ki klere nou anwo,
ki souleve lanmè,
ki fè loray gwonde,
ki kache nan yon nyaj.

Tande mwen byen, zòt.
Li la ap gade nou,
Li wè tou sa blan fè.

Boukmann's Prayer

God who created the sun
which shines on us from above,
who raises the sea,
who makes thunder rumble,
who hides in a cloud.

Hear me well, all of you.
He is there watching us,
He sees all that whites do.

Bondye blan mande krim,
pa nou mande bèl jès.
Bondye ki si bon,
Li mande nou vanjans.
Li va kondi nou,
Li va ban nou asistans.

Jete nan raje
pòtre Bondye blan an:
Li swaf dlo nan je nou twòp.
Koute pito libète
k ap bat nan kè nou:
Bip . . . bip . . . bip . . . bip . . .
(Dumesle 1824; Fouchard 1972: 529; Fuertès 1992: 23–24)

The white God asks for crimes,
ours asks for good deeds.
God who is so good,
He asks vengeance of us.
He will lead us,
He will give us assistance.

Throw into the jungle
the image of the white God:
He is too thirsty for the tears in our eyes.
Listen rather to the freedom
that is beating in our hearts:
Boom . . . boom . . . boom . . . boom . . .

Chan lagè

Mounsoundi, n a fè lagè!
Eya, eya, eya!
Nou se nanchon lagè.
Ou pa tande kanno tire?
(Courlander 1960: 132; Fuertès 1992: 21)

War Song

Mounsoundi, we will make war!
Eya, eya, eya!
We are war nations.
Don't you hear the cannons fire?

Batay la angaje

Batay la angaje,
an mil senk san twa,
yo pran nou nan Ginen,
yo mete chenn nan ren nou
pou nou ka fè esklav pou yo.
Zanfan yo, nou tande, an nou met tèt ansanm
pou nou sove peyi a, batay la angaje!
Yo di fò n gen lafwa,
yo di fò n batize,
yo di fò n konvèti,
yo di se demon nou ye!
Zanfan yo, nou tande, an nou met tèt ansanm,
pou nou sove peyi a, batay la angaje!
Nou fè Bwa Kayiman nou,
nou fè revolisyon nou,
nou kreye drapo nou
pou n ka genyen libète vre.

The Battle Continues

The battle continues,
in 1503,
they took us from Ginen,
they put chains around our waists
so that we could work as slaves for them.
Children, you hear, let's work together
to save the country, the battle continues!
They say we have to have faith,
they say we have to be baptized,
they say we have to convert,
they say we are demons!
Children, you hear, let's work together
to save the country, the battle continues!
We did our ceremony at Bwa Kayiman,[1]
we did our revolution,
we created our flag
so that we could truly have freedom.

Zanfan yo, nou tande, an nou met tèt ansanm,
pou nou sove peyi a, batay la angaje!
Sou prezidan Jefra,
yo monte yon konkòda,
yo di y ap fè lekòl,
pou yo ka sivilize nou vre la.
Zanfan yo, nou tande, an nou met tèt ansanm,
pou nou sove peyi a, batay la angaje!
An mil nèf san kenz, blan vin pran peyi a.
Vodou a pa kontan, li voye Chalmay,
li voye Batravil, yo touye toulede.
Yo di se Makanda yo ye la a!
Zanfan yo, nou tande, an nou met tèt ansanm,
pou nou sove peyi a, batay la angaje!
Sou prezidan Vensan,
reyaksyonè legliz yo,
yo pouse Lachanm pou yo pran yon lwa
pou yo di Vodou a se maji vre l ap fè la a.
Zanfan yo, nou tande, an nou met tèt ansanm,
pou nou sove peyi a, batay la angaje!
Sou prezidan Lesko,
yo kanpe lame yo,
yo pran rejete yo,
yo koupe pyebwa yo,
y arete Bòkò yo,
yo di se demon nou ye vre la!
Zanfan yo, nou tande, an nou met tèt ansanm,
pou nou sove peyi a, batay la angaje!
Kwak mouche
Divalye te di se pèp li ye,
li di se Vodou l ye, li fon w twa rekòlt,
li masakre kochon nou,
li vann peyi a ven milyon an.
Zanfan yo, nou tande, an nou met tèt ansanm,
pou nou sove peyi a, batay la angaje!
Apre sèt fevriye,
relijyon yo dechennen,
yo masakre Bòkò,
yo touye Manbo,
yo kraze hounfò, yo vyole tifi,
yo di se travay Bondje vre y ap fè la a!
Zanfan yo, nou tande, an nou met tèt ansanm,
pou nou sove peyi a, batay la angaje!
Gen yon jou ka rive,

Children, you hear, let's work together
to save the country, the battle continues!
Under president Geffrard,[2]
they arranged a concordat,
they said they were going to make schools
so they can truly civilize us here.
Children, you hear, let's work together
to save the country, the battle continues!
In 1915, whites took over the country.
Vodou was not happy, it sent Charlemagne,[3]
it sent Batraville, they killed them both.
They said they're evil sorcerers!
Children, you hear, let's work together
to save the country, the battle continues!
Under president Vincent,[4]
the church's reactionaries
pushed the National Assembly to make a law
so they could say Vodou is truly about magic.
Children, you hear, let's work together
to save the country, the battle continues!
Under president Lescot,[5]
they took their army,
they started their persecutions,
they cut down Vodou trees,
they arrested Vodou priests,
they said we're truly demons here!
Children, you hear, let's work together
to save the country, the battle continues!
Even though mister
Duvalier[6] said he was of the people,
he said he was Vodou, he did three harvests,
he massacred our pigs,[7]
he sold the country for pennies on the dollar.
Children, you hear, let's work together
to save the country, the battle continues!
After the seventh of February,[8]
the religious extremists were unchained,
they massacred Vodou priests,
they killed Vodou priestesses,
they destroyed temples, they raped girls,
they said they were doing the work of God!
Children, you hear, let's work together
to save the country, the battle continues!
There is a day that will come,

n a sonnen ason nou,
n a pale ak zansèt yo.
N av al jete dlo,
peyi a pa pou AMÈN,
se peyi ABOBO li ye!
Zanfan yo, nou tande, an nou met tèt ansanm,
pou nou sove peyi a, batay la angaje! (ter)
ABOBO, ABOBO, ABOBO!
Peyi a pa pou AMÈN,
se peyi ki moun li ye? ABOBO!
(Beauvoir 2008b: 130–131)

we will shake our sacred rattles,
we will speak with our ancestors.
We are going to pour out water libations,
the country is not for AMEN,
this country is for ABOBO!
Children, you hear, let's work together
to save the country, the battle continues!
ABOBO, ABOBO, ABOBO!
The country is not for AMEN,
this is the country of which people? ABOBO!

CHAPTER 3

Jacques Roumain's, Werner A. Jaegerhuber's, and Jean Price-Mars's Songs

THIS CHAPTER assembles an assortment of Vodou songs, most from Jacques Roumain's *Le sacrifice du tambour-Assôtô(r)* (1943) but also a few from Werner A. Jaegerhuber's *Complaintes haïtiennes* (1950) and Jean Price-Mars's *Formation ethnique, folk-lore et culture du peuple haïtien* (1956). Roumain includes a diversity of songs and texts that accompany Vodou rituals. He collected them in the course of various ceremonies dedicated to the enormous *asòtò* drum and its lwa, Asòtò. In this chapter, I synthesize some of Roumain's descriptions of the rituals and activities that accompany the songs for the Asòtò, in addition to those for the lwa Ogou, since they are mixed together.[1]

Song 1 in the Roumain collection is sung at the baptismal ceremony for the *asòtò* drum. The family that will offer a sacrifice lays out a white cloth onto which the *asòtò* is laid on its side. The drum wears a white dress and bonnet. The pegs are decorated with multicolored ribbons, and drumsticks are placed alongside the drum. A vèvè composed of the flours of wheat, corn, Ginen flour, and coffee consecrates the location. The four cardinal points are evoked, and seven *parenn* (godfathers) and *marenn* (godmothers), with candles in hand, circle around the drum. The candles are blown out at the end of the circumambulation, and each person bows to the drum. Then song 1 is sung.

Song 2 is sung for Ogou Feray at the same ceremony. Possessed by Ogou, the oungan traces the lwa's vèvè and plants a red-hot iron bar in the middle of it. The iron bar is called the *fòj Ogou* (Ogou's forge) and represents Ogou's association with iron, metallurgy, war, and defense. Text 3 is a Rada oath to Ogou sworn by the Vodou family (Roumain 1943: 20). As the text is delivered, the members of the community light pieces of *kanpèch* (logwood). The head of the family carries a red rooster and a chicken. The oungan shakes the chickens over the members of the family as they shout out, "*Gras lamizerikòd* (Grace and mercy)." Subsequently vigorous possessions occur, and Ogou appears with a thundering voice. The *laplas* (master of ceremonies) is presented with one of Ogou's icons, a saber, which he embraces. In accordance with Ogou's color code, he is dressed in red attire, and red handkerchiefs are tied to his arms. The lwa is ceremoniously seated, and the members of the family kneel before him and offer him a cigar and a bottle of rum; he drinks the rum copiously, puffs the cigar, and provides advice and news from deceased family members.

The animals are oriented to the four cardinal directions while text 4, an invocation, is spoken by the oungan. The names of Ogou are cited. The rooster and the chicken are given to Ogou, who tears their heads off and drinks blood from the severed neck. He consecrates his forehead with the blood, and three drops are dripped onto Ogou's forge so "it may absorb the soul of the sacrificed animals" (Roumain 1943: 25). Next, the oungan consecrates the ceremony for Ogou by exploding gunpowder in three small cups. The audience shouts "*Abobo!* (Praise be to Vodou!)," and the members of the Vodou family sign themselves with the sacrificial blood. The *ounsi* (initiates) prepare the poultry with rum and spices but not garlic and parsley, which are taboo in this instance. Other traditional dishes are prepared. The head of the rooster, wings, liver, and thighs are reserved for the one possessed by Ogou (Roumain 1943: 25). *Yanvalou* and *nago* rhythm and dance ensue accompanied by song 151 in the Marcelin chapter.[2] All of the food ingredients are placed in a vase while song 6 is sung and danced by everybody. Food is offered to the four cardinal directions, and those who are possessed begin to eat and are offered rum, bitter coffee, and cigars. The bones of the sacrificial birds are buried so that Ogou can resurrect them whenever he wants to eat. The oungan traces a vèvè while everybody sings song 7.

The members of the family dig a hole oriented toward the east; it is dug either in front of Ogou's forge or in the ground of the *ounfò* (temple) itself. Money offerings, a red scarf, a bottle of rum, a cigar, a piece of iron, and the bones are deposited there. Everybody dances around the hole while singing song 8. The hole is filled with dirt, and the oungan plants in the filled center of the hole three lit candles, of which one must be red. Everybody dances, claps their hands rhythmically, and sings song 9 so that the lwa Ogou will depart from the ceremony and make way for the next lwa. The Vodou priest, holding a lit candle, circles the drum and sprinkles it with holy water. A vase with cakes, bread, and grilled corn and alcoholic beverages in a bowl are placed before the *asòtò* drum. A few chunks of cake and corn seeds are placed on the drum, which is covered with a cloth. The drum is saluted with flags that are crossed over it. Finally, the *asòtò* drum is placed upright and baptized and receives a soul (Roumain 1943: 32).

Regarding the rest of Roumain's material, songs 10–14 are from ceremonies for the lwa Legba; songs 15–19 are from ceremonies for the lwa Ayizan; and songs 20–29 are from ceremonies for lwa Loko. Songs 30–42 are for the sacrifice of the Asòtò, a ritual accompanied by songs, prayers, invocations, and animal sacrifice in honor of the lwa and drum. Song 43 is sung when the lwa Asòtò possesses his horse; songs 44–47 request the departure of the lwa Asòtò.

Jaegerhuber's songs were originally published with the accompanying sheet music. Here I reproduce the lyrics only, without the musical notation, and I provide an English translation. Along with Courlander 1939, Jaegerhuber 1950 is one of the first efforts to seriously document and study the lyrics and musical structure of Vodou songs. Jaegerhuber, son of a Haitian mother and an American father, lived most of his life in Germany and became an academician and administrator at the Conservatory Von Bernuth, as well as the director of the music faculty in Spetzgart. He directed several orchestras and gave concerts in many European towns. In 1937, he abandoned Adolf Hitler's Nazi Germany and returned to his native Haiti, where he dedicated himself to the collection of Vodou songs. Jaegerhuber felt that the publication and popularization of Vodou and folkloric songs would help the Haitian people advance their artistic aspirations and attain the summits of civilization.[3] Although it would not come to be, Roger E. Savain notes in his introduction to Jaegerhuber's book that Jaegerhuber planned to produce a school textbook of folkloric songs for three voices.[4] At this point in time, little has been published about the technical aspects of Vodou music, aside from the contributions of Harold Courlander (1939, 1960), Gerdès Fleurant (1987), and Lois Wilcken (1992).[5]

The Price-Mars collection, a reprint of the 1936 edition, offers three songs, which follow a three-page introduction titled "Commemorative Ceremonies." There he writes that he attended a ceremony on a farm a good distance from his home in Pétionville. The ceremony commemorated the memory of twins who were the victims of the slave trade (Price-Mars 1956: 57). A propitiatory sacrifice was also offered to all of the children who had perished since independence from the plagues that afflict Haiti's "shamefully abandoned" rural regions (Price-Mars 1956: 57). The three songs address the feeling of abandonment that parentless twins and children must have felt in slavery. When one thinks of the earthquake on January 12, 2010, or the impact of AIDS—brought to Haiti by U.S. sex tourists in the 1970s (see Farmer 1999)—one can see that the plague of parentless children continues and that the message to the Marasa is as pertinent as ever: "I don't have family, / Who is going to speak for me? / The Divine Twins, oh yeah!"

Chante Jak Woumen

1.
Asòtò Micho.
N ape rele Jan.
Jan Asòtò, n ape rele
pou nou batize tanbou Asòtò.
Dye le Pè, Dye le Fis,
Dye le Sent Espri.
Apre Bondye, m ap batize.
Ou sòti nan Ginen,
ou vini wè kreyòl la yo,
nou kontan wè Asòtò Micho.
M ap batize Asòtò.

2.
Kimalada sanble,
Se pa mwen sèl o ki pou sèvi lwa.
Bolada yo sanble.
Bolada Kimalada, o Kimalada,
ou kanni laflè Vodoun,
ou kanni laras Velekete,
flè Vodoun.
A kriye: Abobo,
Sodyeme Vodoun, an tout Dye.

3.
Nou Rada deja, nou deja Rada.
Se pa mwen sèl ki pou sèvi Ogoun Feray;
fanmi anpil, se mwen youn.[6]

4.
Ogoun Feray, men sa m ape ba w,
san rankin, san rankin,
Papa Ogoun. Ogoun Badagri.
Ogoun Chango. Ogoun Batala.

5.
Wòy, wòy,[7]
Ogoun Chango, nèg Feray o.
San vèse, Feray o, san vèse,
Ogoun Feray touye.
Koklo Feray okon o.

Jacques Roumain's Songs

1.
Asòtò Micho.
We are calling Jean.
Jean Asòtò, we are calling
for you to baptize the Asòtò drum.
God the Father, God the Son,
God the Holy Spirit.
After God, I'm baptizing.
You come from Ginen,
you come to see the Creoles,
we are happy to see Asòtò Micho.
I'm baptizing Asòtò.

2.
Kimalada has gathered,
Oh it is not me alone who should serve the lwa.
The Bolada have gathered.
Bolada Kimalada, oh Kimalada,
you gave birth to the Vodoun flower,
you gave birth to the race of Velekete,
flower of Vodoun.
Ah, cry out: Abobo,
Sodyeme Vodoun, God in all ways.

3.
We are Rada already, we are already Rada.
I'm not alone in serving Ogoun Feray;
the family is numerous, I am one of them.

4.
Ogoun Feray, here is what I'm offering you,
without bitterness, without bitterness,
Papa Ogoun. Ogoun Badagri.
Ogoun Chango. Ogoun Batala.

5.
Oh my, oh my,
Ogoun Chango, oh Feray man.
Blood is shed, oh Feray, blood is shed,
Ogoun Feray kills.
Oh Feray's rooster is sacrificed.

N ape ba w donon, Feray o.
Sanyan, sanyan, sanyan.
Gad jan nou touye koklo a,
sanyan, sanyan, sanyan.

We are giving you food, oh Feray,
Bleed, bleed, bleed.
Look at how we killed the rooster,
bleed, bleed, bleed.

6.

Ogoun Fè, prete m terin la
pou m ale dine.
Achade, m poko dine.
Achade, m poko dine.
Achade, m ape dine.
Olicha, prete m terin la,
Obatala, pou m ale dine.
Ogoun Fè, pou m ale dine.
Olicha, m poko dine.
Ogoun Fè, Ogoun Feray.
Ogoun vle manje.
M poko dounon, mwen prale dounon.
Abobo!

6.

Ogoun Fè, lend me the vase of dead souls
so that I may go dine.
Achade, I haven't yet dined.
Achade, I haven't yet dined.
Achade, I'm dining.
Olicha, lend me the vase of dead souls,
Obatala, so that I may go dine.
Ogoun fè, so that I may go dine.
Olicha, I haven't yet dined.
Ogoun Fè, Ogoun Feray.
Ogoun wants to eat.
I haven't eaten yet, I'm going to eat.
Abobo!

7.

E, lorye, se mwen Ogoun o.
Mwen lorye.
Dawomen dakò, e.
Se mwen Ogoun.
Se mwen, se mwen, se mwen, Olicha.
Nèg Batala, nèg Achade, bòkò,[8]
se mwen, se mwen Ogoun, se mwen.
Abobo!

7.

Hey, laurel, it's me oh Ogoun.
I'm laurel.
Hey, Dawomen agrees.
It's me Ogoun.
It's me, it's me, it's me, Olicha.
Man of Batala, the man Achade, bòkò,
it's me, it's me Ogoun, it's me.
Abobo!

8.

Twou a, twou a,
Olicha, n ap ofri w.
N ape fouye twou, Olicha.
Pou nou fouye twou Olicha.
Pou nou ba li manje.
N ape fouye twou Ogoun
pou nou ba li manje.
N ape fouye twou Chango.
Twou a, o twou a,
twou Olicha.
Abobo!

8.

The hole, the hole,
Olicha, we're offering it to you.
We're digging a hole, Olicha.
We should dig a hole, Olicha.
We should give him food.
We are digging the hole of Ogoun
so that we can give him food.
We are digging the hole of Chango.
The hole, oh the hole,
the hole of Olicha.
Abobo!

9.

L ale, l ale, li pa di m.
Ogoun Fè ki monte lanmè,
li p ap tounen.
L ale, l ale, li pa di mwen.
Batala ki monte lanmè, li p ap tounen.
L ale, l ale, li pa di mwen.
Olicha ki monte lanmè, li p ap tounen.
L ale, l ale, li pa di mwen.
Aochè Nago!
O Papa Ogoun, o Papa Ogoun o!
Mwen prale lakay mwen,
chwal mwen sele.

9.

He went, he went, he didn't tell me.
Ogoun Fè who went out to sea,
he isn't returning.
He went, he went, he didn't tell me.
Batala who went out to sea, he isn't returning.
He went, he went, he didn't tell me.
Olicha who went out to sea, he isn't returning.
She went, she went, she didn't tell me.
Aochè Nago!
Oh Papa Ogoun, oh Papa Ogoun, oh!
I'm going to my house,
my horse is saddled.

10.

Papa Legba, louvri bayè a pou mwen, ago ye.
Papa Legba, louvri bayè a pou mwen,
pou mwen pase.
Lò m a tounen, m a remesye lwa yo.
Vodoun Legba, louvri bayè a pou mwen.
O louvri bayè a pou mwen, pou mwen pase.
Lò m a pase m a remesye lwa yo.

10.

Papa Legba, open the gate for me, ago yeah.
Papa Legba, open the gate for me,
so that I can pass through.
When I return, I'll thank the lwa.
Vodoun Legba, open the gate for me.
Oh open the gate for me, for me to pass through.
When I have passed through I'll thank the lwa.

11.

Legba fè yo wè sa.
Alegba-se, se nou de.
Se nou de, Katawoulo.
Se nou de.
Se nou de, vanyan Legba, se nou de.
Legba, fè yo wè sa.
Alegba-se, se nou de, e!
Se nou de, Legba, se nou de la.
Legba, fè yo wè sa.
Legba-se, se nou de, a!
Se nou de, Katawoulo.
Vanyan Legba, se nou de o!
Kriye abobo, Atibon Legba,
se nou de la a, a!
Legba, fè yo wè sa.
Legba-se, se nou de e!
Se nou de Atibon, se nou de, a!

11.

Legba makes them see that.
Alegba's divine force, it's us two.
It's us two, Katawoulo.
It's us two.
It's us two, courageous Legba, it's us two.
Legba, make them see that.
Alegba's divine force, it's us two, hey!
It's us two, Legba, it's us two here.
Legba, make them see that.
Legba's divine force, it's us two, ah!
It's us two, Katawoulo.
Courageous Legba, oh it's us two!
Cry out abobo, Atibon Legba,
it's us two here, ah!
Legba, make them see that.
Legba's divine force, hey it's us two!
It's us two, Atibon, it's us two, ah!

12.
Santa Maria Gratia,
Toni, rele Kongo.
O Santa Marya,
o Toni, rele Kongo.
Toni, rele Kongo,
Santa Maria Gratia.

12.
Holy Mary of Grace,
you need to call on the Kongo.
Oh Holy Mary,
oh Toni,[9] call on the Kongo.
Toni, call on the Kongo,
Holy Mary of Grace.

13.
Senyen, senyen, senyen!
Gade, nou senyen koklo la.
Senyen, senyen, senyen!
Voyez, nous avons saigné le koklo.

13.
Bleed, bleed, bleed!
Look, we bleed the rooster here.
Bleed, bleed, bleed!
Look, we have bled the rooster.

14.
Poul la,
O . . . poul la,
poul la make non mwen.
Poul la make non Alegba.
Poul la make non li vre.
Poul la, poul la,
poul la make de me plè.
Poul la make non mwen,
vanyan Legba.
Li make non Katawoulo.
Li make non vanyan Legba.

14.
The chicken,
Oh . . . the chicken,
the chicken is marked with my name.
The chicken is marked with the name Alegba.
The chicken truly marks his name.
The chicken, the chicken,
the chicken is marked for my pleasure.
The chicken is marked with my name,
courageous Legba.
It is marked with the name Katawoulo.
It is marked with the intimate name of Legba.

15.
Ayizan-De,
Hountò-Legui, se lajan.
Yo vini gade m
pou yo pote m ale.
Ayizan-De, w a di Hountò-Legui, se lajan.
Ayizan e, Hountò-Legui gen lajan.
Agasou-Miwa, Hountò-Legui, se lajan.
Yo vini gade mwen
pou yo pòte m ale.
Yo vini veye mwen
pou yo pòte m ale.
Ayizan-De, w a di Hountò-Legui, se lajan.
Abobo!

15.
Ayizan-De,
Hountò-Legui, it's money.
They come to look at me
so that they can carry me away.
Ayizan-De, you'll tell Hountò-Legui, it's money.
Hey Ayizan, Hountò-Legui has money.
Agasou-Miwa, Hountò-Legui, it's money.
They come to look at me
so that they can carry me away.
They come to watch me
so that they can carry me away.
Ayizan-De, you'll tell Hountò-Legui, it's money.
Abobo!

16.

Ayizan o, Ayizan o.
Ayizan e, Ayizan e.
Nèg sòt mare chwal li,
nèg lespri di l a lage l.
Ayizan, nou wè sa,
ou pa wè nou mare?
Ayizan e, Ayizan e.
Ayizan mare chwal li,
nèg lespri di l a lage l.
Ayizan, nou wè sa,
ou pa wè nou mare?

16.

Oh Ayizan, oh Ayizan.
Hey Ayizan, hey Ayizan.
The stupid man ties up his horse,
the wise man says he'll untie it.
Ayizan, you see that,
don't you see we're tied up?
Hey Ayizan, hey Ayizan.
Ayizan ties up her horse,
the wise man says he'll untie it.
Ayizan, you see that,
don't you see we're tied up?

17.

Vèvè dlo.
Se hounsi ki fè houngan, vèvè dlo.
Houngan tonbe, hounsi leve, vèvè dlo.
Konbyen hounsi ki fè houngan, vèvè dlo?
Konbyen hounsi ki fè houngan, vèvè dlo?
Depi nan Ginen hounsi trayi houngan,
vèvè dlo.
Konbyen hounsi ki fè houngan, vèvè dlo?
Vèvè dlo, lakòt Ginen, vèvè dlo.
Abobo!

17.

Water vèvè.
It's hounsi who become houngan, water vèvè.
The houngan falls, the hounsi rises, water vèvè.
How many hounsi become houngan, water vèvè?
How many hounsi become houngan, water vèvè?
Since Ginen hounsi have betrayed houngan,
water vèvè.
How many hounsi become houngan, water vèvè?
Water vèvè, the coast of Ginen, water vèvè.
Abobo!

18.

Ayizan, e, e, e!
Likè tounen dlo lakay Ayizan.

18.

Ayizan, hey, hey, hey!
Liquor turns to water with Ayizan.

19.

Zo, kouman sa ye?
Ayizan, papa, kouman sa ye?
Si hounsi tonbe la, pinga kite li gate.
Anvan yo fouye twou li,
mwen di: zo, kouman sa ye?
A, zo ki fè houngan mwen,
kouman sa ye?
Si hounsi tonbe la, o pinga kite li gate.
Anvan w fouye twou li,
fouye twou zo Klimo.
Zo Klimo, hounsi kanzo, Ladegwesan.
Sofi Badè, Okominawe Velekete.
Okomalada,
O ou kanni laflè Vodoun.

19.

Bones, how is it going?
Ayizan, oh wow, how is it going?
If the hounsi falls here, don't let her spoil.
Before they dig her hole,
I say: bone, how is it going?
Ah, bones which make my houngan,
how is it going?
If the hounsi falls here, don't let her spoil.
Before they dig her hole,
dig the hole for Klimo's bones.
Klimo's bones, hounsi kanzo, Ladegwesan.
Sofi Badè, Okominawe Velekete
Okomalada,
Oh you gave birth to the flower of Vodoun.

20.
Vè, Atisougwè,
men Yanvalou Loko,
Atisou ki mande paran l yo.
Atisou o, men fanmi an yo,
Loko-Atisou, papa, men fanmi an yo.
Y ape sèvi Loko
pou nou ba Loko manje.
A Loko Atisou,
men Yanvalou Loko.

20.
Vè, Atisougwè,
here is Yanvalou Loko,
Atisou who asks his parents.
Oh Atisou, here is the family,
Loko-Atisou, papa, here is the family.
They're serving Loko
we should can give Loko food.
Ah Loko Atisou,
here is Yanvalou Loko.

21.
Yanvalou Priyè Ginen
M mande w padon,
Papa Loko, m mande w padon.
Papa, m mande w padon.
Papa Loko, mwen se pitit ou deja,
pinga w mòde m jous nan zo.
M mande padon, Loko Atisou.
Papa Loko, papa, mwen mande padon.
A Loko, m se pitit ou deja,
o pinga w mòde m jous nan zo.
O padon, lwa mwen yo,
mwen mande nou padon.
Padon Ginen, padon lesen.
A Loko, nou se pitit ou deja.
O pinga w mòde nou jous nan zo.
Kriye: abobo Loko Atisou!
O kriye abobo o, houngan mwen.
O kriye abobo, hounsi kanzo.
Houngan mwen, e!
Mwen kriye abobo,
laplas kay la.
Houngan mwen, o,
Papa Loko, n a prale, dakò?
Papa Loko, papa, nou prale, dakò?
Yo poko houngan.
O kreyòl yo di kon sa
yo va manyen vèvè Loko.
Se kreyòl jodi
ki montre Ginen chanson kreyòl.
Mwen kriye: abobo!
Papa Loko, papa, n a prale, dakò?
Pou nou sakre sèvis la,

21.
Yanvalou Ginen Prayer
I ask you for forgiveness,
Papa Loko, I ask you for forgiveness.
Papa, I ask you for forgiveness.
Papa Loko, I am your child already,
don't you bite me all the way to the bone.
I ask for forgiveness, Loko Atisou.
Papa Loko, papa, I ask for forgiveness.
Ah Loko, I'm your child already,
oh don't you bite me all the way to the bone.
Oh sorry, my lwa,
I ask you for forgiveness.
Sorry Ginen, sorry saints.
Ah Loko, we are your children already.
Oh don't you bite us all the way to the bone.
Cry out: Abobo Loko Atisou!
Oh cry out abobo, my houngan.
Oh cry out abobo, hounsi kanzo.
My houngan, hey!
I cry out abobo,
master of ceremonies of the house.
Oh my houngan,
Papa Loko, we're heading off, okay?
Papa Loko, papa, we're heading off, okay?
They are not yet houngan.
Oh the Creoles say that
they're going to touch Loko's vèvè.
It's the Creoles today
who show the Ginen Creole songs.
I cry out: abobo!
Papa Loko, papa, we're heading off, okay?
In order to bless the service,

sèvis sila, sèvis Adanyi,
Adanyi Sobo, Sobokeson Bolojè Atisougwè.
Men Yanvaloujyè,
gwo Loko, men Yanvalou mwen.
N ape mande yo kote hounsi yo ye?
N ape mande yo
kote houngan kay la ye?
O sali o, houngan mwen.

that service, the service of Adanyi,
Adanyi Sobo, Sobokeson Bolojè Atisougwè.
Here is Yanvaloujyè,
big Loko, here is my Yanvalou.
We're asking them where the hounsi are?
We're asking them
where is the houngan of the house?
Oh greetings, oh my houngan.

22.

A Loko Atisougwè o,
o men Yanvalou Sègwèlo, se nou de.
A Loko, o Kisigwe,
Papa Loko-Kisigwe,
o men Yanvalou Sègwèlo, se nou de.
O bèf la mouri,
li kite mizè pou poul li.
An Loko,
o gade mizè n a pou pase.
Papa Loko mouri,
li kite mizè pou poul li, ago ye!
A Loko, o Kisigwè,
o men Yanvalou Sègwèlo, se nou de.
Dyòl anwo, dyòl anwo, dyòl anba, dyòl anba,
o Papa Loko kite mizè pou poul li.
Kriye: abobo Loko Atisou!
Kriye: abobo Azanblou, Azanblou Kidi!
Kriye: abobo hounsi yo!
Abobo lesen yo!
Abobo Ginen an yo!
N ape rele yo, o vini dounou ak nou.
Nou kriye: abobo houngennikon o!
O laplas kay la,
nou rele abobo, Papa Loko, Papa nou,
Papa Loko, Papa nou, nou kriye: abobo!

22.

Ah Loko Atisougwè oh,
oh here is Yanvalou Sègwèlo, it's us two.
Ah Loko, oh Kisigwe,
Papa Loko-Kisigwe,
oh here is Yanvalou Sègwèlo, it's us two.
Oh the cow died,
it left misery for its chicken.
Ah Loko,
oh look at the misery we'll have to traverse.
Papa Loko died,
he left misery for his chickens, ago yeah!
Ah Loko, oh Kisigwè,
oh here is Yanvalou Sègwèlo, it's us two.
Face up, face up, face down, face down,
oh Papa Loko left misery for his chickens.
Cry out: abobo Loko Atisou!
Cry out: abobo Azanblou, Azanblou Kidi!
Cry out: abobo for the hounsi!
Abobo for the saints!
Abobo for the Ginen!
We're calling them, oh come eat with us.
We cry out: oh abobo houngennikon!
Oh master of ceremonies of the house,
we cry out abobo, Papa Loko, our Father,
Papa Loko, our Father, we cry out: abobo!

23.

Ayayay, Loko, Papa Loko, Papa, n aprale.
Papa Loko, papa, n aprale.
Boutèy ki boutèy, rat manje l,
ki dire kalbas o.
Eskize n, Loko, n aprale,
Lafanmi an yo, m remesye n.
Lafanmi an yo, remesye Loko, m prale,

23.

Oh my, Loko, Papa Loko, Papa, we're going.
Papa Loko, papa, we're going.
Rats eat actual bottles,
oh not to mention calabash.
Excuse us, Loko, we're going.
Members of the family, I thank you.
Members of the family, thank Loko, I'm going,

boutèy o, kalbas o.
Boutèy ki boutèy, rat manje l,
ki dire kalbas o.
Nan Ginen sa a, n aprale,
nan Ginen sa a, n aprale,
Alèkile kreyòl pa sèvi Loko ankò.
Loko di nou Ginen l aprale, l aprale.
Papa Loko di, boutèy ki boutèy, rat manje l,
ki dire kalbas o.
Eskize Loko, n aprale.
Bòn sante Loko, n aprale.
Eskize Loko, n aprale.

oh bottle, oh calabash.
Rats eat actual bottles,
oh not to mention calabash.
To that Ginen, we're going,
to that Ginen, we're going,
These days Creoles don't serve Loko anymore.
Loko tells us he's going to Ginen, he's going.
Papa Loko says, oh rats eat actual bottles,
oh not to mention calabash.
Excuse us, Loko, we're going.
Good health to you, Loko, we're going.
Excuse us, Loko, we're going.

24.

Leve, leve, leve, o Gwimakou,
houngan m ape travay.
Loko ape dòmi,
Leve, leve, leve, leve, o Gwimakou,
houngan m ape travay o.
Loko ape dòmi, ape dòmi,
Djahountò, l ape dòmi,
leve, leve, leve, hounsi kanzo.
Hounsi bosal, bay lè pou hounsi,
kanzo pase.
Leve, leve, leve, o Gwimakou,
houngan m ape travay.
Loko m ape dòmi.
Abobo.

24.

Get up, get up, get up, oh Gwimakou,
my houngan is working.
Loko is sleeping,
Get up, get up, get up, get up, oh Gwimakou,
oh my houngan is working.
Loko is sleeping, is sleeping,
Djahountò, he's sleeping,
get up, get up, get up, hounsi kanzo.
Hounsi bosal, leave the hounsi alone,
the kanzo ceremony is over.
Get up, get up, get up, oh Gwimakou,
my houngan is working.
Loko, I'm sleeping.
Abobo.

25.

Salye manbo,
o salye manbo kay la, m aprale.
Sa ki bezwen wè, mache pou yo wè.
Sa ki bezwen tande, mache y a tande.
Salye manbo,
salye manbo kay la, n ap antre.
Salye manbo kay la.
Hounsi temerè,
o laplas kay la,
mwen di: salye manbo.
O salye manbo kay la, eya!
M ap antre.
Sa ki bezwen wè, mache pou wè e.
Sa ki bezwen tande, mache, y a tande.

25.

Greetings manbo,
oh greet the manbo of the house, I'm going.
Whoever needs to see, walk so they may see.
Whoever needs to hear, walk and they'll hear.
Greetings manbo,
greet the manbo of the house, we're entering.
Greetings manbo of the house.
Hounsi temerè,
oh master of ceremonies of the house,
I say: greetings manbo.
Oh greetings manbo of the house, oh yeah!
I'm entering.
Whoever needs to see, hey, walk to see.
Whoever needs to hear, walk, they'll hear.

Salye manbo, ey!
O salye manbo kay la, eya!
Nou rantre.
Abobo!

Greetings manbo, hey!
Oh greet the manbo of the house, oh yeah!
We're entering.
Abobo!

26.

Loko gen fanm jodi a,
Danyiso.
Dawomen Loko-si,
Dawomen an, Dawomen.
M ap mande kote Danyiso Loko?
Dawomen, Dawomen.

26.

Loko has women today,
Danyiso.
Dahomian Loko-si,
the Dahomian, Dahomian.
I'm asking where is Danyiso Loko?
Dahomey, Dahomey.

27.

Abobo, mwen kriye,
abobo, Loko Atisou.
Atisou sa a, Atisou, vanyan gason.
Mwen kriye abobo, nèg Agasou-miwa,
Nèg Kotoli.
Eya! Poto a plante, nèg Atisou.
Ye Vodounsi, ye Okimalada,
lanfanmi,
ou kanni Vodoun.
Ya Vodoun Djohoun te pale Makandal;
li pa te vle koute.
Se nan moute desann
kay Loman,
yo fè l dousman, o lwa mwen yo.
Toulejou, toulejou,
m ape pale, Loko Atisou.
Li pa vle koute, ago!
Toulejou, toulejou,
li pa vle tande, ago!
Papa Loko pale, yo pa vle koute.
Gade jan yo fè li dousman,
Dousman, Loko Atisou,
o dousman.
Mwen kriye abobo, Jan Pyè Desalin,
Kongweya!
Mwen kriye abobo, Loko Atisou o!
Nou kriye abobo Loko-de,
a, Loko Atisou.
Mwen kriye pou Santayi Loko,

27.

Abobo, I cry,
abobo Loko Atisou.
That Atisou, Atisou, courageous man.
I cry out abobo, mister Agasou-mirror,
Kotoli man.
Eya! The post is planted, mister Atisou.
Ye Vodou initiates, ye Okimalada,
members of the family,
you give birth to Vodoun.
Ya Vodoun Djohoun spoke with Makandal;
he didn't want to listen.
It was by going up and down from
Loman's house,
that they killed him, oh my lwa.
At all times, at all times,
I'm speaking, Loko Atisou.
He didn't want to listen, ago!
At all times, at all times,
he didn't want to listen, ago!
Papa Loko spoke, they didn't want to listen.
Look at how they killed him,
They took his life, Loko Atisou,
oh they took his life.
I cry out abobo, Jean Pierre Dessalines,
Kongweya!
I cry out abobo, oh Loko Atisou!
We cry out abobo, Loko-de,
ah, Loko Atisou.
I cry out for Santayi Loko,

a Loko Azanblou.
Mwen kriye abobo Loko vanyan-vanyan,
lè nou rive, fò nou remesye Loko, ago!
Nou rive, Jan Pyè Desalin,
nou rive, onon Loko Atisou.
Nèg Bakousou Alade Olomla.
Atisou di l ape janbe,
abobo!

ah Loko Azanblou.
I cry out abobo, Loko most courageous,
when we arrive, we must thank Loko, ago!
We have arrived, Jean Pierre Dessalines,
we have arrived, in the name of Loko Atisou.
Mister Bakousou Alade Olomla.
Atisou says he's crossing over,
abobo!

28.

Ki nanchon w, papa?
—Loko Atisou.
Nou byen kontan wè w.
Èske w kontan ak pitit ou yo?
—Wi, m kontan, pitit mwen yo.

28.

What nation are you, papa?
—Loko Atisou.
We're very happy to see you.
Are you happy with your children?
—Yes, I'm happy, my children.

29.

Pinga Loko,
Loko manyen wanga cho.
Pinga Loko,
Loko manyen manje cho.
Pinga Loko.

29.

Watch out for Loko,
Loko touched a hot talisman.
Watch out for Loko,
Loko touched hot food.
Watch out for Loko.

30.
Le sacrifice de l'Asòtò

Dieu le Père, Dieu le Fils,
Dieu le Saint-Esprit.

Waye, Asòtò Micho,
m ape fouye twou a.
Twou Asòtò Micho,
twou sila, twou Asòtò Micho,
Asòtò Micho Oliban.

30.
The Sacrifice of the Asòtò

God the Father, God the Son,
God the Holy Spirit.

Waye, Asòtò Micho,
I'm digging the hole.
The hole of Asòtò Micho,
that hole, the hole of Asòtò Micho,
Asòtò Micho Oliban.

31.

Asòtò Micho Tokodoum Vodoun.
E! Plante poto.
Plante poto.
E! Plante pote.
Asòtò Micho plante poto li.
E! Plante poto,
Abobo.

31.

Asòtò Micho Tokodoum Vodoun.
Hey! Plant the post.
Plant the post.
Hey! Plant the post.
Asòtò Micho plants his post.
Hey! Plant the post,
Abobo.

32.

Priyè Ginen

A, se yon Micho,
m ap rele w, kote w ye?
Ou nan Ginen,
se nan Ginen ou te ye,
kreyòl Ginen k ape rele w.
Laras ou kanni Ginen.
Vini sove nou,
donnou an pare.

32.

Ginen Prayer

Ah, it's a Micho,
I'm calling you, where are you?
You're in Ginen,
you were indeed in Ginen,
the Creole Ginen are calling you.
Your race was born in Ginen.
Come to save us,
the food is ready.

33.

Dezyèm Priyè Ginen

Asòtò Micho,
men manje m ap ba w.
Se Asòtò ki mande manje.
Ane a bout,
men manje m ap ba w,
Sodyeme, an tout, Dye.

33.

Second Ginen Prayer

Asòtò Micho
here is the food I'm giving you.
It's Asòtò who asks for food.
The year is over,
here is the food I'm giving you,
Sodyeme, in all, God.

34.

Alegba Micho, Asòtò Micho,
louvri bayè a pou mwen
pou mwen pase.
Lè m arive m a remèsye lwa yo.

34.

Alegba Micho, Asòtò Micho,
open the gate for me
so that I can pass through.
When I arrive, I'll thank the lwa.

35.

Simeyon Solèy,
M evoke w pou w desann asiste
seremoni sila a.
Pou mwen, silvouplè, nonmen Micho,
Asòtò Micho.

35.

Simeyon Solèy,
I invoke you to come down and attend
this ceremony.
For me, please, name Micho,
Asòtò Micho.

36.

Priyè Ginen

Se lapriyè Ginen
ki mennen Asòtò Micho.
Asòtò Micho nan Ginen,
In nomino Patri spiriti sancto amen.[10]

36.

Ginen Prayer

It's the Ginen prayer
which leads Asòtò Micho.
Asòtò Micho in Ginen,
In nomino Patri spiriti sancto amen.

37.

Santa Maria Gratia, Larèn Ginen.
Nou Ginen, plezi a bèl,
Gratia Santa Maria, Gratia.

37.

Santa Maria Gratia, Queen of Ginen.
We're Ginen, the pleasure is beautiful,
Gratia Santa Maria Gratia.

38.
Do-Do,
M a rele Do-Do.
Vin adore Do.
Adore Do.
N ape adore
pou Asòtò Micho.
Do, m a rele Do.
Do, m a rele Do-Do.

38.
Do-Do,
I'll call Do-Do.
Come worship Do.
Worship Do.
We're worshiping
for Asòtò Micho.
Do, I'm calling Do.
Do, I'm calling Do-Do.

39.
Asòtò, siyanyan, o.
Ay Micho!
Asòtò siyanyan.

39.
Asòtò, oh bleed.
Hey Micho!
Asòtò bleed.

40.
Manje lwa:
Atoutou.
Yanm wouj.
Yanm-Ginen (nwa).
Yanm-Frans (blanch).
Yanm-Sigwin (jòn).
Yanm-Ibo (vyolèt).
Yanm-Masòkò (jòn).
Malanga (nwa e jòn).
Bannann-matehen.
Bannann-Ginen.
Fig-Ginen.
Kalalou-Ginen.
Lalo.
Vyann (esepte vyann kochon).
Pwason nèg (nwa).
Pwason pewokèt (wouj).
Sadin Ginen.
Poul ki gen plimay tout koulè.

40.
Lwa's Food:
Corn flower.
Red yams.
Ginen-yams (black).
French-yams (white).
Sigwin-yams (yellow).
Ibo-yams (violet).
Masòkò-yams (yellow).
Malanga (black and yellow).
Matehen-plantains.
Ginen-plantains.
Ginen-bananas.
Ginen-Okra.
Jute.
Meat (except pork).
Black fish (black).
Red fish (red).
Ginen sardine.
Chicken with multicolored plumage.

41.
Zo Klimo, papa, kouman sa ye?
O Zo Klimo, papa, kouman sa ye?
Si Asòtò tonbe, pinga kite l gate
anvan yo fouye twou li.
Mwen di: Zo, kouman sa ye?
Zo Klimo, papa, kouman sa ye?
Si Asòtò tonbe, pinga kite l gate

41.
Zo Klimo, papa, how is it going?
Oh Zo Klimo, papa, how is it going?
If Asòtò falls, don't let him spoil
before they dig his hole.
I say: Zo, how is it going?
Zo Klimo, papa, how is it going?
If Asòtò falls, don't let him spoil

anvan yo fouye twou li, ago ye!
Mwen kriye: abobo!
pou Asòtò Micho.
Si Asòtò tonbe, pinga kite l gate
anvan yo fouye twou li.

before they dig his hole, ago yeah!
I cry out: abobo!
for Asòtò Micho.
If Asòtò falls, don't let him spoil
before they dig his hole.

42.

Ogoun Asòtò Micho Oliban,
o Dye, nou prale anbake,
o Dye, o Dye, o Dye,
nou prale anbake.
Asòtò Micho, pitit mwen malad,
m voye chache fèy.
Pitit mwen grangou,
m voye chache manje.
Alèkile yo pa bezwen m ankò.
Yo di m manje moun.
Se paske mwen inosan.
Yo di m manje moun.
M pa gen manman,
m pa gen fanmi,
m pral anbake.
Kreyòl yo reponn: kote w prale?
Asòtò di: se nan Ginen m prale.
Abobo, Kreyòl!
Ago, Ginen!

42.

Ogoun Asòtò Micho Oliban,
oh God, we're going to embark,
oh God, oh God, oh God,
we're going to embark.
Asòtò Micho, my child is ill,
I sent for leaves.
My child is hungry,
I sent for food.
Now they don't need me anymore.
They say I victimize people.
It's because I'm innocent.
They say I victimize people.
I don't have a mother,
I don't have a family,
I'm going to embark.
The Creoles reply: where are you going?
Asòtò says: I'm going to Ginen.
Abobo, Creoles!
Ago, Ginen!

43.

Asòtò Micho,
men manje y ap ba w.
Se Asòtò ki mande manje.
Men manje m ap ba w.
Ane a bout.
Men manje m ap ba w.
Sodyeme, an tout, Dye.

43.

Asòtò Micho,
here is food they're giving you.
It's Asòtò who asks for food.
Here is the food I'm giving you.
The year is over.
Here is food I'm giving you.
Sodyeme, in all, God..

44.

Asòtò, yo di w manje moun
paske w inosan.
Tout moun manje moun.
Se ou menm ki gen move tèt.
Ou prale nan Ginen.
Kreyòl yo mande, kote w a prale?

44.

Asòtò, they say you victimize people
because you're innocent.
Everybody victimizes someone.
You yourself have a bad temper.
You're going to Ginen.
The Creoles ask, where are you going?

Asòtò reponn: l a prale nan Ginen.
Kreyòl pa vle wè l.
Abobo Asòtò! Abobo Kreyòl! Ago.

Asòtò replies: he will go to Ginen.
Creoles don't want to see him.
Abobo Asòtò! Abobo Creoles! Ago.

45.
Adye, Asòtò,
N ekspedye vou pou jamè. Je renonce.

Ki disait n aprale?
Mwen di, nan Ginen mande pou nou,
N ape se fué,[11] pou nou ale,
yo me voy.

45.
Oh my, Asòtò,
We expel you forever. I renounce.

Who said we're going?
I say, Ginen has asked for us,
We're going, we need to go,
I'm going.

46.
E, konble li, Poto.
Asòtò Micho, konble li, Poto.
Poto plante, li konble.
E, konble li, Poto.

46.
Hey, fill it up, Post.
Asòtò Micho, fill it up, Post.
The post is planted, it's filled up.
Hey, fill it up, Post.

47.
Lafanmi kaba.
Asòtò ale,
li pa kite dèyè.
Se regrè.
Amen.

47.
The family is finished.
Asòtò is gone,
he didn't leave anything behind.
It's regrettable.
Amen.

Chante Werner A. Jaegerhuber

1.
Èzili malad
We, Èzili malad o.
We, nanpwen dlo nan syèl o.
Solèy boule tè o.
Èzili malad o,
nou pa gen chans, mezanmi o.

Èzili e! Èzili e! Sa o!
M pa genyen chans, mezanmi,
yon sèl pitit mwen genyen o!
Èzili e! Èzili e! Sa o! O o o!
We, Èzili malad o!
Yon sèl pitit mwen genyen,
Èzili e! Èzili e! Sa o!

Werner A. Jaegerhuber's Songs

1.
Èzili Is Sick
Help, oh Èzili is sick.
Help, oh there is no water in the sky.
Oh the sun burns the land.
Oh Èzili is sick,
we don't have luck, oh my goodness.

Èzili hey! Èzili hey! Oh my!
I don't have luck, my goodness,
oh I have only one child!
Èzili hey! Èzili hey! Oh that! Oh oh oh!
Help, oh Èzili is sick!
Oh I have only one child,
Èzili hey! Èzili hey! Oh my!

2.

M Agwe Tawoyo

M Agwe Tawoyo,
Di m kote m demere.
Timoun pa pase la, Agwe o!
Nan lanmè m te ye.
Nan zile m te ye.

2.

I'm Agwe Tawoyo

I'm Agwe Tawoyo,
Tell me where I dwell.
Children don't come here, oh Agwe!
I was in the sea.
I was on the island.

3.

Envokasyon pou Danbala

Danbala o!
Danbala, non sakre o!
Danbala, Danbala Wèdo,
Danbala, non sakre o!
Danbala o!
Danbala, non sakre o!
Danbala, Danbala Wèdo,
Danbala, non sakre o!
Danbala o!

3.

Invocation to Danbala

Oh Danbala!
Danbala, oh sacred name!
Danbala, Danbala Wèdo,
Danbala, oh sacred name!
Oh Danbala!
Danbala, oh sacred name!
Danbala, Danbala Wèdo,
Danbala, oh sacred name!
Oh Danbala!

4.

Gwo lwa mwen

Gwo lwa mwen, gwo lwa mwen,
Simbi nan dlo.
Gwo lwa mwen, gwo lwa mwen,
Papa Simbi.
Batiman mwen chita nan bè,
li pa sa janbe.
M ap mande ki bagay sa?
M pa sa pale.
M pa sa pale o.

4.

My Great Lwa

My great lwa, my great lwa,
Simbi in the water.
My great lwa, my great lwa,
Papa Simbi.
My boat is sitting in the bay,
it can't cross over.
I'm asking what is this thing?
I can't talk about it.
Oh I can't talk about it.

5.

Èzili O! Èzili Sa!

Èzili o! Èzili sa!
Èzili e! Èzili sa! Enhen!
Nan lanmè kannòt mwen vle chavire.
Fò n priye Bondye
pou moun pa neye.
Èzili e! Fanm chans, Èzili sa!
Èzili manman, fanm chans,
Èzili sa! Enhen!
Nan lanmè kannòt mwen vle chavire.
Fò n priye Bondye
pou moun pa neye.

5.

Oh Ezili! That Ezili!

Oh Ezili! That Ezili!
Hey Ezili! That Ezili! Oh yeah!
On the sea my canoe wants to flip over.
We have to pray to God
so that people won't drown.
Hey Ezili! Good luck woman, that Ezili!
Mother Ezili, good luck woman,
That Ezili! Oh yeah!
On the sea my canoe wants to flip over.
We have to pray to God
so that people won't drown.

6.
Marasa eyo!
Eyo, eyo, eyo,[12]
mwen se pitit,
mwen pa genyen kay pou mwen.
Marasa eyo.
M pa gen papa.
M pa genyen manman.
Marasa eyo, eyo, eyo, eyo.
Marasa eyo.
M pa gen papa.
M pa genyen manman.
Marasa eyo, eyo, eyo, eyo.
Marasa eyo.
M pa gen papa.
M pa gen manman.
Marasa eyo, eyo, eyo, eyo.

6.
Marasa eyo!
Family, family, family,
I'm a child,
I don't have a house of my own.
Marasa is family.
I don't have a father.
I don't have a mother.
Marasa is family, family, family, family.
Marasa is family.
I don't have a father.
I don't have a mother.
Marasa is family, family, family, family.
Marasa is family.
I don't have a father.
I don't have a mother.
Marasa is family, family, family, family.

Chante Jean Price-Mars

1.
M sòti nan Ginen,
M pa genyen fanmi.
Marasa eyo.
M pa genyen papa.
M pa genyen manman.
Marasa eyo!

2.
M pa genyen fanmi,
sa k va pale pou mwen?
Marasa eyo!
M pa genyen pèsonn
pou pale pou mwen.
Marasa eyo!

3.
Fanmi mwen yo tout ale Jelefre.
Marasa eyo!
M pa genyen,
M pa genyen zanmi.
Marasa eyo!

Jean Price-Mars's Songs

1.
I come from Ginen,
I don't have family.
Marasa is family.
I don't have a father.
I don't have a mother.
Marasa is family!

2.
I don't have family,
who is going to speak for me?
Marasa is family!
I don't have anybody
to speak for me.
Marasa is family!

3.
My entire family went to Africa.
Marasa is family!
I don't have,
I don't have friends.
Marasa is family!

CHAPTER 4

Milo Marcelin's Songs

BENJAMIN HEBBLETHWAITE
and JOANNE BARTLEY

THIS CHAPTER includes all of the Haitian Creole texts from Milo Marcelin's *Mythologie Vodou (Rite Arada)* (Marcelin 1950a, 1950b). These source texts shed light on a diverse range of Vodou songs and provide an introduction to the religion and its pantheon, mythology, and philosophy. Marcelin collected these songs in various Vodou temples, and some of them can be found in identical or variant forms in Max Beauvoir's *Le grand recueil sacré ou répertoire des chansons du vodou haïtien* (2008) or Jacques Roumain's *Le sacrifice du tambour-Assôtô(r)* (1943). This fact suggests that some of the songs are widely disseminated and have been used uninterrupted for well over sixty years. These songs are both old and new. Their age is reflected in their preservation of *langaj* (West African language fragments) of Fon, Yorùbá, and Kikongo origin, among other languages. Their newness is expressed in the unique glimpses they provide into Haiti of the 1940s and their revelations about the lwa. The spelling has been normalized to the standard form.

The commentary on the songs that Marcelin (1950a, 1950b) collected forms an important source for Appendix A: Dictionary of Vodou Terms. The chapter includes songs dedicated to the following lwa: Atibon Legba, Ayizan Velekete, Loko Atisou, Danbala Wèdo, Ayida Wèdo, Metrès Èzili, Lavyèj Karidad, Sent Elizabèt, Grann Èzili, Agwe Tawoyo, Metrès Lasirèn, Agasou Gnenen, Ogou, Ogou Badagri, Ogou Feray, Chango, Azaka Mede, Agawou Tonnè, Sobo Kèsou, Badè, the Marasa, Gede, Bawon Samdi, Grann Brijit, and Gede Nibo. This list of twenty-five lwa includes the most significant ones in Vodou, and the order of the lwa and their songs closely reflects the order that one would encounter in a ceremony.

After Catholic texts and songs have been read or sung, a ceremony dedicated to a given lwa will greet between twenty and twenty-five lwa with three songs for each one, and the order in which the lwa are greeted will proceed consistently. Therefore, Atibon Legba will receive the first cycle of three songs, Ayizan Velekete will receive the second cycle of three songs, Loko Atisou will receive the third cycle of three songs, and so forth, until all of the appropriate lwa have been greeted. While each lwa receives three songs, the actual songs themselves may differ from ceremony to ceremony, since each lwa has a significant catalogue of songs that can be drawn from. The ordering of the lwa in Vodou ceremonies is conventional and usually follows an established sequence. The ordering of songs reflects the importance of *regleman* (order) in Vodou ritual, and the priests, priestesses, and oungenikon (choir leaders) of Vodou take this very seriously. These songs and the order in which they are presented provide valuable means for the study of *regleman* in Vodou ceremonies and offer precious insights into the mythology and characteristics of the lwa.

Chante Milo Marcelin

I. Atibon Legba

1.

Atibon Legba, louvri bayè pou mwen, ago e!
Papa Legba, louvri bayè pou mwen,
pou mwen pase.
Lò m a tounen m a salye lwa yo!
Vodou Legba, louvri bayè pou mwen,
pou mwen sa rantre.
Lò m a tounen m a remesye lwa yo,
Abobo!

2.

Atibon Legba, rive nan bayè a,
nou vye, o!
Papa Legba nan kalfou,
ou pa wè nou vye, o!
Papa Legba, nou vye!
Atibon rive nan chimen,
nou vye!

3.

Alegba, mache non!
N ape pote Atibon Legba,

Milo Marcelin's Songs

I. Atibon Legba

1.

Atibon Legba, open the gate for me, ago e!
Papa Legba, open the gate for me,
so that I can pass through.
When I return I'll greet the lwa!
Vodou Legba, open the gate for me,
so that I can enter.
When I return I'll thank the lwa,
Abobo!

2.

Atibon Legba, arrives at the gate,
you are so old!
Papa Legba is in the crossroads,
don't you see how old you are, phew!
Papa Legba, you're old!
Atibon arrives on the path,
you're old!

3.

Alegba, get walking already!
We're carrying Atibon Legba,

n ape pote potomitan!
Alegba, mache non!
Kote n bouke, se la n a poze
poto ki nan do n.

we're carrying the center post!
Alegba, get walking already!
When we are tired, we'll set down
the post that is on our backs.

4.
Vye zo o! Vye zo o! Papa Legba!
Ou pa wè nou san zo!

4.
Oh old bones! Oh old bones! Papa Legba!
Don't you see we're without bones!

5.
Mwen ta pran makout Alegba,
kwoke li nan do mwen.
E! e! e!
Makout Alegba,
kwoke li nan do mwen.
Eee, eee, eee!
Makout Alegba,
kwoke li nan do mwen.

5.
I would take Alegba's straw bag,
sling it over my back.
Ey! ey! ey!
Alegba's straw bag,
sling it over my back.
Hey, hey, hey!
Alegba's straw bag,
sling it over my back.

6.
Papa Legba nan ounfò mwen!
Atibon Lebga nan ounfò mwen!
Alegba Papa nan ounfò mwen!
Ou menm ki pote drapo nan Ginen!
Ou menm ki pote chapo nan Ginen!
Se ou menm k a pare solèy pou lwa yo.

6.
Papa Legba is in my temple!
Atibon Legba is in my temple!
Alegba Papa is in my temple!
It's you who bears the flag in Ginen!
It's you who wears the hat in Ginen!
It's you who will block the sun for the lwa.

7.
Alegba rete l ap gade m,
nou pa wè l, li wè n;
gade nou pa wè l.
Tout sa ki di byen,
li la, l ape koute.
Tout sa ki di mal,
li la, l ape koute.
Yo siyen non mwen Alegba,
yo pa siyen pye m.
M mande kote y a wè m.

7.
Alegba stops, he's looking at me,
we don't see him, he sees us;
look we don't see him.
All those who speak well,
he's there, he's listening.
All those who speak badly,
he's there, he's listening.
They sign my name Alegba,
they can't sign my tree.
I'm asking where they'll see me.

8.
Papa Legba m poko rive,
y ap nonmen non m!
Ankò m se wa,
jalouzi a pote pou mwen!

8.
Papa Legba I have not yet arrived,
they are calling my name!
Once again I am king,
jealousy is directed at me!

Ankò m se wa,
ankò m se wa,
jalouzi a pote pou mwen!

Once again I am king,
once again I am king,
jealousy is directed at me!

9.

Alegba, men yanvalou mwen, ago ye!
Mwen poko rive la,
men lennmi bare mwen.
Alegba nou poko rive la,
men lennmi bare mwen.
Ago! Ago! lwa yo.
Mwen poko rive la,
men lennmi bare mwen.

9.

Alegba, here's my yanvalou rhythm, ago yeah!
I have not yet arrived,
but enemies block me.
Alegba we have not yet arrived there,
but enemies block me.
Ago! Ago! The lwa.
I have not yet arrived there,
but enemies block me.

10.

M di: nan baryè sa a, pouki yo nonmen non m?
Nan baryè sa a, pouki yo nonmen non m?
Kan mwen rive nan baryè sa a,
Alegba, m pral regle afè sila yo.
Alegba Kinan, Kinan,
bo imaj Toto,
o byento n a wè yo.
Sa ki chèche va twouve.

10.

I said: at this gate, why do they call my name?
At this gate, why do they call my name?
When I have arrived at this gate,
Alegba, I will deal with these issues.
Alegba Quignan, Quignan,
kiss the image of Toto,
oh soon we will see them.
Those who seek will find.

11.

Ou manje poul la,
ou pa ban mwen.
Poul sila a,
poul Alegba.
Ou manje poul la, ou pa ban mwen.
Koklo sila a, se koklo Alegba,
Legba-si, Legba-sinyanyan, abobo.
Vanyan Legba,
sèt Legba Katawoulo yo.
Vanyan Legba,
Alegba-se, se nou de,
ago, ye!

11.

You ate the chicken,
you did not give me any.
This chicken here,
Alegba's chicken.
You ate the chicken, you did not give me any.
This rooster is Alegba's rooster,
Legba-si, Legba-signangnan, abobo.
Courageous Legba,
the seven Legba of the Katawoulo.
Valliant Legba,
Alegba's divine power, it is the two of us,
ago, yeah!

II. Ayizan Velekete

12.

Grann Ayizan, salye Legba ey!
Alèkilè lajan kase wòch!
M ape mande kouman nou ye?
Salye Legba ey!

II. Ayizan Velekete

12.

Granny Ayizan, greet Legba yeah!
At this time money breaks rocks!
I am asking how you are doing?
Greet Legba yeah!

Kreyòl yo sonde miwa Legba!
Ayizan vye, vye!
Kreyòl yo sonde
miwa Atibon Legba.

The Creoles are challenging Legba's mirror!
Ayizan is old, old!
The Creoles are challenging
Atibon Legba's mirror.

13.

Ayizan! Ayizan! Ayizan mache!
Ayizan mache, Ayizan pwonmennen!
Ayizan! Ayizan! Ayizan pwonmennen!

Ayizan De,
Ayizan ale pwonmennen!
Li mache, l al pwonmennen!
Ayizan De!

Ayizan, Ayizan Belekou o!
M di: Ayizan, Ayizan Belekou o!
Ou se ye, o! Se la nou ye!
Ayizan Belekou mache.

13.

Ayizan! Ayizan! Ayizan walks!
Ayizan walks, Ayizan strolls!
Ayizan! Ayizan! Ayizan strolls!

Ayizan De,
Ayizan went for a stroll!
She walked, she went for a stroll!
Ayizan De!

Ayizan, Ayizan Belekou oh!
I say: Ayizan, Ayizan Belekou oh!
It is you! We are here!
Ayizan Belekou walks.

14.

Mache, mache! Ayizan mache!
N a wè ki jan Ayizan mache!
Ayizan mache, n a wè ki jan, ago e!
Ayizan mache!
Ayizan mache, pou wè kichòy!
Ayizan mache!
Mache, mache, mache Ayizan, aochè Nago!

14.

Walk, walk! Ayizan walks!
We will see how Ayizan walks!
Ayizan walks, we will see how, ago yeah!
Ayizan walks!
Ayizan walks to see something!
Ayizan walks!
Walk, walk, walk, Ayizan, aochè Nago!

15.

Ey Ayizan,
Santayi, lese yo fè.
Santayi, papa, yo kontrarye nou.
Ayizan, papa, yo kontrarye nou.
Ayizan, lese yo fè.
Nanpwen anyen la pase Bondye.
Ayizan,
ou pa wè kreyòl kontrarye nou?
Santaye lese yo fè.
Nanpwen anyen la pase Bondye.
N ap gade o!
N ap gade, manbo Ayizan.
N ap gade yo la,
Ayizan-Gwèto, lese yo fè,
nanpwen anyen la pase Bondye o!

15.

Hey Ayizan,
Santayi, let them do what they want.
Santayi, man, they trouble us.
Ayizan, oh my, they trouble us.
Ayizan, let them do what they want.
There is nothing here except God.
Ayizan,
don't you see that the Creoles trouble us?
Santaye let them do what they want.
There is nothing here except God.
We're watching, oh!
We're watching, manbo Ayizan.
We are watching them here,
Ayizan-Gwèto let them do what they want,
oh there is nothing here except God!

Kreyòl kontrarye mwen.
Apre Dye, m ap ranje pou mwen gade o!
Mwen gade lakòt Ginen.
Après toi, notre Seigneur suprême,
fòk nou gade lesen.
Ayizan sa se lwa Ginen.
Nan Ginen, lakòt Ginen.
Nan Ginen o! Abobo!

16.
Sa m a di o!
Sa m a di Ayizan?
Sa m a di?
Se Bondye
ki ban mwen sen an kenbe.
Sa m a di lesen o!
Sa m a di?
Se Bondye ki ban mwen lwa a kenbe.
Sa m a di lwa a, sa m a di o!
Sa m a di Lavyèj Mari,
Dosou, Dosa.
Se Bondye ki ban mwen lwa a kenbe.
Sa m a di lakòt Ginen?
Sa m a di yo? Abobo!

17.
Rele Ayizan pou mwen!
Ayizan ou menm ki pote lorye blan!
Rele Ayizan pou mwen!
Badè Awannen m, Wannen m, Ayizan o!
Sobo Awannen m, Wannen m, Ayizan o!
Ayizan ou menm ki pote lorye blan!
Rele Ayizan pou mwen! Abobo!

18.
Manbo Ayizan,
ounsi la yo dozado!
Ounsi-kanzo, ounsi-bosal,
pale, ounsi kreyòl yo!
Manbo Ayizan,
ounsi la yo dozado!

The Creoles are troubling me.
After God, oh I'm getting ready to watch!
I watch the coast of Ginen.
After you, our Supreme savior,
we must look to the saints.
This Ayizan is a lwa from Ginen.
In Ginen, on the coast of Ginen.
Oh in Ginen! Abobo

16.
Oh what shall I say!
What shall I tell Ayizan?
What shall I say?
It is God
who gave me the saint to hold on to.
Oh what shall I tell the saints!
What shall I say?
It is God who gave me the lwa to hold on to.
What shall I tell the lwa, oh what shall I say!
What shall I tell the Virgin Mary,
Dosou, Dosa.
It is God who gave me the lwa to hold.
What shall I tell the coast of Ginen?
What shall I tell them? Abobo!

17.
Call Ayizan for me!
Ayizan, it's you who brings the white laurel!
Call Ayizan for me!
My Badè Awannen, my Wannen, oh Ayizan!
My Sobo Awannen, my Wannen, oh Ayizan!
Ayizan it's you who brings white laurel!
Call Ayizan for me! Abobo!

18.
Manbo Ayizan,
the temple members are back to back!
Ounsi-kanzo, ounsi-bosal,
speak, Creole temple members!
Manbo Ayizan,
the initiates are back to back!

19.

Ayizan-konplo pi fò pase wanga!
Gade m chita, mezanmi,
yo vle manje rezon mwen!
Ayizan-konplo pi fò pase wanga!
Dechouke, yo vle manje rezon mwen!
M di: Ayizan-konplo pi fò pase wanga.
Mwen di: Ayizan-konplo.
M poko rive pou m pale pawòl la.
Kreyòl manje rezon mwen!
Sa nou wè la a, nou pa sa pale o.
Ayizan-konplo,
nou poko rive pou m pale pawòl la,
Kreyòl manje rezon m!

19.

Ayizan-plotting is stronger than wanga!
Look at me sitting here, my goodness,
they want to devour my sanity!
Ayizan-plotting is stronger than wanga!
Uprooted, they want to devour my sanity!
I say: Ayizan-plotting is stronger than wanga.
I say: Ayizan-plotting.
I have not yet arrived to speak the words.
Creoles devoured my sanity!
What we saw here, oh we cannot speak of it.
Ayizan-plotting,
you have not yet arrived to speak the words,
Creoles devoured my sanity!

20.

Rele Ayizan pou mwen.
Ayizan, nou pral rele lwa anba dlo!
Rele Ayizan pou mwen.
Nou pral rele lwa anba dlo!

20.

Call Ayizan for me.
Ayizan, we will call the lwa from the water!
Call Ayizan for me.
We will call the lwa from the water!

21.

Yo ban mwen zen an.
Pote tou mare!
Yo ban mwen zen an,
zen an deja fele!
Yo ban mwen zen an.
Pote tou mare.

21.

They gave me the clay vessel.
Bring it all tied up!
The gave me the clay vessel,
the clay vessel was already cracked!
They gave me the clay vessel.
Bring it all tied up.

III. Loko Atisou

22.

Solèy o! Ati Dan, Ibo Loko! Solèy o!
Papa, mwen pa moun isit
Atchango, mwen sòti lwen, solèy o!
Papa Loko, m pa t vin pou rete.
Atò m pa kab travèse, solèy o!

23.

Loko De, abobo!
Loko De, a Loko De, Wa De.
Loko Miwa, o Loko De.
A! Loko De, Wa De.
O Loko Miwa o!

III. Loko Atisou

22.

Oh sun! Ati Dan, Ibo Loko! Oh sun!
Father, I am not from here.
Atchango, I come from afar, oh sun!
Father Loko, I didn't come to stay.
At this point I cannot cross over, oh sun!

23.

Loko De, abobo!
Loko De, ah Loko De, King De.
Loko-mirror, oh Loko De.
Ah! Loko De, King De.
Oh Loko-mirror, oh!

Lanperè Desalin o!
Kle ounfò a nan men nou, Loko De.
A! Loko De, Wa De, Loko Miwa.
O Loko De.
Lanperè Desalin o!
O kle ounfò a nan men nou.
Kle ounfò a nan men Agasou Miwa.
Kle ounfò a nan men nou.

Oh Emperor Dessalines!
The temple keys are in your hands, Loko De.
Ah! Loko De, king-De, Loko-mirror,
Oh Loko De.
Oh Emperor Dessalines!
Oh the temple keys are in your hands.
The temple keys are held by Agassou-mirror.
The temple keys are in your hands.

24.

O nou dija Ginen dija.
Nou pa sa gate.
O kreyòl yo di kon sa yo va gate Loko.
O, zòt manti, Agaza.
Nou dija ayè, nou dija.
Nou pa sa gate.
O kriye: Abobo!
Nou kriye: Abobo!
A! Loko Atisou!
O mangnanva!
Abobo.

24.

Oh we are already Ginen already.
You cannot ruin that.
Oh the Creoles say they will spoil Loko.
Oh, you tell lies, Agaza.
We are already yesterday, we are already.
You cannot spoil it.
Oh cry: Abobo!
We cry: Abobo!
Ah! Loko Atisou!
Oh mangananva!
Abobo.

25.

M te kite Loko veye kay pou mwen!
Loko rele Dawomen!
M te kite Loko veye kay pou mwen!
Loko rele Dawomen!

25.

I left Loko to watch the house for me!
Loko called Dahomey!
I left Loko to watch the house for me!
Loko called Dahomey!

26.

Men Yanva Loko!
Yo rayi oungan mwen.
Yo renmen wanga l!
Kote sèvitè Loko yo?
Vin salye l!
Yanvalou, kote sèvitè Loko?
Vin salye l!

26.

Here is Yanva Loko!
They hate my Vodou priest.
They love his magic charms!
Where are Loko's servants?
Come to greet him!
Yanvalou, where are Loko's servants?
Come to greet him!

27.

Nan oryan:
Pa pouvwa Sen Jozèf.
Pa pouvwa papa Loko.
Pa pouvwa Loko Atisou.

Nan oksidan:
Onon Loko Azanblou Gidi.

27.

To the east
By the power of Saint Joseph.
By the power of father Loko.
By the power of Loko Atisou.

To the west:
In the name of Loko Azanblou Gidi.

Onon Loko Dawomen.
Onon Loko, wa Nago.

Nan sid:
Onon Loko De.
Onon Loko Kisigwè.
Onon Loko Yay.

Anfen, nan nò a:
Onon de Azagon Loko,
Onon de Loko Dan Yiso,
Onon de Loko, ponm Adan
(ou lanmou).
Ago, ago isi, ago la!

In the name of Loko Dahomey.
In the name of Loko, king of Nago.

To the south:
In the name of Loko De.
In the name of Loko Kisigwè.
In the name of Loko Yai.

Finally, to the north:
In the name of Azagon Loko.
In the name of Loko Dan Yiso.
In the name of Loko, apple of Adam
(or love).
Ago, ago here, ago there!

28.

Sonnen klòch la, papa, men Gede!
M ape vini tout an nwa
pou jwenn Papa Loko!
Ti Wawè, vini tout an nwa
jwenn Papa Loko!
Ti Wawè vini tout an nwa
jwenn Papa Loko-Atisou!
Ti Wawè. Abobo.
Mèt Loko Atisou,
ounfò a mande drapo!

28.

Ring the bell, man, here is Gede!
I'll come all dressed in black
to find Father Loko!
Little Wawè, come all in black
to find father Loko!
Little Wawè, come all in black
to find father Loko Atisou!
Little Wawè. Abobo.
Master Loko Atisou,
the temple requires flags!

29.

Papa Loko, fanm vye,
fanm mande pwòpte.
Fanm pa janm vye.
Kadyamisou di fanm Loko vye.
Fanm pa janm vye.
Douvan wòb fanm
mande pwòpte.
Kote fanm Loko
konnen vye?
Douvan wòb fanm
mande pwòpte.
Depi fanm mande pwòpte,
li pa janm vye.
Mwen di vye,
Kadyamisou di fanm Loko vye.
Fanm pa janm vye, larenn o!
Ayayay larenn, n ap pale.

29.

Father Loko, women are old,
women ask for cleanliness.
Women are never old.
Kadyamisou says that Loko's women are old.
Women are never old.
The front of women's dresses
require cleanliness.
Where have Loko's women
been known as old?
The front of women's dresses
demand cleanliness.
When a woman asks for cleanliness,
she is never old.
I say old,
Kadyamisou says Loko's women are old.
Women are never old, oh queen!
O my goodness the queen, we're talking.

Fanm pa janm vye.
Fanm vye, fanm pa janm vye.
Depi fanm genyen pwòpte,
fanm pa janm vye.
Loko Atisou di madanm Loko vye.
Li pa vye.
Fanm vye, fanm pa janm vye, larenn o.
Denpi yon fanm gen pwòpte,
li pa janm vye.

Women are never old.
Old women, women are never old.
As long as women are clean,
women are never old.
Loko Atisou says Loko's wife is old.
She isn't old.
Old women, women are never old, oh queen.
As long as a woman is clean,
she is never old.

30.
A! Loko di yo!
Papa Loko di yo sa, ey!
Loko, ki sòti lan Jakmèl,
l ap gaye nouvèl ban nou!

30.
Ah! Loko told them!
Father Loko told them this, hey!
Loko, who comes from Jacmel,
he will spread the news to us!

31.
Van, van, van, Loko!
Loko mande van, ey! Loko!
Aleba Loko mande van, ey!
Van, van, van, Loko!
Loko mande van, ey! Loko!
Aleba Loko mande van, ey!

31.
Wind, wind, wind, Loko!
Loko asks for wind, hey! Loko!
Aleba Loko asks for wind, hey!
Wind, wind, wind, Loko!
Loko asks for wind, hey! Loko!
Aleba Loko asks for wind, hey!

32.
Loko, Loko di yo.
Se papa Loko sa ye.
M pral chache fanmi mwen yo
O mi owa, owa.
Loko, enhen.
M pral chache fanmi mwen yo.

32.
Loko, Loko tells them.
This is Father Loko.
I will find members of my family.
O mi owa owa.
Loko, oh yeah.
I will find members of my family.

33.
A! Loko voye chache m.
Papa ou voye chache m.
Kote m te ye a, m te byen la.
Voye rele m Loko Atisou.
Loko Atisou, ou voye chache m.
Kote m te ye a, m te byen la.

33.
Ah! Loko has sent to find me.
Father, you sent to find me.
Where I was, I was good there.
Call for me Loko Atisou.
Loko Atisou, you sent to find me.
Where I was, I was good there.

34.
Men Yanva Loko.
Loko, enhen!
Men Yanva Loko.
Loko, enhen!

34.
Here is Yanva Loko.
Loko, oh yeah!
Here is Yanva Loko.
Loko, oh yeah!

Se Yanva Loko!
Se pa Loko sa?
Kite m chache fanmi mwen!
Men Yanva Loko!
Loko, enhen!

It is Yanva Loko!
Isn't that Loko?
Let me look for my family!
Here is Yanva Loko!
Loko, oh yeah!

IV. Danbala Wèdo

35.
Koulèv, koulèv o!
Danbala Wèdo, Papa, ou koulèv o!
Koulèv, koulèv o!
O Danbala Wèdo,
Ou koulèv o!
M ape rele koulèv o!
Koulèv pa sa pale!
Danbala, Papa, ou se koulèv o!

36.
M di: syèl o, salye latè, ey!
Oso, ey!
Danbala Wèdo m granmoun, o ey!

37.
Danbala Wèdo se koulèv dlo!
Chèche Danbala, ki bò w a wè li?
Papa Danbala se koulèv dlo,
li plonje anba dlo!

38.
Ala lwa mache nan dlo,
se Danbala o!
Ala lwa mache nan dlo,
se Danbala o!
Papa Danbala se tèt dlo!
Papa Danbala se tèt dlo! Abobo!

39.
Papa Danbala,
mwen bezwen benyen la a.
Dlo a nan basen mwen,
O Danbala Wèdo.
M bezwen benyen la a.
Dlo a nan basen lwa yo.

IV. Danbala Wèdo

35.
Oh snake, snake!
Danbala Wèdo, Papa, oh you are a snake!
Oh snake, snake!
Oh Danbala Wèdo,
Oh you are a snake!
Oh I am calling the snake!
The snake cannot speak!
Danbala, Papa, oh you are a snake!

36.
I say: oh heavens, greet the earth, hey!
Oso, hey!
My Danbala Wèdo is grown up, oh hey!

37.
Danbala Wèdo is the water snake!
Look for Danbala, where will you see him?
Papa Danbala is the water snake,
he dives under water!

38.
Look how the lwa walks on water,
oh it is Danbala!
Look how the lwa walks on water,
oh it is Danbala!
Papa Danbala is the water's spring!
Papa Danbala is the water's spring! Abobo!

39.
Papa Danbala,
I need to bathe right here.
The water is in my pond,
Oh Danbala Wèdo.
I need to bathe right here.
The water is in the pond of the lwa.

40.
Danbala o, siyale o!
Siyale o, lwa mwen o!
Papa Danbala o,
Siyale o, anye o!

40.
Oh Danbala, oh signal!
Oh signal, oh my lwa!
Oh Papa Danbala,
Oh signal, oh my!

41.
Danbala ey!
Danbala, nou sakre!
Danbala ey!
Danbala, nou sakre!
Danbala Wèdo!

41.
Danbala hey!
Danbala, you are sacred!
Danbala hey!
Danbala, you are sacred!
Danbala Wèdo!

42.
Lè yo bezwen m, yo rele m papa.
Jou yo pa bezwen m,
yo di m se koulèv o!
Danbala Wèdo, sa m fè yo?
Papa m se move tèt o!
Kite m navige!
Papa, yo salye tout moun,
pouki yo pa salye mwen!
Papa yo salye tout moun,
pouki yo pa salye mwen!
Papa m se move tèt o!
Kite m navige!

42.
When they need me, they call me papa.
The days they do not need me,
oh they say I am a snake!
Danbala Wèdo, what have I done to them?
Oh my father is angry!
Let me navigate!
Papa, they greet everyone,
why don't they greet me!
Papa they greet everyone,
why don't they greet me!
Oh my father is a mad head!
Let me navigate!

43.
Danbala Wèdo,
tout moun kontan,
Ou menm fache!
Danbala Wèdo,
tout moun kontan,
ou menm fache!
O si nou wè Danbala pase,
karese l pou mwen!

43.
Danbala Wèdo,
everyone is happy,
You are angry!
Danbala Wèdo,
everyone is happy,
you are angry!
Oh if you should see Danbala pass by,
caress him for me!

44.
O miwaze!
Danbala se granmoun o!
Ou pa wè nou prale!
O miwaze!
Danbala se granmoun o!
Ou pa wè nou prale!

44.
Oh mirror of the egg![1]
Oh Danbala is grown up!
Don't you see that we are leaving!
Oh mirror of the egg!
Oh Danbala is grown up!
Don't you see that we are leaving!

V. Ayida Wèdo

45.

File m ap file.
Fanm Danbala Wèdo se koulèv o!
File m ap file.
fanm Danbala Wèdo se koulèv o!

46.

Vodou lakansyèl.
O Vodou lwa m.
O Vodou Lakansyèl.
Lakansyèl, Vodou lwa m.

47.

Si nou wè koulèv, ou wè Ayida Wèdo!
Ayida Wèdo se yon koulèv o!
Si ou wè koulèv, ou wè Danbala!
Ayida Wèdo se yon koulèv o!

48.

Nou tout ble, ble, Danbala Wèdo.
Danbala Wèdo rele Wanki.
N ape rele navige, papa.
O nou tou ble o!
Basen sa, basen Danbala Wèdo.
Basen sa, basen Ayida Wèdo.
O nou tout ble, ble.

49.

Fiyole pou Danbala.
Ayida Wèdo, fiyole.
Kondi m ale nan ounfò mwen.
Danbala Wèdo, fiyole.
Mete mwen lan ounfò mwen.
Danbala, voye m al nan ounfò mwen.

50.

Pouswiv o! Vivan ape swiv mwen.
Y ap pouswiv o!
M chita la, m pa fè pèsòn anyen.
M chita, m pa di pèsòn anyen.
Y ap pouswiv mwen.
Se mwen menm, Danbala Wèdo.

V. Ayida Wèdo

45.

I'm indeed slithering.
Oh the wife of Danbala Wèdo is a snake!
I'm indeed slithering.
Oh the wife of Danbala Wèdo is a snake!

46.

Vodou of the rainbow.
Oh my Vodou lwa.
Oh Vodou Rainbow.
Rainbow, my Vodou lwa.

47.

If you see a snake, you see Ayida Wèdo!
Oh Ayida Wèdo is a snake!
If you see a snake, you see Danbala!
Oh Ayida Wèdo is a snake!

48.

We are all blue, blue, Danbala Wèdo.
Danbala Wèdo cries Wanki.
We cry sail on, man.
Oh we are all blue!
This basin is Danbala Wèdo's basin.
This basin is Ayida Wèdo's basin.
Oh we are all blue, blue.

49.

Wipe the face for Danbala.
Ayida Wèdo, wipe the face.
Take me to my temple.
Danbala Wèdo, wipe the face.
Put me in my temple.
Danbala, send me to my temple.

50.

Oh pursuit! The living are pursuing me.
Oh they are in pursuit!
I sit here, I have done nothing to anyone.
I sit, I don't tell anyone anything.
They are pursuing me.
It is me, Danbala Wèdo.

Se mwen menm, Ayida Wèdo.
Nou pa janm wè
kote m tounen koulèv o!

It is me, Ayida Wèdo.
Oh you have never seen
where I turn into a snake!

VI. Metrès Èzili

VI. Mistress Èzili

51.

Mwen pa genyen chans, mezanmi o!
Mwen pa genyen chans!
Mwen pa genyen chans, mezanmi o!
Mwen pa genyen chans!

Yon sèl ti pitit mwen genyen.
L ale navige lan lanmè.
Kannòt chavire avèk li!
Lan lanmè, kannòt chavire!

51.

I am out of luck, oh good grief!
I am out of luck!
I am out of luck, oh good grief!
I am out of luck!

One lone, small child that I have.
He went off to sail the seas.
The canoe flipped over on him!
In the sea, the canoe flipped over!

52.

Èzili mari ou dòmi deyò!
O Metrès Èzili, mari ou
dòmi deyò!
Èzili mari ou dòmi deyò.
Kote sa li pote pou ou?

52.

Èzili your husband slept away from home!
Oh Mistress Èzili, your husband
slept away from home!
Èzili your husband slept somewhere else.
Where is what he brought for you?

53.

Èzili Freda o! Kote ou ye?
M pa wè ou lan dlo.
Si ou bezwen m, mache lakay.
W a wè m Èzili.

Èzili o! Kote ou ye?
Ala ou lan dlo!
Kote ou ye bèl fanm?
Mache lakay! Mache lakay o!
Manbo Freda Dawomen.

53.

Oh Èzili Freda! Where are you?
I don't see you in the water.
If you need me, come home.
You will see me Èzili.

Oh Èzili! Where are you?
Look you are in the water!
Where are you beautiful woman?
Come home! Oh come home!
Manbo Freda Dawomen.

54.

M angaje o!
Èzili voye rele lwa yo
pou m wè si m a sove!
Ala ennan sis mwa
mwen sou lanmè!
Anyen pa sa fè m!

54.

Oh I am in trouble!
Èzili send for the lwa
so that I may be saved!
Oh for one year and six months
I have been at sea!
Nothing can trouble me!

Èzili voye rele lwa yo
pou m wè si m a sove o!
Èzili o! Èzili sa!
Se sou lanmè kannòt mwen t ap neye!
Nou pa gen chans Èzili, nou pa gen chans!
Se sou lanmè, kannòt mwen t ap neye.

Èzili send for the lwa
oh so that I may be saved!
Oh Èzili! This Èzili!
It was in the sea that my canoe was sinking!
We are out of luck Èzili, we are out of luck!
It was in the sea that my canoe was sinking.

55.
Mwen mande ou padon,
Metrès Èzili Freda.
Mwen mande ou padon.
Metrès nou se pitit Bondye fè.
Nou p ap mòde ou jis lan zo.

55.
I ask you for forgiveness,
Mistress Èzili Freda.
I ask you for forgiveness.
Mistress, we are children that God created.
We will not bite you right to the bone.

56.
Èzili o! Èzili o!
Kay ou mande wouze!
Si nanpwen losyon,
n a wouze avèk dlo.

56.
Oh Èzili! Oh Èzili!
Your house needs to be sprinkled!
If it doesn't have lotion,
we will sprinkle it with water.

57.
Èzili Freda Dawomen,
se ou ki bèl,
se ou ki bon,
Èzili Ayida Wèdo.
Mwen santi m ape moute,
o bèl metrès kay mwen.

57.
Èzili Freda Dahonmen,
it is you who is beautiful,
it is you who is good,
Èzili Ayida Wèdo.
I feel that I am being possessed,
oh beautiful mistress of my house.

58.
Èzili o! Apa Èzili sa!
Èzili o! Apa Èzili sa! Abobo!

58.
Oh Èzili! If it isn't that Èzili!
Oh Èzili! If it isn't that Èzili! Abobo!

59.
Ala yon bèl fanm se Èzili!
Metrès, fò m fè ou yon bèl kado
anvan ou ale! Abobo.

59.
What a beautiful woman Èzili is!
Mistress, I must make you a nice gift
before you leave! Abobo.

60.
Èzili Ayida Tokan,
Tout pitit ou yo lan men ou!
Èzili o! Metrès kay mwen!
M prale, m prale, kan m a tounen,
sa k a resevwa mwen?

60.
Èzili Ayida Tokan,
All your children are in your hands!
Oh Èzili! Mistress of my house!
I'm going, I'm going, when I have returned,
who will receive me?

61.

M ape rele Metrès Èzili o!
Prete m yon chèz
pou m rakonte ou mizè m!
M ape rele Èzili Freda o!
Prete m yon chèz
pou m rakonte ou mizè m!

VII. Lavyèj Karidad ak Sent Elizabèt

62.

Yo te voye m Kiba
pou mwen te mouri!
Vyèj Karidad di non,
m p ape mouri o!
Karidad ki kote ou ye?
Karidad ki kote ou ye, manman?
Kou yon pawòl pale
yo di se mwen menm!

63.

Elizabèt lwa mwen,
Nouvèl voye rele ou.
M pa konn sa pou l fè ou.
Rele Sen Nouvèl, rele Elizabèt,
M pral pran pwen depa.

Nouvèl o! Nouvèl o!
Tanbou Vodou m rele Nouvèl o!
Nouvèl o!
Nouvèl ale,
Nouvèl tounen!
O! Tanbou Adja rele Nouvèl o!

VIII. Grann Èzili

64.

Èzili Fre, Èzili Freda,
Dawomen kò a li ye,
Èzili Freda Dawomen!
Èzili Fre, Èzili Freda,
Grann Èzili kò a li ye!
Èzili Freda manman Vodou o!

61.

Oh I am calling Mistress Èzili!
Lend me a chair
so that I may tell you of my misery!
Oh I am calling Èzili Freda!
Lend me a chair
so that I may tell you of my misery!

VII. The Virgin Caridad and Saint Elizabeth

62.

They sent me to Cuba
in order to die!
The Virgin Caridad said no,
oh I will not die!
Caridad where are you?
Caridad where are you, mother?
As soon as a word is spoken
they say that it is me!

63.

Elizabeth my lwa,
Nouvèl is calling for you.
I don't know what he wants with you.
Cry Saint Nouvèl, cry Elizabeth,
I will get a spell to vanish.

Oh Nouvèl! Oh Nouvèl!
Oh my Vodou drums call Nouvèl!
Oh Nouvèl!
Nouvèl has gone,
Nouvèl has returned!
Oh! Adja's drum calls Nouvèl oh!

VIII. Granny Èzili

64.

Èzili Fresh, Èzili Freda,
She belongs to Dahomey,
Èzili Freda Dawomen!
Èzili Fresh, Èzili Freda,
Granny Èzili is who she is!
Oh Èzili Freda mother of Vodou!

Dawomen kò a li ye!
Èzili Fre, Èzili Freda,
Dawomen kò a li ye.

She belongs to Dahomey!
Èzili Fresh, Èzili Freda,
She belongs to Dahomey.

65.

M di Èzili, o!
M pral rele Grann Èzili!
Kote y a wè m?
Èzili kouche sou do!
Mande kote y a wè m?

65.

Oh I say Èzili!
I am going to call Granny Èzili!
Where will they see me?
Èzili is resting on her back!
Ask where they will see me?

66.

Èzili, o! M san zo, ey!
Èzili m san zo!
M san zo lan tout kò m!
Èzili, o! M san zo, ey!
M san zo lan tout kò m!
Èzili o! M san zo.

66.

Oh Èzili! Hey, I have no bones!
Èzili I have no bones!
I have no bones in my entire body!
Oh Èzili! Hey, I have no bones!
I have no bones in my entire body!
Oh Èzili! I have no bones.

67.

Mwen tande yon kannon ki tire,
mezanmi o! M ape mande sa li ye?
Batiman Agwe Tawoyo derape.
Batiman, Koki Lanmè, derape.
Èzili malad o!
Papa va trete li.

67.

I hear a cannon that has fired,
oh my goodness! I am asking what it is?
Agwe Tawoyo's boat has departed.
The boat, Seashell, has departed.
Oh Èzili is ill!
Papa will treat her.

68.

Mwen pa genyen chans, mezanmi o!
Mwen pa genyen chans!

Èzili o! Apa Èzili sa a!
Èzili marye, li pa genyen chans!
Èzili fè jennès, li pa genyen chans!
Yon sèl pitit li genyen.
L ale lan lanmè,
kannòt chavire avè li!
Lan lanmè, kannòt chavire avè li!

68.

I had no luck, oh good grief!
I had no luck!

Oh Èzili! Oh that Èzili!
Èzili got married, she had no luck!
Èzili prostituted herself, she had no luck!
She had one sole child.
She went into the sea,
the canoe flipped over on her!
In the sea, the canoe flipped over on her!

69.

Grann Èzili do ba ye.
M ape pale,
yo pa vle koute m.
M ape pale zanfan la yo,

69.

Granny Èzili has a hunched back, yeah.
I am speaking,
they don't want to listen to me.
I am speaking to these children,

yo pa vle koute m la.
Èzili do ba ye.
M ape pale,
yo pa vle koute m.

they do not want to listen to me here.
Èzili has a hunched back.
I am speaking,
they do not want to listen to me.

70.

Jete dlo a pou mwen.
W a jete dlo a pou mwen.
Grann Èzili Freda,
w a jete dlo a pou mwen.
Grann mwen te pale ou ase,
w a jete dlo a pou mwen.

70.

Pour out water for me.
You will pour out water for me.
Granny Èzili Freda,
you will pour out water for me.
My Granny spoke to you enough,
you will pour out water for me.

71.

M di: Èzili ou granmoun o!
O lonje men, lonje men bay zanfan yo!
Mwen di: Èzili ou granmoun o!
Èzili o! Ou granmoun o!

M di: Grann o! M ape rele Grann o!
Grann Èzili, Grann dantan!
M a lonje men bay zanfan la yo!

71.

I say: oh Èzili you are grown up!
Oh lend a hand, lend a hand to the children!
I say: oh Èzili you are grown up!
Oh Èzili! You are grown up!

I say: oh Granny! Oh I am calling Granny!
Granny Èzili, Granny of old!
I will lend a hand to the children!

72.

Ala ennan sis mwa
mwen pa manje!
M ape mande Èzili ki kote ou ye o?
Èzili ki kote ou ye o?
Grann Èzili, ki kote ou ye, manman?
Kou yon pawòl, yo di se mwen.

72.

Oh for one year and six months
I haven't eaten!
I am asking Èzili oh where are you?
Oh Èzili where are you?
Granny Èzili, where are you, mother?
When a word is spoken, they blame me.

73.

Mwen di Grann bonjou, bonjou Grann.
M ape mande kouman ou ye?
Mwen di Grann bonjou, bonjou Grann.
M ape mande kouman ou ye?
M ape chèche Grann.
Sobo, mwen pa jwenn Grann.
M ape chèche Grann.
Sobo, mwen pa jwenn Grann.
Men Yanvalou mwen, Sobo, m a sove.

73.

I say to Granny good day, good day Granny.
I am asking how are you?
I say to Granny good day, good day Granny.
I am asking how you are?
I am looking for Granny.
Sobo, I have not found Granny.
I am looking for Granny.
Sobo, I have not found Granny.
Here is my Yanvalou, Sobo, I'll be saved.

74.
Èzili o! Èzili o!
Èzili o! Kay la mande wouze!
Èzili, si pa genyen dlo?
Vin wouze lan pye m!

74.
Oh Èzili! Oh Èzili!
Oh Èzili! The house needs sprinkling!
Èzili, if there is no water?
Come sprinkle on my feet!

IX. Agwe Tawoyo

75.
Ala yon bèl pwason
ki sòti lan lanmè!
Si ou koute pwason sa a,
w a mouri malere!

76.
Agwe, Agwe, m di Agwe, Agwe!
Agwe Tawoyo, Desalin o!
Desalin rete la,
Li tire kanon, se pou Agwe!
Agwe, Agwe, Agwe Tawoyo, Desalin o!

77.
Agwe o! Siyen lòd ou!
Jou m angaje, m a rele Agwe!
Agwe Woyo, m pa prese!
Koki Lanmè, m pa prese!
Genyen yon kou dèyè!
Papa, m a pare tann yo!

78.
Agwe rete sou lanmè, li tire o!
Li tire o, Agwe Tawoyo!
Agwe rete sou lanmè, li tire o, li tire o,
Agwe Tawoyo!

79.
Agwe Tawoyo,
kote m demere, timoun pa demere la.
Lan letan m te ye.
Lan zile m te ye.
Kote m demere, timoun pa demere la,
Agwe Tawoyo.

IX. Agwe Tawoyo

75.
What a beautiful fish
that comes from the sea!
If you listen to this fish,
you will die poor!

76.
Agwe, Agwe, I say Agwe, Agwe!
Agwe Tawoyo, oh Dessalines!
Dessalines stays here,
He fires the cannon, it is for Agwe!
Agwe, Agwe, Agwe Tawoyo, oh Dessalines!

77.
Oh Agwe! Sign your order!
The day I am in trouble, I will call Agwe!
Agwe Woyo, I am in no hurry!
Koki Lanmè, I am in no hurry!
There is plotting behind us!
Man, I'll be ready and waiting for them!

78.
Agwe stays at sea, oh he fires!
Oh he fires, Agwe Tawoyo!
Agwe stays at sea, oh he fires, oh he fires,
Agwe Tawoyo!

79.
Agwe Tawoyo,
where I stay, children do not stay there.
I was in the lake.
I was on the island.
Where I stay, children do not stay there,
Agwe Tawoyo.

80.

Vi m asire, Agwe Tawoyo!
Agwe Tawoyo, vi m asire!
Sou lanmè Doki, lanmè fò.
Ago! Ago! Ago!

Agwe Woyo,
sobagi m asire devan lwa yo!
Aprè Dye,
m pa gen manman ki pou pale pou mwen!
M pa gen papa isit ki pou pale pou mwen!
Agwe Woyo,
sobagi m asire devan lwa yo!

80.

My life is assured, Agwe Tawoyo!
Agwe Tawoyo, my life is assured!
On Doqui's sea, the sea is rough.
Ago! Ago! Ago!

Agwe Woyo,
my sanctuary is assured before the lwa!
After God,
I don't have a mother to speak for me!
I don't have a father here to speak for me!
Agwe Woyo,
my sanctuary is assured before the lwa!

81.

Siyale Wodo Wam we-le-o, papa!
Siyale n ape siyale o!
Agwe Tawoyo, Papa! Siyale!

81.

Signal Wodo Wam we-le-o, Papa!
Oh we are fully signaling!
Agwe Tawoyo, Papa! Signal!

82.

Lan lanmè m t ale peche, Agwe Woyo!
M pèdi zaviwon lwa mwen!
M ape mande sa m a soupe.
Koki Lanmè, sa m a soupe?

Sou lanmè m te ye!
Sa m a soupe, Teta lan dlo?
Sa m a soupe, Koki Lanmè?
M ap navige! Sou lanmè m te ye!
M ap navige, Agwe Tawoyo!
M pèdi zaviwon lwa mwen!
M ape mande Awoyo, sa m a soupe?

Agwe,
ou pa wè m pèdi zavi lwa mwen!
M ape mande, Papa, sa m a soupe?
Sa m a soupe, Agwe Tawoyo?
Sa m a soupe?
Ou pa wè kannòt mwen chavire!
M ape mande Agwe Tawoyo sa m a jwenn!
M ape mande sa m a soupe.

82.

In the sea I went fishing, Agwe Woyo!
I lost my lwa's paddle!
I'm asking what I will eat for supper.
Seashell, what will I eat for supper?

I was on the sea!
What will I eat for supper, water Tadpole?
What will I eat for supper, Seashell?
I'm navigating! I was on the sea!
I will navigate, Agwe Tawoyo!
I lost my lwa's paddle!
I ask Awoyo, what will I eat for supper?

Agwe,
don't you see that I lost my lwa's paddle!
I'm asking, Papa, what will I eat for supper?
What will I eat for supper, Agwe Tawoyo?
What will I eat for supper?
Don't you see that my canoe has flipped over!
I'm asking Agwe Tawoyo what I will find!
I'm asking what I will eat for supper.

83.
Mèt Agwe, kote ou ye?
Ou pa wè mwen nan resif?
Agwe Tawoyo, kote ou ye?
Ou pa wè mwen sou lanmè?
M gen zaviwon nan men mwen,
M pa sa tounen dèyè!
M douvan deja, m pa sa tounen dèyè!
Mèt Agwe Woyo kote ou ye non?
Ou pa wè mwen nan resif?

83.
Master Agwe, where are you?
Don't you see that I am having difficulty?
Agwe Tawoyo, where are you?
Don't you see that I am at sea?
I have a paddle in my hand,
I cannot turn back!
I'm already out at sea, I cannot turn back!
Master Agwe Woyo where are you, huh?
Don't you see that I am having difficulty?

84.
Malere, Agweta, ala lanmò ki rèd
se lanmò malere!
M a di: chante jodi a. M a di: va demen!
Ala lanmò ki rèd
se lanmò malere!

84.
Poor, Agweta, what a terrible death
is the death of a poor person!
I'll say: sing today. I'll say: go tomorrow!
What a terrible death
is the death of a poor person!

85.
Agwe, mwen lan Ginen.
M ape di Agwe Tawoyo,
mwen lan Ginen la.
M ape mande
sa k a ban nou dlo a pou nou jete.
Agwe Tawoyo,
sa ki pou ban nou dlo a pou nou jete.
Ayibobo pou lwa yo.

85.
Agwe, I am in Ginen.
I say Agwe Tawoyo,
I am here in Ginen.
I'm asking
who will give us water to pour out.
Agwe Tawoyo,
who will give us the water for libations.
Ayibobo for the lwa.

X. Metrès Lasirenn

86.
Lasirenn o! Se ou menm ki Balenn o!
Apre sen, se mwen k ap koumande!

87.
Metrès o!
Pinga ou nonmen non m!
Si ou nonmen non m,
kanon va tire o!
Metrès, bèl fanm o!
Pouki ou nonmen non m?
Si ou nonmen non m!
Metrès, kannon va tire o!
Kannon va tire o!
Kannon va tire, Metrès o!

X. Mistress Lasirenn

86.
Oh Lasirenn! Oh it is you who is the Whale!
After the saints, it is me who commands!

87.
Oh Mistress!
You'd better not speak my name!
If you speak my name,
oh cannons will fire!
Mistress, oh beautiful woman!
Why do you speak my name?
If you speak my name!
Oh Mistress, cannons will fire!
Oh cannons will fire!
Cannons will fire, oh Mistress!

88.

Mwen pa wè Metrès Lasirenn.
M ape mande Agwe Tawoyo pou li.
Lasirenn, nou la,
n ape gade ou.
Nou pa wè ou.
M ape mande Agwe Tawoyo pou ou.
Nou la, n ape gade ou.

Balenn o! Rele Sirenn o!
Nanpwen zanmi tankou Sirenn o!
Mwen di: nanpwen zanmi tankou Balenn o!
Balenn o! Rele Sirenn o!

88.

I don't see Mistress Lasirenn.
I ask Agwe Tawoyo for her.
Lasirenn, we are here,
we are watching for you.
We don't see you.
I ask Agwe Tawoyo for you.
We are here, we are watching for you.

Oh Balenn! Oh call Sirenn!
Oh there is no friend like Sirenn!
I say: oh there is no friend like Balenn!
Oh Balenn! Call Sirenn!

89.

Amwa, Kong de Labalenn e de la Lasirenn!
Sa ki nonmen non mwen?
Amwa, Kong de Labalenn e de Lasirenn!
Sa ki nonmen non mwen?
W a di yo,
w a di yo mwen angaje.

89.

Oh my, Eel of Labalenn and Lasirenn!
Who spoke my name?
Oh my, Eel of Labalenn and Lasirenn!
Who spoke my name?
You will tell them,
you will tell them I am in trouble.

90.

Metrès Lasirenn,
m prale, m prale!
Lasirenn, Lasirenn,
rete sou lanmè, li tire kannon.

90.

Mistress Lasirenn,
I am leaving, I am leaving!
Lasirenn, Lasirenn,
stays at sea, she fires cannons.

XI. Agasou Gnenen

91.

Agasou o! M prale lan Ginen!
Kretyen vivan pa Bondye!

Agasou ale lan Ginen!
Agasou Gnenen ale lan Ginen!
Kretyen vivan pa Bondye!

92.

Agasou Do Miwa ey!
Agasou Yeme Do Miwa ey!
Agasou Do Miwa ey!
Ago! Ago! Ago!

XI. Agasou Gnenen

91.

Oh Agasou! I am going to Ginen!
Living beings are not God!

Agasou went to Ginen!
Agasou Gnenen went to Ginen!
Living beings are not God!

92.

Agasou Do Miwa[2] hey!
Agasou Yeme Do Miwa hey!
Agasou Do Miwa hey!
Ago! Ago! Ago!

93.

Agasou Yeme pale zanfan ou yo!
Sen Agasou Yeme, pale pitit ou yo!
Genyen yon jou, genyen yon tan!
O n a wè sa!
Ago! Ago! Ago!

93.

Agasou Yeme, speak to your children!
Saint Agasou Yeme, speak to your children!
There is a day, there is a time!
Oh we will see this!
Ago! Ago! Ago!

94.

Agasou Yeme, m se granmoun o!
Silibo Vevou mwen, ago, ago!
M te pale zanfan yo,
m te pale pitit yo,
yo pa vle koute.
Agasou Yeme, m se granmoun o!
Silibo Vevou mwen, ago! ago!

94.

Agasou Yeme, oh I am an adult!
My Silibo Vevou, ago, ago!
I counseled the children,
I counseled the infants,
they did not want to listen.
Oh Agasou Yeme, I am grown up!
My Silibo Vevou, ago, ago!

95.

Agasou o! Yeme o!
Silibo eya, nan tan m!
M prale, Papa Agasou!
Silibo eya, nan tan m!

95.

Oh Agasou! Oh Yeme!
Silibo eya, in my time!
I'm going, Papa Agasou!
Silibo eya, in my time!

XII. Papa Simbi

96.

Simbi Lasous o! Wayo!
Simbi Lasous lan peyi mwen!

96.

Oh Simbi of the Spring! Wayo!
Simbi of the Spring is in my country!

97.

Simbi rele m pou m vini pran dlo!
Simbi rele m pou m vini keyi yon fèy!
M pran dlo a,
o dlo a tonbe lan men m!
M keyi fèy la,
o fèy la tranble lan men m!

97.

Simbi calls me to come and take water!
Simbi calls me to come and pick a leaf!
I take the water,
oh the water falls from my hands!
I pick the leaf,
oh the leaf trembles in my hands!

98.

Se mwen, Simbi dlo!
Se mwen, tèt dlo!
Bèl timoun, kouman yo rele ou?
Ou vini wè Papa Simbi?
Simbi va resevwa ou byen, enhen!
Enhen! Simbi va resevwa ou byen!

98.

It is I, Simbi of the water!
It is I, spring of water!
Beautiful child, what do they call you?
Have you come to see Papa Simbi?
Simbi will receive you well, yeah!
Yeah! Simbi will receive you well!

Ti milat vin wè Papa Simbi!
Enhen! Simbi va resevwa l byen, enhen!
Enhen! Enhen! Enhen!

Little mulatto come see Papa Simbi!
Yeah! Simbi will receive him well, yeah!
Yeah! Yeah! Yeah!

99.
Grann Simba Wayo!
Grann Simba sòti lasous,
Li tou mouye!

99.
Granny Simba Wayo!
Granny Simba comes from the source,
She is all wet!

100.
Simbi Lawouze!
Nèg sòt mare chwal li lan so!
Nèg espri mare chwal li anba so!

100.
Simbi of the Dew!
The stupid man ties his horse to a waterfall!
The wise man ties his horse inside a waterfall!

101.
Mwen sòti lan dlo!
Mwen tou mouye!
Se mwen menm, Papa Simbi,
Mwen tou mouye!
M prale la
kote yo konnen mwen!
M pral rele Papa Simbi o!
Mwen tou mouye!

101.
I come from the water!
I am all wet!
It is me, Papa Simbi,
I am all wet!
I am going there
where they know me!
Oh I will cry Papa Simbi!
I am all wet!

102.
Simbi mwen se gwo nèg.
Ou pa wè mwen se gwo nèg ase!

102.
Simbi I am a powerful man.
Don't you see that I am powerful enough!

103.
Bi ale Simbi, bi ale!
Bi ale Simbi, bi ale!
Simbi Andezo sòti anba dlo
ak tout Dosou Marasa, bi ale!
Pale langaj ou pou mwen tande!

103.
Hey go Simbi, hey go!
Hey go Simbi, hey go!
Simbi Andezo comes from under the water
with all the Dosou twins, hey go!
Speak your mystical words so that I may hear!

104.
Legba, Papa, ouvri baryè a pou mwen, ago ye!
Papa Legba ouvri baryè a pou mwen,
ouvri baryè a pou mwen, Papa,
pou mwen pase.
Lò m a pase, m a remèsye ou.

104.
Legba, Papa, open the gate for me, ago ye!
Papa Legba open the gate for me,
open the gate for me, Papa,
so that I may pass.
When I have passed, I will thank you.

105.
Lafanmi sanble.
Si ou bezwen bon gangan,
Se kay Gwo Wòch pou ale.

105.
The family assembles.
If you need a good Vodou priest,
you should go to the house of Gwo Wòch.

106.
Fèy nan bwa, nou asire!
Lènmi bare mwen!
Fèy nan bwa sove nou!

106.
Leaves in the woods, we are secure!
The enemy caught me!
Leaves in the woods save us!

107.
Nan ounfò o!
Twa fèy tonbe!
Nan ounfò o!
Simbi Moyo, twa fèy tonbe!
Mwen nan dlo o!
Twa fèy tonbe nan ounfò a!
Fèy yo sekwe nan ounfò a!
Lafanmi sanble nan ounfò o!
Zila Moyo, ajenou nan ounfò o!
Twa fèy tonbe nan basen!

107.
Oh in the temple!
Three leaves fell!
Oh in the temple!
Simbi Moyo, three leaves fell!
Oh I am in water!
Three leaves fell in the temple!
The leaves shook in the temple!
Oh the family assembled in the temple!
Oh Zila Moyo, kneeling in the temple!
Three leaves fell into the basin!

108.
Simbi o! O gangan ou ye!
M sòti larivyè o!
Lènmi bare mwen!

108.
Oh Simbi! Oh you are a Vodou priest!
Oh, I leave the river!
The enemy blocks me!

109.
Simbi dlo, ya ye!
Simbi poko konnen mwen!
Simbi dlo, ya ye!
M mande kote yo konnen mwen?
Simbi dlo, ya ye!

109.
Simbi of the water, yah yeah!
Simbi doesn't know me yet!
Simbi of the water, yah yeah!
I ask where do they know me?
Simbi of the water, yah yeah!

XIII. Ogou yo

110.
Nago, vini wè kote m demere!
Si ou wè kote m demere,
w a twoke dola pou sa!
Nago, Nago, vini wè kote m demere!

XIII. The Ogous

110.
Nago, come and see where I stay!
If you see where I stay,
you will swap dollars for that!
Nago, Nago, come see where I stay!

111.
Mwen se nèg Nago.
Tout tan tanbou Nago pa bat
lapli p ap tonbe!
Mwen se nèg Nago!

111.
I am a Nago man.
As long as the Nago drum isn't beaten
rain will not fall!
I am a Nago man!

112.
Nago, Nago, ey!
Vin wè kote m demele!
Si ou wè kote m demele,
w a peye bonbon pou sa!
Nago, Nago, ey!

112.
Nago, Nago, hey!
Come see where I make ends meet!
If you see where I make ends meet,
you'll pay for cookies for the opportunity!
Nago, Nago, hey!

113.
Mèt Ogou, bwè li bwè,
janmen sou!
Ogou Feray bwè li bwè, janmen sou!
N a rele Olisha o!
Ogou bwè li bwè, janmen sou!
Ou wè si nou mare!
Sobo, m a lage!

113.
Master Ogou, he drinks hard,
he's never drunk!
Ogou Feray drinks hard, he's never drunk!
Oh we will call Olisha!
Ogou drinks hard, he's never drunk!
You see if we are in trouble!
Sobo, I'll be untied!

XIV. Sen Jak Majè a

114.
Nèg Sen Jak,
n a monte chwal nou.
Ogou Badagri,
N a moute chwal nou,
n a moute chwal nou devan dèyè!
Si m manke ou, m a pran ou!
Nèg Sen Jak, nou la!
Ogou Badagri, nou la!
Nèg awoyo,
si m manke ou, m a pran ou!

115.
Si m te gen yon byen pou m fè,
mren t av al fè li ak chen mwen!
Lò m gen yon byen pou m fè,
m av al fè li avè chen mren!
Ou mèt wè chen mren anraje,
li p ape sa mòde m!
Mèt Ogou o!

XIV. Saint James the Greater

114.
Saint James the man,
we will mount our horses.
Ogou Badagri,
We will mount our horses,
we will mount our horses backwards!
If I miss you, I will take you!
Saint James the man, we are here!
Ogou Badagri, we are here!
Furious man,
if I miss you, I will take you!

115.
If I had a good deed to do,
I[3] would go do it with my dog!
When I have a good deed to do,
I'm going to do it in the company of my dog!
You may see that my dog is enraged,
he isn't able to bite me!
Oh Master Ogou!

Konsa yo ye, moun sa yo!
M a viv ak yo!

That is how they are, these people!
I will live with them!

116.

Sen Jak pa la, papa:
se chen an ki la.
Sen Jak pa la:
chen an mòde mren.

Saint James is not here, man:
it's the dog that is here.
Saint James is not here:
the dog bit me.

117.

Ogou o! Nèg gè!
Kannon tire, fizi tire!
Nou pa pè lagè!
Ogou o! Nèg gè!

Oh Ogou! Man of war!
Cannons fire, rifles fire!
We do not fear war!
Oh Ogou! Man of war!

118.

Sen Jak o, pase wè mren!
Gason lagè, Sen Jak Majè,
pase wè mren!
Gason lagè, Sen Jak o!
Pase wè mren!

Oh Saint James, come and see me!
Young warrior, Saint James the Greater,
come and see me!
Young warrior, oh Saint James!
Come and see me!

119.

Sen Jak o, vini wè mren!
M gason lagè!
Sen Jak Majè vini wè m!
M gason lagè!
Sen Jak w a voye di yo,
Sen Jak vini kenbe m!
Sen Jak, o! W a voye kenbe m!
Sen Jak ou se nèg lagè!

Oh Saint James, come and see me!
I am a young warrior!
Saint James the Greater come and see me!
I am a young warrior!
Saint James you will send to tell them,
Saint James, come and support me!
Oh Saint James! You will send me support!
Saint James you are a man of war!

120.

Sen Jak o, m blese!
O Sen Jak, o mwen blese!
M blese, m pa wè san an!
Ogou Badagri, Papa, ou wè m blese!
Papa Ogou o, m blese!
M blese-e-e, m pa wè san an!

Oh Saint James, I am wounded!
Oh Saint James, oh I am wounded!
I am cut, I don't see the blood!
Ogou Badagri, Papa, you see I am wounded!
Oh Papa Ogou, I am wounded!
I am wounded-ded-ded, I don't see the blood!

121.

Sen Jak o!
Trete li pou mren!
Ou menm ba li vè,

Oh Saint James!
Treat him for me!
You who gave him worms,

trete li pou mren!
Ou menm ba li maleng lan do,
trete li pou mren!
Li mèt genyen vè,
li mèt genyen maleng lan do,
trete li pou mren!

treat him for me!
You who gave him a sore on his back,
treat him for me!
He may have worms,
he may have sores on his back,
treat him for me!

122.
Salye Nago ey!
O Nago rive o!
Li lè, li tan, o Batala!
Li lè, li tan, Batala!
Salye Nago jodi sa ey!

122.
Greet Nago hey!
Oh Nago has arrived oh!
It is the hour, it is the time, oh Batala!
It is the hour, it is the time, Batala!
Greet Nago this day hey!

XV. Ogou Badagri

123.
M kriye, m kriye:
M sèvi Badagri!
M di ey!
Apa mouche Ogou sa?
M pa vle lwa touye m!

124.
Jou m an kòlè!
Mwen di: jou m an kòlè,
m a vomi san sou yo!

125.
Mren pral pile wanga mren:
kote y a wè mren?
Mwen pral fouye mazi mren:
kote y a wè mren?
Kote y a wè mren, rele:
Ogou o! Rele Ogou o!
Sove y a sove,
kote y a wè mwen . . . ?

126.
Depi tan m la!
Ogou Badagri!
M di n ap lage m!
Depi tan m la!
Kòd mare kòd!

XV. Ogou Badagri

123.
I cry, I cry:
I serve Badagri!
I say hey!
Isn't that mister Ogou?
I don't want lwa to kill me!

124.
The day that I am angry!
I say: the day that I am angry,
I will vomit blood on them!

125.
I will grind my charm:
where will they see me?
I will rummage through my hovel:
where will they see me?
Where they will see me, shout:
Oh Ogou! Oh shout Ogou!
They will save themselves,
where will they see me . . . ?

126.
I've been here for ages!
Ogou Badagri!
I say you are forsaking me!
I've been here for ages!
Cords tie cords!

Depi tan m la!
Yo pa konnen m se Ogou!
Depi tan m la!

I've been here for ages!
They don't know I am Ogou!
I've been here for ages!

127.

Mwen blese, m blese o!
Jodi yo kontan wè m,
Demen y a fache!
Ogou Badagri,
Nèg Nago, Woyo!

127.

I'm wounded, oh I'm wounded!
Today they are happy to see me,
Tomorrow they will be upset!
Ogou Badagri,
Man of Nago, Woyo!

128.

M se zèb atè,
yo pa konnen sa ki lan kè mwen!
Pile Badagri ki sòt lan dlo!
Ogou Badagri ki sòt lan dlo,
yo pa konnen sa ki lan kè l!
Pile o! Yo wè m, yo pa konnen m!

128.

I am the grass on the ground,
they don't know what is in my heart!
Stomp, Badagri who comes from the water!
Ogou Badagri who comes from the water,
they don't know what is in his heart!
Oh stomp! They see me, they don't know me!

129.

Ogou Badagri, se nèg politik o!
Lè ou antrave, se lese koule!
Ogou Badagri, se nèg politik o!
Pa kite nèg touye ou!
Tanpèt mare, lanmè move!
Ogou Badagri o! Se nèg politik!
Glise koule, glise ale fè wout ou!
Ogou Badagri, se nèg politik o!

129.

Oh Ogou Badagri is a politician!
When you are in a bind, let go!
Oh Ogou Badagri is a politician!
Don't let men kill you!
The storm is raging, the sea is troubled!
Oh Ogou Badagri! He is a politician!
Slip away, slip away and be on your way!
Oh Ogou Badagri is a politician!

130.

Ogou Badagri,
M ap sèvi lwa mren,
m pa gen èd o!
Pase mren p ap pale,
yo di mren pa la o!
Ogou Badagri,
m ap sèvi lwa mren,
mren pa gen èd, o!

130.

Ogou Badagri,
I am serving my lwa,
oh I don't have help!
Because I will not speak,
Oh they say I am not here!
Ogou Badagri,
I am serving my lwa,
oh I don't have help!

131.

Ey! Lorye, se mren Ogou o! Mren lòrye.
Dawomen dakò ey! Se mren, Ogou.
Se mren, se mren, Ogou, se mren, lòrye,
Abobo!

131.

Hey! Laurel, oh it is I Ogou! I am laurel.
Hey Dawomen agrees! It is I, Ogou.
It is I, it is I, Ogou, it is I, laurel,
Abobo!

XVI. Ogou Feray

132.
Ogou o! Feray o! Ann ale avè m!
M di: Ogou o! Feray o!
Ann ale avè m!
Kannon te mèt tire, fizi te mèt tire,
pinga ou vini gade!
An n ale avè m!

133.
Ogou Feray o!
Ou se nèg politik!
Kouman yo rele sa?
M pa mele Sen Jak!

134.
Ogou travay o! Ogou pa manje!
Tout lajan Ogou fè,
se pou li pote bay bèl fanm!
Yè oswa,
Ogou dòmi san soupe!

135.
Ogou travay o!
Ogou pa manje!
Ogou pase jounen deyò!
Li achte bèl wòb bay fanm li!
Yè oswa,
Ogou dòmi san soupe!

136.
Ogou travay o!
Li pa manje!
Li sere lajan
pou l dòmi kay bèl fanm!
Yè oswa,
Feray dòmi san soupe!

137.
Ogou Feray o!
Men sa n ape ba ou!
San rankin, san rankin,
san rankin, Papa Ogou!

XVI. Ogou Feray

132.
Oh Ogou! Oh Feray! Come along with me!
I say: oh Ogou! Oh Feray!
Come along with me!
Cannons could fire, bullets could fire,
you'd better not come to watch!
Come along with me!

133.
Oh Ogou Feray!
You are a politician!
What do they call this?
I don't mess with Saint James!

134.
Oh Ogou works! Ogou doesn't eat!
All of the money Ogou earns,
is for him to bring to beautiful women!
Yesterday evening,
Ogou slept without supper!

135.
Oh Ogou works!
Ogou doesn't eat!
Ogou spent the entire day out!
He bought beautiful dresses for his women!
Yesterday evening,
Ogou slept without supper!

136.
Oh Ogou works!
He doesn't eat!
He saves money
to sleep with beautiful women!
Yesterday evening,
Feray slept without supper!

137.
Oh Ogou Feray!
Here is what we will give you!
Without grudge, without grudge,
without grudge, Papa Ogou!

138.
Fè, Ogou Fè, Ogou Fè, Ogou Fè, o!
Danbala, m ap tire kannon, o!
Fè, Ogou Fè, Ogou Fè, Ogou Fè, o!
Danbala, m ap tire kanon, o!

138.
Oh Iron, Ogou Iron, Ogou Iron, Ogou Iron!
Oh Danbala, I will fire cannons!
Oh Iron, Ogou Iron, Ogou Iron, Ogou Iron!
Oh Danbala, I will fire cannons!

139.
Feray o! Fè lè!
Ogou Balindjo, nou poko rive,
yo tire kannon pou nou.

139.
Oh Feray! Take your time!
Ogou Balindjo, we have not arrived yet,
they fire cannons for us.

140.
Feray o!
Lan men ki moun ou lese
badji lwa m yo?
Feray o!
Lan men ki moun ou lese zanfan la yo?
Kou ou wè m,
m a rete, m sonje Ogou Feray,
m a konsole, m a pran kouraj o!
Rele Aleman, Leman, sobadji n asire!
Lan Gita o! Gita sobadji!
M a rele Papa Ogou, sobadji n asire!

140.
Oh Feray!
In whose hands did you leave
the sanctuary of my lwa?
Oh Feray!
In whose hands did you leave the children?
As soon as you see me,
I'll stay, I remember Ogou Feray,
I will be consoled, oh I will have courage!
Call Aleman, Leman, our sanctuary is secure!
Oh in Gita! Gita sanctuary!
I will call Papa Ogou, our sanctuary is secure!

141.
Ogou o! Lese n salye ou!
Devan badji a n ap salye ou!

141.
Oh Ogou! Let us greet you!
In front of the altar, we will greet you!

142.
Ogou o! Feray o!
Feray ann ale!
Mande kote ou kite Nago?
Fiyole
pou lwa m yo!
Feray o!

142.
Oh Ogou! Oh Feray!
Feray let's go!
Ask where you leave Nago?
Wipe the face of the one possessed
for my lwa!
Oh Feray!

XVII. Lòt Ogou

143.
Pito, pito rele Achade!
Achade se granmoun o!
Mwen pa vle lwa yo touye mwen!

XVII. Other Ogous

143.
Instead, instead call Achade!
Oh Achade is grown up!
I don't want the lwa to kill me!

144.
Achade o!
Achade, m pa genyen paran isit
ki pou pale pou mwen!
Achade, mwen pa genyen paran isit
ki pou pale pou mwen la!
Achade o, Ogou move o!

144.
Oh Achade!
Achade, I don't have parents here
to speak for me!
Achade, I don't have parents here
to speak for me here!
Oh Achade, oh Ogou is angry!

145.
Feray pa la,
Yo di y ap touye mwen!
Balindjo pa la,
Yo di y ap manje mwen!
O Papa Bakouson Achade!
O! Sove mwen!

145.
Feray is not here,
They say they will kill me!
Balindjo is not here,
They say they will eat me!
Oh Papa Bakouson Achade!
Oh! Save me!

146.
Salye Papa Ogou Achade!
M ape salye Papa Ogou Achade!
Li lè, li tan, Achade, o!
Papa Ogou pa te la,
men li rive!

146.
Greet Papa Ogou Achade!
I'm greeting Papa Ogou Achade!
It is the hour, it is the time, oh Achade!
Papa Ogou was not here,
but he has arrived!

147.
Achade m se granmoun o!
Achade se granmoun o!
Gade m chita lakay mwen,
timoun yo ap anbete mwen!

147.
Oh my Achade is grown up!
Oh Achade is grown up!
Look at me sitting at my house,
the children are annoying me!

148.
Kou yo malad o, yo rele Achade.
O kou yo geri kò yo,
Achade se demon.

148.
Oh once they are sick, they call Achade.
Oh once they're healed,
Achade is a demon.

149.
Olicha, sa fè mren lapèn!
M ta kriye!
Olicha, sa fè mren lapèn!
M ta rele!

149.
Olicha, this makes me sorrowful!
I could cry!
Olicha, this makes me sorrowful!
I could shout!

150.
Sa m fè pou yo rayi mwen?
Enhen! Olicha!
Sa m fè pou yo rayi mwen?
Olicha, mren move!

150.
What did I do for them to hate me?
Yeah! Olicha!
What did I do for them to hate me?
Olicha, I am angry!

151.
Salye Nago ey! Nago rive o!
Li lè, li tan,
O Batala
Salye Nago jodi a, ayibobo!
Li lè, li tan,
Olicha!
Ayibobo!
Kriye abobo pou
Nèg Olicha Badjita Wangita!
Achade, Nèg bòkò Olicha!

151.
Hey greet the Nago! Oh Nago has arrived!
It is the hour, it is the time,
Oh Batala
Greet the Nago today, ayibobo!
It is the hour, it is the time,
Olicha!
Ayibobo!
Cry ayibobo for
the Man Olicha Badjita Wangita!
Achade, bòkò Man of Olicha!

152.
L ale, l ale, li pa di m!
Ogou Fè ki monte lan mè,
li p ap tounen!
L ale, l ale, li pa di mwen!
Batala ki monte lan mè,
li p ap tounen!
L ale, l ale, li pa di mwen!
Olicha ki monte lan mè,
li p ap tounen!
L ale, l ale, li pa di mwen!
Aoche Nago,
Papa Ogou o! Papa Ogou o!
Mwen prale lakay mwen,
chwal mren sele!

152.
He left, he left, he didn't tell me!
Ogou Iron who went out to sea,
he will not return!
He left, he left, he didn't tell me!
Batala who went out to sea,
he will not return!
He left, he left, he didn't tell me!
Olicha who went out to sea,
he will not return!
He left, he left, he didn't tell me!
Aoche Nago,
Oh Papa Ogou! Oh Papa Ogou!
I am going to my house,
my horse is saddled!

153.
Ogou Balindjo,
li di l ap sele chwal la!
Sele o! Bride!
Balinjo di l ap pile pase!

153.
Ogou Balindjo,
he says he will saddle the horse![4]
Oh saddled! Bridled!
Balindjo says he will stomp on by!

154.
Ale, ale Balindjo, ale, mwen p ape tounen.
Ale, ale, nèg Nago.
Ale, mwen p ape tounen.
Mwen se nèg Nago, mwen se nèg manchèt.
Kan m kenbe, Balindjo, mwen pa lage.

154.
Go, go Balindjo, go, I am not returning.
Go, go, man of Nago.
Go, I am not returning.
I am a man of Nago, I am a machete man.
When I hold, Balindjo, I don't let go.

155.
Balindjo, Ogou, wa, wa!
M pa manje manje
ki pou touye chwal an mwen.

155.
Balindjo, Ogou, wah, wah!
I don't eat food
that will kill my horse.

Balindjo, Ogou, wa, wa!
M pa bwè bwason
ki pou touye chwal an mwen.
Balindjo, Ogou, wa, wa!

Balindjo, Ogou, wah, wah!
I don't drink drinks
that will kill my horse.
Balindjo, Ogou, wah, wah!

156.
Balindjo, Ogou wa, wa!
Se pa manje ranje
ki pou touye chwal an mwen.
M griye mayi mwen, se pou Balindjo!
M griye pistach mwen, se pou Balindjo!
Se pa manje ranje
ki pou touye chwal an mwen.

156.
Balindjo, Ogou wah, wah!
It is not poisoned food
that will kill my horse.
I grilled my corn, it is for Balindjo!
I grilled my pistachios, they are for Balindjo!
It is not poisoned food
that will kill my horse.

157.
Balindjo, Ogou wa, wa!
Se pa manje ranje
ki pou touye chwal an mwen!
Chwal an mwen byen poudre,
chwal an mwen byen benyen,
chwal an mwen santi bon!
Se pa manje ranje
k a touye chwal an mwen!

157.
Balindjo, Ogou wah, wah!
It is not poisoned food
that will kill my horse!
My horse is well powdered,
my horse is well bathed,
my horse smells good!
It is not poisoned food
that will kill my horse!

158.
Osanj o! Lese koule Mèt Osanj.
O lese koule!
Yo pran ason Osanj sèvi gerizon.
O lese koule!
Yo pran badji Osanj sèvi gerizon.
O lese koule Mèt Osanj!
Osanj o! Lese koule Mèt Osanj!

158.
Oh Osanj! Let it be Master Osanj.
Oh let it be!
They take Osanj's rattle to heal.
Oh let it be!
They take Osanj's altar to heal.
Oh let it be Master Osanj!
Oh Osanj! Let it be Master Osanj!

159.
Osanj o, ou ban mwen je a
pou mwen gade yo!
Yo rayi Osanj, yo renmen wanga l!
Osanj o! Prete m ason ou a!
Osanj o! Prete badji ou a!
Ason pa pou mwen, ason Balindjo!
Badji pa pou mwen, badji Balindjo!
Sa ki di sa? Se msye Osanj!
Lajan kawo tè ou la.

159.
Oh Osanj, you gave me the eye
for me to see them!
They hate Osanj, they love his charms!
Oh Osanj! Lend me your rattle!
Oh Osanj! Lend your altar!
The rattle is not mine, it is Balindjo's rattle!
The altar is not mine, it is Balindjo's altar!
Who says this? It is mister Osanj!
The money for your acres of land is here.

160.
Mèt Osanj o!
Yo rayi wè mwen!
Yo rayi wè mwen, Osanj.
Se mwen y a wè!
Yo pa vle wè mwen.
Se mwen y a wè!
Apre Bondye lan syèl,
m a viv ak yo!

160.
Oh master Osanj!
They hate to see me!
They hate to see me, Osanj.
It is me they will see!
They don't want to see me.
It is me they will see!
After God in heaven,
I will live with them!

161.
Osanj Batala kase fèy.
Kouvri kanari lwa yo.
Osanj kase fèy.
Kouvri kanari lwa yo.

161.
Osanj Batala breaks leaves.
Cover the jars of the lwa.
Osanj breaks leaves.
Cover the jars of the lwa.

162.
Ogou o! Ogou o!
Ala lontan m pa wè ou.
Ogou Chalode, m gen dizan depi
m pa wè bèl chè ti papa.
Ala lontan m pa wè Ogou sila a.

162.
Oh Ogou! Oh Ogou!
It's been a long time since I've seen you.
Ogou Chalode, it has been ten years since
I've seen the dearly beloved little father.
It's been a while since I've seen this Ogou.

XVIII. Chango

163.
Wòy, wòy!
Ogou Chango, nèg Feray o!
San vèse, Feray, san vèse!
Ogou Feray touye,
koklo Feray okon o.
N ape ba ou donon,
Feray o!
Sanyan, sanyan, sanyan!
Gad jan n touye koklo la!
Sanyan, sanyan, sanyan!

164.
Chango nou rele!
Ogou Badagri, nou Chango!
Nou rele twa fwa.
Nou Chango, nou rele!
M rele m Chango!

XVIII. Chango

163.
Oh my, oh my!
Ogou Chango, oh man of Feray!
Blood is shed, Feray, blood is shed!
Ogou Feray killed,
oh Feray's rooster is killed.
We will give you food,
Oh Feray!
Bleeding, bleeding, bleeding!
Look how he killed the rooster!
Bleeding, bleeding, bleeding!

164.
Chango we shout!
Ogou Badagri, you are Chango!
We shout three times.
We are Chango, we shout!
I call myself Chango!

M rele twa fwa, Ogou Badagri,
Nou rele twa fwa, nou Chango!
Chango, nou rele!

I shout three times, Ogou Badagri,
We shout three times, you are Chango!
Chango, we call!

XIX. Azaka Mede ak Kouzen Zaka

165.
Minis Odan mache o!
O Minis Zaka mache o!
Mache pou n al konniye!
O Minis Odan, n ap konniye!
Odan, n ap konniye!
Azaka, n ap konniye!

166.
Azaka Mede, m ape di ou bonjou!
Mwen di ou bonjou, o Minis o!
Azaka Mede, kote ou prale la a?
Azaka Mede, m pral lan pakoti!

167.
Papa Zaka, ki kote ou prale?
Minis Zaka, ki kote ou prale?
Mren di: o! Minis o!
M pral lan pakoti!

168.
Minis Zaka isi, Minis Zaka la!
O Minis Zaka isi, Minis Zaka la!
Minis Zaka Mede!
Lese m chèche rezon m!

169.
Azaka Gweli o!
O enhen! Enhen o!
Azaka Gweli o!
Kannòt an mwen chavire!

170.
Azaka Gweli o!
Kannòt an mwen chavire!
Mren sòti Miragwàn,

XIX. Azaka Mede and Cousin Zaka

165.
Oh Minister Odan walks!
Oh Minister Zaka walks!
Walk so that we can slither and dance!
Oh Minister Odan, we will slither and dance!
Odan, we will slither and dance!
Azaka, we will slither and dance!

166.
Azaka Mede, I am saying to you good day!
Oh I say to you good day, oh Minister!
Azaka Mede, where are you going?
Azaka Mede, I am going in cheap duds!

167.
Papa Zaka where are you going?
Minister Zaka where are you going?
I say: oh! Oh Minister!
I am going in cheap duds!

168.
Minister Zaka here, Minister Zaka there!
Oh Minister Zaka here, Minister Zaka there!
Minister Zaka Mede!
Let me find my reasons!

169.
Oh Azaka is a sacred lwa![5]
Oh yeah! Oh yeah!
Oh Azaka is a sacred lwa!
My canoe flipped over!

170.
Oh Azaka is a sacred lwa!
My canoe flipped over!
I came from Miragoâne,

an arivan, mwen lan Leyogàn,
kannòt an mwen chavire!
Sent Azaka Gweli o!

upon arriving, I was in Leyogann,
my canoe flipped over!
Oh Saint Azaka is a sacred lwa!

171.
Kouzin o! Kouzen o!
Kouzin, m p ap pran kouzen mwen, tande!
De gouden pa lajan!
Senkant santim pa lajan!
Kouzin o! Kouzen o!
Kouzin, m p ap pran Kouzen mwen, tande!

171.
Oh Cousin! Oh Cousin!
Cousin, I won't take my cousin, you hear!
Two gourdes is not much money!
Fifty cents is not much money!
Oh Cousin! Oh Cousin!
Cousin, I will not take my Cousin, you hear!

172.
Zaka ki lide ou la?
Tonnè boule!
Kouzen, ki lide ou la?
Tonnè boule!
Ou pito mande charite pase ou vòlò!
Kouzen Zaka ki lide ou la?
Tonnè!

172.
Zaka what are your intentions here?
I swear to God!
Cousin, what are your intentions here?
I swear to God!
You would rather beg than steal!
Cousin Zaka what are your intentions here?
I swear!

173.
Abitan, leve non!
Kwi mayi m tonbe!
Abitan, leve non!
Kwi tchoka m lan solèy!

173.
Farmer, get up!
My corn bowl has fallen!
Farmer, get up!
My bowl of ground coffee is in the sun!

174.
Kouzen, kouri non!
Vin pran mayi boukannen!

174.
Cousin, run already!
Come and take roasted corn!

175.
O pinga mayi m boule!
Ou wè mayi m pile?
O pinga mayi m boule!
Ou wè mayi m kase?
Ou wè mayi m pile?
O pinga mayi m boule!

175.
Oh my corn better not burn!
You see that my corn is ground?
Oh my corn better not burn!
You see that my corn is dehusked?
You see my corn is ground?
Oh my corn better not burn!

176.
Zaka, weya, weya, pay mayi a boule!
Pay mayi a boule!
Zaka, weya, weya, pay mayi a boule!

176.
Zaka, weya, weya, the corn straw is burned!
The corn straw is burned!
Zaka, weya, weya, the corn straw is burned!

177.
Ounsi la yo pran kouraj o!
N ape pase Zaka lan betiz o!
Ounsi la yo pran kouraj o!
N ape pase Zaka lan betiz o!
Sipòte n ap sipòte.
Sipòte n a prale sipòte.
N ape pase Zaka lan betiz o!

177.
Oh Vodou initiates take courage!
Oh you ridicule Zaka!
Oh Vodou initiates take courage!
Oh you ridicule Zaka!
We're putting up with it.
We're going to be putting up with it.
Oh you ridicule Zaka!

178.
Kouzen Zaka, ou anraje!
O dyab o!
Kouzen, ou anraje!
O dyab la!
Ou vle kite fanm de byen
pou al viv ak vakabon!
Kouzen Zaka, ou anraje!
O dyab o!

178.
Cousin Zaka, you are out of your mind!
Oh dyab[6] oh!
Cousin, you are out of your mind!
Oh the dyab!
You want to leave a good woman
to go live with delinquents!
Cousin Zaka, you are out of your mind!
Oh dyab oh!

179.
Kouzen Zaka sòti anwo, l ap desann.
O ti gout dlo Kouzen mande!
Kouzen Zaka sòti anwo, l ap desann,
O ti gout dlo Kouzen mande!
Lestomak li fè l mal,
lanpwen gode pou Kouzen bwè!

179.
Cousin Zaka comes from above, he descends.
Oh Cousin asks for a little drop of water!
Cousin Zaka comes from above, he descends,
Oh cousin asks for a drop of water!
His chest hurts him,
there is no cup for cousin to drink from!

180.
Minis o! Enhen nou la!
Azaka yo pral nonmen m depite!
Azaka yo pral nonmen m senatè!
Enhen! Nou la!

180.
Oh minister! Yeah we are here!
Azaka they will name me deputy!
Azaka they will name me senator!
Yeah! We are here!

181.
Minis o! Enhen! Nou la!
O Minis Zaka o! Gade nou la o!
Zaka, yo nonmen m depite!
Enhen! Nou la!

181.
Oh Minister! Yeah! We are here!
Oh Minister Zaka! Oh look we are here!
Zaka, they named me deputy!
Yeah! We are here!

XX. Agawou Tonnè

182.
Misan, Misan wòy!
Agawou Tonnè, kreyòl mande wè ou!

XX. Agawou Thunder

182.
Misan, Misan oh my!
Agawou Thunder, the Creoles ask to see you!

Gade, m a prale!
N a prale, monchè Misan, n a prale!
N a prale, Potokoli, n a prale!
N a prale, Potokoli,
kote yo bezwen m!

Look, I am going!
We are going, mister Misan, we are going!
We are going, Potokoli, we are going!
We are going, Potokoli,
to where they need me!

183.

Li lè, li tan o! M a prale!
Agawou Tonnè o!
Kreyòl mande mwen!
Nou pa wè m di m a prale!
Agawou Loray, m a prale!
Agawou Zeklè, m a prale!
Agawou De o! Kreyòl mande mwen!
Ou pa wè m di m a prale!

183.

It is the hour, oh it is the time! I'm leaving!
Oh Agawou Thunder!
The Creoles ask for me!
Don't you see I say I'm leaving!
Agawou Thunder, I'm leaving!
Agawou Lightning, I'm leaving!
Oh Agawou De! The Creoles ask for me!
Don't you see I say I'm leaving!

184.

Agawou, vante, vante!
Li vante Nòde,
Li vante Sirwa!
Agawou se pa moun isit!
Agawou gwonde, gwonde,
Li gwonde loray!
Agawou vante, vante,
Li vante van!
Agawou sòti lan Ginen,
li vante, li gwonde!
Yo pa bezwen m ankò!
Yo rele vye bagay!

184.

Agawou blows, blows!
He blows the northeastern wind,
He blows the southeastern wind!
Agawou is not from here!
Agawou rumbles, rumbles,
He rumbles the thunder!
Agawou blows, blows,
He blows the wind!
Agawou comes from Ginen,
he blows, he rumbles!
They don't need me anymore!
They shout bad things!

185.

Agawou leve, leve non!
Vin wè si n fè byen!
Agawou leve, leve non!
Vin gade si n fè byen!

185.

Agawou get up, get up already!
Come see if we've done well!
Agawou get up, get up already!
Come see if we've done well!

186.

Sonde yo vini sonde!
M di yo vini sonde m la!
Agawou, bèt san san,
nou p ap pale tout pawòl o!
Gade, y ap sonde m!

186.

They are really trying to challenge me!
I tell them to come and challenge me here!
Agawou, animal without blood,
oh we won't say all the words!
Look, they are challenging me!

187.

Pa pouvwa Msye Agawou Tonnè,
Agawou Wèdo, Agawou Misan Wèdo,
Agawou Potokoli, Agawou Konbe,
Agawou Kata, Agawou Zeklè,
Agawou Loray,
Agawou Bèt san San,
Nèg gwo, gwo, gwo. Ago, Ago-si, Ago-la.

XXI. Sobo Kèsou ak Badè

188.

Sobo Kèsou, m di mren prale, enhen o!
Kay la boule, m a fè lòt!
M a gaye nouvèl la ba yo!

189.

Yanvalou mwen, Sobo Kèsou o!
Sobagi Sobo,
se mwen, Manzè file!

190.

Ala move fanmi Sobo genyen!
Yo kite mwen la,
yo pral sèvi
kay etranje!
Lafanmi sa yo!
Tan mal kou sa ye, yo kite mwen la.
Yo pral sèvi etranje!
Lafanmi sa yo!
Tan mal kou sa ye!
Yo kite mwen la!
Yo pral sèvi etranje!
Gen yon tan y a bezwen mren!

191.

Sobo, m granmoun o!
Se mren n a wè!
Papa Sobo, nou granmoun o!
Se mren n a wè!
Nèg Sobo, nou granmoun o!
Se mren n a wè!

187.

By the power of Mister Agawou Thunder,
Agawou Wèdo, Agawou Misan Wèdo,
Agawou Potokoli, Agawou Konbe,
Agawou Kata, Agawou Lightning,
Agawou Thunder,
Agawou Beast without Blood,
Great, great, great Guy. Ago, Ago-si, Ago-la.

XXI. Sobo Kèsou and Badè

188.

Oh hey! Sobo Kèsou, I say I'm leaving!
The house burned down, I will make another!
I will spread the news to them!

189.

Oh my yanvalou, Sobo Kèsou!
Sobo of the inner sanctuary,
it's me, Miss Shooting Star!

190.

What a mean family Sobo has!
They left me here,
they are going to serve
at the homes of foreigners!
These family members!
As bad as this time is, they left me here.
They are going to serve foreigners!
These family members!
As bad as this time is!
They left me here!
They are going to serve foreigners!
There will be a time when they will need me!

191.

Oh Sobo, I'm grown up!
It's me you will see!
Papa Sobo, oh we are grown up!
It is me you will see!
Mister Sobo, oh we're grown up!
It is me you will see!

192.
Ogou pa la; mwen menm, mwen la!
Ogou pa la, chen an mòde mren!
Ogou pa la, mwen menm, mwen la!
Mwen menm, Sobo, fè chen li mòde ou,
Mwen menm Sobo!

192.
Ogou is not here; me, I am here!
Ogou is not here, the dog bit me!
Ogou is not here, me, I am here!
I, Sobo, made his dog bite you,
I, Sobo!

193.
An nou mache,
n a jwenn kichoy atè a!
O an nou mache!
N a jwenn kichoy atè a!
Kichòy atè a Sobo,
n a ranmase jodi a.

193.
Let us walk,
we will find something on the ground!
Oh let us walk!
We will find something on the ground!
Something on the ground Sobo,
we will pick it up today.

194.
Papa Sobo ou ale!
Ou kite mwen la!
Lan men ki moun
ou a kite pitit la yo?
Ou a kite zanfan la yo?
Kite pitit la yo lan men Bondye,
tanpri souple!
Sa k dèyè, ranmase l pou mwen!

194.
Papa Sobo, you went away!
You left me here!
In whose hand
will you leave your children?
Will you leave your children?
Leave the children in the hands of God,
I beg you please!
Those who are behind, gather them up for me!

195.
Kafe Vodou Sobo, kafe!
Kafe Vodou Sobo!
Byenere, pitit yo k a keyi!
Ayida Wèdo, pinga kafe m tonbe!

195.
The coffee of Vodou Sobo, coffee!
The coffee of Vodou Sobo!
Happy, the children can harvest!
Ayida Wèdo, my coffee had better not fall!

196.
Badè-Si ki di: y ap sonde m!
M pa mango sou bwa
pou yo sonde m!
M pa mango; m pa kalbas;
m pa melon!
Si yo sonde m,
y a sonde loraj o!
Si yo sonde m,
y a sonde zeklè o!

196.
Badè-Si who says: they challenge me!
I am not a mango on a branch
for them to challenge!
I am not a mango; I am not a calabash;
I am not a melon!
If they challenge me,
oh they will challenge thunder!
If they challenge me,
oh they will challenge lightning!

197.
Badè o! Badè o!
Li vanyan gason.
Men domaj!
Li vanyan gason, men l san zo!

197.
Oh Badè! Oh Badè!
He is a brave man.
But it is unfortunate!
He is a brave man, but he is without bones!

198.
Fanm Badè a dòmi deyò, ey!
Fanm Sobo a dòmi deyò, ey!
O lan Ginen, n a souke yo!

198.
Hey, Badè's wife slept with someone else!
Hey, Sobo's wife slept with someone else!
Oh in Ginen, we will shake them!

199.
Badè o! Badè o!
Badè vanyan gason, jamè li tonbe!
O Topi Badè ki bwè,
gade, li pa sou o!

199.
Oh Badè! Oh Badè!
Badè is a brave man, he never falls!
Oh Topi Badè who drinks,
oh look, he is not drunk!

200.
Sobo wi nou la!
Badè wi nou la!
Sobo Kèsou, n ape navige!

200.
Sobo, yes, we are here!
Badè, yes, we are here!
Sobo Kèsou, we are navigating!

201.
Badè m se granmoun o!
Ey! Sobo, n ape navige!

201.
Oh Badè, I am grown up!
Hey! Sobo, we're navigating!

202.
Badè nou la o!
Sobo nou la o!
Papa Badè ki voye bonjou pou nou!
Papa Sobo ki voye bonjou pou nou!
L ap mande kouman nou ye!
Ago! Ago! Ago!

202.
Oh Badè we are here!
Oh Sobo we are here!
Papa Badè who bids us good day!
Papa Sobo who bids us good day!
He asks how we are!
Ago! Ago! Ago!

203.
Badè o! Nou sèl o!
O Sobo, nou sèl o!
Papa Badè, gade n ape neye!
Papa Sobo, gade n ape neye!

203.
Oh Badè! Oh we are alone!
Oh Sobo, oh we are alone!
Papa Badè, look, we are drowning!
Papa Sobo, look, we are drowning!

204.
Je m, je m la! M ap gade l!
O Papa Badè ki ban m
kwa a pou m pote!

204.
My eyes, my eyes are here! I am looking at it!
Oh Papa Badè who gives me
the cross to carry!

Je m, je m la!
M ap gade l!

My eyes, my eyes are here!
I am looking at it!

205.
Papa Badè, m a prale o!
Gonayiv o! M a prale o!
Rele Gonayiv o!
Badè ou inosan, di yo!

205.
Papa Badè, oh I am leaving!
Oh Gonaïve! Oh I am leaving!
Oh shout Gonaïve!
Badè, you are innocent, tell them!

206.
O Papa Badè-Si, papa m,
sòti Gwomòn o!
M prale lan kafou Ege!
M pa vini pou m mize!
Mwen vini gade zanfan yo!
Badè-Si, wi nou la,
n ap gade ou prale!

206.
Oh Papa Badè-Si, my papa,
oh coming from Gros-Morne!
I am going to Ege crossroad!
I didn't come to dawdle!
I came to see the children!
Badè-Si, yes we are here,
we are watching you leave!

207.
Badè-Si, ankò yo wè m!
O pase yo wè m, Papa,
yo di mren Badè!

207.
Badè-Si, again they see me!
Oh because they see me, Papa,
they say that I am Badè!

208.
Onon Msye Sobo Kèsou,
Annannan Vodou, Sobo Badè,
Badè-Si Wanman,
Nèg Badè-Si-Kwa-La-Wonsi,
Nèg-Lànye-Tingi,
Ago, Ago-si, Ago-la.

208.
In the name of Mister Sobo Kèsou,
Annannan Vodou, Sobo Badè,
Badè-Si Wanman,
Badè-Si-Kwa-La-Wonsi-Guy,
Lànye-Tingi-Guy,
Ago, Ago-si, Ago-la.

XXII. Marasa yo

209.
Dosou Marasa, ede m!
Marasa, ede m!
M ap bay ou manje
pou sa ede m!

210.
Marasa, pànye kouvri pànye!
Marasa, men manje, men dlo!
Marasa, men dlo, men manje!

XXII. The Divine Twins

209.
Dosou Marasa, help me!
Marasa, help me!
I will give you food
so that you will help me!

210.
Marasa, the basket covers the basket!
Marasa, here is food, here is water!
Marasa, here is water, here is food!

211.
Lafanmi sanble, o sanble nou!
Pou n pale pawòl nou.
Lafanmi sanble!

211.
The family gathers, oh gather your selves!
So that we may speak our words.
The family gathers!

212.
Lafanmi sanble.
Sanble nou tout.
Lafanmi sanble.
Men nou sanble pou pale pawòl nou!
Lafanmi sanble! Abobo!

212.
The family gathers.
Gather all together.
The family gathers.
Here we gather to speak our words!
The family gathers! Abobo!

213.
Lafanmi sanble!
O kreyòl nou la ey!
Lanpwen Ginen ankò!
Lanfanmi sanble o!
Lanpwen Ginen ankò!
O kreyòl nou la ey!

213.
The family gathers!
Oh hey, Creoles, we are here!
Ginen is over and done with!
Oh the family is gathered!
Ginen is over and done with!
Oh hey, Creoles, we are here!

214.
Lapriyè pou sen yo!
Kriye abobo pou lwa yo!
Mwen sèvi lesen avè Marasa!
Mwen sèvi Marasa avè lesen!
Lapriyè pou sen yo!
Bondye k a gide nou!

214.
Pray for the saints!
Cry abobo for the lwa!
I serve the saints and the Marasa!
I serve the Marasa and the saints!
Pray for the saints!
It is God who will guide us!

215.
Marasa enhen! Marasa enhen!
Marasa, mete tèt ansanm!
A nou de!
Eya Marasa!

215.
Yeah Marasa! Yeah Marasa!
Marasa, put your heads together!
Between us both!
Eya Marasa!

216.
Marasa, men dounou!

216.
Marasa, here is your food!

217.
Marasa, m ape mande,
sa ou wè la, si ou kontan.
Ago ey!
Marasa de, twa, kat, m ape mande
sa ou wè la, si ou kontan.
Ago ey!
Marasa kay, Marasa bwa,

217.
Marasa, I am asking,
if you are happy with what you see here.
Hey ago!
Twins two, three, four, I am asking
if you are happy with what you see here.
Hey ago!
Twins of houses, twins of the woods,

Marasa kafou, m ape mande,
sa ou wè la, si ou kontan.
Abobo!

Twins of crossroads, I am asking,
if you are happy with what you see here.
Abobo!

218.
Marasa la yo, nou tout vyèy!
Danbala Wèdo, nou tout vye!
Ayida nou tout vye!

218.
Those Marasa there, you are so old!
Danbala Wèdo, you are so old!
Ayida you are all old!

XXIII. Gede yo

XXIII. The Gedes

219.
Papa Gede bèl gason!
Gede Nibo bèl gason!
L abiye l tout an blan
pou l al monte Palè a!
Lò l abiye l tout an nwa,
li potrè yon depite.
Lò l abiye l tout an jòn,
li potrè yon senatè.

219.
Papa Gede is a handsome fellow!
Gede Nibo is a handsome fellow!
He dresses himself all in white
to go to the palace!
When he dresses himself all in black,
he looks just like a deputy.
When he dresses himself all in yellow,
he looks just like a senator.

220.
Papa Gede bèl gason!
Gede Nibo bèl gason!
L abiye l tout an blan,
pou l al monte o Palè!
Lò l abiye l tout an nwa,
li pòtre yon depite.
Lò l abiye l tout an blan,
li pòtre yon jasmen doub.

220.
Papa Gede is a handsome fellow!
Gede Nibo is a handsome fellow!
He dresses himself all in white,
to go up to the palace!
When he dresses himself all in black,
he looks just like a deputy.
When he dresses himself all in white,
he looks just like an Arabian jasmine.

221.
M rive o! Mwen rantre!
Bawon Samdi,
Bawon Simityè,
Bawon Lakwa,
Nèg simityè!
Mezanmi, nou pa janm wè sa?
Koulèv janbe Lento!

221.
Oh I have arrived! I have entered!
Bawon Samdi,
Bawon of Cemeteries,
Bawon of the Cross,
Man of cemeteries!
My goodness, have you never seen that?
The snake crosses over to Lento!

222.
Bawon Samdi, se ou m a di!
Seklekite, se ou m a di!
Balewouze, se ou m a di!
Bawon Samdi

222.
Bawon Samdi, it is you I will tell!
Seklekite, put it aside, it is you I will tell!
Balewouze, it is you I will tell!
Bawon Samdi

ki di li fò pase Bondye!
Gede Nibo, se ou m a di, y a wè!
Bawon Simityè
ki di li fò pase Bondye!
Gede Nibo, se ou m a di, y a wè!
Bawon Lakwa
ki di li fò pase Bondye!
Gede Nibo, se ou m a di, y a wè!
Ayibobo!

who says he is stronger than God!
Gede Nibo, it is you I will tell, they will see!
Bawon of Cemeteries
who says he is stronger than God!
Gede Nibo, it is you I will tell, they will see!
Bawon of the Cross
who says he is stronger than God!
Gede Nibo, it is you I will tell, they'll see!
Ayibobo!

XXIV. Bawon yo

223.
Bawon m ap fè priyè m,
m pa envite ou lan priyè m!
M ap fè sèvis mwen,
m pa envite ou lan sèvis mwen!
Si ou pran malonèt, se pou kò ou.
M ap fè priyè m,
m pa envite ou lan priyè m!

224.
Yo ban mren kleren an!
Sèvi m kleren an, Bawon,
lan gode san lave!

225.
Si ou wè koulèv o!
Ou wè Danbala Wèdo!
Danbala Wèdo se koulèv o!
Li se koulèv o! Danbala Wèdo!
Danbala Wèdo se koulèv o!

226.
Koulèv, koulèv o!
Danbala Wèdo, ou se koulèv o!
Mwen rele koulèv,
koulèv pa sa pale!
Danbala Wèdo, ou se koulèv o!

227.
Danbala Wèdo, kote mwen ye!
Ago ey!
Men mwen, manman.

XXIV. The Bawon

223.
Bawon I am saying my prayers,
I didn't invite you to my prayer!
I am having my service,
I didn't invite you to my service!
If you are treated unkindly, it's your problem.
I am saying my prayers,
I didn't invite you to my prayer!

224.
They give me the raw rum!
Serve me the raw rum, Bawon,
in an unwashed cup!

225.
Oh if you see a snake!
You see Danbala Wèdo!
Oh Danbala Wèdo is a snake!
Oh he is a snake! Danbala Wèdo!
Oh Danbala Wèdo is a snake!

226.
Snake, oh snake!
Oh Danbala Wèdo, you are a snake!
My name is snake,
the snake cannot speak!
Oh Danbala Wèdo, you are a snake!

227.
Danbala Wèdo, where am I?
Hey ago!
Here I am, mother.

O di mwen kote mwen ye!
Men mwen, papa.
O di mwen kote mwen ye!

Oh tell me where I am!
Here I am, father.
Oh tell me where I am!

228.

Yo vin sonde mren—
pou yo pote m ale!
Yo vin gade mren—
pou yo pote m ale!
Malè pote pou yo!
Yo pa sa pote m ale!

228.

They came to challenge me—
to take me away!
They came to watch me—
to take me away!
Unfortunately for them!
They cannot take me away!

229.

M te chita chita m.
Yo vin atake mren!
M a monte anwo.
Zafè m va regle!
M te mande jouda yo,
sa m genyen ak yo!

229.

I was sitting around.
They came to attack me!
I will climb up above.
My affairs will be handled!
I asked the gossips,
what do I have to do with them!

230.

Yo mete wanga lan baryè mwen,
pou m pa pase!
Samdi youn, dimanch de,
lendi m a fè yo vole
anba maji!

230.

They put wanga on my gate,
so that I can't pass!
Saturday one, Sunday two,
Monday I will make them jump
from the magic!

231.

Bawon kenbe moun yo!
Bawon kenbe moun yo!
Pinga lage!

231.

Bawon hold these people!
Bawon hold these people!
Don't let go!

232.

Bawon kenbe moun yo!
O pinga lage yo!
Bawon Lakwa, kenbe moun yo!
O pinga lage!

232.

Bawon hold these people!
Oh don't let them go!
Bawon of the Cross, hold these people!
Oh don't let go!

233.

Bawon Lakwa, kondi l ale!
O Bawon kondi l ale!
Kondi l ale lan simityè!
Grann Brijit k ap mare granmoun o!
Bawon Vil o!
Kondi l ale lan simityè!

233.

Bawon of the Cross, lead him away!
Oh Bawon lead him away!
Lead him away to the cemetery!
Oh Granny Brijit who spellbinds adults!
Oh Bawon of the City!
Lead him away to the cemetery!

XXV. Grann Brijit

234.
Ou di Manman Brijit kouche,
l ap dòmi!
Ou di Manman Brijit kouche,
l ap dòmi!
Lò l a reveye, dènye ounsi do ba!
Dlo lan je Manman Brijit!
Lò l a reveye, dènye ounsi do ba!

235.
Manman Brijit ale, geng, gong!

236.
Brav o!
Ale rele Manzè Brijit pou mwen!
M pral Tomazo!
M pa genyen manman ki pou pale pou mwen!
M pa genyen papa ki pou pale pou mwen!
Brav o!
Ale rele Manzè Brijit pou mwen!
M pral Tomazo!

XXV. Granny Brijit

234.
You say Mother Brijit is lying down,
she is sleeping!
You say Mother Brijit is lying down,
she is sleeping!
When she wakes, every last initiate will bow!
Water in the eyes of Mother Brijit!
When she wakes, every last initiate will bow!

235.
Mother Brijit leaves, ding, dong!

236.
Oh Brave!
Go and call Miss Brijit for me!
I am going to Tomazo!
I don't have a mother who can speak for me!
I don't have a father who can speak for me!
Oh Brave!
Go and call Miss Brijit for me!
I am going to Tomazo!

XXVI. Gede Nibo

237.
Sa ki mande pou Gede a, l a rive!
Gede Nibo se nèg Miragwann o!
Gede Nibo, li mache ak ponya l!
Gede Nibo, li mache ak djara l!
Sa ki mande pou li a, l a rive!
Gede Nibo se nèg Miragwann o!

238.
Lafanmi san yo,
gen jou y a bezwen mren!
Lafanmi san yo,
gen jou y a chache mren!
Gen jou y a chache m, mesye!
Ankò yo wè mren, yo kwè m se vagabon!
Ankò yo wè mren, yo kwè m se sanzave!
Yon jou, y a bezwen m, mesye!

XXVI. Gede Nibo

237.
Those who ask for the Gede, he will come!
Oh Gede Nibo is a man of Miragoâne!
Gede Nibo, he walks with his dagger!
Gede Nibo, he walks with his djara!
Those who ask for him, he will come!
Oh Gede Nibo is a man from Miragoâne!

238.
Blood families,
there are days when they will need me!
Blood families,
there are days they will look for me!
There are days they will look for me, sirs!
Again they see me, they think I am worthless!
Again they see me, they think I am a bum!
One day, they will need me, sirs!

239.
Sa k mande pou Gede Nibo?
Apa li!
Gede Ousou, li mache ak ponya!
Gede Nibo se nèg Miragwann, o!
Sa k mande pou Gede Nibo?
Apa li!
Trase-Fouye k ap mache ak kouto l!
Gede Nibo se nèg Miragwann, o!

239.
Who asks for Gede Nibo?
Here he is!
Gede Ousou, he walks with a dagger!
Oh Gede Nibo is a man from Miragoâne!
Who asks for Gede Nibo?
Here he is!
Trace-Dig who walks with his dagger!
Oh Gede Nibo is a man from Miragoâne!

240.
Dèyè lakwa a, Gede!
Gede Nibo rete dèyè lakwa!
Gran mèsi, Bondye la a!
Gede ret dèyè lakwa! Gede!

240.
Behind the cross, Gede!
Gede Nibo lives behind the cross!
Great thanks, God is here!
Gede lives behind the cross! Gede!

241.
Gede Nibo
ki di l dèyè lakwa a! Gede!
Bawon Samdi
ki di l devan lakwa a! Gede!
O gran mèsi Lavyèj!
Gede Nibo
ki di l dèyè lakwa a! Gede!

241.
Gede Nibo
who says he's behind the cross! Gede!
Bawon Samdi
who says he's in front of the cross! Gede!
Oh great thanks Virgin!
Gede Nibo
who says he lives behind the cross! Gede!

242.
Gede Nibo, men lajan.
M ape ba ou lajan
pou gade zanfan lwa yo!
O Seklekite, Balewouze,
M ape ba ou manje
pou gade zanfan lwa yo!
Gede, men lajan.
M ape ba ou manje
pou gade zanfan lwa yo!

242.
Gede Nibo, here is some money.
I will give you money
to look after the children of the lwa!
O Seklekite, Balewouze,
I will give you food
to look after the children of the lwa!
Gede here is some money.
I will give you food
to look after the children of the lwa!

243.
Kou yo bezwen m, yo rele m papa!
Lò yo pa bezwen m,
yo di m se tafyatè!

243.
Once they need me, they call me papa!
When they don't need me,
they say I'm a drunkard!

244.
Gede Nibo, m pa dra!
Si m te dra, m ta kouvri pou yo!
Kou yo malad, yo rele Gede!
Lò yo geri, Gede se demon!

244.
Gede Nibo, I am not a cloth!
If I was a cloth, I would cover for them!
When they are sick, they call Gede!
When they are healed, Gede is a demon!

245.
Gede Nibo genyen yon redengòt,
yon bò wo, yon bò ba!
Gede Nibo genyen yon koma,
yon bò wo, yon bò ba!
O si nou wè sa, Jan Simon,
n a mande prete l!

245.
Gede Nibo has a coat,
one side high, one side low!
Gede Nibo has a tophat,
one side high, one side low!
Oh if you see that, John Simon,
you will ask to borrow it!

246.
Gede mache ak foula nwa o!
Enhen, enhen! Tomazo!
Papa Gede mache ak foula nwa!
Tomazo!
Enhen, enhen! Tomazo!

246.
Oh Gede walks with a black scarf!
Yeah, yeah! Tomazo!
Papa Gede walks with a black scarf!
Tomazo!
Yeah, yeah! Tomazo!

247.
Viv Gede o!
Se pa Gede sa?
Viv Gede o!
Gede Nibo!

247.
Oh long live Gede!
Isn't that Gede?
Oh long live Gede!
Gede Nibo!

248.
Gede tchou kanèl!
Gade mache Gede!
Gede tchou kanèl!
Gade mache Gede!

248.
Gede cinnamon butthole!
Look at Gede's gait!
Gede cinnamon butthole!
Look at Gede's gait!

249.
De moun pa mete woy!
De moun pa mete, l a chire!
De moun pa mete, l a pete!
De moun pa mete woy!

249.
Whoa, two people cannot put it on!
Two people cannot put it on, it will tear!
Two people cannot put it on, it will blow!
Whoa, two people cannot put it on!

250.
Gede Nibo, li bèl,
li bèl anraje!
Jan Simon, li bèl,
li bèl anraje!

250.
Gede Nibo, he is handsome,
handsomely out of his mind!
John Simon, he is handsome,
handsomely out of his mind!

Lò l ap danse, li gouye jis atè!
Lò l ap danse, li danse jis atè!
Gede Nibo, li bèl,
li bèl anraje!
Jan Simon, li bèl,
li bèl anraje!

When he is dancing, he grinds to the floor!
When he is dancing, he dances to the floor!
Gede Nibo, he is handsome,
handsomely out of his mind!
John Simon, he is handsome,
handsomely out of his mind!

251.
Abram leve twa mren!
Benefis se pou malere!
Si yon fanm gouye pase m,
venn dèyè li a demonte!
Si yon fanm gouye pase m,
venn dèyè li a devise!

251.
Abraham raises three like me!
The benefits are for the poor!
If a woman grinds better than me,
her Achilles tendon will fall apart!
If a woman grinds better than me,
her Achilles tendon will unravel!

252.
Plim o! Plim o!
Se plim o! M mande!

252.
Oh feather! Oh feather!
Oh it is the feather! I ask!

253.
Tout manman ki gen pitit fi,
sere l lan malèt o!
Samdi lò Bondye leve,
sa va pi rèd o!

253.
Every mother who has a daughter,
oh keep her in a trunk!
Saturday when God gets up,
oh it will be worse!

XXVII. Lòt Gede

XXVII. Other Gedes

254.
Men oungan, mwen malad o!
Gedevi, mache ak Gede!
Gede Nibo, mache ak Gede sa a!
Men oungan, mwen malad o!
Gede sila, mache ak Papa Gede!
Men oungan, mwen malad o!
Papa Gede, mache ak Gede sila!
Men oungan, mwen malad o!

254.
Here is the oungan, oh I am sick!
Gedevi, walk with Gede!
Gede Nibo, walk with this Gede!
Here is the oungan, oh I am sick!
This Gede, walk with Papa Gede!
Here is the oungan, oh I am sick!
Papa Gede, walk with this Gede!
Here is the oungan, oh I am sick!

255.
Mwen di brav o!
Rele Brav, o gason temerè.
Bout bannann, li temerè.
Moso poul, li temerè.
Yon kou d kleren, li temerè.
Moso patat, li temerè.

255.
I say oh brave!
Call the Brave, oh bold boy.
Piece of plantain, he is bold.
A piece of chicken, he is bold.
One shot of rum, he is bold.
A piece of his sweet potato, he is bold.

M ape rele Brav Gede.
Vini sove zanfan la woy!
Brav o, rele Brav!
Gason temerè.

I will cry Brave Gede.
Come save the children here oh my!
Oh brave, call the Brave!
Bold boy.

256.

Jan Simon, yo di ou se wa.
W a rele Bondye!
Gede Nibo, Papa, yo di ou se wa.
W a rele: Bondye!
Jan Simon, yo di ou se wa.
Fò ou rele Bondye!

256.

John Simon, they say you are king!
You will call for God!
Gede Nibo, Papa, they say you are king.
You will call for God!
John Simon, they say you are king!
You must cry for God!

257.

Ankò se mwen
ki fè yo fè mwen sa!
Ankò se mwen, Gede Masaka
ki fè yo fè mwen sa!
Lalin nouvèl,
espri malen bare mwen.
Malentespri bare mwen!

257.

Again it is me
who makes them do this to me!
Again it is me, Gede Masaka
who makes them do this to me!
The new moon,
cunning spirits block me.
Evil spirits block me!

258.

Kaptèn Zonbi se yon nonm!
Jou malè,
Kaptèn Zonbi se yon nonm!
Kaptèn Zonbi se yon nonm tou!

258.

Captain Zombie is a man!
On days of misfortune,
Captain Zombie is a man!
Captain Zombie is a man too!

259.

Ti Gede, Ti Gede! Bèt nwa.
Ti Gede, Ti Gede, bèt nwa!
Ti Gede, kote ou prale?
M pral kay yaya.
Vouvou ou.

259.

Little Gede, Little Gede! Black insect.
Little Gede, Little Gede, black insect!
Little Gede, where are you going?
I am going to yaya's house.
Your flying beetle!

260.

Gede Loray o!
Gede ipokrit o!
Kite medizan yo pale!

260.

Oh Gede of the Storms!
Oh Gede, hypocrite!
Let the slanderers talk!

261.

Lenjistis yo fè m,
Ti Ware, papa m!
Pwason pouri ki pa bon pou bay kochon,

261.

They did an injustice to me,
Little Ware, my papa!
Rotten fish that are not fit for pigs,

se li yo bay Gede, ankò se mwen!
Ti Ware, papa m, lenjistis yo fè m!
Pwason kraze ki pa bon pou bay kochon,
se li yo bay Gede, ankò se mwen!
Gede Ti Ware, papa m,
lenjistis yo fè m!
Aran kraze ki pa bon pou bay kochon,
se li yo pran pou bay li, ankò se li!
Ti Ware, papa m, lenjistis yo fè m!

262.

Gede Nouvavon gen yon pye mango!
Se yon pye repozwa!

is what they give to Gede, again it is me!
Little Ware, my papa, they did me wrong!
Crushed fish that are not fit for pigs,
is what they give Gede, again it is me!
Gede Ti Ware, my papa,
they did an injustice to me!
Crushed herring that is not fit for pigs,
is what they take to give him, again it is he!
Little Ware, my papa, they did me wrong!

262.

Gede Nouvavon has a mango tree!
It is a lwa's resting tree!

CHAPTER 5

Laura Boulton's Songs

BENJAMIN HEBBLETHWAITE
and JOANNE BARTLEY

BOULTON'S MATERIALS come from a typed manuscript transcription that I located in the Archives of Traditional Music in 2002 while I was working on a doctorate in French linguistics at Indiana University. Dating from 1947, these transcriptions include songs, liturgy, and discourse from a Vodou ceremony. The songs are interspersed with citations from the participants of the ceremony, including the oungan (priest), the oungenikon (choir leader), ounsi (initiates and choir members), and individuals possessed by the lwa (e.g., Gede). In some places in the text, the spoken word and song are interspersed in a call-and-response structure; in other places, songs are grouped together and numbered. The final section of the manuscript is a lengthy dialogue among the participants and the audience at a ceremony. These transcriptions shed light on the kinds of discourse the Vodou community engages in during ceremonies. The materials Boulton recorded reveal the depth and organization of Vodou ideas and language as they emerge through communal worship, and they are entirely different from the content found in the other chapters.

Chante Laura Boulton

1.

Wèdo, rele Wèdo ey.
Wèdo, gade Wèdo ey.
N a prale wè yo.
Si n a dakò, Wèdo wè mwen.
Laplas, rele

Laura Boulton's Songs

1.

Wèdo, hey call Wèdo.
Wèdo, hey look at Wèdo.
We are going to see them.
If we shall be agreed, Wèdo sees me.
Master of ceremonies, call the

ogantye.
Segondye rele
boulaye.
Boulaye pale ak
manman tanbou a pou mwen.
Wèdo, rele Wèdo ey.
N a prale wè si n a dakò.

cowbell percussionist.
The segondye drummer calls
the boula drummer.
Boula drummer talk with
the mother drum for me.
Wèdo, hey call Wèdo.
We are going to see if we shall agree.

2.

Siwo, rele siwo vèvè, siwo.
Danbala Wèdo, Ayida Wèdo, n ape rele,
siwo vèvè, siwo.
Siwo, rele siwo vèvè, siwo.
Ayida Wèdo, Papa Danbala, n ape rele,
siwo vèvè, siwo.

2.

Syrup, call for the syrup vèvè, syrup.
Danbala Wèdo, Ayida Wèdo, we are calling,
syrup vèvè, syrup.
Syrup, call for the syrup vèvè, syrup.
Ayida Wèdo, Papa Danbala, we are calling,
syrup vèvè, syrup.

3.

Danbala Kyesou ey, mwen kriye, ago ago!
Depi tan mwen la;
pèsonn pa konnen mwen.
Se mwen menm, Sent Elizabèt, ago ago.
Se mwen menm, gwo koulèv Agouye, ago ago.
Depi tan mwen la,
pèsonn pa konnen mwen.

3.

Hey Danbala Kyesou, I cry, ago ago!
For a long time I have been here;
no one knows me.
It is me, Saint Elizabeth, ago ago.
It is me, the big snake of Agouye, ago ago.
For a long time I have been here,
no one knows me.

4.

Ago, Danbala; ago, Danbala;
ago, Papa Misan Ewe.
Ago ey, Danbala;
nou se pitit Sobokyesou.
Danbala, ago, Papa Misan Ewe.

4.

Ago, Danbala; ago, Danbala;
ago, Papa Misan Ewe.
Ago hey, Danbala;
we are Sobokyesou's children.
Danbala, ago, Papa Misan Ewe.

5.

Danbala Sayiti, ede mwen.
Ede mwen, Danbala Wèdo, ede mwen.
Goumen, goumen, Danbala; ou kòve, goumen.

5.

Danbala of Saiti,[1] help me.
Help me, Danbala Wèdo, help me.
Fight, fight, Danbala; you struggle, fight.

6.

Van vante van.
Ki kote l sòti?
Agouye Tawoyo, ou deja devan.
Van vante van.
Ki kote l sòti?
Ako Zangi, ou deja devan.

6.

Wind blows wind.
Where did it come from?
Agouye[2] Tawoyo, you are already ahead.
Wind blows wind.
Where did it come from?
Ako Zangi, you are already ahead.

7.

Anonse zanj dlo, Bakosou Moula,
Manman Lawe.
Mwen di, mwen prale anba lavil Okan;
peyi a chanje.
Mwen di, peyi a chanje, nèg Nago,
Bakosou Alade; peyi a chanje.

7.

Announce the water angel, Bakosou Moula,
Mother of Lawe.
I say, I'm going down to Lavil Okan;
the country has changed.
I say, this country has changed, Nago guys,
Bakosou Alade; the country has changed.

8.

Lali anwo; mwen di ey! Pòv Lali ey.
Mwen di, ey! Pòv Lali o.
Chemen Nago bouche,
Lamenzo Batala, an ey o.

8.

Lalue up there; I say, hey! Hey poor Lalue.
I say, hey! Oh poor Lalue.
The Nago way is blocked,
Lamenzo Batala, oh yeah.

9.

Abobo! Mwen di. Mwen di, Abobo!
Nou pa tande; mwen di, Abobo!
Silans! M ap chante.
Kan m vole, mwen rele Ogoun o.
Kan m vole, Ogoun Badagri kite m vole.
Kan m vole, mwen vole twò wo, tonbe atè,
lwa pran mwen.

9.

Abobo! I say. I say, Abobo!
You don't hear; I say, Abobo!
Silence! I am singing.
When I fly, oh I call Ogoun.
When I fly, Ogoun Badagri lets me fly.
When I fly, I fly too high, fall to the ground,
the lwa takes me.

10.

Abobo (pale).
Bann maledve,
mwen pa envite nou ale lakay nou.
Mwen pale nou, pa vini nwi mwen.
Vya, vya, vya, vya,
kou w a manke,
vya, vya, vya, vya.
M achte chen mwen, karese chen mwen.
Mwen ba li non pote; kan l anraje,
li refize mòde.
Fanm Sobokyesou dòmi deyò ey!
Tengendeng masouke.

10.

Abobo (spoken).
Band of ill-bred,
I do not invite you to go to our house.
I tell you, don't come and give me trouble.
Choo, choo, choo, choo,
you'll avoid a beating,
choo, choo, choo, choo.
I bought my dog, stroked my dog.
I gave him a name; when he's mad,
he refuses to bite.
Hey, Sobokyesou's wife sleeps around!
Tengendeng masouke.

11.

Se dwòl o, se dwòl o,
se dwòl o.
Se dwòl o, se dwòl o, Lakahe,
fanm nan koupe lavi m;
m ap lese peyi a ba yo.
Tout lajounen, tout lannuit, zanmi m,
m ap danse Tanbou a.

11.

Oh that's strange, oh that's strange,
oh that's strange.
Oh that's strange, oh that's strange, Lakahe,
the women cut up my life;
I'm leaving the country for them.
All day, all night, my friend,
I'm dancing to the Drum.

12.

Van vante van o.
Van vante van o.
Van vante van nò o.
Van vante van o.
O, mwen vante van, van vante nò.
Van vante van o, van vante;
van ale.

13.

Rele Ti Kite Alzade, rele Bondye ey.
Rele Ti Kite Alzade, rele.
Ou pa wè medam?
Gade y al pale Bondye.
Gade li; se Blake o, rele.
Pi gwo bouzen, gade l pale.
Rele Ti Kite Alzade, rele.

14.

Ti nèg Bèlè vin sonde vi mwen.
W a di li mwen fò anpil.
Gran mèsi Bondye, vi mwen fò.
Fè m chonje, fè m chonje,
fè m chonje; mwen pale fanm nan;
fanm nan joure manman ane a, an.
Sanba, mwen pale avè ou, li joure Lolo.
Fè m chonje, fè m chonje.
Woy, depi lòt jou Fansilis
ta pale avè li, li joure Lolo.
Fè m chonje, fè m chonje,
fè m chonje; mwen pale fanm nan;
fanm nan joure manman ane a, an.
Se kon sa ti gason, m ape pale avè li.
Se kon sa nèg anba, m ape pale avè li.
Se pa konsa Jòj,
mwen pale avè li.
Fransilis o, mwen pa ta pale avè li.
Nan Choda, mwen ta danse avè li,
anye o!

15.

Se dwòl o, Irani, se dwòl o, se dwòl o,
Irani, se dwòl o.
Irani gen yon matla; Bouki dòmi ladan.
Se dwòl, se dwòl o.

12.

Oh wind blows wind.
Oh wind blows wind.
Oh wind blows the northern wind.
Oh wind blows wind.
Oh, I blow wind, wind blows north.
Oh wind blows wind, wind blows;
wind goes away.

13.

Call Ti Kite Alzade, hey, call God.
Call Ti Kite Alzade, call.
Don't you see the ladies?
Watch them go speak to God.
Look at him; oh it's Blake, call out.
Grossest floozy, look at her speak.
Call Ti Kite Alzade, call.

14.

Little Bel-Air guy comes to challenge my life.
You'll tell him I am very strong.
Great thanks to God, my life is strong.
Make me remember, make me remember,
make me remember; I spoke with the woman;
the woman insults her mother this year, oh.
Minstrel, I speak with you, she insults Lolo.
Make me remember, make me remember.
Whoa, since the other day Fansilis
would speak with her, she insulted Lolo.
Make me remember, make me remember,
make me remember; I speak with the woman;
the woman insults her mother this year, huh.
It's like this little boy, I'm speaking with her.
It's like this poor guy, I'm speaking with her.
It's not like this George,
I'm speaking with her.
Oh Fransilis, I wouldn't speak with her.
Oh my, in Choda, I would dance with her,
my oh my!

15.

Oh that's strange, Uranie, oh that's strange,
Uranie, oh that's strange.
Uranie has a mattress; a sucker sleeps on it.
That's strange, that's strange.

16.

San pale, mwen pa mouri mal o,
san pale.
San pale, mwen pa mouri mal o,
san pale.
Nou deja devan san pale.
M pa mouri mal o;
pou m pale Bondye.

16.

Without talking, oh I won't die badly,
without talking.
Without talking, oh I won't die badly,
without talking.
We are already ahead without talking.
Oh I won't die badly;
let me talk to God.

17.

Aganman,[3] Ibo lele, lele, lele.
Aganman, Obo lele,
ou pile pye m;
ou pa di m padon.
Sa padon an fè pou ou?
Aganman, Ibo lele, lele, lele.
Aganman, Obol lele, ou pile pye m;
ou pa di m padon.
Aganman, Ibo lele, lele, lele.

17.

Chameleon, Ibo cries out, cries out, cries out.
Chameleon, Obo cries out,
you stomp on my foot;
you don't say pardon.
What does saying pardon do to you?
Chameleon, Ibo cries out, cries out, cries out.
Chameleon, Obo cries out, you stomp on my foot;
you don't say pardon.
Chameleon, Ibo cries out, cries out, cries out.

18.

Abobo.
Mache pran youn, Èzili; nou pa genyen chans.
Mache pran de, nou pa genyen chans.
Yon sèl ti pitit mwen genyen pou m navige;
avè li lan lanmè, kons chavire.
Èzili, se pa Èzili sa.
Èzili ey! Se pa Èzili Fawon!
Lan lanmè, kons chavire;
si se pa te Bondye, tout moun ta neye.

18.

Abobo.
Walk and take one, Èzili; we're not lucky.
Walk and take two, we are not lucky.
Only one child do I have to navigate the sea;
the boat turns over in the sea with him.
Èzili, that's not Èzili!
Hey Èzili! It's not Èzili Fawon!
In the sea, the boat turns over;
if it wasn't for God, everyone would drown.

19.

Papa Legba,
ouvè bayè pou m pase.
Papa Legba,
ouvè bayè pou m pase.
Papa Legba,
ouvè bayè pou m pase.

19.

Papa Legba,
open the gate for me to pass through.
Papa Legba,
open the gate for me to pass through.
Papa Legba,
open the gate for me to pass through.

20.

Legba lan bayè mwen, Legba laye mwen,
Legba Kita, bayè mwen.
Se ou ki pote drapo;
drapo k ap pare solèy pou lwa yo.

20.

Legba is at my gate, Legba flips me,
Legba Kita, my gate.
It's you who carries the flag;
the flag that blocks the sun for the lwa.

21.

Feray o,
lan men ki moun, ou kite bagi yo la?
Kan m rete, chonje Ogoun Feray;
konsole, m ap pran kouraj o.
Rele Alanman;
ounsi malad o, kwanye
Angita, Angita o, kwanye!
M ape rele Alanman, o Lemisou;
sobagi n asire.

21.

Oh Feray,
in whose hands have you left the sanctuary?
When I stop, remember Ogoun Feray;
consolation, oh I take courage.
Call Alanman;
oh the Vodou initiates are sick, be calm!
Angita, oh Angita, be calm!
I am calling Alanman, oh Lemisou;
your sanctuary is safe.

22.

Chabodo.
Simbi Andezo, sa yo di moun?
Simbi Andezo, sa y a fè mwen?
Sa y a di m?
Mwen prale lan simityè;
mwen prale chache pwen mwen.
Mwen prale chache pwen Makaya;
mwen prale chache pwen Simbi Andezo.
Mwen prale chache anba, nèg;
mwen prale chache pwen.

22.

Chabodo.
Simbi Andezo, what do they say to people?
Simbi Andezo, what will they do to me?
What will they tell me?
I'm going to the cemetery;
I'm going to seek out my magic charm.
I'm going to seek out Makaya's charm;
I'm going to seek out Simbi Andezo's charm.
I'm going to seek down yonder, brother;
I'm going to seek out a charm.

23.

Abobo.
Se jodi vivan latè
ap pale sou do mwen.
Se pa poutèt sa,
pou m al tiye tèt mwen.
Mwen kriye, ago, mwen rele Bondye.
Ago, ago, mwen rele Bondye pi fò.
Mwen kriye, ago, mwen rele Bondye.
Pawòl la fè mwen mal;
dlo kouri lan je m.
Pawòl la fè m mal; san m ape koule.

23.

Abobo.
It is today that earthlings
are talking behind my back.
That's no reason
for me to go kill myself.
I cry, ago, I call on God.
Ago, ago, I call God harder.
I cry, ago, I call on God.
The word hurts me;
tears pour from my eyes.
The word hurts me; my blood is spilling out.

24.

Si m gen byen pou m fè,
m ap fè l ak chen mwen.
Si m gen mal pou m fè, m ap fè l ak pechè yo.
Mwen di, ey! Mache lannuit o;
vivan ki rayi mwen an mèt veye mwen.

24.

If I have good to do,
I'm doing it with my dog.
If I have bad to do, I do it with the sinners.
I say, hey! Oh walking in the night;
the one who hates me can look out for me.

25.
Imamou Lèmizo, kay mwen boule.
Imamou, bèl bato mwen,
kay mwen boule.

25.
Imamou Lemizo, my house burned down.
Imamou, my beautiful boat,
my house burned down.

26.
Do, do, do, pitit mwen,
manman li ale larivyè,
papa li ale chache krab.
Do, do, ti pitit, manman li,
manman li ale larivyè.
Papa li ale chache bwa pou li,
pou li kuit manje pou pitit li.
Manman li ale larivyè,
papa li ale vil la l chache
yon ti bonbon pou ti pitit manje.
Do, do, pitit, manman li.
Do, do, ti pitit, do, do,
ti pitit, do, do, pitit mwen;
chat mawon va manje ou.
Do, do, pitit mwen, do, do pitit mwen.
Do, do, pitit mwen; dòmi an lan je ou.
Do, do, pitit mwen;
toutalè m a ba ou manje ou;
do, do, do pitit mwen.
Do, do, ti pitit, do, do, pitit mwen;
chat mawon va manje ou,
do, do pitit mwen.

26.
Sleep, sleep, sleep, my little child,
her mama went to the river,
her papa went to look for crabs.
Sleep, sleep, little child, her mama,
her mama went to the river.
Her papa went to look for wood for her,
to cook food for his child.
Her mama went to the river,
her papa went to town to look for
a little cake for the little one to eat.
Sleep, sleep, little child, her mama (says).
Sleep, sleep, little child, sleep, sleep,
little child, sleep, sleep, my child;
the wild cat's going to eat you.
Sleep, sleep my child, sleep, sleep my child.
Sleep, sleep my child; the sleep's in your eyes.
Sleep, sleep my child;
in a moment I'll give you your food;
sleep, sleep, sleep my child.
Sleep, sleep, little child, sleep, sleep, my child;
the wild cat's going to eat you,
sleep, sleep my child.

27.
Manman, mani, wa, wi, wa;
kenbe li ban mwen, wi, wa.
Ti poul sove, wi, wa;
kenbe li ban mwen, wi, wa.

27.
Mama, mommy, wa, wi, wa;
catch him for me, wi, wa.
Little chicken got away, wi, wa;
catch him for me, wi, wa.

28.
Wa, wa, pitit kon ou;
Nelyo vole pijon.
Nelyo vole pijon;
sere l anba levit.

28.
King, king, small like you;
Nelyo stole the pigeon.
Nelyo stole the pigeon;
he keeps it under his coat.

29.
Fèzè ratè la, ou pa konnen
sa ki lan kè m kirye?

29.
You trouble maker, don't you know
what is in my heart is curious?

Fèzè ratè la,
ou pa konnen sa ki lan kè m kirye?
Papa Pyè, mwen se zèb pa tè;
si l te konnen sa ki lan kè m,
mwen kirye o.
Serye pran konnen nou la.
Lwa Ibo, Sen Ibo, lafanmi anpil.
Vini, cheri, lwa mwen,
w a gade lan rasin nan;
w a wè lwa Ibo a kanpe.

30.
Nago, se ou ki mennen m isi;
pran ka m.
Pran ka m, pran ka m.
Nago, se ou ki mennen m isi;
pran ka m.

31.
Bling sou bling; lakay Manbo Zili;
mwen tande bling sou bling;
kana m sou dlo, ago ey!
Èzili o, konsa nou ye, Èzili;
konsa nou ye, bling sou bling;
kana mwen sou dlo.

32.
Prezidan pa te la;
l ap antre nan lamezon.
Prezidan pa te la;
l ap antre nan gouvènman.
Prezidan pa te la;
l ap antre respekte nou.

33.
Papa Legba, ouvè bayè.
Ouvè bayè, Atibon;
nou bezwen pase, voye.
Papa Legba, ouvè bayè.

34.
Sen Jak pa la;
Dye ki fè, se mwen ki la.

You troublemaker,
don't you know what is in my heart is curious?
Papa Peter, I am grass on the earth;
if he knew what is in my heart,
oh I'm curious.
The serious find out we're here.
Lwa Ibo, Saint Ibo, the family is numerous.
Come, dear, my lwa,
you'll look to the roots;
you'll see the lwa Ibo standing there.

30.
Nago, it is you who brought me here;
take care of me.
Take care of me, take care of me.
Nago, it is you who brought me here;
take care of me.

31.
Ping on ping; at Manbo Zulie's;
I hear ping on ping;
hey ago, my duck is on the water!
Oh Èzili, that's how we are, Èzili;
that's how we are, ping on ping;
my duck is on water.

32.
The president was not there;
he is entering the house.
The president was not there;
he is entering the government.
The president was not there;
he is entering to respect us.

33.
Papa Legba, open the gate.
Open the gate, Atibon;
we want to pass through, throw.
Papa Legba, open the gate.

34.
Saint James is not here;
it is God who made me be here.

Sen Jak pa la;
se chen ki la; ou pa wè? Pou n ale.
Sen Jak pa la;
se chen ki la.
Sen Jak pa la; ou pa wè?
Chen move; n a prale.

Saint James is not here;
it's a dog that is there; don't you see? Let's go.
Saint James is not there;
it's a dog that is there.
Saint James is not there; don't you see?
This dog is mean; we'll get going.

35.

Dawomen ey wa,[4] oungenikonn mwen!
Dawomen ey wa, oungenikonn, atò!
Dawomen ey wa,
kreyòl rayi rezon lwa!
Kan m ape pale yo, ey,
yo pa vle koute m.
Chache, Dawomen ey wa,
oungenikonn, atò.
Dawomen ey wa,
kreyòl rayi rezon lwa!

35.

Dawomen the beautiful,[5] my choir leader!
Dawomen the beautiful, choir leader, at last!
Dawomen the beautiful,
the Creoles hate the motives of the lwa!
When I'm speaking to them,
they don't want to listen to me.
Find, Dawomen the beautiful,
the choir leader, right now.
Dawomen the beautiful,
the Creoles hate the motives of the lwa!

36.

Danse o, ala yon bèl dans!
Se dans Papa Gede.
Danse o manman mwen, ki bagay sa?
Se dans Papa Gede.
Apiye sou pye, pran kouraj,
se dans Papa Gede.
O o, ki bagay sa?
Se dans Papa Gede.

36.

Oh dance, what a fine dance!
It's the dance of Papa Gede.
Oh dance my mother, what is this?
It's the dance of Papa Gede
Lean on your feet, take heart,
it's the dance of Papa Gede
Oho, what is this?
It's the dance of Papa Gede.

37.

Chande. Savalou mwen, Papa Pyè;
Savalou mwen, Mèt Feray, Savalou mwen.
Jaden mwen lwen;
mayi m ape kase, ago ey!
Si m pran yon fanm ki pa pote pànye
lan tèt, ago ey, Papa Pyè!
Achade, Savalou mwen, Monchè Pyè;
Savalou mwen, Azagon, Savalou mwen,
mèt Feray, Savalou mwen la!
Jaden mwen lwen,
mayi m ape kase, rele ey
Si m pran yon fanm ki pa pote pànye
lan tèt, ago ey, Papa Pyè.

37.

Chande. My Savalou, Papa Peter;
my Savalou, Master Feray, my Savalou.
My garden is far;
my corn is breaking, ago hey!
If I take a wife who doesn't carry a basket
on her head, oh hey, Papa Peter!
Achade, my Savalou, my dear Peter;
my Savalou, Azagon, my Savalou,
master Feray, my Savalou is here!
My garden is far,
my corn is being broken, shout hey!
If I take a wife who doesn't carry a basket
on her head, ago hey, Papa Peter

38.

Voye rele Banda pou mwen,
Banda ale lakay ey.
Banda o, Banda mouri san pale
Voye rele Banda pou mwen;
Banda ale lakay ey.

38.

Go and call Banda for me;
hey, Banda's going home.
Oh Banda, Banda dies without speaking.
Go and call Banda for me;
hey, Banda's going home.

39.

Annou mache, Pyè; m pral chawonyen yo;
an nou mache.
Papa Pyè, kite m chawonyen yo.
Annou mache, Pyè; kite m chawonyen yo.
Papa Pyè, kite m chawoule lwa.
M nya bobo, kite m chawonyen yo.
Annou mache, Pyè; n ap chawonyen yo.

39.

Let's walk, Peter; I am going to annoy them;
let's walk.
Papa Peter, let me annoy them.
Let's walk, Peter; let me annoy them.
Papa Peter, let me bother the lwa.
M nya bobo, let me annoy them.
Let's walk, Peter; we are going to annoy them.

40.

Bling sou bling;
lakay manbo kay,
mwen tande bling sou bling;
kanna mwen sou dlo,
Èzili o, kon sa m ap di yo, Èzili o;
kon sa nou ye, bling sou bling;
kanna mwen sou dlo
Mwen di, ey, Èzili; frè mwen, bling sou bling;
kanna mwen sou dlo.
Tande, mwen di bling; manbo kay
pale bling; mèt Sansan,
mwen di bling lakay Manbo Èzili,
mwen tande bling sou bling;
kanna mwen sou dlo
Èzili Freda, konsa nou ye,
Èzili o, konsa nou ye, bling sou bling;
kanna mwen sou dlo.

40.

Ping on ping;
at the house of the manbo's assistant,
I hear ping on ping;
my duck is on the water,
Oh Èzili, I'm telling them this way, oh Èzili;
this is how we are, ping on ping;
my duck is on the water.
I said, hey, Èzili; my brother, ping on ping;
my duck is on the water.
Listen up, I say ping; the manbo's assistant
says ping; teacher Sansan,
I say ping at Manbo Èzili's house,
I hear ping on ping;
my duck is on the water.
Èzili Freda, this is how we are,
oh Èzili; this is how we are, ping on ping;
my duck is on the water.

41.

a.

Jwe non Zaka, jwe; jwe non Zaka, jwe;
Azaka, m pral pote plent
pou Agwe Wèdo; jwe Zaka jwe.
Azaka vin fè m rapò
poutèt Zaka Mede; jwe Zaka jwe

41.

a.

Play now, Zaka, play; play now, Zaka, play;
Azaka, I'm going to make my complaint
to Agwe Wèdo; play, Zaka, play.
Azaka comes to me to make a report
about Zaka Mede; play, Zaka, play.

b.

Azaka vin fè m rapò poutèt
Zaka Tonde; jwe, Zaka, jwe.
Azaka, yo pote m plent;
se pou Zaka Mede; jwe, Zaka, jwe.
Azaka, m pral fè on rapò
pou Gaswèmen; jwe Zaka jwe.
Mede vin pote on plent poutèt
Gaswèmen; jwe, Zaka, jwe.
Mede vin fè on rapò, gade;
fè m yon travay; jwe, Zaka, jwe.
Zaka vin fè on rapò pou
Agwe Wèdo la; jwe Zaka, jwe.

b.

Azaka comes to me to make a report about
Zaka Tonde; play, Zaka, play.
Azaka, they bring me complaints;
they are for Zaka Mede; play, Zaka, play.
Azaka, I'm going to make a report
about Gaswemen; play, Zaka, play.
Mede comes to make a complaint about
Gaswemen; play, Zaka, play.
Mede comes to make a report, you see;
make some work for me; play, Zaka, play.
Zaka comes to make a report for
Agwe Wèdo; play, Zaka, play.

c.

Azaka vin pote on plent,
se pou Azaka Tonnè; jwe, Zaka, jwe.
Azaka, ki Zaka ou ye? Se Zaka Mede;
jwe, Zaka, jwe.
Azaka, yo pale nou mal;
se pou Azaka Tonnè; jwe, Zaka, jwe.

c.

Azaka brings a complaint,
it is for Azaka Tonnè; play, Zaka, play.
Azaka, which Zaka are you? It is Zaka Mede;
play, Zaka, play.
Azaka, they speak badly of us;
it is for Azaka Tonnè; play, Zaka, play.

42.

Oungenikon
M di, minis Zaka,
m ape di ou, bonjou o;
m di, bonjou o, minis o.
Azaka, ki kote nou prale,
w a di yo, bonjou?
M pral lan pakoti ey.

Koral ounsi
Minis Zaka, m ape di ou, bonswa o,
bonswa o, minis o.

Oungenikon
M di, Azaka Mede di nou, bonjou o.

Koral ounsi
Bonswa o, minis o.

Oungenikon
Azaka, ki kote nou a di yo?
M pral lan pakoti ou.

42.

Choir leader
I say, Minister Zaka,
I'm telling you, oh good morning;
I say, oh good morning, oh minister.
Azaka, where are you going,
will you tell them, good morning?
Hey, I'm going in rags.

Chorus of initiates
Minister Zaka, tell us, oh good evening,
oh good evening, oh minister.

Choir leader
I say, Azaka Mede tells us, oh good morning.

Chorus of initiates
Oh good evening, oh minister.

Choir leader
Azaka, where shall we tell them?
I'm going in rags.

Koral ounsi
Azaka, ki kote nou prale?

Chorus of initiates
Azaka, where are you going?

43.
Oungenikon
Nago, Nago, vin wè kote m demere.
Si nou wè kote m demere,
n a peye dola pou mwen.

Koral ounsi
Nago, Nago, vin wè kote m demere.
(a) . . . n a voye dola ban mwen.
(b) . . . fòk n anvi peye dola.
(c) . . . fòk n anvi rale dola.
(d) . . . n a peye lajan pou mwen.
(e) . . . fòk n anvi peye lajan.
(f) . . . n a voye lajan ban mwen.
(g) . . . fòk n anvi voye rele m.
(h) . . . fòk n anvi voye chache m.
(i) . . . fòk n anvi peye yo la.

43.
Choir leader
Nago, Nago, come and see where I live.
If you see where I live,
you'll pay me dollars.

Chorus of initiates
Nago, Nago, come see where I live.
(a) . . . you'll send me dollars.
(b) . . . you'll feel compelled to pay dollars.
(c) . . . you'll want to pull out dollars.
(d) . . . you'll pay me money.
(e) . . . you'll feel compelled to pay money.
(f) . . . you'll send me money.
(g) . . . you have to want to send for me.
(h) . . . you have to want to send for me.
(i) . . . you have to want to pay them now.

44.
Oungenikon
Nago, yo pile pye m,
manyen pou pwal mwen, manyen kò.
Jeneral Nago, ki manyen kò mwen?
Kè li sote.

Koral ounsi
Nago, pile pye m,
Jeneral Nago,
ki manyen kò mwen? Kè li sote.

44.
Choir leader
Nago, they pound my foot,
reach for my hair, touch my body.
General Nago, who touches my body?
His heart leaps.

Chorus of initiates
Nago, pounding on my foot,
General Nago,
who touches my body? His heart leaps.

45.
Oungenikon
Kay o, kay o,
kay mwen santi foula,
Tata Maoumbe ey.
Kay mwen,
ki santi foula mwen,
Tata Maoumbe.
Kay mwen, ki santi foula,
Tata Maoumbe ey.

45.
Choir leader
Oh house, oh house,
my house smells of sprayed rum,
hey Tata Maoumbe.
My house,
which smells of my vaporized rum,
Tata Maoumbe.
My house, which smells of vaporized rum,
hey, Tata Maoumbe.

Koral ounsi
Kay o, kay o,
kay mwen santi foula,
Tata Maoumbe ey.

Chorus of initiates
Oh house, oh house,
my house smells of vaporized rum,
hey Tata Maoumbe.

46.
Oungenikon
Bagay la koumanse
Ti Kita mwen, vanyan gason,
chenn lan ren.
Vanyan gason, chenn lan ren.

Koral ounsi
Vanyan gason, chenn lan ren,
ti Kita.

46.
Choir leader
Let's get started.
My little Kita, brave man,
chain around the waist.
Brave man, chain around the waist.

Chorus of initiates
Brave man, chain around the waist,
little Kita.

47.
Oungenikon
Orelyen chante.

Oungenikon
Ibo lele, lele, lele,
Ibo lele.
Nan chan Ibo, sa ou genyen konsa?
Ibo lele ey.

Koral ounsi
Ibo lele, Ibo lele,
sa ou genyen konsa?
Genyen konsa?
M di ey! Ibo lele, lele, lele.

Oungenikon
Ayanman sa, konsa, Ayanman,
konsa m danse Ibo.

Koral ounsi
Ayanman, konsa, konsa, Ayanman.

Oungenikon
Kon sa m danse Ibo.

47.
Choir leader
Orelyen sings.

Choir leader
Ibo cries out, cries out, cries out,
Ibo cries out.
In the Ibo song, what's going on with you?
Hey, Ibo cries out.

Chorus of initiates
Ibo cries out, Ibo cries out,
what's going on with you?
Going on with this?
I say hey! Ibo cries out, cries out, cries out.

Choir leader
That Ayanman, like this, Ayanman,
that's how I dance Ibo.

Chorus of initiates
Ayanman, like this, like this, Ayanman.

Choir leader
I dance Ibo like this.

48.

Oungenikon
Lenba, ti pilon sa,
m ap pile yo, Lenba.
Men ti pilon, m ap kraze yo.

Koral ounsi
Lenba, ti pilon sa,
m ap pile yo, Lenba.

48.

Choir leader
Lenba, my little mortar,
I am pounding them, Lenba.
Here is the little mortar, I am crushing them.

Chorus of initiates
Lenba, that little mortar,
I am pounding them, Lenba.

49.

Oungenikon
Men, ti pilon sa, m ap pile yo.
Simbi Kita, lawouze ki mennen mwen

Koral ounsi
Simbi, lawouze ki mennen mwen.

Oungenikon
Twa kout bagi
lan ounfò lwa ki mennen mwen.

Varyasyon:
(a) Papa Simbi, lawouze sa
ki mennen mwen.
(b) Papa Simbi lan ounfò sa
ki mennen mwen.
(c) Papa Simbi, lawouze
ki pote m la.
(d) Simbi lan dlo, lawouze
ki mennen m la.

49.

Choir leader
Here, little mortar, I am pounding them.
Simbi Kita, it's the dew that brings me.

Chorus of initiates
Simbi, it's the dew that brings me.

Choir leader
Three strikes of the drumstick
in the temple of the lwa that brings me.

Variations:
(a) Papa Simbi, it's this dew here
that brings me.
(b) It's Papa Simbi in that temple
who brings me
(c) Papa Simbi, it's the dew
that carries me here.
(d) Simbi in the water, it's the dew
that brings me here.

50.

Oungenikon
Prese, pou m pa prese ey!
Prese, pou m pa prese, dyab mwen an!
Nanpwen gangan pase Bondye
lan peyi a
Si m mare, m a lage la devan Bondye

Koral ounsi
Prese, prese o, prese, pa prese!
Nanpwen gangan pase Bondye
lan peyi a.
Si m mare, m a lage o.

50.

Choir leader
Hurry, oh I can't be hurried!
Hurry, I can't be hurried, my dyab!
There's no Vodou priest greater than God
in this country.
If I'm bound, I'll be untied there before God.

Chorus of initiates
Hurry, oh hurry, hurry, don't hurry!
There's no Vodou priest greater than God
in this country.
If I'm bound, oh I'll be free.

51.

Moun ki posede ak Gede
Bonswa, bonswa, bonswa,
mesyedam.

Koral
Kouman nou ye?

Moun ki posede ak Gede
M prale, m prale;
sa m a di lakay?

Koral ounsi
Kouman nou ye?

Moun ki chwal Gede
M ale o, m ale;
sa m a di lakay?

51.

Person mounted by Gede
Good evening, good evening, good evening,
ladies and gentlemen.

Chorus of initiates
How are you?

Person mounted by Gede
I'm going, I'm going;
what shall I say at home?

Chorus of initiates
How are you?

Person possessed by Gede
Oh I'm going, I'm going;
what shall I say at home?

52.

Lawouze o, pale lapli pou mwen;
Atoutan mwen la,
nou poko tonbe, vre.
He, Pò Mago la,
se la genyen bon gangan.
N a tiye yo, kan yo merite.
Lawouze, rele lapli pou mwen.
Atoutan mwen la, nou pa sa tonbe
Lawouze, se bon,
Lawouze, pale solèy pou mwen.
Atoutan mwen la ey, nou poko tonbe.
Pò Mago a, se la genyen bon gangan.
N a tiye yo, kan yo merite l.

52.

Oh dew, speak to the rain for me;
As long as I'm here,
we haven't truly fallen yet.
Hey, Port-Margot is here,
that's where good oungan are.
We'll kill them, when they deserve it.
Dew, call the rain for me.
As long as I'm here, we can't fall.
Dew, it's okay,
Dew, speak to the sun for me.
Hey as long as I'm here, we haven't yet fallen.
Port-Margot, that's where good oungan are.
We'll kill them, when they deserve it.

53.

Latibonit o, men gade: yo voye di mwen
nou wè solèy malad.
Latibonit o, Balodi.
Latibonit o, gade jan nou voye di mwen
nou wè solèy malad
Kan m te rive Latibonit o,
mwen jwenn solèy kouche.
Se regretan sa, pou m antere solèy.

53.

Oh Latibonit, take a look: they let me know that
you see that the sun is sick.
Oh Latibonit, Balodi.
Oh Latibonit, look how you let me know
that you see that the sun is sick.
Oh when I arrived in Latibonit,
I found the sun had set.
That is unfortunate, for me to bury the sun.

54.

Byen mal pa lanmò, ey.
Ey Zoblezo, byen mal
pa lanmò pou mwen.
Zoblezo, Zoblezo, lanmò fè lapenn o.
Mwen poko rive, Sovèt,
nou tande rele, "konpè"!
O Zoblezo mwen,
byen mal pa lanmò vre;
Zoblezo, Zoblezo, lanmò sa fè lapenn o.

54.

Hey, thoroughly bad isn't death.
Hey Zoblezo, thoroughly bad
isn't death for me.
Zoblezo, Zoblezo, oh death hurts.
I have not yet arrived, Sovet,
we hear them cry, "old friend"!
Oh my Zoblezo,
thoroughly bad isn't really death;
Zoblezo, Zoblezo, oh that death is hard.

55.

Ti Charl o, anko nou malere la.
Ti Charl o, gade jan nou malere.
Ti Charl mouri, l ale.
O Sen Charl mouri, l ale la.
Pantalon ble akonpanye ale.

55.

Oh little Charles, we are still poor here.
Oh little Charles, look how poor we are.
Little Charles died, he went away.
Oh Saint Charles died, he went there.
Blue pants accompanied his departure.

56.

Dokwala, Dokwala ey, men nou te tou konnen,
fò malè ta rive yo
poutèt Mangousa.
Dokwala chita chita li;
li trayi lesen.
Dokwala chita la; gade l trayi Bondye.
Men nou te tou konnen,
fòk malè ta rive yo
poutèt Mangousa.
Mwen di Dokwala, Kenken, Zando, Dokwala,
Dokwala, Bebe Lyan,
Dokwala, Manman Mari Malo, fè byen,
granmèsi, nanpwen Dokwala.
Mwen te tou konnen, fòk malè ta rive
yo poutèt Mangousa.
Dokwala, ou chita la;
gade jan yo trayi Bondye

56.

Dokwala, hey Dokwala, but we knew better,
misfortune must happen to them
for Mangousa's sake.
Dokwala sat out;
he betrayed the saints.
Dokwala sat there; look he betrayed God.
But we knew better,
misfortune has to happen to them
for Mangousa's sake.
I say Dokwala, Kenken, Zando, Dokwala,
Dokwala, Baby Lyan,
Dokwala, Mama Mari Malo, do good,
great thanks, there is no Dokwala.
I knew better, misfortune had to happen
to them for Mangousa's sake.
Dokwala, you sat there;
look how they betrayed God.

57.

Sa ki vle ale, yo va ale;
sa ki vle rete, yo va rete.
M ape rete, Kimanga,
pou m veye kay mwen.
Kite m rete, Kimanga,
men nou prale veye kay sila;
sa ki vle ale, yo va ale.

57.

Those who want to go, they will go;
those who want to stay, they will stay.
I am staying, Kimanga,
so I can watch my house.
Let me stay, Kimanga,
but we are going to watch this house;
those who want to go, they will go.

M di ey, sa ki vle ale,
Kenji Palmando va ale;
sa ki vle rete va rete;
m ape rete pou veye kay;
kite m rete, Dyamega,
pou mwen veye kay.

I say hey, those who want to go,
Kenji Palmando is going;
those who want to stay are going to stay;
I'm staying on to watch the house;
let me stay, Dyamega,
so I can watch the house.

58.

M pa renmen fanm anbisye;
mwen pa bezwen gason fè jalou twòp o.
Gouvènè Kola, siyen lòd la pou mwen
Enperatris menm balanse de lo;
pou n ale.
Gouvènè Kola, tou sa ou wè la se
betiz o; m ap prale chemen mwen.
M ap prale chemen mwen,
pou m ganyen lavi mwen.

58.

I do not like ambitious women;
oh I don't need guys who are too jealous.
Governor Kola, sign the order for me
The empress herself sways from side to side;
we should go.
Oh governor Kola, everything you see here
is ridiculous; I'm going on my way.
I'm going on my way,
to earn a living.

59.

Oungenikon	*Koral*
Imamou lele o!	Kò aniye![6]
Bo Imamou lele!	Kò aniye!
Imamou Agwe Tawoyo!	Kò aniye!
O Imamou, mwen lele!	Kò aniye!
Imamou, dlo sale sila!	Kò aniye!
O Imamou, mwen lele o!	Kò aniye!
Imamou Bako Zangi!	Kò aniye!
O Imamou lele!	Kò aniye!
Imamou Batiman Aton!	Kò aniye!
O Imamou, mwen lele!	Kò aniye!

59.

Vodou choir leader	*Chorus*
Oh Imamou cries out!	Stay calm!
Bo Imamou cries out!	Stay calm!
Imamou Agwe Tawoyo!	Stay calm!
Oh Imamou, I'm crying out!	Stay calm!
Imamou, that salty water!	Stay calm!
Oh Imamou, oh I cry out!	Stay calm!
Imamou Bako Eel!	Stay calm!
Oh Imamou cries out!	Stay calm!
Imamou Aton Boat!	Stay calm!
Oh Imamou, I'm crying out!	Stay calm!

60.

Oungan (pale)
M fè espre menm mwen di,
tou sa ladan ni. Mete tou sa.
Genlè se jwe nou vin jwe
enposib. Si se pa jwe!
Nou vin jwe, "Okipe zafè nou."

Ounsi (pale)
Koumanse? Koumanse?

Duklos (pale)
Se kounye a ou di koumanse;
depi tan sa ou ta fè?

60.

Vodou priest (speaking)
I did just as I said,
all that's involved. Put it all in.
It seems we've really come to play
the impossible. If it's not play!
We came to play, "Mind your own business."

Ounsi (speaking)
Are we starting? Starting?

Duklos (speaking)
So now you say let's get started;
what have you been doing all along?

61.

Duklos (pale)
Sa ou di?

Duklos (chante)
Prepare, ounsi Ladogwèsan,
n a prepare vre;
prepare, nou pral regle zafè nou.
N a prepare, Koskora; n a prepare,
n a prepare divinite a, prepare, men
prepare pou n ale regle zafè nou vre.
Prepare, ounsi Ladogwèsan,
n a prepare, prepare zafè nou.
Prepare, ounsi Ladogwèsan,
n a prepare la; men prepare;
nou prale regle zafè nou.
Prepare; kote ounsi a yo?
N a prepare, vre; men prepare,
pou n regle zafè nou.

61.

Duklos (speaking)
What did you say?

Duklos (singing)
Prepare, ounsi of the heritage.[7]
we shall truly prepare;
prepared, we shall set our things in order.
We shall prepare, Koskora; we shall prepare,
we'll prepare the divinity, prepare, now
prepared, we shall set our things in order.
Prepare, ounsi of the heritage,
we shall prepare, prepare our things.
Prepare, ounsi of the heritage,
we shall prepare here; now prepared;
we are going to set our things in order
Prepare; where are they, those ounsi?
We shall truly prepare; now prepared,
so we may set our things in order.

62.

Duklos (pale)
Kote ounsi yo ye?

Duklos (chante)
Sanble pou m wè yo;
men kote ounsi Ladogwèsan ye?
Sanble, n a wè yo.
Sese, wanzen mwen! Yo ki leve
lamen an devan sobagi o!
Sese wanzen sila! Yo ki leve
lamen devan ountògri lwa!
M pa di anyen; sanble,
pou m wè yo sobagi
Sese wanzen sila yo!
Oungan pa di anyen;
sanble, n a wè yo.
M di ey! Sanble, pou m wè nou,
divinite a; n ap wè yo, Koskora,
n ap wè yo; kote pitit la yo?
Ey la, sanble, pou m wè yo.
Sese mason, ki leve lamen vre!
Sese wanzen la, yo ki leve
lamen devan ountògri sila!

62.

Duklos (speaking)
Where are the ounsi?

Duklos (singing)
Gather so I may see them;
oh where are the ounsi of the heritage?
Gather, we'll see them.
Sister, my wanzen! Oh those who raise
their hands before this sanctuary!
Sister wanzen there! Those who raise
their hands before the drums of the lwa!
I'm not saying anything; gather round
so I may see them in the sanctuary.
Those sister wanzen there!
The oungan doesn't say anything;
gather around, we'll see them.
I say hey! Gather so that I may see you,
divinity; we will see them, Koskora,
we will see them; where are the children?
Hey there, gather around, so I may see them.
Sister masons, who truly raise their hands!
Sister wanzen there, those who raise
their hands before that drum!

M pa anyen; sanble, n a wè yo.
Medam, pwoche fè vit non!

I'm nothing; gather around, you'll see them.
Ladies, step right up!

63.

M tande youn, medam jenès,
ki fini anraje.
Men se mwen menm Lasirèn, ki kote
mwen bezwen; ou pa prale a!
M ap achte yon sèl; m ap sele;
m achte yon brid; m ap bride!
Men si m bride yon salòp,
se ponpe w a ponpe dèyè yo.

63.

I hear someone, a female prostitute,
who got mad.
But I am Lasirenn, wherever I need to be;
you're not going there!
I am buying a saddle; I'm saddling up;
I am buying a bridle; I'm bridling up!
But if I bridle a slut,
you'll really be pumping behind them.

64.

Se voye yo voye yo;
si ou pale, m pale o.
Si ou pale pawòl sila, n a mouri nan prizon.
Se mwen menm, Manzèl Ilali Kande;
ala m leve lendi maten, pral lan travay;
mwen wè yon vye vèmin ki rete lari,
pou l konprann l ap fè m eksplikasyon.
Mwen konnen m se yon jenn debyen;
mwen pa janm pale nan lari.
Se mwen menm, Ilali Kande; ala m leve,
m ap okipe zafè mwen,
m wè vèmin nan vini, pou l anbisi m.
Mwen konnen, pa janmen nan rapò ak
vèmin o

64.

They really sent them;
if you speak, oh I speak.
If you speak those words, we'll die in jail.
It's me, Miss Eulali Konde;
look, I get up on Monday morning, go to work;
I see a nasty scumbag who lives in the street
who thinks she can put me down.
I know I'm a well-bred youth;
I never talk in the street.
It's me, Eulali Kande; look, I get up,
I mind my own business,
I see the scumbag coming to bug me.
Oh I know, never deal with
scumbags.

65.

Varyason:
Mwen janmen betize.
Mwen janmen vagabon.
M konnen pa janm ri avè pèsonn o.
Mwen machann gaz.
Mwen machann salezon.
Ki vin pou pokire m dezagreman?

65.

Variation:
I never play around.
I'm never bumming around.
I know to never laugh at anyone.
I'm a gas seller.
I'm a vendor of salted meat.
Who comes to bring me trouble?

CHAPTER 6

J.L.'s Songs

BENJAMIN HEBBLETHWAITE
and CHRIS BALLENGEE

THIS CHAPTER is a collection of Haitian Creole texts collected and composed by a Vodouist in his late teens. It reflects an individual, and not a collective, view of Vodou. I met J.L., a Haitian refugee, in West Lafayette, Indiana, in 1996, and in the course of our friendship and discussions about Vodou he entrusted me with a photocopy of his remarkable handwritten manuscript. He had lost both of his parents during Hurricane Gordon in 1994 and was adopted by a U.S. family. These texts include Vodou materials that he acquired through his family's domestic traditions and their close association with a temple. There are also poems about J.L.'s personal experiences in Vodou. They include nonreligious texts about his mother, his philosophy, and his life experiences.

The young author, who painfully suffered the loss of his mother, expresses a mixture of anger and commitment to the lwa. J.L.'s texts provide an intimate window into the life and ideas of a young Vodouist. Texts are dedicated to the lwa Legba, Gran Bwa, Alomi, Papa Loko, Sen Jak Majè, Simbi Makaya, Agwe Tawoyo, Sobo, Badè, Ogou Badagi, Èzili, Dan Petwo, Genbo Makaya, Anminan, Bawon Samdi, Grann Silibo, Kouzen Zaka, and Dyobolo Bosou. There are texts that praise the local Catholic priest for his support during J.L.'s personal crisis; there are songs to Our Lady of Mount Carmel, the Virgin Mary, and Jesus. Portraits of women as mothers, religious figures (saints or manbo [Vodou priestesses]), lovers, friends, and sexual objects co-mingle in J.L.'s collection. He addresses relationship problems, rivalries, and disagreements with neighbors. His texts address notions such as *gad* (guardian lwa, guard, protector lwa), *pwen* (spells empowered by lwa), and *maji* (magic). Some texts are dedicated to his *konpa* music group, others to Ginen (Africa). Ethical, philosophical, and moral aspects of life resonate in his writing. Several texts are in the genre of the *chante pwen* (songs of reproach). Catholic orientations are inextricably combined with songs extolling the lwa and Vodou. In several texts, J.L. describes his pursuit of Bondye (God) *and* the lwa—both approaches to the divine are considered essential. J.L.'s texts are different from the others in this book because they provide a personal view of the Vodouist's inclusive and multilayered relationship toward Vodou and Catholicism, and they explore the many parts of life that link into spirituality.

Chante J.L.

1.
Rèn o Selisa. Selisa di l pa manje
moun ankò, mache bonè o.
Si yon nèg santi,
gason mache san w pa bezwen o.
M di Rèn o Selisa, aswè a nou pran moun.

2.
Wi, gen on jou m gen pou m mouri.
Lè m mouri sa k ap ranplase mwen,
m a rele manman;
si Roz ban m yon pitit gason,
avan mwen mouri, m a montre l chante sèl,
k ap kenbe kò n nan.

3.
Rezye w, frè m, ou pa bezwen kriye.
Zafè lanmò a
pa egzanp pesòn o.
Se tout moun sou latè ki gen pou mouri,
ou pa bezwen kriye.

4.
Lwa ki lwa ou e,
se lwa leman e, o zo.
M di lwa ki lwa ou e.
Papa Ogou o se lwa leman e.

5.
Inosan, gad jan
mwen inosan malgre m.
Inosan, nèg yo pale an,

J.L.'s Songs

1.
Oh Queen Selisa. Selisa says she doesn't eat
people anymore, oh walk early.
If a guy smells,
oh the guy walks unnecessarily.
Oh I say Queen Selisa, tonight we get people.

2.
Yes, there is an hour for my death.
When I die the one who replaces me,
I will call mother;
if Rose gives me a little boy,
before I die, I alone will teach him to sing,
that will give us strength.

3.
Deal with it, my brother, you don't need to cry.
Oh the event of death
is an example to nobody.
Everyone on earth has to die,
you don't need to cry.

4.
Hey the lwa who is your lwa,
is a protective lwa, hey, oh bones.
I say a lwa who is your lwa, yeah.
Oh Papa Ogou is a protective lwa.

5.
Innocent, look at how
I'm innocent in spite of myself.
Even though I'm innocent, oh, the guys talk,

o mwen.
M di medizan malpalan sispann o.
Si w pa vle rete, Ti Mal,
malè va rive w.

oh me oh my.
I say stop, you backbiters and slanderers.
If you don't want to stop, Ti Mal,
misfortune will befall you.

6.
Kouvè Legba pare,
sèvis la pral kòmanse,
men moun yo vle gate sèvis la,
se bon, o!
Papa Legba
pa nan betiz o!
Lese yo fè,
men Legba nan baryè a.

6.
Legba's food is ready,
the ceremony is going to start,
but the people want to spoil the service,
oh great!
Oh Papa Legba
does not put up with foolishness!
Let them try to do it,
but Legba is at the crossroads.

7.
Neg yo pote kòd sou kòd pou yo mare mwen.
Gran Bwa mande,
sa m fè yo pou yo mare mwen?
Gran Bwa ou, o Gran Bwa.
Jan w wè m piti an,
m santi m danble o.

7.
The men carry lots of rope to bind me.
Gran Bwa asks,
what I did to make them bind me?
Your Gran Bwa, oh Gran Bwa.
Even though you see me as small,
oh I feel protected!

8.
M pral nan Gran Bwa,
mesye dèyè on rezon.
Lè m a retounen, m ava ranmase lwa yo,
Adye, o, ay dyab la,
Rezon gwo lwa yo
pa nan betiz o!

8.
I'm going to Gran Bwa,
the men are after an excuse.
When I will return, I will pick up the lwa,
Oh heavens, whoa the dyab,
Oh the reason of great lwa
is no joke!

9.
M sot Leyogann, m pral lavil o,
menm si pwen an lou.
M a woule rive, m a rive.
Moun yo pale mwen mal o!
Mwen chèche pwen an
pou m wè longè moun sa yo.

9.
I left Leyogann, oh I'm going to town,
even if the charm is heavy.
I will arrive soundly, I will arrive.
Oh people speak badly of me!
I sought the charm
to see what they're made of.

10.
Alomi o, kote manman mwen?
Alomi,
mwen mete jenou m atè devan ounfò
epi m sèmante sèt fwa,
fò m jwenn jistis mwen.

10.
Oh Alomi, where is my mother?
Alomi,
I kneel on the ground before the temple
and I swear seven times over,
I must find my justice.

11.
Gran Bwa nan ayi pilon m sa,
maji a pare.
Gran bwa,
maji a pare kote zanfan yo vini.
Mache dogwe, men maji a pare.

11.
Gran Bwa prepares magic in my sacred mortar.
the magic is ready.
Gran Bwa,
magic is ready where the children come.
Do a ritual curtsey, here the magic is ready.

12.
Papa Loko pral fè yon wout o,
w a pale moun yo pou mwen,
lavi a long o!
Jèn gason de byen pa byen bon.
Ase souvan de byen
se bat bouda w.

12.
Oh Papa Loko is going to make a path,
you will tell the people for me,
oh life is long!
The well-to-do boy isn't really good.
Often enough the well-to-do boy
is beating your ass.

13.
Sen Jak Majè, m vin pale w;
pou moun yo, se chita m chita;
m ap travay, moun yo vin anmegde mwen.
M di Sen Jak,
w a lage chen yo dèyè yo.
Si l pran yo la, devore yo.
Si l pa pran yo, n a pare tann yo.

13.
Sen Jak Majè, I've come to talk to you;
according to the people, I'm just sitting around;
I'm working, people come bother me.
I say Sen Jak,
you will release the dog behind them.
If he gets them there, devour them.
If he doesn't get them, we will wait for them.

14.
Pè Larak, m ap di w mèsi,
se pa lajan w ban mwen.
M vin di w mèsi.
Se vre lakou a ban m rele lwa yo.
Lè m rele lwa yo, lwa yo tande mwen.
Lè m pal a lwa yo, yo regle
zafè mwen.

14.
Father Larak, I'm thanking you,
it's not about the money you gave me.
I came to thank you.
It's true the yard gave me the calling of the lwa.
When I call the lwa, the lwa hear me.
When I speak to the lwa, they take care of
my problems.

15.
Gade yon lavi, se lavi malere.
Tou sa ki pa bon,
yo lage l sou do malere.
Avan n mouri,
malere wi n ap pase pa nou.

15.
Look at this life, it's the life of poverty.
All that is no good,
they throw upon the backs of the poor.
Before we die,
we will indeed pass through our poverty.

16.
Vyèj mirak Sodo,
m vin lapriyè w.
Mwen vin mande w
pou bay moun sa yo travay.

16.
Virgin miracle of Sodo,
I have come to pray to you.
I come to ask you
to give these people work.

Men nuit kou jou, mesye,
y ape pale mal.
Mwen santi m about o!

But night and day, the men,
they have been speaking unkindly.
Oh I'm at the end of my tether!

17.

Sak Poura,
rasin nan pou l pa lage.
M konnen chenn ki chenn, li kase,
ale wè pou yon ti kòd pit.
O pou l pa lage.

17.

Sak Poura,
it's the root that should not be forgotten.
I know that a strong chain is broken,
not to mention a little sisal rope.
Oh he must not let go.

18.

Sayira, Sayira, jan w wè m granmoun la,
m ka fè sèvis lwa yo.
Devan pewon an, Silibo vin jèn o.
Sayira, m pral fè sèvis lwa yo.

18.

Sayira, Sayira, you see me as an old person,
I can do a service for the lwa.
In front of the altar, oh Silibo became young.
Sayira, I am going to do a ceremony for the lwa.

19.

Gran Bwa e, men moun;
yo rayi mwen o, sa m fè yo?
M pa manje nan men yo;
m pa bwè dlo lakay yo.
Amwa, m Gran Bwa,
m deja Gran Bwa nan kò m.
Mwen konnen yo; m ap fout viv avè yo.

19.

Hey Gran Bwa, here are the people;
oh they abhor me, what did I do to them?
I don't eat among them;
I don't drink water at their home.
As for me, I'm Gran Bwa,
I am already Gran Bwa in my body.
I know them; I'm fucking living with them.

20.

Selisa, Selisa, ale resevwa moun yo.
Dyab la nan baryè a,
Selisa o ki rèn lakou a.
Ale resevwa moun yo;
men dyab la nan baryè a.

20.

Selisa, Selisa, go receive the people.
The dyab is at the gate,
oh Selisa who is queen of the yard.
Go receive the people;
here the dyab is at the gate.

21.

Mache chèche pa janm dòmi
san soupe nan lakou lakay.
Nan mache chèche o,
ay, Rawoul pran nan zip.
Papa l a korije l.

21.

Those who seek never sleep
without eating supper in the home yard.
Oh, in searching all around,
oh my, Rawoul got into trouble.
His father will correct him.

22.

Jan w wè m piti an, m sèvi gwo lwa.
Nan demanbre m lakou
lakay granmoun: granmoun, timoun,
timoun.

22.

You may see me as puny, but I serve great lwa.
In my family's ceremony in the yard
at the home of the elders: elders, children,
children.

23.
Mesye jèn gason pa maltrete fanm yo paske
gen de jou nan jou,
yo pliske manman nou.
Yo fè manje, yo lave, yo pase.
Lè solèy kouche, n rele yo manman.

23.
Young men don't mistreat women because
there are days when
they are more than our mothers.
They make food, they wash, they iron.
When the sun sets, we call them mother.

24.
Jèn gason k ap mache renmen,
m pral ban nou yon konsèy.
Pa janm pran fanm pou n ba l abitid,
li p ap bon pou nou.
Abitid se yon gwo maladi ki gen nan renmen.
Jèn gason fò n pran prekosyon
anba fanm sa yo.

24.
Young boys who are falling in love,
I am going to give you some advice.
Never take a woman and make a habit of it,
it is not going to be good for you.
Habits are a big sickness in love.
Young boys, you must be careful
in the company of these women.

25.
Sispann kriye, salòp, jalouzi pa bay.
Si w pa gen afèksyon,
ou p ap gen mari, salòp.
Gason yo se bebe, si w bat bouda yo,
y a dòmi.
Si w pa gen afèksyon,
w p ap gen mari, salòp.

25.
Stop crying, slut, jealousy gets you nothing.
If you don't show affection,
you won't find a husband, slut.
Boys are babies, if you pat their butts,
they'll sleep.
If you don't show affection,
you won't find a husband, slut.

26.
Depi m piti m ap pase mizè mwen.
Nan mitan fanmi mwen,
zanmi m pase, yo wè m,
zanmi m pa rele mwen.
M p ap dekouraje,
tou sa se lavi a.

26.
Since I was a child, I have been in misery.
In the middle of my family,
my friends stop by, they see me,
my friends don't call me.
I am not going to be discouraged,
all that is part of life.

27.
Mache nan nwit o, mache lajounen o,
Simbi Makaya o!
M resi wè moun yo.
Makaya o, yo se levanjil,
Kou l lanjelis, Simbi,
moun yo chanje po yo.

27.
Oh walking at night, oh walking in the day,
oh Simbi Makaya!
I can see the true nature of people.
Oh Makaya, they're Protestants,
As soon as dusk falls, Simbi,
people change their skin.

28.
Mache nan nwit, mesye, mache lajounen,
depi l minwi,

28.
Walking at night, sir, walking in the day,
as soon as it's midnight,

m tounen sa m vle nan peyi a.
Anhan—hahan—anhan, o dyab, o pwen an mache nan nwit.

I turn into what I want in this country.
Yeah—hey—yeah, oh dyab, oh the magic works at night.

29.
Byen viv o, mal viv o, m ta pito
mande charite devan sobagi lwa m nan.
Moun yo di lwa pa ban m lajan,
men l proteje lan mwen.
Li sove lavi m e l sove lavi
zanfan yo lè nèg yo vle manje mwen.

29.
Oh, good life, oh dreadful life, I would rather
ask for charity in front of the temple of my lwa.
The people say the lwa doesn't give me money,
but she protects me within.
She saves my life and she saves the lives
of children when men want to destroy me.

30.
Fè m toujou, men gen yon tan,
mesye o, y a bezwen mwen.
Lè y a bezwen mwen, y a rele m papa.
Mesye, m p ap okipe yo
nan gran chimen.

30.
Hurt me as you wish, but a time will come,
oh sirs, when they'll need me.
When they'll need me, they'll call me father.
Sir, I will not take notice of them
on the main road.

31.
M al dousman o pou m ka viv de jou o;
jan ou wè m piti an,
pwen m nan andire
M ale dousman
pou m ka viv de jou nan peyi an.
Toupiti m, toupiti m,
pwen m nan andire.

31.
Oh I go peacefully so I can live a while oh;
you may see me as small,
but my magic charm endures.
I go peacefully
so that I can live a while in this country.
My little means, my little means,
my magic charm endures.

32.
Agwesi manbo,
pawòl nou t ap pale a, men nou wè l.
Nèg la tiye fanm li pou lajan,
se enjistis o!
Makomè, w ale, sa fè mwen mal,
men m nan tonbo.
A, w a sonje m te pale w
pou nèg sila.

32.
Oh Vodou priestess of Agwe,
the matter we were discussing, here it is.
The guy killed his woman for money,
oh it's an injustice!
My friend, you're gone, that hurts me badly,
here I'm in the tomb.
Ah, you'll remember I spoke to you
about that guy.

33.
Mwen gen lontan m ap travay,
gade m pa manje.
Malgre m pa manje,
moun yo di m pa travay.
Vyèj mirak Sodo,

33.
I have been working for a long time,
but look I don't eat.
Even though I don't eat,
the people say I don't work.
Virgin of the miracle of Sodo,

di yon mo pou mwen.
M pa konn kisa o pou m fè ak moun sa yo.
Moun yo twò odasye.

speak a word for me.
Oh I don't know what to do with these people.
The people are too outrageous.

34.
Granmoun nan pa te la,
li rantre Alouba do ba sou baton l.
Gad jan on granmoun telele.
Mwen di Alouba, li telele,
m di Aloumandya, li telele.
Alouba Aloumandya o, grann telele.

34.
The old woman was not here,
she returned as Alouba bent over on her cane.
See the way an old woman is dancing.
I say Alouba, she's dancing,
I say Aloumandya, she's dancing.
Oh, Alouba Aloumandya, dancing granny.

35.
Similò, nèg yo mare pwen an, jou
pwen an lage, va gen rele.
Jou mwen lage pwen, Similò,
w ava tande rèl bò isit,
w ava tande rèl bò lòt bò,
Similò, men dyab la andyable.

35.
Similò, the men fix the charm, the day
the charm is set loose, there will be shouting.
The day I release the charm, Similò,
you will hear wailing on this side,
you will hear wailing from the other side,
Similò, look the dyab is enraged.

36.
Lajounen o, m se youn o,
leswa o m se yon lòt o.
men dyab la tounen blengendeng
lè l sou devosyon l.
Bakoulou baka, ayayay, dyab la nou se kaliko.

36.
Oh in the daytime, oh I am one,
oh at night I am another.
The dyab became an evil spirit
when he was serving him.
Wicked demon, oh my, our dyab are fickle.

37.
Moun yo voye rele m—Ale m prale.
Sa ki bezwen koulèv—Mache prese.
Nou pa bezwen kriye—Si n wè l ale.
Pa jodi, pa demen—L ap tounen vin
fè sèvis lwa yo.

37.
The people call me names—I am heading off.
Who needs snakes?—Walk fast.
We don't need to cry—If we see him going.
Not today, not tomorrow—He will return to
do a service for the lwa.

38.
Gad jan moun yo fè yo wè
kisa yo ye, Mirabo, li lè pou w sispann
fè anbochay.
Pa chaje sa w pa ka pote.
Mirabo li lè pou w sispann fè anbochay.

38.
Look at how the people make them see
what they are, Mirabo, it's time to stop
recruiting
Don't take on loads you can't carry.
Mirabo it's time to stop recruiting.

39.
M sot nan Gran Bwa,
m plante figye nan lakou a.

39.
I came from Gran Bwa,
I planted a fig tree in the yard.

Mwen vle figye grandi;
figye di, mwen pa mèt li.
Ane sila, figye tèlman gen fanmi,
lè figye mouri,
m pa kwè l ap gen antèman.

I want the fig tree to grow;
the fig tree says, I'm not his master.
This year, the fig tree has such a big family that
when the fig tree dies,
I don't believe it'll have a burial.

40.

En, de, twa—tande sa yo fè mwen.
Kat, senk, sis—ti nèg nwè engra o.
Ala yon move bèt se bèf o.
Tann dat m ap swen bèf la,
kounye a l vle devore mwen,
m p ap fè byen ankò.

40.

One, two, three—listen to what they did to me.
Four, five, six—oh, little black ingrates.
Oh what awful animals cows are.
For ages I've been caring for the cow,
now it wants to devour me,
I won't do good again.

41.

Va toutou, chen toutou,
sa k fè w jape konsa o, chen an?
Se pa tout chen k jape
pou w vire do w ba li, anhan.
Chen toutou,
m p ap okipe w, men mwen.

41.

Go puppy, puppy dog,
oh what makes you bark like this, dog?
It's not every dog who barks
that you turn your back on, get it.
Puppy dog,
I'm not paying attention to you, here I am.

42.

Mwen kale chen an pou dezòd mèt chen an,
m fache pou gwo nèg.
Pouki w p ap pale chen an,
pouki w pa t mare chen an?
Toutan w pa pale chen an,
jwèt la pe kontinye.

42.

I beat the dog for the dog's master's unruliness,
I'm angry about the big guys.
Why are you not talking to the dog,
why did you not tie up the dog?
As long as you don't talk to the dog,
the game can continue.

43.

Bèf la gwonde, m pa deranje.
Chen an jape, m pa panike.
Bèt ki gen pye pa ka ban m pwoblèm.
Se pa yon ti koulèv madlèn
ki pou ta panike m.

43.

The cow grumbles, I'm not bothered.
The dog barks, I'm not panicking.
Animals that have feet can't give me problems.
It would take more than a little green snake
to make me afraid.

44.

Sa ki mande pou mwen an,
di yo mwen la twa fwa.
Gran Bwa k te la li toujou la e,
men Gran Bwa.
Pa nan betiz o, di yo mwen la.

44.

Whoever asks for me,
tell them three times I'm here.
Gran Bwa who was there is always there, yeah,
here is Gran Bwa.
Oh don't fool around, tell them I'm here.

45.

Mila, Mila, Mila, Mila, pa pale m mal.
Pale mal la, se lapriyè jouda yo,
kite yo pale.
Nou menm, n ap travay yo, lavi a long o!
Nou la pou n wè yo.

45.

Mila, Mila, Mila, Mila, don't speak badly of me.
Speaking badly, it's the prayer of the gossiper,
let them talk.
As for us, we are working, oh life is long!
We are here in order to see them.

46.

Etwal mwen file;
men moun yo fè vèy mwen.
Palmannan, gade mwen la e,
jou a poko rive.
Men Ginen pa mouri mal o.
Pa janm pale nan zafè moun,
w a viv pou lontan.

46.

My star is shooting;
here the people are having my wake.
Hey Palmannan, look I'm here,
the day hasn't yet come.
Oh but the Ginen don't die badly.
Never speak badly about people's business,
you'll live a long time.

47.

Jwi m, zanmi m, jwi m,
jwi m o, sa k vle jwi m.
Mezanmi, gen yon jou m p ap la o.
Yo lonmen non mwen.
M pwofite jwi mwen avan m ale.

47.

Take pleasure in me, my friends, enjoy me,
oh enjoy me, those who want to enjoy me.
Oh my dear, one day I'm not going to be here.
They call my name.
I try to enjoy myself before I go.

48.

Se vye m vye, m itil o.
Se lè m pa la y a wè valè mwen.
Se vye m vye, m itil o.

48.

How very old I am, oh I'm useful.
When I'm not here they'll see value in me.
How very old I am, oh I'm useful.

49.

Ti gason, m ape ba w yon konsèy:
pa janm koute nèg sòt k ap pran pwen
pou w pa jwi lavi w demen.
Gen Bondye; genyen lwa
k ap ba w tousa w bezwen.
Se konn regleman, ti papa,
zafè w va mache toubònman.

49.

Little boy, I will give you advice:
never listen to an idiot who is getting charms
so you cannot enjoy your life tomorrow.
There is God; there are the lwa
who are giving you all you need.
You should know the rules, little guy,
your business is going to go all the way.

50.

Ou se Ginen, li se Ginen,
pouki nou nan konkirans?
Pou ki nou pa met tèt ansanm o,
pou n met rasin nan pi devan.
O se konsa zòt a respekte nou,
y a wè vrèman Vodou pa dyab o.

50.

You are Ginen, he is Ginen,
why are we competing with each other?
Oh why don't we collaborate
so we can advance the roots religion.
Oh that's how others will respect us,
oh they'll truly see Vodou isn't diabolical.

51.
Charite m ape mande, vin gad jan de
moun k ap lage nan kwi mwen.
Lwa rasin yo, nou fè m mal o.
Se ta sèl nou k pou fè m mande
moun sa yo.

51.
I'm asking for alms, come see the kind of
people who are offering to my gourd bowl.
Roots lwa, oh you are doing me wrong.
It could only be you who make me beg
those people.

52.
M te panse m te pòv, m te pòv o;
lè m gade, mwen wè gen pi mal;
M pran kouraj o.
Pandan m t ap kabicha
sa k te pi mal la vòlè kwi a.
Gad se nan kwi a
li fè tout afè li nan lavi sa.
Pa janm di ou pi mal,
genyen pi mal.

52.
I thought I was poor, oh I was poor;
when I looked, I saw there were worse off.
Oh I mustered my courage.
While I was napping
the one worse off stole my calabash bowl.
Look it's in the calabash bowl
that he takes care of all his business in this life.
Never say you're the worst off,
there are those who are even more worse off.

53.
Lèse m pale pawòl Ginen an
—pale, pale w.
Lèse m chante chante Ginen an
—chante, chante w.
Lwa Ginen se pa lwa achte
—se verite.
Lèse m mache selon Ginen an
—konsa, konsa.

53.
Let me speak the words of Ginen
—speak your words.
Let me sing the Ginen songs
—sing your songs.
The Ginen lwa aren't purchased lwa
—it's true.
Let me walk according to the Ginen
—like this, like this.

54.
Moun yo mare m sèt fwa
pou m pa lage.
A wi m lage sèt fwa devan Bondye.
Woy, ti vagabon,
adye ti vagabon.
Pa rayi m pou sa w pa ka fè a,
ti vagabon.

54.
The people tie me up seven times
so I don't get loose.
Ah yes, I'm set free seven times before God.
Whoa, little scumbag,
what a pity, little scumbag.
Don't hate me for what you can't do,
little scumbag.

55.
Nasyon m yo, tanpri ede mwen.
Pou m ret kay moun
pou yon lwa reklame m, mezanmi.
Kondisyon sa, m pa ka sipote l.

55.
My nations of lwa, please help me.
Staying at someone else's house
and being claimed by a lwa, my goodness.
That condition, I cannot accept it.

56.
Si m se vi w, lwa,
se pou lè m gen pwoblèm.
Se pa pou bèl non
pou m adore mistè lakay mwen.
Si m sèvi yon lwa,
fò l ka regle zafè mwen.

56.
If I am your life, lwa,
it is for when I have problems.
It isn't for renown
that I worship the mysteries of my house.
If I serve a lwa,
she must be able to take care of my business.

57.
Si w wè kote m ap fè maji mwen,
w a kontan, w a remesye lwa yo.
Gad la tate kofre pwen an,
myan myan.
Si w wè kote m ap fè maji mwen,
w a kontan, tout gangan pa menm o.

57.
If you see where I am making my magic,
you will be happy, you will thank the lwa.
The lwa tried to snuff out the spell,
myan myan.
If you see where I am making my magic,
you'll be happy, oh all oungan are not the same.

Manman

58.
Manman mwen, si ou wè mizè m ap pase,
se rèl o.
Mwen mache lè m pa dwe mache,
m dòmi kote m pa t dwe dòmi.
Adye manman mwen, kote ou ye,
tounen vin chèche mwen,
san pa sa m ap mouri o.

59.
Gen de lè, m fin ri,
m anvi kriye daprè lavi m.
O manman, ou mete m sou tè a
epi w ale kite mwen.
Kenpòt kote w ye, w ka tande plenn mwen,
m santi m pa ka kenbe.

60.
Valè mizè m pase,
m p ap ka bliye l,
sitou lè m sonje manman mwen
dlo kouri nan je mwen.
Sa k pa gen manman yo,
pran ka yo.
Sa k pa gen manman yo,
pran kouraj, pi gwo kado a l pote n

Mother

58.
My mother, if you see the misery I'm enduring,
oh it's wailing.
I go around when I shouldn't go around,
I sleep where I shouldn't sleep.
What a pity, my mother, wherever you are,
come and find me,
oh without that I'm going to die.

59.
There are times when I'm done with laughing,
my life makes me want to cry.
Oh mother, you put me on the earth
and you left me.
Wherever you are, you can hear my groaning,
I feel as though I can't stand it.

60.
The amount of misery I have endured,
I won't be able to forget it,
especially when I remember my mother
tears flow from my eyes.
Those who don't have their mothers,
take care of them.
Those who don't have their mothers,
take heart, the biggest gift is that she carried us

nèf mwa nan vant,
aprè Bondye nan syel la ban nou lavi o.

nine months in her womb,
oh after God in heaven gave us life.

61.

Lè m te piti,
m pa t konn valè manman mwen.
Kounye a vin gran,
m vle karese manman mwen.
Sa k pi fè m mal la
lè fèt manman rive . . .
Tout moun ap fete, mwen menm,
mwen dlo nan je mwen, manman . . . lavi sa . . .
o hay . . .
Pa gen pèsòn ki ka ranplase manman mwen.

61.

When I was a child,
I didn't appreciate the value of my mother.
Now that I'm grown up,
I want to hug my mother.
What hurts me the most
is when Mother's Day comes . . .
Everyone is celebrating, myself,
tears are in my eyes, mother . . . this life . . .
oh, heavens . . .
There is no one who can replace my mother.

62.

Manman cheri m nan,
kisa pou m ta ba ou ane sa?
Sa w fè pou mwen, manman,
m p ap janm fin
peye w sa malerezman.
Pou moun ki pa gen manman yo,
pa dekouraje paske Bondye avèk nou.

62.

Mother my dear,
what could I give you this year?
What you did for me, mother,
I am unfortunately never going to finish
repaying you for that.
For people who have lost their mothers,
don't lose heart because God is with you.

63.

Mwen gen yon bagay m ap kalkile,
chak fwa m sonje l, li fè dlo kouri nan je m.
Mwen gen yon bagay m ap kalkile,
lè m sonje jan m pèdi manman mwen,
bagay la fè mwen mal o.
Dominasyon sa, pa jodi pa demen,
li k ap mennen m al jwenn manman mwen.

63.

I have something I'm thinking about,
each time I recall it, it makes me cry.
I have something I'm thinking about,
when I recall how I lost my mother,
oh the thought hurts me.
This preoccupation, not for days or for weeks,
is leading me to go find my mother.

64.

M p ap fè yo byen—Way!
M p ap fè yo mal—Way!
Sa k te kase fèy nan Gran Bwa
—Gran Bwa rive.
Men Gran Bwa ale nan demanbre m.

64.

I'm not going to do them good—Hey!
I'm not going to do them bad—Hey!
Whosoever broke leaves in Gran Bwa
—Gran Bwa arrives.
Here Gran Bwa goes to my home ceremony.

65.

Si n wè m pran yon pwen,
pa kritike m lè m te nan pa bon an.
N te pale m mal o.

65.

If you see me get a charm,
don't criticize me when I was in bad shape.
Oh you spoke badly of me.

Kounye a n rele m papa o devan pwen an.
Si yo vle bon gangan
n ap fè pou yo toutan n kapab o.

Oh now you call me papa in front of the charm.
If they want a good oungan,
oh we can do it for them as long as we're able.

66.

Mwen rele pwen an,
m pa wè pwen an.
Ou pa bezwen kriye,
ou konn jou a prèske rive.

66.

I call the charm,
I don't see the charm.
You don't need to cry,
you know the day is almost here.

67.

Gade kriye siklòn Godòn nan
kite nan mitan fanmi yo.
Se yon gwo lapenn lè w abitwe ak
fanmi ou san l pa malad.
Yon jou l ale kite ou, manman,
Godòn, o hay.
Anverite, m p ap janm ka fin kriye, non.

67.

Look at the weeping hurricane Gordon
left in the midst of the families.
It's a great sorrow when you're used to
your family being without illness.
Oh my, one day it went and took you, mother,
oh no, Gordon.
In truth, no I can never stop crying.

68.

M p ap se lwa ankò o,
M ta prefere pa sèvi lwa
ankò o.
Si m gen gwo lwa lakay
pou yon lougawou fè m sa l vle o,
m ta mare lwa lage l nan lanmè an.
m pa sèvi lwa ankò o.

68.

Oh I am not into the lwa anymore,
Oh I would prefer not to serve the lwa
anymore.
Oh if I have a great lwa at home
and then a warlock does what he wants to me,
I would tie up the lwa and throw him in the sea.
Oh I don't serve lwa anymore.

69.

Leyogàn se la m t al chèche
pwen an,
lè m retounen maji a bèl o.
Chèche fouye pou w jwenn
sa w bezwen o.
Leyogàn se la m t al chèche
pwen an, maji a solid o.

69.

Leyogann is where I was going to search for
the charm,
oh when I returned the magic was beautiful.
Oh seek and dig to find
what you need.
Leyogann is where I was going to search for
the charm, oh the magic is strong.

70.

Ti pa o n a rive,
ti pa ti pa n a rive.
Si gen moun ki bezwen devan,
ba yo devan o.
Ti pa ti pa n a rive.

70.

Oh step by step we'll get there,
step by step we'll get there.
If there are people who need to lead,
oh let them lead.
Step by step we'll get there.

71.
Ogou o w manniganse pwen an.
W a prete m manchèt ou,
m pral vanje a moun yo.
Ogou o, w manniganse pwen an.

72.
Sa k ap manje kann nan ban n ti mòso
anba kabann nan;
m tande, way, m pa ka pale.
Mazaka Lakwa se yon lwa
ki dous konsa solèy leve.
Se way solèy kouche, se way, ala w bon lwa
ki dous konsa, lwa Mazaka.

73.
Ti Mari sa k fè w konyen konsa;
se manman m ki mouri kite lwa Gede
ki fè m konyen konsa.
Koko pa ti chodyè, Ti Mari,
konyen byen.
Tann dat w ap konyen, Ti Mari,
kot dantan koko w?

74.
Vin mete mwen deyò, m prale;
m a rele, m pa ka sipòte manman
mete m deyò, m prale.
Paske m pa gen fanmi an,
gade sa yo fè mwen.
M di m a rele, m pa ka sipòte,
o manman mete m deyò, m prale.

75.
Jan w wè m pale a
se pa konsa pwen an pale.
Gad Anminan, gad Anminan, m a rele.
Simbi Andezo, gad la move.

76.
Tan e tan fè tan
e ala rele o dyab o.
Ti nèg pa Bondye.
Nèg k ap mache pran pwen

71.
Oh Ogou, you control the charm.
You'll lend me your machete,
I'm going to avenge the people.
Oh Ogou, you control the charm.

72.
Those who are eating the cane give us a little
under the bed;
I hear, oh my, I can't speak.
Mazaka Lakwa is a lwa
who rises as sweetly as the sun.
As wow as the sunset, so wow, what a good lwa
who is so sweet, lwa Mazaka.

73.
Little Mary what makes you fuck like that;
my mother who died left me with the lwa Gede
who makes me fuck like that.
Pussy is not a little cooking pot, Little Mary,
fucking is good.
For ages you have been fucking, Little Mary,
where are your pussy's ancestors?

74.
Come and put me out, I am going;
I will cry out, I can't take my mother
putting me out, I'm going.
Because I don't have family,
see what they do to me.
I say I will yell, oh I can't take it,
oh mother put me out, I'm going.

75.
The way you see me speak
is not how the spell speaks.
Guard Anminan, guard Anminan, I will call.
Simbi Andezo, the guard is angry.

76.
This much and that much makes this much
And oh what yelling oh dyab.
The little man isn't God.
The men who are going around taking charms

kay gangan pou yo ka
pi bon nan rasin, se bon o.
M di tan e tan
fè tan e m a rele, o dyab o,
pinga jou regleman.

at the oungan's house so that they can be
stronger in roots religion, oh it's good.
I say this much and that much
makes this much and I'll cry out, oh dyab oh,
watch out for the day of settlement.

77.

Mwen p ap janm bliye lontan . . .
Jan ti peyi m te bèl . . .
Te gen richès tou, n te viv . . .
Se kolon blan yo
ki lage n nan mizè.

77.

I am never going to forget the past . . .
How my little country was beautiful . . .
It had riches too, we lived . . .
It's the white colonialists
who left us in misery.

78.

Estil kè kal fanatik rele yon
"*nonbè wòn.*"
Ane sila nou "*nonbè wòn*" nan kanaval.
Estil kè kal se don nou, chak ane pou n
fè moun danse.
Estil kè kal se don nou; granmoun, timoun
fin awoyo nan estil kè kal.

78.

The relaxed style that the fans call
"number one."
This year we are "number one" in carnival.
The relaxed style is our gift, each year we need
to make people dance.
The relaxed style is our gift; grownups, kids
go over the top for the relaxed style.

79.

Manman zanfan yo, pale timoun yo,
alèkile peyi a malouk o.
Depi se timoun ki pa koute
granmoun, malè gen pou rive yo.
Manman zanfan yo, pale timoun yo.
Si yo pa tande,
yo gen pou y al dwat anndan simityè.

79.

Mother of the children, speak to the children,
right now, oh the country is vicious.
As long as there are children who don't listen
to adults, misfortune will come to them.
Mothers of the children, speak to the little ones.
If they don't listen,
they will end up six feet under.

80.

Gen kat bagay ki divize n:
se lajan, lafanm, ladwòg, latè,
ki mete n nan divizyon.
Men yo tout se vanite o.
Kòb se van, fanm pa byen,
dwòg se dyab.
Men latè a pa erityе pèsòn o;
tande sa pou n antann nou.

80.

There are four things that divide us:
it's money, women, drugs, the land,
that drive us apart.
Oh but they all are vanity.
Money is wind, loose women are no good,
drugs are the devil.
Oh the earth is not the inheritance of anyone;
listen to this so that we can get along.

81.

Nou menm rasin Gran Bwa . . .
Nou se papa tout bwa ki gen o

81.

We ourselves are Gran Bwa's roots . . .
Oh we are the fathers of all the trees

nan Gran Bwa.
Lè Bwa Kayiman . . .
rasin Gran Bwa te la.
Boukmann o . . .
rasin Gran Bwa nan men ou.

in Gran Bwa.
At the time of Bwa Kayiman . . .
Gran Bwa's roots were there.
Oh Boukmann . . .
Gran Bwa's roots are in your hands.

82.
Lafanmi o, an n rasanble
nan demanbre a,
n pral fè seremoni an.
Limen balenn nan—o an n rele lwa yo.
Sonnen ason an—rele Papa Legba.
Nan kafou a, o nou angaje.
Papa Legba—louvri baryè pou lwa yo.

82.
Oh my kith and kin, let's assemble
in the home ritual,
we're going to do the service.
Light the candle—oh let's call the lwa.
Shake the rattle—call Papa Legba.
At the crossroad, oh we're in trouble.
Papa Legba—open the gate for the lwa.

83.
Mari ou sen, ou se manman Bondye;
nou se pechè, o lapriyè pou nou.
Avan n ap sèvi lwa yo,
n rele Bondye avan.
Mari ou sen, ou se manman Bondye.
Nou se pechè, o lapriyè pou nou.

83.
Mary, you are holy, you are God's mother;
we are sinners, oh pray for us.
Before we are serving the lwa,
we call upon God first.
Mary, you are holy, you are God's mother.
We are sinners, oh pray for us.

84.
Nan Ginen,
ann tande sa yo fè mwen.
M mande o, sa m fè moun yo
ki fè yo rayi mwen.

84.
Those in Ginen,
let's hear what they did to me.
Oh I ask, what did I do to the people
that makes them hate me.

85.
Papa Legba, ouvè baryè pou mwen,
m bezwen rantre pou n al ranmesi lwa yo.

85.
Papa Legba, open the gate for me,
I need to return so that we can thank the lwa.

86.
Twa Patè, o twa Ave Mariya, nou kwè nan
Dye a ki ban nou lavi a, men gen Ginen.
Nan Ginen, o genyen lwa, genyen lwa o
nan Ginen lafanmi o, an nou met
tèt ansanm pou n ka sove peyi a.

86.
Three Paters, oh three Hail Marys, we believe in
the God who gave us life, but there is Ginen.
In Ginen, oh there are lwa, there are lwa oh,
oh the family is in Ginen, let's put
our heads together so we can save the country.

87.
Respekte granmoun,
pa pale nan sa k pa mele w,
koute konsèy granmoun,

87.
Respect elders,
don't speak about what doesn't concern you,
listen to elders' advice,

m di se yon pwen.
Pawòl gratis sa . . .
koute chè pou sa k konnen n.
Sa k vle tande l, tande l,
sa k vle koute l, koute l,
Anverite, tout moun ki swiv chemen sa,
w deja sove.

I say it's a charm.
This free advice . . .
costs much for those who understand it.
Those who want to hear it, hear it,
those who want to listen to it, listen to it,
In truth, everyone who follows this path,
you are already saved.

88.

Nou pa bezwen kriye.
Nou pa bezwen rele.
Nou tout se pasaje sou latè,
se yon tan n ap viv o, adye!
Kriye rele a pa leve lanmò a.
Nou mèt konsole nou
menm lè sa fè nou mal o.

88.

We don't need to cry.
We don't need to shout.
We all are passengers on earth,
oh, it's a short time we are living, what a pity!
Crying and shouting don't raise the dead.
Oh we may console ourselves
even though this hurts us.

89.

Nan pwonmennen gade,
m rive nan Zandò.
Voye pale moun yo di
men Koulou rive
Apre Dye, m granmoun o,
Frè Innèl,
o voye pale moun yo di
Zandò reveye.

89.

While walking and looking around,
I arrive at Zandò.
Send word to the people saying
Koulou has arrived here.
After God, oh I'm an adult,
Brother Innèl,
oh send word to the people saying
Zandò is awake.

90.

Pa swiv mwen, pa swiv mwen.
Mwen Agwetawoyo, menm si m ap navige,
Pa swiv mwen, pa swiv mwen,
pa swiv mwen.
Mwen Agwetawoyo a, w pa wè mwen asire?

90.

Don't follow me, don't follow me.
I'm Agwetawoyo, even if I am sailing,
Don't follow me, don't follow me,
don't follow me.
I'm Agwetawoyo, don't you see I'm secure?

91.

Pa wè ke w gen pwoblèm pa w,
pou w di w gen
plis pwoblèm dan lavi;
lavi sa pa nan paspouki,
chak moun gen pwoblèm pa yo.
Gen moun ki gen lajan
ki pa ka manje.
Pwoblèm m pale, sa depann de
fason ke l fè kòb li.

91.

Don't you see that you have your own problems;
for you to say you have
more problems in life;
this life doesn't play favorites,
each person has problems of his own.
There are people who have money
who can't eat.
I'm talking about problems that depend on
the way in which he makes his money.

Gen moun ki gen manje,
men ki pa gen kote pou l dòmi.
Tout se problèm o; sa depann de fason
ke l mennen vi l.
Pwoblèm pa w, pwoblèm pa l,
tout se pwoblèm o.
Se sèl Granmèt la ki konn moun
ki gen plis pwoblèm.

There are people who have food,
but don't have a place to sleep.
Oh all are problems that depend on the way
that he leads his life.
Your problems, his problems,
oh all are problems.
It's only the Lord who knows people
who have more problems.

92.

Pandan ke m pa te la,
m konn sa k rive o.
Gen sa k pale byen,
sa k pale mal sou do mwen.
Bondye fè m miyò pase yo.
Yo mèt ranje kò yo,
ane sila Gran Bwa nan bouda yo.

92.

During the time I was gone,
oh I know what happened.
There are those who speak well,
those who speak badly behind my back.
God makes me better than them.
They'd better get ready,
this year Gran Bwa is after their asses.

93.

M se yon vye chemen o
ki pa genyen bout o.
Yo mèt mache de san mil an,
mwen vye chemen sa,
yo p ap janm wè bout mwen.

93.

Oh I'm an old path
that has no end oh.
They can walk for two hundred thousand years,
I'm that old path,
they're never going to see my end.

94.

Gade yon konplo
k ranje sou do m.
M p ap pran Bondye devan,
Ginen dèyè.
Koulou, gade m nan mitan yo.
Bondye fè m konnen m inosan,
kite m nan mitan yo.

94.

Look at a conspiracy
which is going on behind my back.
I'm not choosing God in front,
Ginen behind.
Koulou, look I'm in between them.
God lets me know that I'm innocent,
leave me in between them.

95.

Yanvalou

Nou mèt fè konbinezon,
konplo sou konplo,
Rasin Gran Bwa nan bwa deja fòme,
ala l p ap ka kraze.
Se twa gwo bwa nan bwa
k fòme rasin Gran Bwa.
Rasin Gran Bwa
nan bwa deja fòme,

95.

Yanvalou

You may make a plot,
conspiracies upon conspiracies,
Gran Bwa's roots in trees are already matured,
oh be assured that he cannot be crushed.
It's three big trees in the forest
that form Gran Bwa's roots.
Gran Bwa's roots
in the forest are already matured,

ala l p ap ka kraze.
Sobo, o Badè, kay manbo Lis o,
wonsi yo dogwe doba o
nan dyèvò a.
Kolye vèvè sa
nou pote sou do nou se pa blag o.
M di manbo Lis, o w a pale wonsi yo
pou yo gen sekrè pou pa pale pawòl la.
Mesye dam pa prese
si n vle wè longè lavi a dousman o.
Mache prese, jènjan,
pa louvri jou.
Dousman, dousman, jèn gason, n a wè lavi a.

oh be assured that he cannot be crushed.
Sobo, oh Badè, oh at the house of manbo Lis,
Oh the ounsi dogwe doba is
in the initiation hut.
Oh this vèvè necklace
We wear on our backs is no joke.
I say to manbo Lis, oh you'll speak to the ounsi
so they'll keep secrets under wraps.
Oh people don't be rushed
if you want to see the length of life gently.
Walking quickly, young man,
doesn't open up the day.
Gently, gently, young boy, you will see life.

96.
Djòlè, pale moun yo pale,
n pa okipe yo.
Si nou toujou la
se paske nou se fran Ginen.
Moun yo mache pale,
yo di Vodou soudevlope.
Men lè nou frape, moun yo pran rele o.

96.
Loudmouth, people talk their talk,
we don't pay attention to them.
If we are still here
it is because we are pure Ginen.
The people go around talking,
they say Vodou is underdeveloped.
But when we strike, oh they start to shout.

97.
Rasin sa se nan san nou l ye,
depi tanbou frape,
tout moun leve danse.
Depi tanbou frape
tout moun leve danse.
Men rasin sa,
m pral limen yon balenn nan pye w o.

97.
This root it's right in our blood,
as soon as drums beat,
everyone gets up to dance.
As soon as the drums beat
everyone gets up to dance.
Here are these roots,
oh I'm going to light a candle at your feet.

98.
Alantou a sou kote,
ou pa wè m nan mitan yo.
Dat moun sa yo ap pale mal,
mwen miyò pase yo.
Mwen pral Kwa Bosal.
Mwen pral achte mamit
san konte pou m ba yo travay o.

98.
Those on the side and around,
don't you see I'm among them.
They've been forever speaking badly,
I'm better than them.
I'm going to Kwa Bosal.
Oh I'm going to buy foodstuff
without the thought of putting them to work.

99.
Latibonit, mesye, m t al achte yon pwen,
lè m retounen, mesye,

99.
To Latibonit, sirs, I went to buy a charm;
when I returned, sirs,

m bliye non pwen an.
Lè m reflechi,
m sonje l rele Koure.
Jeneral Koure
pral raboure moun yo.

I forgot the name of the charm.
When I thought about it,
I remembered he was called Koure.
General Koure
is going to plow over the people.

100.

Amwa, m Koure—amwa m Koure,
m deja Koure nan labou a.
Koure nan labou a,
n p ap ka manje rezon li.
Amwa, m Koure, papa o, nan labou a.

100.

As for me, I'm Koure—as for me, I'm Koure,
I'm already Koure in the mud.
Koure in the mud,
you won't be able to eat his reason.
As for me, I'm Koure, oh man, in the mud.

101.

M gen yon lwa ki reklame mwen . . .
Pandan m nan somèy,
m gen w lwa ki reklame m o.
M gen yon lwa ki reklame mwen.
Ogou Batagi se yon lwa ki danjere.

101.

I have a lwa who claims me . . .
While I'm sleeping,
oh I have a lwa who claims me.
I have a lwa who claims me.
Ogou Batagi is a lwa who is dangerous.

102.

Ogou o, kafou a danjere.
Papa Ogou o,
kafou a danjere.
Ogou o, kafou a danjere.
Pandan m nan kafou a, papa,
Lwa Ogou a pran mwen.

102.

Oh Ogou, the crossroads are dangerous.
Oh Papa Ogou,
the crossroads are dangerous.
Oh Ogou, the crossroads are dangerous.
While I was in the crossroads, man,
The lwa Ogou took a hold of me.

103.

M achte yon bèl manchèt pou Papa Ogou o.
M achte yon boutèy wonm pou Ogou fè ray.
M achte yon bèl mouchwa
pou Papa Ogou o.
Bèl mouchwa sa
se pou l mare ponyèt li.

103.

Oh I buy a beautiful machete for Papa Ogou.
I buy a bottle of rum so Ogou can rage,
Oh I buy a beautiful handkerchief
for Papa Ogou.
This beautiful handkerchief
is for him to wrap around his arms.

104.

Si ou wè m malere, pa kritike mwen.
Si ou wè m bwè kleren,
pa fawouche mwen.
Se yon lwa Ogou
k ap fè m pase mizè sa.
Li vle m sèvi l,
men m poko vle sèvi l.

104.

If you see that I'm poor, don't criticize me.
If you see that I'm drinking rum,
don't harass me.
It's an Ogou lwa
who is making me endure this misery.
He wants me to serve him,
but I don't want to serve him yet.

105.

Papa Ogou, Papa, se mwen menm sèl,
o m a rele m.
Se pitit Ginen,
anyen pa ka fè mwen.
Moun yo mache ti pa pou yo tiye mwen.
M konn aprè Bondye,
m gen yon gwo lwa lakay la.

105.

Papa Ogou, Papa, it is me alone,
oh I will call myself.
I'm a child of Ginen,
nothing can do me wrong.
They silently go around trying to kill me.
I know that after God,
I have a great lwa at home.

106.

Ogou

Ogou o, mande sa m fè moun yo.
Mwen konnen ti nèg pa Bondye,
Aprè Bondye nan syèl,
Neg nwè pa ka tiye mwen.

106.

Ogou

Oh Ogou, ask what I did to the people.
I know the little men are not God.
Next to God in heaven,
Black men cannot kill me.

107.

Agwe

Bato m sou dlo, m ap vwayaje.
Nan dòmi yo di m lanmè a move.
Pandan m nan somèy
yo di m lanmè a move.
Agwetawoyo, ou pa wè m ape nwaye?

107.

Agwe

My boat's in the water, I'm traveling.
In my sleep they tell me the sea is rough.
While I'm sleeping
they tell me the sea is rough.
Agwetawoyo, don't you see that I'm drowning?

108.

Bato m chaje, m ranpli kou ze,
m pral demare nan lanmè wouj la,
migèla migole.
M rele mèt Agwe pou vin sove lavi mwen.
Nan lanmè wouj la, migèla migole.

108.

My boat is packed, I'm full like an egg,
I'm shoving off in the red sea,
migèla migole.
I call on Agwe to come save my life.
In the red sea, migèla migole.

109.

Mande sa k pase la o sou lanmè.
Agwetawoyo sòti nan dlo,
li pa mouye.
M mande sa k pase k fè l pa mouye.

109.

Oh ask what happened here on the sea.
Agwetawoyo comes out of the water,
he isn't wet.
I ask how it could be that he isn't wet.

110.

Bato a koule o,
bato a koule o, bato a koule
Sou lanmè a, fanmi mèt Agwe yo trankil o.

110.

Oh the boat sinks,
oh the boat sinks, the boat sinks.
On the sea, oh Agwe's family is calm.

111.
Bò lanmè a m t ap chèche lavi mwen.
Agwetawoyo mennen m anba dlo.
M di anba lanmè genyen lwa e.
M sot anba lanmè a.

111.
I was going to earn my living by the sea.
Agwetawoyo led me under the water.
Hey I say under the sea there are lwa.
I come from under the sea.

112.
Lè mwen retounen m tounen
ak ason nan men m.
Sou lanmè a m te ye, chapo m tonbe,
Lasirenn o.
W a ranmase li pou mwen.
Sou lanmè a, chapo m tonbe.
Lasirèn o k te sou lanmè a, chapo m tonbe.
Gade, l ranmase li pou mwen.

112.
When I return I come
with a priest's rattle in my hand.
I was on the sea, my hat fell off,
oh Lasirenn.
You will pick it up for me.
On the sea, my hat fell off.
Oh Lasirenn who was on the sea, my hat fell off.
Look, she picked it up for me.

113.
Èzili
Èzili Dantò o, fanm chans mwen,
m ape rele w, manbo,
pou n salande pwen an.
Manbo Èzili a k ape kòmande pwen an.
Èzili Dantò o, fanm chans mwen,
m ape rele w, maji ap salande.

113.
Èzili
Oh Èzili Dantò, woman of my good luck,
I am calling you, priestess,
for you to bless the charm.
The priestess Èzili controls the charm.
Oh Èzili Dantò, woman of my good luck,
I'm calling on you, the magic is spreading.

114.
Èzili Dan Petwo,
nou pral pike moun yo.
Èzili o, Mètrès o.
An n montre moun yo
n sèvi gwo lwa lakay nou.

114.
Èzili Dan Petwo,
we are going to sting the people.
Oh Èzili, oh Mistress.
Let's show the people
we serve great lwa at our house.

115.
Bale kay la, Èzili nan wout o.
Wouze kay la, Èzili nan wout o.
Pafimen kay la, Èzili nan wout o.
Manbo Èzili se yon fanm ki tou limen.

115.
Oh sweep the house, Èzili is on the way.
Oh water the house, Èzili is on the way.
Perfume the house, Èzili is on the way.
Manbo Èzili is a woman who's all lit up.

116.
Èzili Dantò fanm Dan Petwo
elan he, mwen angaje.
M rele Zili, m pa wè Zili elan he.
Ala m pa gen chans; o jou m angaje a,
Èzili malad o.

116.
Hey, Èzili Dantò is the wife of Dan Petwo,
elan hey, I'm in trouble.
I call Zili, hey I don't see Zili, elan hey.
I'm out of luck; oh the day I'm in trouble,
Èzili is sick.

117.

Èzili o, moun yo di ou manje moun.
M pral wè o si se vre.
M pral wè o si se vre.
Èzili Dantò se yon fanm ki kriminèl.

117.

Oh Èzili, the people say you eat people.
Oh I'm going to see if it's true.
Oh I'm going to see if it's true.
Èzili Dantò is a woman who is criminal.

118.

Mètrès o, moun yo pa vle rete,
sa pou n fè yo?
Kite y ale, kite y ale,
chemen an long, li laj.
Lè l rive,
l a wè sa k gen devan.

118.

Oh mistress, the people don't want to stop,
what can we do to them?
Let them go, let them go,
the path is long, it's broad.
When she arrives,
she will see what is in front of her.

119.

Genbo Makaya, sa ki bezwen,
o n ap ba yo pase.
Makaya, nou pa prese o.
Makaya Genbo, an n ba yo pase la,
Pi devan n ap pran o.

119.

Genbo Makaya, those who need to,
oh we're going to let them through.
Oh Makaya, we don't rush.
Makaya Genbo, let's give them passage,
Further ahead we will take them.

120.

Genbo Makaya,
nou tout se moun o, hay.
Genbo Makaya, nou tout se moun o.
Men gen de lè nou tout pa menm o.

120.

Oh Genbo Makaya,
we are all people, oh my.
Oh Genbo Makaya, we are all people.
Oh but it appears that we aren't all the same.

121.

Si yon nonm pa gason,
ou pa sèvi pwen Makaya o, hay.
Makaya mache nan nwit o, devan rezon an
l tounen sa l vle o.

121.

Oh if a man isn't brave,
you don't serve Makaya's charm, oh my.
Oh Makaya walks at night, faced with the cause
he turns into anything he wants.

122.

Simbi Makaya,
m konn pouki moun yo pa vle wè mwen,
se poutèt don rasin nan.
M pa konn al lakay ti nèg o
pou ban n don rasin o.
M di se gwo lwa nan bitasyon mwen
ki ban mwen don rasin nan.

122.

Simbi Makaya,
I know why the people don't want to see me,
it's because of the gift of the Vodou roots.
Oh I don't go to the home of the little guy
to give him the gift of Vodou roots, oh.
I say there are great lwa on my land
who give me the gift of Vodou roots.

123.
Andezo pwen an, o hay, Andezo o hay.
Men nèg yo fè konplo
pou yo tiye chwal la.
Dyab la rete souke tèt li,
li ri kra kra.
Alantou a o sou kote a,
Koulou nan mitan yo.

123.
Andezo the charm, oh my, Andezo oh my.
Look how they make a plot
to kill the possessed one.
The dyab keeps shaking his head,
he laughs ha, ha.
Oh those on the side and around,
Koulou is in the middle of them.

124.
Andezo va lite; yo lite pou
yo sonde chwal la.
Aprè Bondye nan syèl la, m gwo nèg o.
Yo mèt mache;
mwen pa t okipe yo.
Devan rezon an,
m pa pè pèsonn o.

124.
Andezo is going to struggle; they struggle so that
they can challenge the possessed one.
After God in heaven, oh, I'm a big man.
They can walk off;
I didn't pay any attention to them.
In the face of the cause,
oh I'm not afraid of anyone.

125.
Gen de lè m rete, m santi foula,
lè kon sa m santi m pral vole.
Bann mannan yo ranje kò nou,
Makaya nan wout o.
Gran Bwa pral vole.

125.
There are times I stay, I feel the vaporized rum.
At those times I feel like I'm going to fly.
The bunch of beggars had better watch out,
oh Makaya is on the path.
Gran Bwa is going to fly.

126.
M pral vole mare Ogou Badagi a,
o m pral vole.
Se nou ki ban mwen pwen sa
pou m mache nan nwit o.
M pral vole, m a rele Ogou,
m pral vole;
w a pare tann mwen.

126.
I'm going to fly to tie up Ogou Badagi,
oh I'm going to fly.
Oh it's you who gave me this charm
so that I can walk at night.
I'm going to fly, I will call Ogou,
I'm going to fly;
you will prepare and wait for me.

127.
M pral foula e, an han,
m pral foula e.
Anminan m rele gad la,
se konsa mache pwen an.
Foula e, gad la,
m pral foula e pwen an.

127.
I'm going to vaporize rum, hey, oh yeah;
I'm going to vaporize rum, yeah.
My lwa Anminan calls the guard,
that's how the charm works.
Hey, vaporize rum, protector lwa,
Hey, I'm going to vaporize rum on the charm.

128.

Peye gad la elan he o peye gad la,
elan he o, peye gad la.
Se pou jou n angaje.

128.

Pay for the guard, oh yeah, pay for the guard,
oh yeah, pay for the guard.
It's for the day we're in trouble.

129.

Si nèg yo te konnen,
yo ta peye pwen an.
Si yo te konnen,
yo ta peye pwen Andezo.
Lè y angaje,
pwen an ta fè pou yo.

129.

If the men knew,
they would pay for the charm.
If they knew,
they would pay for Andezo's charm.
When they're in trouble,
the magic charm would work for them.

130.

Pa gad sa m fè pou w di w ap fè.
Pa gad sa m fè pou w di w ap fè.
Pa gad sa m fè pou w di w ap fè sa,
ti vagabon.
Andezo se pa lwa achte, pa vin
tenten la devan rezon lwa m nan.

130.

Don't look at what I do only to say you'll do it.
Don't look at what I do only to say you'll do it.
Don't look at what I do only to say you'll do it,
little scumbag.
Andezo is not a purchased lwa, don't come
act stupidly here before the motives of my lwa.

131.

Sousou Pandyanmen, han, han, han.
Sousou Pandyanmen, lè m ap balanse gad la,
se timoun kou granmoun k andile,
lè m ap balanse gad la.

131.

Sousou Pandyanmen, hey, hey, hey.
Sousou Pandyanmen, when I put the guard to use,
it's children and adults who undulate,
when I put the guard to use.

132.

Sa m fè moun yo, o gwo chen mwen,
moun yo pase sou pase;
yo pa rele mwen.
Se yo santi m nan,
ki fè moun rayi moun o.
Kòb pa fè moun, mesye,
l p ap janm fè moun,
men l fè moun rayi moun o.

132.

What did I do to the people, oh my big dog,
the people keep passing by;
they don't call me.
It's that they sense me,
which makes people hate each other.
Money doesn't make a person, sir,
it'll never make a person,
but oh it makes people hate each other.

133.

M p ap fè lach devan lavi,
lavi gen revè, m p ap lach.
O pou m al volè.
Paske pou m ta volè,
m ta pito mande charite.
Lavi a di o, vi a difisil,
fò n aprann pran kouraj o.

133.

I'm not going to be a coward in the face of life,
life has two sides, I'm not going to be a coward.
Oh to go thieving.
Because instead of stealing,
I would rather ask for charity.
Oh life is hard, life is difficult,
oh we must learn to take heart.

134.

Podyab se bon zanmi mwen nèg isit,
se kon sa yo ye o.
Devan w, y ap di podyab,
dèyè w yo di se bon.
Men jan de moun sa yo, se konsa yo ye,
ala m ka viv avè yo.

134.

The poor fellow is my good friend here
oh, that's how they are.
In front of you, they are saying poor fellow,
behind you they are saying it's good.
Here are some of these people, they are like that,
oh how I'm living with them.

135.

Manman, manman, manman, se pa po m sa.
A wi pitit, sa se po w sa.
Manman m di w se pa po m sa a,
wi pitit, se po w sa.
M di se po w sa,
gade w di se pa po w la.
Debouye w chèche po w la.

135.

Mother, mother, mother, this is not my skin.
Ah yes, child, this is your skin.
My mother tells you this is not my skin,
ah yes child, this is your skin.
I say this is your skin,
look at you saying it isn't your skin there.
Hurry up and look for your skin.

136.
Bawon

Bawon Samdi,
ou menm ki wa nan simityè.
W a jije rezon m.
Yo di mwen kwa,
men m konnen m pa kwa.
Ou menm ki wa nan simityè;
w a ban mwen rezon mwen.

136.
Bawon

Bawon Samdi,
you are indeed king of the cemetery.
You'll judge my motives.
They say I'm the cross,
but I know I'm not the cross.
You indeed are king of the cemetery;
you'll give me my motives.

137.

Bawon Samdi mèt simityè.
Èske gen moun sou latè
k pa ka mouri?
Moun yo mache pale,
yo di yo se towo.
Nan sèkèy la, Bawon,
n a wè longè yo.

137.

Bawon Samdi is the master of the cemetery.
Is there anyone in the world
who can't die?
The people go around talking,
they say they're are bulls.
In the coffin, Bawon,
we'll see how big they are.

138.

Bawon o, se ou k mennen m isi a.
Bawon o, se ou k voye chèche mwen.
Bawon o, moun yo manje rezon mwen.
M a rele, mennen m ale lakay mwen.

138.

Oh Bawon, it's you who led me here.
Oh Bawon, it's you who sent for me.
Oh Bawon, the people devoured my reasoning.
I will cry out, lead me away to my house.

139.

Bawon, jou a rive,
Bawon o, jou a rive,
Bawon, jou a rive devan Bondye.
Si w konnen w te dwe Chango,
ou pral peye Chango.

139.

Bawon, the day arrives,
oh Bawon, the day arrives.
Bawon, the day arrives before God.
If you know you owe Chango,
you are going to pay Chango.

140.

Moun sa yo di Bawon konnen yo . . .
way.
Moun sa yo di simityè konnen yo . . .
way-way.
Moun sa yo di Bawon konnen yo . . .
way.
Moun sa yo di simityè konnen yo . . .
Bawon konnen moun yo,
konnen Bondye.
Bawon o, se ou ki kondi sèt mò
nan simityè.
Bawon o konnen moun yo, konnen Bondye.

140.

These people say Bawon knows them . . .
oh sorrow.
These people say the cemetery knows them . . .
oh sorrow of sorrows.
These people say Bawon knows them . . .
oh sorrow.
These people say the cemetery knows them . . .
Bawon knows the people,
knows God.
Oh Bawon, it's you who leads the seven dead
to the cemetery.
Oh Bawon knows the people, knows God.

141.

Ala yon lavi o, ala yon mizè,
m ap pase ak yon lwa m achte o.
Men lwa sa se yon lwa kriminèl,
li vle manje tout moun lakay mwen.
Lenglensou o benyen nan basen san.

141.

Oh what a life, oh what misery,
I'm going through with a lwa I've purchased.
But this lwa is a criminal lwa,
he wants to eat everyone in my house.
Oh Lenglensou bathes in a basin of blood.

142.

Lenglensou m nan lwa kriminèl la.
Lenglensou m nan, lwa kaliko m nan.
Lenglensou o di l pa manje moun o.
Inosan o ki pou sove w.

142.

My Lenglensou is a criminal lwa.
My Lenglensou, my fickle lwa.
Oh Lenglensou says he doesn't eat people.
Oh innocence is what saves you.

143.

Lajan malediksyon sa,
kilès ki kreye w.
Nonm nan sòt,
li sòt pase yon pla pye.
Men lè l ap ri, li ri an franse.
Lajan malediksyon sa, kilès ki kreye w.

143.

That cursed money,
who is it that created you.
The man is stupid,
he's more stupid than the sole of a foot.
But when he is laughing, he laughs in French.
That cursed money, who is it that created you.

144.

Mwen gen yon bagay nan tèt mwen,
se lè m angaje.

144.

I have something in my head,
it's when I'm in trouble.

Y a wè sa ki nan tèt mwen.
M pral wè sa ki nan tèt mwen.
Men lè m angaje,
lwa manman m yo dechennen.

They will see what's in my head.
I'm going to see what's in my head.
But when I'm in trouble,
my mother's lwa are unchained.

145.

Nèg yo rele mwen pou yo sonde
chwal la.
Annarivan mwen, towo pouse kòn o.
Towo kriminèl yo
vle sonde pwen an.

145.

The guys called me to challenge
the one possessed.
Upon my arrival, oh, the bull grew horns.
The criminal bulls
want to challenge the magic charm.

146.

Manbo Èzili a, kote ou ye?
Nou anba kòd o . . . oh sorrow.
Nèg yo mare Gran Bwa sèt ne
pou l pa lage.
Manbo Èzili a ki mache nan nwit o,
w a va lage li pou mwen.

146.

Manbo Èzili, where are you?
Oh we are all tied up . . . hey.
The guys bind Gran Bwa with seven knots
so he can't get away.
Oh Manbo Èzili who goes around at night,
you will free him for me.

147.

Mache pou wè, chita pou tande, devan maji m,
pa ko wè kou Leyogàn.
Depi w gen lajan, ou ka mache;
w ap jwenn sa w bezwen.
Mache chèche o, chèche fouye,
wi w a jwenn sa w bezwen
nan Leyogàn o.

147.

Walk to see, sit to hear, before my magic,
not yet seen like Leyogann.
As long as you have money, you can walk;
you are finding what you need.
Oh go searching, seek high and low,
oh yes you will find what you need
in Leyogann.

148.

Moun sa yo di y ap tiye mwen.
Avan yo tiye mwen,
m pral mande Bondye sa m fè yo.
Men Bondye, mwen inosan e.
Avan yo tiye mwen,
m pral mande Bondye sa m fè yo.

148.

These people say they'll kill me.
Before they kill me,
I am going to ask God what I did to them.
But God, hey I'm innocent.
Before they kill me,
I'm going to ask God what I did to them.

149.

Grann Silibo, manman moun yo,
mwen poko sa.
M pral fout travay pou dyòl yo.
Sa se yon egzanp o, pou m pa fè byen.
Lè m fè yo byen, byen an tounen mal o.

149.

Grann Silibo, the people's mother,
I'm not that yet.
I'm going to fucking work for their mugs.
Oh this is an example, for me not to do good.
When I do them good, oh the good turns bad.

150.
M pral vwayaje an Afrik o
pou m ka konn nannan rasin nan,
kote l ye o.
Chak grenn Ginen se yon branch o.
Nannan rasin nan se nan san nou l ye.

150.
Oh I'm going to travel to Africa
in order to know the inner roots,
oh where it is.
Oh each individual Vodouist is a branch.
The inner root is right in our blood.

151.
Kay lwa m boule, li tounen sann o.
M ape mande sa k ap ranmase lwa m yo.
Kay lwa m boule;
demanbre a la o.
An n rasanble pou n ka ranmase lwa yo.

151.
My lwa's house burned, oh it turned into ashes.
I'm asking what can restore my lwa.
My lwa's house burned;
oh the ceremony there.
Let's get together so we can gather up the lwa.

152.
M rantre nan lakou a,
seremoni lwa m nan pral bèl o.
Sonnen ason an pou n rele lwa yo,
seremoni an pral bèl.

152.
I enter the yard,
oh my lwa's ceremony is going to be beautiful.
Shake the rattle to call the lwa,
the ceremony is going to be beautiful.

153.
Yo mare mwen pou yo al tiye mwen.
Kou l fè minwi, towo,
chenn kase chenn, l ale.
Moun yo wè mwen, men yo pa konnen mwen.

153.
They bind me so they can kill me.
At the stroke of midnight, bull,
chains break chains, it goes.
The people see me, but they don't know me.

154.
Anmwe o, m rele anmwe o,
tou sa m fè nan vi m tounen mal
o ewa ewa.
M ap mande si se yon kondisyon
pou m pase mizè mwen.
Anmwe, m rele anmwe pou sa m pa wè.

154.
Oh help, oh I'm calling for help,
all that I have done in my life is turning bad,
oh my, oh my.
I'm asking if it's a condition
that I experience my misery.
Help, I call for help for what I can't see.

155.
Pye w mache, valè mache w mache
avan m jwenn rezon an.
Mwen monte mòn o
pou n jwenn rezon an.
Mwen fin jwenn rezon an,
m prale mache pou n jwenn devosyon an.

155.
Your feet walk, oh how much you walk
before finding the reason.
Oh I climb mountains
so that we can find the reason.
I've finally found the reason,
I'm going to walk so we can find the devotion.

156.
M ale o, m ale, m ale o, m ale.
Aprè Bondye nan syèl, melevi mele dyò o.

156.
Oh I go, I go, oh I go, I go.
Before God in heaven, oh melevi mixes dyò.

157.

Y al chèche kòd pou yo mare Ti Jan,
Ti Jan nan kay la,
men yo pa wè Ti Jan.
Yo vire kay la,
yo pa wè Ti Jan, yo tounen kay la.
Yo pa wè Ti Jan;
Ti Jan, veye zo w,
moun yo pa renmen w.

157.

They go search for rope to bind Ti Jan.
Ti Jan is in the house,
but they don't see Ti Jan.
They turn the house inside out,
they don't see Ti Jan, they return to their house.
They don't see Ti Jan;
Ti Jan, you better watch out,
the people don't love you.

158.

Moun yo fè konplo pou yo tiye nou;
kanibal, sonje genyen Bondye.
Ou manje manman w,
manje papa w, manje pitit.
Kanibal, sonje ane a bout o.

158.

The people make a plot to kill us;
remember, cannibals, there is a God.
You eat your mother,
eat your father, eat children.
Oh cannibals remember the year is at an end.

159.

Valè mache m mache
pou m jwenn yon jan pou viv.
Ginen montre chemen;
nèg yo vle manje mwen.
Bondye o, sa m fè yo?
Depi m piti, gwo lwa yo reklame mwen
pou m fè sèvis Ginen an.
M pa konn pouki, mesye,
nèg yo vle manje mwen.

159.

The lengths I walk
to find a way to live.
Ginen shows the way;
the guys want to destroy me.
Oh God, what did I do to them?
Since I was a child, great lwa have claimed me
in order that I hold Ginen services.
I don't know why, sir,
the guys want to destroy me.

160.

Rasin Gran Bwa, pran kouraj o.
Avèk pasyans, gen yon lè n a va rive.
Yo pran rasin nan,
yo fè l tounen bwa dan yo;
yo pran atis yo,
yo fè l tounen tòchon yo.
Avèk pasyans, gen yon lè n a va rive.

160.

Oh roots of Gran Bwa, take heart.
With patience, there is a time we'll arrive.
They take the roots,
they make them into toothpicks;
they take the artists,
they turn them into dirty rags.
With patience, there is a time we'll arrive.

161.

Rasin Gran Bwa gen yon pàn estatè,
jou va jou vyen,
gen lè l a derape.
Atis yo, n se mekanisyen, si n vle travay,
gen yon lè n ap derape.

161.

Roots of Gran Bwa has a broken starter,
days come and go,
it seems like it will start.
Artists, you are mechanics, if you want work,
a time will come when we'll start.

162.

Ayayay, papa, yo pale nou mal o,
sa n fè yo?
Nou vire yo, n pa wè yo,
n chèche yo, n pa wè yo.
Ayayay, papa,
moun yo pa vle wè nou.
N ap rele Sen Jozèf,
pale l pou moun yo.

162.

Oh my goodness, man, they speak badly of us,
what did we do to them?
We turn them around, we don't see them,
we search for them, we don't see them.
My goodness, man,
the people don't want to see us.
We are calling Saint Joseph,
talk to him for the people.

163.

Se lwa k fè m sa, se lwa mwen.
Si m te pran ka lwa m,
m ta vire kò m.
M ta tounen kò m o.
Èzili Je Wouj la
se lwa k fè m sa o.

163.

It's a lwa that did this to me, it's my lwa.
If I took up the cause of my lwa,
I would spin myself around.
Oh I would turn myself around.
Oh Èzili Je Wouj
is the lwa who did this to me.

164.

Gramèt la inosan e, se bòn nouvèl la
li t ap bay, l inosan e.
Pou twa o ti pyès lajan
Jida vann Granmèt la.
Malgre l kloure sou lakwa,
l inosan e.

164.

Yeah the Lord is innocent, that's the good news
he was sharing, he's innocent yeah.
Oh for three pieces of silver
Judas betrayed the Lord.
Even though he was nailed on a cross,
hey he's innocent.

165.

Ann rasanble pou n fete nwèl o.
Se nan nich pay la
Mari te fè Jezi.
Se menm lè sa,
yon gwo etwal klere Bètleyèm
pou twa wa maj yo.
Mesye, n p ap ka bliye l o.

165.

Oh let's gather to celebrate Christmas.
It was in a nest of hay
that Mary gave birth to Jesus.
At the same time,
a great star shone upon Bethlehem
for the three Magi.
Sirs, oh we can't forget it.

166.

Siklòn Gòdon sa ki pote doulè a.
Siklòn Gòdon sa ki pote chagren an.
Siklòn Gòdon sa ki pote tristès la.
Lakay fanmi yo, papa, se rèl o.

166.

Hurricane Gordon that brought the pain.
Hurricane Gordon that brought the sorrow.
Hurricane Gordon that brought the sadness.
In the homes of families, oh man, it's weeping.

167.

Avan yè swa,
m t ap fè yon seremoni.

167.

The day before yesterday,
I was doing a ceremony.

M gen yon bon zanmi
k te vle gate seyans lan.
Mwen se yon ti zo
k nan mitan senkant chen.
Niche y a niche mwen,
yo p ap ka kraze mwen.

I have a good friend
who wanted to spoil the event.
I am a little bone
who is in the midst of fifty dogs.
For all their licking,
they can't break me.

168.

Se don mwen, se don mwen poutèt m ap fè
mizik mwen, men nèg yo vle manje mwen.
Se don mwen, se don mwen.
Gen moun ki wè m ap fè mizik,
yo konn se blag o.
Fè mizik se don, respekte sa, Ti Mal,
pa gad sa m fè
pou w di w ap fè tou.

168.

It's my gift, it's my gift because I am making
my music, but the guys want to destroy me.
It's my gift, it's my gift.
There are people who see me making music,
oh they think it's a joke.
Making music is a gift, respect it, Ti Mal,
don't look at what I do
only to say you'll do it too.

169.

Moun yo di y ap manje mwen;
yo pa konn lè m te fèt
men yo di y ap manje mwen.
Aprè Dye, m granmoun o.
Si n panse m pa granmoun,
mache sonde mwen pou nou wè.

169.

The people say they are going to destroy me;
they don't know when I was born
but they say they're going to destroy me.
After God, oh I'm a fully grown man.
If you don't think I'm a fully grown man,
start challenging me so that you can see.

170.

Nan kafou a nèg yo mare pwen an,
m di m prale wè, papa,
si m a lage li.
O nan kafou a
nèg yo mare pwen an.
M di m prale wè, papa,
si m a lage li.

170.

At the crossroads the guys tie up the charm,
I say I am going to see, man,
if I'll be able to release it.
Oh in the crossroads
the guys tie up the charm.
I say I'm going to see, man,
if I'll be able to release it.

171.

Kouzen o, se chak jou yon kwi
nan men w, w ap mande charite.
Kwi sa, kwi sa, konpè o.
Si jodi a se pou mwen, demen se pou ou.

171.

Oh cousin, every day there's a calabash bowl
in your hands, you are asking for charity.
This cup, this cup, oh old friend.
If today it's for me, tomorrow it's for you.

172.

Kouzen o,
paske w te fè m travay sila,
pito w te tiye mwen.

172.

Oh Cousin,
because you made me work like this,
I would rather you had killed me.

Ou voye m al mande moun yo,
moun yo pi mal pase mwen.
Kouzen o,
tan pou te fè m travay sila,
pito w te tiye mwen.

173.
Men gade mizè m ap pase o
nan peyi mwen.
M pa gen manman,
m pa gen papa nan peyi mwen.
Azaka m pral chèche lavi mwen
kote yo konnen mwen.

174.
Fanm sa, ou di ou se fanm chans mwen,
men manman fanm mwen li la,
ou pa konnen li.
Li ban m lajan, l ban m bijou,
l ban m afeksyon nan fè bagay,
Èzili se "nonbè wòn."

175.
Kite m viv o sosyete malpalan,
kite m viv o.
Mwen gen manman mwen, gen papa
se pou m viv o.
Kite m viv o sosyete dyòl ansanm,
kite m viv o.

176.
Viv pwen an,
viv dyab la nan demanbre m.
Anorzo nou pral salande
nan demanbre m.
Viv pwen,
viv dyab la nan demanbre m.

177.
Dyobolo Bosou mwen o, m a prale,
Anminan, sa k ap kenbe Gran Bwa
lè mwen pa la.
Moun yo voye rele mwen
pou zanfan ki malad.

You send me to go ask the people,
the people are worse off than me.
Oh Cousin,
rather than make me work like this,
it would be better if you had killed me.

173.
Oh look at the misery I am going through
in my country.
I don't have a mother,
I don't have a father in my country.
My Azaka is going to seek out a living
where they know me.

174.
That woman, you say she's my lucky woman,
but the mother of my woman is there,
you don't know her.
She gives me money, she gives me jewels,
she gives me affection in sex,
Èzili is "number one."

175.
Let me live, oh slanderous society,
oh let me live.
I have my mother, I have my father,
oh let me live.
Let me live, oh society of mouths in unison,
oh let me live.

176.
Long live the charm,
long live the dyab in my family ceremony.
Anorzo we are going to do Vodou
in my family ceremony.
Long live the charm,
long live the dyab in my family ceremony.

177.
Oh my Dyobolo Bosou, I'm going,
Anminan, the one who is keeping Gran Bwa
when I'm not here.
The people send for me
on account of the sick children.

Se mwen k manman papa zanfan la yo,
si yo malad, mezanmi,
se pou m ale pou m al bay o lavi o.

I'm the mother and father of the children,
if they are sick, my goodness,
oh I need to go in order to make them well.

178.
Gad jan m ap viv avèk nou,
nou pa konnen valè mwen.
Gen yon jou nan jou o n a bezwen mwen;
lè nou pa wè mwen,
lè sa n a wè valè mwen.

178.
Look at the way I'm living with you,
you don't know my value.
Oh there will be a day you will need me;
when you don't see me,
that's when you'll see my worth.

179.
Mwen se towo, lè m angaje
m konn pouse kòn mwen, m konn begle.
Amwa, m deja towo,
m konnen m ka begle.
Si w wè m pa begle, paske m pa angaje.

179.
I'm a bull, when I'm in trouble
I push out my horns, I bellow.
As for me, I'm already a bull,
I know I can bellow.
If you see I don't bellow, then I'm not in trouble.

180.
Paske m se malere,
yo mennen m nan prizon;
yo kondane mwen san jije.
Si mwen te gen lajan,
m t ap jwenn jistis o.
Malere ak chen se marasa nan peyi nwa yo,
pa gen jistis o.

180.
Because I am poor,
they lead me to prison,
they convict me without a trial.
If I had money,
oh I would find justice.
The poor and dogs are twins in black countries,
oh there is no justice.

181.
Nan pwonmennen m t ap chèche lavi mwen.
Nan chèche lavi mwen, gade s ak rive,
m vin wè sa lavi a fè mwen.
Moun yo pa respekte mwen,
tou sa se lavi a.
Nan pwonmennen m t ap chèche lavi mwen.
Nan chèche lavi mwen, gade s ak rive,
m vin wè sa lavi a fè mwen,
lavi a dwòl o.

181.
By walking I was seeking out a living.
In seeking out my living, look at what happened,
I came to see what this life did to me.
The people don't respect me,
all that is life.
While walking I was seeking out a living.
In seeking out my living, look at what happened,
I came to see what this life did to me,
oh life is strange.

182.
Adelina bèl fanm,
pawòl la pale.
Manman m voye m larivyè
al chèche mouchwa nwa.
Mouchwa pèdi avan lari konnen,
an n voye l ale.

182.
Adelina, beautiful woman,
the words are spoken.
My mother sent me to the river
to go search for a black handkerchief.
The handkerchief was lost before everyone knew,
let's send it away.

183.
Sen Jak o,
w a pale moun yo pou mwen.
Jan yo wè m fasil la,
se kon sa m danjere.
Sen Jak pa janm fache,
lè l fache, l danjere.
Sen Jak o,
w a pale moun yo pou mwen.
Jan yo wè m fasil la,
se kon sa m danjere.

183.
Oh Sen Jak,
you will speak to the people for me.
The way they see me as easy,
is how I'm dangerous.
Sen Jak is never angry,
when he's angry, he's dangerous.
Oh Sen Jak,
you will speak to the people for me.
The way they see me as easy,
is how I'm dangerous.

184.
Mwen koupe sèt chemen,
sèt kafou avan m jwenn pwen an.
Alèkile, si nèg yo vle manje m,
m ap fout rele pwen an pike kè yo.

184.
I cut seven paths,
seven crossroads before I found the charm.
At this point, if the guys want to destroy me,
I will fucking tell the charm to pierce their hearts.

185.
M pa towo bèf yo mennen m labatwa;
mesye pou y al tiye mwen.
Si yo te jije m o,
yo ta wè m inosan;
jij la ta ban m lavi o.

185.
I'm not a bull they lead to the slaughterhouse;
the guys are out to kill me.
Oh if they judged me,
they would see I'm innocent;
the judge would give me my life, oh.

186.
Annavan devan regleman
pwen an ki mande sa.
Pwen an di m, gad devan,
piga w vire dèyè, si mwen vire dèyè,
malè va rive mwen, sila moyo.

186.
March onward before the requirements
of the charm that asks this.
The charm tells me, look ahead,
don't turn around, if I turn around,
misfortune will come to me, sila moyo.

187.
Èzili mande dlo.
Kay la mande wouze la.
Si pa gen dlo,
n ap wouze l avèk losyon.

187.
Èzili asks for water.
The house needs to be sprinkled.
If there isn't water,
we're going to sprinkle it with lotion.

188.
Sa k pa kapab la,
ou te mèt ale o.
Nou deja rive la deja;
s ak gen pou l fèt la fò l fèt.

188.
Those who aren't able to be here,
oh you could have gone.
We have already arrived here already;
what has to be done here, it must be done.

189.

Kolobri fouye tou li,
se pou l pa move; mwen menm,
m fè afè mwen, se pou respè mwen.
Lapli tonbe sèt fwa, li pa move,
tyan gan nann, tyan gan nann o,
pa w se pa w, se mwen k ap komande l.

189.

The hummingbird digs his hole,
it's so he won't be angry; as for me,
I do my business, it's for my self-respect.
Rain fell seven times, it wasn't angry,
oh tyan gan nann, tyan gan nann,
what's yours is yours, I'm commanding it.

190.

Move tan pase, kay mwen koule,
kouman m pral fè
avèk vye zanfan yo.
Granmesi w, kwizin kite nan lakou a,
m te pare lapli a pou jou k demen,
ki fè mwen move.

190.

Bad weather came by, my house collapsed,
how am I going to make do
with the poor children.
Thanks to you, a kitchen in the yard,
I could hide from the rain until the next day;
that makes me mad.

191.

Lapli move mwen, solèy seche mò,
kalamite sa pi rèd o.
Manman mwen, papa mò anba tribilasyon sa,
m pa ka sipote l.

191.

My angry rain, the sun dried the dead,
oh that calamity is harder.
My mother and father dead in this tribulation,
I can't handle it.

192.

Pou w se Ginen, fò w gen fyèl o,
pou w sèvi lwa, fò w pa wont o.
Gen lwa k otan mechan
anvan pou w bon,
l ka fè w mande charite.

192.

To be a Ginen, oh you have to have courage,
to serve the lwa, oh you must not be ashamed.
There are lwa who are so mean
that before you're in a good position,
he can make you beg.

193.

Paske se mwen an ki fè yo fè mwen sa,
moun yo manje rezon mwen pou anyen o.
A wi gen yon tan m a wè yo.
Jou sakrifis la,
se yo k ap peye gay la.

193.

Because it's me who makes them do this to me,
oh the people destroy my motives for nothing.
Yes there is a time when I will see them.
The day of sacrifice,
they're the ones who will pay for the rooster.

194.

Moun sa yo di yo se Ginen,
y ap jwe rasin
epi yo nan konkirans.
Nou rasin Gran Bwa, nou sèmante
swansan disèt fwa pou n pale sa nou konnen,
tou sa nou wè, ak sa ki regade nou.

194.

These people say they are Ginen,
they are playing roots music
and they are competing.
We roots of Gran Bwa, we swear
seventy seven times to speak what we know,
all that we see, and what concerns us.

195.

De bra dèyè,
m pral ak moun yo, Kafou o.
M mande lese pase o
pou m al ak moun yo.
Kafou o, kay la manke moun o.
Kafou o, lese m ale ak moun yo,
de bra dèyè o.

195.

Two arms behind me,
I'm going with the people, oh Crossroads.
Oh I ask to be let through
so that I can go with the people.
Oh Crossroads, oh the house lacks people.
Oh Crossroads, let me go with the people,
oh two arms behind me.

196.

Ti zwazo kote w a prale o;
mwen prale kay fiyèt la;
depi m te toupiti,
yo di l manje timoun.
Ti zwazo, al kouche nan nich ou;
ret dousman pou w ka vin de jou o.

196.

Oh little bird where are you going;
I'm going to the house of the sorceress;
since I was small,
they say she devours children.
Little bird, go to sleep in your nest;
oh stay calm so that you can turn two days old.

CHAPTER 7

Benjamin Hebblethwaite's Songs

THIS CHAPTER includes songs that I collected during trips to Haiti in 1999, 2000, 2008, and 2009. Several of the songs were also shared by Oungan Nelson Marcenat during interviews with him.

Chante Hebblethwaite

Piti koudjay, 9 janvye, 2000

1.

Avoudayi, Itavila, Kongo,
lè moun nan fache, kote l chita?
Atè a.

Larèn Kongo a,
woule kongo a pou mwen,
Larèn Kongo a, woule kongo a,
m pral fè kongo a mache.
Larèn Kongo a, woule kongo a
pou n fè kongo a mache.

2.

Salwe, salwe Lavyèj Mari.
Salwe, salwe Lavyèj Mari o.
Sa k mande pou mwen,
men mwen prezante,
vin pale avè m.

Hebblethwaite's Songs

Small Celebration, January 9, 2000

1.

Avoudayi, Itavila, Kongo,
when a person is upset, where does he sit?
On the ground.

Queen of the Kongo,
roll the kongo for me.
Queen of the Kongo, roll the kongo,
I will make the kongo work.
Queen of the Kongo, roll the kongo
so that the kongo works.

2.

Greetings, greetings Virgin Mary.
Oh greetings, greetings Virgin Mary.
Those who call for me,
here I am before you,
come speak with me.

3.

Bawon Lakwa

Bawon konnen moun yo, konnen Bondye.
Mèt Bawon Lakwa
konnen moun yo, konnen Bondye.
Bawon o! Bawon Lakwa,
Bawon o konnen moun, konnen Bondye.
Bawon Papa konnen moun yo,
konnen Bondye.

—Sa se rit rasin Ginen!

3.

Bawon Lakwa

Bawon knows the people, knows God.
Master Bawon Lakwa
knows the people, knows God.
Oh Bawon! Bawon Lakwa,
Oh Bawon knows people, knows God.
Bawon Papa knows the people,
knows God.

—That was the rhythm of the roots of Ginen!

4.

Ogou

M ap vole, m ap rele Ogou o.
M pral vole, lè m vole,
m vole twò wo.
Si ou pa pare, pa rele Ogou sa.
M ap rele, m ap rele Ogou o.
Lè m vole, m vole twò wo.

Ogou travay o, Ogou pa manje.
Ogou travay o, Ogou pa manje.
Ogou sere lajan pou l achte yon bèl rechanj.
Bèl rechanj o, Ogou dòmi san soupe.
Ogoun pran chwal li
pou l achte yon bèl rechanj.
Bèl rechanj o,
pou l dòmi san soupe.

Tanbouyè n pa manman,
tanbouyè n pa papa.
Pase bagèt kote ou jwenn,
woule bagèt, pase bagèt.
Abobo!

4.

Ogou

I will jump, oh I will call Ogou.
I will jump, when I jump,
I jump too high.
If you aren't ready, don't call this Ogou.
I will call, oh I will call Ogou.
When I jump, I jump too high.

Oh Ogou works, Ogou doesn't eat.
Oh Ogou works, Ogou doesn't eat.
Ogou saves money to buy a beautiful suit.
Oh beautiful suit, Ogou sleeps without supper.
Ogoun takes his horse
to buy a beautiful suit.
Oh a beautiful suit,
so he'll sleep without supper.

Our drummer is not a mother,
our drummer is not a father.
Strike the drumstick where you find one,
roll the drumstick, strike the drumstick.
Abobo!

5.

Danbala

Danbala, men lwa koulèv la, ye!
Danbala, men lwa koulèv la, ba li siwo!
Danbala, men lwa koulèv la, ba li siwo!

5.

Danbala

Danbala, here is the snake lwa, yeah!
Danbala, here is the snake lwa, give him syrup!
Danbala, here is the snake lwa, give him syrup!

6.

Fèy yo

Fèy yo, sove lavi mwen nan mizè mwen ye o.
Fèy yo, sove lavi mwen nan mizè mwen ye o.
Pitit mwen malad, mwen kouri kay gangan,
Simbi o.
Si ou bon gangan,
sove lavi mwen nan mizè mwen ye o.

6.

Leaves

Oh leaves, save my life from the misery I'm in.
Oh leaves, save my life from the misery I'm in.
My child is ill, I run to the house of the gangan,
oh Simbi.
If you're a good gangan,
oh save my life from the misery I'm in.

7.

Lafanmi

Lafanmi vin fè san.
Vin fè san.
Seremoni an bèl o.

7.

Lafanmi

Family come be marked with blood.
Come be marked with blood.
Oh the ceremony is beautiful.

8.

Move Tan

Se mwen menm, Move Tan, o k pral pase.
Li bwote dlo pou touye dife sa.
Se mwen menm, Move Tan, o k ap pase.

8.

Move Tan

Oh it is I, Move Tan,[1] who will pass.
He carried water to extinguish this fire.
Oh it is I, Move Tan, who is passing.

9.

Peye san

Dèt la m te dwe a, dèt la peye.
M di dèt la m te dwe a, dèt la peye
pou m ale.

9.

Pay for the Sacrificial Blood

The debt that I owed, the debt is paid.
I said the debt that I owed, the debt is paid
in order for me to go forward.

10.

Danbala

Li syèl e dlatè, solèy yo,
Danbala Wèdo m solid o!
Li syèl o e dlatè, solèy yo,
Danbala Wèdo m solid o, wi!
Li syèl e dlatè, syèl e delatè,
Danbala Wèdo m solid o!

10.

Danbala

He is of the sky and of the earth, the suns,
Oh my Danbala Wèdo is strong!
Oh he of the sky and of the earth, the suns,
Oh my Danbala Wèdo is strong, yes indeed!
He of the sky and of the earth, sky and earth,
Oh my Danbala Wèdo is strong!

CHAPTER 8

Harold Courlander's Songs

BENJAMIN HEBBLETHWAITE
and ERICA FELKER-KANTOR

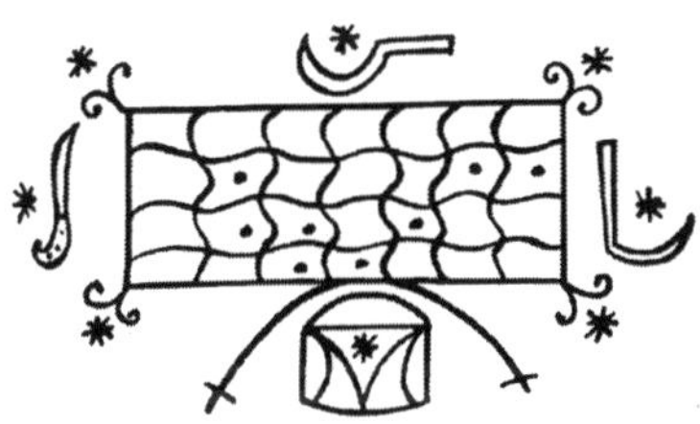

WHILE ATTENDING the Haitian Studies Association's meeting at Indiana University in Bloomington in 2009, I was able to investigate a few manuscripts I had found in the database of the Archives of Traditional Music. To my amazement, I discovered that the Harold Courlander collection of recordings made in Haiti in 1939–1940 included a 366-page manuscript of song transcriptions and translations. Courlander completed this undertaking over the two years that followed his fieldwork. He is well known for his important works in Haitian ethnomusicology and culture, *Haiti Singing* (1939) and *The Drum and the Hoe* (1960). According to a note attached to his manuscript, some of the songs in his corpus later appeared in *The Drum and the Hoe.* I have exclusively selected and edited materials from the manuscript (Courlander 1939–1940) because the songs were superbly transcribed, and it includes extensive footnotes about the meanings of the songs and the terminology within them. Although we have used some of Courlander's insights as endnotes in this chapter, many of his notes have been incorporated directly into Appendix A: Dictionary of Vodou Terms because they address notions that belong to the lexicon of the religion at large.

Courlander's corpus includes several genres, including children's songs, political songs, *chante pwen* (songs of reproach), and popular songs. However, the majority of the material is Vodouist. Here I include only Vodou songs. Only 50 of the approximately 150 in his corpus were incorporated because of space limitations. The songs in Courlander's corpus were collected as solos, duets, or arrangements with a song leader, a chorus, and rhythm instrumentation. Some of the songs were recorded outside the Vodou ritual context, while others were recorded in the course of Vodou services either at homes or at temples.[1]

Courlander's meticulous transcription methodology captures the slightest variations in the lyrics as a song cycles through repetitions and gradual embellishments. His method (Courlander 1939–1940) is empirical but consumes space that a work of this nature does not allow. Here we follow the more compact presentation of Vodou texts as they are found in Max Beauvoir's *Lapriyè Ginen* and *Le grand recueil sacré ou répertoire des chansons du vodou haïtien* (Beauvoir 2008a, 2008b). His method captures the songs' basic cycle of lyrics, which allows for the reproduction of a larger sample of songs.

We have updated Courlander's orthography, which employs the French conventions typical of the 1930s and 1940s. We have kept his frequent exclamation marks because they help represent the emotion and strength of these texts. Vodou songs are sung with a force that mirrors that of the Vodou system, with its thundering drums and powerful manifestations of the lwa. Courlander's exclamation marks capture an important truth about the *emphatics* of Vodou music and worship. Many of the songs refer to people who are calling the lwa or are being spoken through by the lwa. The vivid words and imagery represent the community's devotion to the lwa and express the power the lwa have in Vodou.

Chante Hawòl Koulèndè

1.

Ogoun Balindjo,
yo vini gade m
pou y ale pale o!
Ogoun Balindjo a,
je wè, bouch pe o!
Ogoun Balindjo,
ou pa wè yo vini gade mwen?

Ogoun Balindjo Sogo,
yo vini gade mwen
pou n ale pale o!
Ogoun o,
je wè, bouch pe!
Ago e ago e!

Harold Courlander's Songs

1.

Ogoun Balindjo,
oh they come to look at me
so they can go away and talk!
Ogoun Balindjo,
oh the eyes watch, the mouth is shut!
Ogoun Balindjo,
don't you see they come to look at me?

Ogoun Balindjo Sogo,
they come to look at me
oh so they can go away and talk!
Oh Ogoun,
the eyes watch, the mouth is closed!
Ago e ago e!

2.
Papa Ogoun, gade mizè!
Mèt Ogoun, gade mizè!
Gade mizè,
Papa Ogoun, gade mizè la!

Ogoun o, gade mizè!
Papa Ogoun sila, gade mizè!
O Soudjamen sila, gade mizè
Papa Ogoun sila, gade mizè!
O Soudjamen sila, gade mizè!
Abobo!

2.
Papa Ogoun, look at my misery!
Master Ogoun, look at my misery!
Look at my misery,
Papa Ogoun, look at my misery here!

Oh Ogoun, look at misery!
Papa Ogoun there, look at misery!
Oh that Soudjamen, look at misery!
That Papa Ogoun, look at misery!
Oh that Soudjamen, look at misery!
Abobo!

3.
Kondui m ale o!
Kondui m ale djab nan Twou Fouban,
kondui m ale!

3.
Oh lead me!
Lead me to the djab in Twou Fouban,
lead me away!

4.
Ogoun o, m se nèg Panama!
Yo vini gade!
Yo vini gade o!
O Ogoun o, m se nèg Panama!

Ogoun o Ogoun, Sogo kite!
Ogoun o, m se nèg Panama e!
Ogoun o, m se nèg Panama o!

Ogoun o, m se nèg Panama e!
Kata non!
Ogoun o, m se nèg Panama e!
Yo vini gade!
Yo vini pale o!
O Ogoun o, m se nèg Panama!
Ayibobo!

4.
Oh Ogoun, I am the Panama guy![2]
They come to look!
Oh they come to look!
Oh Ogoun oh, I am the Panama guy!

Ogoun oh Ogoun, Sogo is leaving!
Oh Ogoun, I am the Panama guy hey!
Oh Ogoun, I am the Panama guy oh!

Oh Ogoun, I am the Panama guy hey!
Beat the drums harder!
Oh Ogoun, I am the Panama guy hey!
They come to look!
Oh they come to talk!
Oh Ogoun oh, I am the Panama guy!
Ayibobo!

5.
Va Loko Yenvalo!
Va Loko Yenvalo!
Va Loko Yenvalo!
Mèt Ogoun Fè, Yenvalo!

Yenvalo, Mèt Ogoun Fè, Yenvalo!
Abobo!

5.
Go away Loko Yenvalo!
Go away Loko Yenvalo!
Go away Loko Yenvalo!
Master Ogoun Fè, Yenvalo!

Yenvalo, Master Ogoun Fè, Yenvalo!
Abobo!

6.
Abobo!
Adja, nou mele, o Adja o!
Adja, nou mele!
Nou mele, Papa Loko,
nou mele jodi a!

Adja, nou mele, o Adja o!
Adja, nou mele!
O nou mele Sedje, ase,
nou mele jodi a!

O nou mele, Kile Oude, nèg Sobo,
nou mele jodi a!

O nou mele, Sèklekite,
nou mele jodi a!
Nou mele wi, Sobo,
nou mele jodi a!
Nou mele, Bawon Samdi,
nou mele la!
Nou mele wi, nèg Parenn,
o nèg Feray,
nou mele jodi a!
Adja, nou mele, o Adja o!
Adja, nou mele!
Abobo!

6.
Abobo!
Adja, we are all mixed up, oh Adja oh!
Adja, we are all mixed up!
We are mixed up, Papa Loko,
we are all mixed up today!

Adja, we are all mixed up, oh Adja oh!
Adja, we are all mixed up!
Oh we are mixed up Sedje, enough,
we are all mixed up today!

Oh we are mixed up, Kile Oude, Sobo Guy,
we are all mixed up today!

Oh we are mixed up, Sèklekite,
we are all mixed up today!
Yes, we are mixed up, Sobo,
we are all mixed up today!
We are mixed up, Bawon Samdi,
we are all mixed up here!
Yes, we are all mixed up, Godparents,
oh Feray Guy,
we are all mixed up today!
Adja, we are all mixed up, oh Adja oh!
Adja, we are all mixed up!
Abobo!

7.
Ogoun Balindjo,
O Ogoun o!
Ogoun Balindjo,
O Ogoun o!
Se pa manje ranje
ki pral touye chwal mwen!

7.
Ogoun Balindjo,
Oh Ogoun oh!
Ogoun Balindjo,
Oh Ogoun oh!
It's not poisoned food
that's going to kill my horse!

8.
Lakarantèn, twa dam, twa vyèj,
priyè pou sen yo,
lapriyè pou lesen mache!

Lakarantèn, twa dam, twa vyèj,
priyè pou sen yo,
Lapriyè pou lesen mache!

8.
Forty days, three women, three virgins,
pray for the saints,
pray for the saints to walk!

Forty days, three women, three virgins,
pray for the saints,
Pray for the saints to walk!

Priyè pou lesen yo!
Priyè pou lwa yo,
Sent Antwàn o,
n ape mande padon!

Pray for the saints!
Pray for the lwa,
Oh Saint Anthony,
we are asking for forgiveness!

Lakarantèn, twa dam, twa vyèj,
Priyè pou sen yo,
lapriyè pou lesen mache!
Lakarantèn, twa dam, twa vyèj,
priyè pou lesen yo,
lapriyè pou lesen mache!
Priyè pou lwa yo!

Forty days, three women, three virgins,
Pray for the saints,
pray for the saints to walk!
Forty days, three women, three virgins,
pray for the saints,
pray for the saints to walk!
Pray for the lwa!

9.
Sen Jak mare chwal li,
li pa di pèsonn o,
veye li pou mwen!
Li mèt genyen vè,
li mèt genyen maleng nan do,
Sen Jak o!
Ba li lavi pou mwen!

9.
Saint James ties his horse,
oh he doesn't tell anyone,
watch him for me!
He might have worms,
he might have sores on his back,
Oh Saint James!
Give him life for me!

10.
Ogoun vole, Achade!
Ou vole, papa!
Nago o!
Anago!
Ogoun vole, Achade!
Nago Sobo!
Ogoun vole!
Anago!

10.
Ogoun flies, Achade!
You fly, man!
Oh Nago!
Anago!
Ogoun flies, Achade!
Nago Sobo!
Ogoun flies!
Anago!

11.
Nan Ginen genyen lwa o!
Èvo èvo ounsi kanzo!
Nan Ginen genyen lwa, ayibobo!

11.
Oh in Ginen there are lwa!
Èvo èvo ounsi kanzo!
In Ginen there are lwa, ayibobo!

12.
Danbala Wèdo, o se san e!
Danbala Wèdo, o se san e!
Danbala mande tèt kabrit,
se san li mande!
O ase!

12.
Danbala Wèdo, oh it's blood, hey!
Danbala Wèdo, oh it's blood, hey!
Danbala asks for the head of a goat,
it's blood he asks for!
Only that!

13.

O Adja manje bounda dèmijon!
Adja vye kò, vye kò!
Adja manje bounda dèmijon!
Adjasou a, vye kò, vye kò!

13.

Oh Adja eats glass!
Adja, the old one, the old one!
Adja eats glass!
The Adjasou, old one, old one!

14.

Lakaye nou la, nou la!
Lakaye, koulèv vale wanga!
Koulèv vale wanga mwen!
Koulèv vale wanga mwen sa!

Ti gason, men zobòp, wye wye,
men zobòp!
Ti gason, men zonbi, wye wye,
men zonbi!
Abobo Abobo Abobo!

14.

Lakaye,[3] we're here, we're here!
In Lakaye, a snake swallowed my wanga!
A snake swallowed my wanga!
A snake swallowed my wanga there!

Little boy, here is the zobòp, wye wye,
here is the zobòp!
Little boy, here is the zombie, wye wye,
here is the zombie!
Abobo Abobo Abobo!

15.

Lafanmi, li fè sa!
Lazile Ibo volonte!
Lafanmi, li fè sa! O eya!
Lafanmi, li fè sa! Li fè sa!
Lafanmi, li fè sa!
O taybo!

15.

The family, it does this!
Lazile Ibo decides!
The family, it does this! Oh yeah!
The family, it does this! It does this!
The family, it does this!
Oh what a beautiful gesture!

16.

Chache lwa yo! Nou bare lwa yo!
Nou chache lwa yo! Nou bare lwa yo!
Èzili Freda kote lwa yo ye?
Yo mare Leyogàn o!
Èzili Freda, sa fè mwen lapenn o!
Mwen kriye!

16.

Look for the lwa! We bar the lwa!
We look for the lwa! We bar the lwa!
Èzili Freda, where are the lwa?
Oh they're tied down in Leyogann![4]
Oh Èzili Freda, that hurts me!
I cry!

17.

Jan Zonbi, o wi wa, kondwi m ale!
M pa bwè tafya, m pa bwè siwo!
Kondwi m ale, Jan Zonbi, o wi wa!

Wòy! Jan Zonbi, vini wè mwen,
kondwi m ale!
M pa bwè tafya pou nou fè tenten!
Devan hounfò mwen, kondwi m ale!
M pa bwè tafya pou nou fè tenten!

17.

Jan Zombie, oh wi wa, take me away!
I didn't drink rum, I didn't drink syrup!
Come take me, Jan Zombie, oh wi wa!

Oh my! Jean Zombie, come see me,
take me away!
I didn't drink rum so that you could act stupidly!
Before my hounfò, come take me away!
I didn't drink rum so that you could act stupidly!

18.

Dawomen i wa oungenikon o!
Dawomen i wa genikon e!
Danwomen i wa, yo fè manje rezon mwen!
Lè mwen vle pale, ou pa vle mwen pale!
Lè mwen vle chante, ou pa vle mwen chante!
Dawomen i wa, yo fè manje rezon mwen!

Dawomen i wa, oungenikon e!
O Sobagi i wa, oungenikon i wa!
Dawomen i wa, yo fè manje rezon mwen!
Lè mwen vle pale, ou pa vle mwen pale!
Lè mwen vle jwe, ou pa vle mwen jwe la!
Dawomen i wa yo fè manje rezon mwen!

18.

Oh Dawomen i wa oungenikon!
Dawomen i wa genikon hey!
Dawomen i wa, they do me wrong![5]
When I want to speak, you don't allow me to speak!
When I want to sing, you don't allow me to sing!
Dawomen i wa, they do me wrong!

Dawomen i wa, oungenikon hey!
O Sobagi i wa, oungenikon i wa!
Dawomen i wa, they do me wrong!
When I want to speak, you don't want me to speak!
When I want to play, you don't want me to play!
Dawomen i wa, they do me wrong!

19.

M ape rele, mwen anba paviyon lwa mwen!
Lese m demele mwen anba paviyon Dereya!
Jou m ale, pinga yo lonmen non mwen!

Demele demele anba paviyon mwen!
Lese m demele anba paviyon Dereya!
O jou m ale o, pinga yo lonmen non mwen!

Lese m demele mwen!

19.

I am calling, I am under my lwa's pavilion![6]
Let me figure it out under Dereya's pavilion!
The day I go, they had better not call my name!

Let me figure it out under my pavilion!
Let me figure it out under Dereya's pavilion!
Oh the day I go, oh they better not call my name!

Let me figure it out!

20.

Sende, Sende Makaya!
Chache yon fanm ki bèl o!
Sende, Sende Makaya!

20.

Sende, Sende Makaya!
Oh look for a beautiful woman!
Sende, Sende Makaya!

21.

Èzili Fre, Èzili Freda,
kote w kite kò an nou ye?
Èzili Fre, Freda Dawomen,
kote w kite kò an nou ye?

21.

Èzili Fre, Èzili Freda,
where have you gone?
Èzili Fre, Freda Dawomen,
where have you gone?

22.

Ban mwen, m a pran!
Se kon sa ou vle ban mwen!
Ban mwen, m a pran!
E se kon sa ou vle ban mwen!

22.

Give it to me, I will take it![7]
You want to give it to me like that!
Give it to me, I will take it!
And you want to give it to me like that!

23.

Nèg Nago, w a vini wè mwen!
Nèg Nago, w a vini wè mwen!
Nèg Nago, w a vini wè mwen la,
o Sen an!

Nèg Nago, w a vini wè mwen!
Ochan Nago, w a vini wè mwen!
Nèg Nago, w a vini wè mwen la,
o sen an!
Avotayi!

23.

Nago Guy,[8] you will come see me!
Nago Guy, you will come see me!
Nago Guy, you will come see me here,
oh Saint!

Nago Guy, you will come see me!
Praises to Nago, you will come see me!
Nago Guy, you will come see me here,
oh the saint!
Avotayi!

24.

File n a file, Danbala Wèdo, vini wè mwen!
File n a file, Nèg Nago, vini wè m la!
File n a file, Papa Wèdo, vini wè mwen!

24.

We'll slither indeed, Danbala Wèdo, come see me!
We'll slither indeed, Nago Guy, come see me here!
We'll slither indeed, Papa Wèdo, come see me!

25.

Mèt Agwe soti nan lanmè,
kanon m chaje e!
Mèt Agwe soti nan lanmè,
kanon m chaje o!
Kanon m chaje pou m tire, Mèt Awoyo!

25.

Master Agwe comes from the sea,
my cannon is loaded hey![9]
Master Agwe was born in the sea,
oh my cannon is loaded!
My cannon is loaded to fire, Master Awoyo!

26.

Ou poko hounsi o!
Ou di m ou se houngan!
Ou poko hounsi!
Ou di m ou se houngan, se sa!
O pay atè!
Pouse ale!
O Alada malad o!

26.

Oh you are not a hounsi yet!
You tell me you are a houngan!
You are not a hounsi yet!
You tell me you are a hougan, yeah right!
Oh straw on the ground!
Push away!
Oh Alada is ill oh!

27.

Laye, laye!
Laye, laye o vye kò!
Tanbouyè bouke!
Laye, laye o!
Tanbouyè bouke!

O laye, laye o vye kò!
Laye, laye Dawomen!
Tanbouyè bouke la!
Laye, laye, vye kò!

27.

Dance, dance!
Dance, oh dance old friend!
The drummers are tired!
Dance, oh dance!
The drummers are tired!

Oh dance, oh dance old friend!
Dance, dance the Dawomen!
The drummers are tired!
Dance, dance, old friend!

Laye, laye Dawomen!
Vye mouche bouke, frè mwen!

Dance, dance the Dawomen!
The old man is tired, my brother!

Laye, laye!
O laye, laye vye kò!
M pote ou sou do m, Dawomen!
Vye manman bouke, papa!

Dance, dance!
Oh dance, dance old friend!
I'll carry you on my back, Dawomen!
The old mothers are tired, man!

Tanbouyè bouke!
Tanbouyè bouke, oungan!
Peye lajan vye kò!
Tanbouyè bouke o!

The drummers are tired!
The drummers are tired, oungan!
Pay the money old friend!
Oh the drummers are tired!

28.

Wanga sa, o wanga sa!
O lè pou peye m, pinga w fache!
Ou mande m wanga la, ou kontan!
Men lè pou peye m, pinga w fache!

Wanga sa, wanga sa cho!
Lè pou peye li, pinga w fache!
Ou renmen wanga la, ou kontan!
Ou mande m wanga la, ou kontan!
Lè pou peye li, pinga w fache!

28.

This wanga, oh this wanga!
Oh when it comes time to pay me, don't get angry!
When you ask me for the wanga, you are happy!
But when it comes time to pay me, don't get angry!

This wanga, this wanga is hot magic!
When it comes time to pay for it, don't get angry!
You like the wanga, you are happy!
When you ask me for the wanga, you are happy!
When it comes time to pay for it, don't get angry!

29.

Si nou wè kote m demere,
fò m peye bon bon pou sa!
Anago Nago!
Vin kote m demere!

29.

If you see where I live,
I must pay well for that!
Anago Nago!
Come see where I live!

30.

Nago rive e!
Boulicha Nago rive e!
Nago rive e!
Boulicha Nago rive e!
Li lè, li tan, bata la!
Nago rive jodi a, o enhen!

30.

Nago arrives hey!
Boulicha Nago arrives hey!
Nago arrives hey!
Boulicha Nago arrives hey!
It is the hour, it is the time, beat the drums!
Nago arrives today, oh yeah!

31.

Ogoun Yèkè Yèkè Nèg Kenizon e!
O toulejou n ape pale
Ogoun mal!
Ogoun pa konn betize!

31.

Ogoun Yèkè Yèkè Kenizon Guy hey!
Oh every day you're speaking
badly about Ogoun!
Ogoun doesn't like joking!

32.

Ogoun e, o mwen blese!
O Feray, o monchè, o mwen blese!
Apa m blese!
M pa wè san mwen!
M pa wè san m, Badagri,
Mwen pa wè san mwen!
Mwen pa wè san poto plante,
mwen pa wè san m ankò!

32.

Ogoun hey, oh I am hurt!
Oh Feray, oh my friend, oh I am hurt!
Look I am hurt!
I do not see my blood!
I do not see my blood Badagri,
I do not see my blood!
I don't see blood at the planted centerpost,
I do not see my blood anymore![10]

33.

Yabofe monchè, yo pa bezwen mwen!
M prale wè mitan
si n ap djagwe!
Yabofe monchè, yo pa bezwen mwen!
M prale wè mitan
si m a djagwè!
Yabofe monchè,
yo pa bezwen mwen ankò!
M prale wè mitan
si y a djagwe!

33.

Yabofe my friend, they don't need me!
I'm going to the center post to see
if we're going to writhe!
Yabofe my friend, they don't need me!
I'm going to the center post to see
if I will writhe!
Yabofe my friend,
they don't need me anymore!
I'm going to the center post to see
if they will writhe!

34.

Se pase n ap pase la!
Se pase m ap pase la!
E hounsi bosal e, yo lonmen non mwen!
Yo lonmen non mwen, yo lonmen non mwen!
Yo rele hounsi kanzo!
Yo rele Dawomen!
Yo rele mwen!

Se pase n a pase, Nèg Dawomen, n a pase!
N a pase, Sèklekite, n a pase!
Gede sa, n a pase!
Nèg ason, n a pase!
Se pase!
N ape pase la!
Mwen pase!
Yo di yo lonmen non mwen!

Se pase, Sobo, n a pase!
Se pase mwen di m a pase la!
Pou wè m pase!
Yo di y ap lonmen non mwen!

34.

We are passing here!
I am passing here!
Hey hounsi bosal hey, they call my name!
They call my name, they call my name!
They call the hounsi kanzo!
They call Dawomen!
They call me!

We will pass, Dawomen Guy, we will pass!
We will pass, Sèklekite, we will pass!
That Gede, we will pass!
Guy with the sacred rattle, we will pass!
We pass!
We are passing here!
I pass!
They say they called my name!

We pass, Sobo, we will pass!
I say I will pass here!
To see me pass!
They say they are calling my name!

Lonmen non mwen, ase, lonmen non mwen!
Lonmen non hounsi kanzo,
lonmen non mwen,
nèg Dawomen, lonmen non mwen!
Se pase mwen di m ap pase!
Mwen pase!
Yo di yo lonmen non mwen!

Se pase, Nèg Dawomen, n a pase!
N a pase, Sèklekite, Nègès Kreyòl,
n a pase!
N a pase, Jan Bato, n a pase,
Nèg Dawomen, n a pase, Nèg Feray,
n a pase!
Se pase n ape pase la!
Mwen pase!
Yo di yo lonmen non mwen!

Call my name, enough, call my name!
Call the hounsi kanzo's name,
call my name,
Dawomen Guy, call my name!
I say I am passing!
I pass!
They say they called my name!

We pass, Dawomen Guy, we will pass!
We will pass, Sèklekite, Creole Beauty,
we will pass!
We will pass, Jean Bato, we will pass,
Dawomen Guy, we will pass, Feray Guy,
we will pass!
We are indeed passing here!
I pass!
They say they called my name!

35.

Èzili Nennen o!
Èzili o, se mwen Yagaza!

Èzili n ap mache, n ap koute,
n ap pale,
poutan y ap pale pawòl mwen!
Èzili Nennen o!
Èzili Freda o, Nennen o!
Èzili Freda o, se mwen Yagaza!

Medam nan yo chita nan kay la,
Yo vle djaye o
tout tan solèy pa leve!
Medam yo pase,
y a tonbe atè ajenou,
y ape plenyen lesò yo!
Èzili Nennen o!
Èzili o, se mwen Yagaza!

Lawouze fè banda tout tan solèy pa leve!
Èzili Nennen o!
Èzili Freda o, kote mwen bò Yagaza!

35.

Oh Godmother Èzili!
Oh Èzili, I am Yagaza!

Èzili we are walking, we are listening,
we are speaking,
at yet they are speaking my words!
Oh Godmother Èzili!
Oh Èzili Freda, oh Godmother!
Oh Èzili Freda, I am Yagaza!

The women are sitting in the house,
They want to dance in trance
as long as the sun hasn't risen!
The women pass,
they will fall to the ground on their knees,
they are complaining about their troubles!
Oh Godmother Èzili!
Oh Èzili, I am Yagaza!

The dew glistens as long as the sun hasn't risen!
Oh Godmother Èzili!
Oh Èzili Freda, I'm on Yagaza's side!

Èzili Freda, Nèg Sobo, Nèg Gran Chimen,
nèg Bale Wouze, Sèklekite, abobo sa!
Èzili Nennen o!
Èzili Freda kote w ye, mwen la Yagaza!

Èzili Freda, Sobo Guy, Gran Chimen Guy,
Bale Wouze Guy, Sèklekite, that abobo!
Oh Godmother Èzili!
Èzili Freda, where are you, I'm here Yagaza!

Medam nan yo pase nan bout kay la,
yo jete ajenou,
y ape plenyen mizè yo!
Medam nan yo pase nan kay la,
y a plenyen mizè yo!
Èzili Nennen o!
Èzili sa, kote mwen Yagaza!

The women go to the end of the house,
they fall to their knees,
they are complaining about their misery!
The women are passing through the house,
they are complaining of their misery!
Oh Godmother Èzili!
That Èzili, I'm on Yagaza's side!

36.
Danbala!
Danbala e!
Danbala Wèdo!
Danbala konsakre!
Danbala enhen!
Danbala konsakre!
O Danbala!

36.
Danbala!
Danbala hey!
Danbala Wèdo!
Danbala is consecrated!
Danbala yeah!
Danbala is consecrated!
Oh Danbala!

37.
Ibo lele! Ibo lele!
Pile pye m, ou mande m padon!
Sa padon la va fè pou mwen?

37.
Ibo is crying out![11] Ibo is crying out!
You step on my foot, you ask for my apology!
What will the apology do for me?[12]

38.
Mari Lwiz Kanga, nou mele!
Mari Lwiz, o nou mele!
Kote sa w ban mwen pou m ale?

38.
Mari Lwiz Kanga, we are mixed up!
Mari Lwiz, oh we are mixed up!
Where is what you give me for me to go?

39.
Nou vle wè oungan!
O nou vle wè o!
Nou vle wè o!
Si y a kite kay la tonbe!
Ngan o!

Nou vle wè Yaminyan an!
Nou vle wè!
Nou vle wè msye Dou a!
Nou vle wè!
Nou vle wè fèy bwa sa!

39.
We want to see the oungan!
Oh we want to see oh!
We want to see oh!
If they'll let the house fall!
Oh Ngan!

We want to see the Yaminyan!
We want to see!
We want to see mister Dou!
We want to see!
We want to see those leaves in the woods!

Nou vle wè, pale moun yo pou mwen!	We want to see, speak to the people for me!
Nou vle wè, aye!	We want to see, oh hey!
Nou vle wè o, si y a kite kay la tonbe!	Oh we want to see if they will let the house fall!
Nou vle wè Bondye!	We want to see God!
Nou vle wè o!	Oh we want to see!
Nou vle wè o!	Oh we want to see!
Si y a kite kay la tonbe!	If they'll let the house fall!
Ngan o!	Oh Ngan!
Nou vle wè Yaminyan sa!	We want to see that Yaminyan!
Nou vle wè!	We want to see!
Nou vle wè Balindjo!	We want to see Balindjo!
Nou di nou vle wè!	We say we want to see!
Si-Azaka, nou vle wè!	Si-Azaka, we want to see!
Kanga Twa, nou vle wè, aye!	Kanga Twa, we want to see, hey!
Nou vle wè Kanga Twa, nou vle wè!	We want to see Kanga Twa, we want to see!
Machè Danbala Vè!	My dear Danbala Vè!
Nou pral chache Kokinandlo	We're going to look for Kokinandlo
pou n al fè travay nou!	so we can go do our work!
Fè travay Takwa, travay o!	Do the work Takwa, oh work!
N a fè travay la!	We will work here!
Wi, nou vle wè nan dekou!	Yes, we want to see at the new moon!
Nou vle wè moun sa yo!	We want to see those people!
Ngan o!	Oh Ngan!
Nou vle wè o!	Oh we want to see!
Nou vle wè sa, si y a kite kay tonbe!	We want to see this, if they will let the house fall!
Ngan o! Di o!	Oh Ngan! Oh say!
Monchè Takwa a nou vle wè!	My friend Takwa we want to see!
Nou vle wè Dansi Osou, o nou vle wè!	We want to see Dansi Osou, oh we want to see!
Yaki Bosan, nou vle wè o!	Yaki Bosan, oh we want to see!
Ngan o!	Oh Ngan!
Nou vle wè Akwa a, nou vle wè o!	We want to see Akwa, oh we want to see!
Nou vle wè si y a kite kay tonbe!	We want to see if they will let the house fall!
Ngan o!	Oh Ngan!
40.	**40.**
Makaya Boumba Boubma!	Makaya Boumba Boumba!
Leve danse!	Get up and dance!
Makaya Boumba!	Makaya Boumba!
Kaya Boumba, leve danse!	Kaya Boumba, get up and dance!

Mèt Boumba, vini danse!
Boumba, monchè, vini danse!
Mèt Boumba, m prale danse!
Mèt Boumba, nou prale danse!

Master Boumba, come and dance!
Boumba, my friend, come and dance!
Master Boumba, I will dance!
Master Boumba, we will dance!

41.

O mwen Loko,
kote hounsi mwen yo!

Kote hounsi mwen yo,
mennen m nan hounfò,
m ap djaye!
  Hounfò o,
  kote hounsi mwen yo!

Mennen m nan hounfò Loko,
mennen m nan hounfò,
m ap djaye!
  Nan hounfò Loko,
  kote pitit mwen yo!

Kote pitit mwen yo,
mennen m nan hounfò,
m ap djaye!
  Apa Loko,
  kote pitit mwen yo!

41.

Oh I am Loko,
where are my hounsi!

Where are my hounsi,
bring me to the temple,
I am trembling in the spirit!
  Oh temple,
  where are my hounsi!

Bring me to Loko's temple,
bring me to the temple,
I am trembling in the spirit!
  In Loko's temple,
  where are my children!

Where are my children,
bring me to the temple,
I am trembling in the spirit!
  Here is Loko,
  where are my children![13]

42.

Fèy nan bwa, kon sa nou ye!
Nanpwen renmen pa mande kite!
Simbi Andezo
ki sòti anba dlo,
gade sa yo fè mwen!
M di Lolo, ban mwen nouvèl pou m ba yo!

42.

Leaves in the woods, that's how we are![14]
There is no love that asks to break up!
Simbi Andezo
who comes from under the sea,
see what they do to me!
I tell Lolo, give me the news to give to them!

43.

Papa Danbala, ou se koulèv o!
Pouki w pa neye?
Pouki w pa neye?
Danbala, pouki ou pa neye nan dlo?

Papa Danbala, ou se koulèv o!
Pouki w pa neye?
Danbala Wèdo, se koulèv o!

43.

Oh Papa Danbala, you are a snake!
Why don't you drown?
Why don't you drown?
Danbala, why don't you drown in the water?

Papa Danbala, oh you are a snake!
Why don't you drown?
Danbala Wèdo, oh you are a snake!

Pouki w pa neye?
Danbala, pouki w pa neye nan dlo?

Domisi Wèdo, se koulèv o!
Ayida Wèdo, se koulèv o!

Papa Danbala, Ayida Wèdo se koulèv!
Pouki w pa neye?
Danbala Wèdo, se koulèv o!
Pouki w pa neye?
Pouki w pa neye?
Danbala, pouki w pa neye nan dlo?
Abobo!

Why don't you drown?
Danbala, why don't you drown in the water?

Oh Domisi Wèdo is a snake!
Oh Ayida Wèdo you are a snake!

Papa Danbala, Ayida Wèdo, you are snakes!
Why don't you drown?
Danbala Wèdo, oh you are a snake!
Why don't you drown?
Why don't you drown?
Danbala, why don't you drown in the water?
Abobo!

44.
Moundong o yè, yè, yè!
Moundong o!
O Moundong, o yè, yè, yè!
Moundong o!
O Moundong manje kabrit boule!
Moundong manje kabrit boukannen!

44.
Moundong oh yeah, yeah, yeah!
Oh Moundong!
Oh Moundong, oh yeah, yeah, yeah!
Oh Moundong!
Oh Moundong eats grilled goat!
Moundong eats roasted goat!

45.
Kote w pase, n a ba w manje,
o Moundong nan!
Kote w pase, n a ba w manje,
O ti Moundong nan!

45.
Wherever you go, we will give you food,
oh the Moundong!
Wherever you go, we will give you food,
oh the little Moundong!

46.
Maryani o!
O adye Moundong!
O Maryani!
Kote m pase!
Mwen pase bò isi!

Maryani o!
Adye Moundong o!
Maryani o!
Moundong!
Rele Maryani—e!—o!
Moundong o!
Maryani la!
Kote m pase!
Mwen pase!
Mwen kite la!

46.
Oh Maryani!
Oh farewell Moundong!
Oh Maryani!
Where I pass!
I pass over here!

Oh Maryani!
Oh farewell Moundong!
Oh Maryani!
Moundong!
Call Maryani—hey!—oh!
Oh Moundong!
Maryani is here!
Where I pass!
I pass!
I leave here![15]

47.

Fèy nan bwa rele mwen!
O fèy nan bwa rele mwen!
O depi m piti, m ap danse la!
Fèy nan bwa e, rele mwen e!
O fèy nan bwa e rele mwen o!

Ago-Tchi!
Ago-Tchi!
Loko-Tchi, Loko-Tchi!

O fèy nan bwa rele mwen o!
O depi m piti, m ap rele!
Fèy nan bwa!
Rele mwen!
Fèy nan bwa e!

47.

Leaves in the woods call me!
Oh leaves in the woods call me!
Oh since I was small, I have danced here!
Leaves in the woods hey, call me hey!
Oh leaves in the woods hey, oh call me!

Ago-Tchi!
Ago-Tchi!
Loko-Tchi, Loko-Tchi!

Oh leaves in the woods call me!
Oh since I was small, I have cried out!
Leaves in the woods!
Call me!
Leaves in the woods hey!

48.

File n a file!
Danbala Wèdo, se koulèv o!
File n a file, se koulèv o!

48.

We shall slither!
Danbala Wèdo, oh he is a snake!
We shall slither, oh he is a snake!

49.

Van, van, van!
Loko Sende mande van e!
Van, van, van!
Loko Sende mande van e!
Abobo!

49.

Wind, wind, wind!
Loko Sende asks for the wind hey!
Wind, wind, wind!
Loko Sende asks for the wind hey!
Abobo!

50.

Kay mwen foula!
O kay mwen foula!
Kay mwen santi foula!
Santi Makaya!

50.

My house has received vaporized rum!
Oh my house has received vaporized rum!
My house smells of vaporized rum!
It smells of Makaya!

Oungan Nelson Marcenat with his *ason* (sacred rattle) and *klòch* (bell).

Marcenat in front of his *pewon* (altar).
(Courtesy of Keeley Forrestel.)

The upper portion of Marcenat's *pewon*. The knotted ropes are used to "tie up" illness.

A *Ginen* (skull of a Vodouist) at the base of Marcenat's *pewon*. The skull is used for ritual, medicine, and memorializing the ancestors in Vodou.

The three-section *plat Marasa* (Marasa plate) placed on the top level of Marcenat's *pewon*.

Marcenat's altar in 2008.

Assorted items on Marcenat's altar in 2009, including the *ason,* human bones, dolls, a faded chromolithograph of Saint Peter (i.e., Legba), and the Bible in French. The chromolithograph deteriorated significantly in the year between 2008 and 2009, after Haiti was struck by four hurricanes.

Marcenat's Bible on his *pewon*, opened to the Epitre de Jacques (Epistle of James). Saint James is assimilated with Ogou, one of Marcenat's principal lwa.

A Vodou mobile that hangs above Marcenat's *pewon*.

A symbolic tomb just below the top layer of Marcenat's *pewon*. The tomb is the residence of the lwa Gede and Bawon.

A wooden cross next to Marcenat's *pewon*.

Marcenat's *pewon* in 2008. The woman in the framed image is Jezebel, whom Marcenat links with the lwa Rèn Siyèt.

A rooster being raised in the *pewon* for cockfighting.

An outside view of Marcenat's altar room.

The entrance to Marcenat's altar room.

Marcenat, his wife, and members of his family outside his home. *(Courtesy of Don Miller.)*

The tobacco leaves that Marcenat grows, cures, and sells to supplement his income. *(Courtesy of Keeley Forrestel.)*

A Vodou temple located near Leyogann.
(Courtesy of Keeley Forrestel.)

The exterior of the Leyogann temple. The priest of this temple refers to himself as a bòkò rather than an oungan because he serves "cool" and "hot" lwa.

The exterior of the Leyogann temple. The mural shows Boukmann Dutty's Bwa Kayiman ceremony of 1791. The manbo is about to sacrifice a pig.

The Leyogann temple. Above the crown is written "Wa Lesifè" (King Lucifer) and below the figure, "Metrès Lesifè" (Mistress Lucifer).

A figure with a cross painted on an interior wall of the Leyogann temple.
(Courtesy of Keeley Forrestel.)

The lwa Lasirenn (the Mermaid) painted on the wall at the Leyogann temple. *(Courtesy of Keeley Forrestel.)*

The altar of the Leyogann bòkò. The words painted on the wall read "*Fouye w a jwenn*" (Seek [and] you will find). *(Courtesy of Keeley Forrestel.)*

Figures, bottles, and statues on the Leyogann bòkò's altar. *(Courtesy of Keeley Forrestel.)*

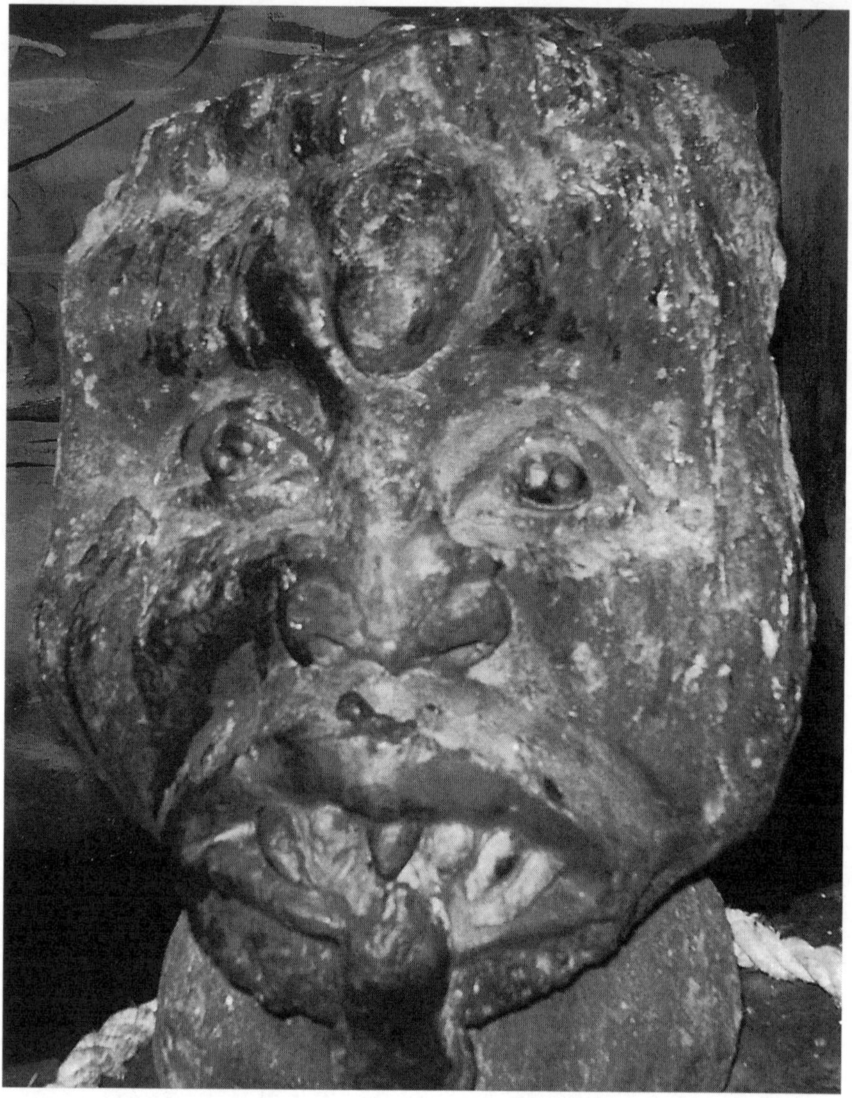

A Vodou statue in the Leyogann temple.
(Courtesy of Keeley Forrestel.)

APPENDIX A

Dictionary of Vodou Terms

BENJAMIN HEBBLETHWAITE,
with contributions from Joanne Bartley,
Andrew Tarter, Quinn Hansen, and Kat Warwick

THIS APPENDIX provides an extensive dictionary of Haitian Vodou terms. The work was begun by extracting all of the Vodou headwords found in Bryant Freeman's *Haitian-English Dictionary* (2004) and Albert Valdman, Iskra Iskrova, Jacques Pierre, and Nicolas André's *Haitian Creole-English Bilingual Dictionary* (2007). Many songs, interviews, monographs, and articles on Vodou were used to expand the list and to provide accurate definitions and explanations. A great effort was made to discover the roots of Haitian Vodou terms in the Fon, Yorùbá, and Kikongo languages, among others. The entries for the lwa are encyclopedic to provide the user with in-depth information in a single body. We have attempted to collect and explain a wide array of Vodou-related terms found in the literature. To improve readability, our sources are given in the footnotes. In light of the great diversity in the spelling of important terms, we have imposed uniformity on the orthography of various words.

101 Nanchon The 101 ethnic groups and their lwa that are woven together in Haiti.[1] An unknown number of African cultures blended in Vodou. The number 101 follows the pattern of 21 *nanchon* (nations) and pantheons of 251 lwa or 401 lwa.[2] The pattern symbolizes the idea that one more nation or lwa can always be added to the Vodou system.

abobo *See* **ayibobo**.

Achade *See* **Bosou Achade**.

Adanyi *See* **Sobo**.

Adja An old lwa who compels the *chwal* (possessed, horse of the lwa) to eat glass. This tradition is found in Haiti and Benin.[3]

adjida *See* **agida**.

adorasyon An "adoration" is a money offering and a song for the cult of the dead.[4]

adore To "adore" is to make a money offering.[5]

adoumaya A rare barrel type of drum.[6]

Aganman Chameleon; the name of a lwa.[7] The chameleon is the symbol of the dual Supreme Being Lisa. *See* **Mawou-Lisa**.

Agasou Gnenen; Agasou Alada; Djeme; Agasou Gweliye; Agasou Do Miwa; Agasou Mede; Silibo Vevou; Agasou Yeme Do Miwa; Agasou-miwa; Agasou Yeme This lwa is served in the Danwonmen, Petwo, and Rada rites and is associated with bodies of water. He rides all the great Vodou oungan and is known for his healing. The lwa's *repozwa* (resting tree) is the mango tree. Agasou is represented by means of a large crab called the *banbara-tayba*; the lines in Agasou's vèvè resemble crab claws.[8] The water in the springs where Agasou dwells cannot be used for domestic purposes but may be drawn from for medicinal purposes.[9] A man addressing Agasou used this invocation at the Plezans spring: "Mister Agasou Gnenen, Saint Agasou, guy coiffed by Dantò, Silibo Vavoun guy, ago, ago-si, ago-la, we draw water from the spring."[10] He then reached into a hole and pulled out a big *banbara-tayba* crab, and the spring water began to flow. When Agasou appears in services, a jar or goblet of water is placed on his head, and sometimes he will dance with it balanced there. Agasou is classified as a "climbing" lwa because those possessed by him climb the *potomitan* (center post) or the vines that hang from trees nearby springs.[11] For some followers, Agasou is white, while for others, he is black. Offerings to Agasou take place at the springs favored by the lwa and consist of white rice, plantain, speckled chicken, liqueurs, among other food and drink offerings. Agasou is sometimes considered a minor lwa of the Rada rite and is classed as an earth lwa.[12] He incarnates the ferocity of a wild beast, and the Vodouist possessed by him displays claws in the position of attack. In the Fon culture, Agasu is the offspring of a sacred panther and the princess Aligbonon. Agasu is the founder of the royal dynasty of the town Allada, Benin, and he disseminated the myth of the panther.[13] Agasu remains the panther-ancestor of the royal families of Allada, Abomey, and Porto-Novo.[14] Agasu is also a *vodun* (lwa) venerated by the Adja-Fon people of Benin. *See* **Bosou Achade**.

Agawou; Agaou; Agawou Bèt san San; Agawou Kata; Agawou Konbe; Agawou Loray; Agawou Mede; Agawou Misan Wèdo; Agawou Tonnè; Agawou Wèdo; Agawou Zeklè; Agawou Zetwal; Nèg sèpèt; Agawou Potokoli A Vodou lwa represented by storms, wind, lightning, thunder, and earthquakes.[15] Agawou is served in the Danwonmen, Petwo, and Rada rites; he is terrestrial and aquatic. Agawou is linked to the Holy Spirit or Saint Augustine and is considered powerful.[16] His possession events are intense and violent; consequently, oungan and manbo must take precautions to control the *chwal* (horse).[17] Vodou songs reflect his link to nature: "Agawou blows the wind, he blows the Nor'easter."[18] Agawou is the brother of Azaka Mede, and both are represented by the *soud* (biting lizard).[19] In an ounfò, a pre-Columbian *pyè tonnè* (thunder stone), which is an arrowhead, ax, or polished stone, represents him. The *kenèp* (Spanish lime) is Agawou's resting tree. His days are Friday and Saturday, and his colors are black, white, and red. Agawou is associated with Saint Rock, Saint Michel, or a small black figure praying in a boat who appears in the chromos of the Virgin of Charity, depending on who is asked.[20] In certain regions of northern Haiti, the mythology is different in the sense that Agawou is linked to Saint John the Baptist and is called Agoun Tonnè or Ogoun Tonnè.[21] He is the brother of Ogoun Balindjo. Those possessed by Agawou announce themselves with expressions such as, "Damn lightning! . . . It's me Agawou Lightning! . . . It's me the lightning, damn it! . . . It's me, damn it, the cannon officer of God! When I grumble, the sky and earth tremble! M-hou-ou (×3)."[22] Agawou's *chwal* (horse) sometimes spits in the faces of observers, shakes their hands vigorously, and scales trees.[23] There are also stories like the one of a former Vodouist convert to Protestantism who could not resist sitting in the audience of a Vodou ceremony. Suddenly she was possessed by Agawou and injured herself to the point of bleeding and fleeing from the temple, causing jubilation among the Vodouists. Some Haitians, when threatened, will say, "Agawou says if God wants it," with the index finger in the air. Failure to serve Agawou can result in severe punishment or death.[24] Agawou protects his servants against fires and lightning. Agawou distrusts humans.[25] Agawou and his brother, Azaka Mede, receive offerings such as *tòm-tòm* (sweet potatoes, malanga, plantains, okra).[26] Farmers say prayers to Agawou if too much rain has fallen.[27] The Vodou priest buries a bottle of rainwater or ties knots in vines to tie up the rain. In Dahomey, Agawou was the title of the chief of the army of Allada, a position held by Toussaint Louverture's father, Gawou Ginou.[28]

agida; adjida A curved stick used for playing the *segon* drum in the Rada rite.[29] They are made of hard wood because they need to remain intact for several hours during a ceremony.[30] The Fon language has the same word and meaning: *agidà*.[31]

Agiwa-Lensou A Vodou lwa in the Petwo rite.[32]

ago; ago e; agosi; agola Used frequently in songs, this term requests permission to pass through to the world of the lwa.[33] *Ago* is an interjection uttered when someone stumbles on an obstacle, and it expresses warning or demands attention. *Ago* (or *agoò*) in Fon means "I am here!" or "Attention!" or "Watch out!"[34] *Ago e* is also a call-and-response device that the oungenikon (choir leader) uses to signal the chorus to return to the whole text of a song.[35]

agoudjalaa A Vodou acclamation meaning "Yeah! Yes!"[36]

agoye *See* **ago**.

agwesan A scapular worn by a newly initiated *ounsi kanzo*.[37]

Agwe Tawoyo; Agwetawoyo; Agwetawoyo Gweliye; Mèt Agwe The lwa Agwe Tawoyo is the husband of Lasirenn and the supreme master of the sea and all islands.[38] Agwe is served in the Kongo, Petwo, and Rada rites.[39] He is represented as a handsome white man, and his vèvè is a warship named Imamou. In temples dedicated to Agwe, a small boat is suspended from the ceiling. Ceremonies for Agwe take place by the seaside and at sea. The *bak Agwe* (a small Agwe barque) with food and drink offerings is released into the water. Those possessed by Agwe produce the sound of waves and, sitting astride in a chair, imitate rowing.[40] Some possessed by Agwe throw themselves on the ground and mime the movements of swimming; their cheeks puff in and out as if they are breathing like fish.[41] Agwe's *repozwa* is the calabash tree, and his symbol, the *lanbi* (conch shell), may be blown into or displayed on an altar.[42] Tuesday and Thursday are Agwe's days, and his colors are white, green, and rose. White attire is typical for his services. Agwe is identified with Saint Ulrich because he is represented in chromolithographs with a fish in his hand. During World War II, images of Saint Ulrich were unavailable, so merchants identified Agwe with Saint Ambroise, drawing a fish in the saint's hand.[43] In temples dedicated to Agwe, a fish and a boat are painted on the wall. Sometimes he is represented with a green trident on which appear the vertebrae of a marine animal. Agwe is said to help his followers escape from difficult circumstances, especially on the sea. In the colonial period, slaves believed that dead comrades would return to Ginen on the backs of fish.[44] Agwe also presides over fresh water. Workers perished one after the other because they failed to ask Agwe permission for digging the reservoir of Pétionville.[45] Agwe is an admiral and the minister of the Navy. When a warship salutes as it enters a port, it is to Agwe. Emperor Dessalines saluted Agwe with cannonfire.[46] Agwe is violent, angry, and fearless. Agwe lives at sea in *lan zile* (in the islands) or in *twa zile* (three islands).[47] Fishermen offer a ceremony for Agwe each year that lasts for several nights and coincides with the full moon. The ceremony thanks him for protection at sea and for good catches.[48] After meeting at a temple, the Vodouists walk to a covered hut on the seashore. In the hut, a small boat is hung for display, and under the *potomitan* a table with a white tablecloth is covered with *kwi* containing boiled fish drizzled with olive oil, bread, bananas, and roasted chicken. Around the *kwi* are arranged oranges, melons, raisins, and other food. Orange syrup, cola, and cups of coffee are set out. The oungan uses wheat flour to trace a vèvè dedicated to the lwa. A formula invokes Agwe: "By the power of Mister Agwe Tawoyo, Master Agwe Woyo, Seashell Guy, tadpole of the pond Guy, eel Guy, saltwater Guy, arm of strength Guy, Guy on the sea, after God, after God, after God."[49] The oungan and several followers of Agwe then become possessed while the laplas (master of ceremonies) enters the water to his waist and returns waving his sword to ward off all evil. After these rites, the congregation enter boats to deliver the offerings to Agwe. The boats are festooned, and the one designated for Agwe's offering is lit up with candles. Agwe's offerings are placed on the offering tray, which is placed on a current that takes it to *twa zile*. If the *bak* returns to the shore, however, Agwe is not satisfied and requires another service to be appeased.[50] Ceremonies for Agwe can be carried out by the sea or at rivers, ponds, or lakes. If a boat is in peril, Agwe is invoked.[51] Agwe protects contemporary boatpeople who attempt to enter the United States.[52] Agwe has his own "gracious" dance and rhythm called *dans Agwe,* but he accepts *yanvalou, rada,* and other rhythms. The *dans Agwe* involves movements that evoke swimming and the ebb and flow of the tide.[53] Agwe Tawoyo is one of the four principal lwa who preside over the initiation of oungan or manbo, and they often wear his necklace.[54] Agwe is Èzili's lover, and he is associated with Saint Expédit.[55] In the Fon language, *Agbétò* is "the sea, the ocean, and the seaside." In Wéménu-Fon, the deity is called Agbè. When compounded, *Agbétò Awoyo* refers to the divinity of the sea. Ague is also the name of a fishing village in Benin and the *vodun* (lwa) venerated there. In the region of Allada, Benin, Agbè or Agbé töawoyo is the *vodun* of the sea.[56] In Fon, Agbetawoyó is onomatopoeia for the sound of the sea.[57] *See* **Imamou; Lasirenn**.

ajikan; ajikann *See* **badjikan**.

akasan siwo A cornmeal or manioc porridge with added sugar served to the lwa.[58] *See* **doukounou**.

aksyon de gras Thanksgiving prayers borrowed from Catholicism that open a Vodou ceremony.[59]

akwezi A Vodou cross formed by two daggers or two pieces of metal.[60] *Aklúzù* is the Fon word for cross.[61]

Alada A town in southern Benin, the name of a lwa, and the source of the term *Rada,* which refers to one of Vodou's major rites.[62] *See* **Danwonmen; Ginen; Rada**.

alamyèt A Vodou ceremony without drums.[63]

alkòl Alcohol is poured out for libations, sprayed in the ritual *foula* (pulverizing mouthfuls of rum), and consumed by celebrating participants.[64] A Vodou dance is festive, and drinking alcohol in moderation is appropriate but not required. *See* **kleren**.

Aloumandya; Grann Aloumandya A Nago lwa who is the same as Lasirenn.[65] *See* **Lasirenn**.

Altagracia; Altagrasya; Our Lady of High Grace; Virgin of Higuey Altagracia is often used to represent Èzili. She is otherwise the patron of the Dominican Republic. Our Lady of High Grace is a title given to the Virgin Mary.[66] *See* **Èzili**.

Anago Nago The name of a lwa.[67]

Anayiz; Anaïs This lwa is the daughter of Èzili Dantò.[68]

anba dlo *See* **dlo**.

andezo; an de zo The *an de zo* lwa are of "two waters or substances" and therefore are worshiped in both Rada and Kongo-Petwo rites.[69] Legba and Simbi are examples of *an de zo* lwa.

andwaye The "blessing and naming of an infant" is a ritual that Oungan Nelson Marcenat conducts two weeks after he has delivered a child. In Nago (Yorùbá) culture, the name is chosen on the ninth day.[70] *See* **non vanyan**.

angaje The lwa are called by those who are *angaje* (in trouble).[71]

angajman A pact, positive or negative, with a lwa.[72]

anj *See* **zanj**.

Anmin; Anminan A Vodou rite and lwa.[73] *Anmin* and *Mina* were Portuguese terms for the Akan people.[74] The reference to *Anmin Kongo* suggests the lwa Anmin has fused with Kongolese influences. Anminan is a "great" and "sacred" lwa.[75]

anpoul A magic spell.[76]

ansyen bon "Good elders"; those who have tremendous knowledge and wisdom.[77]

Antwàn Lan Gomye A Vodou priest who lived in the village Lan Gomye in the hills surrounding Jeremie in the nineteenth century. His fame came from his skills in divination and clairvoyance. His renown is fixed in the Haitian proverb "Antwàn Lan Gomye himself cannot see what I see for you." His abilities in divination were so great that he is said to have known in advance when a client would come by. Antwàn Lan Gomye is said to have served only with his right hand, thus having a primarily Rada orientation and an aversion to harming people.[78]

anvoutman An evil spell.[79]

anvwa mò To send spirits of the dead to harm or kill the living.[80]

aochè Nago; awo che Nago; awo ache Nago A ritual Vodou cry[81] that refers to the Nago rite and is still common in Nigeria.[82] This acclamation is commonly heard before or after a Vodou song and marks the relevant rite. *Awo* or *lawo* is "lwa," *ache* is "force," and *Nago* refers to the Yorùbá people; hence, together it means "by the power of the Nago lwa."[83] *See* **ayibobo; bilolo**.

arestasyon; arèt A magic charm or ceremony for warding off evil lwa. The *arèt* can involve dots of paint applied to a wall or some surface to keep *lougawou* and evil away.[84]

arètman A protective talisman against the dead and a ritual to prevent the blood-sucking of the *lougawou.*[85]

asagwe A type of Voodoo dance.[86]

asen A tall iron candlestick that is sometimes used to support ritual objects.[87] In the Wéménu-Fon language, the *asen* is a portable metallic altar that represents a family's dead. In the Fon culture, food, sacrificial blood, and alcohol are placed on the *asèèn*. The *asèèn* are used for Fa divination, offering sacrifices, and success in war or rituals.[88]

asogwe; asogwemen The highest-ranked Vodou initiate and the final ritual of the *wosman* (promotion to the priesthood) in Vodou. This final promotion is the vesting of the *ason* (sacred rattle), which the oungan or manbo use to call forth or placate the lwa.[89] Vodou priests sometimes refer to themselves as *oungan asogwe,* which means that they passed through the *asogwe* ritual.[90] Someone who is *asogwe* can prevent the lwa from possessing himself or others by means of the *ason.*[91] *Asògwe* is the Wéménu-Fon term for the gourd shaker that is called the *ason* in Haitian Creole.[92] *See* **ason**.

ason A ritual calabash shaker or rattle held by the oungan or manbo. The ason is made of a small calabash gourd and is laced with beads and snake vertebrae. The *ason* is used by the priest to call and to send away the lwa. The *ason mèt* (master rattle) is the principal sacred rattle and must never leave the temple. An *ason òdinè* (ordinary rattle) is used by a visiting priest or priestess. When an individual chooses to *pran ason* (take the ason), he or she becomes a Vodou priest or priestess. *Sonnen ason* (to sound the ason) is to call the lwa. The *ason* must not be placed on a bed because "power implements" do not belong where children are made.[93] The priest or priestess is an orchestral conductor and uses the *ason* to change the tempo of the rhythm or to stop it.[94] The Fon in Benin call the rattle the *asò, asògò,* or *asògwe,* and it is also covered in snake vertebrae, shells, pearls, or beads. In Benin, the *asòxotò* is a musician who shakes the *asògo* to appease the *vodun* (lwa).[95] *See* **asogwe**.

asòtò; Asòtò The largest of all of the Rada drums. The *asòtò* is used only on very special occasions. The drum is 2 meters tall and is made of oak, mahogany, cedar, or kapok trees because they have a lot of *san* (blood/sap). They are cut during the full moon period and the skin needs to be attached precisely at midnight.[96] The lwa Asòtò dwells within the drum. Several initiates beat the drum together; non-initiates may not touch it. The *asòtò* drum is owned by very few temples, and those that have one house it in a special room and bring it out on rare occasions with much pomp.[97] Possession by the lwa Asòtò is said to be so violent that very few adepts can handle it. Roumain (1943) provides an account of the songs and ceremony for the dedication of the *asòtò* drum. Many *asòtò* drums were destroyed during the *campagne anti-superstitieuse* (anti-superstition campaign) of 1941–1942 organized by the Catholic church and the Haitian government of President Elie Lescot.[98] The Fon word *sátó* (huge and elaborately carved drum) is related to the Haitian Creole *asòtò*.[99] *See* **ountò; rejèt**.

asyèt Ginen A decorated gourd bowl used for food offerings for the lwa.[100]

Ati In Haitian Creole, Ati serves as a titular prefix for respected Vodou leaders. In the Fon language, *Ati* means "tree, forest."[101] The term *atimèvodu,* in Wéménu-Fon, refers to a group of *vodun* (lwa) who reside in a tree.[102] The expression "Ati Max Beauvoir," for example, literally means "the Tree Max Beauvoir," which figuratively means "the most honorable Max Beauvoir." Some lwa, like Loko Atisou, also share the title. *See* **Loko; pyebwa**.

Atibon Legba *See* **Legba**.

Ati Dan In the Fon language, *Ati* is "tree" and *Dan* is "serpent" and refers to the snake deity Dan in Benin and Danbala in Haiti. The term may refer to a serpent lwa who dwells in a tree.

Atisougwè Probably a Vodou honorific term. It appears in the following lyric: "Papa Ogou speaks, / They say it's white rum he drinks ago, ago. / Atisougwe, that's how they're dangerous."[103] *See* **asogwe; Ati; Loko**.

atoutou A ball of hot flour squeezed by Vodou initiates.[104]

avotayi; avoudayi; afoutayi A ritual Vodou acclamation that means "Let's salute the earth."[105] *Afon a* (let's salute) and *ayi* (the earth) are Fon expressions.[106] The expression is used in a call-and-response formula. The priest shouts: *Avoudayi!* The audience shouts: *Yi!* The priest shouts: *Bilabila!* The audience shouts: *Kongo!* The priest shouts: *Lè bounda fache, kote l chita?* (When an ass is angry, where does it sit?) The audience shouts: *Atè!* (On the ground!). This formula is commonly used at the beginning of songs. *See* **ayibobo; bilolo**.

Awida Wèdo A serpent lwa associated with the town of Wida (Ouida), Dahomey. *See* **Danbala**.

awo che Nago *See* **aochè Nago**.

ayabonde *See* **ayibobo**.

ayibobo; abobo A ritual Vodou praise acclamation of the Rada rite.[107] Vodouists shout *Ayibobo!* between songs. The acclamation is sometimes accompanied in Haiti by the smacking of the mouth with the fingers.[108] Robert Faris Thompson suggests that the word may be related to the Kikongo expressions *abu mpya* or *abubu mpya*, which mean "the end of a song."[109] The most likely etymology is found in the contemporary Fon word *awòbóbó*, an acclamation of joy that is also made with the tapping of the lips.[110] *See* **agoudjalaa; aochè Nago; bilolo**.

Ayida Wèdo The name of a lwa represented by the rainbow. Ayida Wèdo and her husband, Danbala Wèdo, were the first lwa God created.[111] Ayida Wèdo, like her husband, is a snake associated with fertility. In Benin, Ayidohuèdó is a *vodun* (lwa) linked to the sky and represented by the rainbow; she is symbolized by two pieces of iron in the form of a snake.[112] The serpentine form of the river Wo in Benin also represents this lwa.[113] *See* **Danbala Wèdo; Domisi Wèdo**.

ayizan Palm leaves cut into strips that ward off evil in Dahomey.[114] *Ayizan* are believed to have purifying and prophylactic powers. The *ayizan* are the strips of palm leaf the *ounyò* (new initiates) wear as a hat at the *leve kanzo* ceremony. The strips of palm leaf flow down over their faces. The use of the *ayizan* is well documented in Benin, Togo, and Haiti.[115] In Fongbe, *àzã* refers to the fringes of the palm leaf.[116] *See* **Ayizan Velekete; chire ayizan; fwèt ayizan; leve kanzo**.

Ayizan Velekete; Ayizan Belekou; Ayizan Belekounde; Ayizan Imamou; Ayizan Keke; Ayizan-konplo; Ayizan Velekete; Manbo Ayizan The Vodou lwa of temples, markets, public places, doors, gates, and roads.[117] Ayizan is the protector of the Vodou temple.[118] Through the *chire ayizan* she is centrally represented in the *leve kanzo* (initiation ritual). She is served in the Danwonmen, Kongo, Petwo, and Rada rites. In Vodou mythology, she is the wife of Loko.[119] Ayizan is the protector of ritual purity and the defender of morality, and she does not tolerate corruption and negative influences.[120] She is linked to fresh water. She does not appreciate the vulgarity of the Gede lwa. The royal palm tree and the *mestiyen beni* (castor oil plant) are her resting trees, and she gives those trees the power to thwart evil spirits. Her vèvè includes the representation of palm fronds. Those possessed by Ayizan wear white attire with a necklace made of woven palm-tree leaves.[121] Ayizan is considered one of the most ancient lwa.[122] Those possessed by Ayizan walk hunched over and are short of breath because of her advanced age. Ayizan provides her devotees with power and authority. Her symbol is the *palmis* (palm tree), a ubiquitous tree in coastal Africa and Haiti. The leaves of palm trees are used to cover Vodou temples, and during ceremonies dedicated to her the faithful carry a palm branch called a "piece of Ayizan." Women who are ill, pregnant, or menstruating may participate in a Vodou service only if they are under the protection of Ayizan. Ayizan's vèvè is traced from corn or wheat flour and represents a palm. The vèvè includes the initials "A. V." of the lwa, which illustrates forms of literacy woven into Vodou ritual.[123] Ayizan is associated with exorcism and purification. Vodouists identify Ayizan with Christ and, in particular, with the representations of Christ's baptism by John the Baptist found in popular Catholic chromolithographs. Ayizan is considered a great manbo. Legba, Ayizan, and Loko are linked together. One formula of invocation for Ayizan is "By the power of Granny Ayizan, Manbo Ayizan Velekete, Ayizan Poumgwe, Uprooting, Ayizan-plotting, Beautiful Black Woman, sisaflè-vodoun, old, old, old Ayizan. Ago, agosi, agola."[124] Ayizan is offered plantain, sweet potato, malanga, pumpkin, millet, *salezon* (salted meat), white rice, cake, cane syrup, a clay vessel of water and, cinnamon-colored chickens. Offerings are ordinarily placed in a *makout* (woven straw bag) and hung on one of Ayizan's favorite trees.[125] Ayizan and those possessed by her consume no alcohol, which explains Roumain's song 18, in which liquor turns into water with Ayizan. In the Wéménu-Fon language of Benin, Ayizan and Àvlèkètè are two distinct *vodun* (lwa). Ayizan is the *vodun* of Ouidah, Benin's marketplace and the brush, whereas Àvlèkètè is a lwa of the sea and lagoons.[126] Ayizan is one of the most important *vodun* in the town of Allada and among the Pedah people of southern Benin.[127] Àvlèkètè inhabits the length of beaches and is honored by those who live nearby. Àvlèkètè is also the name of a port in southern Benin that was active in the slave trade.[128] Therefore, it is possible that Haiti's Ayizan Velekete is the fusion of two originally distinct lwa or a lwa plus a toponym.

Azagon; Azagon Loko; Azagou Loko The name of a lwa recognized for the ability to predict, anticipate, and "see far." In Fon, *Lòkó Azagun* is the large African teak tree that serves as the shelter of sorcerers and "where they receive offerings to *liberate* someone."[129] The expression *loko azangùn* in Fon refers to the big *loko* tree where Loko resides or to "Loko's forest."[130] *See* **Loko Atisou**.

Azaka Mede; Azaka Tonnè; Azaka Gweliye; Minis Azaka; Kouzen Zaka; Minis Agrikilti; Zaka; Si-Azaka The lwa of agriculture and farmers and the protector of travelers. Azaka is represented by Saint Charles Borromeo. Azaka is served in the Djouba, Kongo, Matinik, and Rada rites. Azaka is received affectionately, and he enjoys gossiping and poking around in other people's personal business. He is an old farmer and smokes a pipe, wears denim, carries a *dyakout* (straw bag), and dons a straw hat. He is not a Gede lwa; however, the lwa Gede Nibo is his brother. He has a huge appetite and his vèvè is typically traced from cornmeal, his favorite food. His vèvè includes a large rectangle with many small squares representing rice paddies;

each paddy has a grain of rice in its center, which symbolizes his agricultural orientation.[131] During possession, he listens to requests and gives advice.[132] Azaka's resting tree is a *serizye* (cherry tree) or an aloe plant, and he is represented by the *soud* (biting lizard).[133] Wednesday, Friday, and Saturday are his days of the week, and blue and red are his colors. Azaka is associated with thunder. Azaka is referred to as the minister of agriculture.[134] Azaka needs some time to himself to get his thoughts together.[135] Azaka is called on at sea in times of need.[136] One *chante pwen* (song of reproach) chides Azaka: "Adults don't fool around, it's children who fool around here! / Azaka Mede, be more serious about your business."[137] Azaka is one of the lwa, along with Ayizan, Danbala Wèdo, and Ayida Wèdo, who are connected to the *manje yanm* ceremony, an autumn harvest celebration for which *gonbo* (corn flour, red beans, and okra) and *mousa* (manioc flour dumplings) are prepared in honor of the lwa. The placement of the food on the altar is called the *kouche yanm.* The basic accoutrements of Azaka are his straw hat, straw bag, clay pipe, sickle, and machete. Popular modern *rasin* (roots) music also dedicates songs to Azaka.[138] Azaka was served by the Mede people, who were reputed for their rice production.[139] *See* **Kouzen Zaka; tchaka**.

azè A Vodou symbol in cast iron.[140]

azètò; azetò A rare word for sorcerer in Haitian Creole.[141] In Fon culture, the *azètó* is also a sorcerer, magician, and manufacturer of charms who is distinct from the *bòkònò* (Vodun fortune-teller). The *azètó* uses animals such as the owl, cat, or vulture to seize the soul of his victims and cause their death. The *azètó* is detested, feared, and sometimes killed.[142] The *azètó* works with evil spirits.

babako A "feast" in honor of a Vodou lwa.[143] *See* **demanbre; kandjanhoun**.

baboul A variety of Vodou dance.[144]

bada A chant to ward off an unwelcome Vodou lwa.[145]

Badagri *See* **Ogou**.

Badè; jeneral Badè; Badè Awannen; Sofi Badè The lwa Badè is a military general. He presides over the wind, storms, and lightening.[146] He is so old that he is "without bones."[147] He and his brother, Sobo, are considered cuckolds.[148] Like Ogou, he loves to drink, but he does not get drunk.[149] Badè and Sobo are twin brothers and hence are always invoked together. Badè may ask his servant to bear a cross or burden.[150] Badè declares his innocence with respect to the complaints.[151] Badè comes from the northern town of Gwomòn.[152] Badè shows off about being recognized.[153] Badè is represented with orange, and his resting tree is the *bwadòm* (bastard cedar). Badè's days are Wednesday and Friday, and he is offered white rice, plantains, a white chicken, and white or Madeira wine. He is represented by Saint Paul or Saint Peter.[154] Badè originates in Dahomian tradition.[155] *Sofi Badè* means "Badè of Lightning" in the Fon language.[156] *See* **Sobo**.

badiyèt-konn A special drumstick for the largest of the three Rada drums.[157]

badji; bagi; sobadji The inner sanctuary of a Vodou temple containing one or several altars covered with sacred objects and religious symbols and images.[158] Some people walk into the *badji* backward.[159] The *badji* sometimes has a basin for Danbala and other compartments and dwelling places for lwa. This room is also a vestry where the accoutrements of the lwa are kept until a *chwal* (horse) is possessed and enters to retrieve them.[160] The *badji* is decorated with bones or images of skeletons to evoke the memory of the ancestors.[161]

badjigri A magic charm.[162]

badjikan; badjigan; badjikanz; adjikan; adjikann The person who maintains and guards the *badji* and ceremonial accessories and helps with collecting ritual and medicinal herbs.[163]

Badjo; nan Badjo A Vodou temple near Gonaïves that is dedicated to the Nago lwa of Yorùbá origin.[164]

badjougan A secret informant for a Vodou priest or priestess.[165]

badyèt kòn The curved pipe or horn-shaped drumstick used on the *manman tanbou.*[166] *See* **manman tanbou**.

bagèt; badyèt Drumsticks. *See* **badyèt kòn**.

bagi *See* **badji**.

baka Goblin, or a type of Vodou spirit with negative attributes, such as Èzili Je Wouj or Ti Jan Pye Chèch.[167] Another possible translation of *baka* is "red ogre of the night."[168] The following lyrics show that baka-type lwa inspire fear: "I come from Ginen, / oh I have encountered a baka lwa, the lwa frightens me."[169] Vèvè can be used to block the negative influence of *baka.*[170] The Mbaka are an ethnic group who live in the forest in the Kongo. They are short people, which is why Haitians sometimes call each other *ti baka* (little baka).[171] *See* **Bakoulou baka; dyab; gwo baka; lougawou; mazanga; ti baka**.

bak Agwe The Agwe barque is a small platform or tray that contains food and drink offerings that is released into the sea to honor the lwa. *See* **Agwe Tawoyo**.

Bakoulou baka Ancient Elder of Yore; a Vodou lwa of Kongolese origin.[172] The Kikongo word *ba-kúlu* is composed of the plural prefix *ba-* and the noun *nkúlu* (elder).[173] Some in Haiti consider Bakoulou baka an evil and mischievous demon nourished by human flesh.[174] In songs dedicated to Bakoulou baka, the lwa is referred to as a *dyab* (fiery lwa) and as a *pwen* (a lwa or charm that provides protection and good luck).[175]

balanse The first lessons given to Vodou initiates.[176]

bale A *pase bale* (to sweep with a broom) is a Vodou trial by ordeal.[177]

Balewouze The name of a lwa.[178]

Balmannan; Balmannan Banda; Balmannan Lenmba; Balmannan Malouk; Balmannan Penmba A female lwa sometimes referred to as *manman* (mother) and rooted in the Kongo-Petwo rite.[179] Balmannan is associated with magic and is a fearsome lwa, as these lyrics suggest: "Balmannan angry head, what kind of a lwa are you? . . . Balmannan terrible head, what kind of lwa are you?"[180] *See* **Kongo; Petwo**.

Banbara A group or *nanchon* of lwa.[181] Bambara is also a language and ethnic group in modern Mali. The *banbara-tayba* crab symbolizes the lwa Agasou. *See* **Agasou Gnenen; nanchon**.

banbocha A Vodou dance to the dead.[182]

banda A sexually suggestive dance for the Gede lwa.[183]

baryè; bayè A "gate" that Legba opens between the human and the lwa; a door to another world.[184]

basen Basins filled with water inside or near a Vodou temple to represent water lwa such as Danbala, Simbi or Agwe. Ponds, reservoirs, and springs are considered the dwelling places of lwa. A bòkò in Leyogann informed me that an actual snake habitually would lounge in the basin located in his *badji* (sanctuary).

Basen Ble Blue Basin, an important Vodou-Catholic pilgrimage site near Jacmel in Haiti's southern peninsula. Vodouists go on pilgrimages to the waterfall and basin called Basen Ble to seek renewal and connection with the lwa.[185] *See* **Sodo; Twou Ogou; Twou Sen Jak**.

batèm A baptism; a Vodou consecration of people, lwa, temples, drums, and necklaces involving prayers, songs, libations, vèvè, and the sprinkling of water.[186]

batize To baptize; an important ritual in Vodou. The Vodou priest can baptize newborn babies in the *andwaye* ritual. The lwa that possess individuals can be considered *lwa batize* (baptized lwa) if they are benevolent and sanctioned; for Marcenat, this refers to *lwa rasin* (roots lwa) or *lwa Ginen* (Ginen lwa) who are inherited through the family and community. New Vodou drums are baptized before they are used. Offerings, prayers, candles, and vèvè accompany the selection and felling of the tree, the carving of the drum, and the boring of the drum peg hole.[187] The baptism invests the lwa Ountò in the drum and involves purification rites in the course of which the drums are dressed in white sheets, the Rada color.[188] *See* **andwaye; asòtò; ountò**.

baton The walking stick that represents the old age of lwa such as Legba, Danbala, Kouzen Zaka, and Gede in possession events.[189] Legba's stick crosses the horizontal line in his vèvè to show his connection between the living and the ancestors; the stick is also linked to Dahomian royalty.[190]

batri An evil fetish or ensemble of charms or spells. The *batri masonnik* (masonic rhythm) is a rhythm produced by the clapping of hands or the beating of drums. A *kout batri* is the dispensing of an evil spell.[191]

bat tanbou To beat drums; to hold a Vodou service.[192]

bawon A grave digger.[193]

Bawon Samdi; Bawon Gede; Bawon Lakwa; Bawon Simityè; Bawon Gran Bwa; Bawon Kafou; Bawon Kara; Bawon Kriminèl; Bawon Lento; Bawon Loray An important Vodou lwa of life and death and the guardian of the cemeteries. Bawon Samdi is served in the Banda, Bawon, and Petwo rites. He and Grann Brijit (Granny Brigitte) are responsible for the passage between life and death. Small masonry constructions alongside the road in Haiti are symbolic tombs and his altar.[194] Bawon Samdi, the father and head of the Gede lwa, is the master of the cemeteries.[195] His symbol is the cross, and he is represented as a robust black man with a long white beard. Those possessed by him wear a frock coat and don a formed tall hat. He always carries a *koko makak* stick and a bottle of white rum, and his emblem is a black cross. His offerings are placed in black boxes. Bawon Samdi is identified with Saint Expédit, who is represented in the Catholic religion with a cross in hand and a helmet at his feet; for the faithful, this helmet is a skull. Bawon Samdi is also identified with Saint Radegund, the founder of the monastery of the Holy Cross at Poitiers, France. On Bawon Samdi's days of consecration, Monday and Saturday, his devotees congregate in the cemeteries; light black wax candles at the foot of the cross, his resting place; and recite the prayers and speeches of Saint Radegund. To improve their situation, Bawon Samdi's servants make wishes to the lwa. On the day that wishing commences, they compose a prayer or speech in their rooms. While they pray, the faithful bring a fabric shirt made of Siam, on which small black crosses are applied, and a black dress. They sleep on the ground and abstain from sexual relations. Offerings to Bawon Samdi are ordinarily made at a temple or at the foot of his resting tree. In the countryside, offerings are made in front of a cross that guards the entrance of cemeteries or on his resting tomb. Vodouists light a black candle and offer him *tafya* (white rum) and calabash bowls containing sweet potatoes, plantain, pieces of cassava, corn, grilled pistachios, and cookies. Vodouists sacrifice a cock with black feathers to Bawon Samdi. On days of important ceremonies, a black goat is sacrificed. For the celebration of the dead, black fabric and a skull and bones are placed next to Gede's cross, resting tree, or symbolic tomb. Bawon Samdi is egotistical and murky. He believes that he is the strongest of the lwa and that Vodouists should dedicate offerings and services only to him. A service was once done for Danbala Wèdo, Mistress Èzili, and Agwe Tawoyo at which Bawon Samdi appeared. To keep from being recognized, he borrowed the gestures of Agawou Tonnè and sang that lwa's song. However, his nasal voice betrayed him. Someone noticed that it was Bawon, and in fury he spewed orders and insulted everybody. Because he is a lwa of life and death, he informed the people who were present that he would deal with them one day. To alleviate him, they offered Bawon a goblet of white rum. He swallowed a big mouthful, grimaced, and sang. They dedicated three flattering songs and dances to him, and he danced to them. Bawon Samdi is represented with a black wooden cross and dresses in a frock coat and a fake collar. A string with a bottle containing *tafya* is attached to the horizontal bar of his cross. On the cross, a black wax candle burns. In front of the niche are crosses and fasteners, a spoon, and a knife. A black stick and an *ason* (rattle) rest on the vertical bar of the cross. In temples consecrated to the Gede, an altar is built to the honor of the Gede. It consists of a small table on which the following are placed: a great black cross, a chromolithograph of Saint Expédit, a black candle lit for Gede, three small crosses and three black wax candles, bottles, and a small cross in a bottle of white rum. (The horizontal bar of this cross is larger than the neck of the bottle.) Bawon Lakwa is also called Azagon Lakwa (see also Azagon Loko). His role is to seek the dead in mortuaries and accompany them to the cemetery. When they recognize the burial, certain Vodouists kneel at the cross that symbolizes Bawon Lakwa and request that the mysteries not seek them. Bawon Lakwa can be seen by people and animals before a person dies. Dogs howl because they see Bawon Lakwa passing as he seeks someone dying. Big black butterflies are messengers of Bawon Lakwa. Bawon Lakwa is represented in the cemeteries by a small wooden cross or by iron found on the tombs. Bawon Simityè (Baron Cemetery) guards cemeteries. He receives the dead from Bawon Lakwa. Like the other Bawon, he is demanding. His resting place, the elm wood (*Guazuma ulmifolia* Lam), is often placed in the cemetery. His days of consecration are Monday and Saturday, and his color is black. Vodouists make the same offerings to him that they make to Bawon Samdi. The first child buried in a cemetery is Bawon Samdi.[196] Bawon Samdi, Bawon Simityè, and Bawon Lakwa form a triad of related attributes. In vèvè symbols, Bawon Samdi is represented in the center by a cross on a hillock; to his right and left are the crosses of Bawon Simityè and of Bawon Lakwa on their own hillocks. At the two horizontal ends are three marked points similar to those of the Freemasons; they represent tombs.[197] On farms, Bawon Samdi is represented by a tomb in masonry with a black cross rising above it. On days of consecration, Vodouists place their offerings on the resting tomb. The Bawon lwa are conceited.[198] They think of themselves as more powerful than all of the other lwa, and they claim that the Christian God is beneath them. *See* **Gede**.

bebe The smallest of the three Rada drums.[199] *See* **boula**.

bèf Rada A bull with a reddish or white-speckled hide destined for sacrifice in a Rada ceremony.[200]

begi A ritual Vodou name for a goat.[201]

Belekou The patron lwa of people who raise cows and the name of a town in Mali.[202]

benison A chant for the dead performed during ritual food offerings.[203]

beny A ritual protective Vodou bath or any rubbing on the body with magic liquids for health or luck.[204] Handfuls of seven types of leaves in the bath symbolize the seven original lwa created by God.[205] A *beny fèy* refers to a ritual bath made of leaves and herbs. A *beny santi* refers to a foul-smelling bath used to ward off evil spirits.[206] In the Fon culture, water, herbal, or mud baths are also important for ritual, healing, and protection. The *lè fá* (Fa bath) is a ritual bath taken after the first initiation to the cult of Fa.[207]

benyè An undertaker or washer of corpses.[208]

benyen To bathe; refers metaphorically to involvement in Vodou. To *benyen nan gwo dlo* (bathe in big waters) or *byen benyen* (to be well bathed) means to be well protected by Vodou powers.[209]

betiz Profanity; a minor trope in Vodou songs and a major one in *rara* processional songs. Beauvoir (2008b) has numerous examples of a sexual nature. Some are "Pussy doesn't have a reverse side; its reverse side is a cock" or "I'm fucking women until the sun comes up / My cock is rubbed red / Congratulations, congratulations, the lesbian's clitoris, you have no need of a candle to light it up!" or "Yoyo, yoyo, a woman who has a big clitoris / Her clitoris shines more than a sheet of corrugated metal!"[210] Because Vodou ceremonies are lengthy celebrations, the atmosphere and the themes of the songs can vary considerably.

beze (tè) Kissing the ground as a sign of respect and submission.[211] Vodouists may kiss the ground before the oungan or manbo, before the drums, before the *potomitan,* before the altar, or before the vèvè.

bi An acclamation uttered by the congregation.[212] *See* **bilolo**.

bila A table or tent used in Petwo rites.[213] Bila is a temple for the Kongo lwa. The expression *bila, bila Kongo* is common before Petwo Vodou songs.[214] In Kikongo, *bila* is a verb (to praise, to honor, or to boast about) and a noun (origin, intention, or tabou). The expression *bila, bila Kongo* means "great praises to the Kongo" or "true Kongo origins."[215] *See* **manmanbila; ounfò**.

bilolo; bilobilo An enthusiastic acclamation of the Petwo rite.[216] *Bilolo* is a peremptory word in Kikongo that means "prepare to hear the decision" or "people get ready to listen."[217] *See* **bi**.

bitasyon The *mèt bitasyon* (master of the farm) is a Vodou spirit who protects a homestead.[218]

biyanbi A small metal whistle used in Vodou ceremonies and *rara* bands.[219]

Bizango; Makanda; Chanpwèl; Sanpwèl; Zobòp, Vlengbedeng; Sosyete Konvwa; Gbon Sante; Kongo; Sanmanman; Soukouyan; Makori; Sendenden; Mazanza; Kanibal; Karibal A Vodou rite and secret society.[220] Many Haitians assert that Bizango are involved in evildoing; however, this seems to be more folklore than fact.[221] One of the objectives of the Bizango is to protect the Vodou community from outside meddling and violence; such prejudice has been carried out by the Haitian government, the Catholic Church, and, more recently, Protestants.[222] Members of Bizango are said to have magical powers, such as not getting wet in the rain.[223] Secret societies are also found in West Africa. The Zangbétò in Porto-Novo, Benin, functions as the police and watchmen of the community. The members protect villagers from thieves and enemies, keep an eye on the crossroads that enter town, and make sure that people keep their holdings tidy.[224] The Gelede is a secret society of Yorùbá origin that is run by women who use rituals attended by men to ensure that the community witches engage in magic that is favorable to the local population.[225] The Gelede employ masks and the society has a religious and educational function.[226] The Oló, which has Yorùbá origins and is found in the Ouémé valley in Benin, is another secret society.[227] The Sanpwèl (Hairless) are members of the Sosyete Bizango (Bizango Society). The word *Bizango* may derive from the Bissango community that dwelled in the archipelago near the coast of Kakonda, between Sierra Leone and Cape Verde.[228] Many of the first Africans in colonial Saint-Domingue were Bizango.[229] *See* **Sanpwèl**.

blan "White" is the color of the ancestors.[230] *See* **nwa**.

Bòde Nasyonal The National Organization of Vodouists.[231]

bohoun A Vodou funeral rite and funeral chant.[232] *See* **desounen**.

bòkò A Vodou priest who deals with both *frèt* (cool) and *cho* (hot) lwa. A *bòkò* is also a healer. The term designates a Vodou priest with a portfolio of practices that differ from the *oungan*. The *bòkò* deals with inherited and purchased lwa while the *oungan* deals primarily with inherited lwa. *Bòkò* sell lwa to clients. *Bòkò* use cards for divination and fortune-telling. In Benin, the *bokónon* does divination and fortune-telling by interpreting the *Fa* (palm kernels) which are thrown and read. The *bokónon* is a healer and philosopher.[233] Divination is a diagnostic aspect of traditional medicine.[234] *Bokónon* means "master of *bo* or knowledge."[235] The *bòkò* is criticized for working for personal interests.[236] *See* **oungan**.

Bolojè *See* **Sobo**.

bonba A dance of the Petwo rite.[237]

Bondye; Bondje "God" is the Supreme Being in Vodou. Since *Bondye* is disconnected from human matters, the lwa are viewed as essential intermediaries. God is too great to dance, like the lwa, "in the heads of earthlings."[238] In Vodou thought, God is not envious that humans worship the lwa because God has no vices like jealousy and because God is indisputably the greatest power.[239] After the catastrophic earthquake of January 12, 2010, the *oungan* Max Beauvoir pointed out that God did not cause the earthquake in Haiti because God does not meddle in human affairs.[240] Spatial imagery is common in comparing God to the lwa: God is *anwo* (above) and *lezany* (the angels/lwa) are *anba* (below). God is *devan* (in front) and *lèsen* (the saints/lwa) are *dèyè* (behind).[241] While all Vodou songs assert the primacy of Bondye, the lwa work lockstep with him.[242] Other songs describe dual alliances: "I serve God, I serve the Charm . . . / I serve God, I serve the Three Marasa bowls."[243] These lyrics are characteristic: "After God, it's us [the lwa] who are commanding."[244] One song reads, "The soothsayer isn't God, at some point he'll die."[245] Another song points out God's power over magic: "When I'm doing the magic, it's God I'm afraid of."[246] The notion of a Supreme God is widespread in West Africa: for example, *Mawou-Lisa* in Fon and Ewé and *Olódùmarè* in Yorùbá cultures.[247] As in Haiti, God receives no direct address in African societies, has no temples, no priests, no image, and no cult. God does not bless or get involved in human lives.[248] *See* **Gran Mèt; Mawou-Lisa**.

bone An action taken to prevent an evil spirit from inflicting harm or taking possession of someone.[249]

bonnanj *See* **gwo bonnanj; ti bonnanj**.

bosal "Wild" or "untamed" refers to an uninitiated servant of the lwa.[250] A *lwa bosal* refers to a violent and unidentified lwa. An *ounsi bosal* refers to an uninitiated Vodouist.[251] In Haitian history the *bosal* slaves were born in Africa and the *kreyòl* slaves were born in Haiti. The *bosal* slaves spoke Creole as a second language and did not share the same norms or culture as the *kreyòl* slaves and free people. The *kreyòl* slaves were assimilated and the *bosal* were not. Likewise, the *kreyòl* slaves had better skills and status while the *bosal* slaves were employed in the most difficult physical labor. Today *bosal* in Haitian Creole refers to anything "wild, savage, fierce, brutal, violent" and, in the context of Vodou, the "uninitiated" or "of lower rank."[252] Likewise, a *lwa bosal* is a "wild lwa" who has the potential to harm its *chwal* (horse).

Bosou A Vodou rite associated with the lwa Kadya Bosou.[253] *See* **Kadya Bosou**.

Bosou; Bosou Achade; Bosou Dlo; Bosou Kalendjo; Bosou Towo; Bosou Twa Kòn Kandonble; Achade Bòkò; Djobolo Bosou Bosou is served in the Danwonmen, Petwo, and Rada rites and he is represented in vèvè and *drapo* as a bull with three horns.[254] The three horns represent the three classes of lwa: those in the sky, on the ground, and under the water.[255] Some statues represent Bosou Twa Kòn with a beard, a pipe, and a snake slithering from his genital area.[256] Bosou represents fertility and provides protection. Bosou is powerful and endowed with the ability to transform into any animal, particularly the bull. In the Petwo rite, Bosou can be violent so precautions must be taken to restrain him. His master, Legba Kalfou, enjoins him to behave and to recall that the lwa must do good and not evil. Ceremonies for Bosou occur at dawn and attract crowds due to the availability of food.[257] Dahomey, the Kongo and France are possible progenitors of the three horned lwa. Bosou is sometimes represented by the triple-rayed halo of "El Cristo Rey"[258] in which Jesus wears a tripartite crown of gold, carries the cross, and bleeds from a wounded knee.[259] Bosou Achade, king of Dahomey from 1740–1774, was the son of Kadya Bosou. To maintain his power, he promulgated the myth that his family line inherited its authority from the lwa Agasou, one of the founding *vodun* of Dahomey.[260] Achade paid officers of the state and Vodou priests to advance this myth. Like his father Kadya Bosou, Bosou Achade got involved in the slave trade to acquire weapons from Europeans that would assure his power. In the Fon language, *Bòsú* is one of the names of the *vodun* (lwa) Sakpata who is the master of the earth and the source of life and death; he smites the living through smallpox, skin disease, and AIDS. Sakpata is feared and scarcely named.[261] *See* **Djobolo Bosou; Kadya Bosou**.

botanika In the Haitian Diaspora, a *botanika* is a shop of Vodou supplies. Chromolithographs of the saints/lwa, ritual clothing, herbs, traditional medicine, potions, dolls, cards, Vodou CDs and DVDs are sold and card-readings are given. Many *botanika* are also owned by *manbo* (priestesses) or *oungan* (priests). In some *botanika* in Miami, it is common to see chickens and pidgins walking and fluttering freely within the business for protection.[262]

bouji Lit "candles" evoke the lwa. The phrase *limen bouji dèyè yon moun* "to light a candle behind someone" means to put a hex on that person.[263]

Boukman Dutty; Boukmann The Jamaican-born Vodou priest, also known as Zamba, who, with *manbo* Cécile Fatiman, led the Bwa Kayiman Vodou ceremony on August 14, 1791, and took part in the revolts the following week. This ceremony ignited the Haitian Revolution and Boukman remains a central figure in Haitian history.[264] He was a Maroon leader and a *papalwa* (Vodou priest). Boukman worked as a *konmandè* (slave leader/driver) on the Celement plantation which was one of the first burned to the ground.[265] He was captured, executed and had his head impaled shortly after the start of the revolt. *See* **Bwa Kayiman; papalwa**.

boula The *boula* drum is the smallest of the three used in the Rada rite. The *boulaye* sits and holds the drum vertically. The *boula* is struck with two sticks.[266] *See* **manman tanbou; segon**.

boulaye The name for the person who plays the *boula* drum. *See* **boula**.

boule zen The ceremony *boule zen* ends the period of seclusion in the *ounsi* initiation.[267] The *boule zen* are clay or metal pots containing ritual food consecrated to specific lwa. The *ounyò* (initiates), who are the (servants of the *zen* clay pots), *beze tè* (kiss the ground) upon receiving them. The main ritual involves the initiate dipping his or her fingers three times into a warm infusion of wine, oil, and *monben* leaves. *Ounyò* (initiates) must finally pass their hand and foot through flames rising from the *zen* (clay pots). These rituals are not tests of courage but confer *nanm* (supernatural power), health and good luck on the initiate. After these rituals, the flames are intensified with oil and the initiates sing and become the *chwal* (horses) of their lwa. The *boule zen* is also a ceremony to consecrate a new ounfò and the lwa who will protect it. Additionally, the *boule zen* can be a funeral ceremony for important initiates such as *oungan, manbo,* or *ounsi kanzo.* In the ceremony, the vèvè called *zen* is traced next to the vèvè of the main lwa that the deceased served. The *boule zen* occurs between 15 and 40 days after the *desounen.*[268] *See* **desounen; kouche; lave tèt; mèt tèt; ounsi; ounyò; zen**.

Boulicha Nago The name of a Yorùbá lwa.[269]

Boumba The name of a lwa and a people from the Kongo region and hence a part of the Petwo rite.[270] Boumba is located near Mondong and Lenba, other toponyms that became lwa in Vodou.[271] A rhythm and dance in the Petwo rite.[272] The Kikongo etymon *búmba* refers to a medicine bag.[273] *See* **Lenba; Moudong; Petwo; Zandò**.

Boumba Mazwa A Vodou rite.[274] *See* **Marinèt-Bwa-Chèch**.

boutèy The terms *boutèy gad* and *boutèy mavangou* refer to a buried bottle containing a magic potion to protect one's home.[275]

Brijit *See* **Grann Brijit**.

Brize Penmba; Brize Loupenmba A lwa who is invoked in the Kongo, Makaya, Mayonmbe, Mondong, Penmba, and Petwo rites.[276] Brize Penmba is the offspring of Briz Montay and Manman Loupenmba who were sources of hot Petwo energy in the Haitian war of independence (1791–1803). Tradition holds that Brize Penmba was called to protect the Maroons who were freedom fighters throughout the 1700s. He was also present at the Bwa Kayiman ceremony in 1791. Brize Penmba is courageous, bold, and brutal.[277]

Briz Montay The union of Briz Montay and Manman Loupenmba has produced a family of related lwa: Brize Penmba, Brize Makaya, Brize Nèg, Penmba Loupenmba, Loupenmba Gouloufre, Nèg Loupenmba, Penmba Zile, among others.[278]

Bwa Kayiman Bwa Kayiman is the name of the village and forest in Haiti's northern plain where a Vodou ceremony was held that prepared the way for a violent insurrection and helped ignite the war of independence. On August 14, 1791, a preliminary meeting with slave leaders from more than one hundred plantations was held to make preparations for the insurrection.[279] One week later, the Vodou priest Boukman Dutty and the Vodou priestess Cécile Fatiman presided over a ceremony to consecrate the participants and seek the aid of the lwa prior to launching the revolt. The Bwa Kayiman ceremony took place in a location named Caïman (Aligator) near the Marquis de Choiseul's plantation.[280] During what was probably a Petwo warrior ceremony, Manbo Cécile Fatiman, possessed by Èzili Kawoulo, plunged a dagger into a black pig and poured its blood into a bowl to be drunk by all present as an oath to fight for freedom, destroy slavery or die trying.[281] The *Lapriyè Boukman* (Boukmann's Prayer) in this volume is attributed to the ceremony. The expression *koupe tèt, boule kay* (cut heads, burn houses), was the rallying cry that emanated from the ceremony. The sacrificial black pig, the consumption of its blood, the warrior ambiance, the oath to overthrow slavery or die trying, and the calling of the lwa all point to a military-religious event.[282] Participants took hairs from the pig as protective amulets.[283] The insurrection broke out the next night and sequentially spread to other plantations.[284] *See* **Boukman Dutty**.

Bwa Nan Bwa The lwa Bwa Nan Bwa is associated with Bosou, as the following lyric suggests: "Bosou Bwa Nan Bwa, your mother calls."[285] *See* **Bosou**.

bwason lwa A medicine or a drink prepared for a Vodou deity.[286]

call and response *See* **rèl ak repons**.

chalode From Yorùbá, *chalode* (to run away from the shackles) is found in a few Vodou songs—for example, "Nago people hurry, disperse. Loko we are going to run from our shackles."[287]

cham A Vodou charm, philter, or love potion.[288]

chame To charm, bewitch, or hex.[289]

chandèl To *fè yon chandèl* (make or light a candle) is to consult a Vodou priest.[290]

Chango The lwa Chango is powerful and is associated with storms, thunder, lightning, and spitting fire. Wednesday is the day dedicated to him, and his resting tree is the *kòk-chango* (*Lobelia assurgens*).[291] Chango belongs to the Ogou group, and he is sometimes called Ogou Chango. Marcelin's song 163 shows how Chango and Ogou Feray are assimilated. The reason for this is that Chango is the Ogou of the Yorùbá people.[292] Yorùbá traditions dominate in Cuba, where Chango is of greater importance. In Cuba, Chango is a hermaphrodite. In Haiti, Chango is a great general, and the oungan or manbo who organize a Vodou service in his honor wear a *kolye-jeneral* (general's necklace), which represents twenty-one different *nanchon* (Vodou nations and their lwa).[293] Chango brings good luck, keeps illness and trouble away, improves the situation of the downtrodden, and corrects errors. Marcelin recounts an incident in which Chango—riding his possessed *chwal* (horse)—cautioned a member of the community that he had wasted too much of his money.[294] At the same service, Marcelin also notes that prostitutes requested more business from Chango. The prostitutes filled two halved oranges with plant oil, placed two wicks in the oil, and lit a flame. Once the oil was very warm, Chango rubbed the prostitutes' genitalia with the halved oranges. In Haitian Creole the expression *lajan Chango* (Chango's money) refers to giving money with the intention of getting it back.[295] Historically, Shango was the king of Ọ̀yó in Yorùbáland around the year 1100. Because of the king's skills in managing money, Chango controls the money offered to the lwa.[296] Shango's shrine contains a leather wallet and a gourd rattle.[297] In Benin, Shangô is still referred to as an *orisha* (and not by the local word, *vodun*), in keeping with the Yorùbá roots of the spirit. In Porto-Novo, Benin, there is a famous priestess of Shangô called the Yaworitcha.[298] *See* **Dyakata; Sobo**.

Chanpwèl *See* **Sanpwèl**.

chansi A tin rattle used in Vodou.[299]

chante The Creole and Vodou word for "song."

chante pwen The *chante pwen* or *voye pwen* (challenge song or song of reproach) is used to criticize members of the community or to encourage a lwa to *desele* (leave its *chwal* [horse]) and depart from the ceremony. The *chante pwen* typically exerts indirect criticism.[300]

chantrèl The terms *renn chantrèl, larèn chantrèl* (the queen of the vocal cord), and *metrès chantrèl* (mistress of the vocal cord) refer to a female singer in a Vodou ceremony.[301]

chapit Literally meaning "chapter," *chapit* involves foreseeing the future of a client by letting a candle flame flicker over water.[302]

chay Charge; magic power used to change a course of events.[303]

chèf gato Chief cake; offered to the lwa and placed in the middle of the offerings.[304]

chemen dlo Water path; a route by which the lwa arrive and depart from a service.[305]

chire ayizan The *chire ayizan* involves making and wearing hats composed of torn palm strips that cover the faces of the *ounyò* (novices) in the *ounsi* initiation period and represent the lwa's hair.[306] The palm strips are carried into the *djèvo* (initiation room) and placed on Ayizan's vèvè. In Benin, the *vodun* (lwa) Ayizan is represented with small mounds encircled by strips of palm leaves called *azan*.[307] At a *leve kanzo* (initiates' coming-out celebration) in Little Haiti, Miami, four initiates emerged from the *djèvo* wearing straw hats adorned with *ayizan* palm strips covering their faces and a white sheet held over them by the *ounsi*.[308] In Benin, however, the *hunsi yòyò* (novices) are completely covered with palm leaf body masks.

chita tann ban m pase Sit and wait, let me through; a Vodou charm that makes someone do something for you.[309]

chodyè A cooking pot or cauldron used by oungan or manbo to compose *gad* (protective charms/lwa) for clients from their personal items.[310] *See* **gad.**

chòdyè bwaze A cooking pot used to prepare offerings for the lwa.[311]

chofe Heat up; a cultural notion that refers to the encouragement of intensity, energy, and, in the case of Vodou, possession by the lwa. The encouragement takes the form of patronal drumming or singing for a given lwa.[312]

chromolithograph; chromo A color reproduction of a painting that depicts a Catholic saint and is taken to represent a Vodou lwa. For centuries, Vodouists used the Catholic images to camouflage the lwa because Vodou was illegal. Initially, Catholic missionaries encouraged the practice because they thought it drew Africans into the church's sphere of influence. Later, when missionaries realized that Vodouists took no interest in the Catholic dimensions of the images, they recommended their suppression. Today one still does not see chromolithographs at Catholic churches. Note that the lwa are associated with Catholic chromolithographs by people, but the lwa do not recognize themselves in the images.[313] An upside-down chromolithograph on an oungan's or manbo's altar indicates that a lwa is at work for a client. Petwo altars tend to have fewer chromolithographs than Rada ones.[314] Chromolithographs of saints/lwa are sold in Haiti and in the Haitian diaspora at *botanika* Vodou shops.

chwal Horse; the Vodou term for a Vodouist possessed or ridden by a lwa. The term is a metaphor that describes the process of being *monte* (mounted or ridden) or *sele* (saddled) by the lwa. The term reflects the submission of the Vodouist to the lwa who possesses her or him. The *chwal* has no recollection of the possession event because the person's *ti bonnanj* migrates to Ginen (Africa) during the possession event.[315] *See* **gwo bonnanj; lwa; ti bonnanj.**

cyclicality; cyclicity A basic structure in Vodou music that involves the repetition of musical or lyrical structure to emphasize notions and encourage trance or possession states.[316]

Dahomey *See* **Danwonmen**.

Danbalasi A spouse of Danbala; someone who primarily serves Danbala.[317]

Danbala Wèdo; Danbala Flanbo; Danbala Ewa; Danbala Mezi; Danbala Vè; Danbala Yenou; Danbala Wèdo Ogan; Danbala Wèdo Eya; Dan; Dansi Osou; Pyè Danbala; Sèpan Dan Danbala Wèdo, along with Ayida Wèdo, were the first lwa created by God. Danbala is associated with the Kongo, Nago, Petwo, and Rada rites. He and his partner, Ayida Wèdo, represent conception, birth, life, family, love, sexuality, fertility, inspiration, good fortune, movement, continuity, harmony, wisdom, and destiny.[318] He is married to Ayida Wèdo but loves Èzili and other females. Some say that Danbala is the father and Ayida Wèdo the mother of all other lwa.[319] Danbala likes things to be pure and clean; he avoids illness.[320] Danbala and Ayida are represented as two snakes in their vèvè. They wind up their bodies under the water to support the weight of the earth.[321] A white egg represents Danbala, and a rainbow represents Ayida—hence, their epithets Miwaze (Mirror of the Egg) and Lakansyèl (Rainbow). In a *leve kanzo* initiation ceremony in Miami, a white egg was cracked open for Danbala below a vèvè that was situated at the "crossroads," a role served by the street entrance to the ounfò. Initiates covered by a large white sheet took part in rituals over the vèvè. When possessed, servants of Danbala manifest snake-like movements, climb trees, and do not speak but hiss and dart their tongues in and out. A basin with water is found in ounfò dedicated to this couple.[322] Danbala dwells in freshwater springs and is associated with large snakes. Danbala encircles the globe and is a wise and successful man.[323] He is represented as Saint Patrick, who is pictured in chromolithographs driving snakes out of Ireland. His color is white; his offerings include syrup, eggs, milk, flour, rice, and hens, and all of these must be white.[324] Marcelin recounts the story of a man's uncle who was possessed by Danbala. Danbala explained that he required a service dedicated to him annually and the sacrifice of a cow, a sheep, or a gray goat, plus the offering of drinks and desserts.[325] In one oral tradition, a man lit a candle in honor of Danbala and found three jars full of golden coins. Danbala instructed the man to take the money and leave the region because of jealous family. When the lwa departed in a puff of smoke, Danbala and Simbi emerged from the ground in the form of snakes.[326] *Dansi* refers to a follower of Danbala.[327] Danbala in Haiti and Dan in Benin are both linked to the provision of wealth. In Benin, Dan inhabits spatial reality and manifests in the rainbow. Dan ensures the perpetuity of humankind.[328] In Benin, the lwa Dan àìdóhuèdó appears to be a single lwa, whereas in Haiti, Danbala Wèdo is the husband of Ayida Wèdo, suggesting that the original lwa was split into two in Haiti. The Fon word "*Danbadahwèdó*," a clear source for Haiti's lwa Danbala Wèdo, means "rainbow."[329] "Wèdo" may be derived from the name of the town Widah, Benin.[330] Dan is said by some to be the son of the good serpent, Dangbè. Others claim that Dan is the transformation of the python into a rainbow.[331] Dan is reflected in all of the movement of matter; thus, the river Ouémé is called Dan.[332] Snake excrement is used in Dan talismans to procure wealth and happiness.[333] Dan is the guardian of life and movement on earth and in the heavens. Several oral traditions also link Dan to the procurement of wealth and to common sense and instruction.[334] In Benin, Dan is often represented as a snake biting its own tail. Danbala is seen stretching around the earth and supporting it. Dan accompanied Mawu-Lisa as they created the world. His influence is over the water and sea. In his role as an agent of Xèbioso, Dan brings lightning, death, fire, and destruction.[335] Dan provides wealth and fish for fishermen, and he is present at birth in the form of the umbilical cord, which, as in Haitian traditions, should be buried near the home to ensure the long life of the newborn. In the Fon language, Dangbé refers to a *vodun* serpent. The town of Widah is the current seat of Dan worship in Benin, and there are three types and sizes of Dangbé, each venerated in a different neighborhood.[336] In Dahomey, kings had "serpent ditches" in the form of a snake dug into the palace grounds to render them sacred. The Allada area of Benin contains 16,000 kilometers of "serpent ditches."[337] *See* **Ayida Wèdo; Domisi Wèdo**.

Danmisi *See* **Domisi Wèdo**.

Dan Petwo; Don Petwo The name of a lwa, a Vodou priest, and the name of a king in the Kongo. The following proverb is known by most Haitians: "The mapou tree falls, goats eat its leaves, Dan Petwo."[338] The proverb refers to the fall of the unified Kongo under Dan Petwo in 1716; thereafter, regional leaders (i.e., the "goats") fought a bitter battle for power.[339] Dan Petwo is remembered for his opposition to slavery. *See* **Petwo**.

danse nan tèt The lwa "dancing in the head"; a reference to possession.[340]

dans lagè War dancing. Vodou in the colony used *dans lagè* to build up the reflexes needed for combat. War dancing carries on for hours and builds strength and endurance. The tradition continues in Africa. I observed several hours of uninterrupted war dancing at a Rastafari gathering in South Africa in 1994. In Haiti, it continues in the form of *gagann* fighting during Carnival. *Gagann* is a kind of karate from the Kongo.[341]

dans Vodou Vodou dance; a ceremony in honor of the lwa. It is called a "dance" because drumming, singing, and dancing are the primary activities in Vodou worship.

Dantan The ancestors who are served because they are "ancient family who worked with God."[342] White is the color of the ancestors, and black is the color of the living. The ancestors are more active at night because Haiti's nighttime is Africa's daytime.[343] *See* **blan; nwa; zansèt**.

Danwonmen; Dawome; Dawomen A Vodou rite that includes lwa such as Danbala Wèdo, Ayida Wèdo, and Sakpata.[344] Danwonmen also refers to Dahomey, the former name of the West African state Benin and the surrounding regions and countries where the Dahomian state and empire established itself. Dawome represents the historical roots of many Vodouists, as well as a mystical land.[345] Haitian Vodou emanates in part from this empire and from the communities it conquered and sold into slavery. Dahomey exposed itself to the European slave trade and gained economic and military strength but also lost an enormous population and weakened itself. Dahomey ultimately collapsed under the French invasion and colonialism in the late nineteenth century. The systematic nature and strength of Vodou in the Fon-Dahomey empire produced cadres of ritual experts who carried with them a highly developed religion and a tendency to exert power over others to maintain the faith and their livelihoods.[346] In the Fon language, Dawome was the ancient kingdom of Abomey, which is still a town in southern Benin. Originally, the word referred to the palace of Akaba, which was built on the stomach of Dan, the serpent lwa. Gradually, the term came to refer to the town, the surrounding region, and, eventually, the kingdom and empire.[347] The expression *Dawome* or *nèg Dawomen* (Dahomian people) is common in traditional or popular *rasin* (roots) Vodou music.[348] *See* **Danbala Wèdo**.

Dawomen debout The upright Dawomen; a Rada song.[349]

Dawomen zepòl The Dahomian shoulder; a rapid dance.[350]

debatman A struggle between the *ti bonnanj* (good little angel) and the lwa over the possession of a Vodouist *chwal* (vessel of the lwa).[351] *See* **soule**.

debòde chwal li Overwhelm her or his *chwal* (horse); a lwa exhausting a possessed person.[352]

dechoukaj Uprooting. The persecution and destruction of Vodou. *See* **rejèt**.

degradasyon A Vodou ceremony.[353]

degrade mò A ritual to separate a dead person from his or her principal lwa.[354] *See* **desounen**.

degre A magical protective device.[355] *See* **pwen**.

deka An object used by a Vodou priest or priestess to call the lwa.[356] *See* **ason**.

dekanpe A substance that wards off evil spirits.[357]

dekoupe The middle size of the three Rada drums.[358] *See* **segon**.

demanbre; demanbwe A sacred place where the family ancestors are buried.[359] A *demanbre* is a gathering of extended family to feast and honor ancestral Vodou lwa.[360] It is also a sacred piece of land in which the lineage of ancestors is buried.[361] *See* **babako; kandjanhoun; lakou**.

demann A prayer request written on paper and placed on an altar. The *demann* is submitted to the lwa with a lit candle in hand.[362]

derechanj, derechany *See* **rechanj**.

desele Unsaddled; when the *chwal* (horse) is no longer ridden by the lwa.[363]

desounen A ceremony at which the principal lwa is separated from the head of the deceased. The ritual is an example of a rite of passage that a Vodou priest or priestess officiates at death.[364] The sacrifice of a chicken is usually part of this ceremony.[365]

Dessalines, Jean-Jacques/Desalin, Jan Jak A tireless general and warrior for the Haitian people who declared the independence of Haiti from France on January 1, 1804. Dessalines became Haiti's first leader after he secured the final victory over the French. His Constitution of 1804 was the first to allow the freedom of religions. He was assassined in 1806, and that provision was removed from subsequent Constitutions until 1987.[366] Dessalines was first the president but then declared himself emperor.[367] The following song lyric suggests Dessalines's important place in Vodou culture and Haitian history: "Jan Pyè Ibo, oh Emperor Dessalines! This country is not for whites, this country is for blacks, you hear."[368] Dessalines is a lwa in some communities, a fact that fits Vodou's pattern of honoring heroic ancestors.[369]

deven A Vodou priest who specializes in divination.[370] *See* **bòkò; manbo; oungan.**

devlòpman Social and economic development; a central concern of Vodouists.[371]

disip A disciple or follower of Vodou; a protective Vodou spirit.[372]

divinò; divine; divinèz A seer, diviner, or soothsayer; a Vodou priest;[373] a Vodou seer who has undergone the same training as an oungan.[374]

Djahountò; Dyahountò The name of a lwa. Djahountò is known as Ajáhùtó in Dahomey.[375] In the Fon language, *Ajáhùtó* means "king of the Adya nation." He was the son of King Bosou Achade, who promoted the idea that his family descended from the leopard lwa, Agasú.[376] Ajáhùtó assassinated his brother, who had taken the throne from him, and fled to the east. Ajáhùtó is at the origin of the royal dynasties of Allada, Abomey, and Porto-Novo.[377] *See* **Agasou Gnenen.**

djandjoukou A Vodou priest.[378] The Fon words *jánján* (solid) and *jangbanjangbàn* (vigorous) suggest a connection with Benin.[379] The adjective *djanm* (strong) is found in Haitian Creole.

djaweton Drums used for *rara.*[380]

djaye *See* **djayi.**

djayi Trembling and convulsing as one enters a possession trance.[381] The word *jayi* has the same meaning in Fon.[382]

djevo; djèvo; djèvò; dyevo; dyèvò A sacred Vodou initiation room into which one walks backward.[383] One song suggests that the *djevo* be kept under lock and key, a reference to the seriousness of initiation.[384] The *djevo* is also a storeroom for the accoutrements of the various Vodou lwa.[385]

djò The breath that encircles the earth.[386] *Djò* is the space that encircles the globe and is filled with spiritual beings. *Djò* is a wing that surrounds the universe.[387] The word is associated with ceremonies that do not involve animal sacrifice. The expressions *frè djò* (*djò* brothers) or *sè djò* (*djò* sisters) refer to the people who undergo initiation together. A *priyè djò* is a general prayer to the Vodou nations, lwa, and dignitaries.[388] In the Fon language, *jo* means "to restitute, render, give back, consecrate." The verb is used in the context of Vodun in the expression "*jo mè nú vodun* (to consecrate someone to Vodou)."[389]

Djobolo Bosou The name of a lwa that dwells in lakes. Djobolo belongs to the Bosou family, which includes lwa such as Kadja Bosou and Bosou Ile.[390] In the region near Lake Miragwann in southern Haiti, the road near the lake was flooded by Djobolo because the appropriate sacrifices to him had not been carried out. Those who travel alongside or over that lake should offer coins to Djobolo. Some Haitian politicians arrange for offerings at Lake Miragwann. Djobolo sometimes swallows boats into the lake. Djobolo is variously called a lwa, a *dyab* (a hot lwa), and a *gad* (Guard) in the songs collected in Beauvoir, a fact that underlines his complexity.[391]

djoukoujou A musical instrument used in Vodou ceremonies.[392]

dlo Water; an important metaphor in Vodou. The lwa and ancestors such as Danbala and Simbi live *anba dlo* (under the water). Many Vodou pilgrimages are to places where water flows (e.g., Sodo and Basen Ble). Water is a metaphor for spirituality, mysticism, renewal, and purity. Water also refers to insight into mysticism. Under ritual conditions, Vodouists become possessed when they make contact with water because lwa dwell in water. Some Vodou priests with impressive healing powers are said to have lived for a period of seven years under water or in the sea. Eminent oungan and famous political figures are said to spend lengthy periods under water, where they receive directions from lwa.[393] *Dlo demanbre* (ceremonial water) refers to magically poisoned water. *Dlo Ginen* describes consecrated water used in sacrificial ceremonies. The terms *dlo repiyans* and *dlo repouse* (repulsive water) refer to magic potions used to ward off evil. *Dlo santi* (smelly water) is a magic potion, and *dlo mò* (water of the dead) refers to liquid used in remedies.[394] Water is used for libations in Haiti and in the Fon culture of Benin.[395]

doba Low back; a traditional Vodou dance similar to *dans jenou*.[396]

doge To protect a child against evil; a ritual term for the sacrificial ram or goat.[397]

dogwe The triplet child born after the Marasa in the same pregnancy.[398] In Fon, *dokpwe* means "to assemble together."[399] The *dogwe* gives people the power to sojourn under water.[400] *Dogwe* is also defined as a ritual curtsey made for a senior priest and to the lwa.[401] *See* **dosa; dosou; Marasa**.

dole A term that refers to heritage that is found in the Gbe languages—for example, "The drum is the heritage, father Sobo answers, we shall all be the heritage."[402]

dòmi Sleeping; replaces death in the *ounsi kanzo* initiation. Sleeping is travel into the domain of the lwa and the ancestors. Dreams are therefore serious revelations.[403]

Domisi Wèdo; Danmisi Wèdo The name of a lwa; the daughter of Danbala Wèdo.[404] *Ayidawedo* is the Fon term for the rainbow, and at its end is a treasure called Domisi, born from the union of Danbala and Ayida.[405] *See* **Ayida Wèdo; Danbala Wèdo**.

donon; dounon; dounou A Fon word that refers to the feeding of a lwa through the sacrifice of an animal. The expression *dù nu* literally means "to eat."[406] *See* **koklo; okon**.

dosa Girl born after twins.[407] In the Fon language, *dosi* has the same meaning.[408] *See* **dogwe; dosou; Marasa**.

dosou Male born after twins.[409] Dosou is also a lwa associated with lakes, springs, and rivers.[410] The term *Dosou* belongs to the Petwo rite.[411] In the Fon language, the word *dosú* similarly refers to the male child born after twins.[412] *See* **dogwe; dosa; Marasa**.

doukounou A pastry made of cornmeal and wrapped in a banana leaf that is favored by the Kongo lwa.[413] *See* **akasan siwo**.

doundoun The smallest of the three Rada drums.[414]

drapo A Vodou ceremonial flag or banner.[415] Symbolic and decorative flags made from shiny beads are stitched onto fabric and used for rituals and ceremonies in Vodou. A flag may be displayed in a temple in honor of a lwa or the temple itself. *Pòt drapo* and *drapo kò* (flag corps) refer to flag bearers.[416] At a *leve kanzo* ceremony in Miami, two female *pòt drapo* wrapped themselves in shiny beaded Vodou flags, one representing Ogou and the other the society. The *pòt drapo* were playfully chased around the *potomitan* in a ritual dance by the male laplas who carefully held Ogou's sword. Beaded flags are also common in the Vodun of Benin.[417]

dwòg Drug; a magic charm or Vodou potion.[418]

dyab; djab Etymologically related to *diable* (devil) in French but in Haitian Creole sometimes a reference to malicious, mean, difficult, or mischievous Vodou lwa.[419] At other times, *dyab* is synonymous with lwa and does not express negative attributes. *Dyab* is often used in a benign way because Africans did not divide the world of spirits in the Judeo-Christian manner. For example, one song says, "The Djab wants to enter the ceremony / It's a gift, nothing is disturbed."[420] Africans did not believe that there was a war between God and his angels and Satan and his demons.[421] In other contexts, *dyab* are considered willing to accomplish a goal by any means and have high expectations of the person making a request. *Dyab* are said to be cruel and have a taste for evil. For example, Èzili Je Wouj is considered a jealous and angry *dyab*: "Oh Èzili red eyes, if she takes you she'll devour you."[422] Marinèt-Bwa-Chèch is known for having her followers walk through fire. Makandal, the oungan who poisoned hundreds of French colonists, is considered a *dyab* endowed with magical power.[423] Other *dyab* include Petwo Je Wouj, Ti Jan Pye Sèk, Ti Jan Zandò, and Bakoulou baka. These lwa are called *dyab* because of their rage and negativity, and they are often associated with the Petwo rite. The lwa are sometimes asked to protect the community or temple from *dyab.*[424] *See* **lwa; satan.**

Dyakata The name of a Dahomian lwa linked to thunder and lightning. *Lakataw* in the proverb "Lakataw goes boom, in Ginen they hear it" may be linked to Dyakata.[425]

Dyekle Klite The name of a lwa.[426]

dyèvò *See* **djevo.**

dyouba; djouba; jouba A dance and a special Vodou drum used for the lwa Azaka Mede and more generally at carnival time.[427] The dance tends to lose its religious character.[428] The word derives from *dyoula* in the Mede language.[429]

Ebyoso; Ebyosou; Kebyoso The Vodou lwa of thunder who is specially honored at Souvnans.[430] Note also that Héviosso (or Xèvioso, Xèbioso, Khèviôsô) is the *vodun* (lwa) of thunder and lightning in Benin.[431] The original sanctuary of Xèbyoso/Xèvioso/Khèviôsô is in Khèvié (Xèvie), in southern Benin.[432] The name Khèviôsô literally means "the thunder or lightning from Khèvié." The *vodun* (lwa) is feared because he can destroy life in an instant flash.[433] In Benin, Xèbyoso's lightning is a negative cosmic element. However, when accompanied by rain, Xèbioso is a positive source of fecundity. His emblem is a stylized double-headed ax; those who serve him carry an ax whose blade is shaped like a goat's head and spits a lightning bolt or flames. Xèbyoso's ritual language is a Nago (Yorùbá) dialect. When someone is killed by lightning, Xèbyoso is said to be involved in the death.[434] In Benin, the family and community will not bury a victim who has been killed by lightning under the ground; instead, they leave the body exposed in the forest.[435] In traditional African religion, those who die of smallpox, leprosy, madness, or childbirth, and those who have committed suicide, are dumped in the "evil forest," not buried in the earth, because the earth forbids "ceremonial uncleanliness."[436] *See* **Souvnans.**

Ege The country of the lwa.[437] *See* **Ginen.**

enstale A ritual introduction of the lwa into a new Vodou temple.[438]

eritye Heirs or inheritors, a term that refers to those who receive the lwa and Vodou traditions through their family lineage.[439] The following song shows that unity is highly valued: "Where there are heirs, let's work together closely."[440] *See* **lafanmi.**

eskalabaha A cry to call forth Vodou lwa.[441]

esklav Slaves. The French transported 800,000 *esklav* to Saint-Domingue between 1695 and 1791.[442]

eskòt An escort, troupe, flock, family, or group of Vodou lwa that are linked together.[443] *See* **twoupo.**

espedisyon; ekspedisyon The sending of *dyab* or evil magic substances against an enemy.[444] Such magic is the domain of the bòkò. A *seremoni espedisyon* (expedition ceremony) involves freeing oneself from obligations to the lwa.[445]

espedye; ekspedye To send away or placate a lwa; a powder used in remedies.[446]

Èzili; Èzili Anmin; Èzili Balyang; Èzili Boumba; Èzili Dan Petwo; Èzili Dantò; Èzili Doba/Dowa; Èzili Freda Danwonmen; Èzili Freda Badè; Èzili Imado; Èzili Jewouj; Èzili Kawoulo; Èzili Mabenge; Èzili Makanda; Èzili Makaya; Èzili Mapyang; Èzili Mayonèt; Èzili Nennen; Èzili Siniga; Èzili Towo; Èzili Wangòl; Grann Èzili; Manbo Èzili; Metrès Èzili One of the most important families of Vodou lwa. The Èzili family represents love, affection, grace, beauty, motherhood, devotion, and self-sacrifice. Èzili is associated with the Danwonmen, Kongo, Petwo, and Rada rites.[447] She takes several forms, including Dantò (the Black Erzulie), Freda (the White Ezrulie), Je Wouj (a lwa associated with jealousy), and Grann (a crippled old woman). Some of the Petwo Èzili include Boumba, Dantò, Kanlikan, Kè-Nwa, Kokobe and Mapyang.[448] The lwa of beauty, coquettish comportment, and love, Èzili Freda is represented as a mulatto with long hair; she is voluptuous, seductive, and richly clothed. Her vèvè is a heart pierced by a knife, a symbol of her jealousy over betrayal.[449] Her resting tree is a *cirouellier.* Her days of the week are Tuesday and Thursday, and her colors are pale rose and white. Two white chickens or two white pigeons are sacrificed for her.[450] Èzili Freda is associated with the Mater Dolorosa, who in Catholic chromolithographs is represented as an attractive woman wearing pearls and gold, many bracelets, rings, and a heart pierced by a golden sword. Èzili is also linked to two black Virgins: La Altagracia (also called the Virgin of Higüey after a Dominican town) and Our Lady of Mount Carmel. Èzili is luckless, and her love life is plagued with misfortunes. Her tragedy is the loss of her only son at sea, the lwa of war Ogou Badagri. Based on the chromolithograph of the Mater Dolorosa, some Vodou followers believe that Èzili has a daughter named Urzule. Èzili has various lovers among the lwa, including Danbala Wèdo, Agwe Tawoyo, Ogou Badagri (her son to some), and Ogou Feray. Èzili and Ayida Wèdo are *matlòt*—that is, women who share a male partner, Danbala Wèdo. When they simultaneously possess their servants, they argue. Nibo, lwa of death, flirts with Èzili and sometimes appears in ceremonies after Èzili, where he sniffs the air recognizing her lingering scent. Èzili is the mistress of the lwa of the sea, Agwe Tawoyo, and is called on by fishermen in danger.[451] Some temples close to the sea are dedicated to Metrès Èzili because they provide access to her lover, Agwe.[452] Sometimes a faithful Vodouist will marry Èzili and, during a special ceremony, will put a golden ring on his or her finger. The follower's initials and the name of Èzili are engraved on it. After such mystical marriages, the follower may no longer marry or take a common-law spouse (*plase*). A follower who is already married must stay away from his or her marital bed on days dedicated to the lwa (Tuesday and Thursday). When under the protection of Èzili, the follower must not engage in sexual activity, consume alcohol, smoke, gamble, or dance on her day.[453] In *Of Men and Gods,* a documentary about a homosexual Vodouist subculture, Èzili is said to *gate* (spoil) men and make them homosexual. Gay Vodouists hold Èzili in high esteem.[454] One of Marcelin's informants stated that he never again consumed alcohol after being confronted by Èzili about his habitual drunkenness.[455] Èzili corrects and heals people. Followers of Èzili display the *ogatwa* (home shrine) with toiletry items, bouquets of basil, and a small pot of olive oil. Followers of Èzili place her chromolithograph in their ogatwa. Under their beds they keep a basin filled with water, colt's-foot herb, basil leaves, and a handful of grilled peanuts.[456] Temples dedicated to Ezili always have luxurious toiletry items because she is said to have refined taste. On days that Èzili is supposed to be honored, one's house is not supposed to be cleaned, but perfume and lotions should be sprinkled around. On special days dedicated to Èzili Freda, one may not drink or smoke in the ounfò. Altars are adorned with mangos, watermelons, bananas, grenadine juice, sugarcane juice, macerated pineapple juice, vermicelli with milk, wheat flour, eggs, and many other types of food and feminine objects, such as skirts and makeup.[457] In ceremonies dedicated to Èzili, her vèvè, in addition to those of her lovers Agwe, Danbala Wèdo, Ogou Badagri, and Ogou Feray, are traced by the oungan or manbo. The *ounsi* get on their knees and kiss the vèvè three times. In all ceremonies, Legba is first addressed in song, followed by the other lwa in a fixed order, with three songs dedicated to each. As the ceremony begins to focus on Èzili, the manbo is eventually mounted by her. The lwa is invited to sit on a straw couch to receive special attention. Makeup, perfume, fingernails, hair, and rings, each representing her lovers, are provided to the coquettish lwa. Èzili rises and haughtily walks around the *peristil,* where she looks down on the women and flirts with the men. Marcelin tells the story of a manbo, mounted by Èzili, who selected a man to caress her privately. Satisfied with his touches, Èzili (the manbo) gave the man thirty Haitian dollars. The next day, after Èzili had departed from her, the manbo woke up with no memory of the event and thirty Haitian dollars poorer. The man who had caressed her refused to return the money. The manbo brought him before a judge but lost the case because the judge agreed that under Èzili's influence, she had given the money away.[458] According to a Vodou priest, one may invoke Èzili by means of the vèvè of her lovers. Èzili is related to the Wéménu-Fon *vodun* (lwa) Ázlì, who is linked to Lake Agonvè in Benin.[459] *Freda* (princess) refers to the "Kingdom of Freda," another name for the "Kingdom of Wida," a town in modern Benin.[460] Ezili Freda, who receives small and expensive presents such as soap, perfume, and flowers, expresses a "stagey exuberance" that imitates bourgeois culture.[461] Her possession events sometimes involve nervous breakdowns and manic-depressive weeping.[462] *See* **Grann Èzili**.

Èzili Dantò; Èzili Mabenge Considered Dahomian in origin but classed with the Kongo-Petwo rite because of her aggressiveness. Èzili Dantò is said to be the mother of all Petwo lwa.[463] She is a gorgeous black woman who dresses in dark blue attire with a red scarf tied around her neck, symbolic of her role in the Bwa Kayiman ceremony and the Haitian revolution and as the "mother of freedom."[464] She represents the devotion and protectiveness of mothers for their children.[465] As a Petwo lwa, her vèvè are traced from ground hot chili and pepper powders. She is associated with Our Lady of Perpetual Sorrow.[466] French soldiers cut out Èzili Dantò's tongue during the Haitian Revolution.[467] Her *chwal* (horse) cannot speak but violently stutters "*ke, ke, ke*!"[468] Services in honor of Èzili Dantò require the sacrifice of a black pig and the preparation of pork.[469] The fertility of pigs represents her own fertility. Èzili Dantò's son is Ti Jan Dantò. Her rival marked her with two scars on her right cheek. She is jealous and punishes those who displease her, as this song points out: "Èzili Dantò, I know you're angry. . . . Oh look how the guys vomit blood, it's Dantò who stabbed them."[470] Her vèvè includes daggers, and when Èzili possesses her *chwal* (horse), she holds a dagger in each hand, the point turned to her sides. Anayiz is her daughter. Those married to her must sleep apart from their spouses on Tuesdays or Thursdays. The following song reveals her culinary preferences: "Fried pork, plantain, that's what Dantò eats."[471] Her followers offer her jewelry, dresses, scarves, perfume, cigarettes, and rum.[472] The possession events of Èzili Dantò (plus Èzili Je Wouj and Èzili Mayanèt) are more intense than those of Èzili Freda and involve kicking, screaming, and stuttering rages.[473] Èzili was important for the Dahomian and Kongolese populations in Saint-Domingue because of their common Nòk ancestors.[474] *See* **Èzili.**

Èzili Je Wouj Èzili Red Eyes; an angry and jealous lwa.

Èzili Kawoulo An ancient and severe manifestation of Èzili. Èzili Kawoulo unleashes lightning and thunder and mounted the elderly manbo, Cécile Fatiman, who sacrificed a black pig at the Bwa Kayiman ceremony of 1791 and offered sips of its blood in a pact against the criminal French slave culture.[475] *See* **Bwa Kayiman.**

Èzili Mapyang The name of a lwa who is very similar to Èzili Dantò, including scars on her cheeks. She is considered a *gad* (guard), a protector lwa. The vèvè of this Petwo lwa is a pentagram with an omniscient eye traced in its center.[476] *See* **Èzili Dantò.**

Èzili Petwo A Petwo manifestation of the lwa Èzili. In one song, Èzili first asks for and receives a drink offering and then asks for but is denied a human offering: "Èzili, if you ask me for a person / I will pull out now." There are things, such as human sacrifice and murder, that one should *not* do for the lwa.[477] *See* **Èzili.**

Èzili-Zila *See* **Èzili.**

Fa; Ifa Fa and the divinatory traditions associated with this *vodun* (lwa) stem from the town of Ife in Nigeria. The Ifa is a system of divination that shapes human destiny. The priest of Fa, the *bokònòn,* interprets the language of the divinities by means of palm nuts on a special tray.[478] Yorùbá Ifa diviners train for ten years in Ifa divination. Ifa is also a rich Yorùbá poetic corpus that serves as the repository of Yorùbá cultural values.[479] The Fon *bokònòn* and Haitian bòkò soothsaying traditions both stem from Ife.[480] Oungan-Bòkò Alisma in Miami also noted that one of the skills he teaches his initiates to the priesthood is the reading of cards for divination and treatment. *See* **bòkò; Gelefre; Ginen; Ife.**

fanmi A group of Vodou lwa.[481] *See* **eskòt; twoupo.**

farin Ginen Ginen or Guinean flour; any of the powders used by the oungan or manbo to trace vèvè. Ground coffee, wheat flour, cornmeal, charcoal ashes, canon powder, talc, sand, and other powders are used according to the rite or the lwa.[482] *See* **file farin; trase vèvè; vèvè.**

fent A ruse or sudden temporary change in Vodou rhythm.[483] *See* **kase.**

Fèt Demò; Fèt Gede The Feast of the Dead/Gede, which takes place on November 1–2 in Haiti. Ceremonies for the dead continue throughout the month.[484]

fèy Leaves; plants, leaves, and herbs that are used for healing and ritual in Vodou. *Fèy* (leaves) are consumed, rubbed on the body, and bathed in. The use of trees and plants in Vodou healing practices is well founded; today, 40 percent of pharmaceutical products derive from those natural resources.[485] *Fèy nan bwa* (leaves in the woods) refers to members of a temple. The terms *pitit fèy* (leaf child) and *ti fèy* (little leaf) refer to an initiated member or a patient of a Vodou healer.[486] In the Fon language, *hunmà* (leaves of the *vodun*) is the leaf of a lwa that is used in a bath for a new recruit.[487] In the Fon language, *tuwùn amà* (to know leaves) refers to having skills in traditional medicine.[488]

fig *Bon fig* (a good fig) refers to a good and faithful Vodou servant. A *move fig* (bad fig) refers to an untrustworthy Vodou servant or person.[489]

file farin To string flour, referring to the use of flour to draw or trace the lines that form a vèvè.[490] *See* **farin Ginen; trase vèvè; vèvè**.

fimen Smoking; blowing tobacco smoke as a form of consecration in ceremonies. *See* **foula**.

fiyole To wipe the face of someone possessed by a lwa with a handkerchief, a practice carried out by the *ounsi*.[491] On hot nights, the servants of the lwa gently dab each other's sweat in the course of worship and celebration.

flags *See* **drapo**.

flè A *bèl flè* (beautiful flower) refers to a wandering and evil Vodou spirit, as well as to a Vodou rattle devoid of magical power.[492]

fòj Ogou Ogou's forge; an iron bar or rod planted in the ground that represents the lwa Ogou. *See* **Ogou**.

foula A ritual gesture that involves the Vodou priest or priestess pulverizing mouthfuls of water, alcohol, or perfume in a fine spray to consecrate ritual space. *Foula* are also made to the four cardinal directions in honor of the lwa.[493] Lwa in the Èzili family like to have perfume *foula* around the *potomitan*. *Foula* is also a technique that involves spraying a fine mist on a patient for healing.[494] The *foula* consecrates Vodou objects and produces an intense religious atmosphere. The *foula* produces possession in some cases.[495] The ritual gesture of *foula* is mentioned in several Vodou songs.[496] *See* **fimen**.

fran Ginen Pure Ginen; a grassroots Vodouist who, uncorrupted by outside influences, exclusively follows Ginen traditions. This refers to the Rada lwa and hereditary Vodou.[497] *See* **Ginen**.

fwèt; fwèt kach Whip used in Petwo ceremonies to attract the lwa.[498] In a ceremony for Èzili Dantò, I observed various individuals cracking a whip intermittently.

The Ogous are also attracted by the snap of a whip.[499] The whip is cracked at the *leve kanzo* (coming-out celebration for new initiates) as they return to the temple from the *kafou* (crossroads). The cracking whip symbolizes the importance of devotion to the *mèt tèt* (main lwa). In a ceremony in Bizoton, an oungan stretched a whip out on the ground, and the *ounsi* jumped over it.[500] The whip is cracked three times to remember what "Grandma" endured during slavery.[501]

fwèt ayizan Ayizan whip made of palm foliage and used in Vodou initiations.[502] *See* **ayizan**.

gabyèn A variety of Vodou dance.[503]

gad A spiritual guard or protection to preserve an individual from harm.[504] The scarification found in West African Vodou is a form of *gad.*[505] A *gad* is a lwa who protects a Vodouist.[506] Some consider a *gad* to have been a human who died as a martyr and subsequently transformed.[507] *Gad* are obtained to protect children from the evil eye and from *lougawou* (werewolves).[508] The *gad* also belongs to Haitian figural tradition.[509] The term *gad* is possibly borrowed from the French *garde.* However, note the Fon term *gãdida* (protective amulet).[510] *See* **lwa; pakèt Kongo; pwen**.

gadelovi A variety of Vodou dance.[511]

gaj An obligation or pledge made to a Vodou priest or priestess.[512]

Ganga Kalounga The name of a lwa.[513]

gangan; ganga A diminutive or intimate term for oungan.[514] *Gangan* is related to the Kikongo term *ngànga* (healer, ritual expert).[515] Another simultaneous influence may be the reduplication of the Fon word *gan* (chief) which is also found in the Fon term, *houngan* (priest). *See* **manbo; oungan**.

gangans Ritual courtesies exchanged between Vodou priests or priestesses at ceremonies; a bow or curtsey by a Vodou priest or priestess toward the four cardinal points.[516]

gate To spoil; a reference to how Èzili or Jeneral Piman render men or women homosexual.[517]

gate [English] *See* **baryè**.

gate san To spoil blood; to immunize a child's blood against *lougawou.*[518] *See* **lougawou**.

Gbon Sante *See* **Bizango; Sanpwèl**.

gè A *bat gè* (war beating) is a Vodou rite in which forks are struck against plates.[519]

gede A sexually suggestive Vodou dance to the Gede.[520]

Gede; Gede Drivayè; Gede (Ti) Fatra; Gede Honsou; Gede Kriyòl; Gede Lensou; Gede Loray; Gede Nibo; Gede Nouvavou; Gede Pikan; Gede Ramase; Gede Rounsou Mazaka; Gede Ti Wawè; Gede Ti Pis Lakwa; Gede Wonsou; Gede Yèhwe A Vodou rite and the lwa of life and death.[521] Death is not an endpoint for Gede, because life and death are a revolving cycle. As the decider of life and death, Gede is seen as good and bad.[522] The Gede lwa are cold because they emanate from the dead. When they possess people, they warm themselves up by rubbing hot pepper on their bodies and by consuming alcohol infused with hot pepper. The Gede dab white powder on their faces and stuff their ears and nostrils with cotton. They may be wrapped up in cloth like cadavers. The Gede are sometimes mischievous and obscene. They are associated with death but are not the souls of the dead, *lèmò.* Gede Honsou is called a *defansè* (defender).[523] Gede is also the general name for assistants of Bawon Samdi. The Gede are the lwa of the cemeteries and govern the good and the bad.[524] When passing in front of the cemeteries, followers stop, uncover themselves, and say prayers and speeches while lighting black candles.[525] At Vodou ceremonies, the Gede lwa are called on last, immediately following the Ogou flock. Their dance, the *banda,* is performed solely in couples, without distinction of sex. The dance, which originated in the Kongo, involves movements of the hips and the buttocks.[526] At the start of November, the Gede celebrate royally in the villages and the countryside. A number of followers possessed by them circulate in the cemetery, the streets, and the markets. They dress in old frock coats and wear tophats. They appear with cotton in their ears and nostrils, cigars in their mouths, and a bottle of alcohol in one hand and a *koko makak* (beating stick) in the other, and they speak in nasal tones.[527] Rather than a frock coat, men wear a mauve shirt and women wear a dressing gown or mauve *karako* dress. On the night of the celebration of life and death, Vodouists sell drinks and food in the cemeteries. They also sing and make music while the Gede lwa dance. While most lwa appear when called on, the Gede lwa, like death itself, can appear without notice.[528] The Gede family is composed of many members—most notably, Bawon Samdi, Bawon Simityè, Bawon Lakwa, Grann Brijit, and Gede Nibo.[529] In the Fon language, *gede* refers to someone who is complicated and difficult. *See* **Gedevi.**

Gede Nibo An important spirit in the Gede family.[530] Like other lwa, Gede Nibo has the ability to encounter water without getting wet: "The rain fell seven times, he isn't wet!"[531] Gede Nibo is the protector of the living and the dead.[532] His resting tree is a lime tree, and his sacrifice is generally a black cock or a black goat. Many Vodouists identify Nibo with Saint Louis de Gonzague, others with Saint Gerard of Majella. The latter is represented in the Catholic religion wearing a long black cassock and holding a large crucifix. Next to the saint, resting on a small table covered with a red tablecloth, is a skull and an open book.[533] Gede Nibo is associated with the Banda, Bawon, and Petwo rites. Nibo's vèvè has a large cross that represents death. Nibo's feast day, like the other Gede lwa, is November 2, and Vodouists dress in black or white and conduct ceremonies in cemeteries.[534] Gede Nibo governs graveyards and tombs, particularly those of children. To obtain a degree of mystical power, Vodouists address Nibo. On an infant's tomb, they trace a cross on which they make an offering and drink white rum. They then make an engagement or commitment to him.[535] In the Vodou temple, Nibo's altar is a small tomb placed in front of Bawon Samdi's cross. Vodouists light a black candle behind the cross of Gede Nibo. On Nibo's tomb are placed cigars, a bottle containing spices, bottles of alcohol, and other ingredients for healing treatments.[536] Vodouists call on Nibo to receive news of parents who reside in far provinces or abroad. They invoke him to communicate with the recently deceased. For people who have been deceased for long periods of time, the oungan goes to the cemetery at midnight and, after receiving permission from Bawon Samdi, invokes Nibo, who brings him into contact with the dead.[537] Nibo dresses in black and ordinarily wears tatty pants, a worn frock coat, and a deformed hat. He has a black scarf tied around his neck and a cigar at the corner of his mouth. Like Gede, Gede Nibo also carries a *koko makak* (beating stick) in one hand and a bottle of spiced *tafya* (unrefined white rum) in the other.[538] Gede Nibo's possession events are marked by rude behavior and vulgar language. The Gede are known to appear in services dedicated to other lwa to eat, drink, cavort, and curse, and they can be promptly expelled by oungan and manbo.[539] Nibo is the name of a town in the Ibo region of Nigeria.[540] *See* **Gede; Gedevi**.

Gede Petwo A Vodou rite that includes Kaptèn Zonbi and Gede Welo.[541]

Gedevi; Gede Vi; Gedevi Yawe The son of Gede Nibo. In Fon, *vi* means "child"; thus, Gede Vi means "child of Gede."[542] In Haitian Vodou, Gedevi is a healing lwa who assists his father when someone is sick. Gedevi's days and meals are the same as those of Gede Nibo.[543] The Gedevi were the indigenous inhabitants of Abomey, today in Benin, when the Aladoxonù and Doko-Donu population invaded in the seventeenth century. The *vodun* (lwa) Gede was the patron deity of the Gedevi people. The Gedevi population was sold to slave merchants and mostly transported to Haiti.[544] *See* **Gede; Gede Nibo**.

Gelefre A name used for Africa in some Vodou songs.[545] Gelefre is the dwelling place of the Vodou lwa.[546] *See* **Danwonmen; Ginen; Ife; Vilokan**.

genbo *See* **gonbo**.

geri tout Heal all; a powder used in remedies.[547]

gerizon Healing of physical and psychological ailments through herbs, prayer, and psychotherapeutic methods; one of the principal activities of the *oungan/manbo rasin* (roots Vodou priest or priestess).

Ginen; Gine A word with many meanings that can refer to the lwa, the dwelling place of the lwa, the servants of the lwa, and the afterlife paradise where the souls of Vodouists return. It generally refers broadly to Africa. Historically, the term *Ginen* is a reference to West Africa's Guinea region. Several songs refer to *lakòt Ginen* (the coast of Guinea/Ginen/Africa).[548] Ginen refers to precolonial African spiritual roots and to people who work to preserve African culture and traditions. Ginen also refers to a priest or priestess of the Rada rite (e.g., *oungan Ginen* or *manbo Ginen*).[549] Oungan Nelson Marcenat is an *oungan Ginen* because he entered the priesthood through his family. For Marcenat, *Ginen* also refers to the skull at the base of his *pewon* (altar) or the *kwi* (calabash offering bowl), which suggests that the term can be used for any Vodou cultural object. *Sèvi Ginen* (to serve the Ginen) is the same as *sèvi lwa* (to serve the lwa). To *retounen nan Ginen* (return to Ginen) means to die and depart from the earth. *Pale Ginen* (or *langaj*) involves mystical ritual phrases originating from African languages. *Liv Ginen* is a book from Africa and is intelligible to only Vodou priests and priestesses. *Nèg Ginen* (Ginen Guy) is an upstanding individual with good principles.[550] Beauvoir's *Lapriyè Ginen* is an important and ancient Haitian Vodou liturgical text that he reconstructed through research with several Vodou priests. *Ginen* can also refer to ash used to trace vèvè.[551] *See* **Fran Ginen; Gelefre.**

God *See* **Bondye; Gran Mèt; Mawou-Lisa.**

gonbo An expensive ceremony with a lot of food in honor of a Vodou lwa.[552]

Gougoun The name of a lwa associated with Ayizan.[553] The name is possibly linked to Ogoun because prominent syllables in a name are often doubled in Haitian Creole hypocoristics.

gout The phrase *jete twa gout dlo* (pour out three drops of water) refers to libations for the lwa.[554]

gouyad; yayad A pelvic dance.[555]

govi An earthenware jug containing the essences of Vodou lwa and ancestors.[556] The *govi* are used to communicate with the lwa or the ancestors. The Fon word *gozí/gozín,* which refers to earthenware ritual pottery that holds water for purification, is a possible source of the word *govi.*[557]

grajman A dance to chase away unwelcome lwa.[558]

Gran Bwa; Granbwa; Granbwa Nago; Granbwa Yeye; Granbwa Zile; Mèt Granbwa Ile Great Forest; the Vodou lwa of the forest and owner of the leaves.[559] Gran Bwa is associated with the Petwo and Rada rites. Ceremonies for Gran Bwa are secret and by invitation only. Gran Bwa is mentioned with the greatest respect.[560] The *pilon* (pestle) is connected to Gran Bwa's *maji* (magic).[561] Deformed himself, Gran Bwa understands suffering and uses leaves for medicine.[562] Gran Bwa is linked to the Bwa Kayiman ceremony.[563] Offerings to Gran Bwa are leaves from the woods that are placed in a *makout* (woven straw bag) and carried back to the ounfò .[564] One lyric reads, "Gran Bwa, oh I'm a snake!" Gran Bwa is considered a tree-climbing lwa.[565] Gran Bwa has healing powers but can also express wrath. Those possessed by Gran Bwa tell salty jokes. Bon Manbo Racine reports that Gran Bwa was amused by the Catholic Church's recent inclusion of the drums in masses because drums have twenty-one lwa dwelling within them.[566] Gran Bwa is the "self-forest . . . ever lurking, virgin, opening towards unexplored realms."[567] *See* **Loko Atisou.**

Gran Mèt Great Master; a common Haitian Creole term for God that probably came from the Freemasons.[568] *See* **Bondye; Mawou-Lisa.**

Grann Brijit; Brijit; Manman Brijit; Madmwazèl Brijit Granny Brigitte; the wife of Bawon Samdi and the mother of the Gede.[569] Grann Brijit is as powerful as her husband. She is associated with the Banda, Bawon, and Petwo rites. She, her husband,

and Gede Nibo are in charge of the passage between life and death. If the first person buried in a cemetery was a woman, then Grann Brijit is in charge of the cemetery. Those possessed by Grann Brijit lie prostrate as if dead and take on nasal tones.[570] She is a very old black woman. Grann Brijit is identified with Saint Brigid, the patron of Ireland.[571] Her resting tree is a *cirouellier* or a cursed brown fig tree (*Clusia rosea* Jacq.), and in the cemeteries she is represented by a pile of stones. Her days of consecration are Monday and Friday, and her color is black.[572] Grann Brijit rarely possesses an individual, but when she does, the individual becomes like the dead. Vodouists wrap the possessed person's jaw with a black scarf, put cotton in the ears and nostrils, cover her in a white cloth, sprinkle white rum, and chant for her. Grann Brijit never speaks. When she removes herself from her possessed *chwal* (horse), the audience chants. Sometimes Grann Brijit and Bawon Samdi appear together. He sits down on a bed where he awaits his wife. He does not speak or drink or smoke. Worshipers watch him as they watch the dead at a wake. Grann Brijit's ritual meal is composed of potatoes, plantain, salted herring, grilled cod, corn, grilled pistachios, and a sacrificed black chicken.[573] *See* **Bawon Samdi; Brijit**.

Grann Èzili; Èzili Freda; Èzili Freda Dawomen The lwa of fresh water and protector of homes. Grann Èzili is identified with Saint Anne.[574] She is represented as a crying, pale-skinned mulatto bent over in old age. Her followers venerate her devotedly. She is associated with lakes and with Basen Ble (Blue Basin), an important pilgrimage destination.[575] She is known as Grann Èzili Freda Dawomen Manman Vodou (Granny Èzili Freda Dahomian Mother of Vodou).[576] She is also known as the "good Èzili." Grann Èzili is old and constantly sick. Songs in Chapter 4 portray her in various ways. She has difficulty appearing among her followers because she is bedridden; she no longer has bones; sometimes Papa Agwe Tawoyo cares for her. Those possessed by Grann Èzili have hunched-over postures; sometimes they are stricken with paralysis because of the divinity's advanced age.[577] Grann Èzili lost her only child, Urzule, at sea. Urzule's father was the lwa of war, Ogou Badagri, and since Urzule's death, Grann Èzili has been in perpetual mourning—hence her identification with the Mater Dolorosa, who is represented in chromolithographs as a weeping woman. Grann Èzili is wise and sometimes reproaches her children for not following her advice. She requires water libations. Many prostitutes place themselves under the patronage of Grann Èzili in the hope that she will bring them to repent. She is called on for help. Grann Èzili likes cleanliness.[578] She is associated with Danbala Wèdo and does not consume alcohol. Marcelin describes a scene in which Grann Èzili's *chwal* (horse) was accidently served alcohol. As soon as she tasted the drink, she became furious and threatened to kill her *chwal*. Danbala, who was also present, came to the *chwal*'s rescue and calmed Grann Èzili down before she executed her plan. Grann Èzili receives food offerings of bread, cassava flatbread, corn, grilled nuts, candy, plantains, biscuits, dry cake, eggs, wheat flour, sugar, rice, milk, sweet coffee, and orange syrup and rosewater for her perfume. Two white pigeons are sacrificed in her honor. Tuesday and Thursday are consecrated for Grann Èzili, and blue and white are her colors. In services, those possessed by the lwa ordinarily wear a blue marine dress and a blue headscarf.

grenadye Grenadier. A grenadier lwa is one who does not jump into *ma dlo* (mud-pits). *See* **ma dlo; sòtè**.

griz Ritual Vodou clothing.[579]

Gwètò *See* **Ayizan Velekete**.

gwevo The inner sanctuary of a Vodou temple containing an altar.[580] *See* **badji; djèvò**.

gwo baka The big goblin; the larger of the two Kongo-Petwo drums. Its rhythm generally punctuates choreography and dancing like the *manman tanbou* drum in the Rada rite.[581] In some regions, the *gwo baka* is also called the *manman* (mother). *See* **manman tanbou; rale; ti baka**.

gwo bonnanj The big good angel; the divine particle and breath of life in all beings. The presence of this divine particle is the reason all individuals deserve respect.[582] The *gwo bonnanj* gives the *kò kadav* (cadaver body) life.[583] At the time of death, the *gwo bonnanj* returns to God.[584] *See* **Bondye; kò kadav; ti bonnanj**.

gwo chemen The wide path; a reference to reliance on inherited lwa as opposed to the more risky purchased ones.[585] *See* **lwa Ginen; lwa rasin**.

gwonde Rumble; the middle-size drum of the three Kongo rite drums. This drum is similar to the *tenbal*.[586]

Gwo Wòch Big Rock; the name of a lwa.[587]

horse *See* **chwal**.

houngan *See* **oungan**.

houngennikon *See* **oungenikon**.

hounla; hounli A variety of rudimentary drum.[588]

hounsi *See* **ounsi**.

hountoli The player of a *hounli*.[589]

hounyò *See* **ounyò**.

Ibo; Ibo Bibi; Ibo Bwa; Ibo Ewa; Ibo Ewa Zanzan; Ibo Kanman; Ibo Kata; Ibo Kilibwa; Ibo Lazil; Ibo Swaman; Ayanman Ibo Lele; Grann Ibo A Vodou rite, lwa, and dance.[590] The Ibo is a *nanchon* (nation) of Vodou lwa that originates among the Igbo people of Nigeria. Ibo Lele is served in the Ibo, Makaya, and Mondong rites. She is the guardian of historical traditions and is in close contact with the ancestors, especially Emperor Dessalines. Ibo warrior rhythms accompany ceremonies dedicated to her. Ibo Lele is independent, ambitious, and aloof, and even though she is the lwa of language, those possessed by her speak in monosyllables.[591] In the center of her vèvè a *kanari* (clay vessel) is traced surrounded by Haitian flags; within the *kanari* is the soul of the initiate.[592] The Ibo is also a dignified and reserved dance with two steps to the right followed by two steps to the left. An *ibo* is also a type of drum.[593] The Ibo rite has been subsumed by the Rada rite.[594] The Ibo (Igbo) people still inhabit southern Nigeria, and Elele is the name of an Ibo town. Wars with the Dahomian empire caused many Ibos to be sold into slavery.[595] *See* **nanchon; Petwo; Rada**.

Ife The dwelling place of Vodou's most prominent lwa and a kind of "Vodou Olympus."[596] Ife is a town in Nigeria that serves as the religious capital of the Yorùbá people. *See* **Fa**.

Imamou The name of a sea lwa.[597] Imamou is the name of Agwe's boat, and it is inscribed on its side. A model of the boat Imamou is displayed in some temples. Some speculate that the word *imamou* is related to the Arabic word for holy.[598] *Imamou* refers to various lwa (e.g., Legba Gwètò Imamou and Alovi Imamou).[599]

iniyoun A magically poisoned liquid.[600]

Islam There are living traces of Islam in Vodou. The Hausa, Fulah, and Senega populations were exposed to Islam before the slave trade.[601] Non-Catholic traditions such as Islam, Vodou, and Protestantism were banned during the colonial period. The Qu'ran was outlawed, and Islam gradually disappeared.[602] The Vodou community in the village of Balan, known as Maromet (Mohammed), has more than a thousand members still "wedded" to Islam.[603] Songs for Allah are mixed with those for the saints. Memories of Mandingo origins persist in Balan—the Mandingo people hail from Senegal, Gambia, and Guinea. The community is more closely aligned with the veneration of the ancestors than possession by the lwa. In Balan, an a cappella recitation of the Muslim profession of faith is standard. A notebook was also used for writing "ancestral messages." In other communities described by Métraux when the lwa Siniga possesses someone, traces of Muslim salutations can be detected:[604] *Annandiza sandriyo-hibi-wadhauminan anlahim-kalabudu* or *Salama salay genbo.* *See* **Siniga**.

Jan Bato John Boat; the name of a Rada lwa.[605]

janbe dlo/lanmè To cross the water or sea; to consult a Vodou priest or priestess.[606]

Jan Petwo The name of a lwa in the Petwo rite.[607]

jany *See* **zanj**.

Jan Zonbi; Jean Zombie A mulatto who killed white French settlers under the orders of Dessalines during the colonial period.[608] Jan Zonbi exemplifies how a historical figure and ancestor can turn into a lwa.[609] He is still considered ferocious.[610] *See* **Makandal; zonbi**.

je To *bay je* (provide eyes) is to enlighten or inform mystically. The term also refers to endowing someone with the gift of clairvoyance. *Je wouj* (red eyes) indicates a fiery lwa. *Kat je* (four eyes) refers to the ability to foresee the future. To *pran je* (take eyes) is to foresee the future.[611] *See* **Èzili Je Wouj**.

Jeneral Piman Hot Pepper General; the name of a lwa who turns men or women into homosexuals.[612] *See* **Èzili**.

jete dlo To consult a Vodou priest or priestess. To *jete dlo* can also mean to employ supernatural methods. The expression also refers to sprinkling water on the ground to welcome a guest or a Vodou lwa.[613] *See* **fimen; foula; vèse; wouze**.

jete twa (de)gout dlo pou To pay homage to the lwa by pouring out three drops of water.[614]

Jezabèl *See* **Renn Siyèt**.

kabrit tomazo Tomazo goat; a Vodou backslider or someone who has turned to using Vodou for selfish purposes.[615]

kachimbo A clay pipe that the lwa Azaka smokes.[616] *See* **Azaka Mede**.

Kadya Bosou; Kadya Dosou; Dyobolo Bosou The king of Dahomey (r. 1708–1740) and today a lwa.[617] Under his rule, Dahomey went from being a tiny kingdom to an enormous empire. Kadya Bosou seized Allada in 1724 and Wida in 1727, giving him control over Atlantic commerce.[618] Kadya Bosou was furious with the concessions that King Abangla made to the Catholic Church. After the invasion, he expelled all missionaries and confined Europeans to the port. He made his wife, Wanjile, the head of religion.[619] He and his family line were involved in the slave trade because of Dahomey's need for modern weapons to defend itself from Europeans.[620] His child was Bosou Achade. *See* **Bosou Achade; Djobolo Bosou**.

Kadyamisou The name of a lwa who seems to be the antagonist who says that Loko's wife is old in Marcelin's song 29.

kakofè A woman who is both Vodou priestess and midwife.[621] *See* **matwòn**.

kalbas A ritual Vodou dance.[622] The *kalbas* (calabash) is a tropical tree that produces fruit the size of soccer balls that is halved, dried, scraped clean, and used as ritual bowls called *kwi.* In some parts of northern Haiti, the *kalbas* are varnished and used as drums while thimbles on the fingers strike the surface.[623] Among the Fon people in Benin, the *ká* (calabash) is associated with the fecundity of women and deities. The *vodun* (lwa) are born inside the calabash or communicate with humans through the calabash.[624] *See* **kwi**.

Kalfou; Kafou The crossroads where two paths meet; the domain of Legba. Represented by a cross, the crossroads is one of Vodou's fundamental symbols. The crossroads represents the encounter of the living and the ancestors and lwa. Many vèvè have an underlying cross.[625] *See* **vèvè**.

kalinda Nocturnal dances performed before the Haitian Revolution that may have been used to conceal outlawed Vodou ceremonies.[626]

kanari; kannari A clay jar that is linked to the Ibo traditions. *Kase kannari* (breaking the *kanari* clay jar) refers to the breaking of a consecrated jar at a funeral rite.[627] The important ritual is conducted in September and involves filling the clay jar with corn and soup, digging a hole, lining the hole with white sheets, and placing the *kanari* in the hole. Members of the community then take sticks and break the *kanari* while singing.[628]

kanbiz A *chèf kanbiz* is a person in charge of offerings and ritual accessories in a temple.[629]

Kandèl The name of a lwa that is likely Yorùbá, given song references to the Nago.[630] *See* **Nago**.

kandjanhoun A domestic Vodou ceremony and celebration. *See* **babako; demanbre**.

Kanga; Kanga Twa A subcategory of lwa from the Kongo.[631] Kanga is associated with healing.[632] Kanga Twa is an Ibo-Kanga lwa.[633] *Kanga* means to "tie together," a metaphor for healing and protection from the lwa.[634] In modern Kikongo, *kànga* is a polysemous word with meanings like "to tie, bandage, attach, harden, persevere, walk slowly, etc." The word *kanga* (with no accent) means "to deliver, liberate or save."[635]

Kanibal *See* **Bizango; Sanpwèl**.

kank A special necklace used in Vodou.[636]

Kann Chèch Dry Sugarcane; the name of a lwa who is linked with Jan Kita and Twa Ile.[637] *See* **Kita; Twa Ile**.

kanpelwen Stay far; a foul-smelling liquid used as a spell to keep people or evil spirits away.[638]

kansonnen To sprinkle consecrated water during a service to honor the spirits of the dead.[639]

kanzo An initiation led by an oungan or manbo that involves isolation and is the path to knowledge about Vodou and the lwa. The spiritual goal of the *kanzo* is to have the peace, quiet, and sleeping conducive to contact with the lwa and ancestors.[640] The *ounsi kanzo* is "the Vodou servant who has the light of the ancestors."[641] The *kanzo* culminates in a fire or heat ritual. *Kanzo* also refers to someone who, possessed by a lwa, can touch fire without being burned.[642] The *ounsi kanzo* rank is under the priesthood. The *kanzo* initiation ritual requires seven days of isolation and fasting in the *djèvò* (initiation room) of a priest or priestess. The ritual is for empowerment, training, purification, personal growth, and prestige. Preparations for the *ounsi kanzo* ritual entail the purchase of special objects, the payment of a significant fee to the priest, the undertaking of pilgrimages to sacred Vodou-Catholic sites, and the study of Vodou songs and mythology. The minting of *hunsi* in Benin takes a similar form. They are selected at the annual *hunhwè* feast in early December. During that feast, the *vodun* (lwa) Sakpata "slays" one or several women who are wrapped in burial cloth and laid to rest in isolation for seven days. Participation is voluntary and determined at Vodou convents. After the seven days of isolation, the women's "corpses," still wrapped in burial cloth, are resurrected by the *vodun* (lwa) Sakpata in a dramatic public ceremony.[643] The key underlying notions are asceticism and discipline. Fire, smoke, and heat rituals are also common in the practices of the Fon people. The *ahuã* requires initiates to jump over smoking pottery; the *ahuãdídá* ritual for *hunsi* initiates involves purification by fire, which requires pulling cooked food from a boiling pot, passing arms and legs over the pot, and, finally, jumping several times over a pot of flaming cooking oil.[644] These Fon rituals encourage the participants' *vodun* (lwa) to descend on them. The word *kanzo* means "a person who unites with light."[645] *See* **kouche; ounsi**.

kapital Capital; a repository of lwa in found altars such as sacred trees, caves, cliffs, or unusual natural formations.[646] *See* **repozwa**.

kaplata; kaprelata Magic protection or a particularly effective Vodou priest or sorcerer.[647] *Kaplata* also means "Vodou priest" and was common from the colonial period until the nineteenth century.[648] The famous nineteenth-century proverb "The *kaplata* gives you a charm, but he doesn't tell you to curse God" preserves the word.[649] *See* **bòkò; Kaplaw; manbo; oungan**.

Kaplaw; Kaplaw Kanga A rite or subcategory of lwa from the Kongo that includes lwa such as Papa Fatra, Ti Zo, and Zoklimo.[650] *See* **Kanga; kaplata**.

kaprelatè A person who makes Vodou charms.[651] *See* **kaplata; wangatè**.

Kaptenn Zonbi Captain Zombie, the name of a lwa in the Gede family.[652]

kase A break or offbeat phrasing in drum rhythm that insists on the appearance of the lwa.[653] The *kase* pounds the lwa into the head of someone on the verge of possession.[654] A *kase* (bow while bending the knees) is a deferential curtsey.

kata The smallest of the three Rada or *batri maskawon* drums. *Kata* is also an onomatopoeic word that describes the beating of the drum.[655] The *kata* drum sometimes appears in the Petwo rite.[656] *See* **gwo baka; ti baka**.

katabou The smallest of the three drums of the Kongo rite, sometimes referred to as *ti kongo*.[657]

katalyè, katayè The person who marks the rhythm by playing the *kata* drum.[658] *See* **tanbouye**.

Katawoulo The name of a lwa. In the Fon language, *kata* refers to a drum and Vodouists.[659] Katawoulo appears in the following lyric, "Legba Great Path Katawoulo, we're crossing over with the lwa/Papa Legba, open the gates."[660]

Katolik fran Pure Catholics. The *Katolik fran* are Catholics who do not participate in Vodou religious culture.

kat pwen kadino The four cardinal points. Gestures that address *kat pwen kadino* are a fundamental part of Vodou ritual. Gestures with the *ason* to the north are associated with mountains, soil, and the lwa Guidi Aloufa; gestures to the south are associated with fire and the lwa Azaka Mede; gestures to the east are associated with the sky, rain, and the lwa Lenba; and gestures to the west are associated with the ocean, water, and the lwa Agwe.[661]

kavo Burial vault. The *kavo* is important in Haiti. It is typically an impressive structure where entire families are gradually buried. Once bodies have decomposed, the remaining bones are eventually thrown into a pit under the vault. The burial vault, following West African custom, is built on the family compound. The Yorùbá people dig graves inside or in front of the home of the deceased because the dead protect and communicate with the living.[662] *See* **lèmò**.

kay, ka House. In the expressions *kay depo, kay lwa, kay manbo, kay oungan, kay sen,* and *kay lofis, kay* refers to a Vodou temple or complex. A *kay mistè* (house of mysteries) is the inner sanctuary of a temple and includes an altar. A *pitit kay* (child of the house) is a member of a temple.[663] *See* **ounfò**.

kenbe To hold or grip. Some lwa are known to hold or grip a person in a state of illness or crisis to bring about an apology or a change in behavior. A sentence such as "a lwa holds her or him" suggests that a lwa is making a person sick.[664] *See* **lage; sèp**.

Kikit The name of a lwa of the Gede family.[665]

kimanga; kiman A ritual alcoholic liquid made from rum and spices that is especially used in Petwo services and is usually vaporized from the mouth.[666] *See* **foula**.

Kinsou Lavalas The name of a lwa.[667]

Kita; Ti Kita Manbre; Ti Kita Vanyan; Jan Kita A Vodou rite and family of lwa that includes Grann Simba, Marinèt-Bwa-Chèch, and Simbi Kita in the Zandò nation. One song accuses him, "Lwa Kita e / Has the habit of causing sores, Lwa Kita e!"[668] *Kita* is also a variety of Petwo dance that is characterized by rapid shoulder movements.[669] *Kita sèch* and *kita mouye* are drum rhythms.[670] Ti Kita Manbre is referred to as a *dyab* and is linked to the metaphor of boiling water; his followers have the ability to submerge a bag without getting it wet.[671] *Kita* is found in Kikongo as *Nkíta* (god of the waters, the soul of the dead who dwells in water, ravines, woods and valleys).[672] Kita is also the name of a town in western Mali, and Kita Maninkakan is a language in the Mande family that is spoken in Mali.[673]

Klamèy The name of an albino lwa.[674]

kleren Unrefined raw rum, often used for libations, *foula* (ritual vaporizations), and consumption in Vodou ceremonies.[675] *See* **alkòl; foula**.

klòch; klochèt Bells; an important part of Vodou music in Haiti and Benin.[676] Oungan and manbo have bells attached to their *ason* (sacred rattles) and use them to punctuate Vodou music and communicate with the lwa. *See* **ason**.

kòd A *kòd ne* (knotted cord) is used as a Vodou charm. *Mare kòd* (tying cord) refers to the act of fastening bracelets to ward off evil.[677] Knotted cords often hang from altars to thwart unwanted influences, to count the years until a major ceremony, and for healing rituals.[678]

kò drapo The flag corps; flag bearers in Vodou ceremonies.[679] *See* **pòt drapo**.

kòdwon A *kòdwon penitans* (penitence cloth) refers to a cloth belt worn as a penitence. A *kòdwon ve* (wish cloth) is a cloth belt usually worn in tribute to Èzili Freda.[680]

kòk Rooster. The *kòk* is important in Haitian culture and in Vodou. Because of its protectiveness over its chickens, the rooster represents men's sexual virility. It is a fearless fighter and central to the *gagè* (cockfights) that many Vodouists patronize. The rooster and chicken are passed over patients and clients during healing rituals and to remove bad fortune.[681] Roosters can also be sacrificed to the lwa and cooked and consumed by Vodouists. *See* **koklo**.

kò kadav The cadaver body, a reference to a visible physical body, in contrast to *gwo bonnanj* and *ti bonnanj,* which are aspects of the soul.[682] *See* **gwo bonnanj; ti bonnanj**.

koki Seashells. They are referred to in songs to Agwe and symbolize the power and mystery of the sea. In Benin, Vodou initiates wear necklaces made of seashells.[683] In Haiti, seashells are used by priests and priestesses as symbols of having traveled under the water to gain knowledge from the lwa.[684]

Koki Lanmè; Kokidlanmè Shell in the Sea; another name for Agwe.[685] *Koki* may come from the Hausa word for spirit, *iskoki,* or the French word for shell, *coquille.*[686]

koklo A Fon word for a rooster sacrificed to the lwa.[687] *Koklo* is one of the many Fon words still found and understood in Vodou songs. *See* **donon; okon**.

kolera Cholera. A cholera epidemic broke out in Haiti in October 2010, and thousands had fallen ill or died by December. Although the disease probably originated among Nepalese United Nations peacekeepers, the enemies of Vodou, fueled by foreign and Haitian evangelists, blamed Vodou adepts for the epidemic. As a result, by December 25, 2010, mobs had lynched forty-five Vodou adepts whom they accused of making cholera powder.[688] In Vodou beliefs, people can enlist the assistance of spirits—typically through a bòkò—to heal or cause illness. Given this dimension of Vodou belief, it was no surprise to anthropologists that religious lynchings took place in the context of the cholera epidemic.[689] The lynchings also suggested that Vodou adepts are dwindling in Haiti, since minority groups are often scapegoated for epidemics (e.g., the Jews during the bubonic plague in fourteenth-century Europe).[690] In the long term, Vodou priests and priestesses need to overcome this kind of problem by letting the public know they do not have superhuman powers.[691] This may be difficult for them because such admissions affect their livelihood. Vodou priests need to learn from their Christian counterparts who make their living on earth selling access to heaven—something no living person can ever accuse them of failing to do. Whenever people allow others to believe that they have superhuman powers—as Jesus himself once did—they risk facing the public's wrath and death.[692] *See* **rejèt**.

kolye vèvè; kolye madyòk Vèvè necklaces made with glass beads, wood, shells, and metal such as iron, copper, and gold. They protect against illness or an evil spirit. The *kolye madyòk* protects children from jealously. Shell necklaces that cross in the front and back are common in the Vodou of Benin.[693]

kòn A peg that attaches the skin to a Rada drum.[694] *See* **pikèt; ralba**.

konbinezon A combination; a creature of disparate parts.[695]

kondiktè The guiding lwa for a seer.[696]

kondit The maintenance of a sacred lamp.[697] *See* **lanp etènèl**.

konesans Knowledge. Oungan and manbo are expected to have *konesans* of the lwa and their attributes, rituals, song, and tradition.[698]

konfyans; konfiyans A confidence; an intimate associate and adviser of a Vodou priest. A *konfyans* is a caretaker and key holder of a temple.[699]

kongo A Vodou dance involving minimal foot movement but with sudden rapid turns.[700] A *kongo fran* is an older form of the dance in the Kongo rite. A *kongo payèt* is a sexually suggestive dance in which men and women form separate lines. *See* **ti Kongo**.

Kongo A Vodou rite, *nanchon* (nation), and the name of a lwa associated with Petwo traditions.[701] Kongo-Petwo and Rada traditions are Vodou's two main currents. At least half of the population of Haiti at the time of independence was from the Kongo.[702] Kongo traditions include Simbi, Boumba, Kita, Penba, Pwen, Pakèt Kongo, and Kafou. The Kongo rite is common in the city of Gonaïves.[703] *See* **pakèt Kongo**.

Kongo Fran Pure Kongo; a rite that is distinct from the Kongo rite. It includes lwa such as Larèn Kongo, Manman Penba, and Sansan Pannan.[704]

Kongo Savann Bush Kongo, a Vodou rite that includes lwa such as Bazòl and Wosiyòl.[705]

konpèd A variety of Vodou charm.[706] *See* **gad; pwen; wanga**.

Kosi; Kosi Alada The name of a Dahomian lwa with the surname Alada, a town in Benin.[707] Emperor Soulouque of Haiti is said to have served Kosi.[708] *See* **Soulouk**.

kouche To lie down; to consecrate an object or be initiated. *Kouche* refers to the period of ritual seclusion for novices undergoing the *kanzo* initiation.[709] The *kouche* requires seven days of retreat and is usually undertaken with other novices. The main object of the *kouche* is to establish a formal link between a lwa *mèt tèt* (lwa who is the head's master) and the Vodouist. The *kouche* is a symbolic death during which the initiate goes under water to visit the ancestors and lwa.[710] *See* **kanzo; lave tèt; leve kanzo; mèt tèt; ounsi; rantre kanzo**.

koud; kout *Koud lanp* (lamp strike), *koud poud* (powder strike), and *koud zè/koudè* (air strike) refer to hexes.[711]

koudjay; koudyay A big Vodou ceremony.[712] Koudjay is also an important *rasin* (roots) music group.

koumba A dance.[713]

kounaye A lwa.[714]

Koure The name of a lwa who likes to roll in the mud.[715] *See* **sòtè**.

kou vire Twisted neck; a reference to killing a sacrificial bird by wringing its neck.[716]

Kouzen Zaka (*See* **the Azaka songs**) Kouzen Zaka (Cousin Zaka) is the younger brother of Azaka Mede.[717] He is represented by a *mabouya* lizard. He is an oungan and a peasant in the rural mountains. His emblem is a machete, and like his brother, his resting plant is the aloe plant. Kouzen Zaka also wears a straw hat, carries a straw bag, smokes a clay pipe, carries farming implements, and wears peasant clothes. He is associated with Saint Isidore, who is also represented as a farmer in the chromolithographs. Azaka and Kouzen Zaka are rich and greedy. The Marcelin songs in this book convey various notions about Kouzen Zaka: Song 171 reproaches him for offering a prostitute a meager two cents; song 172 indicates that Kouzen Zaka does what he can to *appear* poor; songs 173–176 ridicule Kouzen Zaka for being a peasant; and in song 177, Kouzen Zaka replies angrily. Kouzen Zaka has his own dance and enjoys the *dyouba* and *matinik* rhythms. Those possessed by Kouzen Zaka mime working the soil and adopt the speech and gestures of peasants. As a peasant, Kouzen Zaka is always in a hurry and constantly complains about his lot. He is frightened of police, and members of an audience will pretend that the police are coming to tease him. In response, his *chwal* (horse) will run and hide. Song 178 notes Kouzen Zaka's reputation for abandoning respectable women to sleep with loose ones. In song 177, he complains about not having enough water to drink during a long trek typical of the Haitian peasant. In song 180, he, like his brother Azaka Mede, enters politics. The identities of Azaka Mede and Kouzen Zaka converge in various ways. Kouzen Zaka is offered boiled corn, bread with olive oil drizzled on top, *afiba* (dried cow intestines), cassava bread and rapadou syrup, herring, and absinthe. As a peasant of limited means, Kouzen Zaka is said to be concerned about money, and he counts it with great care.[718] He also distorts various Creole words (e.g., *pale* [to speak] becomes *poule*, and *bagay* [thing] becomes *bougay*).[719] Those served by Kouzen Zaka must eat with their hands.[720] Kouzen Zaka, Ogou, and Gede tend to appear last and stay for a long time. As a vulnerable peasant, Kouzen Zaka begs for and receives money from participants in a ceremony.[721] *See* **Azaka Mede**.

Kouzin The consort of Azaka.[722]

Kowonabo Named after the leader of the Native American Tainos in early colonial Saint-Domingue. Kowonabo now refers to a lineage of Taino spirits maintained in northern Haiti.[723]

Krabinay The name of a violent Petwo lwa.[724]

krabiye A Vodou dance to chase away unwelcome *dyab* or lwa.[725]

kreyòl; kriyòl In Haitian history, the *kreyòl* slaves were born in Haiti, while the *bosal* slaves were born in Africa. The *bosal* population was associated with Vodou, while the *kreyòl* population was associated with the French language, Catholicism, and prestige. Consequently, the *kreyòl* population is referred to critically in many Vodou songs for not understanding or rejecting Vodou and peasant culture. For example, the lyrics "Danbala Wèdo, Ago, Ago e! The Creoles say that there is no Ginen ever again" may reflect the Creole community's rhetoric that it was useless to practice Vodou in the colony.[726] The *kreyòl* are incredulous: "The Creoles ask to see, don't you see I'm going."[727] The next lyrics reveal the hypocritical attitude of the Creoles: "What makes the Creoles hate Vodou? . . . [W]hat makes the Creoles hate Houngan? . . . They love his charm, they hate the Houngan."[728] Vodou music contains many references of this type, which suggests that anti-Vodou prejudice came from Europeans, mulattos, and some creolized Africans in the colonial period. Sometimes the term *kreyòl* simply refers to all Haitians. The term *kreyòl* also refers to lwa who emerged in Saint-Domingue and Haiti.[729] *See* **bosal**.

krich Marasa Ginen Jugs of the Ginen Twins; triple vessels for serving the Marasa.[730]

Kris; Jezi Kris Christ; Jesus Christ. Because of forced conversion to Christianity during colonialism and subsequent Roman Catholic linkages with the Haitian state, every Haitian has heard of Jesus Christ. However, Jesus has no direct role in Vodou. Images of him represent Vodou lwa. For example, his baptism represents Ayizan Velekete. The chromolithograph of Jesus with a triple crown and a bleeding knee represents the lwa Bosou Twa Kòn (Three Horned Bosou). According to one oungan, Jesus was a Vodou priest and the first zombie because he died, was buried, and rose from the dead.[731] *See* **Ayizan Velekete; Bosou Twa Kòn**.

kriz lwa The crisis of the lwa; a reference to the signs—trembling, swooning, stumbling, falling, shaking, and loss of motor control—that lead to possession.[732] *See* **debatman; soule**.

kwa; kwa kwa The sacred rattle used in the Kongo-Petwo rite. A song for Dosou Marasa contains the lyric "Give me my *kwa*, give me my *kwa* so that I can get going!"[733] In Kikongo, *kwàkwà* refers to the sounds of scratching.[734] *See* **ason**.

Kwa Arèt An iron cross and a mystical limit.[735]

kwa digo Indigo cross; a cross drawn with indigo as a Vodou charm.

kwasiyen Signed cross; to trace ritualistically the sign of the cross on a person, animal, or object.[736] The blood of a sacrificed animal can be used.

kwi A calabash bowl that is used to make offerings to the lwa. The symbol of the lwa can be painted on calabash bowls for specific services. For those dedicated to Agwe, a boat, a fish, or the ocean may appear; for Danbala Wèdo, a snake; for Bawon Samdi, a skull; and for Ogou, a saber, sword, or machete.[737]

Labalenn The name of a Vodou marine lwa who is married to Lasirenn.[738] *See* **Lasirenn.**

Ladegwesan Sofi Badè; Ladogwesan; Ladògwesan The name of a lwa.[739] The expression *ounsi Ladogwesan* (Ladogwesan initiate) means "ounsi of the Heritage."[740] *See* **Badè.**

lafanmi The family; a reference to the community of Vodouists associated with a *lakou* (family compound) or an ounfò. *Lafanmi* is expected to uphold the traditions and values of the family compound or community.[741] *See* **eritye; pitit fèy.**

lage Release from the control of a lwa who *kenbe* (holds) someone in illness or crisis as punishment. After receiving the due sacrifices, offerings, and apologies, the lwa *lage* (releases) the individual. *See* **kenbe; lage; sèp.**

lagranzè A witch.[742] *See* **lougawou.**

Lakansyèl Rainbow; the name of a *djab* who can kill people who are unfaithful or immoral.[743]

lakonfyans *See* **konfyans.**

lakou Family compound; an extended family community where several lineage groups dwell together under the guidance of a Vodou elder.[744] *See* **demanbre; eritye; mazi.**

lakwa The cross symbol in Vodou, which represents the intersection of the living and the ancestors.[745] The cross with a long vertical line and a shorter horizontal one is European, while the equal-sided "Benin cross" is of Edo-speaking Yorùbá origin.[746] The Bakongo also have a cross that represents the intersection around which human souls revolve.[747] Many vèvè have the Benin cross as an underlying structure. *See* **vèvè.**

lanbi The conch, a beloved Haitian food and aphrodisiac; its shell is blown into during ceremonies for the lwa Agwe.[748] The conch shell produces a mid-range pitch. It was used by the *mawon* (freedom fighters) in the eighteenth century for long-distance communication. The instrument is memorialized in the statue of the Marron Inconnu (Unknown Maroon) in Port-au-Prince in which a runaway slave, with chains broken, kneels and blows into the conch in one hand to signal revolt while he clutches a machete in his other hand.[749] The employment of the *lanbi* in Vodou suggests a *mawon* influence.[750]

langaj; langay Mystical ritual phrases.[751] *Langaj* are expressions from West African languages, especially Fon, that oungan and manbo employ. The words and chunks have mostly become incomprehensible to Vodouists and have a ritual or mystical purpose. Beauvoir's *Lapriyè Ginen* (2008a) provides many examples of West African language chunks in Vodou liturgy. In Benin, ritual language is called *hungbe* (heart or blood language).[752] *Langaj* is an excellent means for investigating the specific linguistic and cultural sources of Haitian Vodou. Fon, Yorùbá, Igbo, and Kikongo expressions can be identified in *langaj*—for example, *langaj* dedicated to the lwa Simbi is identified as Kikongo.[753] In the Fon language, *hungbè* (Vodou language) is ritual language that involves the inclusion of several languages. The language spoken where a given *vodun* (lwa) originates appears in set phrases in prayers and songs.[754] *See* **oun**.

Langinen *See* **Ginen**.

lanj *See* **zanj**.

Lan Kanpèch A well-known Vodou site in Haiti's Northern Department.[755]

lanperè The Emperor; the leader of a secret Vodou society.[756]

lanp etènèl; lanp letènèl The eternal lamp, consisting of a bowl and a wick that floats in olive oil and is permanently lit in temples in honor of the lwa.[757]

lanp nwa; lanp dezas A *lanp nwa* (black lamp) or *lanp dezas* (disaster lamp) is used to bring vengeance on someone.[758]

lany *See* **zanj**.

laplas The chief assistant or master of ceremonies to a Vodou priest or priestess.[759] When presenting Vodou *drapo* (flags) in temples, the laplas carries a sword or machete while two female assistants, one wrapped in Ogou's flag and the other in the temple's flag, display these symbols before the community.[760] Flags are also important in Benin's Vodou.

Laplenndinò; Laplèndinò; la Plaine-du-Nord The name of the town that is the location of an annual Vodou pilgrimage dedicated to Sen Jak (Saint James) held on July 25 in Haiti's Northern Department.[761]

Larenn; larèn; renn; rèn, rèn chantrèl The *larenn* (queen) is a woman who leads chanting and dancing in Vodou services.[762] *See* **oungenikon**.

Lasirenn; Lasirèn; Metrès Lasirenn; Grann Aloumandya Lasirenn (the Mermaid) is married to Labalenn (the Whale) and is the consort of Agwe Tawoyo. She rescues the victims of shipwrecks with her spouse. Haitian legend has it that she, like Simbi, attracts women to the shore and draws them under the sea to make them in her image and endow them with the power of healing. She is described as a mulatto with long hair. She originates in Dahomey and is associated with the Danwonmen, Kongo, Petwo, and Rada rites.[763] She has the upper body of an attractive woman and the lower body of the *lanmori* (codfish). Her hair reaches to her waist. She is sometimes identified with chromolithographs of Our Lady of the Assumption, Saint Martha, and Saint Philomena because of the anchors their images include.[764] Tuesday and Thursday are consecrated to her, and white is her color. Lasirenn is said to appear at springs combing her long hair. She loves young boys, and to prevent her from taking them under water, parents do not send boys to fetch water after dark. Although Lasirenn is not as popular as Metrès Èzili, some fishermen are said to invoke her for protection and to keep *sirop d'orgeat* (orange syrup) in their boats to call upon her when they need her. Fishermen regularly spot Lasirenn spread out on a rock, on the banks of an island, leaning on their boats, and singing. Metrès Lasirenn, Labalenn (the Whale), and Metrès Èzili go together. Some Vodou priests say that Lasirenn and Labalenn are married and that Labalenn is one of Agwe's chief assistants. Oungan who serve Lasirenn usually have temples within view of the sea. Lasirenn is jealous of her rival, Metrès Èzili.[765] Songs are sung to invite Lasirenn to possess a manbo at a ceremony dedicated to her.[766] Lotions and toiletries are brought to Lasirenn, who then applies them to herself. Basil leaves are brought to her, and she kisses all of the men present three times. Rice, a white pigeon, and various foods are offered.[767] Lasirenn is patterned on the Yorùbá lwa Aloumandya (Mother of Fish).[768]

lasosyete The society; the members of a given temple who form its congregation. *Lasosyete ounfò* refers to Vodouists who have been initiated in the same temple. *Lasosyete soutyen* refers to the group that helps to run and finance a temple.[769]

laswenyay *See* **swenyay**.

lave tèt The washing of the head, a ritual undertaken during the *ounsi* initiation of novices. The *lave tèt* can also symbolize a promise to become initiated into the priesthood.[770] The ritual involves the washing of the head with medicinal herbs, leaves, bread dipped in wine, grilled corn, cornmeal porridge, syrup, animal blood, and so on. In the case of initiation, the ingredients are also wrapped in *monben* (hog plum) leaves and carried in the fold of a scarf by the initiate until the end of his or her seclusion.[771] The *lave tèt* establishes a link between the Vodouist and his or her principle lwa. In the Vodun religion of the Fon people, the *kló alò* (washing of hands) is used to initiate individuals into secret societies.[772] *See* **kouche; mèt tèt; ounsi**.

Lavyèj Karidad The name of a lwa of the sea considered to be a double of Èzili.[773] Lavyèj Karidad is associated with Agwe, the most prominent *lwa* of the sea. Lavyèj Karidad frequently travels by boat. Some of her devotees have seen her walking on water; she was wearing a white robe with long sleeves, new sandals, and white gloves and held a white handkerchief that flapped in the wind. On her sacred day, her followers place on her altar a white basin, soap, a sealed bottle of lotion, a box of *la créole* powder, and a bouquet of basil. Note that Lavyèj Karidad is identified with Chun in Cuba. *See* **Èzili; Sent Elizabèt**.

laye kongo To sift the kongo; to dance the kongo enthusiastically.[774]

Lazil Ibo; Ibo Lazil The name of an Ibo lwa who is linked to Lazil, a town in southern Haiti.[775]

Legba; Legba Atibon; Legba Avadra; Legba Bwa; Legba Donpèd; Legba Evyesou; Legba Gran Chimen Katawoulo; Legba Kalfou; Legba Keke; Legba Kòklòkosou; Legba Mèt Kafou; Legba Pye Kase; Legba Mèt-bitasyon; Legba lan Bayè; Legba Potomitan; Legba Zandò; Alegba; Atibon Legba; Papa Legba The lwa who rules crossroads and paths, as well as the guardian of all entries.[776] Atibon Legba is also known as Alegba. Legba is served in the Danwonmen, Kongo, Nago, Petwo, Zandò, and, in particular, Rada rites.[777] Although Legba was originally a Nigerian Nago lwa, in Haiti he is mostly associated with the Rada rite of Dahomey, probably because Legba was well established in the Dahomey region before the slave trade. Legba is the barrier between the living and the dead and between the natural and supernatural. Poto Legba refers to the *potomitan* that is associated with him and a few other lwa, such as Danbala.[778] He is one of the most important lwa of Vodou mythology because he allows humankind to communicate with God and all other lwa.[779] Legba is identified with Saint Anthony the Hermit or Saint Anthony of Padua. Oungan make use of the image of Saint Anthony the Hermit in the Rada rite and that of Saint Anthony of Padua in the Petwo rite. Many Vodou followers also identify Legba with Saint Lazarus because he is represented in chromolithographs as an old man with a beard and white hair who is leaning on a crutch and stick and whose wounds are licked by stray dogs.[780] Legba is an old and sexually frigid man who can no longer walk without crutches; his followers are obliged to assist him. Legba's bones have so little consistency that they are virtually nonexistent. Legba is portrayed as a hunched-over elderly man who wears a broad-brimmed straw hat and leans on a crutch and a cane; however, he is extremely strong.[781] He smokes a long terracotta pipe and carries a *makout* (woven straw bag). His broad hat protects the other lwa from the sun.[782] Like all lwa, Atibon Legba is invisible. He supervises roads, paths, gardens, courts, dwellings, and crossroads. He sees all that is done and hears all that is said. Legba believes that the world envies him because he is a king. As a result, he easily utters threats. Legba's day of consecration is Thursday, and his color is black. His resting tree is a *medinyè* (*Atropha curcas* L.) situated in a temple court close to a barrier or in a location between two paths. A *makout* is suspended on one of the branches. Legba's followers go there to place offerings of grilled corn, yams, rice and beans, spices, cigars, tobacco leaves, matches, and so on.[783] The services to celebrate and honor Legba always begin at the entrance to the yard. At a small distance from the barrier, a large wood fire is lit and remains so until the end of the ceremony. An oungan walks toward the entrance of the yard, followed by the laplas, *ounsi-kanzo* (initiates), *ounsi bosal* (novice initiates), drummers, and assistants. The oungan traces a large circle on the ground, and members chant the song of Legba that starts all ceremonies: "Atibon Legba louvri bayè a pou mwen (Atibon Legba, open the gate for me)." Once this is complete, the members approach the front of the resting place of the *mistè* (mysteries). The oungan traces a vèvè at the foot of the sacred tree and plants a black candle in the center of the emblem and lights it. Everybody then kneels to kiss the ground three times. The leader of the family separates from the group of Vodouists, carries a jug filled with water, and kneels in front of the oungan. The oungan takes the leader of the family's hand and has him turn around three times (once to the right, then to the left, then to the right again). The jug is handed to the oungan, who presents it to the four cardinal points. Next water is thrown onto the vèvè. In response, each *ounsi* carries a chicken or a black cock for sacrifice and bows in front of the oungan as he circles them. The cock is Legba's traditional food because Legba is the first lwa called on and the cock is the first animal to call in the morning.[784] The sacrifices are presented to the four cardinal points, and the wings and legs are broken. The oungan finally tears off the heads of the chickens and pours drops of their blood onto the vèvè.[785] In any service, Legba has priority over all other lwa. All *milokan* (a single vèvè for several lwa) include Legba.[786] The first three songs and dances are obligatorily dedicated to him. Legba rarely appears in the services; when he possesses his *chwal* (horse), the person shows aspects of the lwa's old age. To invoke Legba, an oungan places loose stones on the lwa's altar. He traces his vèvè with flour on the sanctuary's ground and in front of the altar. He then recites prayers. Legba's dance is called the *krabiyen* of Legba, and it is very merry. To greet Legba, drummers execute two *mayi* rhythms and one *yanvalou.* Atibon Legba has several manifestations, and his name changes according to his rite and attributes. He is called Legba Kafou (Legba of the Crossroads) or Legba Gran Chemen (Legba Great Path) when he surveys the crossroads and the paths. He is Legba Mèt-bitasyon (Legba Master of the Dwellings) when he governs farm dwellings and Legba lan Bayè (Legba at the Gate) when he watches the enclosed entries. He is Legba Avadra (Wandering Legba) who knows all that occurs when he wanders paths. He is also called Legba Pye Kase (Legba Broken Foot) because he is very old and crippled.[787] The healing properties of Simbi are obtained by seeking permission first from Bondye (God) and second from Legba.[788] Atibon Legba is the most important manifestation of Legba. Legba, Ayizan, and Loko are closely linked and are the first lwa invoked in ceremonies. Legba is said to be the Ruler of Light, and after nightfall he hands power over to the less friendly Mèt Kafou (Master of the Crossroads). Legba is in the Rada rite, and Mèt Kafou is in the Petwo rite.[789] A cross symbolizing a crossroads is Mèt Kafou's symbol. The crossroads represents life and death; it is where one passes from the world of the living to the world of the ancestors. One Haitian proverb says, "If the crossroad doesn't give, the cemetery doesn't eat."[790] Legba's Catholic counterparts are Saint Peter, Saint Anthony, and Saint Lazarus. His colors are purple, red, black, orange, and yellow, depending on the community. In Africa, Legba is considered the inner depth of humankind, the non-conscious part of each person, and the expression of lack where the poor require assistance. Legba is understood to be what has always existed since the beginning of time, and he carries people to other frontiers.[791] In Yorùbá mythology, Èsù-Elegbara is also the guardian of the crossroads.[792] In the Fon language, the *vodun* (lwa) Legba is the spirit who protects the individual, a house, an initiatory space, and the market. Legba is the dispenser of good and evil and the messenger of other *vodun* (lwa). Among the Xwedá, the Legba of the market is named Ayizan. (In Haiti, as noted, Ayizan is a distinct lwa.) In the Fon culture, Legba is also male or female; the male Legba, *asù Legba,* is symbolized by a protruding mound of dirt or stone, and the female Legba, *asì Legba,* is symbolized by pieces of clay strewn around the mound. The word *Atibon* refers to Legba's walking stick and phallus.[793] In the Fon culture, Legba is beneficent for his or her protégés but wrathful to those who disappoint. Legba's support is ensured by the daily libation of the *ja* (water and oil). The Fon proverb "Legba's penis is not as big as the master's" means that the head of the household who erected the Legba mound is more immediate than Legba, and the symbol cannot transcend the master's reality.[794] *See* **baton**.

Legba Kalfou The members of a family of lwa have commonalities and differences. Legba Kalfou is served in the Kongo, Nago, and Petwo rites. Legba Kalfou is young. His possession events can be violent. Legba Kalfou is said to understand the human condition, and he helps his devotees with their problems. Echoing his name Kalfou (Crossroads), Legba Kalfou has ceremonies in actual crossroads. His vèvè is created around intersecting lines. Legba Kalfou works at night and under the moon.[795] *See* **Legba Atibon**.

Legede *See* **Gede**.

lele An Ibo word that means "singing" that is used only in songs of the Ibo rite.[796]

lemò; lèmò; lenmò; mò yo Spirits of the dead; the ancestors. *Lemò* are venerated along with the lwa. *Lemò kenbe li* (the dead hold him or her) means that someone is haunted or tormented by the dead because he did not fulfill his symbolic and ritual duties. A *priyè lemò* (prayer to the dead) refers to a Vodou ceremony for the dead which takes place on the last evening of a novena.[797] The dead are omnipresent: "I say the dead are butterflies. / They're travelling in all parts of the country."[798] *See* **kavo**.

Lenba; Lèmba A lwa and magic spell.[799] Lenba is a Kongolese Vodou society that formed around 1660; it is also the name of a town.[800] Lenba is a Kongo healing cult that had an influence on Vodou during the revolutionary period.[801] In the Kikongo language, *lemba* as a verb means to calm the anger of a *nkisi* (lwa, magical spell) or to pour out purification libations; as a noun it refers to a type of counter-spell.[802] *See* **Petwo**.

Lenglensou; Lenglensou Basen San; Lenglensou Tonnè The name of a dangerous lwa.[803] Lenglensou is referred to as a "criminal" and "bloodthirsty" lwa.[804] King Kessy's album *Voudou Djam* (Vodou Is Strong; 2009) contains a praise song for Lenglensou, suggesting that the lwa has other qualities. Common notions in his songs include *basen san* (blood basin) and *tonnè* (thunder and lightning). "Blood basin" may be a reference to the Middle Passage across the Atlantic.[805] One song says, "Where I reside, misbehavior does not take place there, hey!" which suggests that Lenglensou is strict and authoritarian.[806] Lenglensou is linked to Ebyoso, patron lwa of justice; as judges, these lwa have hard and soft sides.[807] *See* **Ebyoso**.

Lensou The name of a lwa. The term *Lensou* appears in composite forms in Haitian Vodou: Agiwa-Lensou, Gede Lensou, and Lenglensou. In Fon culture, Lènsú is a *vodun* (lwa) whose name means "ram." The *vodun* (lwa) Xèbyoso is also called Agbò lènsú (the great ram) because rams bleat with the same suddenness as a lightning strike. The cult of Lènsú is primarily dedicated to the veneration of the king of Abomey, Agájà, and is still closely linked to the descendants of the royal family. The cult addresses the king, dignitaries of his court, children who perish during breastfeeding and have never tasted salty food, and fetuses that do not reach full term.[808] *See* **Agiwa-Lensou; Gede Lensou; Lenglensou**.

Lento; Jeneral Lento The name of a lwa associated with Bawon Samdi. The lwa is called on for succor in the song "Lento I'm in the dark, the enemy has caught me."[809]

lese m atò Leave me now; a powder used in remedies.[810]

lesen; lèsen The saint or saints; synonymous with the term *lwa*. Because of slavery, colonialism, the illegality of Vodou, forced conversion to Christianity, and the underlying West African culture of assemblage, lwa came to be camouflaged by means of the images of Christian saints.[811] The Catholic Church venerates and honors the Communion of Saints: the faithful on Earth, the souls in Purgatory, and the saints in Heaven.[812] The Vodouist slaves were hiding and protecting the lwa from Christian persecutors by disguising them in Christian images and symbols.[813] The Catholic saints were also co-opted into the service of Fon and Yorùbá religion.[814] The Catholic saints are variants or symbols of the lwa. One or several aspects of the chromolithograph of a saint are linked to a lwa. For example, Saint Patrick is linked to the serpent lwa, Danbala, because Saint Patrick is represented driving snakes into the sea. *See* **gad; lwa; pwen**.

lespri Spirit; synonymous with the word *lwa*.[815] *See* **lwa; mistè; zanj**.

Lespri Sen The Holy Spirit; the Christian representation of the lwa Agasou. *See* **Agasou**.

leve kanzo Raising the kanzo; the ceremony for the new *ounsi kanzo* (initiates) as they emerge from seven days of isolation in the *djèvo*. In Miami, the *leve kanzo* takes place on Sunday. The ceremony lasts four hours in the morning and four hours in the evening, and it is replete with drumming, singing, and rituals. *See* **kanzo; ounsi; rantre kanzo**.

Lèwa The Epiphany, which occurs on January 6 in commemoration of the visit of the three Magi (Kings) to the infant Jesus. Vodou ceremonies are commonly organized on January 6 in Haiti; as one song says, "The day of the Epiphany, is when *oungan* work!"[816]

Leyogàn; Leyogann A town in southern Haiti that is a Vodou center.[817] Many songs confirm this—for example, "Oh Leyogàn, I went there to purchase the djab!"[818]

lezany *See* **zanj**.

lezasistan The assistance; members of a given Vodou temple.[819] *See* **lafanmi; lasosyete; pitit fèy**.

lezenvizib The invisibles; fearsome beings who can be lwa as well as the souls of the dead.[820]

limen balenn To light candles; to consult an oungan or manbo or put a hex on someone.[821]

limyè, lalimyè A *kout limyè* refers to the use of a magical oil lamp to harm someone.[822]

Lisa *See* **Mawou-Lisa**.

loko The sacred iroko tree.[823] In Yorùbá, the term *ìrókò* refers to the tree *Chlorophora excelsa.*[824]

Loko Atisou; Loko Atisou Gwe; Loko Atisougwè; Loko Azanblou Gidi; Loko Aziblokidi; Loko Basiye; Loko Dan Yiso; Loko Dawomen; Loko De; Loko Dewaze; Loko Djandjan; Loko Kilindja; Loko Kisigwè; Loko Lweba; Loko Pilipili; Loko Sendjo; Loko-si; Loko Yay; Azagon Loko; Danyiso Loko; Papa Loko; Ibo Loko; Santayi Loko The name of a lwa of medicinal plants and leaves who is associated with healing. Loko is a king and the guardian of sanctuaries.[825] The lwa Loko presides over initiation and protects the priesthood and its symbol, the *ason.*[826] Loko is served in the Danwonmen, Nago, Petwo, and Rada rites. Loko handles a whip in the Petwo rite to emphasize his protective role. Loko's vèvè includes the letter *L.* Loko has a calm demeanor but will not accept injustice. His wife is the lwa Ayizan.[827] Loko loves women, and women love him. He is the lwa of the trees and forests; offerings to him are hung on a tree.[828] He is identified with Saint Joseph.[829] Loko is also linked to the wind. The *doktè fèy* (herbalist) exerts his or her practice under Loko's patronage. Loko belongs to the Makaya rite.[830] In the Fon language, Lòkó Àtínsú is the tree that dominates all others in the forest. The second part of Loko's name may be linked to important Vodou priests whose names became linked to Loko.[831] Loko is referred to as the Adam's apple. Loko is a sympathetic lwa. He is the son of a black woman and a mulatto man. Loko typically dresses in the attire of a general, carries a big stick in his hand, and has a clay pipe in the corner of his mouth. His symbols include the banana, the chameleon, and the green lizard; in temples, a large stone represents him. Loko dwells in the *médecinier béni* (*Jatropha curcas* L.) or the *verveine* (*Verbena* L.); Tuesday is his day of the week, and yellow is his color.[832] Legend has it that Loko played an important role in the war of independence. Legba, Ayizan, and Loko are linked together. In the Fon culture, Loko is also connected to plants and trees, especially the *iroko* tree, which likely provides the source for Loko's name. When serving as the residence of a *vodun* (lwa), the *iroko* tree itself is considered a *vodun* (lwa).[833]

lougawou By day a human, usually female; by night, a vampire-like witch or warlock.[834] The *lougawou* primarily belong to the imaginative and creative repertoire of Haitian folklore. The *lougawou* is said to remove her skin at night and fly about on a broomstick, devouring or sucking the blood of animals and children. There may be a link between the *àzètò* of Benin and the *lougawou* of Haiti, since both refer to individuals who can turn into maleficent animals.[835] The *àzètò* in Fon is a sorcerer who can "seize someone's double (*yè*) or shadow" and who uses animals for the preparation of magic charms.[836]

loukout A witch or sorceress.[837] *See* **lougawou**.

lwa An immaterial spiritual being, force, or spirit. The lwa are spirits created by God; they are also ancestors of great importance who have become the patrons of specific domains.[838] *Sèvi lwa* (to serve the ancestral spirits) refers to calling the lwa and serving as their *chwal* (horses) in possession; it means to sing, chant, divine, offer food and drink, sacrifice animals, construct shrines, observe taboos, make ritual cuisine, and follow rules.[839] *Afè lwa* (business of the spirits) refers to Vodou practice, and *fè sèvis lwa* is "to conduct a Vodou ceremony." To *gen lwa,* like *monte,* is to be temporarily possessed by a Vodou spirit. A *gwo lwa* refers to any revered Vodou lwa who dates from at least the Haitian Revolution. The terms *lwa achte* (purchased lwa) and *lwa bèlflè* (beautiful flower lwa) refer to fiery lwa called on at a Petwo service. A *lwa bitasyon* (lwa of the farm) is the lwa who is established on a farm to protect it. A *lwa blan* (white lwa) is an undefiled lwa; a *lwa bosal* (wild lwa) is any violent and unidentified lwa. A *lwa djab* (djab lwa) refers to the Petwo rite. A *lwa Ginen* (Guinean lwa) refers to the Rada rite. *Lwa je wouj* (red-eyed lwa) refers to an aggressive Petwo lwa. A lwa who originates in the New World is a *lwa kreyòl* (Creole lwa). A *lwa mèt tèt* is one's principal protective lwa, and he or she receives allegiance. *Lwa pwen* (point lwa) refers to a Vodou spirit who provides special protection or powers. A *lwa rasin* (root lwa) is one's ancestral lwa. *Lwa zenga* is a lwa who is deaf or without ears. A *mare lwa* (tying the lwa) is a ceremony to restrain a troublesome lwa. *Ranvwa lwa* (sending of the lwa) expedites the lwa back to the woods or Africa.[840] Four hundred and one lwa and *orisha* are typically counted in Haitian and Yorùbá tradition, respectively.[841] The pantheon of lwa reflects *xenophilia* and *heterodoxy* in that new lwa are happily incorporated and are so diverse that they defy any acknowledged standard.[842] The lwa can be forces of nature, deceased humans who have been made divine, or mysterious spirits with complex characteristics; they have specific symbolic (e.g., Èzili Dantò's *ponya* [daggers]) and iconographic (e.g., chromolithograph) attributes. Many of these key attributes reflect core aspects of Haitian culture and society (e.g., the symbolic link between Èzili Dantò's daggers and her inspiration of the indigenous army during Haiti's war of independence). The lwa are *sakre* (sacred) and they *pale nan tèt* (speak in the heads) of their servants.[843] The authentic and valued lwa are inherited through the family; as one songs says, "This Lwa is my father's Lwa, / I'm going to beg in order to serve them!"[844] In Yorùbá culture, as in Haiti, failure to serve the *orisha* or lwa causes a *dangerous disorder.*[845] The lwa are usually anthropomorphized because as great ancestors, they have names, personalities, preferences, relationships, children, weaknesses, among other human qualities.[846] In Yorùbá religious philosophy, the deities are immortal even if they have human or natural origins.[847] At the same time, each lwa has extraordinary powers. The expression *lwa danse nan tèt (li)* (a lwa dances in his or her head) refers to possession. In this book, *lwa* is used in the English discussions and the word can be singular or plural. A clue to the origin of *lwa* may be found in the Yorùbá and Fon words for a priest of Ife, Babaláwò (the father of secrets), where *láwò* refers to what is secret and mysterious.[848] *See* **dyab; lesen; lespri; papalwa; Vodou; zanj**.

lwa achte Purchased lwa bought from a bòkò. They bring success but must be served faithfully or else they can be vengeful and cause death.

lwa Ginen Guinean lwa; associated with the Rada rite and inherited in the family.

lwa rasin Roots lwa; associated with the Rada rite and inherited in the family.

Lwa Sosyete A Vodou rite that includes lwa such as Èzili Je Wouj and Danbala Laflanbo.[849]

machann lapli Rain merchant; a rainmaker.[850]

madivin; madivinèz Lesbians, who are welcome in most Vodou communities.[851] *See* **masisi**.

madjoman A term of exclamation meaning "the end" used in Petwo chants.[852]

ma dlo Mudpits, used in Vodou rituals around the towns of Gonaïves, Plaine-du-Nord, and Saut d'Eau, among other locations. Possessed by *lwa sòtè* (jumping lwa), the servants of the lwa jump into the mud where they bathe, dance, and writhe. *See* **grenadye; sòtè**.

madouka The assistant to a Vodou priest or priestess.[853]

magrigri A magic love potion.[854]

maji Magic; an art form and a spiritual law holding that specific words or actions will produce a known effect.[855] *Maji* can refer either to *maji blan* (white or positive magic) or to *maji nwa* (black or evil magic or witchcraft). More generally, *maji* can refer to Vodou dances during the preparation of magic charms. Some people object strongly to the stereotypical racial connotations of the white and black terminology; however, many Vodouists in Haiti, including Marcenat, continue to describe magic in those terms and do so without reference to race. To *retire maji* (withdraw magic) means to dispel a Vodou curse.[856]

maji blan White or positive magic. *Maji blan* is for the benefit of people and is the sphere of the oungan and manbo, as opposed to the bòkò, who will also use *maji nwa* (black magic), which can harm others. *See* **manbo; oungan**.

maji nwa Black or negative magic for harming people and the domain of the bòkò. *See* **bòkò**.

makakri Protective charms.[857]

makandal; makanda An evil charm. A *makandal* can refer to a secret society or members of such a society.[858] Some suggest that this society is composed of evildoers; however, this claim may be a folkloric exaggeration. *See* **Bizango; Sanpwèl**.

Makandal (Franswa) François Macandal was a pre-revolutionary leader who violently opposed slavery and was burned alive in 1758.[859] He was burned for having poisoned thousands of farm animals and French colonists. He was a Vodou priest with extensive knowledge of the helpful and harmful properties of plants. One song suggests that Makandal was instructed by the lwa Ya Vodun Djohoun but failed to listen to him, which resulted in his execution.[860] In Haitian lore, Makandal was an African-born Muslim.[861] Haitian school textbooks state that he transformed into a fly while being burned at the stake.[862]

Makaya A Vodou rite and family of lwa that includes lwa such as Simbi, Ezili Mapyang, Loko Atisou, and Wangita.[863] The word *Makaya* is Kikongo in origin; Makaya is a mountain in Haiti that is renowned for its forest and biodiversity. Makaya is considered a magical forest and the realm of the lwa, Gran Bwa.[864] The term also refers to leaves used in healing practices, an aspect of Makaya suggested in this song: "Makaya hey, oh my life is in your hands!"[865] In the Kikongo language, *makaya* refers to leaves, foliage, medicinal leaves, magical leaves, and the like.[866] *See* **Gran Bwa; repozwa; Sende Makaya**.

Makaya Boumba The name of a lwa in the Kongo-Ginen cycle.[867]

Makori *See* **Bizango; Sanpwèl**.

makousiyen A disreputable Vodou priest.[868]

makout A handwoven bag made from dried latania palm. Offerings to the lwa Loko are placed in the *makout* and hung on Loko's resting tree.[869]

maladi malouk A "nefarious sickness" caused by an evil lwa.[870]

manbo A Vodou priestess, healer, or seer. Manbo hold the same level of authority and prestige as the oungan in Haiti's Vodou culture. Manbo, like oungan, either receive the priesthood through the family or undergo training and initiation. A *manbo achte* (purchased priestess) refers to an uninspired priestess. A *manbo kay* (home priestess) refers to the female assistant to a Vodou priest.[871] The lwa Èzili is referred to as "Manbo Freda Dahonmen." The word *manbo* may be related to the Fon word *nanbo. Nan* (mother) and *bo* (knowledge), when combined, mean "mother of knowledge."[872] The Fon term *nagbó*, "an individual initiated to a *vodun* 'lwa' who has the function of giving life to the *vodun*," may also be related.[873] In the Fon language, the word *nagbo* (great woman) refers to a great *vodunsi* (spouse of the *vodun* [lwa]).[874] She is responsible for resuscitating an initiate who is undergoing a seven-day isolation ritual. In West Africa, women are also essential in religion. They hold leadership positions, perform rites and rituals, establish shrines, control secret societies, are final arbiters and the repositories of wisdom, and are the guardians of traditions, song, and dance.[875] *See* **bòkò; manmanlwa; oungan; papalwa**.

Manbo Ayizan; Manbo Delayi; Manbo Delayi Penmba; Manbo Kalavi; Manbo Lisa; Manbo Lisagbadja; Manbo Sayira; Manbo Sentelèn; Manbo Zila In cases such as Manbo Ayizan and Manbo Lisa, the term *manbo* is a gendered title of respect for a well-established lwa. In other cases, such as Manbo Delayi and Manbo Sayira, the name suggests a deified human manbo. Beauvoir (2008b: 287–291) contains several songs dedicated to manbo. *See* **Mawou-Lisa**.

manbo kay The female assistant to the Vodou priest.[876]

Manden A Vodou rite associated with the lwa Gwawonmèt.[877]

manje Food. The term *manje* has many connotations in Vodou. To *bay (tanbou) manje* is to make a food and drink offering to the lwa. *Manje avwa* refers to a special unsalted food for the dead. A *manje brase* (mixed food) is an offering dedicated to a variety of lwa. *Manje depoze* (laid-down food) refers to a food offering to the lwa. *Manje djak* is a food offering to the lwa involving no animal sacrifice (see *manje djò*). The terms *manje Ginen* and *manje Lafrik* refer to food and drink offerings to the lwa in the Rada rite. *Manje lemò* (food of the dead) is considered a food and drink offering to appease spirits of the dead. *Manje lesen* (food of the saints), *manje lwa* (food of the lwa), and *manje zanj* (food of the angels) are symbolic gestures to nourish, pacify, and thank one or more lwa.[878] *Manje Marasa* (twin's food) is for the Divine Twins. To *manje moun* (eat people) means to kill through sorcery. It also refers to a fatal illness or accident sent by evil lwa or *dyab. Manje pòv* (food of the poor) is the ritual act of charity for the dead and the lwa. A *manje tcham* refers to a food and drink offering that involves no animal sacrifice in the Petwo rite. *Manje tèt* (head food) is a food and drink offering for one's principal protective lwa.[879]

manje de zanj *See* **manje dyak**.

manje djò/dyò A ritual plate of raw and chopped food offered to the lwa.[880] The *manje dyò* is a combination of raw and chopped yam, sweet potato, and pumpkin, along with other tubers. *Manje djò* is offered to the lwa during the initiation rituals of the *ounsi.*[881] The term *dyò* may be related to the Fon verb *do* (make or create) and can be used in the locution *do vòsísá* (to pray).[882]

manje dyak Cooked meat, except pork, offered to the lwa.[883] *See* **manje lwa**.

manje lwa; manje zanj (northern Haiti) A food and drink offering to the lwa in return for protection, healing, soothsaying, and other benefits.[884] Some of this ritual food may be scattered outside the temple, buried in a hole inside the temple, or tied to the *potomitan.* Most of the offering is consumed by the *chwal* possessed by a lwa and the Vodou community. In the case of liquid, the "quick absorption of spilled votive liquid into the clay ground is taken as a sign of prayer taken into the consciousness of the spirit."[885]

manje moun To eat people; a reference to the destruction inflicted on people by *dyab* (malicious lwa).[886] *See* **dyab**.

manje pòv Food for the poor; a ritual act of charity in honor of the dead or the lwa.[887]

manje ranje Fixed food; poisoned food. During the colonial period, Vodou herbalists and botanists, employing their knowledge of tropical flora, used poison to wage war on the French colonial regime and the society of plantation slavery. The making of potions, poisons, anesthetics, and medicine has always been an important part of the vocation of oungan, manbo, and bòkò. *See* **Makandal**.

manje tcham A food and drink offering with no animal sacrifice in the Petwo rite.[888]

manje tèt A food and drink offering to one's principal lwa.[889] *See* **mèt tèt**.

manmanbila A magic charm necklace with a pouch.[890]

Manman Brijit *See* **Grann Brijit**.

manmanlwa A Vodou priestess;[891] mother of lwa, an archaic term for a manbo.[892] *See* **manbo; papalwa**.

manman tanbou The mother drum, the largest of the three drums used in Rada rites. The *manman* is also the larger of the two drums used in the Petwo rite.[893] The *manman tanbou* is played with the left hand and a special pipe or horn-shaped stick called the *badyèt kòn* (horn stick). The drummer sits while the drum inclines at a forty-five-degree angle. The *manman tanbou* is the most important drum of the Rada rite.[894] *See* **boula; segon.**

mapou A large tree with magic and tutelary powers. The *mapou* is commonly called the ceiba, the silk-cotton, or the kapok tree.[895] Mapou is also a lwa.[896] The *mapou* stands out in Haiti because of its large trunk and gnarly roots. Lwa dwell in the *mapou,* and it is not cut down in most Haitian communities. A cottony product is harvested from the seeds of the *mapou* to stuff pillows.[897]

Marasa; Marasa Blan; Marasa Bwa; Marasa Elou; Marasa Kafou; Marasa Lafrik; Marasa Ginen; Marasa Jimo; Marasa Kreyòl; Marasa Lafrik Ginen; Marasa Kay; Marasa Kongo; Marasa Dosou, Dosa, Dogwe; Zensou, Zens; Marasa Mezon; Marasa Zandò; Masa Twin lwa associated with children, human twins, and multiple childbirth.[898] Marasa is sometimes translated as "the Divine Twins" in English. The Marasa are considered the twins of God and are associated with fertility.[899] The Marasa are served in the Danwonmen and Rada rites.[900] *Marasa blan* refers to twins who died before being baptized. *Marasa Ginen* refers to twins of the same sex.[901] Living twins are called *Marasa Kreyòl* (Creole Marasa) and dead twins are *Marasa Ginen* (Guinean Twins).[902] *Marasa Kreyòl* also refers to twins of the same gender, while *Marasa Ginen* are twins of both genders, such as Mawou-Lisa.[903] It is often said that the status of the Marasa in Vodou explains the reverence of Haitians for twins and multiple childbirth. Saint Jacob is the father of the Marasa Ginen, and Saint Claire is the mother of the Marasa Kreyòl. Saint Cosmas and Saint Damien, considered twins, are their icons from the chromolithographs. Saint Lucie is the mother of twin girls. Butterflies are associated with the Marasa; they are also linked to snakes called *koulèv Marasa* and drums called the *tanbou Marasa.* The appearance of the Marasa implies force and virility.[904] The Marasa, as infant lwa, can cause all kinds of trouble; they demand food and sugared water to behave well.[905] By hammering a nail into a plank, one can encourage the Marasa to carry out wicked acts, such as making someone mildly ill or causing a toothache. Two adult human twins were said to have given their brother a toothache to force him to apologize for an offense. Eventually he did so, and they cured him ritually with three leaves. Infant twins may abuse their powers and frighten their families; however, their negative powers can be removed if their parents spank them with cords or plantain bark at the slightest hint of misbehavior.[906] The Marasa can *kenbe* (hold) somebody through illness or death, and they can *lage* (release) somebody after they receive an apology. Marasa twins are excellent oungan or manbo, but they are jealous and do not like people consulting elsewhere. Those possessed by the lwa Marasa imitate the gestures of children, eat constantly, cry, and have temper tantrums.[907] Songs are sung in a family setting on days dedicated to the Marasa.[908] At these celebrations, copious amounts of food and drink are prepared for an offering and feast; a pigeon, chicken, turkey, or goat is sacrificed and prepared.[909]

A sack of food is placed on the floor for all dead twins, and in the afternoon the food is distributed to jubilant children outside the temple. After the ceremony has been completed, the family waits until the following dawn to consume it, thus carrying out a twenty-four-hour fast. One can abandon serving the Marasa by throwing bowls into water, but the Marasa may inflict punishment for that. To appease the Marasa, *pwomès* (promises) can be offered, such as giving coffee and food to the poor outside Catholic churches. One oungan claimed that the Marasa and the dead are older and more powerful than the lwa; he also described the Marasa as *zanj* (angels).[910] The cult of the twins is also important in the Fon culture. As in Haiti, twins are considered *vodun* (lwa).[911] Each Vodou lineage in Benin maintains an *ahoho,* an altar dedicated to the twins.[912] Photographs taken in 1969 show initiates taking a lunch break on their long pilgrimage to Porto-Novo: in one image, a child who has lost his twin brother has a small wooden effigy of his deceased twin next to his lunch bowl.[913] In Benin, Vodou priests instruct clients to give candy to twins they meet in the street.[914] *See* **dogwe; dosa; dosou; kenbe; lage; Mawou-Lisa; plat Marasa.**

mare pwen To tie up a charm; to acquire a Vodou charm or lwa to attack or confront a malefactor or rival.[915]

Mari Lwiz Kanga The name of a lwa from the Ibo-Kanga cycle.[916]

Marinèt-Bwa-Chèch; Marinèt-Limen-Dife; Marinèt-Pye-Chèch A dreaded group of Petwo lwa.[917] Marinèt is married to Kongo Zandò.[918] Those possessed by her twist their mouths and turn their eyelids inside out.[919] *See* **Petwo; Zandò.**

maryaj; maryay A mystical union with a lwa.[920] In the Fon culture, one also marries the *vodun* (lwa).[921] *See* **Èzili.**

masisi Homosexuals, who are welcome in most Vodou communities.[922] *See* **madivin.**

Mason Many Vodou priests are Masons or study Masonic literature. One Vodou song says, "Oh my Dan Petwo, we're all Masons."[923] Freemasonry, the world's largest secret society, was well established during the French colonial period, and it remains popular in contemporary Haiti. Mason symbols in Vodou include the skull and crossbones, the all-seeing eye, and the crossed compasses that are commonly found in Vodou vèvè and on Vodou flags.[924] The "crossed compasses" symbol is known as the Masonic Universal and can be found on the lwa Ayizan's vèvè, among others. *Gran Mèt* (Great Master) is a Masonic and Creole term for God. The lwa Bawon Samdi and Ogou are Masons; Bawon Samdi's tophat, jackets, tails, spats, and trappings such as skeletons and skulls come from the secret chambers of Masonic lodges.[925] Masonic handshakes and secret passwords have been incorporated in ritual greetings by Vodou priests.[926] The first Masonic lodge, Loge de la Verité, was established in Cap Français in 1748, and by 1770 all of the important towns of Saint-Domingue had one.[927]

masoudi A sexually suggestive dance for the spirits of the dead.[928]

matchason A Vodou dance.[929]

Mater Dolorosa; Our Lady of Sorrows Mater Dolorosa's image represents the lwa Èzili because her heart is pierced by a sword in her chromolithographs, just as Èzili's vèvè is composed of a pierced heart. Mater Dolorosa is one of the many titles given to the Virgin Mary because of her trials and sorrow over the death of her son, Jesus.[930] *See* **Èzili; vèvè**.

matinik A variety of both Vodou and secular dance, as well as a special drum used for the spirit Zaka.[931]

Matinik-Djouba A Vodou rite that includes lwa such as Kouzen Zaka, Minis Zaka, and Olicha Oko.[932]

matwòn Some Vodou priests, such as Oungan Marcenat, work as birthing nurses. *See* **kakofè**.

Mawon The Maroons were bands of organized guerrilla-style communities composed of runaway former slaves. The Maroons carved out significant swaths of land in the most mountainous and remote areas of eighteenth-century Saint-Domingue. They are the forefathers and mothers of Haitian independence. They carried out raids and attacks on French colonial posts and properties. Boukman Dutty was said to be a Maroon leader. The Maroons practiced a variety of "hot" Vodou that some believe became one of the main contributors to the Petwo rite.[933] The Maroons blew in *lanbi* (conch shells) to communicate over distances. *See* **Boukman; lanbi; Petwo**.

Mawou-Lisa The Fon name for God. Mawou-Lisa is also found in Haitian Vodou. Mawou is the female upper god who created the sky and the earth. Together with her male partner, Lisa, they form a divine pair.[934] The notion of twin Supreme Beings is reflected in the Marasa (Divine Twins).[935] The oft-cited Fon proverb "*Mawu wè dó vodun* (God created the *vodun*)" shows the supremacy of Mawu and how honoring and serving the *vodun* (lwa) is to honor and serve God.[936] Mawou-Lisa forms a single "double deity."[937] Mawou-Lisa's offspring, the *vodun* (lwa) Agè, is the earth. Mawu is translated as the "Supreme Being, creator God." Lisa is represented by the *aganmà* (chameleon) in Fon culture; note that the Creole word for chameleon is also *aganman*.[938] The Fon and the Haitian people share a fundamental monotheism; the *vodun* or the lwa are branches of that trunk. Fon religion is also monotheistic, because Vodouists are devoted to only one *vodun* (lwa).[939] Lisa and Lisagbadja appear in a few Haitian Vodou songs—for example, "Agawou Mede, oh the creoles call our names, to Lisa we will go!"[940] *See* **Aganman**.

Mayanèt This female lwa is assimilated with the popular Catholic image of Anima Sola (the Lonesome Soul).[941] In Anima Sola's chromolithograph, a beautiful woman burns in flames with one arm reaching upward. Services for Mayanèt require grilled or roasted chicken. Mayanèt is tough and eats pieces of burning charcoal. Mayanèt is a *gad* (guard) in that she protects her followers. She possesses her followers on very rare occasions.[942]

mayetis; manyetis A magic spell.[943]

Mayi A Vodou rite and an extremely rapid Vodou dance.[944] The Mayi people inhabited a region north of Dahomey. They were regularly invaded by the kingdoms of Nago-Oyo and Dahomey.[945] Savalou, a name preserved in Haitian Vodou, was the capital of the Mayi region.

mazanga A type of *lougawou* (werewolf or monster) that digs up bodies in cemeteries.[946] Mazanga is a goblin similar to the *baka.*[947] *See* **baka; lougawou.**

Mazanza *See* **Bizango; Sanpwèl.**

mazi A traditional term for a family compound.[948] *See* **demanbre; lakou.**

mazon; mazòn; mazonn; mazoun; mazann A dance or chant to chase away unwelcome lwa and a rapid drum rhythm.[949]

mele To mix, blend, tangle, confuse, involve; a reference to the inappropriate appearance of several lwa at the same time.[950]

men Left hand; negative Vodou practices. The phrase *travay ak de men* (to work with both hands) refers to a Vodou bòkò who works with both cool and hot lwa and magic.[951]

mete kò li deyò To put one's self outside; consult a Vodou priest or priestess.[952]

Mèt Kafou *See* **Legba.**

mèt kay; mèt ounfò The master of the house; the lwa who is in charge of a given ounfò.[953] *See* **lwa.**

Metrès Èzili *See* **Èzili.**

mèt tèt The master of the head; the particular lwa one is chosen to serve in the *ounsi* seclusion ceremony.[954] This lwa will be the Vodouist's protector and will "dance in her or his head" more than other lwa. The Vodou priest or priestess, through the inspiration of the lwa Loko, may select the lwa, or the lwa of the Vodouist may already be established through possession events that occurred before initiation. The priest or priestess calls the lwa through vèvè and songs: the novice is possessed by the lwa who is the *mèt tèt* (master of the head) in the course of initiation. In Benin, a person serves only one lwa in the course of life, whereas in Haiti the practitioner has one principal lwa but typically serves additional lwa.[955] *See* **kouche; lave tèt; ounsi.**

migan A ritualistic potion prepared with the blood of sacrificed animals, sugar, and spices. *See also* **popouri.**[956] Oungan Marcenat points out that *migan* is a cooked mixture of various roots and plantains, plus sacrificial blood, which children are served during rituals for the Marasa. In a song for Ogou, the link to children is shown: "Oh consolation, the children are going to drink the Migan."[957] *See* **tchiman asòtò.**

milokan; minokan A conglomeration of vèvè traced around the base of the *poto-mitan* in the temple. The *milokan* represents the reunification all of the lwa and sources of Vodou.[958] *Milokan* means "all are one."[959]

minwit; minui; minuit Some songs suggest that midnight or darkness provides the opportune occasion to call on the lwa or *dyab.* The following lyric suggests this: "Oh my! As soon as you hear the dyab singing / Oh! Oh the midnight hour! It's my hour!"[960]

mistè Mysteries. *Mistè* can refer to a guardian lwa, the lwa in general, or a mystery. The *kay mistè* (house of the mysteries) is the inner sanctuary of a Vodou temple containing an altar. To *sèvi mistè* (serve the mysteries) means to practice the Vodou religion.[961]

mistik Mystical; refers to Vodou, magic, or the supernatural.[962]

miwa Mirrors and shiny objects that symbolize the ancestors, because their domain is the reverse of our own.[963]

mò Raising the dead, a ceremony performed to call forth dead spirits for a *manje lemò* (food for the dead). *Mò Ginen* (the dead from Ginen) refers to African ancestors. The phrase *wete mò nan dlo* (raising the dead from the water) refers to a Vodou ceremony in which dead souls are transferred from under the water, where they have remained for at least a year and a day.[964]

monben The yellow mombin or hog plum, a sacred tree in Vodou.[965]

Mondong; Moundong; Mongdong; Moudong A family of lwa that originates in the Kongo.[966] Mondong is classified as Kongo-Ginen.[967] Mondong may also refer to a Vodou dance rhythm.[968] Mondong's vèvè is a dog. Dogs or dog ears are offered to the lwa.[969] Other songs assert that Mondong eats burned goat meat.[970] Living in the southern part of the Kongo, the Mondong people were among the first to be enslaved. Later they became important slave traders because of their location at the mouth of the river Malebo. This may be why the lwa Mondong is said to "eat people" and is associated with the dog, a low life form in Haiti.[971]

monpwen My point; the son or daughter to whom a Vodou priest or priestess transmits his or her secrets and knowledge.[972]

monte Mounted or ridden; being possessed by a lwa. Being ridden by a lwa is the expression of affection for the ancestors.[973] The sentence "*Lwa a monte chwal li* (The lwa mounted her horse) means that the lwa has possessed her or his follower. *Monte batri* (mount a charm) refers to the act of preparing a Vodou charm.[974] *See* **chwal; lwa**.

mouchwa A brightly colored headscarf made of silk that represents a given lwa. The use of *mouchwa* is linked to the textile industry of seventeenth-century Kongo.[975]

Moundong *See* **Mondong**.

Move Tan The name of a lwa. Marcenat points out that Move Tan (Bad Weather) is responsible for lightning, rain, and storms and is capable of killing people through bad weather, especially lightning. *See* **Agawou**.

movezè Evil spirits much like the *lougawou.*[976] *See* **lougawou**.

mwayen Medium; the middle Rada drum that is also known as the *segon.*[977] *See* **boula; manman tanbou; segon**.

Nago A Vodou rite, group, or *nanchon* (nation) of lwa, and a dance.[978] Loko is called the *wa Nago* (king of the Nago). *Nago cho* (hot Nago) refers to a rapid and aggressive Vodou dance. A *Nago gran kou* (big Nago strike) is a Vodou dance of greeting to the lwa Ogou.[979] Haitian Creole preserves the expression "*Yon pa kita, yon pa nago* (One step forward, one step backward)." One song expresses an ambivalent relationship between Vodouists and the lwa—in this case, the lwa Nago: "Oh when they're ill, they run to the house of that Nago! / When you see they're healed, Nago is a demon, hey."[980] *Nago* is the Fon word for the Yorùbá language and culture.[981] In Fon, *anagó* refers to inviduals initiated to a *vodun* (lwa) cult with Yorùbá origins; thus, those initiated to the cults of Sakpata, Mawou, Lisa, Segbo, or Gu are *anagó,* even if they reside in Benin.[982] Nago is also a Yorùbá language and is spoken in coastal Nigeria, Benin, and Togo. Because of their proximity to the Atlantic, the Nago people were often victims of the slave trade.[983] *See* **Kandèl**.

naje nan gwo dlo/gran kouran To swim in big waters or currents; to be well protected thanks to Vodou powers or social and business connections.[984]

nanchon Nation; a grouping, based on ethnic origins, of Vodou lwa. Ibo, Rada, Nago, Kongo are examples of *nanchon* in Vodou. The *nanchon* also correspond to Vodou rites. In the colonial period, many West African nations were forced into slavery by African handlers, French slave traders, and colonialists in Saint-Domingue. In that context, nation-based Vodou emerged in many parts of Saint-Domingue. Today the term does not have a strong political or geographical meaning, even if some of the names of Vodou *nachon* have ethnic and geographical etymologies.[985] *Nanchon* also refer to people initiated into Vodou by the same priest or priestess.[986] The participation in Vodou groups based on one's African family heritage was common in the Haiti of the nineteenth century—for example, in 1841, the majority of "dance companies" described by Victor Schoelcher (1804–1893) were composed of individuals descending from specific regions.[987]

Nanginen *See* **Ginen**.

nanm Soul; spirit or vital force. In Vodou, *nanm* can be an immaterial creature—benevolent or malevolent. *Mete nanm* (putting soul) refers to the process of restoring a soul that has been taken from a body. A *move nanm* (bad soul) can refer to the ghost or a *lougawou* (female werewolf), as they wander around at night. A *nanm zonbi* (zombie soul) refers to the soul of a dead person that has been captured by a *benyè* (undertaker) and sold to an unscrupulous Vodou priest or priestess. To *pran* *nanm* (take soul) refers to the charming, distracting, or capturing of someone's protective guardian angel through evil magic.[988]

nasyon *See* **nanchon**.

Nègès Kreyòl Black Creole Woman, the name of a lwa.[989]

neklesen A metal triangle played in Vodou ceremonies.[990]

Nibo *See* **Gede Nibo**.

nich Nest; a small altar or box containing articles for Vodou worship. A *nich lougawou* refers to a luminous trail left in the sky by a *lougawou.*[991]

noble The act of invoking the lwa by a Vodou priest or priestess.[992]

Nòk A people who inhabited Nigeria 3,500 years ago. The Yorùbá people and a portion of the Kongo's people, through migration, inherited their traditions.[993] The Nòk people were ironsmiths, warriors, and farmers. Population pressure, military strength, and agricultural techniques gave rise to their expansion eastward to the Kongo known as the millennia-spanning Bantu Migration.[994]

non vanyan; non pwen The valiant name or name of courage; an intimate Vodou name one receives from one's parents and Vodou priest or priestess.[995] The lwa have *non vanyan,* too. A sacrificial rooster is marked with Legba's *non vanyan,* Katawoulo: "The chicken is marked with my name, courageous Legba. / It is marked with the name Katawoulo. / It is marked with the intimate name of Legba."[996] The kings of Dahomey used what was the equivalent of the *non vanyan,* the *adanyi,* as their official name once in power.[997] *See* **andwaye**.

Nouvèl The name of a lwa who is married to Saint Elizabeth. He originates in the region of Les Cayes in southern Haiti.[998] *See* **Sent Elizabèt**.

nwa Black, the color of the living.[999] *See* **blan**.

obeyi devan mistè To obey before the spirits; ritually striking one's chest three times.[1000]

oble tanbou An insistent drum rhythm played to hurry the appearance of the lwa.[1001]

ochan A special song or drum flourish to mark the appearance of a lwa or distinguished visitor.[1002] *Ochan* is also a type of praise song used to greet the arrival of a lwa who is riding a follower.[1003]

ogan A rhythmic time-keeping instrument similar to a cowbell. An *ogan* is usually a piece of iron struck with an iron clapper in Rada Vodou ceremonies.[1004] It plays the unchanging "time line," or rhythmic reference, around which the drums improvise.[1005] In the Fon language, the *gã* is also a metallic gong or cowbell that is likewise used to provide cadence.[1006] While the *ogan* is sometimes dispensed with, it is always present abstractly.[1007] The iron of the *ogan* links it to the Nago lwa, such as Ogou.[1008]

ogantye; oganye The player of an *ogan*.[1009]

ogatwa; oratwa; wogatwa A personal home altar; often a box, stand, closet, or table containing or supporting sacred objects.[1010] The establishment of an *ogatwa* is the first step toward becoming a servant of the lwa.

Ogou; Ogoun; Ogou Achade; Ogou Baba; Ogou Bakesou; Ogou Bakoule; Ogou Balisaj; Ogou Balote; Ogou Baltaza; Ogou Batala; Ogou Belizè; Ogou Chalode; Ogou Chango; Ogou Djamsan/Yamsen/Yamsan/Yamson; Ogou Dodè/Lodè; Ogou Fè; Ogou Feray; Ogou Galonnen; Ogou Gounnbasa; Ogou Jenizon/Kenizon; Ogou Je Wouj; Ogou Kelendjo; Ogou Koumandja; Ogou Laflanbo; Ogou Lele; Ogou Mileni; Ogou Nago; Ogou Panama; Ogou Pe; Ogou Temerè; Ogou Tonnè; Ogou Ti Mal/Ti Mal Dede; Ogou Yaba; Ogou Yèkè; Ogou Yemenn; Ogou Sabaho; Ogou Velekete Obakesou; Ougon; Chal Ogou; Sen Jak Majè Ogou represents war, defense, energy, force, iron, any kind of metallurgy, and atomic energy.[1011] The numerous Ogou lwa are considered among the most powerful.[1012] The Ogou lwa are served in the Danwonmen, Petwo, and Rada rites.[1013] The Ogou originate in the Nago *nanchon* associated with the Yorùbá people. In times of war, these lwa are said to be absent from Vodou ceremonies because they are preoccupied with the battlefield. Because of Haiti's successful war of independence, Ogou is prominent in many temples.[1014] The emblems of the Ogou lwa are iron, fire, the machete, the sword, and the saber. His day of the week is Wednesday. The Ogou are represented by red and blue. Wearing a red scarf is said to protect warriors and make them intrepid; wearing blue symbolizes protection.[1015] The *kako* rebels (insurgents who fought the U.S. occupation) sought the protection of the Ogou and displayed red scarves. Wearing red scarves gives powers of invincibility. Ogou provides antidotes against poison.[1016] When German gunships threatened to attack Port-au-Prince in 1897 and Gonaïves in 1902 over the repayment of a loan, an individual in each town dressed himself in red and galloped through the streets to incite resistance. Dessalines may have covered his head with a red headscarf in honor of Ogou. Nago lwa, like the Ogou, tend to be boastful and pretentious. The Ogou lwa are rum drinkers but do not get drunk. Since the Ogou lwa are considered terrifying, their possessions are intense. Their *chwal* (horses) growl like wild animals and speak in thundering tones; they tremble and rear up like horses.[1017] Men possessed by Ogou often dress in military attire, with a red scarf tied around the neck or arms. They carry a sword or a machete and a wooden stick around which a red scarf is tied. Women possessed by Ogou wear red attire and a red headscarf. Some of Ogou's *chwal* handle hot iron.[1018] According to Vodou legend, some Haitian revolutionary generals used the wooden stick to fend off French bullets. The establishment of Ogoun in Yorùbá and Fon consciousness is parallel to the development of metallurgy.[1019] In one Yorùbá myth, Ogou extracted iron ore to hack a path through the chaos so that the other *vodun* (lwa) could reach the world. In Yorùbá society, iron smelters, blacksmiths, hunters, warriors, scarifiers, and barbers revere Ògún because their tools were once smelted from iron. Dogs were traditionally offered in sacrifice to Ògún, which is taken to be a sign that Ògún worship began during a hunting stage of culture.[1020] The equivalent *vodun* (lwa) in the Wéménu-Fon community of Benin is Gu. Gu is also the deity of iron and those who use it. Gu is a civilizing deity who offers techniques to humanity. To honor Gu in Benin, an array of metal tools is laid out and sprinkled with sacrificial blood. Hunting and fishing are the domains of Gu. Gu is also the force that propels sperm and fertility; Gu is present at childbirth and cuts the child's umbilical cord.[1021] Non-Christians and non-Muslims in Yorùbáland swear on an iron implement rather than on the Bible or the Qur'an in courts of law.[1022] *See* **Sen Jak Majè**.

Ogou Achade; Papa Bakouson Achade The name of a lwa who is a powerful bòkò, or "Vodou priest who works with both cool and hot lwa." Ogou Achade has knowledge of medicinal plants, and his resting tree is the avocado.[1023] *See* **bòkò; Bosou Achade; Kadya Bosou.**

Ogou Badagri; Ogou Badagi The name of a lwa identified with Saint George the Dragonslayer or Saint James the Greater. As a fighter, he is the patron saint of warriors.[1024] Ogou Badagri is the patron of soldiers and the lwa of war. Ogou Badagri is served in the Danwonmen, Petwo, and Rada rites. Like the other Ogou lwa, Ogou Badagri is partial to women, rum, and cigars, and he drinks without getting drunk. Rum libations are poured out for him, and the *ounsi kanzo* (initiates) pour rum on their hands and light it on fire without getting burned. Ogou Badagri enjoys the sounds of guns and cannons; he can make his followers invulnerable to bullets.[1025] Badagi is a town in Nigeria located on the Ogou River.[1026] Ogou Badagri is said to be a mulatto and the owner of a large property. He is sometimes feared.[1027] The lwa can have a strong will and make major demands. While possessing a manbo, Ogou Badagri insisted on the sacrifice of seven red roosters, but the community could not afford it and tried to sing several songs to appease him and send him away.[1028] Ogou Badagri has a role in carrying out justice and revenge.[1029] Songs sung by the *chwal* (horse) of Ogou Badagri may complain that the lwa was not welcomed with adequate enthusiasm.[1030] The lwa Agwe reproaches Badagri for having ravished his mistress, Mètrès Èzili. Ogou Badagri gets angry saying that Èzili was his wife and that she bore his unfortunate child, Urzule, who was lost at sea.[1031] In the chromolithographs of Saint George, a young girl is represented close to the horseman; Vodouists consider her to be Urzule. Ogou Badagri is referred to as a "politician."[1032] Ogou Badagri's colors are those of flame and blood. In services dedicated to him, the female *ounsi* wear a red peasant's dress with a red headscarf. A red flag is displayed, and hens and roosters with red feathers are sacrificed. Ogou Badagri's resting tree is a red laurel.

Ogou Balindjo; Ogou Balendjo The name of a sea lwa who works as the captain of Agwe's warship, Imamou.[1033] Ogou Balendjo is served in the Danwonmen, Petwo, and Rada rites.[1034] Ogou Balindjo is associated with Saint Joseph or Saint James the Lesser, and he is a healing lwa and a military general.[1035] The machete is his symbol.[1036] Marcelin's song 155 about Ogou Balindjo appears in a slightly different form in the popular *rasin* (roots) song *Kè m pa sòte* (I'm Not Scared).[1037] *See* **Agwe Tawoyo; Imamou.**

Ogou Bayè The name of a lwa who is the guardian of enclosures and the temple door.[1038] *Bayè* in Haitian Creole means "gate." *See* **Legba lan Bayè.**

Ogou Feray Ogou Feray is the lwa of armies and is identified with Saint Philip, Saint George, and Saint James the Greater.[1039] Ogou Feray is served in the Danwonmen, Petwo, and Rada rites. Ogou Feray, a blacksmith, represents the fusion of metal and fire and their role in power, empire, and civilization. Ogou Badagri is a military extension of Ogou Feray. Ogou Feray is calm, smokes a pipe, wears blue clothes with a red scarf around his neck, and has a machete at his side. His possession events are not marked by violence; however, he shows his strength by picking up members of the audience.[1040] His symbols are the sword, iron, and fire. The scarlet red of flame and blood represents him. Ogou Feray protects the brave and leads soldiers into battle.[1041] Saint Philip, the horseman who wears armor in the chromolithographs of Saint James the Greater represents Ogou Feray. Some claim that Feray is the son of Badagri. Ogou Feray's spoils beautiful women with gifts, but this makes him destitute and hungry.[1042] Ogou Feray is said to have many female followers, and they must set up an *ogatwa* in his honor. Chromolithographs, oils, cotton, red candles, bottles of rum, a cigar, and a branch of basil, among other items, are displayed.[1043] His day is Wednesday, and his female followers abstain from sexual intercourse on that day. Ogou Feray is said to bring wealth on his day. Ogou Feray, the lwa of fire, is the patron of metallurgy and the metallurgist. He presides over the production of weapons, armor, and farming tools. Ogou Feray plays an important part in the *manje yanm* (yam offering). A fire is lit in Ogou Feray's forge on days dedicated to him. The forge is composed of two pieces of iron. Ogou Feray's resting tree is the *bwa pen* (pine). While possessing a follower, Ogou Feray drinks rum and puffs a cigar.[1044] The *pentad* (guinea fowl) is the sacrificial animal offered to Ogou because the Nago people of Nigeria traditionally raised those birds.[1045] In one description, Ogou Feray's *chwal* (horse) took the sacrificial chickens, whirled them in the air, snapped their necks, and sucked blood out of their wounds. Blood drops are placed on Ogou Feray's forge and gunpowder is ignited on the ground while the community sings.[1046] Ogou Feray sings a song in reply.[1047] A song is sung with a *yanvalou* rhythm by the members of the congregation while they dance around the *potomitan*.[1048] The sacrificial chicken is cooked, and Ogou Feray's *chwal* sits down to consume a meal in his honor.[1049] After the meal, the oungan traces a vèvè on the ground, and members of the family dig a hole and place rum, coins, a piece of forged iron, cigars, matches, and the bones of the sacrificed animals in the hole. The oungan covers the hole and lights two white candles and one red candle on top of it while the family sings a song.[1050]

Ogou Kankannikan/Zankannikan The name of a lwa who is a bloodthirsty general like Ogou Badagri. Ogou Kankannikan drinks alcohol and the blood of sacrificed animals. Soldiers are said to seek his protection.[1051]

ogounnen To have the protection of Ogou.[1052]

Ogou Panama A lwa that is linked to President Florvil Hippolyte (1889–1896). Hippolyte was a military man who greatly admired Dessalines and was a devout Vodouist. In his pursuit of his rival, Merizye Janis, his wide-brimmed panama hat fell to the ground. Ominously, he failed to pick it up, and later, after falling from his horse, he died of a heart attack.[1053]

okipasyon A spell that takes the form of an impossible task assigned by a *dyab.*[1054]

Okominawe Velekete The name of a lwa.[1055] *See* **Ayizan Velekete**.

okon The Fon word *okon* means "to kill an animal for a sacrifice." The word occurs in songs dedicated to Ogou Chango and illustrates the retention of Fon language fragments.[1056] *See* **donon; koklo; langaj**.

Olicha The name of a lwa associated with Saint Raymond who is regarded as evil-doing and cruel. Olicha is sometimes classified as one of the "other Ogou lwa."[1057] Olicha is said to be a famous magician who has knowledge of plants that kill and heal.[1058] *Oricha* is the Yorùbá and Cuban Santería term for *lwa* (divinity or deity).[1059] The song *Olicha Nago* shows the Yorùbá origins of the lwa Olicha since the term *Nago* refers to Yorùbá language and culture.[1060]

Onè! Respè! Honor! Respect! A greeting used by all Haitians that is also uttered before some Vodou songs.

Oricha The name of a family of Vodou lwa.[1061] *Oricha* is also the general term for the lwa in Cuban Santería. *See* **lwa**.

oryante; oriyante To present an offering or acknowledgment to the four cardinal points of the compass.[1062]

Osanj; O'zany; O'zany Balogè; O'zany Megi; Osany; Osany Agelingwi; Osany Agenitò; Osany Gegimalò; Osany Batagri; Osany-Batala; Osanyi One of the Ogou lwa.[1063] In a song to O'zany, the lyrics "They took the sacred shaker of the lwa to perform a healing" shows that O'zany is a healing lwa.[1064] In Yorùbáland, Osanj is the patron lwa of leaf remedies. The lwa is blind in one eye and has a broken leg and arm—hence, his sympathy for the ill.[1065]

ougan *See* **oungan**.

oun An important root syllable in many Vodou terms. In the Fon language, *oun* refers to "blood, heart, family, drums, bellows, God, and Vodou," notions that are retained in Haitian Vodou.[1066] The *oun* also refers to the largest of the three Rada drums, synonymous with the *manman tanbou* (mother drum.) In Fon, *hùn* is also the name of a specific *vodun* (lwa).[1067] The expression *so hùn* (take blood or spirit) means to be possessed by a *vodun*. *See* **ountò; ountòki**.

ounfò; oufò A Vodou temple complex or compound under the authority of an oungan or a manbo. *Lasosyete ounfò* (temple society) refers to the members of a given temple.[1068] In the Fon language, the term *hunxò* refers to a Vodou hut and *hunxwé* to the house of a *vodun* (lwa) or a Vodou convent.[1069] *See* **badji; djèvò; pe; peristil; pewon**.

oungan; ougan; houngan; gangan; ngangan A Vodou priest, healer, and seer. The best oungan have wisdom, knowledge, clarity, and discernment of what is good and evil.[1070] The oungan is also a "pastoral guide" who interprets the core cultural mores and values of his society.[1071] The oungan (and manbo) acquire profound knowledge of various lwa. They are ritual experts who know the vèvè and symbols of the lwa. They master the songs, prayers, invocations, rituals, dances, and rhythms of the lwa.[1072] Their contact with the lwa gives oungan authority among Vodouists.[1073] An *oungan ason* is a Vodou priest who has passed through and paid for instruction and initiation. The initiation rites require twenty-one days of seclusion and fasting and are preceded by years of training and apprenticeship. An *oungan diplome* is a Vodou priest who is thoroughly versed in the true traditions of the religion. An *oungan Ginen* is a Vodou priest who has received intuitive initiation through Vodou specialists in the family. An *oungan payèt* or *matoufè* is a Vodou priest with only superficial knowledge. An *oungan achte* refers to an uninspiring Vodou priest. An *oungan pike liv* is a Vodou priest directly inspired by the knowledgeable Kongo lwa.[1074] For Oungan Nelson Marcenat, a *pike liv* is an oungan who employs Catholic mystical writings such as Jacques Coret's *L'ange conducteur dans la vrai dévotion* (1851) and Abbé Julio's *Prières merveilleuses pour la guérison de toutes les maladies* (1896) to perform magic, rituals, ceremonies, or rites of passage such as baptism or burial. As one song explains, the priesthood should be taken seriously: "When a man is becoming an oungan, oh stay the course. / The profession of oungan isn't a joke! If you're fooling around you'll die badly."[1075] It is not uncommon for the oungan to encounter hardships, as this song suggests: "Don't you see I endured misery as a Houngan, oh my! Oh Master Crossroads called, the day is here, oh my!"[1076] The expression "each houngan is his own houngan" refers to the fact that each oungan determines the parameters of his religion.[1077] In the Fon language of Benin, the term *hungã* refers to a Vodou chief and the leader of the drummers.[1078] *Gán* in Fongbe is a "chief" or "leader," and *oun* is, first and foremost, "blood." Thus oungan is literally "a leader of blood sacrifice, a chief of the gods."[1079] The Fon expression *hun gan mè* means "someone with superior power."[1080] The number of *ounsi* (initiates) associated with an oungan represents his relative prestige.[1081]

oungannize To serve as a Vodou priest.[1082] The verb also refers to *becoming* a Vodou priest. *See* **asogwe**.

oungenikon; oungenikonn; andjennikon; houngennikon The leader of songs and dances at a Vodou service and the person in charge of offerings. The oungenikon has extensive knowledge about the repertoire of songs in a given temple and the ability to sing them charismatically. The oungenikon is also an assistant to the oungan or manbo.[1083] An *oungenikon katye mèt* is the person in charge of offerings and ritual accessories in a temple.[1084] In the Vodun of Benin, the *hunjènukòn* is the first initiate who enters seclusion and opens the way for the others who will enter the isolation ritual.[1085]

oungeve; ounjeve; ounge A large necklace with varied inserted stones. The *oungeve* can also refer to the decoration on an *ason*.[1086]

ounsi; ousi; hounsi; wonsi; ounsi bosal; ounsi kanzo; ounsi temerè A Vodou initiate in the first degree of initiation, a member of a particular Vodou temple, or the assistant of a priest or priestess. An *ounsi bosal* refers to an uninitiated novice. An *ounsi kanzo* is a Vodouist who has undergone the second degree of initiation rites involving linkage with a lwa and a symbolic ordeal with heat or flame. *Ounsi temerè* (fearless *ounsi*) is the highest degree that a Vodouist can reach without actually becoming a priest or priestess.[1087] The *ounsi* undertakes considerable preparation and pays a significant amount of money to attain the rank, which culminates in a seven-day period of isolation and accompanying rituals. Prior to isolation, the candidate must visit the local Catholic Church to show piety and receive ablutions. The isolation retreat of the *ounyò* (novices) is called the *kouche* (sleeping, lying down.) A ritual of the *kouche* is the *chire ayizan,* which involves wearing hats made of palm strips that cover the faces of the *ounyò* (novices). The palm tree is the resting tree of the lwa Ayizan Velekete and Haiti's national tree. The *ounsi* initiation is for purification and fortification, and while in seclusion initiates receive the *lave tèt* (head washing) that consecrates the Vodouist to a particular lwa.[1088] The *ounsi* wear all-white robes at Rada ceremonies and make up the choir; devotees of the *òrìsà* (lwa) Obàtálá and Ọ̀sun in Yorùbáland must also dress in white.[1089] The *ounsi* learn a large repertoire of Vodou songs and mythology. In the Fon language of Benin, *hunsi* refers to the individual during the period of initiation. Once initiated, these individuals become *vodunsi.*[1090] During initiation in Benin, the *hunsi* studies the rites, dances, songs, and language appropriate to the one *vodun* (lwa) she or he will serve.[1091] The *hunsi* of Benin also undergo a seven-day isolation ritual.[1092] *See* **Ayizan Velekete; boule zen; chire ayizan; kanzo; kouche; lave tèt; mèt tèt; ounyò.**

ountò; hountò The lwa of drums who governs a drummer.[1093] The *ountò* also refers to the middle size of the three Rada drums, synonymous with the *segon* (second drum). *Ountò* also refers to the drummers. In addition, an *ountò* can refer to a ritual dance or a sacrificial goat.[1094] In the Fon language, the *ountò* (drum father) refers to the drummer.[1095] *See* **oun; ountòki.**

ountòki; ountògi; ountògri; hountògi The smallest of the three Rada drums, the same as the *boula* (little drum). The *ountòki* is also the drummer.[1096] The following is a lyric from a song of greeting dedicated to the *hountòki*: "Drummers, I'm telling you good evening, ayibobo!"[1097] *See* **oun; ountò.**

ountòyi The smallest of the three Rada drums, the same as the *boula.*[1098]

ounyò A novice undergoing an initiation ceremony. The *manman ounyò* refers to the woman who cares for the initiate during the *ounsi kanzo* seclusion.[1099] Beauvoir (2008b: 77) provides a photograph of two *ounyò* wearing their *chire ayizan* (hat of palm leaves that cover their faces). In Wéménu-Fon, the term *hunsi yoyo* also refers to the novice undergoing initiation.[1100] The Fon word *hunjò* is defined as "someone who is born through the power of a *vodun* (lwa)." Because of this, the *vodun* holds authority over the individual's entire destiny.[1101] The Fon word, also *hunyó,* refers to someone initiated to the *vodun* (lwa) Agasú.[1102] *See* **Agasou Gnenen; Ayizan Velekete; boule zen; chire ayizan; lave tèt; mèt tèt; ounsi.**

Our Lady of Mount Carmel; Notre Dame de Mont Carmel Linked to the lwa Èzili. *See* **Èzili; Sodo**.

Our Lady of the Assumption; Notre Dame de l'Assomption Linked to the lwa Lasirenn. The Virgin Mary is given this title by Catholics because of the belief that she was taken into heaven at the end of her earthly life.[1103] *See* **Lasirenn**.

Ozanyen; Ozanyen Agwe; Ozanyen Dan; Ozanyen Meji; Ozanyen Ogou; Ozanj; Osayin; Osanyin The name of a lwa who is closely related to Danbala, Ogou Feray, Agwe, Gran Bwa, and Loko. Ozanyen is served in the Dawomen and Rada rites. Ozanyen's vèvè contains a serpent. Ceremonies for him take place in the woods because he, like Gran Bwa, is the guardian of forests. Ozanyen should be invoked prior to collecting medicinal leaves and plants or he will withdraw his powers.[1104] In Yorùbá tradition, Òsanyìn is likewise the *orisha* (lwa) of herbs, medicine, and language.[1105]

pakèt inisye *See* **potèt**.

pakèt Kongo; pakèt Kongo packet; a talisman that is an important component of Haitian religious and figural tradition. The *pakèt Kongo* synthesizes energy and has psychotherapeutic applications. It is composed of incense, cannon powder, bark, twigs, food, and leaves, among which are the *feuille trois paroles* (leaves of three words), which are also referred to as *twa fèy* (three leaves).[1106] These leaves are said to be the basis of healing remedies.[1107] All the ingredients are crushed together, perfumed, and mixed with a paste made from a sacrificed animal. The *pakèt* is then produced in a ceremony at the time of a new moon for a healing spirit. The ingredients are wrapped in satin or silk cloth and consecrated to an associated lwa or rite (e.g., black for Gede, yellow for Kongo, and red for Petwo). Oungan or manbo next prepare the *pakèt* by sealing the contents in an earthen jar.[1108] The *pakèt* are "guards" that can excite or *chofe* (heat up) the lwa. They are used for protection, healing, and good luck. The power of a *pakèt* can be increased by exposing it to flames in the *boule zen* ritual when novices become *ounsi*.[1109] Although the *pakèt Kongo* is related to the *nkisi* (medicine packet) found in the Kongo, it is creolized with its elegant use of silk and feathers. The Fon people of Benin use non-figural empowerment objects called *bo*. The topping of a *pakèt Kongo* with crosses and crucifixes is a tradition that may come from the arrival of Christianity in the Kongo in the 1400s, but it may also be a Creole addition.[1110] The wrapping of jars with rope and fabric show the community that the contents of the jar reflect the sacred.[1111] *See* **boule zen**.

pakèt Rada The packet of the Rada rite, a simply assembled and tied bag that is more modest than the elaborate *pakèt Kongo*.[1112]

pale Ginen Mystical ritual phrases originating in Africa.[1113] *See* **langaj**.

Papa An honorific that is regularly inserted before the names of revered male lwa (e.g., Papa Legba, Papa Ogou, and Papa Simbi).

papalwa Father of the lwa; a reference to a Vodou priest.[1114] Déita (Mercedes Guignard) defines *papalwa* as a Vodou priest or priestess who receives the vocation directly from the lwa and does not undergo the ritual of *prise de asson* (the obtaining of the sacred rattle).[1115] In the Fon language, *babalawo* is synonymous with *bokónò* (Vodou priest who specializes in divination and interprets the Fa). In the Yorùbá language, *babaláwo* is "father of the Vodou secret."[1116] They receive special powers from Ile-Ife.[1117] *See* **bòkò; Fa; Ginen**.

papiyon Butterflies. They are compared to the dead because they flutter around everywhere.[1118] *See* **lèmò**.

parigol A variety of Rada dance.[1119]

paviyon The courtyard of a Vodou temple complex.[1120]

pe A Vodou altar.[1121] *See* **pewon**.

peman lelwa Payment to the lwa, a Vodou ceremony performed on Christmas Eve to ensure health for the coming year.[1122]

peristil; perestil A covered area partially open at the sides where most Vodou drumming, dancing, chanting, and possession take place.[1123] *See* **badji; ounfò; pe; pewon**.

pè savann; prèt savann A Vodou priest who also carries out rites and rituals using Roman Catholic texts. Roumain provides a literary representation of a *pè savann,* Aristomène, as he officiates at the burial of the murdered hero Manuel using Latin and French Catholic texts.[1124] *See* **pike liv**.

Petwo One of the major rites of Vodou. Petwo was once considered a family of Vodou lwa that originated in Haiti. However, most argue that Petwo is an amalgamation of the "hot" and "seditious" lwa from the Kongo, Angola, and Haiti.[1125] The Petwo lwa (which are hot, dangerous, and evil-attacking) and Rada lwa (which are cool, peaceful, and reflective) are counterbalancing components of the overall Vodou religious system.[1126] The temperament of the Petwo nation is one of "cosmic fury" against displacement, alienation, and slavery.[1127] As hot lwa, they are represented by colors (as opposed to the white of Rada), and in particular, the color red—hence, compounds such as Èzili Je Wouj (Red Eyed Èzili)—and by the flames of fire.[1128] The Petwo lwa reflect the ethos of foreigners and outsiders.[1129] Petwo lwa are aggressive, serious, or violent, and their *chwal* (horses) are known to greedily crush glass in their mouths, walk on hot coals, lick hot embers, and juggle iron reddened in the fire.[1130] Gunpowder is ignited to celebrate the Petwo lwa and to raise the dead.[1131] Other Petwo lwa, such as Èzili Dantò, are stern and carry emblems of power, including daggers. The Petwo lwa require pork offerings. They are *pi rèd* (tougher) than the Rada lwa.[1132] Petwo is a pantheon that opposes, confronts, or challenges the cooler Rada religious attitude.[1133] The followers of the Petwo lwa must also be disciplined in serving them; in exchange, they protect and heal.[1134] *Petwo* is also a dance characterized by extremely rapid foot movement with the left hand placed on the hip and the right arm extended. *Petwo maji* refers to a specific type of dance. The term *Petwo* is sometimes attributed to Don Pedro, the important Vodou priest in Haiti who established a new Vodou sect in 1768.[1135] A more likely origin is the Petwo region of the Kongo. Petwo was also the name of a line of kings, including Don Petwo IV and Jan Petwo, who ruled the Kongo in the late seventeenth century and eighteenth century.[1136] Don Petwo was popular for opposing slavery. He was a Christian convert; hence, Vodouists honor him at Christmas.[1137] *See* **Dan Petwo; Jan Petwo; gwo baka; Mawon; Rada; ti baka**.

Petwo Fran Pure Petwo, a Vodou rite with lwa such as Ogou Je Wouj, Marasa Bwa, or Mèt Gran Bwa Ile.[1138]

pewon A Vodou altar.[1139] *See* **badji; ounfò; pe**.

piga A stick used in Vodou ceremonies, especially in the *gede* dance.[1140]

pike liv; pikèt liv Book stake; a Vodou priest who is literate and employs Roman Catholic or Masonic texts for rites and rituals, especially burial. According to Bryant Freeman, a *pike liv* is also a priest who is inspired by Kongo lwa.[1141] *See* **pè savann**.

pikèt A peg that attaches the skin to a Rada drum. *See* **kòn; ralba**.

pile fèy Crushed leaves, a ceremony in which dry leaves and a sacrificial chicken are crushed in a mortar.[1142]

pinik A variety of Vodou dance.[1143]

pisans Power; a reference to magic power.[1144]

pitit fèy; pitit kay Children of the leaves; the congregants of the temple and those who have been treated and healed by the Vodou priest's or priestess's herbal medicine. *See* **tyovi**.

pla sèk Dry plate; a food offering to the lwa with no animal sacrifice involved.[1145]

plase nanm Placing of the soul. In the course of the ceremony to baptize the *asòtò* drum, the *plase nanm* infuses the drum with a soul.[1146] *See* **asòtò**.

plat Marasa Three-part clay or wooden bowls; a special bowl with food offered to the lwa Marasa and the family. Parents with twins undergo celebrations and rituals involving *plat Marasa.* After eating, all guests wipe their hands on the foreheads of the parents of the twins and remind them of their responsibilities as parents.[1147] The *plat Marasa* are found in Rada, Kongo, and Petwo temples. The three bowls reflect the domains of the lwa: sky, earth, and water. They also link the Marasa to the *dosou* or *dosa* born after them.[1148] Marcenat keeps *plat Marasa* bowls on his altar. In the Fon culture, the Divine Twins are also represented by the *hòxógbán,* an assemblage of two (instead of three) small bowls fused side to side.[1149] *See* **dosou; dosa; Marasa**.

plato A round metal plate on an iron rod inserted into the ground and used for Vodou offerings.[1150] Similar iron standards are used in Benin in shrines for the ancestors.[1151]

po The terms *po kanzo* and *po tèt* refer to a small earthen or china pots containing hair and nail clippings from a living Vodouist. This pot represents a Vodouist's spiritual essence and is placed on the altar of a given temple as a sign of membership. A *po rafrechiswa* is a libation pitcher.[1152] *See* **kwi; potèt; zen**.

popouri A ritualistic potion prepared with the blood of sacrificed animals, sugar, and spices.[1153] *See* **kimanga; migan**.

posede To be possessed by a Vodou lwa. As a noun, it refers to the person possessed by a Vodou lwa.[1154] *See* **chwal; lwa; monte**.

posesyon Possession or property in Vodou culture.[1155]

pòt drapo Flag carriers who bear Vodou flags in ceremonies. *See* **kò drapo**.

potèt; pakèt inisye The "head pots" that represent the novice in the ritual to become an *ounsi.* Several ingredients are sealed within the clay jar: *monben* leaves, hair clippings of the novice, fingernails and toenails, corn porridge, sweets, grilled corn, sacrificial chicken feathers, blood, and so on. The novice keeps the *potèt* nearby during the initiation period. Afterward, it is placed in the altar room and symbolizes the good conduct of the initiate and affiliation with the temple. The *potèt* has power, and the priest or priestess can correct a straying member of the community by using magic on the *potèt.*[1156] Those who do not wish to stay in a sanctuary have been known to carry away their *potèt* and keep it hidden at home. In the Fon language, the term *ta vodun* (head *vodun*) refers to clay jars that *vodunsi* (initiates) carry on their heads during processions.[1157] *See* **ounsi; ounyò; zen**.

potomitan The centerpost around which rituals and ceremonies unfold in a Vodou temple. The *potomitan* is described as the nexus or axis mundi between the spheres of the natural and the supernatural. The *potomitan* represents the tree that reaches into the three domains of the lwa: the sky, earth, and water.[1158] As a great tree it reaches into the heavens, and through its roots it grows deep into Africa.[1159] Danbala Wèdo and Ayida Wèdo, both serpent lwa, are often painted wrapped around the *potomitan,* a reflection of their primacy. The *potomitan* is often decorated. Sacrificed chickens are sometimes crushed against the *potomitan* to encourage the appearance of the lwa. Other terms for the centerpost include the *poto Danbala, poto demanbre, poto gad, poto kabès, poto kontra, poto Legba, poto mèt, poto paviyon,* and *poto pewon.*[1160]

poud Magic powder. Oungan earn money selling powders that purport to provide success in business or love or protection from malicious forces. *Poud* is also associated with poison. A *kout poud* (powder strike) is the use of magical powder to harm someone. The phrase *poud fòk ou vle* (you have to want it powder) refers to love potion. *Poud wanga* (talisman powder) refers to magic powder.[1161] *See* **manje ranje**.

presipite A substance used to force someone to do something quickly.[1162]

Priyè Ginen; priyè Dyò Prayers at the beginning of a Vodou service. *Priyè Ginen* is a prayer consisting of both African and Roman Catholic elements.[1163] They are accompanied by the rhythmic shaking of the *ason* (sacred rattle) but no drumming. Beauvoir (2008a) provides a reconstruction of these lengthy prayers based on the contributions of several oungan. *See* **desounen**.

priz ason; priz klòch Taking the sacred rattle; an initiation ceremony into the priesthood.[1164] *See* **asogwe**.

prizdèzye Obtainment of the eyes, a reference to initiation into the priesthood in some parts of Haiti.[1165] A type of clairvoyance expected of Vodou oungan or manbo.[1166] *See* **asogwe; sou pwen**.

pwa grate A mildly harmful spell.[1167]

pwav ginen Ginen pepper; a mixture prepared by a sorcerer.[1168]

pwazon Poison, a harmful Vodou magic amulet.[1169]

pwen A point; a tangible or intangible Vodou charm used for good effects. A *pwen* can also refer to a contract between a human and a lwa. *Pwen* is a concentration of spiritual power, and it is a spiritual gift.[1170] A *pwen* can be made with a doll that represents an ancestor or a *kwi* (calabash bowl) on the base of which a cross is drawn to represent the *kalfou* (crossroads) where the *pwen* is placed.[1171] *Pwen* is also synonymous with *lwa*. A *pwen* is a "degree of mystical power."[1172] The term *pwen* refers to lwa in the Petwo and Bizango rites.[1173] To *bay pwen* (give point) refers to a ceremony to confer special powers. To *pran pwen* (take point) means to acquire special supernatural powers. A *pwen chans* is a good-luck charm. To have *pwen disparèt* means to have the magical power to become invisible.[1174] A *pwen gad* (guard point) is for protection; one song asserts, "If you see me take the pwen, it's because of the hunger in my belly."[1175] Another song states that a *pwen* is needed to combat sickness.[1176] *See* **asogwe; chante pwen; gad; lwa; pakèt Kongo; pwen cho; sou pwen**.

pwen achte Purchased charms, usually for malevolent purposes.[1177]

pwen cho A hot point made by passing the *pwen* over flame, by painting a red dot on it, or by adding hot pepper to give it symbolic energy.[1178] One type of *pwen cho* is a combination of sulfur, saltpeter, and niter, which creates a chemical reaction that produces heat.[1179]

pwotektè One's protective Vodou spirit.[1180] *See* **mèt tèt**.

pyebwa Trees, which are sacred in Vodou because they are in contact with the three realms of the lwa: the sky, earth, and water. Some Vodouists believe that the lwa are leaving Haiti as the country is progressively deforested.[1181] In many parts of Africa, enormous trees that tower above others, such as the silk cotton tree, the *iroko,* and the baobab, are the harbors of spirits.[1182]

pyè tonnè; pyè loraj; pyè lwa Thunder stones; arrowheads or special stones that represent lwa or provide a resting place for them. These stones are sometimes called *pyè lwa* (lwa stones).[1183] Marcenat has in his possession several *pyè tonnè* that appeared mysteriously under his pillow, led to his calling to the Vodou priesthood, and give him healing powers. The *pyè tonnè* are sent to earth by the lwa Sobo and owned by the lwa Fawo Pyè Dantò.[1184] A *pyè dtè* (earth stone) is used as a head rest during initiations. The term *pyè loraj* (thunder stone) describes an arawak ax head used in Vodou services. *Pyè manman* (mother stone) refers to a large round stone that protects a Vodou homestead. A *pyè solèy* (sun stone) is a magic stone capable of bringing sunshine.[1185]

Rada One of the most widespread Vodou rites in Haiti. Rada comprises benevolent but serious Vodou lwa originating in the Dahomian region, such as Agawou Tonnè, Ayizan Velekete, Danbala Wèdo, Hountò, Legba Atibon, and Agwe Tawoyo.[1186] The Rada lwa reflect family, heritage, coolness, water, the feminine, and the insider disposition; they are gentle and good-natured and promote well-being.[1187] *Rada* also refers to a dance rhythm.[1188] Rada is etymologically related to Allada, the name of a town in southwestern Benin. The religion practiced in Allada had a major impact on the formation of Vodou. Yorùbá religion is also considered part of the Rada rite.[1189] Slaves from the Dahomian Rada region dominated the slave population of Saint-Domingue from 1690 to 1750. Slaves from the Kongo region came to equal them in number by 1791.[1190] *See* **Petwo**.

rad penitans Penitence clothes; ritual clothes constructed by sewing strips of different-colored cloth together. Men make multicolored shirts, and women make dresses. The colors represent various lwa. *Rad penitans* are worn to overcome a sin, at times of crisis, or when Vodou is under attack, such as during the Catholic Church's anti-Vodou pogrom of 1941.[1191] Abstinence is required for those wearing the attire.

rafrechi tèt Head freshening, a ceremony performed to increase the power of one's principal lwa of protection.[1192]

ralba A wooden clasp that ties and tunes the cords of a Petwo drum.[1193] *See* **kòn; pikèt**.

rale The sound of the *manman tanbou* or the *gwo baka*. *See* **gwo baka; manman tanbou**.

rale kò Ginen To draw in the Ginen corps; to call on the lwa. The phrase *rale mennen vini* (to draw in) refers to a charm used to attract customers or a romantic interest.[1194]

ranje To arrange; a spell. The term also means to imbue with a protective magical power or it refers to something that is evil or magical.[1195] *See* **manje ranje**.

ranpli ledevwa To fulfill duty, a private ceremony in honor of one's family lwa.[1196]

rantre kanzo A ritual and celebration held for the *ounsi kanzo* candidates as they enter the *djèvo* (initiation room) for seven days of isolation and training. *See* **kanzo; leve kanzo; ounsi**.

ranvwa A spirit or a ghost. A *ranvwa* also refers to a spell or exorcism against an *espedisyon* by using powerful magic. A *ranvwa mò* refers to practices performed at the death of one Vodouist to prevent death from striking another.[1197] The *ranvwa mò* is also a powerful rite performed immediately after the death of someone to cause the death of another. The expression *fè yon ranvwa lwa* refers to sending a lwa off to the woods or to Africa.[1198] *See* **ranvwaye**.

ranvwaye To send off, chase away; a reference to the sending away of a lwa when her or his time and welcome has expired in a ceremony. *Ranvwaye nanm* (sending off the soul) is to send off a dead soul.[1199]

rapèl The clapping of hands to help call forth the lwa.[1200]

rara (bann) A group that mostly parades during the Lenten period from Carnival until Easter.[1201] Members of the *bann rara* learn a repertoire of songs, many of which are Vodou, and make special costumes and disguises. Instruments used in *bann rara* include drums, the *vaksin* (bamboo pipe), the *tchatchatcha* (shakers), *kònè* (cheap tin trumpets), whistles, clarinets, trumpets, saxophones, and accordions. *Bann rara* are usually affiliated with a Vodou temple, where members meet for activities prior to parading. The *bann rara* must show respect to the ancestors at the cemetery.[1202] *Bann rara* draw in spectators and revelers by poking fun at and criticizing society. The word *rara* may be related to the Kikongo term *wala,* which refers to processions.[1203] The *bann rara* is composed of members who bear military and royal titles (e.g., *majò* [major], *majò jon* [drum major], *wa* [king], *rèn* [queen], *avangad* [front guards], and *aryègad* [rear guards]).[1204] *Bann rara* sing in front of the homes of patrons for money. *Rara* may be related to the Dahomian and Nigerian Egougoun celebration, which also involves disguises and starts at a temple. Because of the "heat" of *rara* and the laced drums used, it may also reflect Kongo-Petwo influences. *See* **vaksin**.

rasanbleman A Vodou ceremony.[1205] *See* **seremoni**.

rasin Roots; hereditary lwa and traditions, as opposed to those lwa and traditions sold by the bòkò. *Rasin* is sometimes associated with the Rada rite, in distinction to Kongo-Petwo rite. The *rasin* Vodou priesthood tend to offer *gerizon* (healing) for lower fees. *Rasin* sometimes refers to the tradition inherited in the family. *Rasin* has also come to refer to modern Vodou music that became popular in the 1990s and continues today. *See* **gerizon; manbo; oungan**.

Rasin San Bout Roots without End, the name of a lwa.[1206]

rebelyon Rebellion; refusal to follow the will of a lwa.[1207]

rechanj; rechany Ritual clothing used in Vodou.[1208]

regleman Ordering; the proper arrangement for addressing the saints and the lwa and the corresponding rituals, songs, gestures, rhythms, and structure in a Vodou ceremony.[1209] *Regleman* is the repertoire of Vodou songs.[1210]

rejèt *Rejèt kanpay* (rejection campaign) and *rejèt mouvman* (rejection movement) refer to anti-Vodou campaigns carried out by the Haitian state, the Catholic Church, or the U.S. military during the U.S. occupation.[1211] For example, in 1835, the Haitian government banned *wanga* (Vodou charms), and Vodou dances became illegal in 1864. Persecution took place in 1896, intermittently between 1915 and 1934 (the U.S. occupation), and in 1941.[1212] The most notorious persecution was carried out by the Catholic Church and the Haitian military under President Élie Lescot's government in 1941. Thousands of Vodou temples, objects, and *repozwa* (resting trees of lwa) were destroyed.[1213] The *rejèt kanpay* came to a quick halt after gun shots were fired in the Catholic Church in Delmas during an anti-Vodou mass on February 22, 1942; Vodouists were not going to allow the persecution to continue.[1214] The period after the departure of President Jean-Claude Duvalier in 1986 was also marked by the destruction of Vodou property and people. Finally, in the weeks after the cholera outbreak that began in October 2010, more than forty-five Vodou priests and priestesses were blamed for the epidemic and hacked to death.[1215] *See* **kolera**.

rejete; rejte To formally renounce one's Vodou beliefs and practices. A *rejete* can also refer to an anti-Vodou campaign.[1216]

reklame To claim; a reference to familial lwa who select someone to be their protector. One lyric suggests the jealousy of a lwa who claims an heir: "Oh I have three lwa who have claimed me, / Oh those lwa don't want me to stay with other people, oh my!"[1217] *See* **eritye; lafanmi**.

rèl ak repons Call and response, a basic structure in Vodou singing and music. *Rèl ak repons* involves a lead singer or musician who provides a line of a song that is responded to in song or music.[1218] The oungan, manbo or oungenikon may sing a lyric, and the *ounsi* choir repeats or responds to it.

rele lwa yo To call the lwa.[1219]

renn Queen; a *renn chantrèl* (singing queen) is a lead female singer in a ceremony. A *renn drapo* (flag queen) is a woman in charge of banners. The *renn kòbèy* (basket queen) refers to the treasurer of a temple. A *renn silans* (queen of silence) is a woman in charge of enforcing order during a service.[1220]

Renn Siyèt; Rèn Siyèt Queen Siyèt, the name of a female lwa whom Marcenat links with Jezabèl (Jezebel). In First and Second Kings in the Hebrew Scriptures, Jezebel, a Phoenician, became the queen of ancient Israel through her marriage to King Ahab of the northern kingdom. She convinced Ahab to worship the Phoenician God, Baal.

repiyans Repugnance; a powder used in remedies.[1221]

repouse To push away; a powder used in remedies.[1222]

repozwa; pye repozwa A temporary repository, such as a tree, rock, cave, or person's head, for a lwa.[1223] A *pye repozwa* (resting tree) is where a lwa dwells when not riding a Vodou servant. Many trees are considered *repozwa* in Haiti, and some are associated with specific lwa (e.g., the palm tree and Ayizan Velekete). The *akasya jòn* (yellow acacia), *ave* (*Petiveria alliacea*), *bazilik* (basil), *flanbwayan* (flamboyant), *mapou* (ceiba), and *sèd* (cedar) are included among the trees and plants that have mystical associations in Haiti.[1224] The *mapou* is "the home of many of the lwa that dance in the heads of the Haitian people."[1225] The *mapou* will not be cut down by Haitians. Some trees are valued for their power to stop evil spirits, such as the *sèd*.[1226] In Belle-Rivière, south of Miragoâne, the enormous *mapou* growing by the cemetery is the dwelling place of the lwa of the cemetery (Bawon Samdi), and the community considers the tree sacred. In the Fon language, the *atimévodun* is a class of *vodun* (lwa) who dwell in trees.[1227] *See* **Ayizan Velekete; lwa; pyebwa**.

resèt Earnings, receipt, or recipe; also a reference to magic power.[1228] The semantics of *resèt* (recipe) might be linked to the notion of combining ingredients to produce an object or talisman with magic power. *Fè resèt* means to utter Vodou incantations.[1229] *See* **gad; maji; wanga**.

resting tree *See* **repozwa**.

rèv Dreams. Along with possession, dreams are important ways by which the lwa communicate with their followers. For example, a lwa such as Ogou Feray may appear in a dream to inform a follower about his impending acquisition of wealth.[1230] The lwa take on the appearance of familiar people or things to communicate in dreams, but they provide clues to their identity—by wearing a red scarf in the case of Ogou or sunglasses in the case of Gede.[1231] Lwa appear in dreams to warn their followers about danger, spells, and poisons and to bless Vodouists and announce their protection and graces. *See* **lwa**.

rit Rite. The lwa and their accompanying rituals are divided into twenty-one rites. Many, but not all, of the rites are toponyms: Danwonmen (Dahomey), Gede (village of Gedevi in Dahomey), Wongòl (Angola), Nago (Nigeria), Mayi (Nigeria), Kita (Nigeria), Ibo (Nigeria), and Kongo (the Kongo). Each rite comprises dozens of lwa.[1232] These days, the Rada and Kongo-Petwo rites are predominant.[1233]

rit tanbou Drum rhythms; the musical foundation of Vodou ritual. Wilcken inventories the following order of rhythms from a single ceremony: *yanvalou, parigòl, zepòl, mayi, fla vodou, dawome, djouba, nago, ibo, abitan, kongo payèt, petwo, banda,* and *kita*.[1234]

Saint Aloysius Gonzaga; Louis Gonzage Associated with Gede Nibo because images show him kneeling next to a skull and an open Bible while holding a crucifix. *See* **Gede Nibo**.

Saint Anne Associated with Grann Èzili because she is depicted as an old woman.[1235] *See* **Grann Èzili**.

Saint Anthony of Padua; Antoine of Padoue *See* **Sent Antwàn**.

Saint Anthony the Hermit; Antoine l'Hermite Associated with Legba. *See* **Legba**.

Saint Augustine Associated with Agasou. *See* **Agasou Gnenen**.

Saint Bridgid of Ireland; Brijit Associated with Grann Brijit. *See* **Grann Brijit**.

Saint Charles Borromeo Associated with Azaka Mede. *See* **Azaka Mede**.

Saint Christopher Associated with Simbi. *See* **Simbi**.

Saint Clare of Assisi Represents the mother of the Marasa. *See* **Marasa**.

Saint Elizabeth *See* **Èzili; Sent Elizabèt**.

Saint Expedite; Expedit Associated with Agwe and Bawon Samdi. *See* **Agwe Tawoyo; Bawon Samdi**.

Saint George the Dragonslayer Associated with Ogou Badagri. *See* **Ogou**.

Saint Gerard Majella Associated with Gede Nibo because he kneels next to a skull in one of his chromolithographs. *See* **Gede Nibo**.

Saint Isidore the Farmer Associated with Kouzen Zaka because he is shown farming in his chromolithographs. *See* **Kouzen Zaka**.

Saint James the Greater; James the Elder Associated with the Ogou lwa. He is sometimes considered the father of the Marasa. His chromolithographs show him brandishing a sword or saber and dressed in a red cloak. The saber and red cloak are taken as emblems of the Ogou. *See* **Ogou; Sen Jak Majè**.

Saint James the Lesser; James the Younger Associated with Ogou Balindjo.[1236] *See* **Ogou Balindjo**.

Saint John the Baptist; Sen Jan Batis The lwa who instructed Jesus in the secrets of Vodou. Sen Jan is celebrated in Miragoâne on June 24. Vegetarian food such as popcorn, farina, mangoes, pineapple, and *kleren* (white rum) are offered in his honor.[1237] Sent Elizabèt (Saint Elizabeth), the mother of John the Baptist and kinswoman of Mary, the mother of Jesus, is also a lwa. Sen Jan is represented in chromolithographs as a tender child among lambs. Saint John the Baptist is also associated with Agawou. *See* **Agawou; Sent Elizabèt**.

Saint Joseph; Sen Jozèf Associated with Loko Atissou and Ogou Balindjo. He is linked with the tree-lwa Loko Atisou because his chromolithographs represent him holding flowers or a staff with flowers bursting from the top. *See* **Loko Atisou; Ogou Balindjo**.

Saint Lazarus; Saint Lazare; Sen Laza Associated with Legba. *See* **Legba**.

Saint Lucy; Lucie Represents the mother of twin girls and is linked to the Marasa. *See* **Marasa**.

Saint Patrick Associated with Danbala, the serpent lwa, because he is pictured banishing serpents from the island of Ireland. Ironically, Saint Patrick traveled throughout Ireland fighting the Druids and eventually converted most of the island to Christianity.[1238] *See* **Danbala Wèdo**.

Saint Paul Associated with Jeneral Badè. *See* **Badè**.

Saint Peter; Simon Peter Associated with Legba and Sobo. *See* **Legba; Sobo**.

Saint Philip Associated with Ogou Feray. *See* **Ogou Feray**.

Saint Philomena; Philomène Associated with Lasirenn because she is represented with an anchor, symbolic of her home in the sea. *See* **Lasirenn**.

Saint Radegund; Radegonde Associated with Bawon Samdi because she carries a scepter like the *koko makak* (stick) of Bawon Samdi. *See* **Bawon Samdi**.

Saint Raymond; Raymond Nonnatus Associated with Olicha because he dresses in red and holds a stalk of leaves. *See* **Olicha**.

Saint Roch; Rock; Rocco; Roque Associated with Agawou. *See* **Agawou**.

Saints *See* **lesen**.

Saint Sebastian; Sen Sebastyen Associated with Gran Bwa (Big Tree) because he is pictured tied and martyred to a tree.[1239] *See* **Gran Bwa**.

Saint Ulrich Associated with Agwe because he holds a fish in his hand. *See* **Agwe Tawoyo**.

sakre Consecration; involves the tracing of a cross with sacrificial animal blood on the forehead of members or family by a Vodou priest or priestess. The ceremony takes place annually or periodically. *Sakre* also means "sacred" or "holy" in Vodou. *See* **san**.

sakrifis Animal sacrifice, the most important way for Vodouists to honor and seek the support of the lwa. In the Rada rite, all animals except the pig may be sacrificed. In the Petwo rite, the pig is the most important animal sacrificed. In Haiti, some of the animal's blood and meat are offered to the lwa, but most is cooked and served to those possessed by the lwa and to members of the community. One song suggests that sacrifices may be performed in exchange for a service, such as the provision of magic.[1240] Another song warns of inappropriate offerings: "Gede Nibo, look at the injustice they do to me. / The old rotten herring even a pig doesn't want to eat, / That's what they give Gede."[1241] In the Fon language, the expression *hù nu nú vodun* means "to offer an animal sacrifice to the *vodun*."[1242]

sakwèt A witch or sorceress similar to a *lougawou*.[1243] *See* **lougawou**.

salange To protect or cherish; derived from the Kikongo *sa lunga*.[1244] For example, "Oh Deblayi, which lwa are you? / The Dyab walks entirely in the night, he's going to provide protection."[1245] Other lyrics read, "I'm going to cherish the Charm."[1246]

salango A variety of Petwo dance.[1247]

salitasyon A greeting between Vodou priests.[1248]

Samdi (Bawon) *See* **Bawon Samdi**.

sa m di se sa What I say is what it is; a powder used as a remedy.[1249]

san Sacrificial animal blood, one of the fundamental aspects of Vodou ritual. Animal blood is shed to feed and please the lwa and Vodouists. Marcenat argues that the consumption of raw blood by someone possessed suggests the manifestation of a *dyab*. Those possessed by the lwa are typically offered cooked and spiced blood. In other Vodou temples, an individual possessed by a blood-consuming type of lwa ingests animal blood after the sacrifice. Some lwa will sacrifice a chicken, for example, using the teeth of the one possessed. The Fon expression *dà hùn* (to make cooked blood) refers to cooked blood for the *vodun* (lwa); it is a ritual for initiates.[1250] Blood is traced in the form of a cross on the forehead or lips of Vodouists. In the Fon culture, the *sá hùn* is blood that is poured on the head of an individual in need of deliverance from impurity or evil.[1251] The Fon expression "*nù vodun* (drink *vodun*)" involves the drinking of sacrificial animal blood for magical purposes. Those who do this together consider themselves blood brothers or sisters.[1252]

sanba; sanmba A Kikongo word that refers to a singer, dancer, composer, and musician who has the ability to open the gates between the living and the ancestors.[1253] Oungenikon are sometimes called *sanba* by extolling worshipers. The *sanba* have "bathed in the leaves of a protector lwa."[1254] The same song describes Boukmann and Makandal as *sanba,* showing that the term also refers to historical Vodou leaders. In Kikongo, *sámba* means "to pray, worship, invoke God, etc."[1255] *See* **Boukman Dutty; Makandal; oungenikon**.

Sanmanman *See* **Bizango; Sanpwèl.**

Sanpwèl; Chanpwèl A secret society whose members are reputed to have the power to change form at will, often into animals.[1256] They have a bad reputation and are often accused of misdeeds in Haitian folklore. Marcelin quotes an informant who claimed that a band of Sanpwèl in Fondeblan had a tradition of sacrificing a child to Èzili Je Wouj.[1257] In 2008 in Belle-Rivière, about ten miles from Fond-des-Blancs, informants told me stories about Sanpwèl bands that sought victims for sacrifice in the wee hours of the night. Many rural and urban people will not go out at night for fear of encountering a Sanpwèl band. The popular Haitian legend overlooks other important aspects of secret societies such as Sanpwèl. They resemble societies in Benin or Nigeria such as the Zangbetò, who are engaged in community policing, protection, and Vodou defense.[1258] The groups arose to protect Vodou heritage from destructive forces.[1259] Sanpwèl's goal is to fight for and defend Vodou and to ensure national and local order. Unlike the *oungan Ginen,* the leader of the Sanpwèl has judiciary functions involving the determination of right and wrong in a community. If someone directly attacks the Sanpwèl or one of its members, the group counters the attack. If harmful deeds (land invasion, theft, selfishness, gossiping, disrespect, etc.) have been committed, the perpetrator can be brought before the Sanpwèl for remediation.[1260] The Sanpwèl typically meets in a temple that includes altars for both the Rada and the Petwo lwa. However, the Sanpwèl honors the most fiery and aggressive of the lwa.[1261] The rarest and most severe punishment executed by the Sanpwèl for the most heinous infractions is zombification.[1262] *See* **Bizango; zonbi.**

sanyan; siyanyan Related to *san* (blood); a reference to the bleeding in animal sacrifice.[1263]

satan Sometimes synonymous with *dyab* (fiery lwa).[1264] *See* **dyab; gad; lwa; pwen.**

Savalou E Savalou is a town in Dahomey and modern Benin. *Savalou e* is commonly employed as an acclamation in Vodou songs and texts.[1265]

se Divine power; a reference to the power that God infused into the lwa.[1266] In the Yorùbá language, the equivalent term is *se* or *achè*. The names of the lwa are sometimes fused with this morpheme (e.g., Legba-se and Loko-se).

segon The middle size of the three Rada drums.[1267] The *segontye* either plays the *segon* with hands and fingers or with one hand and one stick. The drummer sits and holds the drum at an eighty-degree angle.[1268] *See* **boula; manman tanbou.**

segontye Second drummer; the person who plays the *segon* drum.

Sèklekite The name of a lwa.[1269]

sele Saddled. Like *monte* (mounted), *sele* means to have a lwa temporarily take over one's mind and body through the release of the *ti bonnanj* (good little angel).[1270]

sen A Vodou lwa and a Catholic saint.[1271] The two terms are often assimilated in the sense that visual features of the Catholic saint on chromolithographs have come to symbolize the lwa and their mythologies. Many Vodouists recognize only the lwa in such images and have no knowledge of the saint and her or his Catholic tradition. This superimposition originates in the forced conversion of Vodouists to Catholicism during French colonialism and slave trafficking (c. 1680–1803). The lwa themselves do not recognize the Catholic chromolithographs with which their servants associate them.[1272] *See* **lwa.**

Sende Makaya The name of a virile lwa.[1273] Courlander's song 20 is sung for this lwa by young people at a wake or *desounen* ritual.[1274] *See* **desounen; Makaya.**

Sendenden *See* **Bizango; Sanpwèl.**

Sen Jak Majè; Papa Ogou; Jeneral Mèt Ogou; Lwa Sen Jak Saint James the Greater, considered the father and the chief of the Ogou lwa and hence sometimes called Papa Ogou, Jeneral Mèt Ogou, or lwa Sen Jak.[1275] In Catholic chromolithographs, he is represented on horseback brandishing a sword.[1276] Sen Jak is often accompanied by a dog.[1277] He is popular in northern Haiti, especially in Cap-Haïtien. Sen Jak, like Ogou, is a minister of war.[1278] Vodouist warriors call on him when they need support.[1279] If Sen Jak sends an illness, only he can heal it.[1280] Some who seek the help of Sen Jak become rich.[1281] Sometimes Sen Jak has his own temple; at other times, he is represented in the temples of other lwa and on Rada altars. In temples dedicated to Sen Jak, one finds a sword or machete in the masonry, his stone on a clay plate, a red candle, a bell, his ritual rattle, the three-section *krich Marasa Ginen* (Marasa Ginen pitchers), a cauldron with three legs mounted on a *degre Nago* (Nago charm), a piece of forged iron, and his *govi* (clay pot) and those of the lwa who accompany him (Loko, Sobo, and Èzili). Sen Jak's day is Wednesday, and his color is red. The lwa's resting tree is the passionfruit. Songs are sung to welcome the arrival of Sen Jak.[1282] Images of Sen Jak were popular among the Spanish and Portuguese because Saint

James was credited with their victory over the Muslim occupiers in 1492. The Portuguese popularized the image during their invasion and occupation of the Kongo in the mid-seventeenth century, and it spread to Saint-Domingue during the Kongo slavery period that started in the mid-eighteenth century.[1283] *See* **Ogou**.

senmafò Vodou *peristil* (temple).[1284] *See* **ounfò; peristil**.

senp Ritualistic gestures or words that have a supernatural effect. A *senp* is also an incantation, a herbal remedy, a magical cure, or a magical substance used to protect a dead body.[1285]

Sent Antwàn The name of a major lwa linked to the Petwo tradition. King Antwàn (António I) ruled over the Kongo from 1661 until the Portuguese killed him at the battle of Mbwila in 1665.[1286] Under his rule, the Kongo became a safe haven for runaway slaves, and his foreign policy sought the expulsion of the Portuguese.[1287] His namesake, the Catholic Saint Anthony of Padua (1195–1231), was born in Portugal and was heavily promoted in the Kongo by the Portuguese.[1288]

Sent Elizabèt Associated with Agwe, lwa of the sea. Sent Elizabèt was the mother of John the Baptist, one of the main teachers of Jesus.[1289] Since she is served similarly to Èzili, she is her double. Sent Elizabèt's husband is Nouvèl, another lwa closely related to Agwe's escort. Sent Elizabèt is associated with Èzili. *See* **Èzili; Lavyèj Karidad; Nouvèl; Saint John the Baptist**.

sèp A symbolic prison for someone who has not behaved according to a lwa's requirements.[1290]

seremoni A Vodou ceremony.[1291] *See* **demanbre; kandjanhoun**.

seremoni zo A ceremony in which the unbroken bones of the sacrificed animal are buried.[1292]

sèt priz tè Seven clutches of earth; a reference to the procedure for composing *pakèt Kongo* and offerings in *kwi*.[1293] *See* **kwi; pakèt Kongo**.

sèvi To serve the lwa; to be a Vodouist. The lwa are served to gain their protection and help. If ignored, they turn their attention to those who do serve them, or they return to Ginen.[1294] To *sèvi ak de men* (serve with both hands) means to be involved in both cool and hot Vodou.[1295] In the Fon language, *sèn vodun* is to "serve a lwa."[1296]

sèvis Service; a reference to a Vodou ritual or ceremony. To *fè sèvis lwa/Ginen* means to conduct a Vodou ceremony. A *sèvis an blan* (service in white) refers to a Vodou ceremony conducted without drums.[1297]

sèvitè Servant; a follower, disciple, or Vodouist. To *fè sèvitè* (make a follower) means to greet someone by touching his or her forehead.[1298] *See* **Vodouyizan**.

sezi To grab or seize; a reference to being possessed by a lwa.[1299] *See* **monte; sele**.

siflèt Whistles that are blown to communicate with the lwa, the musicians, or singers, and to create an exciting ambiance.[1300] Like whips, whistles are linked to the

Petwo rite, because their shrill sounds "heighten the feelings of dissolution and communality" typical of the Petwo ethos.[1301] Whistles are also common in *rara* parades. *See* **ason; klòch**.

Simba; Grann Simba; Grann Simba Lawouze; Man Simba; Manman Simba Some Vodouists claim that Manman Simba (Mother Simba), the spouse of Papa Simbi (Daddy Simbi), is a beautiful white woman. The servants of Mother Simba consume no alcohol and must not be sexually promiscuous. Songs describe Simba rising wet from a well; hence, she, like Simbi, is a water lwa.[1302] One song suggests that she confers powers of transformation: "Man Simba, come see me / I'm going to change into a frog in the woods."[1303] *See* **Simbi**.

Simbi; Simbi An De Zo/Andezo; Simbi Anpaka; Simbi Bwa; Simbi Dlo; Simbi Donpèd; Simbi Fèy; Simbi Ganga; Simbi Gwo Nèg; Simbi Kita; Simbi Kongo; Simbi Lawoka; Simbi Lawouze; Simbi Mazaka; Simbi Makaya; Simbi Malo; Simbi Maza; Simbi Yaya; Simbi Yandezo; Simbi-Yan-Kita; Simbi Twa Ile; Simbi Twa Kafou; Simbi Vyeno; Simbi Zile; Manzè Simbi; Mouche Simbi; Papa Simbi; Rèn Simbi The name of a healing lwa who is associated with fountains, springs, ponds, and lakes and is the guardian of the coasts. The whale is Simbi's symbol.[1304] Simbi is served in the Kongo, Petwo, and Rada rites. In the Rada rite, Simbi is known for his good disposition. In the Petwo rite, he[1305] is known for his skill in fighting and is a member of Ogou Badagri's army. Those possessed by him display their skills in swimming.[1306] Simbi is associated with Saint Christopher because he is shown in a chromolithograph crossing a river with the baby Jesus on his shoulder.[1307] Simbi originates in the Kongo.[1308] Simbi is the patron lwa of *passeurs* (river crossers). A coin should be offered for safe passage. Simbi is said to capture children who go alone to collect water at a spring.[1309] One story claims that a young mulatto child was taken "under the water" by Simbi for seven years and later returned. At first, people thought he was a *zonbi* (a person deprived of a part of his or her mental faculties), but later he founded a Vodou ounfò that was well frequented and became known for healing incurable diseases.[1310] Simbi presides over the dew.[1311] Simbi can have his own temple or might have a small room or niche dedicated to him. Because he is a water spirit, such spaces have altars and a bowl of water. A chromolithograph of Saint Christopher and Moses crossing the Red Sea are placed on the altar.[1312] The chromolithographs are supposed to be blessed by a Catholic priest in a church before being placed in the room. In the room, there is also a saucer with a white stone on it, an olive oil lamp, some *govi* (earthen jugs), and the *pakèt* (sealed earthen jar) of Simbi. Before invoking Simbi, the Vodou priest or priestess requests permission from Atibon Legba, Loko Atisou, and Ayizan Velekete.[1313] Thereafter, she or he traces a vèvè and becomes possessed by the lwa who sings a song dedicated to himself.[1314] Songs describe Papa Simbi as he emerges in his *chwal* (horse) still wet from having surged out of the water.[1315] When Simbi speaks through a *chwal,* he says that, as an African lwa from Ginen and Kongo, he is frustrated with the Creoles, those born in Haiti.[1316] Marcelin's songs in this volume focus on Simbi's role in the healing of the wounded Ti Jozèf.[1317] While possessing a Vodou priest, Simbi requests permission to heal from Pè Letènèl (Eternal Father) and recites the Catholic texts "Our Father," "I Believe in God," and "I Salute You, Mary." Simbi next seeks permission from Legba, whom he calls "the *potomitan.*" The laplas is summoned to bring sugar, syrup, and ground corn. Simbi traces Legba's vèvè on the ground and pours out libations of syrup while singing a song dedicated to Legba.[1318] Simbi announces that Legba has opened the way, and a song is sung by *lafanmi* (the family) while the *ounsi pòt-drapo* (*ounsi* flag bearers) move forward.[1319] Songs are sung while walking to the woods to collect healing leaves.[1320] The leaf gatherers tell the tree that they were sent by Simbi. Three members of the family pick three leaves, which they bring to Simbi, whose *chwal* (horse) is the oungan.[1321] As the healing ceremony continues, Simbi sings a song referring to the three leaves and water.[1322] Simbi bandages Ti Jozèf with the leaves and departs. Ti Jozèf is entirely healed a few days later.[1323] Simbi's resting tree, a *pomme rose,* is often located near a pond because Simbi, like other aquatic lwa, prefers cool breezes. Anecdotes attributing severity to Simbi exist. Simbi sometimes accompanies Danbala Wèdo and can take the form of a snake.[1324] Roosters sacrificed to Simbi are called *koklo,* the Fon word for chicken.[1325] Children born with curly hair have *pwen Simbi* (Simbi's charm), and dreadlocks are called *cheve Simbi* (Simbi's hair).[1326] The "guardian tortoise" is sacred to Simbi.[1327] In modern Kikongo, *Símbi* is the spirit of a good person who is deceased; *Símbi* is associated with the water, both salty and fresh, precipices and the forest. *Símbi* is not considered mean but he should not be disturbed.[1328] *See* **Simba**.

Simbi an de zo; Simbi Andezo *Andezo* means "in two waters," a reference to the presence of Simbi in both Rada and Petwo Vodou rites.[1329] "In two waters" also refers to the waters between the living and the ancestors that Simbi has the power to traverse.[1330]

Simityè *See* **Bawon Samdi**.

Siniga; Senega; Seneka A rite that includes the lwa Mèt Senega and Èzili Seneka.[1331] Siniga is linked to Senegal.[1332] Mèt Senega cannot be offered pork, evidence of his origin in a Muslim region. Also, when people greet him, they utter the Muslim greeting "*Salamalekòm.*"[1333] *See* **Islam**.

siyale To signal; a ritual gesture extending an offering toward the four cardinal points of the compass while indicating the intended lwa.[1334]

sobagi; sogbagi; badji; bagi The inner sanctuary of a Vodou temple containing an altar.[1335] *See* **badji**.

Sobo; Sobo Aloumandja; Sobo Kebyesou; Sobo Kesou; Sobo Kèsou; Sobo Lele; Sobo Timoso; Sobo Wala Walendjo; Sobo Yangòdò; Sogbo; Adanyi Sobo; Papa Sobo; Sobokeson Bolojè The name of the lwa of lightning who is symbolized by a pre-Columbian ax of jade or obsidian or an arrowhead. A Dahomian spirit of thunder and lightning, Sobo is identified in the Danwonmen, Kongo, Petwo, and Rada rites. In the Vodou military, Sobo reports to Agwe. He is the close friend of Badè, lwa of winds. Sobo, high judge of the ounfò, is important to oungan and manbo because they can punish or reward congregants through his judgment. Those possessed by Sobo wear uniforms, and congregants must stand up in his presence when he addresses his "troops."[1336] Sobo has two wives.[1337] His days are Wednesday and Friday; his colors are white, deep yellow, or green. His resting tree is the *grenadye* or *bwadòm*.[1338] The *pyè tonnè* (arrowheads) are thrown from the sky by Sobo. They represent certain lwa or are used to invoke the lwa. These stones are sometimes called *pyè lwa* (lwa stones). Many servants of the lwa identify Sobo with Saint Peter, who guards the Vodou temple's altar. (Note that Legba is also associated with Saint Peter.) One Vodou priest reported to Marcelin that the Vodou altar had to be built on the "stone" or "rock" of Sobo because Christ had instructed Peter, "You are the rock, and on this rock I will build my Church." Sobo is a warrior who dresses like a soldier, armed with a sword and golden spurs. Sobo is considered a *lwa-oungan* (priestly lwa) who has healing powers and looks after children. Sobo complains about his servants' serving other lwa but expresses certainty that they will return.[1339] Sobo is wise and experienced.[1340] Coffee pickers sing songs dedicated to Sobo.[1341] Sobo is offered a white chicken, white rice, yellow plantains, orangeade, and cola. In the Vodou of Benin, the *vodun* (lwa) Sò, Sè, Sègbo, and Sogbó is also linked to thunder. Sò represents Destiny, and Sègbo represents the Great Destiny (Grand-Destin).[1342] Sogbó's brother is Kpelú.[1343] Note the existence in Benin of the distinct deity Ségbó or Dadá Ségbó (Great Spirit or God). In some legends, Ségbó is the supreme spirit and the creator of the *vodun* couple Mawou and Lisa, who depend on him.[1344] *See* **Agasou Gnenen**.

Sodo Saut-d'Eau waterfall is a pilgrimage destination each July 16 for those who serve Èzili Dantò and Our Lady of Mount Carmel.[1345] *See* **Basen Ble; Twou Ogou**.

Sosyete Ginen; Sosyete Vodou Ginen Society; a reference to the members of a Vodou temple.[1346]

Sosyete Konvwa *See* **Bizango; Sanpwèl**.

sosyete soutyen A support society that provides backing to a Vodou temple.[1347]

sòtè A jumping lwa that compels her or his *chwal* (horse) to spring into *ma dlo* (mud pools), where she or he dances, swims, splashes, and cavorts. Mud baths are purifying. *See* **grenadye; ma dlo**.

sòti anba dlo To rise from the water; a reference to becoming a Vodou priest or priestess.[1348]

souf poud Puff of powder, a Vodou hex.[1349]

Soukouyan *See* **Bizango; Sanpwèl**.

Soukri (Danach); Lakou Soukri Soukri is a village near Gonaïves which is famous for its Kongo and Wangòl rites.[1350]

soule Tipsy; on the verge of possession by a lwa.[1351] *See* **debatman; djayi; kriz lwa**.

Soulouk; Lanperè Soulouk Faustin Soulouque was the president of Haiti in 1847–1849 and the emperor in 1849–1859. He was born into slavery and freed in 1793 by André Rigaud. He served the lwa Kosi (Bonnonm Kosi).[1352] His link to Vodou is memorialized in songs: "Oh inform Emperor Soulouque, / You'll tell them for me now, / The jar is full, Legba is behind them!"[1353] *See* **Kosi**.

soup Ginen Ginen soup; an offering to a variety of Vodou spirits.[1354]

sou pwen On point. In some parts of Haiti, the *sou pwen* refers to the initiation into the Vodou priesthood.[1355] *See* **asogwe; prizdèzye**.

sousèt A witch, sorceress, or *lougawou*.[1356]

sousoupannan A sacrificial animal.[1357]

soutyen The terms *mè soutyen* (support mother) and *pè soutyen* (support father) refer to the financial supporters of a Vodou priest.[1358] *See* **sosyete soutyen**.

Souvnans; Souvenans; Nansouvnans A town and temple near Gonaïves that is famous for the Rada rite.[1359] The Temple Mystique (Mystical Temple) is located there, and during Easter week, ceremonies are held for the *asòtò* drum.[1360] The founders of the Dahomian tradition in Souvnans were originally purchased from Dahomey's royal family to serve as the guards of Henri Christophe, king of northern Haiti.[1361] When Christophe's rule ended, the Dahomian guard migrated to the Artibonite region, and their offspring have maintained the temple at Souvnans since. The Lakou Souvnans temple uses a rhythm named after a Dahomian king, Wegbadya. Ebyeso, an ancient Dahomian lwa, is also served there. *See* **asòtò; Ebyoso; Rada**.

spirit *See* **lwa; zanj**.

swenyay A magic healing bath.[1362]

tab The terms *tab konminyon* (communion table) and *tab metrès* (table of the mistress) refer to a special table laden with food in honor of the lwa.[1363]

tana Consecrated raw rum used in Vodou ceremonies; more commonly called *kleren*.[1364]

tanbou Drum.[1365] Drums are the means to address the lwa and the voice of lwa themselves.[1366] Drums are material in that they are made from tree trunks and hollowed out with fire, and non-material in that they "speak through matter."[1367] A Vodou drum has the lwa Ountò dwelling within it.[1368] The outside of drums are shaped by machete and covered with goat or cow skin. To *bat tanbou* (beat drums) is to hold a Vodou service. The consecration of Vodou drums includes various rituals and baptisms.[1369] The terms *kouche tanbou* (lay down the drums) and *manje tanbou* (drum food) refer to rituals to renew the energy of already baptized Vodou drums.[1370] Drums can be consecrated with blood; vèvè symbols can be traced before them; and Vodouists may bow in front of them, kissing the ground. *See* **manman tanbou; ountò**.

tanboura lwanj Praise drum; a special single-headed Kongo drum.[1371]

tanbouye; tanbourinè Drummers. Of all Vodou personnel, *tanbouye* have the most extensive craft training.[1372] They have an enormous repertoire of rhythms and the ability to detect the correct ones from an equally large set of songs. They also must have sensitivity to the role of rhythm during the onset and period of possession. The community prevents drummers from being possessed because they are such a fundamental part of triggering the possession of Vodou worshippers. *See* **kase; katalyè; ountò**.

tanp Vodou temple.[1373] *See* **ounfò**.

tay The sound produced by the smaller of the two Petwo drums.[1374] *See* **rale; ti baka**.

taybo A figure of dance.[1375]

tchaka Literally, stew with many ingredients. Metaphorically, *tchaka* refers to Vodou's culture of assemblage, which salvages, rebuilds, and synthesizes the cultures it encounters while preserving its roots.[1376] Because it includes corn, the *tchaka* recipe is offered to the lwa Azaka Mede.[1377] In the Fon language, *cáká* also means "to mix."[1378]

tchansi A metal rattle used in *rara* and in some Kongo rites.[1379]

tchatcha(tcha) A sacred calabash rattle used in the Petwo and Kongo rites.[1380]

tchiman asòtò Sacrificial blood that is added to other food offerings made to the lwa of the *asòtò* drum.[1381] *See* **asòtò; manje lwa; migan; ountò**.

temerè *See* **ounsi temerè**.

temple *See* **ounfò**.

tenbal A large, double-headed cylindrical drum. The *tenbal* is the middle size of the three drums of the Kongo rite.[1382]

terin A vase where the souls of the dead are kept.[1383]

tèta Tadpole. One Vodou song suggests that a Vodouist, with the help of lwa Twa Basen (Three Basins), can turn into a "tadpole in water."[1384]

tèt fò Strong head'; someone who has a powerful lwa of protection. *See* **mèt tèt**.

ti baka Little goblin; the smaller of the two Kongo-Petwo drums. The *ti baka* is beaten with bare hands.[1385] The drum skin's tension is secured by a rope system. The *ti baka* is also sometimes known as the *pitit* (child). The smaller *ti baka* is the most important drum of the Petwo rite.[1386] *See* **gwo baka**.

ti bonnanj Good little angel; the part of the human mind dedicated to thought, agency, awareness, and memory. In a possession event, an individual's *ti bonnanj* leaves the body and makes way for the possession by one or more lwa.[1387] Mastery of possession involves learning how to release and retrieve the *ti bonnanj*. The lwa and the *ti bonnanj* of inexperienced *chwal* (horses) sometimes violently struggle, and the priest or priestess may have to placate or send away the lwa by shaking the *ason* (sacred rattle).[1388] Vodou priests seamlessly control the release and return of the *ti bonnanj* and thus have complete mastery over the influence of the lwa.[1389] The *ti bonnanj* returns to the ancestors in Ginen at the time of death.[1390] *See* **Ginen; gwo bonnanj**.

Ti Jan Chanpwèl The name of a lwa associated with the Sanpwèl (Chanpwèl) secret society.[1391] *See* **Sanpwèl**.

Ti Jan Dantò The name of a lwa who is the son of Èzili Dantò.[1392]

ti kongo Small, double-headed cylindrical drum; the smallest of three drums in the Kongo rite.[1393] The *ti kongo* can be played with the hands, with sticks, or with a combination of the two.[1394]

tire vèvè To pull a vèvè; to trace ritual designs for the lwa on the ground.[1395] *See* **file farin; trase vèvè**.

Ti W a Wè Little You'll See, the name of a lwa. Marcenat associates Ti W a Wè with with Papa Loko and Bawon Samdi. Those possessed by Ti W a Wè wear black attire.

tonbe lwa Falling lwa, a reference to possession.[1396] *See* **chwal; monte**.

tonm Tomb, grave, or tombstone. A *resevwa tonm* (tomb reception) refers to a Vodou ceremony to consecrate a tomb. A *tonm repozwa* (resting tomb) refers to a family tomb for the Gede.[1397] *See* **repozwa**.

tonnèl An enclosed area for worship and dance in a Vodou *peristil.*[1398] *See* **peristil**.

Tousen Louvèti Toussaint Louverture was the forerunner of Haitian independence and is remembered in a vèvè called the Louvenkou.[1399] *See* **Dessalines; Soulouk**.

Towo-Twa-Grenn Bull with Three Testicles, the name of a greatly feared Vodou lwa or *dyab* of the Jacmel region.[1400]

trase vèvè To trace a *vèvè*; a reference to the use of grain to trace a symbolic diagram on the ground. *See* **file farin; vèvè**.

twa fèy; twa mo priyè; twa pawòl; twa rasin; twa wòch Three leaves, three words of prayer, three words, three roots, three rocks. Such triple symbols refer to the three realms of the lwa: the sky, earth, and water.[1401] The song lyrics, "All leaves are leaves, three words say it is good" and "All leaves are leaves, three words are better" mean that herbal remedies should be accompanied by prayers to the lwa to augment their efficacy.[1402]

Twa Ile The name of a lwa who is also called Simbi Twa Ile.[1403] Simbi, the lwa of springs, is linked by water with Twa Ile. The word *ile* means "temple" in Yorùbá.[1404] *See* **Simbi; Twa Zile**.

Twa Letan Three Lakes; the name of a lwa.[1405]

Twa Pèl; Twa Pikwa; Twa Wou *See* **Bawon Samdi**.

Twa Zile Three islands; a reference to three reefs near Port-au-Prince used in ceremonies dedicated to Agwe.[1406] *See* **Agwe Tawoyo**.

twòn Throne; a reference to a Vodou altar.[1407] *See* **pe; pewon**.

Twou Ogou; Twou Sen Jak The holes of Ogou; mud basins found in the town Plaine-du-Nord. On July 25, the town celebrates the canonical feast of Saint James (Ogou), which attracts Vodou-Catholic pilgrims from all over Haiti.[1408] The holes represent where Saint James's horse galloped.[1409] Some Vodouists wade into the mud ponds and are possessed by the lwa Ogou. Crowds gather and watch; merchants hock wares; animals are sacrificed; and drums beat constantly. Mud baths are linked to healing and good fortune in Vodou.[1410] *See* **Basen Ble; grenadye; Laplenndinò; ma dlo; Ogou; Sen Jak Majè; Sodo; sòtè**.

twoupo Flock. In the Vodou theology of Oungan Marcenat, a *twoupo* is a grouping of seven lwa—for example, those who make up the Ogou *twoupo*: Ogoun Kafou, Ogou Badagi, Ogou Feray, Ogou Chango, Ogoun Balize, Ogou Fè, and the leader of the flock, Sen Jak Majè. *See* **eskòt; fanmi**.

tyatya(tya) *See* **tchatcha(tcha)**.

tyovi; tchovi A member of a particular Vodou temple.[1411] In the Fon language, *-vi* means "child" and illustrates the kinship metaphors commonly used to represent the relationship between Vodou leaders and their congregants. *See* **pitit fèy**.

Urzule The daughter of Èzili Dantò and Ogou Badagri.[1412]

vaksin A one-noted wind instrument made from cut and hollowed bamboo. The *vaksin* are used by *rara* parade groups linked to Vodou temples.[1413] The *vaksin* may be linked to the *disoso* in the Kongo.[1414] Haiti and the Kongo share similar hocketing techniques, which involve the rhythmic alternation of notes, pitches, or chords. *See* **rara**.

vann To sell; a reference to the lodging of a formal complaint with the judiciary tribunal of the Sanpwèl/Bizango secret society. If the complaint is accepted, the society *achte* (buys) it and takes measures to correct the issue.[1415] *See* **Bizango; Sanpwèl**.

vantaye A ritual involving the passing or whirling of a sacrificial bird over the body.[1416]

vanyan Courageous; a reference to the person designated to throw the "sacred burden" into the sea (presumably in ceremonies for Agwe).[1417] *See* **Agwe Tawoyo; non vanyan**.

vèditè Earthworm; a reference to a human being.[1418] *See* **kò kadav**.

Velekete *See* **Ayizan Velekete**.

ve sak kòlèt Vow to wear burlap underclothing as protection against the evil eye. *Ve sak kòlèt* is also specially colored clothing worn until a particular wish is attained.[1419] *See* **kolye vèvè**.

vèse A ritual pouring of drops of liquid on the ground for the dead.[1420]

vèvè A mystical diagram or cosmogram traced on the ground with the flour of corn, ashes, coffee grounds, hot-pepper powder, sand, and other finely granulated substances. The cross or *kalfou* (crossroads), representing the intersection of the living and the ancestors and lwa, is an underlying element of many vèvè.[1421] Each vèvè represents a particular lwa and serves to consecrate the place of the ceremony, to focus the community visually and spiritually, and to call the lwa to possess his or her followers.[1422] Vèvè and the *potomitan* are gates through which the lwa travel to be with Vodouists.[1423] Vèvè are highly formal diagrams and symbols that represent a given lwa; each lwa has her or his own vèvè. Vèvè are also inscribed on walls, flags, banners, *ason,* clothing, and *govi* (clay jars); they are sometimes traced in the air with swords or *ason.*[1424] The oungan, manbo, or oungenikon traces the vèvè. Various songs are dedicated to vèvè: "I'm going to trace my vèvè! / In front of the slanderers, in front of the backbiters."[1425] The Haitian vèvè may be related to the Fon word *weke.*[1426] The edges of the vèvè capture the particular characteristics of the lwa, while the central axis captures their collective qualities. The vèvè are linked to Dahomian "protective ground squares," which are large rectangular vèvè for healing. The slaves from the Kongo and Angola brought more complex visual traditions to Haiti than the Dahomian traditions.[1427] In addition to the Bakongo culture, neighboring cultures such as the Chokwe, Pende, Teke, Luchazi, and Nsenga employ complex ground signs. *Adinkra* designs from Ghana and the *nsibidi* designs of the Ibo people are also linked to vèvè.[1428] The vèvè may also have Amerindian influences.[1429] Etymologically, the Fon term *vèvè* (supplication) may be related to the Haitian term *vèvè,* even if the drawing style is more Kongolese.[1430] *See* **ason; farin Ginen; file farin; manbo; oungan; trase vèvè**.

Vilokan; Lavilokan Vilokan or Ville-aux-Camps is the mythical capital and place of origin of the lwa in Haiti.[1431] Vilokan is Vodou's Mount Olympus.[1432] Vilokan is located near Port-de-Paix, where some believe the first services to the lwa were held because it was one of the first places West Africans worked as slaves.[1433] Vilokan is called the "first temple of resistance."[1434] Some consider Vilokan synonymous with Ginen.[1435] Morisseau-Leroy (2001) is a lengthy poem about Vilokan. *See* **Danwonmen; Gelefre; Ginen**.

vini nan tèt To come into the head; when a lwa possesses or temporarily takes over one's mind and body.[1436] *See* **monte**.

Virgin of Charity; La Vierge de Caridad del Cobre The small figure in the common chromolithograph of the Virgin of Charity is associated with Agawou because the Virgin is depicted protecting three men during a storm and Agawou is the lwa of storms, wind, and thunder. *See* **Agawou**.

vivi A zombie or soul magically extracted from its body.[1437] *See* **zonbi**.

Vlengbedeng *See* **Bizango; Sanpwèl**.

Vodou A dance to the lwa. To *fè Vodou* (do Vodou) is to perform a Vodou dance.[1438] *See* **sèvi**.

Vodou; Vodoun; vodun Haiti's hereditary religion and philosophy. Vodou has roots in Africa, especially Dahomey (modern-day Benin) and the Kongo. Vodou philosophy emphasizes patience, calm, discipline, respect, and order and is rooted in the veneration of the ancestors and lwa.[1439] Vodou is a dialectical system of inextricable contrasts (life and death, war and defense, calm and aggression), which views life in its entirety. West and Central African and Haitian religions share a dialectical approach to perpetuity and mutability.[1440] Vodou is built out of the mythology and worship of the lwa, the memory of the ancestors, the centrality and distance of God, communion with nature, and the methods of ritual, dance, song, and rhythm to achieve mystical states.[1441] Papa Vodou is the name of a lwa.[1442] The word *Vodou* first appeared in print in the year 1658 in the book *Doctrina Christiana.*[1443] The Fon word *vodun* is translated as *lwa* in Haitian Creole; secondarily, *Vodun* in Fon also refers to the religion dedicated to the *vodun.*[1444] *Vodun* is every manifestation of force that cannot be defined, all that surpasses the imagination and intelligence; *vodun* is mystery.[1445] In Benin, the *vodun* are forces from nature and humanity. The following types of *vodun* are distinguished in the Fon language: *ayì vodun* (deities of the earth; e.g., Gede and Dan); *akò vodun* (deities of the clan, tribe, or family); *atínmèvódún* (deities that reside in a tree; e.g., Loko); *hènnu vodun* (familial deities); *jì vodun* (deities from on high; e.g., Lisa, Mawou, Ji, Xèbyoso); *nùkánmè/zunmè vodun* (deities of the forest; e.g., Fa, Granbwa); *ta vodun* (*vodun* head jar carried on the head in processions); and *tò vodun* (deities of the city, of the country [*tò Legba*]).[1446] In Haiti, the lwa inhabit three domains: the sky; earth, which includes trees and plants; and under the water.[1447] The *vodun* are go-betweens who link humans with God and the divine. In Benin, *vodun,* like the lwa in Haiti, are often reflected in forces of nature such as storms, lightning, water, plants, trees, stones, springs, and animals. The *vodun* encompass the public, the private, the urban and rural, the dead, royalty, the state, and foreign and indigenous expressions.[1448] Vodou is a link between the living and the ancestors.[1449] Vodou is also the reconstitution, beyond the family compound, of the memory of important people and traditions. The Fon meaning of *vodun* (lwa) is retained in some Haitian Creole songs (e.g., *Vodou Danbala Wèdo* [The Lwa Danbala Wèdo], *Vodou Lasirèn* [Lwa Lasirenn], and *Vodou Legba* [Lwa Legba]).[1450] Some authors criticize the use of the term *Vodou* when referring to the religion of serving the lwa. However, this criticism is overstated in that oungan in Haiti use the term neutrally to designate the religion.[1451] In terms of etymology, in the Fon language *vo* refers to what is concealed and inexplicable, while *du* or *dun* refers to divination. Therefore, *Vodou* is the "divination of the mysterious."[1452]

Vodounsi The Fon term for Vodouist; literally, spouse of a Vodun spirit.[1453] *See* **ounsi**.

Vodouyizan; Vodwizan A Vodouist.[1454] *See* **sèvitè**.

voye To send; a reference to the singing of a song by the oungenikon. The choir then responds with the same song.[1455] *See* **rèl ak repons**.

voye mò (sou) To send the dead; to cast an evil spell.[1456]

wanga A magic charm, amulet, talisman or powder used for either good or evil magic.[1457] God gives the oungan the gift of making *wanga* to resolve problems or to bring about some wish, such as having children, good harvests, healing illness, strengthening marriage, or dealing with an enemy.[1458] The *wanga* is made in private. An offended lwa can cause illness, and *wanga*, prayers, and penitence can undo the disfavor.[1459] There are no illusions about the power of *wanga*. One song dedicated to Ayizan employs the proverb "Plots are stronger than *wanga*."[1460] Other proverbs say, "*Wanga* can't cross the sea" and "The day of misfortune, the *wanga* doesn't work."[1461] One proverb suggests that the effectiveness of *wanga* is related to the price paid: "The measure of your money is the measure of your *wanga*."[1462] The expression "Her whole body is a *wanga*" refers to the embodiment of protective powers.[1463] Since clients do not tolerate ineffective *wanga*, the business of making them is risky. *Wanga* is a Bakongo word.[1464] *See* **gad; makandal; pwen**.

wangatè(z) A person who makes use of *wanga*.[1465]

Wangòl; Wongòl A Vodou rite associated with lwa such as Zazi Wangòl and Gao.[1466] Wangòl is linked to Angola.[1467] *See* **rit; Wa Wongòl**.

Wannen; pale wannen *Pale wannen* (to talk with a nasal tone) refers to the Gede lwa who speak using a nasal tone.

Wa Wangòl King Wangòl, the name of an Angolan lwa. He is invoked to honor the African royalty of Haitian ancestors. On his feast day of January 6, the Epiphany, Vodouists and Catholics organize celebrations and serve *gato lèwa* (cake of kings.)[1468]

wete mò anba dlo To bring the dead back from under the water; a ceremony organized one year after the death of a family member that involves inviting the spirit of the dead back into the community of the living as an active ancestor.[1469] *See* **desounen; lemò**.

wete po, mete po Taking skin off, putting skin on; an expression used in secret societies that refers to the "transmutation and mimesis" that lead to higher states of consciousness in Vodou.[1470]

Wida; Ouida A coastal town in Benin that is famous for its temple dedicated to Dan, the serpent lwa.[1471] The name exists in Creole in the expression *Adje Wida!* (Farewell Wida!). The term was a last goodbye that slaves said to Africa as they were shipped away to Saint-Domingue.[1472]

wonsi *See* **ounsi**.

wosman The first initiation into Vodou, the rising to any higher rank, or the final consecration to the priesthood.[1473] In the case of the priesthood, the vesting of the *ason* (sacred rattle) is the final ritual of the *wosman*.[1474]

woumble The ritual sounding of drums and rattles to call forth all of the lwa or participants.[1475]

wouze Sprinkling water as a libation for a lwa.[1476]

wye An exclamation found in song.[1477]

Yabofe The name of a lwa from the Kongo-Ginen rite.[1478]

Yagaza A place in Africa on the other side of the water where Èzili lives.[1479] *See* **Gelefre; Ginen**.

yaminyan A magic bundle made of herbs created in the ounfò.[1480]

yanm Yam; the *manje yanm* (yam offering) is an annual harvest ceremony in which yams, plantains, and dried fish are offered to thank the lwa for a successful crop.[1481] In Yorùbáland, devotees of the agricultural *òrìsà* (lwa) Òrìsà-Oko must not eat new yams until the annual festival for the *òrìsà.*[1482] The *kouche yanm* (setting the yams down) is the initial ritual of the *manje yanm,* when offerings are laid out. The Ibo people of Nigeria are famous for their yam production.[1483] The *leve yanm* (raising the yams) is the closing rite of the *manje yanm,* with sacrifices, cooking, and consumption of the offering.[1484]

Yanva Loko *See* **Loko Atisou**.

yanvalou; Yanvalou; Miyanvalou A traditional Rada rhythm and dance that involves the leaning forward of the body, hands on bent knees, shoulders rolling, and feet sliding sideways, with a pause on the fourth beat.[1485] In the *yanvalou* dance, the spine of the dancer moves like a snake. *Yanvalou* is one of the most important Vodou drum rhythms. In some songs, Yanvalou is also presented as a lwa.[1486] In Alada, Dahomey, the *yanvalou* was a serpentine gesture of respect that people made when they encountered kings; a related a dance in Haiti is called *yanvalou wayal* (royal yanvalou).[1487] *Yanvalou* is also linked to the *agbadza* rhythm of Ewe culture, which has the same bell and drum patterns.[1488] This song highlights the inclusiveness of the *yanvalou* rhythm: "Yanvalou, all the Saints; yanvalou, all the dead."[1489]

Yèhwe; Yehwe; Yahwè The name of a Vodou lwa. Oungan Beauvoir points out that terms such as *Yehwe* and *Yahwè* suggest the "unity of substance and a common identity," presumably because the words are similar to the name for the Hebrew Supreme Being.[1490] In the Fon culture, Yèhwe is also a *vodun* (lwa). *Yèhwenò* originally refered to the priests of Vodun, but over time it has come to refer to Catholic priests, while *vodunò* now refers exclusively to the priests of Vodun.[1491]

yo A personal pronoun in Haitain Creole that usually means "they," "them," or "their." *Yo* is sometimes used as a reference to the Vodou lwa.[1492]

Zaka *See* **Azaka Mede; Kouzen Zaka**.

zakato A magnetic Vodou charm.[1493] *See* **wanga**.

Zandò; Kongo Zandò; Konpè Awoke; Twa Wou Twa Fren A Vodou rite composed of lwa such as Legba Zandò, Mèt Zandò, and Kongo Zandò.[1494] Zandò is associated with the Kongo.[1495] Zandò is regarded as a powerful and sometimes dangerous lwa.[1496] Kongo Zandò is married to Marinèt.[1497] *See* **Marinèt-Bwa-Chèch**.

zanj; zany; any; anj; lezany; lezanj A lwa or the spirit of a dead person. *Zanj* derives from the French *les anges* (the angels). God is *anwo* (above), and *lezany* are *anba* (below).[1498] The term *zanj* is also the northern Haitian Creole variant of *lwa* (Vodou spirit). To *danse zanj* (dance angels) means to participate in a Vodou ceremony. *Manje zanj* refers to a ceremony of ritual food and drink offering to nourish, pacify, or thank one or more lwa. *L'ange conducteur* (The Guiding Angel; Coret 1851) is a French prayerbook and hymnal used in Vodou services and divination. *Zanj rebèl* (rebel angel) refers to Satan.[1499] *Zanj Lan Bwa* (Angels in the Woods) represents the Petwo lwa, while *Zanj Lan Dlo* (Angels in the Water) represents the Rada lwa.[1500] Marcenat argues that the lwa are the rebel angels who were expelled from heaven. *See* **lwa**.

zanj rebèl Rebel angels; a reference to the *dyab*. One song reads, "Those rebel angels, oh I'm going to do the works! Zila Moyo, let my works progress!"[1501]

zansèt Ancestors, who are venerated in Vodou. Great ancestors evolve into lwa.[1502] *See* **dantan**.

Zantray Guts; an acronym for Zanfan Tradisyon Ayisyen (Children of the Haitian Tradition), an organization for the defense of the Vodou religion.[1503] Zantray was formed because of the lynchings of Vodou priests after the departure of President Jean-Claude Duvalier in 1986.[1504]

zany *See* **zanj**.

Zeklè Lightning Bolt; the name of a *djab* who can kill by means of lightning, according to Marcenat.

Zemès Taino Native American gods and their statues.[1505]

zen An iron or clay pot used in *kanzo* initiation rites. A *zen* also refers to water lwa. A *boule zen* is a Vodou ritual of initiation and consecration and a funeral ceremony that accompanies the *ounsi* initiation. A *boule zen lèmò* (burn the clay pot of the dead) is a ritual performed in honor of the dead. To *kouri zen* (clay pot run) means to dance around the *potomitan*. A *poto zen* or *pye zen* is a tripod used to support the *zen* used in *kanzo* rites.[1506] A *zen* is also a vèvè used in services that consecrate oungan, manbo, or ounsi kanzo.[1507] In the Fon language, the *zen* is "pottery that serves as a recipient," and the *àìzen, to-gozen,* and *ahwã zen* are ritual pots made of clay and used to serve food.[1508] *See* **boule zen; kanzo; ounsi; potèt**.

zen-nago A small, three-legged cauldron that burns in honor of Ogou Feray, a Nago lwa.[1509]

zepòl A Rada dance that emphasizes movement of the shoulders.[1510]

zès A category of sexually suggestive dances for the lwa of the dead.[1511]

Zile The lwa Agwe's city under the sea in Ginen.[1512] A *lan zile* (on the island) is a mystical site in the sea where the sun sets. *Zile anba dlo* refers to an "island below the sea" inhabited by Vodou lwa and the souls of the dead.

Zili *See* **Èzili**.

Zo Bones; the word refers to a lwa.[1513]

zobop; zobòp; zòbok; zòbòp A secret society of evildoers, members of the same, a sorcerer, a demon, a man-eating ogre, or a magic spirit contained in a bottle to protect one's house, according to Haitian legend.[1514] Some Haitians allege that *zobop* are cannibals.[1515] *See* **Bizango; Sanpwèl**.

Zoklimo The name of a lwa.[1516]

zonbi Zombie; a body without its soul; a phantom, ghost, mindless slave; the soul of an unbaptized young child; the soul of someone who has accidentally died before his or her prescribed time; or the soul of a woman who has died a virgin. A zombie can refer to a wandering soul, the *ti bonnanj* (good little angel) that is captured in a bottle, or to the victim of a crime involving poison or anesthesia, live burial, and, after brain damage has set in, unearthing and enslavement. In Haitian folklore, the second type of zombie is stereotypically a slave under the command of an evil bòkò.[1517] The enslaved *zonbi* is sometimes called *zonbi jaden* (garden zombie) or the *zonbi kò kadav* (cadaver zombie.)[1518] *Zonbi grenn* (seed zombies) are trained to steal flowers from coffee bushes to graft onto the trees of the zombie's master.[1519] Zombification is the rarest form of punishment that the Sanpwèl or Bizango secret societies impose on those who commit heinous infractions.[1520] The word *zonbi* is related to the Kikongo term *Nzambi* which refers to the Supreme Being who is untouchable by the *nkisi* (lwa) and who has no image or representation.[1521] The Kikongo term *Nzambi* refers to a god who was not pleased with the wicked deeds of his first human creation, so he buried the man and raised a new human being.[1522] In Haiti, zombies are frightening figures, as one Vodou song puts it: "I went to the cemetery, all the zombies frightened me. / Even Bawon frightened me!"[1523] *See* **Bizango; gwo bonnanj; Sanpwèl**.

APPENDIX B

Outline of Haitian Creole Grammar

BENJAMIN HEBBLETHWAITE
and VANESSA BRISSAULT

THIS APPENDIX presents a systematic grammar of Haitian Creole, following the categories and labels in DeGraff (2007) in addition to a few of our own. The grammar is organized and enumerated by means of syntactic categories. In some instances, such as in the case of the definite determiners, we also address important phonological rules. We have tried to include a fairly thorough, if not exhaustive, list of the major structures found in Haitian Creole. Each grammatical category is exemplified by a Haitian Creole sentence, which is translated into English. We have *italicized* the Haitian Creole focus word or phrase and **boldfaced** the nearest English equivalent. Most of the Haitian Creole sentences we have selected are from our own corpus of Vodou songs and texts. However, we have incorporated (and cited as such) sentences from DeGraff (2007) where we believed that they better illustrated the category.

The motivation for this appendix came from research that I conducted at library collections when I was an undergraduate and graduate student of religion. At the time, I became familiar with various bilingual Sanskrit-English and Tibetan-English works of Hindu and Buddhist literature that provided grammatical sketches to help students of the respective traditions progress in the source language of the texts. In the same tradition, we provide a basic grammatical inventory of Haitian Creole. Students of the language are also advised to consult Freeman (1987, 2004), Valdman (1988), and Valdman, Iskrova, Pierre, and André (2007).

This outline of Haitian Creole grammar is composed of the following major categories: (1–7) verbs and verb markers; (8) complementizers; (9) clause types; (10) negation; (11) the passive; (12) adjectives and predicate clefting; (13) the copula; (14) serial verbs; (15) noun phrases; (16) possession; (17) pronouns; (18) coordinating conjunctions; (19) prepositions; and (20) miscellaneous phenomena. Readers can study the categories in any order.

1. Unmarked verbs
    1.1. Statives[1] with non-past reference
        (a) Ounfò a *mande* drapo!
        (The temple **requires** flags!)
    1.2. Non-statives[2] with past reference
        (a) Ou *manje* poul la.
        (You **ate** the chicken.)
    1.3. Non-statives with non-past reference
        (a) Bouki *vann* chat. (DeGraff 2007: 103)
        (Bouki **sells** cats.)

2. Anterior or past tense
    2.1. Statives with past reference
    te + stative verb = past.
        (a) Manbo a *te konn* repons lan (adapted from DeGraff 2007: 103)
        (The manbo **knew** the answer.)
    2.2. Non-statives with (past-before-) past reference
    te + non-stative verb = past-before-past.
        (a) Bouki *te ale* (anvan Boukinèt vini). (DeGraff 2007: 103)
        (Bouki **had left** [before Boukinèt came].)
    2.3. Anterior or past = counterfactual
    si + *ta* = if + had + would = counterfactual.
        (a) Si m *te* gen yon byen pou m fè, m *ta* fè l.
        (If I **had** a good deed to do, I **would** do it.)
    2.4. Anterior (or past) with adjective
        (a) Elifèt *te* malad. (DeGraff 2007: 104)
        (Elifèt **was** sick.)
    2.5. Anterior (or past) with locative
        (a) Lasirèn o k *te sou lanmè.*
        (Oh Lasirenn who **was on the sea**.)

3. Progressive aspect
    3.1. Indicating progressive
    ap + non-stative verb = progressive.
        (a) M *ap* navige!
        (I'**m** navigat**ing**!)

3.2. Indicating future

ap can sometimes be used to indicate the immediate future.

(a) L *ap* gaye nouvèl ban nou!
(He **will** spread the news for us!)

3.3. Anterior plus progressive

te + *ap* = *t ap*, can be used as past progressive or future in the past.

(a) Se sou lanmè kannòt mwen *t ap* neye!
(It's on the sea that my canoe **was** sink**ing**!)

3.4. Progressive with adjective for a future interpretation

(a) Tank chany la fwote soulye a, tank soulye a *ap* pi klere. (DeGraff 2007: 105)
(The more the shoe-shiner rubs the shoe, the more the shoe **will** shine.)

4. Habitual aspect

4.1. Progressive marker for habitual

(a) Mwen gen yon bagay m *ap* kalkile, chak fwa m sonje l, li fè dlo kouri nan je m.
(I have something I'**m** think**ing** about, each time I recall it, it makes me cry.)

4.2. Marker for habitual

The words *konn* and *abitye,* which can also be used as an auxiliary verb in (a)–(b) and a main verb in (c)–(d), are usually used to mark the habitual aspect.

(a) Mwen se towo, lè m angaje m *konn* pouse kòn mwen, m konn begle.
(I'm a bull, when I'm in trouble I **usually** push out my horns, I bellow.)

(b) Kolbè *abitye* vann liv bò isi a. (DeGraff 2007: 106)
(Kolbè **is in the habit of** selling books around here.)

(c) M pa *konn* sa pou l fè ou.
(I don't **know** what he wants with you.)

(d) Bouki *abitye* ak Boukinèt. (DeGraff 2007: 106)
(Bouki **is accustomed** to Boukinèt.)

4.3. Anterior plus habitual (*te* + *konn*; *te* + *abitye*)

(a) Epi granpapa m *te konn* fè yo fè twa jou dòmi.
(And my grandpa **was known** to make them spend three days sleeping.)

(b) Kolbè *te abitye* vann liv bò isi a (DeGraff 2007: 106)
(Kolbè **was in the habit of** selling books around here.)

5. Completive aspect
5.1. *Fin(i)* the main verb
(a) Lè ou *fini,* chòdyè k rete a, ou met sèl ladan n.
(When you **finish**, the cauldron that remains, you put salt in it.)

5.2. Completive only (before/after V)
(a) Mwen *fin* jwenn rezon an.
(I've **finally** found the reason.)

5.3. Completive plus adjective
(a) Bouki *fin* fou. (DeGraff 2007: 106)
(Bouki **has gone** completely crazy.)

5.4. Anterior (or other preverbal markers) plus completive
(a) Mwen *te fin* bati kay la. (DeGraff 2007: 107)
(I **(had) finished** building the house.)

6. Irrealis mode
6.1. Future (= progressive marker)
The progressive marker *ap* can be used to express the future as shown in the examples from sections 3.2 and 3.4.

6.2. Anterior plus irrealis *ta* (t + a)/*ava* (a + va) = conditional
(a) Mwen *ta* vini si m te kapab. (DeGraff 2007: 107)
(I **would (have)** come if I could.)
(b) Si Bondye vle, m *a(va)* monte nan syèl (DeGraff 2007: 107)
(God willing, I **might/will** go to heaven.)

6.3. Anterior plus irrealis = future in the past
(a) Ounsi a mande oungan an ki lè li *t ap* fè seremoni an.
(The *ounsi* asked the oungan when he **would** do the ceremony.)

7. Other combinations of verbal markers
7.1. Anterior plus irrealis plus progressive
(a) Èske ou kwè li *t av ap* danse pandan manman l *ap* chache l toupatou? (DeGraff 2007: 108)
(Do you think he or she **would be** danc**ing** while his or her mother **is** look**ing** all over for him or her?)

7.2. Other auxiliary-like elements

Pral(e) = "go [somewhere]."

(a) M *pral* chache fanmi mwen yo.
(I **am going** to find members of my family.)

(b) M *prale* lan Ginen!
(I **am going** to Ginen!)

Sòt(i) = "leave," "come from" in examples (c) and (d); example (e) = *just.*

(c) Mwen *soti* lwen.
(I **come from** afar.)

(d) M *soti* larivyè o!
(Oh, I **come from** the river!)

(e) Mwen *sòt* wè Mari. (DeGraff 2007: 108)
(I **just** saw Mari.)

Pran/tonbe = "start"

(f) M *tonbe/pran* kriye.
(I **started** to cry.)

Dwe = "owe" can be used to either signify obligation or likelihood.

(g) Poukisa se la ou *dwe* konmanse?
(Why is it here that you **have** to start?)

(h) Si w konnen w te *dwe* Chango, ou pral peye Chango.
(If you knew you **owed** Chango, you are going to pay Chango.)

Vle = "want."

(i) Moun yo *vle* gate sèvis la.
(The people **want** to spoil the service.)

8. Complementizers

8.1. Zero infinitive marker (represented by the null symbol, ø)

(a) Lòt la vle ø chante.
(The other one wants **to** sing.)

8.2. "For" as infinitive marker

Pou = for; to

(a) Mwen pa gen anyen *pou* m ba w.
(I don't have anything **to** give you.)

(b) Li gen lè li *pou* fonksyone avèk li.
(It has its time **to** function with it.)

(c) M gen *pou* m ale.
(I **need** to go.)

8.3. "For" as a (quasi-) modal

(a) Se oungenikon an ki *pou* te vini.

(It's the oungenikon who **had** to come.)

8.4. "For" introducing a tensed clause

(a) Si sila pa t paresèz, kounye la se yon metsen *pou* l te ye.

(If that one wasn't a lazy girl, by now she would have been a doctor.)

(b) Mwen te mande *pou* l te vini. (DeGraff 2007: 109)

(I asked that she come.)

8.5. The null subordinator (represented by the null symbol, ø)

(a) Men depi m wè ø se nan kòt mal la ou kanpe, m fè bak sou ou.

(But as soon as I see **that** you stand on the side of evil, I back away from you.)

8.6. The subordinator *ke*

(a) Epui lè fini pou rele lwa *ke* ou bezwen pou tab la.

(And at last it is necessary to call the lwa **that** you need for the table.)

9. Dependent clauses

9.1. Subordinate clauses (non-embedded)

(a) Lè sa, n a wè valè mwen.

(When this happens, you'll see my worth.)

9.2. Subordinate clauses (embedded)

(a) Toussaint pa te konnen *si tout patriyòt t ap leve goumen.* (DeGraff 2007: 110)

(Toussaint did not know **if every patriot would rise and fight**.)

9.3. Relative clauses (relative pronoun = subject)

Ki can serve two functions. It can be used as a complementizer such as *that/which* in (a) or it can be used as a relative pronoun in the subject position like *who* in (b).

(a) Se yon tradisyon *ki* enpòtan.

(It's a tradition **that** is important.)

(b) Sa se yon Sen *ki* mistik anpil tou wi.

(This is a Saint **who** is also very mystical.)

9.4. Relative clauses (relative pronoun = direct object); (represented by the null symbol, ø). In (a) *chanm* (room) is the direct object.

(a) Yo tout chwazi chanm ø yo vle a.

(They all chose the room ø they wanted.)

9.5. Relative clauses (relative pronoun = object of preposition; represented by the null symbol, ø). Below, *li* is a resumptive pronoun co-indexed with *libète.*

(a) Vodou bay pèp la libète ø yo te goumen pou li a.
(Vodou gave the people the freedom ø they fought for.)

10. Negation

10.1. Single negation (with predicate)

(a) . . . pase si oungan *pa* ka al nan trètman, l ap voye ou.
(. . . because if an oungan ca**n't** go to the treatment, he'll send you.)

(b) Tou sa ki *pa* bon, yo lage l sou do malere.
(Everything that is**n't** good, they throw on the backs of the poor.)

10.2. Negative concord

(a) Nan katye sa a *pèsonn pa* di *pèsonn* anyen. (DeGraff 2007: 111)
(In this neighborhood, **nobody** says anything to **anybody**.)

(b) *Pèsonn pa* konnen mwen.
(**No one** knows me.)

(c) W abitwe ak fanmi ou *san* l *pa* malad.
(You're used to your family *not* being sick.)

(d) M *pa janm* al lopital.
(I **never** go to the hospital.)

11. Passive

11.1. Passive construction

The object *kabann lan* in (b) has been made passive, and the verb *fè* has taken the passive form, *fèt.* Most Haitian Creole verbs, however, do not have a passive form.

(a) Mwen fè kabann lan rapid rapid maten an. (DeGraff 2007: 112)
(I made the bed very quickly this morning.)

(b) *Kabann lan fèt* rapid-rapid maten an. (DeGraff 2007: 112)
(**The bed was made** very quickly this morning.)

11.2. Passive equivalent

The object *sèvis* is made passive in (b) and (c) and the verb does not change in

(a) Yo kraze sèvis la.
(They broke up the service.)

(b) Epi tout *sèvis kraze,* touye dife, bale, al lakay yo.
(And the whole **service was broken up**, the fire put out, swept up, [everybody] going to their homes.)

(c) Sèvis la kraze.
(The service is broken up.)

12. Adjectives

12.1. Preverbal markers before adjectives

For anterior, see sections 2.4 and 2.5; for aspectual and mood markers, see section 4; for completive markers, see section 5; for absence of verbal copula, see sections 2.4, 2.5, and section 13.

12.2. Preverbal markers before nouns

(a) Li *te* yon manbo.
(She **was** a manbo.)

12.3. Preverbal markers before locatives

(a) Li te *devan* ounfò a.
(She was **in front of** the temple.)

12.4. Predicate clefting: (a) adjectives or (b) verbs

(a) Se *malad* Bouki *malad,* li pa mouri. (DeGraff 2007: 113)
(Bouki is **sick**, not dead.)

(b) Se *mache* Bouki te *mache,* li pa te kouri. (DeGraff 2007: 113)
(Bouki had **walked**, not run.)

12.5. Predicate clefting: other verbs

(a) *Se* yon doktè Elifèt *ye,* li pa yon enfimyè. (DeGraff 2007: 113)
(Elifèt **is** a doctor, not a nurse.)

(b) *Se* nan jaden an Elifèt *ye,* li pa nan kay la. (DeGraff 2007: 113)
(Elifèt **is** in the garden, not in the house.)

12.6. Verb clefting which produces a verb + noun structure (V + V = V + N)

(a) M te *chita chita* m.
(I **sat for a while.**)

12.7. Comparison with *pase* (than) with (a)–(b) adjectives and (c)–(e) predicates:

The superlative morpheme *pi* comes before the adjective. *Ke* replaces *pase* in urban varieties of Haitian Creole.

(a) Ayizan-konplo *pi fò pase* wanga!
(Ayizan-plotting is **stronger than** wanga!)

(b) Wanga *mwen* fò *pase* konplo.
(Wanga are **less** strong **than** plots.)

(c) Katolik la *plis pase* Pwotestan.
(Catholics are **more than** Protestants.)

(d) Pwotestan an *mwens pase* Katolik.
(Protestants are **fewer than** Catholics.)

(e) Yon zanmi ki gen *plis* konesans *pase* li.
(A friend who has **more** knowledge **than** him.)

(f) Yon elèv ki gen *mwens* opòtinite *pase* li.
(A student who has **fewer** opportunities **than** him.)

12.8. Equal comparisons with *tankou, kou, konwè, kon,* and so on.

(a) Seremoni Rada bèl *tankou* seremoni Petwo.
(Rada ceremonies are beautiful **like** Petwo ceremonies.)

13. The copula "am, are, is, to be."

13.1. Equative copula (with NP)

(a) Gede Nibo *se* nèg Miragwann o!
(Oh Gede Nibo **is** a guy from Miragoâne!)

13.2. Highlighter *se* with question words

(a) *Se* ki moun ou ye? (DeGraff 2007: 115)
(Who are you?)

13.3. Highlighter with other structures

(a) *Se* ou menm k a pare solèy pou lwa yo.
(**It's** you who will shade the sun for the lwa.)

13.4. Existential ("have" = "there is")

(a) Aprè Dye, m pa *gen* manman ki pou pale pou mwen!
(After God, I don't **have** a mother to speak for me!)

(b) Wi *gen* manbo.
(Yes **there are** manbo.)

(c) Èzili, si pa *genyen* dlo?
(Èzili, if **there is** no water?)

13.5. Non-pronounced null copula (represented by the null symbol, ø)

(a) Men Dje pa nou an ki ø si bon òdonnen nou.
(But our God who **is** so good commands us.)

(b) Sen Jak ø pa la, papa.
(Sen Jak **is** not here, man.)

14. Serial verbs

14.1. Directional with "go"

al = "go"

(a) Manman m voye m larivyè *al* chèche mouchwa nwa.
(My mother sent me to the river **to go** search for a black handkerchief.)

14.2. Directional with "come"

vini = "come"

(a) *Mennen* timoun yo *vini.* (DeGraff 2007: 116)
(**Bring** the children **over here**.)

14.3. Serial "give" meaning "to," "for"

bay = "to," "for"

(a) Yo pral mete l lakay *ba* w.
(They're going to put it at the house **for** you.)

(b) Pwason pouri ki pa bon pou *bay* kochon . . .
(Rotten fish that are not fit **for** pigs . . .)

(c) Se li yo *bay* Gede.
(That's what they **give** to Gede.)

14.4. Serial "pass" meaning "more than"

See section 12.7.

14.5. Three serial verb constructions

(a) *Mennen* timoun yo *vini wè* m. (DeGraff 2007: 116)
(**Bring** the children **to see** me.)

14.6. Serial verb constructions with four or more verbs

(a) *Al pran* machin lan *pote vini* ban mwen. (DeGraff 2007: 116)
(**Go get** me the car and **bring** it **back** for me.)

15. Noun phrase

15.1. Bare nouns that occur with no determiner (generic, definite)

(a) Mwen gen kay. (DeGraff 2007: 116)
(I have a house/houses.)

(b) Wosiyòl manje kowosòl. (DeGraff 2007: 117)
(Nightingales eat soursops.)

15.2. Indefinite article and numeral

(a) Denpi *yon* fanm gen pwòpte . . .
(When **a** woman is clean . . .)

(b) *Yon* sèl ti pitit mwen genyen . . .
(*A* single small child that I have . . .)

15.3. The singular definite article: *la, a, an, lan, nan*

The preceding word ends in a non-nasal consonant = *la*

(a) Ou manje poul *la.*
(You ate **the** chicken.)

The preceding word ends in an oral vowel = *a*

(b) Pitit yo gen dwa chwazi mety**e** *a*.

(The children have the right to choose **the** profession.)

The preceding word ends in a nasal vowel = *an*

(c) Li wè tou sa bl**an** *an* fè.

(He sees all that **the** whites do.)

The preceding word ends in a nasal vowel + non-nasal consonant = *lan*

(d) . . . pou m wè si sila pran kones**ans** *lan* . . .

(. . . to see if that one takes **the** knowledge . . .)

The preceding word ends in a nasal consonant (*m* or *n*) = *nan*

(e) Fan**m** *nan* koupe lavi m.

(**The** woman cut up my life.)

15.4. The plural marker definite article: *yo*

(a) Jou *yo* pa bezwen m . . .

(**The** days they do not need me . . .)

(b) Lonje men bay zanfan *yo*!

(Lend a hand to **the** children!)

15.5. Personal noun plus plural marker

(a) *Bovwa yo* ekri anpil bon liv sou Vodou.

(**The Beauvoir family** writes a lot of good books about Vodou.)

15.6. Demonstrative

sa = "that" (pronounced with short vowel)

sa a = "this one", "that one" (pronounced with long vowel)

sa yo = "these," "those"

(a) Se pa Loko *sa*?

(Isn't **that** Loko?)

(b) Si ou koute pwason *sa a* . . .

(If you listen to **this** fish . . .)

(c) Jèn gason, fò n pran prekosyon anba fanm *sa yo*.

(Young boys, you must be careful in the company of **those** women.)

15.7. Demonstrative plus definite singular or plural

sa a = singular; *sa yo* = plural

(a) E gad *sa a* soti nan lapriyè?

(And **this** guard comes from prayer?)

(b) Konsa yo ye, moun *sa yo*!

(That is how **those** people are!)

15.8. Relative clause followed by definite or plural marker

(a) Mandela se prezidan nou vle *a.* (DeGraff 2007: 118)
(Mandela is **the** president that we want.)

15.9. Prenominal adjective

(a) Bondje nou mande *bèl* jès.
(Our God asks for **good** deeds.)

(b) Papa m se *move* tèt o!
(Oh my father is an **angry** person!)

15.10. Postnominal adjective

(a) Bondje *blan* an mande krim.
(The **white** God asks for crimes.)

16. Possession

16.1. There is no single morpheme for the word *of* in Haitian Creole.

(a) Jete pòtre ø Dje blan an.
(Throw away the image **of** the white God.)

16.2. Possessive pronouns: distinct

(a) Li achte bèl wòb bay fanm *li*!
(He bought a beautiful dress for **his** wife!)

(b) Lestomak *li* fè l mal.
(**His** chest hurts him.)

17. Pronouns: case distinctions

17.1. Personal pronouns: first person singular

mwen, m, pa m = "I" (subject), "me" (object), "my" (possessive), "mine" (possessive noun)

(a) *M* fè siwo a bwè, siwo fèyay, *m* fè tout, *m* fè yo nan bwa.
(**I** make syrups for drinking, leaf syrups, **I** make all kinds, **I** make them in the woods.)

(b) Yo tande *m* chante.
(They hear **me** sing.)

(c) Ou ka tande plenn *mwen.*
(You can hear **my** groaning.)

(d) Se bagay pa mwen, se *pa m* nèt.
(It's my thing, it's entirely **mine**.)

17.2 Personal pronouns: second person singular

ou/wou, w = "you," "your"

(a) *Ou* pa bezwen kriye.
(**You** don't need to cry.)

(b) Maji oungan *w* bon!
(**Your** oungan's magic is good!)

(c) Tab *ou* gwo ase.
(**Your** table is big enough.)

17.3. Personal pronouns: third person singular

li, l, ni, n = "he," "she," "it," "him," "her," "his," "its"

(a) Bèl mouchwa sa se pou *l* mare ponyèt *li.*
(This beautiful handkerchief is for **her** to wrap around *her* wrists.)

(b) *Li* repare *l.*
(**He** repaired **it**.)

Li can become *ni* or *n* when it is preceded by a nasal vowel or consonant.

(c) L ap mennen *ni* kay oungan.
(She's taking **him** to the oungan's house.)

17.4. Personal pronouns: first person plural

nou, n = "we," "us," "our"

(a) *Nou* vye o!
(Oh **we** are old!)

(b) *N* ape pote potomitan *n*!
(**We**'re carrying **our** center post!)

(c) Yo bat ountò yo pou *nou.*
(They beat the Vodou drums for **us**.)

17.5. Personal pronouns: second person plural

nou, n = "you, "your"

(a) M ape mande kouman *nou* ye?
(I am asking how **you** are doing?)

17.6. Personal pronouns: third person plural

yo, y = "they," "them," "their"

(a) Pouki *yo* nonmen non m?
(Why do **they** call my name?)

(b) *Y* ap nonmen non m!
(**They** are calling my name!)

(c) O byento n a wè *yo.*
(Oh soon we will see **them**.)

17.7. Reflexive pronouns: distinct form

(a) M rele *m* Chango!

(I call **myself** Chango!)

(b) L abiye *l* tout an blan.

(He dresses **himself** all in white.)

17.8. Pronoun intensifier: *menm* "self" (mwen menm; ou menm; li menm; nou menm; yo menm).

(a) Anvan l mouri, m kanzo *mwen menm.*

(Before she died, I was kanzo **myself**.)

(b) Mistik la li gen yon pouvwa; apre Bondye, li gen yon pouvwa *li menm.*

(The mystical has a power; after God, it has a power **itself**.)

17.9. Reflexive pronouns: *tèt* + pronoun; *pou kò* + pronoun

(a) M ap mande *tèt mwen,* pouki se mwen?

(I'm asking **myself**, why is it me?)

(b) Li fè kanzo a *pou kò l.*

(She did the kanzo initiation **by herself**.)

17.10. Interrogative pronouns: (a) and (c) are bimorphemic

(a) Lan men *ki moun* ou lese badji lwa m yo?

(In **whose** hands did you leave the sanctuary of my lwa?)

(b) . . . pase ou konn *kisa* l ap vin fè.

(. . . because you know **what** he (the lwa) is going to come do.)

(c) *Kisa ki* kanzo a?

(**What** is the kanzo?)

17.11. Adverbial interrogatives of time and place

(a) *Ki bò/Ki kote* w a wè li?

(**Where** will you see him?)

(b) *Ki lè* seremoni Dantò a konmanse?

(**When** does the Dantò ceremony begin?)

(c) Timoun p ap vin gade *ki jan* granmoun nan ye.

(Children aren't coming to see **how** the elder is.)

(d) *Konben* gangan pratike nan zòn Bèl Rivyè a?

(**How many** oungan practice in the area of Belle-Rivière?)

17.12. Relative pronouns

(a) Siklòn Gòdonn kraze kay *kote* yo te rete a. (DeGraff 2007: 121)

(Hurricane Gordon destroyed the house **where** they used to live.)

(b) Yo pa jwenn moun *ki* t ap fè sèvis.
(They didn't find the people **who** were holding services.)

18. Coordinators and conjunctions

18.1. "And" joining sentences

(a) Ou mete m sou tè a *epi* w ale kite mwen.
(You put me on the earth **and** you went and left me.)

(b) Y ap jwe rasin *epi* yo nan konkirans.
(They are playing roots music **and** they are competing.)

18.2. "And" joining sentence parts: distinct

(a) Gen moun ki vin bat tanbou *ak* chante?
(Are there people who come to play drums **and** sing?)

(b) Mwen sèvi Lesen *avè* Marasa!
(I serve the Saints **and** the Marasa!)

(c) Kwi *avèk* rasin nan gen yon konèksyon?
(The calabash bowl **and** the root have a connection?)

18.3. Important conjunctions for connecting sentences

(a) *Paske* m pa gen fanmi an, gade sa yo fè mwen.
(**Because** I don't have family, look at what they do to me.)

(b) Yo di yo se manbo, *men* se mango yo ye.
(They say they're manbo, **but** they are mangos.)

(c) Li te fè sa *akòz* pwoblèm li yo.
(She did that **due to** her problems.)

19. Prepositions

19.1. General locative prepositions (or post-position)

(a) Moun yo tout ak on kwi *nan* men.
(The people all have a calabash bowl **in** their hands.)

(b) Mete kwi a *sou* pewon an.
(Put the calabash bowl **on** the altar.)

(c) Alomi, mwen mete jenou m atè *devan* ounfò.
(Alomi, I get on my knees on the ground **before** the temple.)

(d) De bra *dèyè* m.
(Two hands **behind** me.)

19.2. Zero preposition with motion verb plus place (represented by the null symbol, ø)

(a) Timoun yo al ø Mache Pòspyewo. (DeGraff 2007: 122)
(The children have gone **to** the Poste-Pierrot market.)

20. Miscellaneous

20.1. Word order: questions SVO

(a) Èske *ou pral ba pitit ou* menm konesans ou genyen?

(Will **you give your children** the same knowledge that you have?)

20.2. Word order: questions OSV

(a) M pa konn *kisa o pou m fè* ak moun sa yo.

(Oh I don't know **what I should do** with these people.)

20.3. Sentence-final -o

(a) N ap gade *o*!

(**Oh** we're watching!)

(b) Nanpwen anyen la pase Bondye *o*!

(**Oh** there is nothing here except God!)

20.4. Sentence-initial emphatics: *ala, apa*

(a) *Ala* yon move bèt se bèf o!

(**Oh what** awful animals cows are!)

(b) *Apa* w la!

(**Why look** you are here!)

20.5. Sentence-initial presentation morpheme

(a) *Men* ason an.

(**Here** is the sacred rattle.)

20.6. The doubling of adverbs for emphasis in Vodou songs

(a) Danbala Wèdo, m *deja* koulèv *deja.* (Beauvoir 2008b: 307)

(Danbala Wèdo, I'm **already** a snake **already**.)

NOTES

——*

Chapter 1. The World of Vodou Songs

1. “Depi m piti m ap chante,” in Racine Bwa-Kay-Iman 2003.

2. The term *lwa* is singular and plural. We have followed Haitian American English practice with this choice. Some authors awkwardly write *lwa*-s, *manbo*-s, and so on, but we think context adequately disambiguates the number of singular or plural nouns.

3. See Wikipedia, s.v. “Second Franco-Dahomean War,” available on http://en.wikipedia.org/wiki/Second_Franco-Dahomean_War (accessed July 19, 2010).

4. Vodou and Islam were sometimes simultaneously practiced on the northern limits of this region: see Breure 2006.

5. Note that Beauvoir capitalizes all important nouns pertaining to Vodou (e.g., Lwa, Houngan, Manbo). In this book, we do not capitalize such terms except when quoting from his texts.

6. For Korean shamanism, see Kim 2003: 72; Sarfati 2007. For Greece, see Homer and Dros 1991; Homer and Lateur 2010. For Rome, see Virgil and D’Hane-Scheltema 2008.

7. See, however, Freeman 2004 and Valdman et al. 2007 for excellent inventories of Vodou terminology.

8. The best exception is the hard-to-find Laguerre 1980 and Gilles and Gilles 2009. The English translations in Rigaud 1953 and Métraux 1958 also give a good number of songs but far fewer than Laguerre 1980.

9. Various research paradigms provide insights into source texts—for example, textual criticism, historiography, linguistic analyses, ethnopoetics, oral-formulaic theory, genre criticism, source, form and redaction criticism, discourse analysis, rhetorical and narratological criticism, literary criticism, canon criticism, and lexicography and textual analysis: Maring 2003; Porter and Clarke 2002.

10. The recording and transcriptions are held by Indiana University’s Archives of Traditional Music and Columbia University.

11. For this paragraph, see Laguerre 1980: 29.

12. Should they wish to read pre-eminent scholarly studies, readers are referred, among many others, to Beauvoir 2006, 2008a, 2008b; Beauvoir and Dominique 2003; Brown 2006; Fleurant 2007; Hurbon 1987; Laguerre 1980; Marcelin 1950a, 1950b; Mbiti 1990; Métraux 1958; Michel and Bellegarde-Smith 2006; Murray 1980, 1984; Richman 2008; Roumain 1943.

13. *Vodun* is the Fon word for lwa. It is spelled variously as *vodoun, vòdún,* or *vodú*” but is rendered as *vodun* in this book.

14. For example, *mouchwa* (headscarves) and clothing are specifically colored to represent particular lwa or the individual’s role in the Vodou community.

15. Vodou and Catholicism overlap in Haiti in various ways. For example, one finds Vodou drum rhythms used for Catholic hymns, just as one finds Catholic saints symbolizing Vodou lwa in *peristil* (temples). When he was a Catholic priest, Father Aristide (who was later president in 1991–1996 and 2001–2004) occasionally wore Vodou vèvè on his ecclesiastical vestment (this is similar to a Catholic priest wearing the Gay Pride rainbow on his vestment in the United States, something I observed once in Bloomington). In recent decades, Protestantism has grown exponentially in Haiti by converting Catholics and Vodouists. Although they are more exclusivist, Protestant sects are not immune to Vodou influence. Some convene at sacred sites in nature, don the white garb of the ounsi initiates, engage in glossolalia, are overcome by the "crisis of possession," are "slain by the spirit," and use Vodou drum rhythms (Romain 1986: 317). However, in spite of these and many other convergences, Vodou and Christianity are distinct and their roles and influences are stratified (Murray 1984: 214).

16. Unlike its English translation, the Haitian Creole expression is used in many exchanges and has a formulaic conditional grammatical connotation in addition to the theological one.

17. Gerald Murray notes that both Africans and Europeans provide models for pantheons that are ruled over by "Greater Spirits." While the African lwa persist in Haiti, Murray argues that servants of the lwa "pay ultimate homage to none other than the Judeo-Christian God—'Bon Dieu'—as the creator and ruler of all" (Murray 1984: 206). The representatives of the Supreme Being in Haiti were almost entirely European Catholics, and most were French citizens until François Duvalier's Haitianization of the Catholic Church in the 1960s (Murray 1984: 207). Murray finds that Vodouists consider Bondye, not the lwa, to be in control of growing crops, blowing the wind, and sending rain and lightning. Bondye creates all life on earth, not the lwa. Bondye has fundamental power, while the lwa have limited power. Oungan Nelson Marcenat (personal correspondence, 2009) notes that, while God is the underlying force of nature, the lwa can increase agricultural yields or employ lightning to punish people, among other powers. Bondye is likely the convergence of European and African notions of the Supreme Being. As recent work on *relexification* in linguistics shows (Lefebvre 1998; Valdman 2001), the etymology of the phonological form of a word does not mean that the syntax or semantics of the word remain French. Indeed, many African concepts and structures are dressed in European lexical forms in Caribbean Creole languages.

18. Today in the Fon language, the word *Máwú* is translated as "Supreme Being; creator God" and, ironically, the term *Máwúsèntò* has come to mean "Christian" (Höftmann 2003: 294; Segurola and Rassinoux 2000).

19. I retain the widely used term *possession,* but one should note that others prefer designations such as *theomorphosis* (Férère 2005) or *epiphany* (Christophe 2004), among others. Sometimes I also use the terms *ridden* and *appearance* to describe how the lwa dance in the heads of Vodouists.

20. According to Marcenat, personal correspondence, 2008, and Rigaud 1953.

21. Marcenat, personal correspondence, 2008.

22. See Matsushita 1997 for examples.

23. Marcenat, personal correspondence, 2008.

24. Brown (2006: 9) and others argue that it is the *gwo bonnanj* that displaces. However, I follow Jil and Jil (2009: 281), who base their analysis on African sources—in identifying the *ti bonnanj* as the element that displaces: see Appendix A: Dictionary of Vodou Terms, s.v. "*gwo bonnanj*" and "*ti bonnanj.*"

25. A *nanchon* also refers to a community of Vodouists who share a common religious outlook: Beauvoir 2008b: 447–448.

26. For an example, see Matsushita 1997.

27. One anonymous reviewer of this book took offense to the terms *maji blan* (white magic) and *maji nwa* (black magic) because of how they have been used to distort and attack Vodou. We leave them here because Marcenat himself refers to the two types of magic with no racial connotations.

According to A. O. Orubu (2001: 122), "black" and "white" are also used in Africa to designate different "negative" versus "positive" magic, and they are not racial terms.

28. Of course, one must wonder how an actual bòkò (instead of an academic) would report on his activities. More research among this class of Vodou specialists is needed.

29. Some of these categories come from Murray 1984: 196.

30. The Fongbe term is *hùnxò* (Höftmann 2003: 230).

31. In terms of death imagery, think, for instance, of the crucifixion in Christianity or of corpse meditation in Buddhism.

32. For instance, while I was conducting interviews with him in 2009, he organized our meetings around the konbit commitments he already had.

33. Other religions, such as Tibetan Buddhism and Catholicism, also encourage the establishment of home altars to help anchor religious practice.

34. Some commentators recognize various ranks among the *ounsi* (e.g., *ounsi temerè* [fearless ounsi], *ounsi kanzo* [ounsi of fire], and *ounsi bosal* [new ounsi]). Note, however, that these sometimes have different meanings or are not used at all depending on the oungan's or manbo's traditions.

35. Rouget (2001: 11) reports that in the Vodou of Dahomey in the 1950s–1970s (now Benin), Vodouists underwent periods of cloistering that lasted as long as three years. This cloistering involved the study of Vodou oral and hymnal tradition in addition to language study related to the ethnolinguistic origins of the vodun served. *Hunsi* isolation rituals in Benin, however, are also seven days.

36. Working in Haitian studies for more than a decade in the United States has given me the opportunity to regularly encounter negative attitudes about animal sacrifice. North Americans and some Protestant Haitian Americans, for example, sometimes claim that animal sacrifice is a form of cruelty or barbarism. They claim, following their Christian tradition, that the crucifixion of Jesus undid the need to carry out animal sacrifice; they argue that Jesus himself was the "ultimate sacrifice." At the same time, many of those same Protestants carry on a supposedly "secular" consumption of animal flesh and wear animal products such as leather. A Vodouist might argue, however, that the abolishment of ritual animal sacrifice is alienating because it takes animal life for granted and ignores the sacred link between animal and human life. A Vodou priest from Benin noted to a European critic that "you put meat wrapped in cellophane out in your shops and then claim that Africans (or Haitians) are ruthless" (Breure 2006: 199). One should think about this in the context of the caging, forced feeding, injecting, and mechanized killing of animals in the slaughterhouses of the industrial countries. In Vodou, the animal's death is mystical, intimate, and tangible, whereas the killings in the slaughterhouses of the industrialized nations are an "inconvenient truth" and hence hidden away in factories that are filled with immigrant workers. The meat products of these slaughterhouses are finally rendered palatable through packaging.

37. See also Appendix A: Dictionary of Vodou Terms, s.v. "*sakre.*"

38. For more information about Ogou Feray's consumption of blood, see Chapter 3 in this volume.

39. Note that *bouden* (coagulated pig's blood) is a regular part of a healthy Haitian diet.

40. See, e.g., Boukan Ginen 1995, 1995; Boukman Eksperyans 1991, 1995; King Kessy 2009.

41. See Deren 2007.

42. See Rouget 1991 for further discussion.

43. See the photograph from Oungan Beauvoir's temple (Beauvoir 2008b: 74).

44. See Orubu 2001: 13 for discussion on rainmakers in African religion.

45. Nago refers to the Yorùbá people of Nigeria.

46. In this volume, words are left in Haitian Creole if they are essential parts of Vodou religion (e.g., oungan, manbo, *ounsi*) or *langaj* (West African language deposits) unfamiliar to me.

47. For this and the next paragraph, see Laguerre 1980: 28.

48. Dessalines and Jan Pyè Ibo are sometimes fused, as in the case of Roumain's song 27, where one finds Jan Pyè Desalin.

49. Métraux (1972: 187) claims that the celebration of the lwa is more important than the actual content of the songs, which he says are often "meaningless, foolish or absurd." The materials collected here suggest, on the contrary, that the songs are spiritual, formal, and meaningful. Métraux (1972: 188) senses the religious majesty of Vodou songs but emphasizes that he considers them "bare" and "impoverished in content."

50. Beauvoir's *Le grand recueil sacré, ou, Répertoire des chansons du Vodou haïtien* (The great sacred collection, or, Repertory of Haitian Vodou songs [2008]) provides 1,763 Vodou songs in Haitian Creole. That formidable collection provides a unique opportunity for researchers to better study Vodou through Haitian Creole source texts.

51. For this paragraph, see Laguerre 1980: 34.

52. For this paragraph, see ibid.: 35–36.

Chapter 2. Historical Songs

1. August 14, 1791.
2. Fabre Geffrard (1806–1878) was president from 1859 to 1867.
3. Charlemagne Péralte (1886–1919) and Benoît Batraville (1877–1920) led the Cacos freedom fighters against the U.S. military, which occupied Haiti from 1915 to 1934.
4. Sténio Vincent (1874–1959) was president from 1930 to 1941.
5. Élie Lescot (1883–1974) was president from 1941 to 1946.
6. François Duvalier (1907–1971) was president from 1957 to 1971.
7. At the insistence of U.S. agricultural authorities, the entire pig population was eradicated due to the emergence of the African swine fever virus in 1978. The loss of the pig was calamitous for Haitian peasants.
8. February 7, 1986, was the day that President Jean-Claude Duvalier (b. 1951), son of François Duvalier, fled Haiti.

Chapter 3. Jacques Roumain's, Werner A. Jaegerhuber's, and Jean Price-Mars's Songs

1. For extensive discussion and interpretation, see Roumain 1943.
2. This song is the same as the one given in ibid., 26.
3. Savain, cited in Jaegerhuber 1950: 2.
4. Cited in ibid.
5. For more about the life and work of Jaegerhuber, see Largey 2006.
6. For this oath, the members of the Vodou family touch an iron bar with fists closed and then touch their chests.
7. The words are accompanied by vocal tremolo with the slapping of the fingers on the mouth.
8. Here the priest hits his chest three times.
9. Toni is likely a reference to the Portuguese-born Saint Anthony, who was adopted as the figurehead of Antonianism, a movement initiated in 1704 by a Kongo visionary called Dona Beatriz, or Kimpa Vita. By consulting directly with the saint, Kimpa Vita proposed that the way to save the Kongo state involved the Africanization of the local Catholic Church. He pushed for the greater incorporation of Saint Anthony, known locally as Toni Malau (Anthony of Good Fortune); Toni Malau was considered the patron of mothers and children and the protector against illness and misfortune (Campbell 2006).

10. Latin for "In the name of the Father and Holy Spirit, amen."
11. Notice the appearance of French and Spanish in this text.
12. Dyeri Jil and Ivwoz Jil, personal correspondence, 2010, suggest that "*eyo*" should read "*henou* (family)."

Chapter 4. Milo Marcelin's Songs

1. *Ze* (egg) may be referenced because white eggs are offered to Danbala.
2. The expression *Do Miwa* either could be an instance of *langaj* or it could mean "[Lwa Agasou with] Mirrors on His Back," especially since mirrors are important in Vodou.
3. *Mren* (I) is a rural pronunciation of the standard *mwen*; we follow Marcelin's spelling.
4. *Chwal* here refers to the one possessed by the lwa.
5. Jil and Jil (2009: 135) offer this translation of *gweli.*
6. A *dyab* is a malevolent or mischievous lwa.

Chapter 5. Laura Boulton's Songs

1. *Sayti* or *Saiti* in English links the hiss of the serpent lwa, Danbala, with the spelling of "Haiti."
2. Possibly a variant of *Agwe.*
3. Dyeri Jil and Ivwoz Jil (personal correspondence, 2010) note that the version of this song that they know begins with "*Ayaman.*"
4. The original document writes *ey wa.* Jil and Jil (personal correspondence) suggest that *ewa* is the correct form.
5. Jil and Jil (personal correspondence) suggest the translation "the beautiful" for *ey wa.*
6. Jil and Jil (2009: 124) note that the expression *kò aniye* or *kwanye* means to "*retire detrès* (remove distress or stay calm)."
7. Jil and Jil (personal correspondence) suggest "followers of the heritage" for *Ladogwèsan.*

Chapter 7. Benjamin Hebblethwaite's Songs

1. "*Move Tan*" literally means "Bad Weather."

Chapter 8. Harold Courlander's Songs

1. For notes about the identities of the singers and the locations of the recordings, see Courlander 1939–1940.
2. See Appendix A: Dictionary of Vodou Terms, s.v. "Ogoun."
3. Lakaye is a small town near Port-au-Prince.
4. Leyogàn (Léogâne) is a midsize town close to Port-au-Prince (Courlander 1939: 50).
5. A literal translation is "They make (people) eat my reason" (Courlander 1939: 71).
6. The pavilion is a straw or palmleaf roof held up by poles. It covers a dancing court next to the temple (Courlander 1939: 75). See Appendix A: Dictionary of Vodou Terms, s.v. "*peristil.*"
7. This song is part of a ritual sacrifice (Courlander 1939: 93).
8. *Nago* refers to the Yorùbá people.
9. Agwe's "cannon" is thunder (Courlander 1939: 103).
10. Ogoun is waiting for the sacrifice dedicated to him.
11. *Lele* is known by Haitians either as part of the lwa Ibo's name or as the expression "Ibo song" (Courlander 1939: 157). *Lele* also means "to cry out" (Jil and Jil 2009: 15).

12. The song is a metaphor for "What good is the excuse after the damage has been done?" (Courlander 1939: 158).

13. This song illustrates the shifting point of view common in Vodou songs. The perspective shifts between the voice of the lwa Loko and the voice of the servants of the lwa (Courlander 1939: 177).

14. "Leaves in the Woods" is a poetic allusion to the "servants of the loa" (Courlander 1939: 178).

15. Courlander (1939: 192) posits that there is a single lwa, Maryani Moundong. Another reading of the song might be that the lwa Moundong is being ushered out of a ceremony, and the lwa Maryani is being ushered in.

Appendix A. Dictionary of Vodou Terms

1. Fleurant 2006b: 52.
2. Beauvoir 2008a; Oungan Nelson Marcenat, personal correspondence, 2008.
3. See Courlander's song 13; Rietmeijer and Drolenga 2003 (Haiti); Matsushita 1997 (Benin).
4. Freeman 2004: 9.
5. Ibid.
6. Ibid.
7. Beauvoir 2008b: 388.
8. Férère 2005: 33.
9. Marcelin 1950a: 127.
10. Ibid., 127.
11. Ibid., 131.
12. Anglade 1998: 41.
13. Segurola and Rassinoux 2000: 20.
14. Brand 2000b: 1.
15. Freeman 2004: 11.
16. Férère 2005: 33; Marcelin 1950a: 127–132.
17. Férère 2005: 30.
18. Beauvoir 2008b: 242.
19. See Marcelin 1950b: 101.
20. Ibid.
21. Ibid.
22. Ibid., 102.
23. See ibid.
24. For the previous sentences, see ibid., 103.
25. See Marcelin's song 186.
26. See Marcelin 1950b: 105.
27. Ibid.
28. Jil and Jil 2009: 110.
29. Freeman 2004: 8.
30. Wilcken 1992: 33.
31. Segurola and Rassinoux 2000: 21.
32. Freeman 2004: 11.
33. Jil and Jil 2009: 83.
34. Segurola and Rassinoux 2000: 24.
35. Wilcken 1992: 97.
36. Freeman 2004: 12.
37. Ibid.
38. See Marcelin 1950a: 103–113.
39. Férère 2005: 34.
40. Ibid.
41. Marcelin 1950a: 104–105.
42. Jil and Jil 2009: 168; Lola and Brown 1995: 235.
43. See Marcelin's song 75.
44. Marcelin 1950a: 104.
45. Ibid.
46. See Marcelin's song 76.
47. See Marcelin's song 79.
48. See Marcelin's song 80.
49. Marcelin 1950a: 109.
50. See ibid., 110.
51. See Marcelin's song 83.
52. Chery 2008: 10–13.
53. Marcelin 1950a: 113.
54. Ibid.
55. Anglade 1998: 43.
56. Brand 2000b: 1.
57. Segurola and Rassinoux 2000: 28.
58. See Mambo Michele, "Haitian Voodoo Glossary Terms," available online at http://www.erzulies.com/site/articles/view/www.erzulies.com (accessed 2010).
59. Ibid.
60. Freeman 2004: 18.
61. Segurola and Rassinoux 2000: 41.
62. Beauvoir 2008b: 240.
63. See Mambo Michele, "Haitian Voodoo Glossary Terms."
64. Jil and Jil 2009: 188.
65. Ibid., 133.
66. Freze 1992: 201.
67. See Courlander's song 29.

68. Lola and Brown 1995: 229.
69. Fleurant 2006b: 47.
70. Jil and Jil 2009: 268.
71. According to Freeman 2004: 34, *angaje* is the act of making a pact with an evil spirit.
72. Ibid.
73. See Beauvoir 2008a: 187; Freeman 2004: 38.
74. Jil and Jil 2009: 32; Métraux 1958: 22.
75. Beauvoir 2008b: 107.
76. Freeman 2004: 41.
77. Mambo Michele, "Haitian Voodoo Glossary Terms."
78. Rigaud 1953: 72.
79. Freeman 2004: 49.
80. Ibid.
81. Ibid., 64.
82. Jil and Jil 2009: 125.
83. Ibid.
84. See Freeman 2004: 54; Thompson 1995: 106.
85. Freeman 2004: 55.
86. Ibid., 54.
87. Ibid., 56; Métraux 1958: 69.
88. See Brand 2000b: 18; Herskovits 1967: 64; Segurola and Rassinoux 2000: 63.
89. Murrell 2010: 85.
90. Lescot and Magloire 2002.
91. Wilcken 1992: 45.
92. Freeman 2004: 88.
93. Brown 1991: 69.
94. Wilcken 1992: 41.
95. Brand 2000b: 18; Freeman 2004: 58; Marcelin 1950b: 63.
96. Roumain 1943: 15.
97. Férère 2005: 37; Freeman 2004: 58; Roumain 1943: 123.
98. See Métraux 1958: 164; Peters 1941; Roumain 1942: 17.
99. See Blier 1995: 71; Brand 2000b: 77.
100. Freeman 2004: 59.
101. Brand 2000b: 3.
102. See ibid., 19, 26.
103. Beauvoir 2008b: 274.
104. Freeman 2004: 61.
105. Ibid., 63; Jil and Jil 2009: 372.
106. Jil and Jil 2009: 372.
107. Freeman 2004: 65; Métraux 1972: 373.
108. Marcelin 1950b: 65.
109. Thompson 1995: 107.
110. Segurola and Rassinoux 2000: 79.
111. Freeman 2004: 65; Jil and Jil 2009: 88.
112. Segurola and Rassinoux 2000: 85.
113. Brand 2000b: 20.
114. Métraux 1958: 175.
115. Rouget 2001: 12 gives photographs of *ayizan* in Benin; Beckwith and Fisher 1995: 105 gives photographs of *ayizan* in Togo; and Beauvoir 2008b: 77 gives gives photographs of *ayizan* in Haiti.
116. Anglade 1998: 56.
117. Férère 2005: 38.
118. Jérôme Soimaud, personal correspondence, 2010.
119. Jil and Jil 2009: 152.
120. Brown 1991: 54; Férère 2005: 38; Jil and Jil 2009: 315.
121. Métraux 1958: 321.
122. Marcelin 1950a: 29.
123. Ibid., 32.
124. Ibid., 32–34.
125. Ibid., 36.
126. Brand 2000b: 3, 20.
127. Segurola and Rassinoux 2000: 88.
128. Anglade 1998: 55.
129. Ibid., 56.
130. Jil and Jil 2009: 153; Segurola and Rassinoux 2000: 89.
131. Jil and Jil 2009: 137.
132. Férère 2005: 94.
133. Freeman 2004; Marcelin 1950b: 85–88.
134. See Marcelin's song 165.
135. See Marcelin's song 168.
136. See Marcelin's songs 169 and 170.
137. Beauvoir 2008b: 203.
138. Listen to "Konbit Zaka," on Boukman Eksperyans 1995.
139. Jil and Jil 2009: 137.
140. Freeman 2004: 66.
141. Ibid.
142. Segurola and Rassinoux 2000: 90.
143. Beauvoir 2008b: 262.
144. Freeman 2004: 68.
145. Ibid., 69.
146. See Marcelin's song 196 in this volume.
147. See Marcelin's song 197.

148. See Marcelin's song 198.
149. See Marcelin's song 199.
150. See Marcelin's song 204.
151. See Marcelin's song 205.
152. See Marcelin's song 206.
153. See Marcelin's song 207.
154. Marcelin 1950b: 117–120.
155. Averill 2009: 105.
156. Jil and Jil 2009: 177.
157. Freeman 2004: 69.
158. Ibid.
159. Jil and Jil 2009: 250.
160. Métraux 1958: 69.
161. Jil and Jil 2009: 325.
162. Freeman 2004: 69.
163. Ibid.
164. Mambo Michele, "Haitian Voodoo Glossary Terms."
165. Freeman 2004: 69.
166. Comhaire-Sylvain 1951: 63.
167. Freeman 2004: 71.
168. Thompson 1995: 106.
169. Beauvoir 2008b: 321.
170. Thompson 1995: 106.
171. Jil and Jil 2009: 271.
172. Ibid., 38.
173. Laman 1936: 11; Jil and Jil 2009: 38; and Schwegler 2002: 157.
174. Freeman 2004: 72.
175. Beauvoir 2008b: 126.
176. Freeman 2004: 73.
177. Ibid., 74.
178. Averill 2009: 104.
179. Ibid., 153.
180. Beauvoir 2008b: 126.
181. Freeman 2004: 75.
182. Ibid., 75.
183. Ibid., 76.
184. Ibid., 79.
185. See Lescot and Magloire 2002.
186. Freeman 2004: 83.
187. Wilcken 1992: 46.
188. Comhaire-Sylvain 1951: 63.
189. Lola and Brown 1995: 235.
190. Jil and Jil 2009: 315.
191. Freeman 2004: 84.
192. Ibid., 82.
193. Ibid., 85
194. Férère 2005: 41.
195. See Consentino 1995: 43; Marcelin 1950b: 153–171.
196. For this entry, see Marcelin 1950b: 153–173.
197. Ibid., 147.
198. Ibid., 147.
199. Freeman 2004: 88
200. Roumain 1943: 140.
201. Freeman 2004: 89.
202. Jil and Jil 2009: 162.
203. Freeman 2004: 93.
204. Ibid., 94.
205. Jil and Jil 2009: 100.
206. Freeman 2004: 94.
207. Segurola and Rassinoux 2000: 328.
208. Freeman 2004: 94.
209. Ibid.
210. Beauvoir 2008b: 413–414, 438.
211. Freeman 2004: 97.
212. Marcelin 1950b: 20.
213. Freeman 2004: 98.
214. See Jil and Jil 2009: 324.
215. Laman 1936: 37 and Swartenbroeckx 1973: 578.
216. Freeman 2004: 99.
217. Thompson 1995: 107.
218. Freeman 2004: 100.
219. Ibid., 101.
220. Beauvoir 2008a: 187.
221. See Hainard, Mathez, and Schinz 2008.
222. See Beauvoir and Dominique 2003.
223. Beauvoir 2008b: 203.
224. Brand 2000b: 97.
225. See Segurola and Rassinoux 2000: 184.
226. Seiderer 2008: 397.
227. Ibid., 398.
228. Davis 1985: 269.
229. Jil and Jil 2009: 160.
230. Jil and Jil 2009.
231. Freeman 2004: 107.
232. Ibid.,
233. Segurola and Rassinoux 2000: 105.
234. Adepegba 2008: 123.
235. Blier 1995: 86; Freeman 2004: 108; Hurbon 1987 (2002): 161.
236. Jil and Jil 2009: 303.
237. Freeman 2004: 110.

238. Jil and Jil 2009: 71.
239. Ibid., 372.
240. Allen 2010; Jil and Jil 2009: 75.
241. Beauvoir 2008b: 297.
242. See Averill 2009: 153.
243. Beauvoir 2008b: 279.
244. Ibid., 220.
245. Ibid., 185.
246. Ibid., 241.
247. Adepegba 2008: 113.
248. Murrell 2010: 26.
249. Freeman 2004: 111.
250. Ibid., 114.
251. Jil and Jil 2009: 325.
252. Valdman, Iskrova, Pierre, and André 2007: 90.
253. Beauvoir 2008a: 187.
254. Férère 2005: 42.
255. Jil and Jil 2009: 107.
256. Hainard, Mathez, and Schinz 2008.
257. Férère 2005: 42.
258. See Consentino 1995: 56.
259. Manbo Elsie Joseph, personal correspondence, 2010.
260. For the next sentences, see Jil and Jil 2009: 104.
261. Segurola and Rassinoux 2000: 402.
262. Jacques Pierre, personal correspondence, 2010.
263. Freeman 2004: 119.
264. Bellegarde-Smith 2006: 101.
265. Murrell 2010: 63.
266. Comhaire-Sylvain 1951: 63.
267. See Métraux 1958: 182–185.
268. Férère 2005: 97.
269. See Courlander's song 30.
270. Métraux 1958: 76.
271. Averill 2009: 153.
272. Fleurant 2006b: 49.
273. Laman 1936: 70; Swartenbroeckx 1973: 33; Guerra and Schwegler 2005: 95.
274. Beauvoir 2008a: 187.
275. Freeman 2004: 127.
276. Férère 2005: 45.
277. Ibid.
278. Ibid.
279. Geggus 2002: 84.
280. Ibid., 85.
281. See Consentino 1995: 25; Murrell 2010: 63.
282. Murrell 2010: 63.
283. Geggus 2002: 88.
284. Ibid., 87.
285. Averill 2009: 104.
286. Thompson 1995: 114.
287. Beauvoir 2008b: 325. The translation is from Jil and Jil 2009; Jil and Jil, personal correspondence, 2010.
288. Freeman 2004: 150.
289. Ibid.
290. Ibid.
291. See Marcelin 1950b: 81.
292. Ibid.
293. Ibid.
294. Marcelin 1950b: 82.
295. Valdman, Iskrova, Pierre, and André 2007: 402.
296. Jil and Jil 2009: 120.
297. Adepegba 2008: 108, 118.
298. Rouget 2001: 83.
299. Freeman 2004: 152.
300. See Averill 1997, 2009: 103; Jil and Jil 2009: 26.
301. Valdman, Iskrova, Pierre, and André 2007: 116.
302. Ibid.
303. Freeman 2004: 157.
304. Roumain 1943: 140.
305. Freeman 2004: 159.
306. Métraux 1958: 175.
307. Ibid., 321.
308. For photographs of the *chire ayizan* in Haiti and Benin, see Beauvoir 2008b: 77; Rouget 2001: 12–14.
309. Freeman 2004: 167.
310. Lola and Brown 1995: 233.
311. Freeman 2004: 168.
312. Averill 1997: 20; Consentino 1995: 51.
313. Oungan Alisma, personal correspondence, 2011.
314. See Consentino 1995: 202.
315. Murrell 2010: 83.
316. Fleurant 2006b: 49.
317. Beauvoir 2008b: 377.
318. Férère 2005: 49; Freeman 2004: 117; Rouget 2001: 78.

319. Soimaud, personal correspondence, 2010.
320. Murrell 2010: 79.
321. Jil and Jil 2009: 86.
322. See Férère 2005: 46; Jil and Jil 2009: 86.
323. Arthur and Dash 1999: 264.
324. Ibid.
325. Marcelin 1950b: 27–28.
326. Marcelin 1950b.
327. Jil and Jil 2009: 88.
328. Segurola and Rassinoux 2000: 121.
329. Ibid.
330. Férère 2005: 49.
331. Brand 2000a: 26.
332. Ibid.
333. See Brand 2000b: 34.
334. See ibid., 28, 42.
335. Ibid., 26–27.
336. Segurola and Rassinoux 2000: 121. For photographs of *Dan* initiates leaving their cloisters in Benin in 1966, see Rouget 2001: 78–79.
337. Jil and Jil 2009: 91.
338. Beauvoir-Dominique 1995: 173.
339. For this and the next sentence, see Jil and Jil 2009: 210.
340. Freeman 2004: 178.
341. For this entry, see Jil and Jil 2009: 265–266.
342. Valdman, Iskrova, Pierre, and André 2007: 133; Jil and Jil 2009: 29, 78, 216.
343. Jil and Jil 2009: 249.
344. Beauvoir 2008a: 187.
345. Anglade 1998: 84; Freeman 2004: 180.
346. Murrell 2010: 19, 70.
347. Segurola and Rassinoux 2000: 122.
348. See, e.g., François 2008.
349. Roumain 1943: 140.
350. Freeman 2004: 180.
351. Valdman, Iskrova, Pierre, and André 2007: 136.
352. Freeman 2004: 182.
353. Ibid., 190.
354. Ibid.
355. Ibid.
356. Ibid., 192.
357. Ibid.
358. Ibid., 195.
359. Jil and Jil 2009: 53.
360. Freeman 2004: 199.
361. Mambo Michele, "Haitian Voodoo Glossary Terms."
362. Lola and Brown 1995: 228.
363. Freeman 2004: 209.
364. Ibid., 210.
365. See Hall 1953.
366. Dayan 1995: 38.
367. See Marcelin's song 23 dedicated to Loko.
368. Beauvoir 2008b: 168. Roumain's song 27 also references Dessalines.
369. Dayan 1995: 33; Jil and Jil 2009: 127.
370. Freeman 2004: 214.
371. See the song "Priyè (Prayer)," on Racine Bwa-Kay-Iman 2003.
372. Freeman 2004: 226.
373. Ibid., 228.
374. Marcelin 1950b: 124.
375. Roumain's song 24 mentions Djahountò (Roumain 1943: 83).
376. Jil and Jil 2009: 90.
377. Segurola and Rassinoux 2000: 35.
378. Freeman 2004: 230.
379. Segurola and Rassinoux 2000: 256.
380. Freeman 2004: 230.
381. Ibid.
382. Jil and Jil 2009: 319.
383. Ibid., 250.
384. Beauvoir 2008b: 308.
385. Wilcken 1992: 120.
386. Beauvoir 2008b: 28.
387. Freeman 2004: 231.
388. Ibid.
389. Segurola and Rassinoux 2000: 268.
390. Beauvoir 2008b: 216.
391. Ibid., 164–165.
392. Freeman 2004: 233.
393. Marcelin 1950b: 123.
394. Freeman 2004: 233–234.
395. Segurola and Rassinoux 2000: 120.
396. Freeman 2004: 236.
397. Ibid., 237.
398. Houlberg 2005: 28.
399. Jil and Jil 2009: 140.
400. Marcelin 1950b: 123.
401. Mambo Michele, "Haitian Voodoo Glossary Terms."
402. Beauvoir 2008b: 211. The translation is from Jil and Jil, personal correspondence.

403. Jil and Jil 2009: 269.
404. See Courlander's song 43.
405. Jil and Jil 2009: 88.
406. Segurola and Rassinoux 2000: 223. See Marcelin's song 163 for Chango and Roumain's song 22 for Loko.
407. Marcelin 1950b: 123; Valdman, Iskrova, Pierre, and André 2007: 187.
408. Anglade 1998: 93; Segurola and Rassinoux 2000: 136.
409. Marcelin 1950b: 123; Valdman, Iskrova, Pierre, and André 2007: 187.
410. Anglade 1998: 92–93.
411. Bellegarde-Smith 2005: 28.
412. See Segurola and Rassinoux 2000: 235.
413. Mambo Michele, "Haitian Voodoo Glossary Terms"; Valdman, Iskrova, Pierre, and André 2007.
414. Freeman 2004: 243.
415. Ibid., 244. For good photographs of Vodou *drapo,* see Hurbon 1993.
416. Freeman 2004: 244.
417. See Rouget 2001.
418. Freeman 2004: 247.
419. See Averill 2009: 106; Métraux 1958: 103–104.
420. Beauvoir 2008b: 377.
421. Jil and Jil, personal correspondence.
422. Beauvoir 2008b: 175.
423. Ibid., 148.
424. Averill 2009: 106.
425. Jil and Jil 2009: 121.
426. Averill 2009: 104.
427. Freeman 2004: 233.
428. Roumain 1943: 142.
429. Jil and Jil 2009: 142.
430. Freeman 2004: 251.
431. Breure 2006: 282.
432. Rouget 2001: 102.
433. Brand 2000b: 93.
434. Segurola and Rassinoux 2000: 499.
435. Breure 2006.
436. Orubu 2001: 11.
437. See Marcelin's song 206.
438. Freeman 2004: 270.
439. Beauvoir 2008b: 205.
440. Ibid., 258.
441. Freeman 2004: 276.
442. Jil and Jil 2009: 43.
443. Freeman 2004: 278.
444. Ibid., 279–280.
445. Roumain 1943: 140.
446. Freeman 2004: 280.
447. Férère 2005: 53.
448. Freeman 2004: 288.
449. Jil and Jil 2009: 96.
450. Marcelin 1950a: 78.
451. Ibid., 79.
452. Ibid., 120.
453. Ibid., 80.
454. Lescot and Magloire 2002.
455. Marcelin 1950a: 80.
456. See ibid., 81.
457. Ibid., 82.
458. Marcelin 1950a: 84.
459. See Brand 2000b: 7.
460. Jil and Jil 2009: 95.
461. Consentino 1995: 33.
462. Ibid., 33.
463. Jil and Jil 2009: 99, 277.
464. Ibid., 99.
465. Ibid., 98.
466. Hurbon 2008: 271.
467. Arthur and Dash 1999.
468. Jil and Jil 2009: 99.
469. Lola and Brown 1995: 228.
470. Beauvoir 2008b: 173.
471. Ibid.
472. See Férère 2005: 50.
473. Consentino 1995: 33.
474. Jil and Jil 2009: 100.
475. Beauvoir-Dominique 1995: 162.
476. Férère 2005: 54.
477. Averill 2009: 154.
478. Seiderer 2008: 398.
479. Murrell 2010: 31, 34, 47.
480. Segurola and Rassinoux 2000: 253.
481. Freeman 2004: 291.
482. Férère 2005: 78.
483. Freeman 2004: 297.
484. Jil and Jil 2009: 221.
485. Ibid., 295.
486. Freeman 2004: 301.
487. Segurola and Rassinoux 2000: 242.
488. Ibid., 57.
489. Freeman 2004: 302.

490. Beauvoir and Dominique 2003: 54–77.
491. Averill 2009: 101.
492. Freeman 2004: 309.
493. Averill 2009: 151; Beauvoir 2008b: 27.
494. Beauvoir 2006: 131.
495. Métraux 1958.
496. Beauvoir 2008b: 278.
497. Freeman 2004: 339; Mambo Michele, "Haitian Voodoo Glossary Terms."
498. Wilcken 1992: 43.
499. Consentino 1995: 51.
500. Jil and Jil 2009: 27.
501. Ibid., 373.
502. Valdman, Iskrova, Pierre, and André 2007: 258.
503. Freeman 2004: 329.
504. Beauvoir 2006: 132.
505. Ibid. See also Rouget 2001 for photographs of such scarifications.
506. See Beauvoir 2008b; Chapter 6 in this volume.
507. Soimaud, personal correspondence.
508. Métraux 1958: 65.
509. Blier 1995: 85.
510. Brand 2000b: 37.
511. Freeman 2004: 330.
512. Ibid., 331.
513. Beauvoir 2008b: 307.
514. Freeman 2004: 333.
515. Thompson 1995: 104; Schwegler, personal correspondence.
516. Freeman 2004: 333. For good examples of *gangans,* see Deren 2007.
517. See Lescot and Magloire 2002.
518. Freeman 2004: 335.
519. Ibid., 336.
520. Ibid.
521. Beauvoir 2008a: 188.
522. Jil and Jil 2009: 219, 220.
523. Beauvoir 2008b: 194.
524. Marcelin 1950b: 145–147.
525. Ibid., 145.
526. Ibid.; Jil and Jil 2009: 215.
527. Marcelin 1950b: 146.
528. Jil and Jil 2009: 218.
529. Marcelin 1950b: 146.
530. Freeman 2004: 336.
531. Beauvoir 2008b: 220.
532. Marcelin 1950b: 181–190.
533. Ibid., 181.
534. Férère 2005: 57.
535. Marcelin 1950b: 182.
536. Ibid., 185.
537. Ibid., 186.
538. Ibid.
539. Férère 2005: 57.
540. Jil and Jil 2009: 148.
541. Beauvoir 2008a: 188.
542. Höftmann 2003: 373.
543. See Marcelin 1950b: 193–194.
544. Brand 2000b: 41.
545. See Price-Mars's song 3 in this volume.
546. Freeman 2004: 379.
547. Ibid., 337.
548. See Marcelin's song 15, 16 and Roumain's song 17.
549. Freeman 2004: 338.
550. Jil and Jil 2009: 30.
551. Roumain 1943: 141.
552. Freeman 2004: 343; Valdman, Iskrova, Pierre, and André 2007: 271.
553. Averill 2009: 106.
554. Freeman 2004: 345.
555. Ibid.
556. Consentino 1995: 58; Freeman 2004: 346.
557. Brand 2000b: 42.
558. Freeman 2004: 346.
559. Ibid., 347.
560. Férère 2005: 58; Chapter 6 in this volume.
561. See J.L.'s song 11.
562. See J.L.'s song 65; Jil and Jil 2009: 316.
563. See J.L.'s song 82.
564. Férère 2005: 58.
565. See the songs for Gran Bwa in Beauvoir 2008b: 198–199.
566. Bob Corbett's List, available online at http://www.webster.edu/~corbetre/haiti-archive (accessed 2010).
567. Beauvoir-Dominique 1995: 159.
568. Consentino 1995: 43.
569. Marcelin 1950b: 177–178.
570. Férère 2005: 61.
571. Marcelin 1950b: 177.
572. For the remainder of the entry, see ibid., 177–178.
573. Ibid., 178.
574. See ibid., 93–98.
575. Beauvoir 2008b: 205.

576. See Marcelin's song 64.
577. For the remainder of the entry, see Marcelin 1950a: 94–96.
578. See Marcelin's songs 64–74.
579. Freeman 2004: 357.
580. Ibid., 358.
581. Fleurant 2006b; Métraux 1958: 162.
582. Beauvoir 2006: 126.
583. Jil and Jil 2009: 278.
584. Ibid., 279.
585. Lola and Brown 1995: 228.
586. Freeman 2004: 359.
587. See Beauvoir 2008b: 354; Marcelin's song 105.
588. Freeman 2004: 362.
589. Ibid.
590. Beauvoir 2008a: 188; Roumain 1943: 141.
591. Férère 2005: 65.
592. Wilcken 1992: 22.
593. Freeman 2004: 363.
594. Averill 2009: 104.
595. Jil and Jil 2009: 318.
596. Wilcken 1992: 46.
597. Freeman 2004: 365.
598. Consentino 1995: 32, 58.
599. Beauvoir 2008b: 243.
600. Freeman 2004: 367.
601. Jil and Jil 2009: 123.
602. Ibid., 361.
603. For the next five sentences, see Honorin 1997: 8.
604. Métraux 1958: 25.
605. See Courlander's song 34.
606. Freeman 2004: 373.
607. Averill 2009: 151; Beauvoir 2008b: 214.
608. Rigaud 1953: 67.
609. Dayan 1995: 37. For a Jan Zonbi song, see Beauvoir 2008b: 215.
610. Courlander 1939: 68.
611. Freeman 2004: 375–378.
612. Marcenat, personal correspondence.
613. Freeman 2004: 382; Valdman, Iskrova, Pierre, and André 2007: 304.
614. Freeman 2004: 382.
615. Ibid., 395.
616. Mambo Michele, "Haitian Voodoo Glossary Terms."
617. Jil and Jil 2009: 104.
618. Ibid., 94, 107.
619. Ibid., 251.
620. Ibid., 106.
621. Freeman 2004: 401.
622. Ibid., 402.
623. Comhaire-Sylvain 1951: 64.
624. Brand 2000b: 55.
625. For this entry, see Jil and Jil 2009: 251.
626. Freeman 2004: 404.
627. Ibid., 410.
628. Lola and Brown 1995: 233.
629. Freeman 2004: 407.
630. Averill 2009: 103.
631. Métraux 1958: 76.
632. Mambo Racine Sans But, "The Ancestors in Haitian Vodou," available online at http://www.africaspeaks.com (accessed 2010).
633. Courlander 1939: 163.
634. Jil and Jil 2009: 331.
635. Laman (1936:213-214).
636. Freeman 2004: 409.
637. See Averill 2009: 150.
638. Freeman 2004: 412.
639. Ibid., 413.
640. Jil and Jil 2009: 268.
641. Ibid.
642. Freeman 2004: 414; Valdman, Iskrova, Pierre, and André 2007: 327.
643. For an important study with photographs, see Rouget 2001: 33–46, 86.
644. Brand 2000b: 11–12.
645. Jil and Jil 2009: 156.
646. Freeman 2004: 415.
647. Ibid.
648. Weaver 2002: 443.
649. Maniga 2010: 19.
650. Beauvoir 2008a: 188; Métraux 1958: 76.
651. Freeman 2004: 416.
652. Férère 2005: 57.
653. Fleurant 2006b: 50; Freeman 2004: 420.
654. Wilcken 1992: 48.
655. Courlander 1939: 66; Freeman 2004: 423.
656. Wilcken 1992: 34.
657. Freeman 2004: 423.
658. Beauvoir 2008b: 406; Freeman 2004: 424.
659. Anglade 1998: 119.
660. Beauvoir 2008b: 243.
661. Soimaud, personal correspondence.
662. Danmolé 2008: 212.
663. Freeman 2004: 428–429.

664. Ibid., 434.
665. Ibid., 437.
666. Ibid., 438.
667. Averill 2009: 106.
668. Beauvoir 2008a: 189.
669. Freeman 2004: 439.
670. Fleurant 2006b: 49.
671. See Averill 2009: 150.
672. Laman 1936: 721; Swartenbroeckx 1973: 446.
673. Ethnologue website, available online at http://www.ethnologue.com (accessed 2010).
674. Freeman 2004: 441.
675. Ibid., 442.
676. Ibid., 49.
677. Ibid., 449.
678. Marcenat, personal correspondence.
679. Consentino 1995: 50.
680. Freeman 2004: 450.
681. Thompson 1995: 112.
682. Freeman 2004: 397.
683. See Rouget 2001.
684. Métraux 1958: 80.
685. Beauvoir 2008b: 321.
686. Jil and Jil 2009: 165.
687. Segurola and Rassinoux 2000: 294. See Marcelin's song 163 for Chango in this volume.
688. BBC, "Haiti Mobs Lynch Voodoo Priests over Cholera Fears," December 24, 2010, available online at http://www.bbc.co.uk (accessed 2010).
689. Gerald Murray, personal correspondence, 2010.
690. Ibid.
691. Jil and Jil, personal correspondence.
692. Ibid.
693. Jil and Jil 2009: 327–328; Rouget 2001.
694. Wilcken 1992: 121.
695. Freeman 2004: 462.
696. Ibid., 463.
697. Ibid.
698. Mambo Michele, "Haitian Voodoo Glossary Terms."
699. Freeman 2004: 465; Mambo Michele, "Haitian Voodoo Glossary Terms."
700. Freeman 2004: 465.
701. Ibid.
702. For the next sentences, see Jil and Jil 2009: 200.
703. Férère 2005: 66.
704. Beauvoir 2008a: 190.
705. Ibid.
706. Freeman 2004: 471.
707. For songs, see Beauvoir 2008b: 314.
708. Rigaud 1953: 46.
709. Célestin-Mégie 2003; Freeman 2004: 486.
710. Jil and Jil 2009: 302.
711. Freeman 2004: 486.
712. Ibid., 487.
713. Ibid., 489.
714. Ibid.
715. See J.L.'s songs 99–100.
716. Freeman 2004: 485.
717. Marcelin 1950b: 91; Soimaud, personal correspondence.
718. Brown 1991: 63.
719. Ibid., 65.
720. Ibid.
721. Ibid., 66–67.
722. Freeman 2004: 498.
723. Mambo Michele, "Haitian Voodoo Glossary Terms."
724. Freeman 2004: 500.
725. Ibid.
726. Beauvoir 2008b: 153.
727. Ibid., 311.
728. Ibid., 438.
729. Roumain 1943: 14.
730. See Marcelin 1950b: 67.
731. See McAlister 2002.
732. Mambo Michele, "Haitian Voodoo Glossary Terms."
733. Beauvoir 2008b: 277.
734. Laman 1936: 349; note that Jil and Jil 2009: 275 suggest that *kwa kwa* is a Hausa word.
735. Roumain 1943: 140.
736. Freeman 2004: 509.
737. See Marcelin 1950a: 104.
738. Freeman 2004: 515.
739. Roumain 1943: 64.
740. See Boulton's song 61. The translation was suggested by Jil and Jil, personal correspondence.
741. Beauvoir 2008b: 234.
742. Freeman 2004: 522.
743. Marcenat, personal correspondence.
744. Hurbon 2008: 267; Jil and Jil 2009: 54.
745. Jil and Jil 2009: 219.
746. Kaplan 2008: 139.

747. Murrell 2010: 29.
748. Wilcken 1992: 43.
749. Ibid.
750. Comhaire-Sylvain 1951: 63.
751. Freeman 2004: 532.
752. Blier 1995: 82.
753. Thompson 1995: 104–108.
754. Segurola and Rassinoux 2000: 240.
755. Freeman 2004: 533.
756. Jil and Jil 2009: 326.
757. Marcelin 1950b: 67.
758. Freeman 2004: 535.
759. Ibid.; Roumain 1943: 142.
760. Jil and Jil 2009: 132.
761. Consentino 2006; Freeman 2004: 539.
762. Valdman, Iskrova, Pierre, and André 2007: 629.
763. Férère 2005: 69; Marcelin 1950a: 119–122.
764. Thompson 1995: 114.
765. See Marcelin's song 87.
766. See Marcelin's song 88.
767. See Marcelin 1950a: 122.
768. Jil and Jil 2009: 132.
769. Freeman 2004: 543
770. Brown 1991: 76.
771. Métraux 1958: 178.
772. Segurola and Rassinoux 2000: 210.
773. Marcelin 1950a: 89–90.
774. Freeman 2004: 549.
775. Courlander 1939: 48.
776. Marcelin 1950a: 15–24.
777. Férère 2005: 70.
778. Freeman 2004: 551; Marcelin 1950a: 16–17.
779. Jil and Jil 2009: 79.
780. Marcelin 1950a: 15–18.
781. Férère 2005: 70.
782. Marcelin 1950a: 17–18.
783. Ibid., 19.
784. Jil and Jil 2009: 81.
785. Marcelin 1950a: 22.
786. Férère 2005: 70.
787. Marcelin 1950a: 24.
788. Marcelin 1950b: 21.
789. Jil and Jil 2009: 238.
790. For the previous sentences, see Jil and Jil 2009: 237–239.
791. See Adoukonou and Bamunoba 1979: 263.
792. Badejo 2008: 195.
793. Jil and Jil 2009: 82.
794. See Segurola and Rassinoux 2000: 329–330.
795. See Férère 2005: 73.
796. Freeman 2004: 553.
797. Ibid., 554.
798. Beauvoir 2008b: 316.
799. Freeman 2004: 554.
800. Jil and Jil 2009: 208; 276.
801. Averill 2009: 153.
802. Laman 1936: 391.
803. Freeman 2004: 555.
804. J.L.'s songs 45–46.
805. Jil and Jil 2009: 172.
806. For several songs dedicated to Lenglensou, see Beauvoir 2008b: 245–247, 262.
807. Jil and Jil 2009: 175.
808. Segurola and Rassinoux 2000: 331–332.
809. Beauvoir 2008b: 219, 251.
810. Freeman 2004: 557.
811. Ibid.
812. Sollier 1908.
813. Blier 1995: 87.
814. Soyinka 2008: 44.
815. Freeman 2004: 555.
816. Beauvoir 2008b: 322.
817. See J.L.'s song 51
818. Beauvoir 2008b: 252.
819. Freeman 2004: 562.
820. Ibid.
821. Ibid., 565.
822. Ibid.
823. Ibid., 570.
824. Sachnine 1997: 153.
825. Freeman 2004: 570; Jil and Jil 2009: 152.
826. Beauvoir-Dominique 1995: 158.
827. Jil and Jil 2009: 152.
828. Férère 2005: 74.
829. Brown 1995: 208.
830. Beauvoir 2008a: 190.
831. See Anglade 1998: 139.
832. Marcelin 1950a: 41–49.
833. Brand 2000b: 64; Segurola and Rassinoux 2000: 339.
834. Freeman 2004: 574.
835. Blier 1995: 86.
836. Brand 2000b: 3–4.
837. Freeman 2004: 574.

838. Jil and Jil 2009: 53, 72, 323.
839. Freeman 2004: 576; Taiwo 2008: 99.
840. Freeman 2004: 576.
841. Beauvoir 2008a: 187; Oyèláràn 2008: 76.
842. Oyèláràn 2008: 76.
843. Beauvoir 2008b: 313.
844. Ibid., 257.
845. Taiwo 2008: 96.
846. See Blier 1995: 67.
847. Taiwo 2008: 107.
848. Brand 2000b: 21.
849. Beauvoir 2008a: 190.
850. Freeman 2004: 538.
851. Conner 2005.
852. Freeman 2004: 584.
853. Ibid.
854. Ibid., 586.
855. Murrell 2010: 48.
856. Freeman 2004: 586.
857. Freeman 2004: 588.
858. Ibid.
859. Ibid.
860. Roumain's song 38.
861. Bellegarde-Smith 2006: 101.
862. See Anonymous 1985: 25.
863. Beauvoir 2008a: 190; Jil and Jil 2009: 206.
864. Beauvoir-Dominique 1995: 159.
865. Beauvoir 2008b: 284; Thompson 1995: 105.
866. Laman 1936: 480.
867. See Courlander's song 40.
868. Freeman 2004: 589.
869. Beauvoir-Dominique 1995: 169.
870. Freeman 2004: 592.
871. Ibid., 597.
872. Blier 1995: 85.
873. Brand 2000b: 70.
874. Segurola and Rassinoux 2000: 362.
875. Murrell 2010: 42–45.
876. Valdman, Iskrova, Pierre, and André 2007: 455.
877. Beauvoir 2008a: 191.
878. Jil and Jil 2009: 183.
879. Freeman 2004: 601–603.
880. Beauvoir 2008a: 27.
881. Métraux 1958: 158–159, 184.
882. Segurola and Rassinoux 2000: 290.
883. Roumain 1943: 111.
884. Beauvoir-Dominique 1995.
885. Thompson 1993: 146.
886. Beauvoir 2008b: 281.
887. Valdman, Iskrova, Pierre, and André 2007: 459.
888. Ibid., 460.
889. Ibid.
890. Freeman 2004: 604.
891. Ibid.
892. Mambo Michele, "Haitian Voodoo Glossary Terms."
893. Freeman 2004: 604.
894. Comhaire-Sylvain 1951: 63.
895. Freeman 2004: 607.
896. Beauvoir 2008b: 296.
897. Séverin 2000: 90.
898. Marcelin 1950b: 123–139; Valdman, Iskrova, Pierre, and André 2007: 464.
899. Soimaud, personal correspondence.
900. Férère 2005: 77.
901. Freeman 2004: 607.
902. Marcelin 1950b: 124.
903. Jil and Jil 2009: 40.
904. Marcelin's song 209.
905. See Marcelin's song 210.
906. For the previous sentences, see Marcelin 1950b: 124–132.
907. Férère 2005: 77.
908. See Marcelin's songs 211–214.
909. Marcelin's song 216 and 217 are sung to the Marasa.
910. Marcelin 1950b: 134–138.
911. Segurola and Rassinoux 2000: 204.
912. Rouget 2001: 102.
913. Ibid., 53.
914. See Matsushita 1997.
915. Beauvoir 2008b: 264.
916. See Courlander's song 38 in this volume.
917. Dayan 1995: 33; Freeman 2004: 610.
918. Averill 2009: 153.
919. Jil and Jil 2009: 271.
920. Freeman 2004: 610.
921. Segurola and Rassinoux 2000: 470.
922. Conner 2005; Lescot and Magloire 2002.
923. Beauvoir 2008b: 373.
924. Consentino 1995: 43–44.
925. Ibid., 44.
926. Murrell 2010: 73.

927. Beauvoir-Dominique 1995: 161.
928. Freeman 2004: 612.
929. Ibid., 612–613.
930. Freze 1992: 207.
931. Freeman 2004: 614.
932. Beauvoir 2008a: 191.
933. Murrell 2010: 76.
934. Breure 2006: 282.
935. Jil and Jil 2009: 40, 68.
936. Segurola and Rassinoux 2000: 345.
937. Ibid., 469.
938. Beauvoir 2008b: 428; Segurola and Rassinoux 2000: 21.
939. Rouget 2001.
940. Beauvoir 2008b: 254, 347.
941. Consentino 1995: 228.
942. Lola and Brown 1995: 228.
943. Freeman 2004: 616.
944. Beauvoir 2008a: 190; Freeman 2004: 617.
945. Jil and Jil 2009: 135.
946. Freeman 2004: 618.
947. Mambo Michele, "Haitian Voodoo Glossary Terms."
948. Jil and Jil 2009: 54.
949. Freeman 2004: 618–619.
950. Courlander 1939: 2.
951. Freeman 2004: 623–624.
952. Ibid., 629.
953. Mambo Michele, "Haitian Voodoo Glossary Terms."
954. See Métraux 1958: 179.
955. Métraux 1958; Rouget 1991.
956. Freeman 2004: 633.
957. Beauvoir 2008b: 185.
958. Férère 2005: 78; Josué and Dubois 2008: 336.
959. Jil and Jil 2009: 158.
960. Averill 2009: 152.
961. Freeman 2004: 636.
962. Ibid.
963. Jil and Jil 2009: 327.
964. Freeman 2004: 639.
965. Mambo Michele, "Haitian Voodoo Glossary Terms."
966. Métraux 1958: 76.
967. Courlander 1939: 188.
968. Freeman 2004: 642.
969. Métraux 1958: 104.
970. See Courlander's song 44 and Beauvoir 2008b: 314.
971. Jil and Jil 2009: 202.
972. Freeman 2004: 643.
973. Jil and Jil 2009: 320.
974. Freeman 2004: 650.
975. Jil and Jil 2009: 170.
976. Freeman 2004: 652.
977. Ibid., 653.
978. Ibid., 655; Roumain 1943: 143.
979. Freeman 2004: 655.
980. Beauvoir 2008b: 227.
981. See Höftmann 2003: 307.
982. Brand 2000b: 15.
983. Jil and Jil 2009: 134
984. Freeman 2004: 655.
985. Beauvoir 2008b.
986. Freeman 2004: 655.
987. Cited in Thompson 1995: 113. For information on Victor Schoelcher, see http://www.senat.fr/evenement/victor_schoelcher/abolitions.html (accessed 2010).
988. Freeman 2004: 656.
989. See Courlander's song 34.
990. Freeman 2004: 660.
991. Ibid., 663.
992. Ibid.
993. See Jil and Jil 2009: 117, 204 for the next sentences.
994. David K. Jordan, "The Bantu Expansion," available online at http://weber.ucsd.edu/~dkjordan/resources/clarifications/BantuExpansion.html (accessed 2010).
995. See Morisseau-Leroy 2001.
996. See Roumain's song 15.
997. Jil and Jil 2009: 111.
998. Marcelin 1950b: 90.
999. Jil and Jil 2009.
1000. Freeman 2004: 671.
1001. Mambo Michele, "Haitian Voodoo Glossary Terms."
1002. Freeman 2004: 672.
1003. Marcelin 1950b: 63.
1004. Freeman 2004: 674; Wilcken 1992: 41.
1005. Wilcken 1992: 40.
1006. Brand 2000b: 37.
1007. Wilcken 1992: 30.

1008. Ibid., 40.
1009. Freeman 2004: 674.
1010. Ibid.
1011. Freeman 2004.
1012. See Marcelin 1950b: 33–78.
1013. Férère 2005: 82.
1014. Jil and Jil 2009: 129.
1015. Ibid., 130.
1016. Courlander 1939.
1017. Marcelin 1950b: 33–35.
1018. Jil and Jil 2009: 130.
1019. Soyinka 2008: 42.
1020. Adepegba 2008: 110–121.
1021. See Brand 2000b: 43.
1022. Orubu 2001: 12.
1023. Marcelin 1950b: 71.
1024. Ibid., 49–54.
1025. Férère 2005: 81.
1026. Jil and Jil 2009: 114; Métraux 1958: 22.
1027. See Marcelin's song 123.
1028. Marcelin's song 124.
1029. Marcelin's song 125.
1030. Marcelin 1950b: 51–53.
1031. Marcelin's song 129.
1032. Ibid.
1033. Freeman 2004: 675.
1034. Férère 2005: 82.
1035. Marcelin 1950b: 74–75.
1036. Marcelin's song 154.
1037. See Boukman Eksperyans 1991.
1038. Marcelin 1950b: 77.
1039. See ibid., 59–68.
1040. Férère 2005: 85.
1041. See Marcelin's song 132.
1042. See Marcelin's songs 134–136.
1043. See Marcelin 1950b: 61.
1044. Marcelin's song 137 is sung as these items are offered to the lwa.
1045. Jil and Jil 2009: 369.
1046. See Marcelin's song 138.
1047. Marcelin's song 139.
1048. Marcelin's song 140.
1049. Marcelin's song 141 is sung for Ogou Feray at that moment.
1050. See Marcelin's song 142.
1051. Marcelin 1950b: 78.
1052. Valdman, Iskrova, Pierre, and André 2007: 516.
1053. Jil and Jil 2009: 128; see Courlander's song 4 in this volume.
1054. Freeman 2004: 676; Valdman, Iskrova, Pierre, and André 2007: 517.
1055. Roumain 1943: 27.
1056. See Marcelin's song 163; Roumain's song 5.
1057. Marcelin 1950b: 72.
1058. See Marcelin's song 7.
1059. See Atwood Mason 2002.
1060. See Fortere, Joseph, and Fevrier 1997.
1061. Freeman 2004: 682.
1062. Ibid.
1063. Marcelin 1950b: 75.
1064. Beauvoir 2008b: 347.
1065. Jil and Jil 2009: 297.
1066. Blier 1995: 82; Brand 2000b: 46.
1067. Segurola and Rassinoux 2000: 239.
1068. Freeman 2004: 685.
1069. Segurola and Rassinoux 2000: 243.
1070. Jil and Jil 2009: 269.
1071. Murrell 2010: 46.
1072. Ibid., 85.
1073. Jil and Jil 2009: 302.
1074. Freeman 2004: 685.
1075. Beauvoir 2008b: 214.
1076. Ibid., 218.
1077. Jil and Jil 2009: 22.
1078. Brand 2000b: 46.
1079. Höftmann 2003: 183.
1080. Segurola and Rassinoux 2000: 179
1081. See Roumain's song 17.
1082. Freeman 2004: 685.
1083. Valdman, Iskrova, Pierre, and André 2007: 25.
1084. Freeman 2004: 685.
1085. See Rouget 2001: 98.
1086. Freeman 2004: 685.
1087. Ibid., 686.
1088. Métraux 1958: 171–189.
1089. Adepegba 2008: 114, 118.
1090. See Brand 2000b: 88.
1091. Segurola and Rassinoux 2000: 471.
1092. Blier 1995: 82; Rouget 2001: 33–46.
1093. Wilcken 1992: 2. Roumain's song 15 is an example of a song dedicated to a drum lwa, Hountò-Legui.
1094. Freeman 2004: 686.

1095. Segurola and Rassinoux 2000: 243.
1096. Freeman 2004: 686.
1097. Beauvoir 2008b: 211.
1098. Férère 2005: 62.
1099. Freeman 2004: 686.
1100. Brand 2000b: 47; Rouget 2001: 12–15.
1101. Segurola and Rassinoux 2000: 241.
1102. Ibid., 243.
1103. Freze 1992: 208.
1104. Férère 2005: 86.
1105. Abiodun 2008: 56; Oyèláràn 2008: 75.
1106. Freeman 2004: 301.
1107. Marcelin 1950b: 16.
1108. Ibid.
1109. Métraux 1958: 275–276.
1110. See Consentino 1995: 30–32 for the previous sentences.
1111. Thompson 1995: 110.
1112. Ibid., 114.
1113. Freeman 2004: 692.
1114. Ibid., 699.
1115. Déita 2004: 401.
1116. Segurola and Rassinoux 2000: 96.
1117. Murrell 2010: 16.
1118. Beauvoir 2008b: 316.
1119. Freeman 2004: 701.
1120. Ibid., 708.
1121. Ibid., 710.
1122. Ibid., 714.
1123. Ibid., 719.
1124. Roumain 1944: 200–207.
1125. Fleurant 2007; Wilcken 1992: 121.
1126. Blier 1995: 86.
1127. Wilcken 1992: 43.
1128. See Jil and Jil 2009: 267, 271.
1129. Murrell 2010: 76.
1130. Jil and Jil 2009: 131; Marcelin 1950b: 35.
1131. Jil and Jil 2009: 212.
1132. Dayan 1995: 292, fn. 70.
1133. Beauvoir-Dominique 1995: 158.
1134. Murrell 2010: 76.
1135. Blier 1995: 86.
1136. Jil and Jil 2009: 200–210.
1137. Ibid., 213.
1138. Beauvoir 2008a: 193.
1139. Freeman 2004: 722.
1140. Ibid., 724.
1141. Ibid., 725.
1142. Ibid., 727.
1143. Ibid., 728.
1144. Ibid., 729.
1145. Ibid., 733.
1146. Roumain 1943: 143.
1147. Marcelin 1950b: 128.
1148. Jil and Jil 2009.
1149. Segurola and Rassinoux 2000: 235.
1150. Freeman 2004: 736.
1151. Herskovits 1967: 64.
1152. Freeman 2004: 741.
1153. Ibid., 748.
1154. Ibid.
1155. Ibid.
1156. Métraux 1958: 178.
1157. Segurola and Rassinoux 2000: 470.
1158. Jil and Jil 2009.
1159. Murrell 2010: 85.
1160. Freeman 2004: 752.
1161. Ibid., 753.
1162. Ibid., 761.
1163. Ibid.; Jil and Jil 2009: 36.
1164. Valdman, Iskrova, Pierre, and André 2007: 591.
1165. Jil and Jil 2009: 268.
1166. Mambo Michele, "Haitian Voodoo Glossary Terms."
1167. Freeman 2004: 766.
1168. Ibid., 767.
1169. Ibid.
1170. Jil and Jil, personal correspondence; Wilcken 1992: 122.
1171. Blier 1995: 85; Jil and Jil 2009: 304.
1172. Roumain 1943: 143.
1173. Beauvoir-Dominique 1995: 167.
1174. Freeman 2004: 768.
1175. Beauvoir 2008b: 158.
1176. Ibid., 315.
1177. Mambo Michele, "Haitian Voodoo Glossary Terms."
1178. Jil and Jil 2009: 306.
1179. Thompson 1995: 112–113.
1180. Freeman 2004: 774.
1181. Jil and Jil 2009: 150, 154.
1182. Orubu 2001: 8–9.
1183. See Marcelin 1950b: 111.
1184. Mambo Michele, "Haitian Voodoo Glossary Terms."

1185. Freeman 2004: 778.

1186. Beauvoir 2008a: 193–196.

1187. Jil and Jil 2009: 131, 276; Murrell 2010: 76.

1188. Freeman 2004: 783.

1189. Thompson 1993: 153.

1190. Jil and Jil 2009: 204.

1191. Thompson 1995: 92.

1192. Freeman 2004: 784.

1193. Wilcken 1992: 122.

1194. Freeman 2004: 786.

1195. Ibid., 788.

1196. Ibid., 790.

1197. Ibid., 791.

1198. Valdman, Iskrova, Pierre, and André 2007: 615.

1199. See Averill 2009: 103; Iskrova, Pierre, and André 2007: 615.

1200. Freeman 2004: 791.

1201. See ibid., 792; McAlister 2002: 200.

1202. Jil and Jil 2009: 255–262.

1203. Thompson 1995: 107.

1204. See Jil and Jil 2009: 255–262 for the next sentences.

1205. Freeman 2004: 793.

1206. Averill 2009: 106.

1207. Freeman 2004: 796.

1208. Ibid.

1209. Ibid., 800.

1210. Josué and Dubois 2008: 327.

1211. Ibid., 800–801.

1212. Hurbon 2008: 266; Jil and Jil 2009: 354.

1213. Jil and Jil 2009: 256–257.

1214. Métraux 1958: 343.

1215. Catholic anti-Vodou polemical literature is illustrated in Peters 1941; Smarth, Souffrant and Gayot 1963. The conciliatory Roman Catholic approach appears more recently in Fils-Aimé 2004; François 2003: 76; Joint 1999: 257–261. Protestants, and not Catholics, are now considered the greatest threat to Vodou.

1216. Freeman 2004: 801. Carrié Paultre (1965, 1971, 1990), who was a pastor, writes Haitian Creole novels on the putative virtues of conversion to Protestantism.

1217. Beauvoir 2008b: 265.

1218. Fleurant 2006b: 49.

1219. Freeman 2004: 804.

1220. Ibid., 808.

1221. Ibid., 810.

1222. Ibid.

1223. Ibid.

1224. Séverin 2000: 23, 28, 30, 44, 90, 114.

1225. Ibid., 90.

1226. Ibid., 114.

1227. Brand 2000b: 3.

1228. Valdman, Iskrova, Pierre, and André 2007: 634.

1229. Freeman 2004: 812.

1230. Marcelin 1950b: 61.

1231. Métraux 1958: 127–128.

1232. Beauvoir 2008a: 187–196 provides a list of 401 lwa and the rite and family to which each belongs.

1233. Fleurant 2006b.

1234. Wilcken 1992: 63–91.

1235. Freze 1992: 234.

1236. Ibid., 237.

1237. Consentino 1995: 48–50.

1238. Delaney 1983: 390.

1239. Ibid., 178.

1240. Beauvoir 2008b: 247.

1241. Ibid.

1242. Segurola and Rassinoux 2000: 470.

1243. Freeman 2004: 829.

1244. Jil and Jil, personal correspondence.

1245. Beauvoir 2008b: 158.

1246. Ibid., 224, 371–372.

1247. Freeman 2004: 830.

1248. Ibid.

1249. Freeman 2004: 827.

1250. Segurola and Rassinoux 2000: 238.

1251. Ibid.

1252. Ibid., 470.

1253. Jil and Jil 2009: 255.

1254. Beauvoir 2008b: 375.

1255. Swartenbroeckx 1973: 553.

1256. Freeman 2004: 835.

1257. Marcelin 1950b: 124–125.

1258. Brand 2000b: 97; Jil and Jil 2009: 115.

1259. Beauvoir and Dominique 2003: 139–181.

1260. Ibid., 172–173.

1261. Ibid., 155.

1262. Ibid., 175.

1263. Roumain 1943: 109.

1264. See Averill 2009: 106.

1265. See, e.g., the lyrics of "Hountò Legba," on Josué 2007, and the title of Beauvoir and Dominique 2003 (*Savalou E*).

1266. Jil and Jil 2009: 59.

1267. Freeman 2004: 841.

1268. Comhaire-Sylvain 1951: 63.

1269. See Courlander's song 34.

1270. Freeman 2004: 844.

1271. Ibid., 845.

1272. Oungan Alisma, personal correspondence.

1273. Courlander 1939: 88.

1274. Ibid.

1275. Marcelin 1950b: 41.

1276. See Marcelin's song 114.

1277. See Marcelin's song 115.

1278. See Marcelin's song 117.

1279. See Marcelin's songs 118–120.

1280. See Marcelin's song 121.

1281. Marcelin 1950a: 44–45.

1282. See Marcelin's song 122.

1283. Jil and Jil 2009: 336.

1284. Freeman 2004: 848.

1285. Brown 1991: 77; Freeman 2004: 848.

1286. See Wikipedia, s.v. "António I of Kongo," available online at http://en.wikipedia.org/wiki/Ant%C3%B3nio_I_of_Kongo (accessed 2010).

1287. Jil and Jil 2009: 231–233.

1288. Ibid., 234; Wikipedia, s.v. "Anthony of Padua," available online at http://en.wikipedia.org/wiki/Anthony_of_Padua (accessed 2010).

1289. Consentino 1995: 51.

1290. Freeman 2004: 850.

1291. Ibid., 852.

1292. Roumain 1943: 140.

1293. Beauvoir-Dominique 1995: 170.

1294. Jil and Jil 2009: 74.

1295. Freeman 2004: 853–854.

1296. Segurola and Rassinoux 2000: 470.

1297. Freeman 2004: 854.

1298. Ibid., 854.

1299. Ibid., 855.

1300. Comhaire-Sylvain 1951: 66.

1301. Wilcken 1992: 44.

1302. See Marcelin's song 99.

1303. Beauvoir 2008b: 287.

1304. Jil and Jil 2009: 243.

1305. Some authors consider Simbi female and others, male. Simbi is generally considered male except when represented with a fish tail and a human upper body with long hair: Jil and Jil, personal correspondence.

1306. Férère 2005: 89.

1307. See Marcelin 1950b: 13–28.

1308. Thompson 1995: 95.

1309. Roumain 1944: 144.

1310. Marcelin 1950b: 16.

1311. See Marcelin's song 100; Roumain 1944 (1946).

1312. Marcelin 1950b: 16.

1313. Ibid., 17.

1314. See Marcelin's song 101.

1315. See ibid.

1316. See Marcelin 1950b: 18; Musiques Paysannes d'Haïti 1997.

1317. See Marcelin's songs 103–109, which were sung for the wounded twenty-two-year-old Ti Jozèf.

1318. See Marcelin's song 104.

1319. See Marcelin's song 105.

1320. See Marcelin's song 106.

1321. Marcelin 1950b: 23.

1322. See Marcelin's song 107

1323. Marcelin 1950b: 22.

1324. Ibid., 24–28.

1325. See Höftmann 2003: 261; Marcelin 1950b: 18.

1326. Jil and Jil 2009: 229.

1327. Thompson 1995: 112.

1328. Laman 1936: 899 and Swartenbroeckx 1973: 578.

1329. See Michel and Bellegarde-Smith 2006: 141.

1330. Jil and Jil 2009: 243.

1331. Beauvoir 2008a: 196; Freeman 2004: 861.

1332. Métraux 1958: 22.

1333. Jil and Jil 2009: 158.

1334. Freeman 2004: 867.

1335. Valdman, Iskrova, Pierre, and André 2007: 60. See Marcelin's song 80 for an example.

1336. Férère 2005: 90.

1337. Beauvoir 2008b: 402.

1338. See Marcelin 1950b: 111.

1339. See Marcelin's song 190.

1340. See Marcelin's song 191.

1341. See Marcelin's song 195.

1342. Ibid.

1343. Segurola and Rassinoux 2000: 422.

1344. Ibid., 406.

1345. Freeman 2004: 869.

1346. Mambo Michele, "Haitian Voodoo Glossary Terms."

1347. Freeman 2004: 873.

1348. Ibid., 874–875.

1349. Ibid., 876.

1350. Jil and Jil 2009: 224.

1351. Beauvoir 2008b: 430; Freeman 2004: 877.

1352. Rigaud 1953: 46. Jil and Jil (2009: 369) point out that the Kikongo word *nkosa* (leopard) became *kosi* in Haitian Creole.

1353. Beauvoir 2008b: 309.

1354. Freeman 2004: 878.

1355. Jil and Jil 2009: 246.

1356. Freeman 2004: 879.

1357. Ibid., 880.

1358. Ibid.

1359. Ibid.

1360. Consentino 1995: 43.

1361. For the next sentences, see Jil and Jil 2009: 113.

1362. Freeman 2004: 883.

1363. Ibid., 885.

1364. Ibid., 888.

1365. Ibid.

1366. Thompson 1995: 99.

1367. Wilcken 1992: 29.

1368. Ibid., 44.

1369. Wilcken 1992.

1370. Ibid., 46.

1371. Valdman, Iskrova, Pierre, and André 2007: 692.

1372. For this entry, see Wilcken 1992.

1373. Freeman 2004: 890.

1374. Ibid., 893.

1375. Courlander 1939: 48.

1376. Beauvoir-Dominique 1995.

1377. Jil and Jil 2009: 138.

1378. Segurola and Rassinoux 2000: 109.

1379. Freeman 2004: 894.

1380. Ibid., 895.

1381. Roumain 1943: 117.

1382. Freeman 2004: 901.

1383. Ibid., 903.

1384. Beauvoir 2008b: 313.

1385. Métraux 1958: 163.

1386. Comhaire-Sylvain 1951: 63.

1387. Note that Brown 2006: 9 claims that it is the *gwo bonnanj* that cedes its place in the body, while Jil and Jil 2009 claim that it is the *ti bonnanj*. We follow Jil and Jil 2009 because the ground of life, the *gwo bonnanj*, should remain embodied during possession.

1388. Brown 2006: 11.

1389. Rouget 2001.

1390. Jil and Jil 2009: 278, 281.

1391. Beauvoir 2008b: 259.

1392. Lola and Brown 1995: 229.

1393. Métraux 1958: 162.

1394. Comhaire-Sylvain 1951: 64.

1395. Freeman 2004: 915.

1396. Jil and Jil 2009: 281.

1397. Freeman 2004: 920–921.

1398. Ibid., 921.

1399. Jil and Jil 2009: 319.

1400. Freeman 2004: 928.

1401. Jil and Jil 2009: 150.

1402. Beauvoir 2008b: 416; Jil and Jil 2009: 297.

1403. Averill 2009: 151.

1404. Ibid.

1405. Beauvoir 2008b: 253.

1406. Freeman 2004: 937.

1407. Ibid., 938.

1408. See Consentino 2006; Freeman 2004: 371.

1409. Jil and Jil 2009: 337.

1410. See Hurbon 1993.

1411. Freeman 2004: 941.

1412. Marcelin 1950b: 53.

1413. See McAlister 2002.

1414. Thompson 1995: 107.

1415. Beauvoir and Dominique 2003: 172.

1416. Marcelin 1950b: 63; Roumain 1943: 144.

1417. Roumain 1943: 144.

1418. Freeman 2004: 952.

1419. Valdman, Iskrova, Pierre, and André 2007: 741.

1420. Freeman 2004: 954.

1421. Jil and Jil 2009: 310.
1422. Roumain 1943: 145.
1423. Férère 2005: 78.
1424. Galembo 2005: 107.
1425. Beauvoir 2008b: 319.
1426. Blier 1995: 84.
1427. Thompson 1995: 102.
1428. Jil and Jil 2009: 310.
1429. Beauvoir-Dominique 1995: 158.
1430. See Segurola and Rassinoux 2000: 462.
1431. Freeman 2004: 957.
1432. Consentino 1995: 30.
1433. Jil and Jil 2009: 123.
1434. Beauvoir-Dominique 1995: 177.
1435. Mambo Michele, "Haitian Voodoo Glossary Terms."
1436. Freeman 2004: 958.
1437. Ibid., 961.
1438. Ibid., 962.
1439. Blier 1995: 80; Jil and Jil 2009: 23.
1440. Badejo 2008: 191.
1441. Anglade 1999: 193.
1442. Freeman 2004: 962.
1443. Blier 1995: 61.
1444. Brand 2000b: 87.
1445. Segurola and Rassinoux 2000: 469.
1446. Ibid., 470.
1447. Jil and Jil 2009.
1448. See Blier 1995: 62.
1449. Anglade 1998: 193.
1450. Beauvoir 2008b: 423–424.
1451. See, e.g., Beauvoir 2008b.
1452. Blier 1995: 79.
1453. The term *vodounsi* occurs in a few Haitian Vodou songs. See, e.g., Roumain's song 27.
1454. Freeman 2004: 962.
1455. Wilcken 1992: 93.
1456. Freeman 2004: 965.
1457. Ibid., 970.
1458. Jil and Jil 2009: 306.
1459. Ibid., 288.
1460. See Marcelin's song 19.
1461. Jil and Jil 2009: 130.
1462. Ibid., 288.
1463. Beauvoir-Dominique 1995: 168.
1464. Jil and Jil 2009: 307.
1465. Freeman 2004: 970.
1466. Beauvoir 2008a: 196.
1467. Métraux 1958: 22.
1468. Férère 2005: 93.
1469. Murrell 2010: 89.
1470. Beauvoir-Dominique 1995: 169.
1471. Métraux 1958: 30.
1472. Casimir 2000: 7.
1473. Freeman 2004: 979.
1474. Murrell 2010: 85.
1475. Roumain 1943: 144; Freeman 2004: 982.
1476. See Marcelin's song 74 for Grann Èzili.
1477. Courlander 1939: 46.
1478. See Courlander's song 33.
1479. See Courlander's song 35.
1480. Courlander 1939: 163.
1481. Valdman, Iskrova, Pierre, and André 2007: 460.
1482. Adepegba 2008: 116.
1483. Jil and Jil 2009: 149.
1484. Freeman 2004: 987.
1485. Ibid.
1486. See Marcelin's song 73 for Grann Èzili.
1487. Jil and Jil 2009: 93.
1488. Thompson 1995: 93.
1489. Beauvoir 2008b: 308.
1490. Beauvoir 2008b, 65.
1491. Segurola and Rassinoux 2000: 527.
1492. Freeman 2004: 989.
1493. Ibid., 992.
1494. Beauvoir 2008a: 196.
1495. Métraux 1958: 76.
1496. Averill 2009: 100.
1497. Ibid., 153.
1498. Beauvoir 2008b: 297.
1499. Freeman 2004: 992–993.
1500. Jil and Jil 2009: 276.
1501. Beauvoir 2008b: 317.
1502. See Jil and Jil 2009: 29.
1503. Freeman 2004: 994.
1504. Hurbon 2008: 270.
1505. Beauvoir-Dominique 1995: 158.
1506. Freeman 2004: 997.
1507. Férère 2005: 97.
1508. Brand 2000b: 2, 12.
1509. See Marcelin 1950b: 67.
1510. Freeman 2004: 999.
1511. Ibid.
1512. Mambo Michele, "Haitian Voodoo Glossary Terms."

1513. Beauvoir 2008b: 442.
1514. Freeman 2004: 1003.
1515. Courlander 1939: 46.
1516. Beauvoir 2008b: 442.
1517. See Frankétienne 1975.
1518. Davis 1988: 60.
1519. Métraux 1972: 283.
1520. Beauvoir and Dominique 2003: 175.
1521. Laman 1936: 821.
1522. Davis 1988: 57.
1523. Beauvoir 2008b: 258.

Appendix B. Outline of Haitian Creole Grammar

1. Examples of stative verbs are *believe, belong, know, like, love, see, smell,* and *think.*

2. Examples of non-stative verbs are *arrive, come, die, drink, drive, eat, get, go, jump, leave, play, read, start, stay, wait,* and *write.*

REFERENCES

——*

Abiodun, Rowland. 2008. "Who Was the First to Speak?" In *Òrìshà Devotion as World Religion,* ed. Jacob K. Olupona and Terry Rey, 51–69. Madison: University of Wisconsin Press.

Adepegba, Cornelius O. 2008. "Associated Place Names and Sacred Icons of Seven Yorùbá Deities." In *Òrìshà Devotion as World Religion,* ed. Jacob K. Olupona and Terry Rey, 106–127. Madison: University of Wisconsin Press.

Adoukonou, Barthélémy, and Y. K. Bamunoba. 1979. *La mort dans la vie africaine.* Paris: Présence Africaine and United Nations Educational, Scientific, and Cultural Organization.

Akíntúndé, Akínyẹmí. 2004. *Yorùbá Royal Poetry: A Socio-historical Exposition and Annotated Translation.* Bayreuth, Germany: Bayreuth African Studies Series.

Anglade, Pierre. 1998. *Inventaire étymologique des termes créoles des caraïbes d'orgine africaine.* Paris: L'Harmattan.

Anonymous. 1985. *Ti Koze sou Istwa Peyi Dayiti.* Port-au-Prince: Editions Henri Deschamps.

Arthur, Charles, and Michael Dash, eds. 1999. *Libète: A Haiti Anthology.* Princeton, N.J.: Markus Wiener.

Atwood Mason, Michael. 2002. *Living Santería.* Washington, D.C.: Smithsonian Institution Press.

Averill, Gage. 1997. *A Day for the Hunter, a Day for the Prey: Popular Music and Power in Haiti.* Chicago Studies in Ethnomusicology. Chicago: University of Chicago Press.

Badejo, Diedre L. 2008. The Pathways of Òsun as Cultural Synergy. In *Òrìshà Devotion as World Religion,* ed. Jacob K. Olupona and Terry Rey, 191–201. Madison: University of Wisconsin Press.

Beauvoir, Max G. 2006. "Herbs and Energy: The Holistic Medical System of the Haitian People." In *Haitian Vodou: Spirit, Myth, and Reality,* ed. Patrick Bellegarde-Smith and Claudine Michel, 112–133. Bloomington: Indiana University Press.

———. 2008a. *Lapriyè Ginen.* Port-au-Prince: Edisyon Près Nasyonal d Ayiti.

———. 2008b. *Le grand recueil sacré ou répertoire des chansons du vodou haïtien.* Port-au-Prince: Edisyon Près Nasyonal d Ayiti.

Beauvoir, Rachel, and Didier Dominique. 2003. *Savalou E.* Montreal: Les Éditions du Centre International de Documentation et d'Information Haïtienne, Caribéenne, et Afro-Canadienne.

Beauvoir-Dominique, Rachel. 1995. "Underground Realms of Being: Vodoun Magic." In *Sacred Arts of Haitian Vodou,* ed. Donald J. Consentino, 153–177. Los Angeles: Fowler Museum of Cultural History, University of California, Los Angeles.

Beckwith, Carol, and Angela Fisher. 1995. "The African Roots of Voodoo." *National Geographic* 188, no. 3 (August): 102–113.

Bellegarde-Smith, Patrick. 2006. "Resisting Freedom: Cultural Factors in Democracy—The Case for Haiti." In *Vodou in Haitian Life and Culture: Invisible Powers,* ed. Claudine Michel and Patrick Bellegarde-Smith, 101–115. New York: Palgrave Macmillan.

Bleek, Wilhelm H.I., and Lucy C. Lloyd. 1911 (1968). *Specimens of Bushman Folklore.* London: George Allen.

Blier, Suzanne Preson. 1995. "Vodun: West African Roots of Vodou." In *Sacred Arts of Haitian Vodou,* ed. Donald J. Consentino, 61–87. Los Angeles: Fowler Museum of Cultural History, University of California, Los Angeles.

Brand, Roger. 2000a. *Cultes vodoun et textes oraux des Wéménou du sud Bénin.* Munich: Lincom Europa.

———. 2000b. *Ethnographie et vocabulaire religieux des cultes vodoun.* Munich: Lincom Europa.

Breure, Marnel. 2006. *Het land van Legba: Voodoo in Afrika.* Amsterdam: Uitgeverij Augustus.

Brown, Karen McCarthy. 1987. "Plenty Confidence in Myself: The Initiation of a White Woman Scholar into Haitian Vodou." *Journal of Feminist Studies in Religion* 3, no. 1 (Spring): 67–76.

———. 1991. *Mama Lola: A Vodou Priestess in Brooklyn.* Comparative Studies in Religion and Society, 4. Berkeley: University of California Press.

———. 1995. "Serving the Spirits: The Ritual Economy of Haitian Vodou." In *Sacred Arts of Haitian Vodou,* ed. Donald J. Consentino, 205–223. Los Angeles: Fowler Museum of Cultural History, University of California, Los Angeles.

———. 2006. "Afro-Caribbean Spirituality: A Haitian Case Study." In *Vodou in Haitian Life and Culture: Invisible Powers,* ed. Claudine Michel and Patrick Bellegarde-Smith, 1–26. New York: Palgrave Macmillan.

Carvalho, José Jorge. 2008. "Yorùbá Sacred Songs in the New World." In *Òrìshà Devotion as World Religion,* ed. Jacob K. Olupona and Terry Rey, 416–435. Madison: University of Wisconsin Press.

Casimir, Jean. 2000. *Ayiti Toma/Haïti Chérie.* Port-au-Prince: Communication Plus.

Castor, Kesner. 1998. *Éthique vaudou.* Paris: L'Harmattan.

Célestin-Mégie, Émile. 2003. *Agasya Chwal Simbi.* Miami: Edisyon Mapou.

Chery, Pierre Michel. 2008. *Bèbè Golgota.* Port-au-Prince: Edisyon Près Nasyonal d Ayiti.

Christophe, Marc. 2004. "Epiphany of the Vodou Lwa in Hërsza Barjon's Painting." In *The Descent of the Lwa,* ed. Claudine Michel. Santa Barbara: Center for Black Studies Research.

Cohen, Richard A. 2001. *Ethics, Exegesis, and Philosophy.* Cambridge: Cambridge University Press.

Comhaire-Sylvain, Suzanne. 1951. "La chanson haïtienne." In *Haïti: Poètes noirs,* ed. Alioune Diop, 61–87. Paris: Éditions du Seuil.

Conner, Randy. 2005. "Rainbow's Children: Diversity of Gender and Sexuality in African-Diasporic Spiritual Traditions." In *Fragments of Bone: Neo-African Religions in a New World,* ed. Patrick Bellegarde-Smith, 143–166. Urbana: University of Illinois Press.

Consentino, Donald. 1995. *Sacred Arts of Haitian Vodou.* Los Angeles: Fowler Museum of Cultural History, University of California, Los Angeles.

———. 2006. "It's All for You, Sen Jak!" In *Vodou in Haitian Life and Culture: Invisible Powers,* ed. Claudine Michel and Patrick Bellegarde-Smith, 199–216. New York: Palgrave Macmillan.

Coret, Jacques. 1851. *L'ange conducteur dans la vrai dévotion.* Paris: A. Audiard.

Courlander, Harold. 1939. *Haiti Singing.* Chapel Hill: University of North Carolina Press.

———. 1939–1940. Unpublished manuscript. Special Collections Library, University of Michigan, Ann Arbor.

———. 1960. *The Drum and the Hoe: Life and Lore of the Haitian People.* Berkeley: University of California Press.

Danmolé, H. O. 2008. "Religious Encounter in Southwestern Nigeria: The Domestication of Islam among the Yorùbá." In *Òrìshà Devotion as World Religion,* ed. Jacob K. Olupona and Terry Rey, 202–221. Madison: University of Wisconsin Press.

Dauphin, Claude. 1986. *La musique du vaudou: Fonctions, structures, et styles.* Sherbrooke, Quebec: Éditions Naaman.
Davis, Wade. 1985. *The Serpent and the Rainbow.* New York: Simon and Schuster.
———. 1988. *Passage of Darkness: The Ethnobiology of the Haitian Zombie.* Chapel Hill: University of North Carolina Press.
Dayan, Joan. 1995. *Haiti, History, and the Gods.* Berkeley: University of California Press.
DeGraff, Michel. 2007. "Haitian Creole." In *Comparative Creole Syntax: Parallel Outlines of 18 Creole Grammars,* ed. John Holm and Peter Patrick, 101–126. London: Battlebridge.
Déita [Mercedes Guignard]. 2004. *La légende des loa vodou haïtien.* Port-au-Prince: Imprimeur II.
Delaney, John J. 1983. *Pocket Dictionary of Saints.* New York: Doubleday.
Desmangles, Leslie. 2006. "African Interpretations of the Christian Cross in Vodou." In *Vodou in Haitian Life and Culture: Invisible Powers,* ed. Claudine Michel and Patrick Bellegarde-Smith, 39–50. New York: Palgrave Macmillan.
Dumesle, Hérard. 1824. *Voyage dans le nord d'Haïti ou révélations des lieux et des monuments historiques.* Les Cayes.
Farmer, Paul. 1999. *Infections and Inequalities: Modern Plagues.* Berkeley: University of California Press.
Férère, Nancy Turnier. 2005. *Vèvè: L'art ritual du vodou haïtien = Ritual art of Haitian vodou = Arte ritual del vodú haitiano.* Boca Raton, Fla.: Nancy Turnier Férère.
Fils-Aimé, Jean. 2004. "L'inculturation de la foi chrétienne au contexte du vodou haïtien: Une analyse de l'oeuvre de trois théologiens protestants haïtiens." Ph.D. diss., Université de Montréal.
Fleurant, Gerdès. 1987. "The Ethnomusicology of Yanvalou: A Study of the Rada Rite of Haiti." Ph.D. diss., Tufts University, Medford, Mass.
———. 1996. *Dancing Spirits: Rhythms and Rituals of Haitian Vodun, the Rada Rite.* Westport, Conn.: Greenwood Press.
———. 2000. "The Music of Haitian Vodun." In *African Spirituality: Forms, Meanings, and Expressions,* ed. Jacob K. Olupona, 416–449. New York: Herder and Herder.
———. 2006a. "The Song of Freedom: Vodou, Conscientization, and Popular Culture in Haiti." In *Vodou in Haitian Life and Culture: Invisible Powers,* ed. Claudine Michel and Patrick Bellegarde-Smith, 51–63. New York: Palgrave Macmillan.
———. 2006b. "Vodun, Music, and Society in Haiti: Affirmation and Identity." In *Haitian Vodou: Spirit, Myth, and Reality,* ed. Patrick Bellegarde-Smith and Claudine Michel, 46–57. Bloomington: Indiana University Press.
———. 2007. "Mizik Vodou ann Ayiti." In *Mozayik: Yon konbit literè,* ed. Woje Saven and Drèksèl Woudsonn, 76–88. Plantation, Fla.: Infinity Publishing.
Fouchard, Jean. 1972. *Les marrons de la liberté.* Paris: Éditions de l'École.
François, Kawas. 2003. *L'Église catholique en Haïti à l'épreuve du pluralisme religieux.* Port-au-Prince: Les Cahiers du Centre de Réflexion et de Recherches Interdisciplinaires.
Frankétienne. 1975 (2002). *Dezafi.* Châteauneuf-le-Rouge, France: Vents d'Ailleurs.
Franswa, Wozilya. 2009. "Anwal, ougan oubyen doktè?" *Bon nouvèl* 42, no. 458: 6.
Freeman, Bryant, and Jowel Laguerre. 1987 (2004). *Ti Koze Kreyòl.* Lawrence, Kan.: Institute of Haitian Studies.
———. 2004. *Haitian-English Dictionary,* 5th ed. Lawrence, Kan.: Institute of Haitian Studies.
Freze, Michael. 1992. *Patron Saints.* Huntington, Ind.: Our Sunday Visitor Publishing Division.
Fuertès, Serge. 1992. *Wòl Vodou nan Bwa Kayiman.* Ottawa: Fabriksiy Kawonabo.
Galembo, Phyllis. 2005. *Vodou: Vision and Voices of Haiti.* Berkeley: Ten Speed Press.
Geggus, David P. 2002. *Haitian Revolutionary Studies.* Bloomington: Indiana University Press.
Gilles, Jerry, and Yvrose Gilles. 2009. *Remembrance: Roots, Rituals, and Reverence in Vodou.* Davie, Fla.: Bookmanlit. [English version of Jil and Jil 2009.]

Guerra, Jesús Fuentes, and Armin Schwegler. 2005. *Lengua y ritos del Palo Monte Mayonbe: Dioses cubanos y sus Fuentes africanas.* Madrid: Iberoamericana.

Hainard, Jacques, Philippe Mathez, and Olivier Schinz. 2008. *Vodou: Kunst en Mystiek uit Haïti.* Amsterdam: Koninklijk Instituut voor de Tropen.

Hall, Robert. 1953. *Haitian Creole: Grammar, Texts, Vocabulary.* Philadelphia: American Folklore Society.

Hebblethwaite, Benjamin, and Jacques Pierre, eds. 2001. *Pyebwa frenn nan/Le fraisne.* Translation of Marie de France. Bloomington, Ind.: Classic Editions.

———, eds. 2005. *The Gospel of Thomas in Haitian Creole, English, and French.* Gainesville, Fla.: Classic Editions.

———, eds. 2010. *Une saison en enfer/Yon sezon matchyavèl* (Arthur Rimbaud's 1873 prose poem). Paris: L'Harmattan.

Herskovits, Melville. 1967. *Dahomey: An Ancient West African Kingdom.* Evanston, Ill.: Northwestern University Press.

Höftmann, Hildegard. 2003. *Dictionnaire Fon-Français.* Cologne: Rüdiger Köppe Verlag.

Homer [Homeros] and Imme Dros. 1991 (2006). *Odysseia (De reizen van Odysseus).* Amsterdam: Athenaeum—Polak and Van Gennep.

Homer [Homeros] and Patrick Lateur. 2010. *Ilias (Ilias Wrok in Troje).* Amsterdam: Athenaeum—Polak and Van Gennep.

Honorin, Emmanuelle. 1997. "Liner Notes." On Musique Paysannes d'Haïti, *Fond-des-Nègres/Fond-des-Blancs.* Buda Musique, Paris.

Houlberg, Marilyn. 2005. "Magique Marasa: The Ritual Cosmos of the Twins and Other Sacred Children." In *Fragments of Bone: Neo-African Religions in a New World,* ed. Patrick Bellegarde-Smith, 13–31. Urbana: University of Illinois Press.

Hurbon, Laënnec. 1987. *Le barbare imaginaire.* Port-au-Prince: Editions Henri Deschamps.

———. 1987 (2002). *Dieu dans le vaudou haïtien.* Paris: Maisonneuve et Larose.

———. 1993. *Les mystères du vaudou.* Paris: Gallimard.

———. 2008. "Globalization and the Evolution of Haitian Vodou." In *Òrìshà Devotion as World Religion,* ed. Jacob K. Olupona and Terry Rey, 263–277. Madison: University of Wisconsin Press.

Jaegerhuber, Werner A. 1950 (1945). *Complaintes haïtiennes.* Port-au-Prince: n.p.

Jahn, Jaheinz. 1961. *Muntu: An Outline of the New African Culture.* New York: Grove.

Jil, Dyeri M., and Ivwoz S. Jil. 2009. *Sèvis Ginen: Rasin, rityèl, respè lan Vodou.* Davi, Fla.: Bookmanlit. [Haitian Creole version of Gilles and Gilles 2009.]

Joint, Gasner, Missionary Oblates of Mary Immaculate. 1999. *Libération du vaudou dans la dynamique d'inculturation en Haïti.* Rome: Editrice Pontificia Università Gregoriana.

Josué, Erol, and Laurent Dubois. 2008. "Le Vodou, miroir de l'histoire." In *Vodou,* ed. Jacques Hainard, Philippe Mathez, and Olivier Schinz, 325–340. Geneva: Infolio Editions.

Julio, Abbé. 1896 (2005). *Prières merveilleuses pour la guérison de toutes les maladies.* Paris: Bussière.

Kabwiku, Nsuka Zi. 1986. *Recueil de littérature orale kongo.* Kinshasa, Congo: United Nations Development Program and United Nations Educational, Scientific, and Cultural Organization.

Kaplan, Flora Edouwaye S. 2008. "Twice-Told Tales: Yorúba Religious and Cultural Hegemony in Benin, Nigeria." In *Òrìshà Devotion as World Religion,* ed. Jacob K. Olupona and Terry Rey, 128–163. Madison: University of Wisconsin Press.

Kim, Chongho. 2003. *Korean Shamanism: The Cultural Paradox.* Aldershot: Ashgate.

Kümmel, W. G. 1972. *The New Testament: The History of the Investigation of Its Problems,* trans. S. McLean Gilmour and H. C. Kee. Nashville: Abingdon Press.

Laguerre, Michel. 1980. *Voodoo Heritage.* Beverly Hills: Sage Publications.

Laman, K. E. 1964 (1936). *Dictionnaire kikongo-français,* 2 vols. Ridgewood, N.J.: Gregg Press.

Largey, Michael D. 2006. *Vodou Nation: Haitian Art Music and Cultural Nationalism.* Chicago Studies in Ethnomusicology. Chicago: University of Chicago Press.

Lefebvre, Claire. 1998. *Creole Genesis and the Acquisition of Grammar: The Case of Haitian Creole.* Cambridge: Cambridge University Press.

Lola, Mama, and Karen McCarthy Brown. 1995. "The Altar Room: A Dialogue." In *Sacred Arts of Haitian Vodou,* ed. Donald J. Consentino, 227–239. Los Angeles: Fowler Museum of Cultural History, University of California, Los Angeles.

Maniga, Maks. 2010. *Sajès ayisyen: Ansyen pwovèb kreyòl.* Coconut Creek, Fla.: Educa Vision.

Marcelin, Milo. 1950a. *Mythologie Vodou (Rite Arada),* vol. 1. Pétionville: Éditions Canapé Vert.

———. 1950b. *Mythologie Vodou (Rite Arada),* vol. 2. Pétionville: Éditions Canapé Vert.

Maring, Heather. 2003. "Oral Traditional Approaches to Old English Verse." *Oral Tradition* 18, no. 2: 219–222.

Mason, John. 1992. *Orin Òrìsà: Songs for Selected Heads.* New York: Yoruba Theological Seminary.

Mbiti, John. 1990. *African Religions and Philosophy,* 2d ed. Portsmouth, N.H.: Heinemann.

McAlister, Elizabeth. 2002. *Rara! Vodou, Power, and Performance in Haiti and Its Diaspora.* Berkeley: University of California Press.

Merlo, Christian. 1940. "Hierarchie fétichiste de Ouidah." *Bulletin de l'Institut Français d'Afrique Noire* 2, no. 1: 1–83.

Métraux, Alfred. 1958. *Le vaudou haïtien.* Paris: Éditions Gallimard.

———. 1972. *Voodoo in Haiti.* New York: Schocken Books.

Michel, Claudine. 2006. "Vodou in Haiti: Way of Life and Mode of Survival." In *Vodou in Haitian Life and Culture: Invisible Powers,* ed. Claudine Michel and Patrick Bellegarde-Smith, 27–37. New York: Palgrave Macmillan.

Michel, Claudine, and Patrick Bellegarde-Smith, eds. 2006. *Vodou in Haitian Life and Culture: Invisible Powers.* New York: Palgrave Macmillan.

Monsia, Marc. 2003. *Religions indigènes et savoir endogène au Bénin.* Cotonou, Benin: Les Éditions du Flamboyant.

Morisseau-Leroy, Félix. 2001. *Kont kreyòl.* Port-au-Prince: Imprimerie Le Natal.

Murray, Gerald. 1980. "Population Pressure, Land Tenure, and Voodoo: The Economics of Haitian Peasant Ritual." In *Beyond the Myths of Culture,* ed. E. Ross, 295–321. New York: Academic Press.

———. 1984. "Bon-Dieu and the Rites of Passage in Rural Haiti: Structural Determinants of Post-colonial Religion." In *The Catholic Church and Religions in Latin America,* ed. Thomas Bruneau, Mary Mooney, and Chester Gabriel, 188–231. Montreal: Centre for Developing Area Studies.

Murrell, Nathaniel Samuel. 2010. *Afro-Caribbean Religions: An Introduction to Their Historical, Cultural, and Sacred Traditions.* Philadelphia: Temple University Press.

Olupona, Jacob K., and Terry Rey. 2008. *Òrìshà Devotion as World Religion.* Madison: University of Wisconsin Press.

Orubu, A. O. 2001. "Elements of the Environment in African Traditional Religion." In *African Traditional Religion,* ed. A. O. Orubu, 1–17. Benin City, Nigeria: Institute of Education.

Orubu, A. O., and O. Omiegbe. 2001 "Witchcraft in African Religion." In *African Traditional Religion,* ed. A. O. Orubu, 116–132. Benin City, Nigeria: Institute of Education.

Oyèláràn, Olásopé. 2008. "In What Tongue?" In *Òrìshà Devotion as World Religion,* ed. Jacob K. Olupona and Terry Rey, 70–83. Madison: University of Wisconsin Press.

Parsons, Elsie Clews. 1933. *Folk-lore of the Antilles, French, and English,* part 1. New York: American Folk-lore Society.

———. 1936. *Folk-lore of the Antilles, French, and English,* pt. 2. New York: American Folklore Society.

Paultre, Carrié. 1965 (2001). *Ti Jak.* Lawrence, Kan.: Institute of Haitian Studies.

———. 1971 (2001). *Mànwela.* Lawrence, Kan.: Institute of Haitian Studies.

———. 1990 (2001). *Lavalas pa ka pote l ale.* Lawrence, Kan.: Institute of Haitian Studies.

Peters, Carl Edward. 1941. *Lumière sur le humfort.* Port-au-Prince: Chéraquit.

Porter, Stanley E., and Kent D. Clarke. 2002. "What Is Exegesis? An Analysis of Various Definitions." In *A Handbook to the Exegesis of the New Testament,* ed. Stanley E. Porter, 3–22. Leiden: Brill Academic Publishers.

Price, Richard. 2002. *First-Time: The Historical Vision of an African American People.* Chicago: University of Chicago Press.

Price-Mars, Jean. 1956 (1936). *Formation ethnique, folk-lore et culture du peuple haïtien,* 2d ed. Port-au-Prince: Imprimerie N.A. Théodore.

Richman, Karen. 2007. "Chante pwen sou kasèt." In *Mozayik: Yon konbit literè,* ed. Woje Saven and Drèksèl Woudsonn, 89–102. Plantation, Fla.: Infinity Publishing.

———. 2008. *Migration and Vodou.* Gainesville: University Press of Florida.

Rigaud, Milo. 1953. *La tradition voudoo et le voudoo haïtien: Son temple, ses mystères, sa magie.* Paris: Éditions Niclaus.

Romain, Charles Poisset. 1986. *Le protestantisme dans la société haïtienne.* Port-au-Prince: Imprimerie Henri Deschamps.

Rouget, Gilbert. 1991 (1980). *La musique et la transe.* Paris: Gallimard.

———. 2001. *Initiatique vôdoun, images du rituel: Chants et danses initiatiques pour le culte des vôdoun au Bénin.* Saint-Maur, France: Éditions Sépia.

Roumain, Jacques. 1942 (2004). *Sur les superstitions.* Montreal: Éditions Mémoire d'Encrier.

———. 1943 (2007). *Le sacrifice du tambour-Assôtô(r).* Port-au-Prince: Éditions Presses Nationales d'Haïti.

———. 1944 (1946). *Gouverneurs de la rosée.* Paris: Les Éditeurs Français Réunis.

Sachnine, Michka. 1997. *Dictionnaire usuel yorùbá-français.* Paris: Karthala.

Saint-Lot, Marie-Jose Alcide. 2003. *Vodou, a Sacred Theatre: The African Heritage in Haiti.* Coconut Grove, Fla.: Educa Vision.

Sarfati, Liora Rivka. 2007. "Performance, Spirituality, Audiences, and Shamans." *Korea Foundation Newsletter,* vol. 16, no. 6, November.

Schwegler, Armin. 2002. "El vocabulario (ritual) bantú de Cuba. Parte I: Acerca de la matriz africana de la 'lengua congo' In *La Romania americana. Procesos lingüísticos en situaciones de contacto,* ed. Norma Díaz, Ralph Ludwig, and Stefan Pfänder, 97–194. Frankfurt: Vervuert Verlag.

Segurola, Basilio, and Jean Rassinoux. 2000. *Dictionnaire Fon–Français.* Madrid: Société des Missions Africaines.

Seiderer, Anna. 2008. "La muséification des objets vodou." In *Vodou,* ed. Jacques Hainard, Philippe Mathez, and Olivier Schinz, 387–408. Geneva: Infolio Editions.

Séverin, François. 2000. *Plant ak pyebwa tè d Ayiti.* Port-au-Prince: Éditions Quitel.

Smarth, William, Claude Souffrant, and François Gayot, eds. 1963. *Église en marche: Pastorale et Vodou.* Port-au-Prince: Catholic Church.

Smucker, Glenn R. 1984. "The Social Character of Religion in Rural Haiti." In *Haiti—Today and Tomorrow,* ed. Charles Foster and Albert Valdman, 35–56. Lanham, Md.: University Press of America.

Sollier, Joseph. 1908. "The Communion of Saints." *The Catholic Encyclopedia,* vol. 4. New York: Robert Appleton.

Soyinka, Wole. 2008. "The Tolerant Gods." In *Òrìshà Devotion as World Religion,* ed. Jacob K. Olupona and Terry Rey, 31–50. Madison: University of Wisconsin Press.

Swartenbroeckx, Pierre. 1973. *Dictionnaire kikongo et kituba-français: Vocabulaire comparé des langages kongo traditionnels et véhiculaires.* Bandundu: Ceeba Publications.

Taiwo, Olufemi. 2008. "Orisa." In *Òrìshà Devotion as World Religion,* ed. Jacob K. Olupona and Terry Rey, 84–105. Madison: University of Wisconsin Press.

Thompson, Robert Faris. 1993. *Face of the Gods: Art and Altars of Africa and the African Americas.* New York: Museum for African Art.

———. 1995. "From the Isle beneath the Sea: Haiti's Africanizing Vodou Art." In *Sacred Arts of Haitian Vodou,* ed. Donald J. Consentino, 91–119. Los Angeles: Fowler Museum of Cultural History, University of California, Los Angeles.

Valdman, Albert. 1988 (2002). *Ann pale kreyòl.* Bloomington, Ind.: Creole Institute.

———. 2001. "Sur les processus lexicogénétiques du créole haïtien." In *Linguistik als Kulturwissenschaft: Festschrift für Bernd Spillner zum 60 Gegurtstag,* ed. Bernd Spillner, Hartmut Schröder, Petra Kumschlies, and María González, 43–53. Frankfurt: Peter Lang.

Valdman, Albert, Iskra Iskrova, Jacques Pierre, and Nicolas André. 2007. *Haitian Creole-English Bilingual Dictionary.* Bloomington, Ind.: Creole Institute.

Verger, Pierre. 1999 (1957). *Notas sobre o culto aos orixàs e voduns na Bahia de Todos os Santos, no Brasil, e na antiga costa dos escravos, na Àfrica* (originally published in French as *Notes sur le culte des Orisa et Vodun à Bahia: La baie de tous les saints, au Bresil et a l'ancienne Côte des Esclaves en Afrique*). São Paulo: Editora da Universidade de São Paulo.

Virgil [Virgilius], and M. D'Hane-Scheltema. 2008. *Aeneis (Het verhaal van Aeneas).* Amsterdam: Athenaeum—Polak and Van Gennep.

Weaver, Karol Kovalovich. 2002. "The Enslaved Healers of Eighteenth-Century Saint Domingue." *Bulletin of the History of Medicine* 76, no. 3: 429–460.

Wilcken, Lois. 1992. *The Drums of Vodou.* Tempe, Ariz.: White Cliffs Media.

Yai, Olabiyi Babalola. 2008. "Yorùbá Religion and Globalization: Some Reflections." In *Òrìshà Devotion as World Religion,* ed. Jacob K. Olupona and Terry Rey, 233–246. Madison: University of Wisconsin Press.

Online References

Allen, Nick. 2010. "Haiti Earthquake: Voodoo High Priest Claims Aid Monopolised by Christians," February 1. Available online at http://www.telegraph.co.uk.

BBC. "Haiti Mobs Lynch Voodoo Priests over Cholera Fears," December 24, 2010. Available online at http://www.bbc.co.uk/news/world-latin-america-12073029.

Bob Corbett's List. Available online at http://www.webster.edu/~corbetre/haiti-archive.

Campbell, Thomas. 2006. "Saint Anthony (Toni Malau)." Available online at http://www.metmuseum.org/toah/works-of-art/1999.295.2.

Ethnologue. Available online at http://www.ethnologue.com.

Jordan, David K. "The Bantu Expansion." Available online at http://weber.ucsd.edu/~dkjordan/resources/clarifications/BantuExpansion.html.

Mambo Michele. "Haitian Voodoo Glossary Terms." Available online at http://www.erzulies.com/site/articles/view/9.

Mambo Racine Sans But. "The Ancestors in Haitian Vodou," December 31, 2003. Available online at http://www.africaspeaks.com/reasoning/index.php?topic=1170.0.

Miami Vodou Temple, Société Roi Linto. "Trois Mysteres Promotions Video," June 18, 2011. Available online at http://www.youtube.com/user/haiti220.

Sénat. "Victor Schoelcher, (1804–1893): Une vie, un siècle." Available online at http://www.senat.fr/evenement/victor_schoelcher/index.html.

Wikipedia. Available online at http://en.wikipedia.org/wiki/Second_Franco-Dahomean_War; http://en.wikipedia.org/wiki/Anthony_of_Padua; http://en.wikipedia.org/wiki/Ant%C3%B3nio_I_of_Kongo.

Filmography

Deren, Maya. 2007 (1947–1955). *The Divine Horsemen, the Living Gods of Haiti.* Microcinema, San Francisco.

Lescot, Anne, and Laurence Magloire. 2002. *Of Men and Gods.* Documentary Educational Resources, Watertown, Mass.

Matsushita, Toshi. 1997. *Voodoo Kingdom.* Cinema Guild, New York.

Rietmeijer, Saskia, and Bart Drolenga. 2003. *Buying the Spirit.* Filmmakers Library, New York.

Discography

Angels in the Mirror: Vodou Music in Haiti. 1997. Ellipsis Arts, New York.

Averill, Gage. 2009. *Alan Lomax's Recordings in Haiti.* Harte Recordings, San Francisco.

Boukan Ginen. 1995. *Jou a rive.* Xenophile, Nashville.

———. 1996. *Rèv an nou.* Xenophilem, Nashville.

Boukman Eksperyans. 1991. *Vodou Adjae.* Island Records, New York.

———. 1995. *Libète (Pran pou pran l).* Island Records, New York.

Chandèl. 2003. *Mea culpa.* Geronimo Records, New York.

Fortere, Jacques, Raoul Joseph, and Sylomene Fevrier. 1997. *Haitian Voodoo.* Sounds of the World, n.p., Portugal.

François, Eddy. 2008. *Djohu.* Solèy Sounds, Port-au-Prince.

Freedom (Christopher Laroche). 2004. *1804 Liberation.* Freedom Recordz, Toronto.

Josué, Erol. 2007. *Régléman,* Mi5 Recordings, Fort Lauderdale, Fla.

Kanpèch. 2001. *Ogou.* Geronimo Records, New York.

King Kessy. 2009. *Voudou Djam* (Vodou Is Strong). Available online at http://KingKessy.com.

Lomax, Alan, Elizabeth Lyttleton, Révolie Polinice, Gage Averill, Anna Lomax Wood, Ellen Harold, and H. P. Davis. 2009. *Alan Lomax in Haiti.* Harte Recordings, San Francisco.

Les 101 nations du vaudou. 2009. Buda Musique, Paris.

Musique Paysannes d'Haïti. 1997. *Fond-des-Nègres/Fond-des-Blancs.* Buda Musique, Paris.

Pierre, Julmis, Monique Pierre, Dieubon Alerte, and Moril Morisseau. 1999. *Ceremonie Gran'n.* Geronimo Records, New York.

Racine Bwa-Kay-Iman. 2003. *Sa m fè moun yo.* Mass Konpa Productions, Miami.

Racine Figuier. 1999. *Dantò.* Geronimo Records, New York.

———. 2002. *Se don nou.* Geronimo Records, New York.

Racine Mapou de Azor. 1999. *Sanba Move 2.* Geronimo Records, New York.

Ram. 1997. *Puritan Vodou.* Island Records, London.

Tokay. 2000. *La Pe* [*Lapè*]. Constant Productions and Planèt Mizik, Hialeah, Fla.

Toto Bissainthe. 1977 (1989). *Toto Bissainthe Sings Haïti.* Arion, Paris.

Wawa and Azor. N.d. Collection 8 and 3. Geronimo Records, New York.

———. N.d. Collection 9 and 1. Geronimo Records, New York.

WaWa and Rasin Kanga. 2005. *The Haitian Roots 4.* Geronimo Records, New York.

INDEX

——*

Page numbers preceded by the letter g *refer to photo gallery pages, which follow text page 204.*

Benjamin Hebblethwaite, who was born in Johannesburg, South Africa, is an Assistant Professor in the Department of Languages, Literatures and Cultures at the University of Florida. He is the coeditor (with Jacques Pierre) of Arthur Rimbaud's prose poem *Une saison en enfer / Yon sezon matchyavèl* (2010). He has published articles in the *Journal of Pidgin and Creole Languages, Bilingualism: Language and Cognition, Cahiers de linguistique, Revue roumaine de linguistique,* and the *Journal of Universal Language.*

——*

Chris Ballengee was born in Newton, North Carolina. He is an Adjunct Lecturer and a doctoral candidate in Ethnomusicology at the University of Florida School of Music, as well as an Adjunct Professor of Music and Technical Theatre at Santa Fe College in Gainesville, Florida. Ballengee holds a bachelor's degree in Music from Lenoir-Rhyne University and a master's degree in Ethnomusicology from Bowling Green State University. His research focuses on folk and popular music in the Caribbean region, especially Indo-Trinidadian tassa drumming.

Joanne Bartley was born in Port-au-Prince, Haiti. She earned a bachelor's degree in English with a minor in Music Performance from the University of Florida. She is the author of the online booklet *Maladi Malarya: Enfòmasyon ou dwe konnen (The Disease Malaria: Information You Need to Know)* and has provided Haitian Creole and English translations for various departments at the University of Florida. She is the recipient of the University of Florida Presidential Scholarship and the Bright Futures Florida Medallion Scholars Award. She is currently studying Medicine at the University of Florida.

Vanessa Brissault was born in Port-au-Prince, Haiti. At the age of nine she moved to the United States with her family. Brissault is a passionate student of Haitian Creole, French, and English. She is currently a University of Florida undergraduate majoring in Linguistics and minoring in Teaching English as a Second Language. Brissault is the recipient of the I. Douglas Turner Grant, a federal Pell Grant, and a Kiwanis Club scholarship.

Erica Felker-Kantor was born in Santa Clara, California, and grew up in Salt Lake City, Utah. She attended Boston University (BU), where she earned a bachelor's degree in Latin American Studies and Spanish. During her time at BU, she spent a year and a half studying and conducting research in Ecuador, Nicaragua, and El Salvador. After graduation, she worked for Oxfam America and ACCION USA, as well as for non-profit organizations in Ecuador, Bolivia, and Costa Rica. At the University of Florida, she pursued graduate coursework on global health and was awarded three U.S. Department of Education Foreign Language and Areas Studies fellowships in Haitian Creole. In the summer of 2011, she traveled to Haiti to coordinate a health education program. Felker-Kantor is currently pursuing a master's degree in Global Public Health at Johns Hopkins University.

Quinn Hansen was born in Salt Lake City, Utah. He earned a bachelor's degree in Spanish and Portuguese Languages and Literatures from the University of Texas, Austin, following earlier studies in Hawaii, Mexico, Portugal, and Spain. He subsequently earned the Grau de Mestre in Linguistics from the Universidade Nova de Lisboa, Portugal, conducting thesis work on a Mayan language spoken in the Guatemalan highlands. After a brief stint as a first-grade teacher in Aleppo, Syria, he returned to the United States and earned a doctorate in Linguistics from the University of Florida, supported in part by a U.S. Department of Education Foreign Language and Areas Studies fellowship in Haitian Creole.

Andrew Tarter was born in Okay, Haiti. His first exposure to Vodou songs was as a seven-year-old child living in rural Haiti, where the sounds of nighttime ceremonies were carried to his ears on the wind. He earned an interdisciplinary undergraduate degree in Environmental Studies from the University of Washington, Seattle, and a master's degree in Cultural Anthropology from the University of Florida, with funding from two U.S. Department of Education Foreign Language and Areas Studies fellowships in Haitian Creole. Tarter is currently pursuing a doctorate in Anthropology at the University of Florida with funding from the National Science Foundation. His research focuses on all subjects related to Haiti and Haitians, with a particular emphasis on human-nature interactions. Tarter has conducted research in Haiti, Costa Rica, the Democratic Republic of Congo, and India.

Kat Warwick was born in Melbourne, Florida. When she was six years old, her parents began a nonprofit organization that brought simple water purification systems to families in the Dominican Republic and Haiti and grew to serve more than a hundred communities. While at the University of Florida pursuing an undergraduate degree in Civil Engineering, Warwick enrolled in several Haitian Creole language and culture courses, and she traveled to Haiti on numerous occasions to conduct research on improving Haitian engineering methods. She is currently pursuing a master's degree in Civil Engineering at Virginia Tech, with the goal of designing structures that will survive the natural hazards that impact Haiti: earthquakes, landslides, and hurricanes.